CANADA'S NATIONAL NEWSPAPER
THE GLOBE AND MAIL

STYLE BOOK

Ninth Edition

A Guide to
Language and Usage

J.A. (SANDY) McFARLANE
AND WARREN CLEMENTS

M&S

National Library of Canada Cataloguing in Publication

McFarlane, J.A. (James Alexander)
    The Globe and Mail style book : a guide to language and usage / J.A. (Sandy) McFarlane & Warren Clements. – 9th ed.

ISBN 0-7710-5685-0

1. English language – Usage – Dictionaries.   I. Clements, Warren, 1952–   .
II. Title.

Z253.P44 2003   428'.003   C2003-904420-3

Typeset in Goudy by M&S, Toronto

McClelland & Stewart Ltd.
The Canadian Publishers
481 University Avenue
Toronto, Ontario
M5G 2E9

1 2 3 4 5   07 06 05 04 03

Printed in Canada

Preface

The Globe and Mail has always aspired to great heights when it comes to the use of the English language. Moreover, writers and editors know that if they allow their standards to slip, readers will bring them up short. Whenever I have made a grammatical error – and I've unfortunately made more than a few – it has inspired a deluge of correspondence from our grammatically minded readers. The advent of e-mail has shortened the response time considerably, providing a rough-and-tumble daily education in the splendid minutiae of our language.

Few of the issues with which we grapple are immutable. Our internal communications systems buzz with regular exchanges and debates about style issues. Should the former Iraqi dictator be referred to in headlines as Saddam or Hussein? At what point do we accept a legal name change designed to confuse the public? And the age-old question: Is it Yukon or the Yukon?

Although we welcome the readers' interventions, the aim of our editors and reporters is to police themselves. Their last line of defence rests in your hands right now. This is the ninth edition of *The Globe and Mail Style Book*. We have been compiling our style points in an organized fashion for decades, but the first detailed version of this book was not born until 1990 under the editorship of two Globe and Mail giants, Sandy McFarlane and Warren Clements. Sandy has since retired, although not before leaving behind notes with suggested revisions. Warren, with help and advice from innumerable colleagues, worked tirelessly to produce this latest update. On many days, I would pass his desk and watch him, eyeglasses pushed up on his forehead, as he pored over page after page of dictionary listings.

The Globe's style book is about much more than spelling and grammar, straying into historical claims to place names and the intricacies of journalistic practice. Still, the most significant change in the 2003 edition is a switch in our official spelling dictionary from the *Nelson Canadian Dictionary* to *The Canadian Oxford Dictionary*. Much else has changed as well since the eighth edition was published in 1998. The world has seen the birth of new countries; Canada has seen the birth of new political parties; medical science has seen the birth of new diseases. Eaton's is gone. The euro is here. Newfoundland is Newfoundland and Labrador. The territories now number three, not two, with the creation of Nunavut. All this and more makes this edition of *The Globe and Mail Style Book* an important step forward.

Edward Greenspon
Editor-in-chief
June, 2003

Introduction

Writing for newspaper readers is a special challenge. Although a few readers have time for leisurely digestion of all that The Globe has to offer, most do not. They have little patience with stories that delay the newest and most important developments; with writing that obliges them to consult a dictionary or pick up a calculator; with writing so murky or disjointed that they lose track of who is being quoted or why they are being told all this.

This book is intended to help writers and editors present their information clearly, accurately and concisely. Doing this in language that also delights the reader raises journalism from a craft to an art, but the craft comes first.

The entries in this guide are in alphabetical order, with cross-references rather than an index. For ease of handling, the book has been designed to lie open flat on the desk. There are general maps of Canada and the world, devised by The Globe's Bernard Bennell, and drawings to break up the text.

On occasion we have broken our own rules to solve the peculiar editorial problems of a style book. As an alternative to a blizzard of quotation marks and other punctuation, we have used devices in ways and to an extent that would not be acceptable in the newspaper, including brackets, boldface and the expressions e.g. and etc. This indulgence should not be taken as a licence to go forth and do likewise.

This guide builds on the work of a long line of editors at The Globe and elsewhere in the community of journalism. We acknowledge in particular the contribution of former deputy managing editor Shirley Sharzer, who began this project and whose experience, insight and research are reflected throughout. We acknowledge as well the valuable work of E. C. Phelan (author of previous editions of *The Globe and Mail Style Book*), Alan Dawson, Martin Lynch and Earle Gill, as well as style-book editors in many other newspapers and wire services. In particular, we have found the style guide of The Canadian Press to be clear and logical, and have adopted some of its style practices. We should also mention the style books of The Associated Press and The Economist, and Roy Copperud's *A Dictionary of Usage and Style*.

Other sources include The Globe and Mail's databases; The Globe's editorial library and its excellent staff; the lawyers of Paterson, MacDougall; various encyclopedias, including *Britannica, Canadian, Canadiana, Americana, Concord* and *Van Nostrand's Scientific*; *The Statesman's Year-Book*; *Colombo's Canadian References*; the Canadian and International *Who's Who*; *The Gazetteer of Canada*; *The Times World Atlas*; Fowler's *Modern English Usage*; Follett's *Modern American Usage*; Strunk and White's *The Elements of Style*; Michael Crawford's *The Journalist's Legal Guide*; the *Canadian Trade Index*; and *Drugs and Drug Abuse*, by the Addiction Research Foundation. The population figures are extrapolated from United Nations and other sources.

While the dividing lines invariably blur in a collaboration of this sort, the writing fell largely to Sandy McFarlane and the editing largely to Warren Clements, who also drew the illustrations and has overseen this revision. We have benefited immensely in preparing this book from the advice and proof-reading of several Globe staff members, and from the guidance of Greg O'Neill and Stan Dellarocca of the newspaper's editorial style committee. Any errors that remain are entirely the responsibility of the authors. Warren Clements welcomes correspondence on that score, care of the editorial department of The Globe and Mail.

a, an

Use **a** before all consonant sounds, including the aspirated h (a hotel, a historic day). The initial silent h, requiring use of **an**, is found in four common words, plus their variants—heir, honest, honour, hour. Use **an** before vowel sounds (an egg), including those in numbers (an eight-year-old), and note that the $ symbol is pronounced after the number (an $11 tab). Do not use **an** before vowels that are pronounced as consonants (a eulogy, a one-time offer).

These rules also apply to the pronunciation of the letters of the alphabet (an H-bomb, an S-hook, an MD, an L-shaped room).

In general, use **a** or **an** instead of per before non-Latin words ($2 a head, five times a year). See per.

A-

Acceptable in headlines as a prefix meaning atomic or nuclear, as in A-bomb, A-power, A-sub, but not to be used in copy.

AA

Acceptable second reference for Alcoholics Anonymous. No periods.

abattoir

Prefer slaughterhouse, packing plant, meat plant.

abbreviations

The initials of television networks, such as the CBC and PBS, and of cable channels known universally by their initials, such as TSN, CNN and A&E, are acceptable as a first reference, with no need to spell out later. Three other sets of initials, MP, RCMP and AIDS, also have this status in stories of all types, as do NDP, MLA, MPP, MNA and MHA in political stories, and HIV if identified in copy as the AIDS virus.

As adjectives only, B.C., PEI and U.S. may be used in first reference without the need to spell out later. They may be used as nouns in headlines, and in second reference as nouns in copy.

Some very familiar initials for long formal names, e.g. BBC, NATO, are acceptable in first reference to avoid bogging down a lead paragraph, but the name must be spelled out as soon afterward as possible.

Do not abbreviate **Fort** or **Mount** in names of places or geographical features, although this is permissible in short headlines.

Acronyms are pronounceable words, such as NATO, formed from initial letters, from syllables or from a combination of letters and syllables. If a term is not pronounced as a word, but rather as a string of letters, as in CBC, then it is merely **initials** and should not be referred to as an acronym. Other definitions: An **abbreviation** is the shortening of a word, name or phrase by any method. A **contraction** is a specific form of abbreviation in which the first and last elements are both preserved, as in Ltd., Mr. We use periods after such contractions.

Initials and acronyms from initial letters are written all caps, no periods.

Acronyms from syllables are written upper and lower, as in Nazi and Candu, or all lower-case, as in radar and sonar. An exception is NORAD, which is all caps by convention.

There is usually no need to supply the initials or acronym in brackets immediately after the name, and indeed this can ruin a good sentence. Simply lapse into the acronym in second reference, provided it appears within a paragraph or two. But if the reader is likely to be confused, we must supply clear signposts, e.g. ACTRA, the Canadian actors union. . . .

Many foreign political parties, guerrilla groups and other organizations are referred to by a familiar domestic acronym that does not jibe with our English translation of the name. In such cases, first reference should include the abbreviation immediately after the name, either in brackets or with a brief explanation. Examples: the National Union for the Total Independence of Angola (UNITA); the Mozambican National Resistance, known by its Portuguese acronym, Renamo. In many instances, a less cumbersome method is to use the abbreviation in first reference with a brief description, as in "the guerrilla group Polisario," and to inform the reader much later that the name refers to the Popular Front for the Liberation of Seguia el-Hamra and Rio de Oro.

A word of caution: Sets of upper-case initials sprinkled too liberally through a story make it look messy and intimidating to the reader. Whenever there is no chance of confusion, revert to a generic term such as the party, the group, the association, the board, the agency.

Also see notes on abbreviations under directions, measurement, months, punctuation (periods in abbreviations), provinces and states, ranks, religion, streets.

abduct

Use this word unless a ransom has been demanded, in which case it is proper to use the word kidnap.

Aberhart, William

The founder of the Social Credit movement, and Alberta premier from 1935 until his death in 1943, was born in Ontario in 1878; he was 32 before he moved west. He should be called Bible Bill only in stories specifically about the religious aspect of his movement.

ABM

For automated banking machine, the widely used term among Canadian banks. The U.S. term is ATM, for automated teller machine.

A-bomb, see A-.

abominable snowman

Lower-case. Prefer **yeti**, and refer to similar reports in Canada about the sasquatch. See sasquatch.

abortion

Emotions run high on this issue, and we must go the extra mile to avoid even the appearance of taking sides. We must never imply that either camp is not acting on honourable beliefs, honestly held.

There is a range of beliefs. Unless it has been clearly established, we should never imply that someone holds one of the extreme views, or that he or she is an activist on the issue or a member of a particular group.

When describing an individual, it is most accurate simply to name a group he or she belongs to, e.g. Campaign Life or the Canadian Abortion Rights Action League. We might also describe the person's specific beliefs, e.g. against abortion except in the case of rape of a minor, or personally opposed to abortion but advocating others' right to choose.

When describing large crowds at demonstrations, or groups presenting briefs and petitions, it is fair to use the term anti-abortion, since this is an accurate description of the beliefs of all activists on that side, beliefs they hold proudly. However, many on the other side are not personally in favour of abortion, but are in favour of giving others access to it if they so choose, so the term pro-abortion is not always accurate. The term pro-choice is accurate to describe the entire camp, but only because of its vagueness.

Those opposed to abortion say they are unfairly cast in an unfavourable light when the negative term anti-abortion is used in close juxtaposition to the positive term pro-choice. There is no getting around the fact that the issue is abortion and they are against it, but we should nevertheless be sensitive to this concern, and reword whenever possible. We might take a cue from the specific purpose of a demonstration, brief or court action, for example, and describe it as advocating laws to restrict abortion or seeking a ruling on the existence of fetal rights.

Those who oppose abortion would prefer the positive label pro-life. This is unacceptable for two reasons: it unfairly demeans their opponents by saddling them with the obvious opposite labels anti-life and pro-death; and it inaccurately identifies the issue as life, rather than the specific question of abortion. If the issue really were the broad one of life, a person's beliefs on capital punishment, euthanasia, killing in self-defence and killing in war would also have to be considered. However, we do not go so far as to eliminate reference to life when it appears in the names of various anti-abortion organizations.

Although the term anti-abortion is acceptable, do not refer to someone who holds this view as an anti-abortionist.

abridgment

abscess

absolute zero

Spell out zero. It is the theoretical temperature at which all substances have no remaining thermal energy, and is the fixed starting point for the absolute scale, also called the Kelvin scale. Absolute zero is considered unattainable in practice, but laboratories have come within a few millionths of a Kelvin. The Celsius equivalent of 0 Kelvin is -273.16.

Abu Dhabi

Federal capital of the United Arab Emirates, which see.

academe and academia

While the words are largely interchangeable, academe refers more to a specific place of learning, school or group of schools, and academia refers more generally to the academic world and to scholastic life.

Acadia

This is the name given by France from about the 1590s to its land on the east coast of North America, what is now New Brunswick, Nova Scotia, Prince Edward Island, southeastern Quebec and eastern Maine. Nowadays, it is applied to regions of the Maritimes with predominantly French roots, and in the abstract to the fact of francophone culture there. **Acadians** is the proper term for francophone Maritimers, who form about 37 per cent of the population in New Brunswick, 14 per cent in PEI and 10 per cent in Nova Scotia. Use the French terms *l'Acadie* and *Acadien* only for colour in features, and sparingly.

a cappella

accelerator

accent and dialect

Accent refers to the speech of people speaking their non-native language, while dialect refers to regional pronunciation and speech patterns among native speakers of a language. Strictly speaking, we should say he speaks with an Italian accent, but she speaks in the Yorkshire (or Calabrian, Bavarian, Bohemian etc.) dialect. However, we do not adhere slavishly to this in the case of such common U.S. references as "southern accent."

Take care with the expression "Newfoundland dialect," which falsely implies that there is only one. There are many, and they can differ markedly.

accents

Use accents on French names, on English words for which the dictionary shows accents and on the rare French common words that are allowed to remain in copy. But we never guess. Words can be checked in a French dictionary, but if a name is unfamiliar and no reference is available, leave the accent off. Use accents on both capital and lower-case letters.

Do not use accents on words or names in other languages, unless there is a problem of ambiguity otherwise. There is a convention in English that an umlaut in German is replaced by

adding an e to the vowel (schoen, Goering), and that in Danish and Norwegian the vowel å is doubled. Note that these rules do not apply to any other languages.

The most common French accents are the acute (é), which makes the vowel e rhyme approximately with bay; the grave (à, è), which produces flat vowel sounds (è as in where); the cedilla (ç), which produces a soft c, as in city; and the circumflex (â, ê, î, ô, û).

See foreign and French words.

access

Do not use it as a verb, with one exception. To conform to a now-general use and in the interest of brevity, the neo-verb is accepted in the context of computers, meaning to gain access to the information on a computer disk or to gain access to a computer system. This should not be extended to other environments, such as obtaining information from files, a government department etc. See noun invaders.

accessible

accident

Use this word to describe the event, but not the result. Say an accident involving her hand, or injury to her hand, but not an accident to her hand; damage to his car, not an accident to his car.

accolade

accommodate

accountant

Note that there are several categories of accountants, the highest of which is chartered accountant. (There are also certified management accountants, general accountants etc.) The U.S. equivalent of a CA is a CPA (certified public accountant). The degree dictates the tasks that the holder is allowed to perform, such as auditing publicly traded companies, and so we must be specific.

accoutre, accoutrement

accumulate

Achilles heel

acknowledgment

acoustics

As a science, it is singular. As shorthand for acoustical properties, it is plural (the acoustics in the Dome are a problem).

acquiescent

acronyms, see abbreviations.

Action Démocratique du Québec

Use this style, without italics, for the Quebec party headed by Mario Dumont. Second reference is the ADQ.

See foreign and French words.

Act of Union

Upper-case the term for each of four acts of Parliament at Westminster: those uniting Upper and Lower Canada in 1840 (proclaimed in 1841) and uniting England with Wales in 1536, with Scotland in 1707 and with Ireland in 1801. See Canada, Upper Canada, United Kingdom.

actor, actress

In theory, there is no reason why both sexes should not be covered by actor. Say that someone is one of the best actors in the world, or that she always wanted to be an actor. In practice, there will be occasions when actress is inescapable – covering the Academy Awards, for instance – and opinion is divided even among actors about whether actress is a word worth defending, with an honourable history, or a belittling subcategory of actor. Be consistent within the story: Don't

refer to a woman as an actor in one paragraph and an actress six paragraphs later. Where actor is used, male actor and female actor are acceptable where necessary to remove ambiguity.

See women and language.

Actors Studio, no apostrophe.

ACTRA

The Alliance of Canadian Cinema, Television and Radio Artists. It may be described as a union.

acts

Upper-case the full titles of statutes, and also titles from which only "Canadian," "of Canada" or some such has been dropped, e.g. the Criminal Code. Lower-case informal references, e.g. the traffic law. See bills, capitalization.

L'actualité

The Quebec magazine. Italics.

AD, no periods.

From *anno domini*, meaning in the year of the Lord. Purists would insist that it always appear before the year (AD 312) without being preceded by the word in, and that it never apply to centuries or millenniums, since they are not years. However, just as the holder of a PhD need no longer have any knowledge of philosophy, the meaning of the initials AD has evolved beyond that of the words. It now means in the Christian or current era, and so we allow such references as the fourth century AD. If AD is attached to a year, do not use the redundant word "year."

Note, however, that use of AD is necessary only to avoid confusion if the story is also dealing with the period before Christ (BC). If we write about the year 79 or the second century, it is assumed to be of the current era unless we say otherwise.

Addis Ababa, capital of Ethiopia.

adjectival expressions

It is worth recasting to eliminate a long adjectival expression used before a noun or name, as in a Southwest Africa People's Organization fighter, a Moose Jaw, Sask., merchant. These are usually easy to turn around.

admissible

admit, admitted

Loaded words. Avoid, unless the person being quoted agrees that there has been wrongdoing. For example, never write that an executive admitted that company profits doubled last year, since that is something of which he or she is justifiably proud. If the person is merely agreeing with a premise offered by a questioner, an editorially neutral word is acknowledged. See quotations.

ad nauseam

adoption

A child who is adopted becomes part of the family, and is as much the new parents' own child as their biological children. Unless their status is relevant to the story, do not single out children as adopted. Do not refer to the birth mother or father as the child's "real" or "natural" parents, suggesting the adoptive parents are false or unnatural. Use the terms "birth mother," "birth parents," "biological parent" or "children by birth." Similarly, do not refer to the siblings of the adopted child as the parents' "natural" children.

Avoid references to "surrendering" or "giving up" a child for adoption, with their clear connotation of an involuntary, forced arrangement, unless we know this to be the case.

adrenalin

Lower-case, the generic form of the manufactured drug with that proprietary name. The natural hormones manufactured by the body's adrenal gland are epinephrine and cortin. Adrenalin is the manufactured form of epinephrine.

advance planning

Is there another kind?

adverse, averse

Adverse means unfavourable or opposing or hurtful, as in adverse winds, fortune, circumstances, publicity. **Averse** is almost exclusively a predicative adjective, found after such verbs as is, was, seemed. It means having a reluctance to or a fixed dislike for, as in He is averse to change.

advise

Do not use merely as a substitute for inform, say or tell. When followed by of, it is acceptable for notify officially (The government advised the court of its intention to appeal), but in general we should confine it to its usual meaning of giving advice or counsel.

adviser, advisory

aerospace

It describes the industry making aircraft, spacecraft, satellites and their components.

aesthetic

affect, effect

When a noun is called for, the choice is always effect. (There is an obscure noun affect, used only in psychological jargon, meaning emotion or feeling, but journalists are unlikely to encounter it.)

When a verb is called for, odds are that the correct choice is affect, meaning to act upon, have an effect upon, influence, or fancy or imitate (affect an English accent). The verb effect means to cause, make possible, accomplish, complete, as in to effect a change.

Be aware of the inherent vagueness in the verb affect; we should often look for a more precise word.

affidavit

Afghanistan

Adjective and people: Afghan. Currency: afghani. Capital: Kabul.

It was a monarchy until 1973, when King Zahir Shah was overthrown in a military coup led by his brother-in-law and cousin, Mohammed Daoud. Daoud in turn was killed in another military coup in 1978 that led to the establishment of a pro-Soviet government, and then to the entry of Soviet forces to prop it up in 1979. Soviet troops completed their withdrawal in 1989, but Soviet advisers remained and aid continued. Various rebel factions finally swept the former communist government from power in April of 1992, but then turned on each other, continuing the carnage. The Taliban religious movement took control of Kabul in late 1996, enforcing its concept of strict Islamic law and consolidating its hold on most of the rest of the country. In March, 2001, the Taliban were widely condemned for the destruction of ancient monuments that the government deemed un-Islamic, including the Buddha statues in the Bamiyan Valley. One of them stood 52 metres and was the world's tallest standing Buddha carved in antiquity into a cliff face. (Note the qualifying word "standing." The tallest antique Buddha carved out of a cliff is the seated Leshan Buddha in China's Sichuan province, which is 71 metres high and was declared a World Heritage Site in 1996. Modern times have seen far taller statues, including a bronze Buddha in Tokyo that stands 120 metres tall.)

After the Sept. 11, 2001, terrorist attacks against the United States by agents of the international radical Islamic network al-Qaeda, a U.S.-led coalition invaded Afghanistan in a bid to crush al-Qaeda, find its leader Osama bin Laden and remove from power the Taliban, identified as the group's protectors. Bin Laden escaped, but the Taliban were overthrown on Nov. 17, 2001. After a meeting of Afghan opposition groups in Bonn, under United Nations auspices, an Afghan Interim Authority was created on Dec. 22, 2001, with Hamid Karzai as its chair. This body held a *loya jirga* (grand council) the following June. Karzai was elected president of the Transitional Islamic State of Afghanistan, with a mandate to hold a countrywide election within 24 months. An international meeting in Tokyo in January, 2002, committed $4.5-billion to a fund for reconstruction, to be administered by the World Bank.

Afghanistan is mountainous, bisected by the Hindu Kush, and extremely arid, with most of its precipitation falling as snow in its bitter winters. Its population is estimated at between 23 million and 27 million, mostly rural and about 90 per cent illiterate. The main ethnic groups are Pashtun (45 per cent) and Tajik (25 per cent). The religion of the great majority is Sunni Muslim, and the main languages spoken are Afghan Persian (Dari) and Pashto.

Afghanistan is in Central Asia, not in the Middle East.

aficionado(s)

AFL-CIO

For American Federation of Labor and Congress of Industrial Organizations. Not AF **of** L, although it is usually given this way in speech.

African Financial Community

Known by its French initials CFA (for *Communauté financière africaine*). Use the English name. Its members' common currency is the CFA franc.

African Union, the

This 53-member regional organization replaced the Organization of African Unity (OAU) on July 9, 2002, at a summit meeting in Durban, South Africa. Its supporters billed it as a tougher, self-policing group that would allow Africans to foster democracy and economic progress without depending on the charity and political whims of other regions.

Where the OAU respected each member's sovereignty, the AU has a "peace and security council" authorized to send in peacekeepers drawn from African armies in the event of any conflict involving crimes against humanity. The body also created an African Peer Review Mechanism to rate nations with political and economic benchmarks, with the goal of attracting foreign investment and aid. In time, the AU expects to have an African parliament, a central bank, an African court of justice and, eventually, an African Economic Community with a single currency. Its economic blueprint is a recovery strategy called the New Partnership for Africa's Development (NEPAD). As the OAU was, the organization is based in Addis Ababa, Ethiopia.

Afrikaans, language; Afrikaners, people.

Afrikaans is not Dutch. It did develop from the southern Dutch dialect of its Boer settlers in the 1600s, but now is a separate language that has also incorporated many words from English, Portuguese, Malay and various Bantu and Hottentot languages. Reserve **Afrikaner** for an Afrikaans-speaking South African. See South Africa.

after

Take care not to use this preposition illogically. It makes no sense to say a person was injured "after" being punched in the face, or people were killed "after" their plane crashed.

afterward (no s).

Aga Khan

Title of the imams (spiritual leaders) of the Nizari Ismaili sect of the Shia Muslims. (They may be called simply Ismailis, or Ismaili Muslims.) The current holder of the imamate is Aga Khan IV, but he may be referred to simply as the Aga Khan.

aged, elderly

Generally avoid these words as descriptions of specific individuals. They conjure up infirm, halting and decrepit, and are offensive to people of retirement age who are healthy and active. As a rule, we should not use them for people under 80 (except occasionally in an ironic way in lighter stories to describe certain sports figures, entertainers etc. who are past their prime). Vital people in their 80s also may resent such descriptions; the type of person and the type of story must guide our choice of words. It will usually be sufficient to give the age or the age range (in her late 60s). If a generic term is unavoidable, **senior** seems to be the least offensive, but as with all generic terms involving people we must avoid any implication that it refers to a homogeneous class. This is another reason to avoid such long and pretentious terms as octogenarian.

ages

Use figures for ages under 10 if they are used as a descriptive label after a name, with no unit of measurement attached, as in Robert Black, 6. But follow the normal rules for numbers when stating a number of years, months etc. Write out six years old, six-year-old Robert Black.

Do not say someone has died at age 92. Say at 92. If you must assure readers that it is an age, write "at the age of 92."

aging (no e), but **ageism**.

agribusiness

Lower-case. This is an acceptable term if we are merely describing agriculture that uses the methods of big business, including large operations, specialization, heavy capitalization and integrated control and management of the various stages of production, distribution, manufacture and sales. We do not use it in a pejorative way in news stories as a way of implying obliquely that it is socially destructive or morally inferior to small farms. If that is the point, we make it directly in an opinion piece, or quote someone else as doing so.

AIDS

For acquired immune deficiency syndrome.

When reporting unfounded panic, discrimination or calls for repressive measures, we must include information of our own that the disease is not spread by even very close physical contact that is not sexual, and so is not a factor in a work or school environment. Avoid the implication that it is a homosexual disease. Preserve the distinction between those who have tested positive for the presence of antibodies (indicating exposure) and those who have actually developed symptoms of the disease. However, note that the distinction has been blurred. Because of new treatments such as drug cocktails, many who are infected proceed from having very high viral loads (full-blown AIDS) back down to zero (virtually devoid of HIV, the human immunodeficiency virus) and up again. Some sources use the term HIV-AIDS as a single entity in which the severity can vary, much as it can with someone with heart disease.

Those with symptoms should be called people with AIDS, not sufferers or victims. If they are under active treatment, they may be called AIDS patients. Those who have tested positive but have no symptoms may be called carriers, an accepted medical term.

AIDS, named a syndrome before its nature was fully explored and HIV was isolated, may properly be called a disease. Because of the new treatments, do not call it a necessarily fatal one. Preserve the distinction between a treatment, which lessens or eliminates one or more symptoms, or checks one of the diseases to which AIDS makes the body vulnerable, and a cure, which would rid the body of the AIDS virus, or neutralize it.

aircraft

Both singular and plural. If we are faced with the plural possessive, the only possible choice is aircraft's, so reword to avoid.

Air-India

akimbo

The term has a specific meaning: "with hands on hips and elbows outward." Use it only in reference to arms, and only for that particular posture. It does not mean splayed or outstretched or flapping about.

Albania

Adjective and people: Albanian. Currency: lek. Capital: Tirana (not the local spelling, Tiranë).

Albania is one of the Balkan states (those on the Balkan Peninsula). It is on the Adriatic, bounded by Yugoslavia on the north and northeast and by Greece on the south and southeast. Most of the population of 3.4 million are rural, living on the narrow coastal plains. The interior is dominated by barren alps and forested foothills. Albania was an original member of the Warsaw Pact, but ended relations with the Soviet Union in 1961, formally withdrew from the pact in 1968, and ended its special relationship with China in 1977, but diplomatic overtures began with the death of General Enver Hoxha in 1985. The Stalinist one-party system began to crumble in late 1990, and public order suffered with the gradual breakdown of police and other state authority. An election in April of 1992 restored the legitimacy of parliament, which in July of that year outlawed the Communist Party.

A 1997 financial crisis caused by the collapse of fraudulent pyramid schemes led to a period of anarchy, the fall of the government and the election of the Socialist Party. In 1999, the Kosovo crisis that led to NATO air strikes on Yugoslav military targets set off a flood of refugees into Albania. Most were repatriated the same year. See Serbia.

Alert

This weather station on the northern tip of Ellesmere Island is the world's most northerly settlement (transient scientific ice stations aside). It is 833 kilometres from the North Pole.

alfresco

Prefer outdoor, or in the open air.

algae

It is plural. The singular is alga, the adjective is algal.

Alger, Horatio

Like Dr. Frankenstein, Alger is commonly confused with his creation: the poor boy who makes good, in such works as *Sink or Swim*, *Ragged Dick*, *Luck and Pluck*. Compare someone to "a Horatio Alger character" or some such, not to Alger himself.

Algeria

Adjective and people: Algerian. Currency: dinar. Capital: Algiers.

It is the second-largest country in Africa, after Sudan. Almost all its 32 million people, who are mostly Muslim Arabs and Berbers, live in the plain between the Atlas Mountains and the Mediterranean. Its other two regions are a narrow plain between Atlas ranges, and a large Saharan district in the south. Eight years of warfare between the French and the National Liberation Front (FLN) ended with Algeria's being declared independent in 1962. A military junta under Col. Houari Boumédienne overthrew the government in 1965, and a new constitution in 1976 officially created a one-party state. A bid to hold the country's first multiparty election was quashed by the army in late 1991, after the Islamic Salvation Front, a party seeking to create an Islamic state, won a large majority in the first round of voting. Years of civil war followed between the party's armed wing, the Islamic Salvation Army, and security forces, resulting in an estimated 100,000 deaths. The armed wing disbanded in 2000 after newly elected President Abdelaziz Bouteflika offered the rebels a general amnesty. Thousands accepted, but thousands more have continued to fight from mountain strongholds.

Algonquian

This is the largest of Canada's broad native language groups, covering more than 250,000 status Indians on reserves from the Atlantic to the Rockies, and many people in cities and in non-status settlements. It comprises several diverse languages, including the various dialects of Cree and Ojibway along with several other languages in Ontario and Quebec (Delaware, Montagnais, Naskapi, Ottawa, Potawatomi etc.) and the Mi'kmaq and Maliseet languages in the east. We should not imply that two Algonquian languages appear similar to anyone but a language scholar; they can be as different as French and Finnish. See native people.

Ali, Muhammad

alibi
A defence in which an accused person says he or she was elsewhere when the crime was committed. Do not use it to mean an excuse or some other proof of innocence.

Alitalia
The Italian state airline does not have the word Airlines in its name.

alkaloids
Not to be confused with alkali and alkaline metals. Alkaloids are narcotic poisons extracted from plants and fungi, which can be deadly or addictive. They are also useful medicines in smaller doses. They include morphine (which can be modified into heroin), codeine, cocaine, caffeine, nicotine, mescaline, quinine, reserpine, ephedrine, coniine and atropine. See drugs.

Allah
Allah is the Arabic word for God (to be precise, al means the, Lah means God), and English translations of the Koran refer not to Allah, but to God. As a rule, just as we translate the French *dieu*, we should translate Allah, unless it appears in a direct quote.

Where we leave it in the Arabic in expressions such as "Allahu al akbar," we offer an accompanying translation, usually in brackets: in this case, "God is great." There is a degree of flexibility in feature and opinion pieces where "Allah" is used for atmosphere or as a political statement, but be aware that many readers see the use of "Allah" in English stories as a subtle way of portraying Muslims as some unknowable, unfathomable Other. See Islam.

All-American
Two caps. An amateur athlete voted best in the United States at his or her event or position.

Allan Cup
Awarded to Canada's Senior A hockey champions. Its Junior A counterpart is the Memorial Cup.

Allan Gardens, Toronto.

All Blacks
The name of this New Zealand rugby team refers to the colour of its uniforms, not its players' skin.

alleged
The word alleged should be used liberally in crime stories as a participle (is alleged to have robbed), and as an adjective to describe a crime (the alleged fraud), but it comes too close to unfair labelling if it is used as an adjective with a class of felon (the alleged murderer said). In any other type of story, when someone other than the Crown is alleging anything other than a criminal offence, the word alleged offers no protection against defamation suits (the allegedly incompetent doctor). See courts.

Allegheny Mountains
This is also the spelling for the river, county and city in Pennsylvania. The mountains can be called the Alleghenies (an exception to our rule on plurals of proper names; see plurals). Note the different spelling of **Allegany** County in New York and Maryland, and **Alleghany** County in Virginia.

all in, exhausted.

allophone
We should explain that it means someone whose first language is neither French nor English. (When relevant, we should also specify that it applies only to people from immigrant

communities; the term is not used for Indians and Inuit.) We should also confine it to stories dealing with language issues in Quebec. A person in Toronto or Vancouver who speaks Chinese should not be described as an allophone, except perhaps in quoting the Official Languages Commissioner. Even in Quebec, when speaking of an individual we prefer such specific descriptions as Italian-speaking, using allophone as a general term encompassing several or all immigrant groups. See anglophone.

all-out

all right (never alright).

all-round, an all-round athlete.

all-star

Use upper-case for baseball's All-Star Game, a proper name, but not for those in other sports.

al-Qaeda

No italics for this Arabic name. The organization was founded in the late 1980s by Saudi-born Osama bin Laden, to bring together Arabs who had fought the Soviet occupation of Afghanistan. It has been described as an international network of loosely related groups of Islamic militants. "Al" means the; "qaeda" means base, referring to a rule or principle from which other concepts are derived.

See Sept. 11, 2001.

alternate and alternative

As adjectives, **alternate** means following by turns, or reciprocal (Toronto and Vancouver are the alternate hosts of the Grey Cup game), while **alternative** involves a choice or a replacement (the caterer offered an alternative menu for the wedding; we have no alternative but to hire her). However, usage dictates that in stories about conventions etc.

we allow the term alternate delegate and the noun alternate. Strictly speaking, alternative refers to one of two mutually exclusive options. If there are more than two ways to go, prefer option, course of action, plan, recommendation.

Aluminum Co. of Canada Ltd.

Controlled by Alcan **Aluminium** Ltd.

alumni

It is the masculine plural, also used in general references to graduates of both sexes (it literally means foster children). The masculine singular is alumnus. The feminine forms, appropriate when only women graduates are being referred to, are alumna, alumnae.

Alzheimer's disease

But note that the organization is the Alzheimer Society of Canada.

a.m.

Means before noon. Write 6:30 a.m., but never add the redundant "in the morning." If the morning angle is already established by the context, replace a.m. with o'clock, or simply use the figure (at 6:30). See numbers, time elements.

America

America is another term for the Americas, the Western Hemisphere, the New World. It comprises North, Central and South America. The habit of many residents of the United States of referring to their country as America is at least mildly resented by most of their neighbours, particularly by those in Latin America but also by many Canadians. Some regard it as a relatively harmless inaccuracy, but others see it as a manifestation of that most insidious aspect of U.S. "cultural imperialism": its unconscious presumption.

The term American is acceptable (see American), but outside direct quotes do not use America to refer to the United States.

American

Acceptable as a noun, meaning a citizen of the United States. Acceptable as an adjective describing people and things (an American lawyer, an American car), but in more formal references involving the government or the national identity, the adjective U.S. is preferred, as in the U.S. embassy, U.S. ships, the U.S. trade representative.

American Revolution, American War of Independence

Both are acceptable to describe the war of 1775 to 1783 that led to the U.S. colonies' independence from Britain. So are the terms War of American Independence and The Revolutionary War.

America's Cup, yachting, but **Americas Cup**, golf.

Amerindian, Amerind

These words were promoted for a time as short forms for American Indian, but did not catch on even among native people. Use American Indian in general references to describe the geographic race (see race). In specific references, say Indian, Inuk, native person etc. or, better still, use the name of the band or language group (a Sarcee, a Mi'kmaq, a Maya). See native people.

Amex

Upper and lower. Acceptable in second reference and in headlines for both the American Stock Exchange and American Express, provided the context makes it clear which is meant.

amoeba, amoebic dysentery

amok

among and between

Fowler dismisses as a superstition the notion that if more than two things are involved, the proper preposition is always among. If the things are acting severally and individually, the proper word is between, as in compromises between the 11 first ministers, in which each is negotiating with the other 10. If they are acting collectively, then the word we want is among, as in a conspiracy among the three criminals.

amorous

ampersand (&)

Use it in the names of companies and firms that have formally adopted it. It is also acceptable in the abbreviations R&B, R&D, R&R, which see. An ampersand between two words or names takes a space on each side, but one between two letters has no space.

Amtrak

(Not -track). Use this official nickname, not the formal National Railroad Passenger Corp. It began operations in 1971 in an attempt to stop the decline of U.S. rail passenger service. Its deficits, underwritten by Congress, had reached $906-million by 1981, when Ronald Reagan imposed a 20-per-cent budget cut for 1982. In 2003, the cumulative debt stood at $4-billion.

analog, analogue

In reference to computers, the spelling is analog. Reserve analogue for those rare, general occasions when you mean something that bears an analogy to something else.

anathema

ancillary

and

In sentences that contain a list of things, some of which are combinations in their own right, we must always check twice to make sure we have not left out an **and**, as we do in this sentence: The pamphlet stresses that smoking areas should be separate, enclosed and have their own ventilation systems. The sentence says the areas should be **be** two things and **have** one thing, and the first element requires an internal and: Smoking areas should be separate **and** enclosed and have their own ventilation systems. A common error.

Andorra

Adjective and people: Andorran. Currency: Andorran peseta and French franc. Capital: Andorra la Vella.

It is a "co-principality" of 465 square kilometres on the French-Spanish border in the eastern Pyrenees, with joint sovereignty exercised by the Bishop of Urgel (in Spain) and the president of France, through local representatives and on the advice of an elected General Council of the Valleys. The official language is Catalan (see Romance languages), but it is spoken by only 30 per cent of the population of 68,000. About 60 per cent speak Spanish, and about 8 per cent speak French.

anemia

anesthetic

anesthetist and anesthesiologist

In Canada and Britain, use anesthetist, meaning a physician who specializes in anesthesia. In the United States, such a physician is called an anesthesiologist, and the term anesthetist is used for someone without a medical degree who is trained to administer anesthetics. Preserve the distinction in U.S. stories, but explain.

aneurysm (not -ism).

It is a bulge or other defect in a blood vessel. The swelling alone can cause considerable damage if the affected vessel is in the brain. Bleeding from a burst aneurysm can kill quickly if it is in the brain, heart or aorta.

anglicize, anglophile, anglophobe, lower-case.

anglophone, lower-case.

In general, confine this term to stories about distinctions between English-speaking and French-speaking Canadians, particularly in Quebec. When other languages are involved, or in foreign stories, prefer the term English-speaking. For example, say that a northern community is part Cree and part English-speaking. See allophone.

Anglo-Saxon

This is not a synonym for white or Caucasian. It applies to only some residents of England or their descendants, and certainly not to those of Scotland, Ireland or Wales. See WASP.

Angola

Adjective and people: Angolan. Currency: kwanza. Capital: Luanda.

This former Portuguese colony, fully independent since 1975, is on the Atlantic in southern Africa, bounded by Zaire on the north and northeast, Zambia on the southeast and Namibia on the south. More than 90 per cent of its 12 million people are in various Bantu tribes, about 86 per cent of them are rural, and a majority are illiterate. Portuguese remains the official language.

A bitter civil war began with independence in 1975, pitting the Marxist government formed by the MPLA (Portuguese initials for Popular Movement for the Liberation of Angola), with Soviet and Cuban backing, against Jonas Savimbi's UNITA (National Union for the Total Independence of Angola), which was backed by the United States and South Africa. A truce in 1991 led to internationally supervised elections in September of 1992, but UNITA refused to accept its defeat in the voting and resumed the civil war. A 1994 peace accord between the government and UNITA led to a national unity government in 1997, but fighting began again in 1998. After Savimbi was shot in February of 2002, an April ceasefire finally ended the 27-year civil war, estimated to have killed one million people and displaced millions more.

animals

We generally use the pronoun **it** for animals, but he and she are permissible if the sex is known and is relevant, particularly for pets and zoo creatures that have been given human names.

animé (for Japanese animation)

No italics.

animism

To be strictly accurate, animism is the belief in a spirit or soul and in the existence of spiritual beings, and is considered the basis of all organized religions. The term animism is also widely used to describe a particular belief that natural forces, animals and possibly inanimate objects possess souls, and we may use it in this sense if the context is clear. If space permits, an explanation would help the reader.

Annex, the

Upper-case. This neighbourhood, annexed by Toronto in 1883, runs from Bloor Street north to the CPR tracks, between Avenue Road and Bathurst Street.

anniversary

Anniversaries must be counted in full years from the original date. Do not speak of a six-month anniversary.

anoint

Antarctica

The continent is roughly circular with two large indentations—a semicircular bite south of the Atlantic called the Weddell Sea, and a boomerang-shaped one south of New Zealand called the Ross Sea. The Ross Sea's McMurdo Sound gives its name to McMurdo Station on the Ross Ice Shelf, which is the largest of more than 30 permanent stations belonging to 10 countries. Several countries make territorial claims. There is some exposed rock on the coast, with some lichen, mosses and fungi, but the interior is permanently covered by an icecap that ranges up to 4,000 metres (14,000 feet) thick. Only the highest mountains, such as the Vinson Massif and Mounts Menzies, Sidley and Victor, peek through it. There are no animals, beyond birds and seals on the coast. Inland, the only life forms are some mites and microscopic organisms.

antennae and antennas

Use the plural antennae for insects, but antennas for TV and other aerials. See plurals.

anterior cruciate ligament

Frequently torn by athletes and others. Spell it out once high up in the story; ACL is fine otherwise.

anthems

O Canada is the national anthem. *God Save the Queen* is Canada's royal anthem.

anthrax

It is caused by a spore-forming bacterium (*Bacillus anthracis*), but is not itself a bacterium. Describe it as an infectious disease, primarily of grazing herbivores, such as cows and sheep, which eat or breathe in spores from the soil.

Humans who contract anthrax do so usually through contact with infected animals or animal products, 95 per cent of the time through the skin, though it is possible to be infected by inhaling spores or eating undercooked meat from infected animals. The spores use the body's defensive mechanism against itself, resulting in the explosive release of bacteria into the bloodstream, and the spread of toxins. Without vaccination or powerful antibiotics, the disease can be fatal.

anti

Use a hyphen after this prefix. Make an exception for antitrust, and for these words, most of which should be self-evident: antibiotic, antibody, Antichrist, anticlimax, anticlockwise, anticoagulant, anticyclone, antidepressant, antidote, antifreeze, antigen, antihistamine, antimacassar, antipasto (the anti means before), antipathy, antiperspirant, antiseptic and a few scientific terms (antimatter, antinucleon, antiparticle, antiserum, antitoxin).

anti-abortion

But never anti-abortionist. See abortion.

Anti-Ballistic Missile Treaty, ABM Treaty

The landmark nuclear-deterrence pact was implemented in 1972 to provide nuclear stability between the United States and the Soviet Union. It expired in June, 2002, six months after U.S. President George W. Bush announced his country would unilaterally withdraw from the treaty so that it might work on a national shield against missile attack, a step forbidden by the treaty.

Anticosti Island

Antigua and Barbuda

Adjective and people: depending on island, Antiguan or Barbudan. Currency: East Caribbean dollar. Capital: St. John's.

This two-island Caribbean country became fully independent from Britain in 1981, after 14 years as an associated state, and is a member of the Commonwealth. Antigua is the largest and most developed of the Leeward Islands, which mark the northeastern boundary of the Caribbean. Both islands, of volcanic origin and low-lying, are among the driest in the West Indies, and their beaches are their greatest resource. The population of 68,000 is heavily dependent on tourism.

any more, any place, any time

anyone and any one

The pronoun is anyone: He might pick anyone. But note that two words are required for He might pick any one of us.

Apalachin, N.Y.

APEC

Asia-Pacific Economic Co-operation. It is not a treaty among countries but a regular meeting, known as a summit, of "economies" – a vague word designed to enable China and

Taiwan to sit at the same table, and to let Hong Kong have a seat separate from China. The group's members are Australia, Brunei, Canada, Chile, China, Hong Kong, Indonesia, Japan, Malaysia, Mexico, New Zealand, Papua New Guinea, Peru, the Philippines, Russia, Singapore, South Korea, Taiwan, Thailand, the United States and Vietnam.

apocalypse
Lower-case for a prophecy or revelation, upper-case when referring to Revelation, the last book of the New Testament. See Four Horsemen.

Apostles
Make Apostle upper-case when referring to the 12 disciples closest to Jesus, given the mission of spreading the Gospel, and three others: Matthias, who replaced Judas, and Paul and Barnabas in recognition of their missionary work. (The word comes from the Greek for "person sent.") Write out the figure in the term Twelve Apostles. Use lower case for later great missionaries described by the Church as apostles, such as Augustine among the English, Patrick of Ireland, Dénis among the French and Boniface among the Germans.

apostrophe
See possessives, punctuation.

Appalachia
A term coined in 1960 by Eastern U.S. governors seeking federal aid for the poor mountainous regions of their states. It now covers 16 million inhabitants of parts of 13 states.

Appalachian Mountains
Not a mountain range, but an entire mountain system stretching from Newfoundland to central Alabama. Includes the Newfoundland Long Range Mountains, Gaspé's Notre Dame and Shickshock ranges, the Green, White and Taconic systems of New England, New York's Catskills, the Lehigh and South ranges, and the Blue Ridge and the Great Smoky Mountains. See mountains.

appall

appraise and apprise
Appraise means to evaluate, usually formally in preparation for a sale or loan, and usually for a fee. In other circumstances, evaluate is better.
Apprise means to notify or inform. Except in direct quotes, it should be avoided as awkward and dated.

approbation and opprobrium
Approbation, from the same root as approve, means approval or praise, but is often misused to mean criticism, disapproval, hatred. Since so many readers also ascribe the wrong meaning to it, it is misleading even when used correctly. It has been confused with opprobrium, which is also now too obscure to be useful in news stories.

approximate
Do not stick Approximately or About in front of an exact number at the start of a sentence. This device to avoid starting a sentence with a figure is foolish with any but rounded-off numbers. See numbers.
Since approximate means close, the expression very approximate makes no sense at all when used to mean far from exact, in such expressions as "these figures are very approximate." The correct sense is "far from approximate," but this would be confusing to readers. Find another term, such as inexact, very rough.

April Fool's Day
From All Fools' Day. Use lower case, April fool, for the victim of a joke on April 1.

aqu-
In English spelling, if it has to do with water or eagles it is spelled aqu,

as in aquarium, aquiline. Otherwise, the spelling is acqu- (acquaint, acquit etc.). However, proper names should always be checked (Aquinas, Aquitaine).

Arab

The general term covers not only the indigenous peoples of the countries of the Arabian Peninsula (Saudi Arabia, Oman, Yemen, the United Arab Emirates, Qatar and Kuwait), but also all those who speak Arabic and identify with the Arab culture. This takes in Algeria, Egypt, Iraq (but not Iran), Jordan, Lebanon, Libya, Morocco, Sudan, Syria and Tunisia. Speak of the Arab culture and the Arabic language in these countries, but be careful not to give the impression we are speaking of Saudi Arabia if this is not the case. Prefer such specific adjectives as Iraqi, Qatari. The overwhelming majority of Arabs are Muslim, but not all (the Christian Arab population ranges from 5 per cent of Palestinians to about 20 per cent of Lebanese). By the same token, most Muslims are not Arabs; neither are the Iranians, Pakistanis and Turks.

Arabic names

Globe style is to retain the al and el in the names of people, as well as in geographic names. This includes second reference: Farouk al-Sharaa would be Mr. al-Sharaa. For names in use in English, use the person's preferred style if known. For names we transliterate from Arabic, our default style is to lower-case the a and e in al- and el-.

The word we transliterate from the Arabic as Abdul or Abdel is not a name in itself. It means slave of, and always appears in combination with an expression meaning God. Examples include Abdulla (Slave of God), Abdul Rahim (Slave of the Merciful One), Abdul Majid (Slave of the Glorious One), Abdul Latif (Slave of

the Kind One), Abdul Nasser (Slave of the Victorious One). Our usual style of using only one given name doesn't apply here; we can't refer to someone as simply Abdul. If it is a surname, we can't say simply Mr. Rahim in second reference. (Often the temptation is removed because the person has hyphenated the transliteration or even rendered it as one word.)

Two others that must always appear in combination are Abu (father of) and Umm (mother of). They are most frequently used in friendly and casual greetings, but are also used as *noms de guerre*, as in Abu Ammar (Yasser Arafat's, meaning father of the builder), Abu Nidal (father of the struggle), and in surnames, as in Hassan Abu Zeidan . . . Mr. Abu Zeidan. Leaving off the Abu in second reference would be akin to leaving off the Mac/Mc or O' from a Scottish or Irish name.

These rules often do not apply in Muslim countries that are not Arabic, such as Pakistan and Afghanistan. The Arabic names adopted there for religious reasons have often been altered over the centuries.

Aransas Bay

In Texas. It is the wintering area of whooping cranes.

Ararat, Mount

arbitrager

It originally meant one who trades in the same stock or currency on more than one market to take advantage of price differences. However, it has been extended to cover any highly speculative trader who rides market volatility, especially in an atmosphere of takeover rumours, and holds stocks for very short periods, sometimes for a few days but sometimes for a few minutes, and makes full use of margin trading and short selling. Some deal not in stocks but in market futures, in effect betting on how a market will perform during a given day or even hour.

arbour
But note that all variants drop the u.

Arc de Triomphe
Does not need italics.

arch-enemy

archeology

Arctic Circle
It is the most southerly band at which there is at least one day when the sun does not rise, and one on which it does not set. At a place directly on the circle, such as Repulse Bay, Nunavut, there is no sunrise on Dec. 22 (in a normal year) and no sunset on June 21. Farther north, the periods of winter dark and summer midnight sun are longer. The exact latitude of the circle is 66 degrees 32 minutes north.

ardour

area
Do not use it standing alone as an adjective, as in Area lawyer disbarred. National readers must know what city is referred to.

Argentia, Nfld.

Argentina
Adjective and people: Argentine. Currency: peso. Capital: Buenos Aires.
It is the second-largest country in South America, after Brazil, occupying almost all of the southern portion of the continent, with the exception of the narrow Chilean strip. However, Chile owns a greater share than Argentina of Tierra del Fuego (which see). Argentina is in economic trouble, but has too sophisticated an industrial base to be classed as Third World. It is unusual among South American countries in that its population of 38 million is up to 98 per cent white, and the country has few symbols of aboriginal heritage. Yet more than a dozen aboriginal groups survive in the hot, humid Chaco region of the north, in the dry northwest, along the Andean cordillera and in Patagonia. Estimates of total numbers range between 460,000 and 1.5 million in a country of 35 million, but analysts say figures are hard to compile because many Indians are forced to move from their homelands to city slums. Many aboriginal Argentines are classed as mestizo, of mixed Guarani and white origin, but there are Quechua speakers in the far northwest, and other language groups in Patagonia.

After years of military rule, the country returned to civilian rule in December, 1983. A new constitution was adopted in August, 1994.

The Falkland Islands, administered by Britain as an overseas territory but claimed by the Argentines (who call them the Malvinas), sit off the east coast of southern Argentina. There are two main islands – West Falkland and East Falkland – and 200 smaller islands. The capital, Stanley, is on East Falkland. The islands have a population of 3,000 and, though the main activity used to be sheep raising, it is now fishing, in particular for squid. On April 2, 1982, Argentina invaded the islands. Britain sent ships to do battle, and Argentina surrendered on June 14 of that year. Our style is to call them the Falkland Islands, not Falkland Islands/Malvinas, as some sources do.

arguably
A buzzword that is innocent enough if used in the sense of "a case can be made for saying," but in news stories it is often used improperly to mean "some say" or "many are of the opinion," to gloss over the fact that the

story does not specify whom. Just as good news writers do not use such fuzzy attributions as "people say" or "rumour has it," they do not use "arguably" to accomplish the same thing.

Argyll and argyle

It is the **Argyll** and Sutherland Highlanders of Canada, the Argylls. However, the diamond pattern on sweaters and socks is spelled **argyle**.

Armenia

Adjective and people: Armenian. Currency: dram. Capital: Yerevan.

A former Soviet republic bordering on Turkey, Iran, Georgia and Azerbaijan, it became independent with the collapse of the Soviet Union in 1991. Its riots and strikes (beginning in 1988) and eventually open warfare with Azerbaijan over Nagorno-Karabakh, populated largely by Armenians, can be said to have hastened the Soviet collapse, revealing as it did that the Soviet military was ill-equipped to deal with civil uprisings. In 1994, having wrested control of Nagorno-Karabakh from Azerbaijan, Armenia forced a ceasefire on that country, but tensions remain. Hopes for a peace agreement between the two nations in 1999 were derailed when gunmen entered Armenia's parliament and killed eight politicians, including prime minister Vazgen Sarkisian.

It became an independent republic in 1918 after Turkey's defeat in the First World War, was occupied by the Red Army in 1920, was folded into the Soviet Union along with Georgia and Azerbaijan as part of the Trans-Caucasian Soviet Socialist Republic in 1922 and became a separate Soviet republic (the smallest) in 1936. Its population of 3.7 million is 90 per cent Armenian, with small Azeri, Russian and Kurd minorities. Mainly mountainous and forested, it produces copper and molybdenum as well as cotton, grains and silk.

The Armenian language, written in an alphabet of 38 characters, is a separate division of the Indo-European family.

The Armenian massacres (note plural; the main massacres were committed in 1895, 1909 and 1915) may be referred to as genocide. Altogether, the Turks killed more than a million Armenians, sent others to die of thirst and starvation in the desert and forced others to flee abroad. Eventually, only 100,000 were left in the area.

See Soviet Union.

armour

But drop the u in **armorial** and **armorist**.

Acceptable for referring to tanks, and also other military armoured vehicles, either wheeled or tracked, when they are acting as a group with tanks, including personnel carriers, reconnaissance vehicles and self-propelled artillery.

Do not assume armour is steel. The British Chobham dissipates kinetic energy more effectively with laminated steel, aluminum, fabric and ceramics.

Body armour is usually fabric. It should not be referred to simply as armour.

armouries

In Canada, this is widely used as both the singular and plural form. Worth preserving. However, note certain proper names such as Moss Park Armoury.

arms, see guns and calibres.

arrant and errant

Arrant means notoriously bad (an arrant scoundrel) or unmitigated (arrant nonsense). **Errant** means wandering, itinerant (a knight errant). Neither means "in error," although errant occasionally carries such a meaning in the sense of straying from the correct course.

arrondissement

In referring to the Parisian neighbourhoods, use the numeral and lower-case arrondissement, without italics. E.g., the 3rd arrondissement, and the 3rd on second reference. For Quebec cities that have arrondissements, the English translation is ward.

art deco

Takes a hyphen as an adjective (an art-deco building). This type of spare, geometrical design, a break from Victorian fussiness, takes its name from the Paris Exhibition of Decorative Arts in 1925. It had a strong influence through the Thirties.

Arthabaska, Que.

Aruba, see Netherlands.

as

In the construction "Light as it was, the minister could not lift his portfolio," the word "as" means "though." Do not write, "As light as it was."

asdic

Lower-case. This name for sonar, used by British and Commonwealth forces during the Second World War, is an acronym for Allied Submarine Detection Investigation Committee. See sonar.

ASEAN

The Association of Southeast Asian Nations, a regional group led by a secretary-general and having 10 members: Brunei, Cambodia, Indonesia, Laos, Malaysia, Myanmar, the Philippines, Singapore, Thailand and Vietnam. In 2001, it signed an agreement with China to integrate their economies and create the world's largest free-trade area (roughly 500 million ASEAN consumers and one billion Chinese consumers) within a decade. See APEC.

Asia

Its traditional boundaries with Europe are the Ural Mountains and River, the Black and Caspian Seas, the Caucasus Mountains, the Bosporus-Dardanelles passage and the eastern end of the Mediterranean. However, most people today would not think of Russia east of the Urals as being part of Asia, and we should specify its inclusion if that is our intent in a particular reference. Likewise, Asia officially includes the countries of the Middle East, including Israel, but we must make a point of specifying that a reference to Asia includes them when this is the case. Asia is separated from Africa by the Suez Canal and the Red Sea. In the east and south, Asia is also taken to include the islands of Japan, Indonesia and the Philippines. The term **South Asia** means India, Pakistan, Bangladesh, Sri Lanka, Bhutan and Nepal, but we must be sure that readers are aware of this. (See East Indian, native people.)

Asians include Inuit, Israelis, Indians, Mongolian herders, oil sheiks, Thai forest people and Korean industrialists – such a variety, in fact, that for all practical purposes they defy being usefully lumped together under the single word "Asian," except in stories planetary in scope. It is somewhat akin to calling someone from anywhere in the Americas an American: inadequate, misleading and, to some, insulting.

If we can't use a specific word (Chinese, Vietnamese, Pakistani, Sri Lankan etc.) when referring to neighbourhoods, stores, gangs etc., the two most common general adjectives are Oriental and South Asian. It might also be relevant to use Southeast Asian to refer to Vietnam, Laos, Cambodia, Thailand, Myanmar (Burma), Malaysia and Singapore. On their own, Vietnam, Laos and Cambodia take the adjective Indochinese.

The term **Asia Minor** applies not to the entire Mideast but to the peninsula that makes up most of present-day Turkey. It is surrounded on three sides by the Black Sea, the Bosporus-Dardanelles passage and the Mediterranean, and extends eastward as far as the upper Euphrates.

as long as, so long as

When the meaning is during the whole time that, for a lengthy period, use as long as. They were happy as long as it lasted. You can stay as long as you like here.

When the meaning is "provided that," both as long as and so long as are correct. She liked new clothes as long as they fit. The box will be fine here so long as nobody upsets it.

Assisi, St. Francis of

assist, assistance

Help is usually better.

Assumption

Use upper case for the official Roman Catholic dogma that the Virgin Mary was "assumed into heaven body and soul" at the end of her earthly life, and for the feast day marking this, Aug. 15. The dogma was officially declared in 1950 by Pius XII.

astrology

We should not make even the slightest implication in a news story that The Globe or any of its staff believe in astrology. See zodiac.

Astroturf, a trade name.

As a generic term, use artificial turf, not simply turf, in first reference.

Athabasca

This is the spelling for the federal and Saskatchewan ridings, the Alberta riding Athabasca-Lac la Biche, and the town, lake, river, oil sands. But note Arthabaska, Que.

Athapaskan

Note this spelling for the large, diverse language group covering Indian peoples across the Northwest speaking many languages. It should not be referred to as a language itself. See native people.

athlete's foot, singular.

Atlantic Ocean

The word Ocean can often be omitted. Upper-case North Atlantic and South Atlantic. Note the lower case in transatlantic.

Atlantic provinces

New Brunswick, Nova Scotia, Prince Edward Island and Newfoundland and Labrador. The first three are the Maritime provinces, the Maritimes.

ATM, see ABM.

at the present time

Say now, or at present.

Attlee, Clement

In references after December, 1955, Lord Attlee.

attorney-at-law

audiotape

Augean stables

auger and augur

For drilling, it's **auger**. **Augur**, as a verb, means foretell, prophesy or be an omen of (it augurs well). In its rare use as a noun, it means one who foretells.

aureomycin, lower-case.

Australia

Adjective and people: Australian. Currency: Australian dollar. Capital: Canberra.

The Commonwealth of Australia, with a population of 20 million, comprises six states (New South Wales, Queensland, Tasmania, South Australia, Victoria and Western Australia) and two territories (Northern Territory and the Australian Capital Territory). Australia also has jurisdiction over several islands, notably Christmas, Norfolk and the Cocos (Keeling) Islands, and about 12 million square kilometres of Antarctica. Its aboriginal people, properly called Aborigines, are considered a distinct race, separate from the Negroid. See race. We do not use the term Aussie in straight news stories.

Note the spelling of the Australian Labor Party. In a referendum on Nov. 6, 1999, 54.87 per cent of voting Australians said the country should remain a monarchy rather than become a republic with a president chosen by the Parliament.

Austria

Adjective and people: Austrian. Currency: euro (had been the schilling). Capital: Vienna.

Vienna (Wien) is in the eastern lowlands on the Danube; the three other physical regions are the Austrian Alps in the west (on the borders of Germany, Switzerland and Italy), a valley-scarred northern plateau between the Alps and the Danube, and a southern granite plateau. The country is almost 40 per cent forest, and iron is the most important mineral resource. Austria is a federal republic of nine provinces, with a population of about 8.3 million. In historical references, refer to Austria or the Austrian Empire until 1867, when it merged with the Kingdom of Hungary to form Austria-Hungary, also known as the Austro-Hungarian Empire. Speak of Austria again after the First World War, when the empire was dissolved. Austria joined the European Union in 1995.

The European Union imposed mild diplomatic sanctions on Austria in February of 2000, after the xenophobic Freedom Party, whose leader Joerg Haider had expressed admiration for some of Adolf Hitler's policies, was included in the national government. Haider was succeeded as leader in May by his deputy chancellor; sanctions were lifted in September.

author, never a verb.

auto pact

This is acceptable in all references to the agreement signed in January of 1965 removing tariffs and other barriers to trade in motor vehicles and parts between Canada and the United States. It should not be called free trade, because it included controls to safeguard Canadian content. In response to a challenge from Japan and the European Union, the World Trade Organization ruled in 2000 that the agreement violated the WTO's rules. Canada dissolved the auto pact on Feb. 19, 2001.

auxiliary

averse, see adverse.

awesome

Confine it to things that are truly awe-inspiring.

axe

Axel, in figure skating.

aye

Aye is the spelling both of the word meaning yes (the ayes have it) and of the word meaning always (Ready, aye ready). Both words are archaic.

AZA

for Aleph Zadik Aleph, the junior B'nai Brith.

Azerbaijan

Adjective: Azerbaijani. People: Azeri (for the dominant ethnic group) or Azerbaijani. Currency: manat. Capital: Baku.

A former Soviet republic bordering on Russia, Georgia, Armenia and Iran, it gained independence with the disintegration of the Soviet Union in 1991. Use Azerbaijani to refer to the country and also to the overall population of eight million, but Azeri to distinguish the majority (about 80 per cent, Shia Muslims speaking a Turkic language) from other ethnic groups, mainly Russian and Armenian.

(There are also about eight million Azeris across the border in Iran, found throughout the country as a powerful middle class but concentrated in two northern Iranian provinces called Eastern and Western Azerbaijan. Family links make the border between Azerbaijan and Iran a fairly porous one.)

Azerbaijan was occupied by the Red Army in 1920 and made part of the Trans-Caucasian Soviet Socialist Republic in 1922, along with Armenia and Georgia. When they were split into separate Soviet republics in 1936, Azerbaijan was given Nagorno-Karabakh, largely inhabited by Armenians. Armenia's campaign to regain the enclave erupted into strikes and riots in 1988 and quickly into open warfare. By the ceasefire of 1994, Azerbaijan had lost control of Nagorno-Karabakh and other territory to Armenia, and was forced to deal with an estimated 800,000 domestic refugees displaced by the fighting.

B

BA

For bachelor of arts. When spelled out, lower-case.

b and e

Do not use this police-blotter jargon for breaking and entering (not break and enter). Note that a break-in is not necessarily a burglary, which refers to entering an occupied dwelling by night.

baby boom, baby boomer

The baby boom in Canada lasted from 1947 to 1966, as the end of the Second World War and a renewed economic optimism led an unusually large number of couples to start families. Although the first wave of children did well economically, opportunities were scarcer for the second wave, born from 1960 to 1966, who are referred to as Generation X (or Generation X-ers, Gen X-ers) after Douglas Coupland's novel *Generation X*.

Note that the U.S. baby boom started and ended earlier, lasting from 1946 to 1964. As demographer David Foot explains, more of the Americans' war effort was in the Pacific, and the Pacific war wound down sooner than the European war, though the European surrender came first. U.S. troops were brought home earlier and began producing babies sooner.

babysit, babysitter

A babysitter looks after children for brief periods in the absence of their parents. It is inappropriate to use the verb or the noun in reference to the mother or father.

baccalaureate

backbencher

Backbench (adjective), the **back benches**.

backstroke

backup. The verb is **back up**.

backward (no s).

backyard

bacteria, viruses

There are major differences between the two. For example, antibiotics are effective only against bacteria. Do not confuse either of them with other disease-causing invaders, including parasites (such as the cyclosporae that contaminate berries), rickettsiae (micro-organisms that have some of the characteristics of both bacteria and viruses and are responsible for such diseases as typhus and Rocky Mountain spotted fever) and prions (invasive proteins such as the one that causes mad-cow disease).

The noun bacteria always takes a plural verb. The singular is bacterium.

Bactrian camel

Upper-case, for the ancient country Bactria. These are the ones with two humps. The Arabian camel, also called a dromedary, has one.

Baden-Powell, Robert

Later, Lord Baden-Powell. Founder of the Boy Scouts and, with his sister, Agnes Baden-Powell, the Girl Guides.

Baedeker, Karl

Author of guidebooks.

Baghdad

Baha'i

The Baha'i faith, a Baha'i, several Baha'is.

Bahamas, the

Adjective and people: Bahamian. Currency: Bahamian dollar. Capital: Nassau.

This commonwealth of about 700 islands and more than 1,000 islets (called cays) is in the Atlantic off Florida. The islands are too far north to be called Caribbean, but can be numbered among the West Indies. (See West Indies.) Half the population of about 305,000 lives in Nassau or elsewhere on the island of New Providence. Next in population are Grand Bahama (about 35,000) and Eleuthera (about 11,000). Britain granted the Bahamas internal self-government in 1964, and full independence as a member of the Commonwealth in 1973.

Bahrain

Adjective and people: Bahraini(s). Currency: dinar. Capital: Manama.

Bahrain is an island group in the Persian Gulf, between the Qatar peninsula and the Saudi coast, to which it is joined by a causeway. (There are also causeways between major islands.) The economy is heavily dependent on oil production and refining, and has made itself an international banking centre. Bahrain, an emirate under a dynasty in power since 1782, was a British protectorate until 1971. In 2001, voters approved a democratization program in a

referendum. In February, 2002, Sheik Hamad bin Isa al-Khalifa, who had been emir, proclaimed himself king and proclaimed Bahrain a constitutional monarchy called the Kingdom of Bahrain. In a municipal election held that May, and in a national parliamentary election that October, Bahraini women were for the first time permitted to vote and run for office. The population of about 650,000 is mostly Muslim Arab.

bailiff

bailiwick

bakeapples

One word. These acidic yellow berries from the bogs of Newfoundland and Labrador are used for pies and jam. Elsewhere, they are called cloudberries.

bakelite

balaclava

Use lower case for the woollen head covering with holes for eyes and mouth. In upper case, and with a k, Balaklava refers to the Crimean port on the Black Sea.

balance of payments, trade

The **balance of payments** involves all of a country's financial transactions with the rest of the world. It includes trade in goods and services, capital movements and unilateral transfers. The **balance of trade**, which Statistics Canada reports as the balance of merchandise trade, measures the difference between exports and imports of goods only.

The **balance of payments**, the broader measure, includes both current and capital accounts. The current account incorporates the balance of trade plus the balance on imports and exports of services, travel spending, interest and dividend payments, and such transfers as the funds of immigrants and emigrants. The capital account, which measures flows of investment capital, includes purchases of stocks and bonds (portfolio investment) and purchases of real assets such as a company or real estate (direct investment). By definition, the current and capital account balances must add up to zero: If Canada spends more for foreign items than foreigners spend for Canadian items, we have a current-account deficit; to pay the difference, we must borrow from abroad, which creates a capital-account surplus.

bale, bail

A bale of hay, but use bail for most other senses: bail out a boat, bail out of an airplane.

Balkans

These are the countries of the Balkan Peninsula, which is enclosed by the Black, Aegean, Mediterranean, Ionian and Adriatic seas, and extends northward to the Danube and Sava rivers. They are Albania, Bosnia-Herzegovina, Bulgaria, Croatia, Greece, Macedonia, Romania, Slovenia, Serbia and Montenegro and the small European portion of Turkey.

ball game

ballistic missile, see missiles.

ballpark, ballplayer

ballpoint pen

baloney, as in malarkey.
The meat is **bologna**.

Baltic

Lithuania, Latvia and Estonia may be called the Baltic republics, but should not be called "the Baltics" (a misconceived parallel with the Balkans).

Band-Aid

A trade name. The generic term is adhesive bandage. For guidelines on use, see trade names.

Bangladesh

Adjective and people: Bangladeshi. Currency: taka. Capital: Dhaka.

A majority of the people are Muslim Bengalis, but not all, so we use the more inclusive term Bangladeshi, referring to the country. It is the former East Pakistan, on the Bay of Bengal in the northeastern corner of the Indian subcontinent. Its demands for autonomy under Mujibur Rahman's Awami League brought an invasion by West Pakistani forces in 1971, and they were overrun in turn by an Indian invasion later that year. The republic set up in 1972 has had a series of coups and two presidential assassinations (Mujibur Rahman in 1975 and Ziaur Rahman in 1981). It has 140 million people in an area slightly larger than Canada's Maritimes, and most of the country is subject to severe monsoon flooding, since it lies in the low Ganges-Brahmaputra Delta.

bank book, bank card

Bank for International Settlements

Often called the central bankers' central bank, acting as their clearing agency in foreign exchange markets, it is based in Basel and holds routine meetings of central bank governors, including that of the Bank of Canada. Formally, members hold shares in the BIS, which makes a profit and pays dividends. For technical reasons, the U.S. Federal Reserve Board is not a member, the U.S. shares being owned by Citigroup, but a senior Fed official attends the meetings.

Bank of Canada

Canada's central bank acts as the federal government's banker and fiscal agent, managing the national debt, regulating the amount of currency and chartered bank deposits, and setting the bank rate, which both influences and reflects market interest rates. (The bank rate is set each Thursday, at one-quarter of a percentage point above the rate for three-month treasury bills.) It issues and redeems federal securities and pays the interest they earn, issues paper currency and acts for the government on foreign-exchange markets to prevent wide fluctuations in the value of the dollar. It is wholly owned by the government and run by a governor and deputy governor and by 12 directors appointed by the finance minister. (The directors, appointed for three-year terms, name the governor and deputy for seven-year terms.) The deputy minister of finance sits in as a non-voting member of the board. In references to a specific governor, upper-case Governor.

The bank began operations (as a private institution) in 1935, in the depths of the Depression, with instructions to regulate credit and currency "in the best interests of the economic life of the nation." Its seven governors have been G. F. Towers (until 1955), James Coyne (who resigned in 1961 in a dispute with the Diefenbaker government), Louis Rasminsky, Gerald Bouey, John Crow, Gordon Thiessen and David Dodge. The Coyne affair produced an amendment to the Bank Act requiring that the central bank obey government directives on monetary policy.

banks
Treat commercial banks as you would other companies. Do not put "the" in front of the bank's name if it is not part of the official name. For example, Bank of Montreal has reported a profit; second reference is BMO. Royal Bank of Canada has hired new staff; second reference is RBC. The article stays with non-

commercial banks: the Bank of Canada, the World Bank, the Bank for International Settlements.

bannock
This is the basic bread, originally unleavened, made by trappers and settlers. The name is Scottish.

Baptist
This is one of the most diverse of the Protestant denominations, and we must not speak of the Baptist Church as a single entity with homogeneous doctrines. Specify the particular church or sect when this is known. All Baptists believe in adult baptism by total immersion, and most share a strong revivalist tradition.

Barbados
Adjective and people: Barbadian. Currency: Barbados dollar. Capital: Bridgetown.
Never "the Barbados." It is in the West Indies and one of the Lesser Antilles. It is in the Atlantic, but may be called a Caribbean island. Occupied by the British since 1627, it was given internal self-government in 1961 and became a sovereign member of the Commonwealth in 1966. Some oil and natural gas reserves were discovered in the late 1970s. Barbados, which, like Canada, is a monarchy with a governor-general, is considered the most British of the West Indies, with a literacy rate of 97 per cent. About 95 per cent of the population of 270,000 is of African descent.

barbecue

barbiturate, see drugs.

Barclays Bank

bar mitzvah, bat mitzvah
Bar for boys, bat for girls.

barrels
See oil.

barrels a day

Use b/d in subsequent references only in technical or tabular material with many repetitions.

Barren Grounds, Barren Lands, the Barrens

The huge area bounded by Hudson Bay on the east, Great Bear and Great Slave lakes on the west, the Arctic Ocean on the north and roughly the 59th parallel on the south. It is not barren. It is a rolling, rock-studded plain carpeted with short grass and several flowering plants. There are also forest areas in the south and trees along river valleys, and so it should not be described as entirely tundra. See tundra.

Basel, Switzerland (not Basle).

basilica and cathedral

Lower-case, except with a proper name. Basilica is both a type of building (a rectangular design in which two rows of columns create side aisles with high windows) and a canonical title bestowed on important Roman Catholic churches. It is not to be confused with a cathedral, of which there is only one in each diocese. The cathedral (which may be of the basilica design but may also be more modest) is where a bishop has his official seat or throne, his *cathedra*.

basis point

A 100th of a percentage point or of a cent. It should be explained or translated in copy. In second reference and in headlines, the word points is sufficient.

battalion

battleship, warship

A warship is not necessarily a battleship. A battleship is the most heavily armed and armoured class of warship, and until the advent of aircraft carriers and nuclear attack

submarines was the biggest and most feared of all ships of war. No one has built a battleship since the mid-1940s.

BC

No periods for "before Christ." We do use periods in the initials for British Columbia, but note an exception, BC Rail.

BCE Inc.

The principal subsidiary of the Montreal-based communications giant is Bell Canada, the country's largest telephone company, which provides telephone, mobile telephone, satellite television and Internet services, and whose holdings include the Internet portal Sympatico Inc. BCE's other major holdings are a 65-per-cent stake in electronic commerce company BCE Emergis and a 68.5-per-cent stake in Bell Globemedia, owner of The Globe and Mail, the CTV television network and several specialty channels. Bell Globemedia has a 15-per-cent stake in Maple Leaf Sports and Entertainment Ltd., whose assets include the Toronto Maple Leafs hockey club, the Toronto Raptors basketball franchise and the Air Canada Centre in Toronto. The newspaper, which BCE purchased in 2000 from Thomson Corp., is published by Bell Globemedia Publishing Inc.

Stories about BCE or its companies should inform readers about the Globe connection.

Beaches, the

A Toronto neighbourhood. We do not use the singular, the Beach, but there is no need to change quotes from neighbourhood old-timers who do so. It runs from Woodbine Avenue east to Victoria Park Avenue. Its northern boundary is open to argument, but Kingston Road is widely accepted.

bedlam

There was no place called Bedlam, except colloquially. The word derived from "Bethlehem" in the Hospital of St. Mary of Bethlehem in London, England, a hospital for the insane.

Bedouin

These are nomadic Arabs of the Arabian and Syrian deserts and the Sahara. They are Muslim, but also retain many pre-Islamic beliefs and ancient tribal hierarchies. See Arab.

beefeater

Lower-case. This nickname is applied to two groups who wear similar costumes—the Yeomen of the Guard and the warders of the Tower of London. The Yeomen, veteran soldiers who appear on state occasions as bodyguards of the sovereign, are Britain's oldest military unit. Their commander is usually a peer.

bees, killer

The individual stings of these African bees, which escaped from a Brazilian research centre in 1957, are no worse than those of other bees, but their swarms sting 24 times a second, six times the rate of European swarms.

beg the question

It means to indulge in a form of faulty reasoning that assumes the truth of the very issue that is in dispute. It does not mean to ignore the main point, or to demand that the question be dealt with. (For this, we need invite, call for or raise the question.)

behaviour, behavioural

Beirut

The Green Line dividing East Beirut (Christian) and West Beirut (Muslim) was dismantled in 1990. See Lebanon.

belabour

Belarus

Adjective and people: Belarussian. Currency: ruble. Capital: Minsk.

A former Soviet republic known as Byelorussia or Belorussia (White Russia), it was one of the three Slavic republics (the others were Russia and Ukraine) whose formation of the Commonwealth of Independent States on Dec. 8, 1991, doomed the Soviet Union. (Minsk was made the CIS administrative centre.) In 1996, Belarus and Russia signed a treaty reuniting them in a political and economic association, with a complete merger stated as the eventual goal. A 1999 treaty authorized Russia's president and Belarussia's president, the autocratic Alexander Lukoshenko, to rule over the two countries jointly and to issue decrees that would supersede national legislation. A single currency is expected by 2005. The population of 10.4 million is about 80-per-cent Belarussian and 12-per-cent Russian, with small Polish and Ukrainian minorities.

More than 100,000 people were shot in mass executions ordered by Stalin beginning in 1937, and the German occupiers during the Second World War left it a virtual moonscape, with more than three million homeless. Minsk, Mogilev, Orsha and Gomel were totally destroyed. In 1989, mass graves containing 30,000 victims of the Stalinist purges were found near Minsk.

Bordering on Russia, Latvia, Lithuania, Poland and Ukraine, Belarus is mainly forest, pasture and bogland, including the Pripet Marshes in the east. Winters are mild, and drained land is very productive. Meat and dairy products account for half the agricultural output, and crops include grains, potatoes, sugar beets and flax. Leather and peat are also important products. Manufacturing includes farm equipment, trucks, fertilizers, glass and textiles. Minsk was the centre of the Soviet computer industry.

See Soviet Union.

Belgium

Adjective and people: Belgian. Currency: euro (had been the Belgian franc). Capital: Brussels.

It is divided between Flemings in the north, who speak Flemish, a Dutch dialect, and French-speaking Walloons in the south. Some German is also spoken. The population is 10.3 million. The area occupied by the Flemings is part of the medieval county of Flanders. Belgium is mostly inland, having a short North Sea coast squeezed between France and the Netherlands. Its principal port is Antwerp. It is one of the three Benelux countries, along with the Netherlands and Luxembourg. The name of this customs union, established in 1944, is useful shorthand for the three countries. In 1993, the Parliament amended the constitution to create a federal state of Belgium, comprising the largely autonomous regions of Flanders, Wallonia and (bilingual) Brussels. It remains a constitutional and hereditary monarchy.

Belize

Adjective and people: Belizean. Currency: Belize dollar. Capital: Belmopan.

The northernmost Central American country, bordering on Mexico and Guatemala, is a member of the Commonwealth. It was known as British Honduras until 1973, and has been independent since 1981. It shares the Yucatan Peninsula with three Mexican states and part of Guatemala. Its 260,000 people, largely of mixed African, European and Indian (Carib and Maya) origin, speak English, Spanish and some Indian dialects.

Bell Canada

Its owner, formerly called Bell Canada Enterprises, is now called BCE Inc. See BCE Inc.

bellwether

A wether is a castrated ram. The image is of a ram with a bell around its neck leading the flock of sheep; thus, of a leading indicator.

belly button

bellyful

Belmont Stakes

beluga

Lower-case. This adjective, from the Russian word for white, is applied to a small northern whale and to the great white sturgeon of the Black and Caspian seas.

bemused

It has nothing to do with amusement, even the quiet, contemplative kind that many use it to convey. Bemused means bewildered, stupefied, and also engrossed, deep in thought. A word that is probably not worth the trouble.

benchmark

benefited, benefiting

Benelux, see Belgium.

Benin

Adjective and people: Beninian. Currency: CFA franc. Capital: Porto Novo, but the principal city and de facto capital is the port of Cotonou.

This narrow country running northward from the Guinea Coast of West Africa, squeezed between Togo and Nigeria, was known as Dahomey until 1975. It was an important kingdom renowned for its bronze sculpture, but its population was greatly reduced by slave raids. It became part of French West Africa in 1904, and was made fully independent in 1960. After six coups, it became a Marxist-Leninist state in 1972, and its name was changed to Benin in 1975.

Free elections were restored in 1991. The population of 6.8 million includes four major tribes.

Bennett, W. A. C.

This B.C. premier (1952-72) should not be referred to as Wacky.

Berbers

They are the principal non-Arab inhabitants of North Africa, the various tribes being farmers, herders or oasis people found mainly in Algeria, Libya, Morocco and Tunisia. The general name comes from their Hamitic language, Berber, of which they speak diverse dialects. We would normally use their tribal names, notably the Beraber, Tuareg, Riff and Shawia.

BERD

Acronym from the French name for the European Bank for Reconstruction and Development. See IMF.

Bermuda

Adjective and people: Bermudian. Currency: Bermuda dollar. Capital: Hamilton.

This British colony in the mid-Atlantic comprises about 150 coral islands, 20 of them inhabited by its 65,000 people. Hamilton is on Bermuda Island. The option of independence from Britain was rejected in a 1995 referendum.

berserk

beryllium

bestseller

bettor, one who bets.

between . . . and

When we are expressing an approximate number, idiom demands between 25 **and** 50 things, never between 25 **to** 50.

Be aware that between . . . and, strictly speaking, excludes the two extremes. When we say something happened between April 30 and May 2, we are saying it happened on May 1. Idiom allows such a construction in informal usage, but if there is a chance of ambiguity or if precision is an issue in the story, say April 30 to May 2.

between and among, see among.

Bhutan

Adjective and people: Bhutanese. Currency: ngultrum, but the Indian rupee is also legal tender. Capital: Thimphu (official), Para (administrative).

This Himalayan kingdom borders on China (Tibet) in the north and is otherwise surrounded by India. Tea grows in the valleys, along with rice and other subsistence crops. About two-thirds of the population of two million are Bhutias, and most of the rest are Nepalese. Lamaism (a form of Buddhism) is the major religion.

biannual, biennial

Biannual means twice a year. **Biennial** means every two years, or living for two years, as in a plant. But since most readers have to stop and think about the distinction, it is better to avoid both words. For biannual, say twice a year or twice-yearly. (Semi-annual is fairly clear but more awkward, and so less acceptable.) Biennial is fine for describing plants, but in other contexts say every two years. Be similarly cautious with biweekly, bimonthly.

Bible, upper-case.

But use lower case for guidebooks and reference works, as in the home buyer's bible, and for the adjective biblical. Do not italicize the Bible.

biceps, triceps, quadriceps

All have s on the singular.

bigamy

Do not apply this term to the taking of two spouses in countries where this is legal. See polygamy.

Big Bang

Upper case for the one that started it all.

Big Ben

It is a bell, the one that strikes the hours in the Westminster Clock Tower. The name should not be applied to the tower itself, nor to the clock (the Great Clock of Westminster), nor to the bells that strike the quarter-hours.

Big Blue Machine

Upper-case, for the efficient and powerful Progressive Conservative Party in Ontario in the 1970s and early 1980s, particularly the advisers and election teams surrounding William Davis. The term, coined in 1971 in the heyday of Cincinnati's Big Red Machine, should not be applied to the current party.

Big Dipper

The preferred term. See Ursa.

biker, cyclist

Use biker for people who ride motorcycles, and cyclist for people who ride bicycles.

bilingual

Under the Constitution, Canada and New Brunswick are officially bilingual. However, it is unclear whether a city, as the creature of a province, has a legal right to declare itself "officially" bilingual without the authority of provincial legislation. In the 1980s, the courts struck down such a declaration by Kapuskasing, Ontario, on the basis that the city did not have the jurisdiction. This does not prevent a municipality from creating a language policy that sets out how French-language services are to be offered or requiring fluency in French when hiring senior staff. However, in the absence of provincial legislative approval, write of a city declaring itself bilingual, not officially bilingual.

billiards

It is singular. The term billiards covers many games, all played on a felt-covered table with side cushions, but not all using pockets. The most familiar games are pool (pocket billiards), snooker, English billiards and carom billiards. The games use various numbers of balls (e.g. 22 in snooker, 16 in pool, three in English billiards).

bills

Government bills are identified by number, according to the order in which they are introduced in a legislative session, such as Bill 65 provincially, or Bill C-65 or S-65 federally (C and S indicate origin in the Commons or the Senate). They are properly referred to in this way while still in the legislative process, although we must also explain what they are about if this is not clear from the story, e.g. Bill 65, amending the Fish and Game Act. After they have been passed they acquire a name, or in the case of amendments simply disappear into the existing statute, and should no longer be referred to by the old number. Indeed, within a year or so that number has been applied to a different piece of legislation. However, some particularly contentious laws remain popularly known for years by the number under which they were hotly debated. In this case, we can say something like "Quebec's language law, commonly referred to as Bill 178." See green paper, white paper.

bird's-eye view

Birks, for Henry Birks & Sons Ltd.

bison

Use this word (not buffalo) for the live animal, but allow buffalo steak, coat, robe, chips, hunter, jump.

black

This is the term preferred by most people of that racial group. Avoid Negro, except in direct quotations. The expression Negro spirituals is still marginally acceptable, but the word spirituals usually suffices. The word coloured is accepted in Bermuda, but we should use it only when quoting others. In stories from South Africa, accompany the word coloured with an explanation that it is applied there to persons of mixed race. Avoid African-Canadian and African-American, which could imply an immigrant from Africa. See race.

black box

Prefer flight recorders (there are two: the flight data recorder and the cockpit voice recorder). They're no longer black, so confine black box to quotes.

Blackfoot, both singular and plural.

blackout, noun. The verb is **black out**.

Black Watch

The formal name is the Royal Highland Regiment of Canada (Black Watch). Do not call it the Black Watch Regiment.

black widow, see spiders.

blatant, flagrant

The words are not interchangeable. Flagrant is by far the more usual in a news setting. It means openly disgraceful or heinous, notorious, as in a flagrant disregard for proper usage. Blatant means blaring, noisy and, by extension, obvious, as in blatantly idiotic. "Blatantly obvious" risks redundancy.

blind

Avoid the term "the blind," implying a homogeneous class of people. See disabled.

blizzard

but do you think it's windy enough for a blizzard?

Technically, a snowstorm with winds above 40 km/h and temperature below -10. We are not quite this restrictive, but we reserve the term for major storms. Readers who regularly experience blizzards resent use of the term to describe a snowfall in fairly still, mild conditions. See weather.

bloc and block

Use **bloc** only for groups of countries, politicians, parties, provinces etc. with a common interest or purpose, usually political, economic or military. Otherwise, use **block**.

Bloc Québécois

Italics not needed. This federal political party that espouses Quebec sovereignty is best called the Bloc in second reference, because BQ invites confusion with PQ. The adjective is Bloquiste.

blond and blonde

Blond is the adjective for both sexes, and the noun when referring to a man. Use **blonde** only as a noun referring to a woman. However, be wary of gratuitous descriptions. See women and language.

blood diamonds

Also known as conflict diamonds. The informal term refers to diamonds that are smuggled out of various African countries and sold abroad to finance terrorism and rebellion.

bloody mary, the drink.

Use upper case for Bloody Mary only when naming a specific person, such as England's Mary I or the character in the show *South Pacific*.

blowtorch

It is a pot-shaped device that produces a weak flame, suitable only for such things as melting lead and stripping paint. In references to cutting through metal (rescues, bank jobs etc.) the appropriate expression is cutting torch (or simply torch, if cutting has already been established).

bluegrass music

blue jay

Also the Toronto Blue Jays. This bird should not be confused with the Canada jay, which is grey.

blueline

Bluenose

This nickname is applied to Nova Scotians, not all Maritimers. It should be used only in lighter stories with no pejorative overtones.

The Lunenburg schooner that has graced the dime since 1936 is properly called Bluenose (no "the"). The copy built in 1963, Bluenose II, has lasted longer than the original, which was launched in 1921, won the International Fishermen's Trophy five times under Captain Angus Walters and sank off Haiti in 1946. It was a two-masted fishing schooner, and should not be called a ship. See ship.

Although it is famous in Canada

for its exploits in East Coast races, we should be wary of calling Bluenose Canada's most famous sailing vessel. Marco Polo, built in 1851 at Saint John, N.B., was in the Australian passenger trade and well known as "the fastest ship in the world." Mary Celeste, built in Nova Scotia in 1861, is a famous mystery ship (commonly misnamed Marie Celeste) found abandoned with cargo intact drifting off the Azores in 1872. See tall ships.

B'nai Brith

bodycheck

bogey, bogie

It is **bogey** in golf, and when referring to a hobgoblin or an unidentified aircraft. Make bogeyman one word. A **bogie** is a railway truck, or an extra wheel used to distribute weight. Humphrey Bogart's nickname is spelled Bogie.

Boleyn, Anne

Bolivia

Adjective and people: Bolivian. Currency: boliviano. Capital: La Paz (administrative), Sucre (legal).

It is one of South America's two landlocked countries, the other being Paraguay, on which it borders. It also borders on Brazil, Peru, Chile and Argentina. About three-quarters of its 8.5 million people live in the west on the Altiplano, the high Andean plain that contains Lake Titicaca (shared with Peru). Bolivia's other two regions are the central Montanas and the Oriente (eastern) lowlands of the Amazon basin, largely rain forest and swamps. The main languages are Spanish, Aymara and Quechua. Chile, which took over Bolivia's narrow link to the Pacific in a war in 1884, has given it certain privileges in the Chilean port of Arica.

bologna, see baloney.

bonjour

bonsoir

booby

No hyphen in booby hatch, prize, trap. Booby hatch is too offensive for use in news stories, except in direct quotes.

boost

Marginally acceptable in headlines and copy when a synonym is needed for raise or increase, although these words are preferred. It is more acceptable when it means support or give a lift to, as in a morale-booster.

Bophuthatswana, a former South African homeland. See South Africa.

border

In general, confine to divisions between countries. For provinces and states, prefer boundary or line. Avoid frontier, which is common overseas but has a different meaning in North America.

boreal forest

Lower-case. See taiga.

born-again Christians

Like all religious labels, this should never be used in a pejorative sense. It is fair to say the concept of a changed or renewed life through an affirmation or reaffirmation of faith is strongest among fundamentalist sects. The reference is to John 3:3, in which Jesus tells the Pharisee Nicodemus that "except a man be born again, he cannot see the kingdom of God." See Christian.

Borneo

A complex corner of the world. The largest island in the Malay Archipelago, marking the southern edge of the South China Sea, is shared by three countries. Along its northern coast are the independent sultanate of Brunei and two states of Malaysia—Sarawak and Sabah. Its southern two-thirds contains four Indonesian states: Central, East, West and South Kalimantan.

borscht

Bosnia-Herzegovina

Adjective and people: Bosnian (but also give specific ethnic group). Currency: dinar. Capital: Sarajevo.

Unless the Herzegovina region is at issue, common journalistic practice is to shorten the name to Bosnia. We do not use the Serbo-Croat spelling, Bosna-Hercegovina.

Along with Croatia, it bore the brunt of Serb resistance to the breakup of Yugoslavia. Its ethnic Serb minority (about 32 per cent) reacted violently to the republic's vote for independence on Feb. 29, 1992, saying they feared that the Muslims (39 per cent), who largely controlled the government, would set up an Islamic state. With heavy support from Serbia, particularly in weapons, they declared a secessionist Serb state called the Republic of Srpska, and undertook a brutal campaign of "ethnic cleansing," seizing control of more than two-thirds of Bosnia-Herzegovina and clearing entire areas of Muslims and Croats. The Croats, a strong minority at about 18 per cent, got help from Croatia as they fought to hold on to their traditional territory, including the Herzegovina region, and were also accused of some atrocities. Before the fighting began, the population of Bosnia-Herzegovina was about 4.4 million; it fell to 3.5 million. Tens of thousands were killed in the fighting, and populations of whole regions were made homeless, forced to flee as refugees or put into Serb-run concentration camps. A United Nations relief operation began in 1992. Internationally brokered peace proposals in 1993 called for 10, then three, ethnically based autonomous regions, but the Dayton accord (actually signed in Paris, on Dec. 14, 1995) set up two entities: a Muslim-Croat federation and the Republic of Srpska. A NATO-led international peacekeeping force (IFOR) was assigned to implement the agreement in 1995-96, and was succeeded by a smaller, NATO-led Stabilization Force (SFOR) with a mandate to keep the peace.

Bosnia is mountainous and isolated, virtually landlocked. Croatia envelops it on the north and west, mostly cutting it off from the Adriatic, and Serbia and Montenegro lie to the east and southeast.

The Bosnian Muslims are Slavs descended from adherents of the Bogomil Christian heresy, who were converted to Islam after the area was incorporated into the Ottoman Empire in the 15th century. Prefer Bosnian Muslim to the term Bosniak, which requires explanation if used.

See Yugoslavia.

Bosporus, the
This strait connecting the Black Sea and the Sea of Marmara separates European and Asian Turkey.

both
It should not be used if two things are acting in reference to each other. Say two people are **both at odds** with a third person, but simply that they are **at odds** (with each other), not both at odds.

Botswana
Adjective and people: Botswanan. Currency: pula. Capital: Gaborone.

This landlocked country in southern Africa, a member of the Commonwealth, was Bechuanaland before independence in 1966. It is surrounded by Zimbabwe, South Africa and Namibia. The Tswana people, after whom the country is named, are the major ethnic group in the population of about 1.6 million,

but it is wrong to refer to all Botswanans as Tswana. English is referred to as the official language, and Tswana as the national language.

bouillon

bourgeois, the bourgeoisie
Too vague, and with too many pejorative connotations, to be useful in a news story. Reserve for direct quotations or discussions of Marxist theory. See proletariat.

Bourgeoys, see St. Marguerite Bourgeoys.

boutonniere

bowdlerize
Lower-case, meaning to zealously remove blasphemous or indecent passages from a text. The reference is to Thomas Bowdler, publisher of the *Family Shakespeare*.

box office, noun. The adjective is box-office.

boy
Use it for males under 16 if pressed, but prefer more specific terms narrowing down the age range. If we cannot give the exact age or grade (a 10-year-old, a Grade 10 student), consider such terms as preteen, adolescent, teenager. See girl, youth.

boyfriend

Boy Scouts, a Scout, see capitalization.

brackets, see punctuation.

braggadocio

Brahman, Brahma, Brahmin
The Hindu idea of the All and One, the essential self of all things, is the concept of **Brahman**. The personification of this is the all-

pervading god **Brahma**. The top rank of the Hindu caste system is the **Brahmin** class. See Hinduism.

Braille

Branson

On May 1, 1998, as one effect of Ontario's Health Services Restructuring Commission, North York Branson Hospital ceased to exist as an independent entity. It became part of North York General Hospital, and should be referred to as the Branson division of North York General Hospital.

bravery, bravado, bravura

Bravado is affectation of bravery, or boastful menace or defiance. **Bravura** is most often encountered as an adjective meaning brilliant or daring, applied to a performance.

bravery decorations

Canada's military decorations for bravery in battle, approved in 1993, are the Victoria Cross, the Star of Military Valour and the Medal of Military Valour. Previously, military personnel had shared with civilians the three Canadian decorations for selfless acts of courage instituted in 1972, the Cross of Valour, the Star of Courage and the Medal of (not for) Bravery. Recipients of these may use the initials CV, SC or MB after their names. The awards are made by the governor-general on the advice of the Canadian Decorations Advisory Committee. We should say the three civilian ranks reflect the degree of peril faced by the recipient, not the quality or level of the person's bravery.

Policemen who commit acts of bravery while on duty receive the federal Police Exemplary Service Medal. Firefighters and others in dangerous jobs are eligible for various provincial and municipal awards.

The Canadian version of the Victoria Cross is inscribed Pro Valore,

Latin for the For Valour of the British original. It is awarded "for the most conspicuous bravery, a daring or pre-eminent act of valour or self-sacrifice or extreme devotion to duty, in the presence of the enemy."

Ninety-three Canadians had received the Imperial VC, the last in 1945.

Bravo!

Include the exclamation point in the name of the Canadian performing-arts cable channel. There is a U.S. cable channel called Bravo.

Brazil

Adjective and people: Brazilian. Currency: real. Capital: Brasilia.

The world's fifth-largest country covers nearly half of South America, has more than 7,000 kilometres of coast and shares boundaries with all countries on the continent except Chile and Ecuador. It is popularly identified with the low Amazon basin, but two-thirds of its area is the mountainous tableland of the south and east known as the Brazilian highlands. Brazilians speak Portuguese, and the races are less distinct than those of Brazil's Spanish-speaking neighbours, the Europeans having intermarried more extensively with blacks and Indians. The Indians of Amazonia number about 200,000, out of a total population of 173 million. Brazil is Latin America's leading industrial power, and despite pockets of severe poverty is not considered part of the Third World. The largest metropolitan areas are Sao Paulo, Rio de Janeiro, Belo Horizonte and Salvador.

The armed forces held power from 1964 to 1985. In 2002, Luiz Inacio Lula da Silva, a former metalworker who was briefly jailed under military rule, was elected president.

breach and breech

Breach is by far the more common, applying to all situations involving breaking—either physically breaking through or violating an agreement. It is also a noun (as in breach of contract, a breach in a dike). **Breech** is a noun referring to the lower part of the body (a breech birth), the lower section of a pulley or the part of a gun behind the barrel. The plural, for trousers, is now rarely used. See **broach**.

breakdown, break-in, breakout, breakup

Nouns. The verbs are all two words.

breaststroke

Breathalyzer

A trade name, so always uppercase. The generic term breath-analysis machine is better if we are not sure of the brand used, especially if the accuracy of a machine is at issue.

Breeders' Crown for harness horses; **Breeders' Cup** for thoroughbreds.

bridegroom

Groom is acceptable when referring to a bridegroom.

Brier, the curling event.

brigadier-general, Brig.-Gen. See ranks.

bring and take

It must reflect the location of the writer, and take is usually the correct choice. Say that parents were asked to take (not bring) their children for vaccination. Say that immigrants bring their traditions to Canada, just as Canadians take theirs overseas. See come.

brinkmanship

The diplomatic tactic of going to the brink of war, or a willingness to court danger in the interest of achieving an objective. Not brinksmanship.

Brink's Inc.; Brink's Canada Ltd.

A **Brink's truck**, but only for this company. Otherwise, use the generic term armoured truck.

Britain

It means the island containing England, Scotland and Wales, formally called Great Britain (a name that once distinguished it from Brittany). But Britain, and the adjective British, are also our preferred terms for the political entity the United Kingdom of Great Britain and Northern Ireland.

Do not use the adjective British with events that predate the Act of Union of 1707. (If there had been things British during the reign of Elizabeth I, we would have difficulty explaining what territory her cousin ruled as Mary Queen of Scots.) However, the term British can be a geographical expression, as in the British Isles, and the prehistoric and ancient peoples of the island of Britain are referred to as British tribes or as Romano-British in their culture.

By the same token, in stories set after 1707 do not refer to the king or prime minister "of England," but rather of Britain.

See United Kingdom.

British Broadcasting Corp.

BBC may be used in first reference in a complex lead, if we set it up soon afterward.

Briton, not Britisher.

Britten, Benjamin

Composer. Later, Baron Britten of Aldeburgh.

broach and brooch

To **broach** a subject is to introduce it for the first time. Broach also means to pierce for the purpose of withdrawing a liquid. As a noun, a broach is a piercing tool, or a roasting spit. A **brooch** is a piece of jewellery.

Brookings Institution (not Institute).

brouhaha

Brundtland report

So called after Gro Harlem Brundtland, prime minister of Norway at the time and chair of the independent commission that released this document in 1987. The formal title was Our Common Future: The Report of the World Commission on Environment and Development. The mandate of the commissioners, from 21 countries including Canada, was to examine how the global economy and development were affecting the natural environment. Ms. Brundtland coined the expression, "think globally, act locally," and the report popularized the concept of "sustainable development."

Brunei

Adjective and people: Bruneian. Currency: Brunei dollar. Capital: Bandar Seri Begawan.

This sultanate on the northwest coast of the island of Borneo, on the South China Sea, is a member of the Commonwealth, fully independent from Britain since Dec. 31, 1983. The Malaysian state of Sarawak surrounds Brunei and splits it into two separate pieces. Brunei has oil, both on land and offshore, and has one of the world's biggest liquefied natural gas plants, its production going mainly to Japan. About half the population of 335,000 speak Malay, and half the rest speak Chinese.

brusque

Brussels sprouts

brutalize

Commonly misused. It does not mean to subject to brutal treatment. It means to make or become brutal, to turn into a brute. It is the cruel secret-

police torturer, the child molester or the wife-beater who has been brutalized, not the victim.

BSE

Common in second reference for bovine spongiform encephalopathy (mad-cow disease). For that reason, avoid its use as a short form for breast self-examination.

Btfsplk, Joe

The character in L'il Abner who carried bad luck with him wherever he went.

buckshot

A shotgun load consisting of very large pellets meant for bringing down deer and other large game, and usually fatal to people. The more usual load for intimidating and scattering crowds is birdshot. If we are unsure which load was used, we use the generic term shotgun blasts.

Buddha, Buddhism, Buddhist

Buddha is not a name but a title, the Buddha, meaning the awakened or enlightened one. His name was Gautama (his lay name had been Prince Siddhartha), and he died in the fifth century BC. His teaching, written from oral tradition as the **Pali canon** shortly after his death, is based on the **Four Noble Truths**. They are that life involves suffering; the cause of suffering is desire; eliminating desire ends suffering; and there is a method or path that must be followed if desire is to be eliminated. This method is the **Noble Eightfold Path**—right vision, right thought, right speech, right action, right way of life, right effort, right-mindedness and right meditation. It leads to **Nirvana**, a state free from the cycle of suffering, death and rebirth. Buddhism no longer exists as a major religion in India, and was changed by local beliefs in every country to which it spread. This has created several schools of thought on the nature of enlightenment and how to achieve it (Zen, Theravada, Amidism, Kuan-yin, Lamaism etc.), and we should be specific. The clergy consists of monks and nuns in monastic communities, some there permanently but some meditating for as little as a few days or months. See Zen.

buildup, noun.
The verb is **build up**; the adjective is **built-up**.

Bulgaria
Adjective and people: Bulgarian. Currency: lev. Capital: Sofia.

It is a Balkan republic (see Balkans) on the Black Sea, bordering on Romania, Serbia and Montenegro, Greece and Turkey. Its name refers to the Bulgar conquerors of the seventh century, but they adopted the language and customs of the indigenous Slavs. Bulgaria was on the German side in both world wars. It was occupied by the Soviet Union in 1944, and the Fatherland Front declared a people's republic in 1946. Bulgaria tried forcibly to assimilate its minorities and its ethnic mix is not recorded precisely, but ethnic Turks are believed to make up more than 10 per cent of its eight million people, with smaller minorities of Roma (Gypsies), Jews, Romanians and Armenians. Dictator Todor Zhivkov resigned under pressure from Communist reformers in late 1989. Zhivkov's party (renamed the Socialists) was defeated in an election in June of 1990 by an anti-Communist coalition, the Union of Democratic Forces. Zhivkov's mismanagement had left Bulgaria one of Europe's poorest countries, ill-equipped to handle the transition to a market economy, and he was jailed in 1992 for embezzling state funds.

In 2000, Bulgaria began talks with the hope of one day joining the European Union and the North Atlantic Treaty Organization.

In 2001, Simeon Saxe-Coburg, who as pretender to the throne had fled Soviet-controlled Bulgaria with his mother 55 years earlier, returned to fight an election as head of the newly formed National Movement for Simeon II, and won. Call him Mr. Saxe-Coburg on second reference.

bullets
These are the heavy dots (•) used to introduce a series of examples or brief points, preceded by a colon. In newspaper jargon the term also refers to the items themselves.

Bullets are meant only for very short, clear summaries. Otherwise, they are confusing and intimidating.

There are two types: those that combine to form one giant sentence, each completing the partial sentence interrupted by the colon; and those that are each a fully independent sentence or paragraph in their own right. In Globe style both types begin with upper case, and neither carries a paragraph indent.

The first type must be introduced by a grammatically incomplete sentence, and all items end with a semi-colon except the final one, which has a period to end the sentence. No item can contain another sentence, except possibly the final one. The items should be similar in structure, usually beginning with the same part of speech. An example of this type:
The students demanded that the government:
• Take steps to end corruption among party officials;
• Institute political reforms leading to more democracy and less authoritarianism;
• Hold talks with student leaders outside the framework of official associations;
• End martial law in the capital.

If the items are more complex, we must use the second type of bullets. These are introduced by a grammatically complete sentence, often containing an anticipatory word tipping off the reader that a list is to follow. Some examples: The students made these demands: The students listed several demands: The students presented a long list of objectives:

These bullet items are each at least one complete sentence. They can contain more than one sentence, but cannot run more than a paragraph. Each item ends with a period.

If only one item of the partial-sentence type requires another sentence by way of explanation, or if only one of the second type requires a second paragraph, the bullet structure may be preserved by moving this longer item to the end of the list and adding the extra information as a next paragraph. If the complications extend further than this, the story is unsuitable for bullets and must be recast. However, it might be a candidate for insertion of a very brief set of bullets up high to make the basic points, to be followed by the explanations and complications in regular paragraph form.

bullpen

bullring

bull session

bull's-eye

bullwhip

bulrush

bunkum

bureaus (not bureaux).

burgle, not burglarize.

Burkina Faso
No useful adjective or word for the people; say citizens of Burkina Faso. (The local word, Burkinabes, is

obscure and confusing.) Currency: CFA franc. Capital: Ouagadougou.

This West African country, landlocked north of Ivory Coast, Ghana, Togo and Benin, became fully independent of France in 1960, as **Upper Volta**. There were coups in 1966, 1980, 1982 and 1983. The name was changed in 1984 to Burkina Faso, meaning land of honest men. The population is 12.6 million. The Mossi are the largest ethnic group at 48 per cent, and their language, Moré, is spoken by many others. French is the official language; the language of commerce is called Dyula.

Burk's Falls, Ont.

burly
Usually unnecessary. Assume that most bodyguards, bouncers etc. fit this description.

Burma, see **Myanmar**.

Burundi
Adjective and people: Burundian. Currency: Burundi franc. Capital: Bujumbura.

It is in eastern Africa, between Tanzania and Congo (formerly Zaire) on the northeastern shore of Lake Tanganyika, bordering on Rwanda. A tiny state, it is the second most densely populated in Africa, after Rwanda. The Tutsi (Watusi) herders are only 15 per cent of the population of 6.6 million, but maintain a social, political and especially military dominance far out of proportion to their numbers. About 1 per cent are Pygmy (Twa) hunters.

The Tutsis ruled the Hutus for 400 years, and were kept in power after independence in 1962 (Burundi had been a German colony, then was administered by Belgium under the League of Nations and United Nations). More than 100,000 were slaughtered after a failed Hutu coup attempt in 1972.

More than 300,000 have been killed in waves of Hutu-Tutsi violence since late 1993. The country's first Hutu president was assassinated by Tutsi paratroops in October, and his successor was killed along with the Rwandan president in a plane crash in April of 1994, another presumed assassination. The late 1990s saw continued domination of weak governments by the Tutsi military and sporadic violence by the army, Hutu insurgents and armed gangs. Despite a power-sharing arrangement in 2000, the two main Hutu rebel groups have continued to fight.

bus, buses, busing

(**Bussing**, referring to kissing, is rarely encountered.)

Bush, George W.

Retain the middle W. (stands for Walker) for the U.S. president elected in 2000, to help distinguish him from his father, George (Herbert) Bush, president from 1990 to 1994. This is consistent with past U.S. practice, which uses a middle name to distinguish between John Adams (1798-1802) and John Quincy Adams (1826-1830). The W explains the second Bush's widespread nickname, Dubya.

Business Development Bank of Canada, BDC

The abbreviation omits the B for Bank.

Butchart Gardens, near Victoria.

Bute Inlet

On B.C. coast. Not Butte.

butterfly stroke, the butterfly

by-election

bylaw

bylines

Avoid more than three names. If four or more writers have collaborated on a story, group their names at the end.

If all the writers were not in the same city, remove the placeline and indicate in the body of the story where the various elements take place.

Remember that the term byline is newspaper jargon. Use it in a news story only if its meaning is clear from the context.

See capitalization.

bypass

byproduct

C

Cabbagetown

This old Toronto neighbourhood, settled from about the time of Confederation through the 1880s by Irish and English working-class immigrants who grew cabbages in their front yards, is bounded approximately north and south by Wellesley and Queen Streets, and east and west by Sherbourne Street and the Don River.

cab driver

Cabot and Cartier

They are often confused. The first landing by southern Europeans in what is now Canada, probably in Nova Scotia, was made by John Cabot, a naturalized English citizen of Italian birth, in the ship Matthew in 1497 (when Jacques Cartier was still a boy of 6 in St-Malo). Cabot also sighted Cape Race, but may not have gone ashore in Newfoundland. (See Discovery Day.) He did not return from a second voyage the next year. Cartier's three voyages, during which he discovered the St. Lawrence, spent two winters in the area and named Mont Royal, were made in 1534, 1535-36 and 1541-42. See L'Anse aux Meadows, Thorfinnson.

cacciatore

cactuses

caddy

Caesar

But **cesarean section**. (**Caesarean** means pertaining to Caesar.)

Caesars Palace, no apostrophe.

caisse populaire, caisses populaires, caisses

This is an exception to our rule that English should be substituted for French and foreign words. To call them credit unions would be misleading to most readers, who would equate them with the fairly small and relatively anonymous saving and lending associations connected with companies and unions. The caisses of Quebec, New Brunswick and parts of the West are truly people's banks, with branches on main streets and a wide range of services.

Caisse de dépôt et placement du Québec

Italics. In second reference, the Caisse is upper-case. If there are two caisses in the story, second reference is the Caisse de dépôt.

Calcutta

Use this spelling, not Kolkata.

Calder Memorial Trophy

For the NHL's top rookie. It is named for Frank Calder, league president from 1917 to 1943.

calèche

calibres, see guns and calibres.

calisthenics

Callander, Ont.
But note there is also a **Kaladar, Ont.**

Callender Street, Toronto.

callous and callus
Callous is an adjective meaning hardened, including impervious to feeling(s). **Callus** is a noun meaning hardened, thickened skin, bone or plant material.

call-up, noun. The verb is **call up**.

Cambodia
Adjective and people: Cambodian. Currency: riel. Capital: Phnom Penh.
It called itself the Khmer Republic from 1970 to 1975, and Kampuchea from 1975 to 1989. It is in Southeast Asia, one of the three countries that make up Indochina (the others are Vietnam and Laos). About 85 per cent of the 13 million people are Khmer, and this is the name of the national language. There are also Chinese and Vietnamese minorities, and several hill tribes (from mountain ranges in the north and south). The Mekong River provides north-south transportation and deposits silt that is excellent for growing rice. Years of warfare have disrupted rubber production.
Prince Norodom Sihanouk's aid to the Viet Cong brought a U.S. attack in 1970 to support a coup by General Lon Nol. (This brought a wave of U.S. protests, including the one on May 4, 1970, in which four students were killed and nine wounded by members of the National Guard at Kent State University.) The Khmer Rouge defeated Lon Nol in 1975. Mass killings by the new regime after Pol Pot became prime minister in 1976 led to a Vietnamese invasion in 1978-79. Most Vietnamese troops left in 1988-89.

A 13-year civil war against the Vietnamese-installed government ended with a peace accord in May of 1991, which called for a massive United Nations civilian and military operation (including Canadian participation) to virtually administer the country, the largest and costliest operation in UN history. The job of the UN, begun in 1992, was to monitor the ceasefire, disarm the forces of the government and three rebel groups (one of which was the reluctant Khmer Rouge, which resisted disarmament), restore government operations, supervise the return of 700,000 displaced persons and supervise fair elections in May, 1993. In September of that year, a new elected government took office and Prince Norodom Sihanouk was restored to the throne as king.
Pol Pot continued to direct a Khmer Rouge insurgency until his support eroded in 1997. He died in a remote forest camp in 1998, at 73. Hun Sen, now prime minister, staged a violent coup in July, 1997, and declared victory in a 1998 election marked by violence and intimidation. Efforts to set up a special court to try those responsible for the killings from 1975 to 1979 have not yet been successful.
When writing Cambodian names, be aware that for a Cambodian named Tan Sam Huoth, Huoth is the given name – the equivalent of Joe or Joanna in Western names. But it is also the name by which the person is formally known, in the way that Canadians are known by their surnames. Therefore, use that name on second reference, preceded by the honorific. Tan Sam Huoth would be Mr. Huoth.
A note of caution: Some Cambodians will give a reversed name order when talking to Westerners because they think it will be clearer. When in doubt, it is acceptable to repeat both (or all three) names on second reference.

camel, see Bactrian.

Cameroon

Adjective and people: Cameroonian, but avoid as awkward. Currency: CFA franc. Capital: Yaoundé.

It is in central West Africa, stretching from the corner of the Gulf of Guinea northward to Lake Chad. It adjoins Nigeria, Chad and four other countries. Its diverse vegetation and rainfall (ranging from very wet in southern coastal areas to near desert in the north) is reflected in the ethnic mix among its 16 million people. There are Pygmy forest hunters and farming Bantu villagers in the south, and various nomadic groups in the north, including Hamitic, Sudanese and Arab.

Canada

Population: 31 million. Since passage of the federal Official Languages Act in 1969, Canada's two official languages have been English and French. Currency: dollar (known colloquially as the loonie). Capital: Ottawa.

Provincial capitals: Victoria (British Columbia), Edmonton (Alberta), Regina (Saskatchewan), Winnipeg (Manitoba), Toronto (Ontario), Quebec City (Quebec), Fredericton (New Brunswick), Halifax (Nova Scotia), Charlottetown (Prince Edward Island), St. John's (Newfoundland and Labrador). Territorial capitals: Whitehorse (Yukon), Yellowknife (Northwest Territories), Iqaluit (Nunavut).

It is impossible to do justice to Canada's history in a short space, but here are a few milestones.

In 1763, four years after the Battle of the Plains of Abraham and the surrender of Quebec (then a French colony) to the British, Quebec became a British possession under the Treaty of Paris that ended the Seven Years' War. In 1791, Britain passed the Canada Act (or Constitutional Act), which divided Quebec into the provinces of Upper Canada and Lower Canada.

In 1841 the Canadas merged into a single Province of Canada, divided administratively into Canada East and Canada West. It was split into Ontario and Quebec under the British North America Act of March 29, 1867. The BNA Act, cornerstone of Canada's current Constitution, united the two provinces with Nova Scotia and New Brunswick as the Dominion of Canada. Manitoba joined Confederation in 1870, British Columbia in 1871, Prince Edward Island in 1873, Saskatchewan and Alberta in 1905, and Newfoundland in 1949. In 1870, Canada acquired Rupert's Land and the North-Western Territory from the Hudson's Bay Company and Britain, and this great expanse of land was over time carved up into Manitoba, Saskatchewan and Alberta (with additional land later added to Manitoba, Ontario and Quebec) and the territories of Yukon and the Northwest Territories. See Northwest Territories, Yukon.

Under the 1931 British Statute of Westminster, Britain gave Canada its legal freedom but retained, at Canada's request, the power to amend the Constitution. In 1981, the federal and provincial governments (with the significant exception of Quebec) agreed to ask Britain to amend the BNA Act and relinquish all powers over it to Canada—a step known as patriation. In 1982, the British Parliament did so: The BNA Act was renamed the Constitution Act, 1867, and was supplemented by the Constitution Act, 1982, which included a Charter of Rights and Freedoms (which see) and, for the first time, a formula for amending the Constitution.

Depending on the change sought, the amending formula requires the unanimous agreement of the federal

Parliament and all provincial legislatures; the agreement of Parliament
and the legislatures of at least seven
provinces containing at least half the
country's population; or the agreement
of Parliament and the province
directly affected by the change.

In 1980 and 1995, the Parti
Québécois (PQ) government of
Quebec, which favoured Quebec's
secession from Canada, held two
plebiscites (usually referred to as
referendums) on whether Quebec
should leave Canada.

The 1980 question: "The
Government of Quebec has made
public its proposal to negotiate a new
agreement with the rest of Canada
based on the equality of nations. This
agreement would enable Quebec to
acquire the exclusive power to make
its laws, levy its taxes and establish
relations abroad – in other words
sovereignty – and at the same time to
maintain with Canada an economic
association including a common
currency. No change in political
status resulting from these
negotiations will be effected without
approval by the people through
another referendum. On these terms
do you give the Government of
Quebec the mandate to negotiate the
proposed agreement between Quebec
and Canada? Yes. No."

The 1995 question: "Do you agree
that Quebec should become sovereign,
after having made a formal offer to
Canada for a new Economic and
Political Partnership within the scope
of the Bill respecting the future of
Quebec and of the agreement signed
on June 12, 1995?"

The percentage of those who voted
No to an independent Quebec was
59.56 in 1980 and 50.6 per cent in
1995. The difference between the two
sides in 1995 was 53,498 votes. Jean
Charest's federalist Liberal Party
defeated the PQ in April, 2003.

In April, 1999, the Northwest
Territories was divided into a smaller
Northwest Territories and the
predominantly Inuit territory
Nunavut. See Nunavut.

The name of the Province of
Newfoundland was formally changed
to the Province of Newfoundland and
Labrador on Dec. 6, 2001. See
Newfoundland and Labrador.

**Canada Customs and Revenue
Agency**
On Nov. 1, 1999, Revenue
Canada (the informal name for the
Department of National Revenue)
officially changed its name to the
Canada Customs and Revenue
Agency. It is now an agency rather
than a department, but continues to
report to the Minister of National
Revenue and to Parliament. Although
the agency prefers to be known on
second reference as CCRA, that form
is unhelpful to readers. Refer instead to
Canada Customs or Canada Revenue,
depending on which element of the
agency is being referred to. Canada
Revenue is the taxation division.
Canada Customs is the customs and
excise division; in addition to
collecting duties, it is responsible for
excise taxes and federal sales taxes.
Except when a story concerns the
agency as a whole, it is acceptable to
use either short form in first reference.
The revenue side must never be called
Internal Revenue, which is the name
of its U.S. counterpart.

Canada Development Corp. (not
Canadian).

Canada Industrial Relations Board
(not Canadian).

Canada Labour Relations Board

**Canada Mortgage and Housing
Corp., CMHC**

Canada Post Corp.
On second reference, **Canada Post**
or **the Post Office**.

Canadian Alliance

The full official name is the Canadian Reform Conservative Alliance, but Canadian Alliance is fine in first reference. The federal party was created in 2000 as the successor to the Reform Party, in an effort to broaden the party's appeal and, it was hoped, persuade members of the Progressive Conservative Party to leave that party for the Alliance. Although the name initially proposed—Canadian Conservative Reform Alliance—lent itself to great sport involving the acronym CCRAP (with P for party), remember that the word party is not in the official name, and there is no reason to tag a lower-case party onto the end.

Canadian Armed Forces

In all instances, **Canadian Forces** is acceptable on first reference. If there are many repetitions, or in a tight headline, it may be shortened to **the Forces**, upper-case. The name takes a plural verb. Also see ranks.

Write Canadian Forces Base Cold Lake, but the Canadian Forces base at Cold Lake. If more bases are named in a story, shorten subsequent names to CFB, as in CFB Cold Lake.

Canadian Broadcasting Corp.

May be referred to simply as the CBC even on first reference. See Radio-Canada.

Canadian Human Rights Commission, Canadian Human Rights Tribunal

Avoid confusing these two bodies. It is the tribunal, not the commission, that hands down rulings in rights cases. The tribunal is a separate, independent body.

Complaints are made to the commission, which is charged with investigating such matters. If warranted, it refers the case to the tribunal, which selects three members from its standing list of about 100

part-time panelists to conduct a hearing and issue a decision. It is the quasi-judicial tribunal, not the commission, that has the power to order that a discriminatory practice stop and that compensation be paid.

The commission does have a role at these tribunal hearings: to act as an advocate (a sort of prosecutor, although we should not use that term) on behalf of the complainant. The commission may also appeal if it is dissatisfied with the decision.

Canadian International Trade Tribunal

An independent quasi-judicial body, the CITT was created on Dec. 31, 1988, the eve of free trade, to replace the Tariff Board, Canadian Import Tribunal and the Textile and Clothing Board. Individuals can go to the CITT to contest Canada Customs and Revenue Agency decisions on either customs duties or federal sales and excise taxes; the Tariff Board used to carry out that job. It also hears dumping cases, a job formerly performed by the Canadian Import Tribunal. If Canada Customs decides that an import has been dumped on the Canadian market or has been subsidized, the CITT holds a hearing to decide whether the imported goods are causing or are likely to cause "material injury" to Canadian producers. If it finds injury, Canada Customs then levies on the imported good anti-dumping or countervailing duties that are equal to the margin of dumping or the subsidy.

Canadian Interuniversity Athletic Union

The CIAU is the governing body of university sports across Canada.

Canadian National Railway Co.

Canada's largest railway may be referred to in second reference simply as **CN**. Formerly a federal Crown corporation, it was privatized on

Nov. 28, 1995, through a sale of public shares that raised $2.2-billion. By then, it had detached itself from such subsidiaries as the ferry company CN Marine (which began operating as a separate Crown company in 1985 and was renamed Marine Atlantic in 1986). The non-rail real-estate holdings that had been managed and developed by the subsidiary CN Real Estate were either sold or held back from privatization by the federal government. CN Exploration, an oil and gas company based in Calgary, was sold early in 1995 to a Calgary company. In references to the former Crown-owned company, be aware that while the official name even then was Canadian National Railway Co., it called itself Canadian National Railways (note the s) for most purposes, including its annual report.

Canadian Pacific

Canadian Pacific Ltd., which was the parent company to such subsidiaries as CP Rail, CP Ships, CP Trucks and Canadian Pacific Hotels, engineered its own breakup in October, 2001. It was replaced with five businesses in the transportation, energy and hotel sectors: Canadian Pacific Railway Ltd., which may be called CPR in second reference; Fording Inc., which in 2003 merged its coal mines with mines owned by Sherritt International Corp. and Teck Cominco Ltd. to become Fording Canadian Coal Trust; Fairmont Hotels & Resorts Inc.; PanCanadian Energy Corp., which merged with Alberta Energy Co. Ltd. in 2002 to form EnCana Corp., Canada's second-largest oil company; and British-based CP Ships Ltd.

Canadian Press

In copy, The Canadian Press. In credit lines, Canadian Press. Describe it as a news co-operative, not as a news service. It is owned by its members.

Canadian Radio-television and Telecommunications Commission

In subsequent references, **CRTC**. Its name can slow down a lead, so consider calling it something like Canada's (or the federal) broadcasting regulator or Canada's communications regulator, depending on the story, and leaving the name to the second paragraph.

Canadian Security Intelligence Service (no **and**).

Insiders pronounce its initials as an acronym, See-sis, and most of our readers would also do so. As a matter of style, omit the definite article with the initials in second reference (say CSIS, not the CSIS). It may also be called the agency, but not the security service if there is any danger of confusion with its predecessor, the security service of the RCMP.

can and may

Can expresses ability; **may** denotes possibility or permission. See may and might.

cancer

This term refers to a group of diseases in which cells start to divide uncontrollably and form a tumour; hence, the proper generic term is often **cancers**. The various types behave differently enough that we should be specific when we know the details. The most common type is **carcinoma**, found in the skin, glands and linings of internal organs and intestines. **Sarcoma** hits muscle, bone and cartilage. **Lymphoma** hits the lymphatic system, as in Hodgkin's disease. Cancerous cells may spread from the original tumour to form secondary colonies, known as **metastases**. **Leukemia** does not involve tumours, but may be described as a cancer of the white blood cells.

candour

Candu

It is upper-and-lower, standing for Canadian deuterium uranium (reactor).

canister

canker and chancre

A **canker** is an ulceration of the mouth or lip, or something that causes decay, especially in plants. A **chancre** is a sore or lesion caused by syphilis. No need to add the word "sore" to either.

cannelloni

canola

It is the name for the strain of rapeseed, developed in Canada, that allowed the use of rape for edible oil.

canon and cannon

A **canon** is a rule or set of rules, usually religious, or a type of musical composition, or a list of literary works, or an Anglican title. See religious titles. A **cannon** is a gun. See guns and calibres.

Canute

King of England from 1016 to 1035, and for part of that time king of Denmark and Norway. He ordered the tide to halt as a way of showing his fawning yes-men that he was not omnipotent. We must not perpetuate the misunderstanding that he believed he could stop the tide.

canvas and canvass

Canvas is a type of cloth. To **canvass** means to seek votes or opinions. A canvass is the act of doing so.

Cape Breton

When speaking of the region, we do not normally attach the word Island to the name.

capelin (not caplin)

Cape Spear, Nfld.

The most easterly point in Canada and North America, at 52 degrees 37 minutes west. (Brazil extends much farther east, to about 35 degrees.)

Cape Town

Cape Verde

No useful adjective. Currency: escudo. Capital: Praia.

This state, which gained full independence from Portugal in 1975, comprises 10 very dry islands (and five islets) in the Atlantic, 620 kilometres off Africa. The nearest mainland countries are Senegal, Mauritania and Gambia. The official language is Portuguese, but the common language spoken on all the islands is called Crioulo. The capital is on the island of Sao Tiago. More than two-thirds of the population of 416,000 are of mixed race, and most of the rest are black. Most exports (canned and frozen fish, bananas, salt) go to Portugal.

capital, Capitol

The **Capitol** is the official building of the U.S. Congress in Washington, D.C., the name of the legislature buildings in many U.S. state capitals, and the temple of Jupiter Capitolinus in ancient Rome. For the seat of government and other uses, the word is **capital**.

capitalization

Entries in this section are broken down into these major headings: political terms; royalty; non-political officeholders; organizations and their members; education terms; arts and publishing; courts and judges; dates, holidays and historical periods; geography; numbered labels (Grade 1, Act 2); police and military; religions and clergy; science, nature and medicine; signs, slogans and mottoes; sports; trade names.

Political terms

Upper-case the names of **legislative bodies** at all three levels, but upper-case the commonly accepted shortened names only at the federal level (Parliament, the Senate, the House of Commons, the Commons, the Alberta Legislature, the legislature, Moncton City Council, the council). Follow the same practice when using these as adjectives (a Commons committee, a council resolution), but note that the adjective parliamentary is lower-case. Upper-case the proper names of foreign political bodies, but not their English translations (the U.S. House of Representatives, but Poland's

parliament, the Sejm). Upper-case such nicknames as the Red Chamber, but lower-case such merely descriptive phrases as the upper chamber, the lower house.

Upper-case the proper names of other **elected or appointed bodies** (the Toronto District School Board, the Wheat Board, the Canada Council), but lower-case their generic second references (the board, the council). Likewise, upper-case only the proper names of **royal commissions** (the Royal Commission on Newspapers; but the Kent commission, a royal commission on the newspaper industry).

Lower-case **government**, **cabinet** and the names of standing committees (the legislature's finance committee, the cabinet's priorities and planning committee). But upper-case the proper names of special committees, formed for a specific length of time and a specific investigation.

Government departments at the federal and provincial level are upper-case, since they have a legal corporate identity for the purpose of contracts etc. (the Department of Finance, the Finance Department, Finance; but the department). Lower-case the word "departments" when naming more than one (the departments of Health and Finance). We do not upper-case departments of municipalities, counties and regions (Vancouver's health department). We use upper case for translations of department names in non-English-speaking countries (the Russian Foreign Ministry, the French Foreign Office). Japan's Ministry of International Trade and Industry is widely known as MITI, which is acceptable in second reference.

Upper-case **political titles** both before and after a name, provided there is only one person holding such a title in that jurisdiction. (Finance Minister Susan Black; Colin Green, Saskatchewan's Minister of Parks,

Recreation and Culture; the Labour Minister, James Brown.) At the federal and provincial levels, such titles are also upper-case without the name if the title stands for a specific person or the personification of a department. (The Finance Minister was applauded. Payment is made to the Revenue Minister.) But when speaking of the position generically, or in the plural with no names attached, use lower case. (He is looking for a new education minister; a meeting of the 11 attorneys-general.) The same rules apply to the translated political titles of office-holders in non-English-speaking countries. Upper-case plural titles appearing before names (an initiative of Mayors Mary Smith and Albert Jones). Qualified terms such as president-elect and premier-designate are lower-case, even before a name: president-elect Chelsea Clinton.

At the municipal level, or when there is more than one person with a political title in the same jurisdiction, we use upper case only before the name. (Alderman Ronald Glover, but Ronald Glover, alderman for Ward 5. The mayor said; the alderman said.) Similarly, lower-case "the minister" used without the name and portfolio, since several people hold that generic title. And lower-case "the ministry" when it stands alone.

Deputy is upper-case only for the official cabinet positions of Deputy Prime Minister and Deputy Premier. **Acting** is always lower-case, and so is the position title accompanying it (acting prime minister Joe Brown). The position title is also lower-case when preceded by the word former or late (former prime minister Pierre Trudeau). Departmental **deputy minister** is lower-case, even before names (deputy finance minister Frederick White). Note that the portfolio name is also lower-case here, unless it is the department itself that is being emphasized and the word could be replaced by the full department

title (Frederick Gorbet, the deputy minister at Finance).

Parliamentary titles, such as Liberal Leader, Opposition Leader, Whip and House Leader, follow the same rules, taking upper case as a title before the name, and also as a description standing alone if it is unique in that jurisdiction. (NDP Whip James Green; the whip said, the three House leaders; the Liberal Leader said, but the leader said.) The titles of their deputies are lower-case, as are those of ministers' parliamentary secretaries. **Speaker** is always upper-case, for clarity, but the word deputy attached to it is not.

Opposition is upper-case when we are referring to the Official Opposition in a British-type parliamentary democracy, meaning the second-largest party or coalition. But it is lower-case when referring collectively to all the non-government parties.

Parliamentary papers and procedures are usually upper-case, as in Question Period, Speech from the Throne, Throne Speech. But lower-case **white paper** when the official title is not used (the minister's white paper on future defence spending). Lower-case the common **stages of legislative passage**, such as second reading, report stage, committee of the whole, royal assent.

The full names of **bills** and **laws** are upper-case, and so are some commonly accepted shortened names (the Criminal Code, the Charter). In generic references without the name, lower-case the words the bill, the act. The **Constitution** is always upper-case when referring to that of Canada, the United States and other English-speaking countries in which that is the document's official title. But do not use upper case in translation (China's constitution).

Political parties and movements, plus their nicknames or shortened names, are upper-case (the Progressive Conservatives, the Conservatives, the

Tories, the Peronistas). But use lower case when referring to general philosophies (conservative, liberal, socialist). Capitalize Communist when referring to a party of that name or an official member, but lower-case communism, communistic and communist philosophy, teaching or leanings.

Ambassador is upper-case only before a name (U.S. Ambassador Edward Ney; but Edward Ney, the U.S. ambassador; the ambassador said). Always lower-case **embassy**, even when it appears with the name of the country (the Iranian embassy).

Crown is upper-case, both as a noun and as an adjective, when referring to the government or the prosecution in court. (The Crown, a Crown corporation, the Crown attorney.) It is lower-case only when referring to the headgear.

Federal and **national** are upper-case only when an integral part of a title (National Employment Service; Federal Bureau of Investigation). They are lower-case as adjectives used merely to distinguish from provincial or state (the federal Finance Department).

Province, State, City, County, Town etc. are upper-case in those rare instances when we must give the official corporate name of a jurisdiction (the Province of Saskatchewan, the City of Hamilton). They are lower-case standing alone, even when referring to the government or corporate entity (he is suing the province), and in their adjectival form even when accompanied by the name (an Edmonton city bylaw, an Alberta provincial inquiry).

Royalty

Upper-case Royal Family and Royal Household (and, by extension, the Royals, which we use only in direct quotes), but only in reference to that of Canada and other Commonwealth monarchies. Lower-case royalty, royal tour, royal car etc. Note that the former Royal Yacht Britannia was an official name, but lower-case "the royal yacht" in second reference.

Upper-case the Queen, the King, the Prince, the Sultan, the Sheik etc. in second reference to a specific person. This applies to all monarchies.

Non-political officeholders

Titles of officers in companies, clubs and organizations and appointed government bodies are lower-case, even before names (Chrysler president Kurt Weiss; CMA chairman Raymond Braun; chief grain commissioner Milt Schwartz). But upper-case first references to high statutory offices that are unique to a jurisdiction, especially those whose incumbents report to Parliament or a legislature. These include Auditor-General, Privacy Commissioner, Ombudsman, Governor of the Bank of Canada and the like. In second reference, upper-case a full title when referring to a specific person (the Auditor-General said) but not a generic word (the commissioner reported).

Organizations and their members

Upper-case the names of organizations and their commonly accepted short forms (the International Brotherhood of Teamsters, the Teamsters, the Grand Orange Lodge of Ontario, the Orangemen). Upper-case the shortened form for people if we are denoting official membership (a Teamster, a Scout), but not if we are merely describing a philosophical leaning or an occupation. (One can be a steelworker without being a Steelworker, a member of the union.)

For **military** organizations, we use lower case for generic or occupational descriptions as opposed to ranks, even when they echo the service's official name (the Royal Marines, three marines; the Canadian Coast Guard, two coastguardmen). But upper-case adjectival forms standing for the organization (a Marine investigation). See ranks.

Education terms

Upper-case the full names of schools at all levels and the full names of their internal colleges, but lower-case the names of faculties, including faculties that call themselves schools (such as schools of law, medicine, nursing). But note Osgoode Hall Law School. Upper-case Professor when it appears before a name as an honorific, but not when standing alone or combined with "emeritus." Lower-case other titles and descriptions: president, principal, freshman, class of '94, alma mater. Lower-case degrees (bachelor of arts) but upper-case their abbreviations (BA, BSc, PhD). Upper-case the full names of chairs, fellowships and awards.

Arts and publishing

In titles of films, TV and radio programs, books, plays, poems, works of art, record albums, tapes, songs and other musical compositions, upper-case the first and last words and all the principal words in between. That is, do not upper-case articles or short conjunctions and prepositions (*Zorba the Greek*, *Breakfast at Tiffany's*). Longer conjunctions and prepositions, such as because, around and through, are jarring in lower case, and so should be capped.

If a title is all caps, we upper-case only the first letters of words. If a title is all lower-case, as in *the fifth estate*, we conform; however, the first word must be upper-case if the title begins a sentence. For titles of French works, follow the style of that language and upper-case only the first word and proper names.

Magazine is upper-case only if it is part of the name (Harper's Magazine, but Maclean's magazine). All-cap names are changed to upper and lower, but we allow names that are all lower-case.

Newspaper names are run with the city included, regardless of whether it is an official part of the paper's name; our treatment of the word "the" indicates whether the name we are using is the official one. Upper-case "The" when the official name includes the city (The Hamilton Spectator) but lower-case it when "the" is not part of the newspaper's official title as used on the front page (the Toronto Star) or when we have inserted the city ourselves (the Montreal Gazette). In second reference, "the" is upper-case only for papers without city names (The Globe, The Gazette, but the Star, the Spectator). Use lower case when the paper's name is used as an adjective (the story in The Globe, but the Globe story).

When reporting **headlines**, subheads, captions, the titles of magazine articles, chapter headings and the like, upper-case the first letter of each word, regardless of the style used in the particular publication.

In **Globe bylines**, writers' names and the word "BY" are upper-case. The prefix Mac or Mc is upper-and-lower if the root name begins with a capital (MacDonald is written BY MARY MacDONALD), but the prefix is all caps if the root name is lower-case (Macdonald is written BY MARY MACDONALD). Other prefixes, such as VAN and DE, are all caps.

Courts and judges

Upper-case the names of all courts and their commonly accepted shortened names, such as Supreme Court, Superior Court, Divisional Court, Court of Appeal (but appeal court), Provincial Court, Family Court, International Court of Justice, the World Court. But lower-case court names in non-English-speaking countries that we have translated into the English equivalent (China's supreme court).

Court and **bench** when standing alone are usually lower-case, but for clarity be prepared to use upper case in direct quotations when the speaker is using the Court or the Bench as personifications, especially in parallel constructions with the Crown.

Upper-case **the Chief Justice** in second reference without the name, for both the federal and provincial levels, but lower-case **the judge** in second reference. Upper-case Your Honour and His Honour (these terms usually arise only in quotes).

Lower-case **jury**, foreman, grand jury, coroner's jury, court reporter, bailiff.

Dates, holidays, historical periods

Upper-case the names of all civic **holidays**, and all days or periods observed by commonly recognized religions (Canada Day, Palm Sunday, Yom Kippur, Holy Week, Ramadan). For clarity, upper-case the English translations of foreign holidays (Lithuania's Independence Day).

Upper-case other special days that are not official holidays but have a similar air, such as Halloween, May Day, April Fool's Day, New Year's Eve. But lower-case more mundane days such as election day, nomination day, enumeration day, garbage day.

Upper-case special names given to days, weeks, months and years for purposes of fundraising, education etc. (Apple Day, Heart Month, the Year of the Child).

Upper-case days and other periods of time that have been given **historical labels** (the Night of the Long Knives, D-Day, the Age of Reason, the Renaissance, the Reign of Terror, the Age of Steam, the Stone Age, the Middle Ages). But note that there have been several ice ages, so these are lower-case. See the note below on geological ages.

Upper-case decades when speaking of them as a distinctive period (the Gay Nineties, the decadence of the Twenties, the Hungry Thirties, the Dirty Thirties). But these same decades can be lower-case when used simply as time periods (He worked at several papers in the twenties, thirties and forties). When the century is included, use figures (the 1930s). Lower-case centuries (the ninth century, the 21st century). See AD, numbers.

Geography

North, south, east and west are lower-case when referring to simple directions (the tanks rolled east), and so are northern, southern, eastern and western when not referring to a district that is distinctive for reasons other than simple direction (the storm moved from eastern Alberta into southwestern Saskatchewan). But upper-case these words when they refer to areas that are commonly considered to be set apart by climate, political administration, economics, language or even outlook. These include the West, the East, Western Canada, Central Canada, Eastern Canada, the North, the Far North, the Far East, Southern California, West Texas, the Eastern Townships, the West End (in London), the South Side (in Chicago). For most provinces, upper-case Northern and Southern. For Ontario, upper-case Northern, Southern, Eastern, Northeastern, Northwestern, Southwestern, Central. Local attitudes and usage are our guide. For example, England has the North and the South, but other directional adjectives are lower-case (southeastern England).

Lower-case the adjectives eastern, western, northern and southern when not attached to a geographical name or a well-defined region (say Western Canadian businessmen, but western businessmen, eastern arrogance, southern cooking, northern hospitality). The exception is the upper-case adjective Western when it means of the Western world or Western alliance.

Lower-case **coast** (north coast, east coast etc.) when referring to actual shorelines (the west coast of Cape Breton, oil shipments along the west coast of Canada). But use upper case when referring to geographical areas (people on the West Coast; he got a job on the Coast). This is especially required in local names for coastal regions that do not lie in the direction that the name implies, such as British Columbia's North Coast and South Coast, which are actually the northern and southern sections of the West Coast. In Nova Scotia, the South Shore faces southeast, running from Halifax to Yarmouth.

Upper-case the names and nicknames of geographical and political regions, such as the Avalon Peninsula, the Mackenzie Delta, the Prairies, the Prairie provinces, the Maritimes, Peace River Country, the Annapolis Valley, Silicon Valley, the Wheat Belt, the Bible Belt, and England's Midlands, Lake District, West Country, Constable Country. But lower-case words such as prairie, delta, valley, peninsula and country when simply referring to physical features or characteristics (the entire Saugeen valley is good pheasant country). When listing the name of more than one geographical feature or street, retain the upper case for the generic noun (Lakes Huron and Erie, Hudson and James Bays, Peel and Sherbrooke Streets).

Upper-case **Greater** in the official name of a city-centred region, such as Greater Vancouver Regional District and Greater London, but not in such merely descriptive terms as greater Chatham.

Upper-case **Dominion**, both as noun and adjective, when referring to Canada.

Numbered labels

In general, upper-case labels that include a number, such as Grade 1, No. 2. In documents such as statutes,

charters and constitutions, and in books and other published material, upper-case formal numbered headings, such as Part 2; Chapter 3; Act 2, Scene 3; Section 205 (d) (iii); but not labels for divisions that are not headings, such as page 162, paragraph 4, line 2. An exception is made for newspaper pages, which are upper-case by convention (Page 1, Page 7). The word **verse** is upper-case for such works as the Bible in which verses are formally numbered, but not when referring to verses of poems and songs.

Police and military

Upper-case the formal names of police and military forces, and those of divisions such as corps, divisions, brigades, regiments, battalions, companies, platoons (D Company, Company A, 52 Division). Also upper-case their nicknames (the Patricias, the Old Contemptibles, the Big Red One). But lower-case names of occupational groups such as a signals squad, a reconnaissance detail, and such police subdepartments as morality squad, traffic section, homicide division. Do not upper-case "police department" without the name of the municipality. Also see ranks.

Religions and clergy

For all monotheistic religions, upper-case the word God, such proper names as Jehovah and Allah (see Allah), and such alternative names as Father, Holy Spirit, Almighty, Saviour, Christ, King of Heaven. Also upper-case alternative names for the principal figures in various religions, such as the Enlightened One referring to Buddha, the Holy Prophet in Islam, the Apostle Paul. Upper-case the Twelve Apostles, but lower-case "the apostle" used without a name. Upper-case Virgin, Blessed Virgin, Madonna and other such references to Mary.

For ancient pagan religions and modern religions with more than one deity, lower-case the word god (the god Jupiter, the goddess Sakti), and also lower-case all pronouns.

Upper-case the names of all modern religions (Christianity, Shintoism, Islam) and all their sects and denominations (Protestant, Anglican, Sunni, Reform). Upper-case shortened forms referring to members (a Witness, a Mormon), but not the terms applied to non-members (gentile) or non-believers (atheist).

Upper-case the names of the sacred books of all modern religions, the names of their various versions, and the words Holy and Sacred when used to modify them (the Bible, the Holy Koran, the King James Version, the Pentateuch). But lower-case such adjectives as biblical and talmudic, and such generic terms as sacred scrolls.

Upper-case major events depicted in religious writings or religious history, such as the Exodus, the Crucifixion, the Resurrection, the Hegira, the Diaspora. But lower-case the regular observances of current adherents, such as mass, holy communion, confession, baptism, compline, seder, minyan.

Lower-case **heaven**, limbo, purgatory and hell, except when used as an appellation for the Deity, as in "I thank Heaven." But upper-case such proper names for heaven and hell as Paradise, Hades, Asgard, Elysian Fields.

Upper-case **Church** in reference to a religion or denomination (The United Church of Canada, the Christian Science Church), but lower-case when standing alone.

Clerical titles are upper-case when accompanied by the person's name (Father Brown, Brother Michael, Rabbi Small). High offices are also upper-case without the name when given in full and referring to a specific person (the Archbishop of Canterbury, the Pope, the Dalai Lama). But in second or generic references to offices held by many people, say the archbishop, a brother, the rabbi, the mullah. See religious titles.

Religious holidays are upper-case. See note above on dates, holidays.

Science, nature, medicine

Latin scientific names have the first letter of only the genus in upper case, even when the name of a subspecies is derived from a proper name, such as that of the Canadian beaver, *Castor fiber canadensis*. They should be in italics. The levels of classification above genus, such as classes and families, are upper-case, e.g. *Mammalia*, *Rodentia*. (We avoid using scientific names in most stories unless the specific species is at issue, but they sometimes appear in direct quotes.)

In **medicine**, Latin names have tended to hang on in everyday jargon more than they have in other scientific disciplines. In considering capitalization, there is a distinction between formal Latin classifications, in which the genus is upper-case as usual, and the same names standing alone or with non-Latin adjectives, in which case they are lower-case. We would say *Streptococcus anaerobius* (italics), but describe it as the war-wound streptococcus (no italics). Say *Streptococcus bovis*, but call the same bacterium Bargen's streptococcus.

Diseases and conditions are lower-case (cancer, chickenpox), but adjectives derived from the names of people and places are upper-case (Kaposi's sarcoma, Parkinson's disease, Parkinsonism, Spanish flu).

The generic English names of **animals and plants**, and common adjectives attached to them, are lower-case (ruby-throated hummingbird, ring-necked gull, rainbow trout, quarter horse, bull terrier, polar bear, morning glory, yellow daisy, winter wheat, durum wheat). But adjectives from the names of countries, regions, cities, races and individuals usually remain upper-case (Labrador retriever, Lab, Pekingese, Great Dane, St. Bernard, German shepherd, Percheron, Holstein, Arctic owl, black-eyed Susan, Queen Anne's lace; but note jack-in-the-pulpit). Developed varieties of fruits, vegetables and grains are always upper-case (Beefsteak tomatoes, Empire apples, Golden Delicious, Red Fife wheat).

The **seasons** are lower-case (spring, autumn), and so are the milestone days in the yearly orbit (spring equinox, summer solstice).

Upper-case **Earth** when naming the planet (Earth's atmosphere), but not when it means soil. In familiar expressions, decide which meaning applies: down to earth; but it costs the Earth. Upper-case the names and nicknames of planets, stars, groups of stars and other **bodies in space** (Mars, the Red Planet, the Big Dipper), and also the adjectives derived from them (Martian, Jovian). But lower-case universe, sun and moon and the adjectives pertaining to them (lunar, helio-), since these words are generic. Lower-case other generic terms such as black hole, supernova, nebula, red giant, quasar, pulsar, even when these are accompanied by a name (The Andromeda nebula is the most distant thing visible to the naked eye).

Upper-case the **signs of the zodiac** and their commonly accepted English names (the Crab, the Twins). See zodiac.

Lower-case the names of the **imaginary lines** dividing Earth, such as equator, meridian, parallel, tropic, unless they have a proper noun attached to them (Tropic of Capricorn, the Arctic Circle). An exception is the International Date Line.

Upper-case the well-defined regions of Earth, such as the Northern Hemisphere, the Arctic, the North Temperate Zone.

Upper-case the names of eras, periods and epochs in the Earth's development (Paleozoic, Carboniferous, Pliocene), and also such informal period names as the

Age of Mammals, the Stone Age. But note that ice age(s) is lower-case.

Signs, slogans, mottoes

Picket and protest signs, commercial signs, official notices and the like come in a variety of capitalization styles, but are most often all initial caps. In reporting them, we upper-case only the first word and proper names ("Ban the bomb"; "Locked out by Eaton's").

The same rule applies to slogans chanted by crowds and to mottoes. (With shouts of "Solidarity forever," the crowd advanced. The corps's motto is "Always faithful.")

Sports

Upper-case official titles of leagues and divisions (the American League, the NHL's Atlantic Division), but lower-case second references and generic uses (the league, both divisions, a grapefruit league, a Class AA league). Lower-case the term major leagues, the majors.

Upper-case such words as Series, Games and Cup when they stand for specific major events (the World Series, the Series; the Pan-American Games, the Games; the World Cup, the Cup). Also upper-case adjectival uses (Games officials; the most confused Cup game since the notorious Fog Bowl).

But lower-case such words as cup and trophy in second reference to the actual hardware (He has won the trophy four times).

Use upper case for baseball's All-Star Game, a proper name, but lower-case all-star in other references.

Use caps when quoting references to Game 1, Game 2 of a series, but in our own writing we prefer first game, second game.

Trade names

Always upper-case registered trade names, unless the official spelling starts with a lower-case letter: eBay, iMac. In such cases, the first letter is upper-case if it begins a sentence. For the trade names of drugs, the Globe library has the standard index for the industry, the *Compendium of Pharmaceuticals and Specialties*, known as the CPS (lower-case generic drug names.) For all other trade names protected in Canada, consult the *Canadian Trade Index*.

The use of upper case implies that the exact brand is involved (Aspirin, Xerox, Fiberglas, Coke, Kleenex). For the sake of safety and accuracy, prefer generic terms (ASA, fibreglass, pain pill, copier, cola, tissue) unless the brand name is at issue in the story. Some exceptions are made for features. See trademark.

Upper-case common nicknames for brand names (Caddy, Jag).

If a trade name is all caps, we upper-case only the first letter of each word. But also use upper case after hyphens (Band-Aid; Jell-O).

Some names have entered the public domain for informal generic references, such as photostat, laundromat and nylon. Some product names have undergone this process in the United States but are still protected brand names in Canada, so it is best to check.

cappuccino

capriccio

captain, Capt. See ranks.

carat
See karat.

carburetor

cardinal
When identifying cardinals of the Roman Catholic Church, use the style Cardinal Given Name/Surname. Thus, Cardinal Aloysius Ambrozic. See religious titles.

careen and career
Careen, from the Latin word for keel, implies dangerous leaning. A sailing vessel is careening if it is leaning precariously in a storm, and is careened when it is purposely tipped on its side for cleaning. By extension, any type of vehicle that comes close to tipping over, particularly because it is cornering rapidly, can be described as careening. Even a swaying drunk can be pictured as careening down the street.

To **career** means to move swiftly and freely, full speed ahead. If a car is speeding straight down Main Street, it is careering through town. If it is veering and swaying, it is careening.

Caribbean
It is important to be aware of the exact boundaries of the Caribbean. It is bounded on the north by the Greater Antilles (Cuba, Hispaniola, Jamaica and Puerto Rico) and on the east by the Lesser Antilles, the arc that runs from the Virgin Islands south to Trinidad, just off Venezuela. That means that the Bahamas, Bermuda and the Turks and Caicos are too far north to be called Caribbean islands, and Barbados is too far east. They are in the Atlantic. (They can, however, be called part of the West Indies.)

Cariboo and caribou
The spelling is **Cariboo** for all uses connected with the Cariboo Mountains of east-central British Columbia, including Cariboo country, Cariboo District, Cariboo gold rush, Cariboo Road, Cariboo Meadows, B.C., and the federal riding of Cariboo-Chilcotin. Cariboo is always upper-case.

Lower-case **caribou** for the animal, and use the same word for both singular and plural. It can be described as the North American reindeer, but we should not imply they are identical. The two North American species are the woodland and the smaller Barren Grounds caribou.

Upper-case Caribou for the twin-engine plane made by de Havilland, and for the Caribou Inuit. (These people, one of the eight major groups of Inuit, occupy the Barrens and hunt caribou.)

The spelling is Caribou for all place names outside B.C., including communities in New Brunswick, Newfoundland, Nova Scotia, Ontario and Yukon. (Note that even B.C. has Caribou Hide.)

caries, singular. Prefer **decay**.

carillonneur

Carleton and Carlton
Carleton is by far the more common, found in place names in Nova Scotia, Ontario, PEI and Quebec, in constituency names in New Brunswick and the Ottawa area, and in the university name.

But note the Ritz-Carlton in Montreal; Carlton, Sask.; and Toronto's Carlton Street.

carry-on (adj.).

Cartier, Sir George-Étienne (not Georges).

casbah (not kasbah)

case, see pronouns.

caseload
One caseload, many cases.

casualties, injuries, fatalities
Casualty means both an accident and the victim of one (or a victim of military action). But this sort of extension does not apply to injury and fatality, which both define events only, not people. It is proper to say there were no fatalities (meaning deaths), but not that both fatalities were from Winnipeg (meaning dead people). Also see homicide.

catarrh

Caterpillar
A trade name. Cat. Lower-case for larvae.

cathedral and basilica, see basilica.

Catholic
Acceptable first reference for Roman Catholic in such obvious references as Catholic school board, but always include Roman if there is a chance of confusion with other sects.

Caulfeild
District of West Vancouver, and old Anglo-Irish name. Not Caulfield.

cause and reason
Careful writers reserve **reason** for describing human reasoning, motive or justification (His need to match the competition was the reason he kept the store open). For non-human agents, use **cause** (The recession was the cause of his bankruptcy, not the reason for his bankruptcy).

cavalcade
Originally a procession of horsemen. It can be applied now to any procession or parade, but not to static shows or events. Do not change such proper names as the Cavalcade of Colours, but when using your own words call it a festival or celebration of fall colours.

cave-in, noun. The verb is **cave in**.

CBC
Acceptable in first reference. No need to spell out Canadian Broadcasting Corp., but we must make sure that later references to "the corporation" are clear.

CCF
Co-operative Commonwealth Federation. See New Democratic Party.

ceasefire, noun. The verb is **cease firing**.

CEGEPs

There is no need to write out the full name, *Collèges d'enseignement général et professionnel*, but we must explain in the story that they are Quebec institutions of postsecondary, pre-university education offering a choice of university preparation or professional training leading to a diploma.

In Quebec, high school is a five-year program equivalent to Grades 7 to 11 in other provinces. After getting a secondary-school diploma, students go on to a CEGEP.

celebrant

Reserve this for one who presides over a religious rite. A maker of whoopee is a **celebrator**.

cellphone

One word.

Celsius

There is no need to specify that a temperature is in the Celsius scale unless the reader might be led to suspect otherwise (e.g. when a U.S. scientist is giving the temperature at which a reaction takes place). Even then, it is enough to establish this with the first temperature in the story. The proper style is 450 C (no period).

Normally, we simply convert temperatures to Celsius, but we must be careful not to imply that the person speaking was using Celsius if this was not the case.

To convert temperatures from degrees Fahrenheit to Celsius, subtract 32 and multiply the result by 5/9 (that is, multiply by 5 and then divide by 9).

For the sake of comprehension by the majority of our readers, always add the Fahrenheit equivalent in brackets when reporting human body temperatures. See measurement.

cement

A sticking or bonding agent. It is only one component of concrete, so say concrete blocks etc., not cement blocks.

censer and censor

A **censer** is a receptacle for incense. A **censor** is one who rules on acceptability.

centenary

This word has largely fallen into disuse, supplanted by centennial. It survives in bicentenary, but even here bicentennial is preferred. The higher levels of centenary (tercentenary etc.) are too obscure for newspaper use. Say 300th, 400th anniversary.

Centers for Disease Control and Prevention

In Atlanta. The tag "and Prevention" was added in 1992. Name is usually preceded by the modifier "national" or "U.S. national."

Central African Republic

No useful adjective. Currency: CFA franc. Capital: Bangui.

This landlocked country on a plateau just north of the equator was called Ubangi Shari when it was one of the four districts of French Equatorial Africa. It became independent in 1960. The Ubangi are one of five ethnic groups, and are not the largest; the Banda make up 45 per cent of the population of 3.6 million. French is the official language, but the national lingua franca is Sango. There are few paved roads, and the major link to other countries is the Ubangi River. The major exports are coffee, timber and diamonds.

Five years after independence, the head of the army, Jean-Bédel Bokassa, seized power from his nephew in a coup, and a decade later declared himself Emperor Bokassa I. His oppressive rule ended only after France, shocked by the massacre of

100 schoolchildren in 1979, staged a bloodless coup while he was in Libya. After another 14 years of misrule, the country elected a civilian government in 1993, headed by Ange-Félix Patasse. He was overthrown in a military coup in 2003.

Central America

It can be described as the narrow arc of land linking Mexico to South America, or the countries found there. (Mexico is part of North America.) Its seven republics are, from north to south, Belize, Guatemala, Honduras, El Salvador, Nicaragua, Costa Rica and Panama. Five of them have coasts on both the Caribbean and the Pacific, but Belize fronts only on the Caribbean and El Salvador only on the Pacific. Panama is aligned east-west, and joins the western coast of Colombia, not the northern coast. The Panama Canal runs north-south. We can say generally that Central America is Spanish-speaking and its people are Indian, white, black and often a mixture of these. But note that English is the official language of Belize (formerly called British Honduras), and that Costa Rica is overwhelmingly white.

centre

Preserve this spelling except in the case of proper U.S. names (e.g. Rockefeller Center).

Centre of Forensic Sciences

Ontario. Not for, and note plural.

centre on (not centre around).

centuries

They are spelled out, lower-case, if the number is below 10 (the ninth century). For 10 and above, the numeral is used (the 21st century). See capitalization, numbers, millennium.

certificates of origin

They establish the country of origin of imported goods, and acquired new importance in Canada when the Canada-U.S. free-trade agreement went into effect on Jan. 1, 1989. Issued by chambers of commerce and similar bodies, they are used by customs officials to determine how goods should be treated for tariff purposes.

cesarean section

CFA

For the *Communauté financière africaine*, the African Financial Community. Its members use a single currency, the CFA franc.

CFA also means chartered financial analyst, acceptable in second reference. In Newfoundland, it also stands for an outsider, meaning come-from-away, but explain.

Chad

Adjective and people: Chadian. Currency: CFA franc. Capital: N'Djamena (formerly France's Fort Lamy).

It is a landlocked country in north-central Africa, extending northward into a mountainous area of the Sahara where it has a disputed boundary with its northern neighbour, Libya. The population of 9 million is split between Arab nomads in the north, including the Wadai and Fulani, and Negroid tribes of the southern savannahs around Lake Chad, notably the Sara. Independence from France in 1960 was followed by 22 years of coups and civil war involving up to 11 factions, including secessionist Arab groups in the centre and north, until a northern army under Hissène Habré gained control over the entire country in 1982. He was ousted in 1990. There are more than 100 languages and dialects, but French serves as an administrative language and Arabic is a lingua franca in all but the south.

chair

It is accepted in most dictionaries, including our own, as a verb for taking the chair or directing a meeting.

It may be used as a noun meaning a person, if there is no risk of confusion with a piece of furniture. Say that she chaired the meeting or was in the chair, that she was the chair, or that the party will choose a new chair. The nouns chairman and chairwoman may be used as well, or chairperson if the reference is generic, with no known gender. See women and language.

chaise longue (not lounge).

Champs Élysées

chancellery

chancre and canker, see canker.

changeover, noun. The verb is change over.

changing the guard

The preposition of is needed in such sentences as The Queen watched the changing of the guard. See trooping the colour.

channel, station, network

Use channel as the generic term to refer to such cable services as Bravo!, A&E and The Learning Channel, even where the formal name (The Sports Network) may suggest otherwise. Channel is the number you punch in on your TV, and so is most relevant to individual viewers (and our readers).

Station properly applies to broadcast outlets that transmit through the air to their local areas. Some are also distributed by satellite or cable as "superstations," such as CHCH, SBK and WGN.

Network means an entity that produces programming for a string of owned or affiliated broadcast stations, such as CBC, CTV, TVO and CBS. It

is usually the signal from one of these local affiliates that is picked up by your local cable company, but we can fairly say it's the network that is being transmitted.

Channel, the

Acceptable even in first reference for the English Channel.

Channel Islands

They should be described as dependencies since 1066 of the English (not British) Crown, and as lying south of England off northwestern France. They are not part of the United Kingdom, being governed according to their own constitutions. There are two main bailiwicks—Guernsey, which also includes the islands of Sark, Alderney, Herm, Brechou, Jethou and Lihou; and Jersey, which also includes Ecrehou Rocks and Les Minquiers.

Channel Islands National Park is off Southern California. Its eight islands are noted for their sea lions.

Chanukah

Use **Hanukkah** instead.

chaperone, noun and verb.

Chappaquiddick

It is an island off Martha's Vineyard, Mass. Senator Edward Kennedy drove off a bridge there in July of 1969; his passenger, Mary Jo Kopechne, drowned. He received a two-month suspended sentence for not reporting the accident until the next morning.

Chapter 11

It should be used only in reference to U.S. bankruptcy-protection provisions. In Canada, the mechanism is the Companies' Creditors Arrangements Act.

chargé d'affaires, chargés d'affaires

charley horse

Charlottetown accord

A package of proposed constitutional amendments agreed to by federal and provincial governments and four aboriginal groups at Charlottetown on Aug. 28, 1992, after a two-year process of consultation and negotiation in the wake of the failure in 1990 of the Meech Lake accord (which see). The package was rejected in a national vote (actually a plebiscite, but universally referred to as a referendum) on Oct. 26, 1992.

Technically, it was two separate votes on the same day: in Quebec under the provincial referendum law, and in the rest of Canada under the federal law.

The national result was about 54 per cent No, 45 per cent Yes. The accord was strongly endorsed only in Newfoundland, New Brunswick and Prince Edward Island. It narrowly passed in Ontario, was narrowly defeated in Nova Scotia, and was strongly rejected in all other provinces and the territories. It was also rejected by native voters.

Meech had been widely criticized as being a backroom deal and as failing to address concerns outside Quebec, including those of native people (it was a native MLA in Manitoba who dealt Meech its death blow in June of 1990). The lessons of Meech resulted in the most open and extensive public consultation in Canada's history for the next attempt, and participation by the four major native groups.

The Quebec Liberal Party's Allaire commission and the provincial Bélanger-Campeau commission both formulated proposals, and the province set Oct. 26, 1992, as its deadline for holding a vote either on a constitutional offer or on sovereignty. The package reached at Charlottetown built on the cross-Canada consultations of the Spicer commission (the Citizens' Forum on Canada's Future); a 28-point package of federal proposals, called *Shaping Canada's Future*, examined by the Beaudoin-Dobbie (originally the Castonguay-Dobbie) joint parliamentary committee; the Beaudoin-Edwards committee on the actual amendment process; commissions in the provinces; and a series of federal-provincial conferences of constitutional ministers and then first ministers.

The package of proposals had five major themes:

(1) A Canada clause, defining the fundamental nature of the country: Key provisions were that Quebec was a distinct society, and that aboriginal governments constituted one of three orders of government (along with the federal and provincial).

(2) Parliamentary reform: A Triple-E Senate (equal, elected, effective) had been a major goal in the West, particularly Alberta. The accord would have given each province six elected senators (in Quebec, the election would be in the National Assembly). The Commons would gain seats to bring it closer to representation by population, with Quebec guaranteed 25 per cent of the members. (This met with particularly stiff opposition in B.C., with its burgeoning population.) The Senate could veto Commons bills on natural resources or "materially affecting" the French language and culture, but defeat of other bills would provoke a joint sitting with the Commons. Quebec would be guaranteed three of the nine Supreme Court judges, who would be selected by Ottawa from lists submitted by the provinces.

(3) Aboriginal self-government, recognized as an inherent right, would be defined in five years of consultations, during which it could not be taken to the courts (it was "non-justiciable").

(4) Division of powers: The accord maintained provincial equality,

rejecting "asymmetrical federalism," but allowed provinces to opt out of national programs, with compensation, if their own programs met national standards. Ottawa would drop out of forestry, mining, tourism, recreation, housing and urban affairs. Culture and labour-market training would be provincial, but Ottawa would keep the CBC and unemployment insurance.

(5) A social and economic union: The proposals for universal social standards and for a Canada-wide harmonized common market were watered down at Charlottetown, emerging as broadly sketched, subject to future political negotiation and with no real enforcement mechanism.

Charter of Rights and Freedoms
The full name is the Canadian Charter of Rights and Freedoms, but it may be called the Charter of Rights and Freedoms in first reference and the Charter (always upper-case) on second reference.

Adopted as part of the Constitution Act, 1982 (see Canada), the Charter requires the federal and provincial governments to respect certain rights and freedoms that are guaranteed to everyone in Canada or, in cases such as democratic rights, every citizen of Canada. The guarantee is "subject only to such reasonable limits prescribed by law as can be demonstrably justified in a free and democratic society." Section 15, the section on equality rights, took effect on April 17, 1985.

Section 33 of the Charter enables Parliament or a provincial legislature to specifically exempt any of its laws from three parts of the Charter: those covering fundamental freedoms, legal rights and equality rights. The exemption automatically expires after five years, but may be renewed. Section 33 is known colloquially as the notwithstanding clause, from its stipulation that an exempted piece of legislation "shall operate notwith-

standing a provision" in the Charter, and may be referred to that way if the context is clear.

Chassidim
Style is **Hasidim, Hasidic**.

chastise
Never chastize.

Cheboygan, Mich., but **Sheboygan**, Wis.

checkered past

checkers, checkerboard
But note Chequers, the official country residence of Britain's prime minister.

checklist

checkmate

checkoff, noun. Verb is **check off**.

cheque, chequebook, chequing account
But the bill received at a restaurant is a check.

cherubs (not cherubim).

chesterfield
Lower-case when it means sofa. A good Canadian word, but sofa's star is rising, particularly in sofa bed.

Chianti

Chibougamau

chief
Lower-case in generic second references to a specific police, fire or Indian chief (the chief said). Upper-case as a rank (police or fire department) before a name, in first or second reference. For the political title of Indian officeholders, we would normally use Mr. or Ms. in second reference, but Chief is acceptable as a

reminder to readers if the second reference is far from the first. Upper-case the Chief in references to former prime minister John Diefenbaker. This will crop up most often in direct quotes, but is also acceptable in features and less sombre news stories.

child

In the context of Canadian courts, someone 11 or younger is called a child (those 12 to 17 are called young persons). In general news stories, we need not be so restrictive. We may use child as a generic to describe those aged approximately 2 to 12, but note that rapid development at this age makes it necessary to find a more descriptive term when speaking of a specific child (a preschooler, a boy in Grade 7) or to use the age. Above 12, we normally use such terms as teenager, adolescent. A large group that includes only a few who are 13 or 14 may be called a group of children.

The term **children** is often used to refer to adult offspring (Mr. Jones, 68, has three children and 12 grandchildren). However, when we know the details we prefer the terms son and daughter.

Chile

Adjective and people: Chilean. Currency: peso. Capital: Santiago.

It measures more than 4,000 kilometres north to south, but only about 400 kilometres at its widest point. It owns the larger share of Tierra del Fuego, including its most southerly point, Cape Horn on Horn Island. Its numerous island possessions also include Easter Island and the Juan Fernandez Islands, west of Valparaiso. It also claims part of Antarctica, and has seven bases there. Most of its 15.5 million people live in the temperate central area. The north is a near-desert, the south is cool and wet. Chile is a major exporter of minerals, notably copper, and of fruit.

In 1973, the country's military overthrew the elected government of Salvador Allende and installed the brutal regime of Augusto Pinochet, who ruled the country until the election of Patricio Aylwin as president in 1990. Pinochet was arrested in England in 1998 and returned to Chile in 2000, where he was charged with the murder or "disappearance" of more than 3,000 people during his rule. A Chilean court ruled in 2001 that he was too sick and confused to stand trial.

chili

For the pepper: **chili sauce**, **chili con carne**.

Chilkoot Pass

Route through the Coast Mountains from the Alaskan Panhandle to Yukon.

Chilliwack, B.C.

Also the spelling for the adjacent area, formerly **Chilliwhack**.

China

Adjective and people: Chinese (never Chinaman). Currency: yuan. (Note that there are two types: the renminbi, people's money, which is not convertible, and foreign exchange certificates, which are. The two currencies are officially worth the same.) Capital: Beijing.

We never call it Red China. There is no need to call it mainland China, since we refer to the country across the Taiwan Strait as Taiwan. In very rare cases when we need to draw fine legal distinctions, or to explain initials used in a quote, the two countries are the People's Republic of China and the Republic of China. (See Taiwan.) China has 21 provinces (it would include Taiwan as a 22nd), plus five autonomous regions (Tibet, Inner Mongolia, Guangxi, Ningxia and Xinjiang) and three municipalities that are directly under the central government (Beijing, Shanghai and

Tianjin). Hong Kong, which reverted to China from Britain on July 1, 1997, is classed as a Special Administrative Region. In an agreement with Britain on Dec. 19, 1984, China undertook to respect a policy of one country, two systems, by which Hong Kong would retain a large measure of autonomy except in defence and foreign relations.

More than 90 per cent of China's population of about 1.3 billion is Han Chinese; the rest is split into 55 ethnic minorities. We may speak simply of the Chinese language (or Chinese) when we mean Mandarin, which is the common language of the country and of government, the schools and the media. (The Chinese word for the Mandarin language is Putonghua, which literally means "common tongue.") Specify regional dialects (such as Cantonese or Shanghainese) if we know they are being used. Cantonese is common among Chinese immigrants to Canada, since most are from Hong Kong.

A Beijing protest against the ruling Communist Party in 1989 culminated in what is commonly referred to as the June 4 Tiananmen Square massacre, in which a great number of Beijing pro-democracy protesters were killed by Chinese security forces. The official Chinese estimate of 300 deaths is unrealistically low. Amnesty International reported in 1990 that the toll was at least 1,000. University of Toronto historian Timothy Brook has estimated it at 2,600.

In April, 2003, Hu Jintao succeeded Jiang Zemin as president of China. Jiang had succeeded Deng Xiaoping, who succeeded Mao Zedong, the first leader of postwar Communist China.

china, lower-case for crockery.

Chinese names

In stories from China, names usually come family name first, followed by the person's given name(s). But watch out if the first name that appears is Lao or Xiao.

It is familiar practice in China to use only the surname and precede it with Lao (old) or Xiao (young or little). If a tradesman, for example, is known as Lao Liu, it is most likely that his family name is Liu, and it would be risky in the extreme to use "Mr. Lao" in second reference. If we can't get confirmation, the safest course is to repeat the entire name in subsequent references in such cases.

To further complicate things, the name that follows Xiao is not always the family name. Xiao is sometimes used as a part of given names, commonly for the youngest in the family, as with Deng Xiaoping. His daughter is widely known as Xiao Rong, but she is neither Ms. Xiao nor Ms. Rong. She is Deng Xiao Rong, and therefore Ms. Deng in second reference.

There is no ironclad rule in China, Taiwan, Hong Kong or Korea on whether the given names are run together as one word, split into two or hyphenated, and so we must be guided by the person's own usage. This is especially true with people of Oriental birth or ancestry who are now living in the West. Many adopt the Western practice of putting the family name last, and writers must take pains to determine the proper second reference. The old method of romanizing Chinese names, Wade-Giles, was replaced by China in 1958 with Pinyin, which is now the international standard. Peking became Beijing, Mao Tsetung became Mao Zedong and Chou Enlai became Zhou Enlai. See Pinyin.

chinook

Lower-case for the wind and the salmon, upper-case for the Chinook helicopter, the Indians at the mouth of the Columbia River, and the Chinook Jargon, the lingua franca of the West Coast fur trade. (The Jargon survives today in many B.C. place names and in such expressions as "high muckamucks," the rich and powerful.)

Chipewyan

Note the spelling of these northern Athapaskan-speaking people who give their name to many geographical names in Alberta. The name is Cree for pointed skins, but the Chipewyan call themselves Dene, meaning people.

Chippawa and Chippewa

Chippawa is the spelling of the community in the Niagara area, of the nearby Chippawa Channel, and of Chippawa Hill on Ontario's Bruce Peninsula.

Chippewa is the spelling for the creek running through North Bay and the community nearby; the bank, river and falls in the Soo area; and the island in Georgian Bay, which contains the Chippewa Island Indian Reserve.

chlorophyll

cholesterol

chord, cord

The chord is a group of musical notes: in search of the lost chord, strikes a responsive chord. The cord is the rope or wire: spinal cord, vocal cords.

Christian

In stories on such subjects as abortion rights, family values, school library controversies, gun control, U.S. political figures and right-wing activist groups, do not use the word "Christian" to carry extra baggage.

The word is often used by evangelical sects in a way that suggests a person cannot be a true Christian without sharing the sect's strict religious (and often social and political) beliefs. In particular, do not add the modifier "devout," as if mainstream Protestants, Roman Catholics, Eastern Rite adherents and others could not be devout Christians.

The word is also used pejoratively by many liberals to imply that all people who regard themselves as devout Christians are automatically right-wing, redneck Bible thumpers and sociopolitical Neanderthals.

We should not abet either side in its effort to steal this word from the general lexicon and bend it to partisan purposes. A Christian is, by the most widely accepted definition, one who believes in the divinity of Jesus Christ. This is often extended to include obedience to Christ's teachings, but this is not mandatory (belief alone is deemed to be sufficient to ensure forgiveness and salvation), and of course it opens up the controversy of exactly what the various lessons and parables imply.

The efforts of propagandists on both sides, coupled with the wide variety of Christianity's permutations, make it difficult journalistically to use the word "Christian" without a modifier of some sort. When we know it, use the sect or denomination (which often would not require adding the word "Christian" at all). Similarly, do not use the unmodified generalization "Christian schools" if the point being made excludes, for example, Ukrainian Orthodox or Roman Catholic Christians.

In choosing modifiers, avoid implying that fundamentalist Christian beliefs are necessarily synonymous with right-wing political ones, particularly in Canada. Many fundamentalist Christians are extremely liberal on social welfare, human rights, refugee aid and similar issues. In fact, literal belief in Christ's teachings, and acting on them, might be regarded in some right-wing quarters as outright communism.

One who seeks religious converts may be described as an evangelical or proselytizing Christian. But one who seeks political converts or pushes a particular political agenda may best be described simply as a right-wing or conservative (or liberal or left-wing) political activist. If the stated underpinning of this political stance is religious, that can be imparted separately, since one does not necessarily follow from the other.

"Christian" can usually safely stand alone when the comparison is with a different religion altogether, particularly in overseas references. Seen from a distance, for example, it is not necessary to describe the Christian militia and political faction in Lebanon as being Maronite, unless the story deals with various other Christian sects there.

Christian Brothers

Be careful when writing of the Christian Brothers notorious for instances of abuse at the Mount Cashel orphanage in Newfoundland. For the sake of accuracy and fairness, we should always use, at least once in the story, the formal name of whichever order we are writing about. It is not fair to associate the Ontario-based Brothers of the Christian Schools with the Newfoundland abuses committed by Christian Brothers, and also unfair to the Christian Brothers (an order based in Ireland and still very much in business) to imply they were involved in cases related to the Ontario reform schools at Uxbridge and Alfred.

Christian name

Use **given name**, and **family name** or **surname**. The term "Christian name" makes an assumption about religion, and the term "first name" disregards cultures where family names come first.

Christmas

Injection of a Christmas angle to make a lead more poignant or heart-warming is a device that should be used sparingly. In addition, we must be watchful for silly references to Christmas in stories about non-Christian countries.

chromosome

chronic

From the Greek word for time, it means long-lasting, lingering. It can also mean recurrent. Applied to disease, it is the opposite of **acute**, which means reaching a crisis quickly.

chronic obstructive pulmonary disorder (or disease), COPD

A persistent obstruction of the airways that results in the slow death of the lungs. The disorder may have many underlying causes, including emphysema, which is an enlargement of the tiny air sacs of the lungs (the alveoli) and the destruction of their walls. However, emphysema and COPD are not synonyms. One is cause, one is effect.

Church of Christ, Scientist

Even in first reference can properly be called the Christian Science Church.

Church of Jesus Christ of Latter-day Saints

Even in first reference can be called the Mormon Church, or the Mormons. In the official name, note that -day is lower-case. Also note that Mormons often shorten it to Church of the Latter-day Saints.

chutzpah, brazen effrontery.

cigarette

Cincinnati

cirrhosis

Liver disease. Do not confuse it with **sclerosis**, meaning the thickening or hardening of tissue.

Citibank

Since 1998, the U.S. bank has been a subsidiary of Citigroup Inc., a financial services company.

cities

For a list of cities that need not be qualified in copy by a province or state, see provinces and states.

citizens band

The U.S. term for what in Canada is GRS, for general radio service. But citizens band is fine.

CITT

See Canadian International Trade Tribunal.

City, the

Upper-case for London's financial district. Otherwise, City is upper-case only in the formal names of municipalities, e.g. the City of Calgary. Such references are rarely needed.

In headlines, do not use the words "city" or "area" as adjectives meaning Toronto, as in Society disbars city lawyer. National readers must be told which city is meant. If a foreign city has a traditional English name, we use it (Munich, not Muenchen; Rangoon, not Yangon; Bombay, not Mumbai).

CITY-TV, Toronto.

Use this style of its official name, not the stylized citytv of its commercial logo.

citywide

civil service

This term applies to only some of those on the public payroll. The term **public service (servant)** is better because it covers the civil service and many others, and in common parlance has an application even wider than that used by government paymasters. The term **public employee** is broader still.

In most news stories not dealing with technical distinctions between types of government workers, the term **public servant** adequately covers direct government employees, and the term **public employee** covers almost

all others. (Technically, however, only one somewhat awkward term applies to every last person paid from taxes: public-sector worker.)

Civil service (servant) is reserved for members of federal or provincial governments' full-time, non-political work forces, entitled to full benefits. It does not include contract or unclassified employees such as ministers' executive assistants. A principal distinction is the restriction on political activity contained in civil servants' terms of employment.

Public service (servant), for the purposes of most news stories, can be taken to mean all direct employees of any government, including municipal governments. (Some municipalities refer to their employees as the civic service, but this term is unfamiliar and confusing to most readers.) In the general public's mind, the term public servant is often also applied to police, firefighters and even teachers. This use may be acceptable in some general stories about a municipal payroll, for example, but should not be used in stories specifically dealing with them. And the term public servant is almost never applied by the public to doctors and nurses, even though technically it fits those who work on salary for provincial institutions such as psychiatric hospitals.

To federal and provincial civil service commissions, the term public service encompasses civil servants plus unclassified, part-time and casual workers who do not qualify for pensions and other civil service benefits.

Crown employees is a term used on the federal and provincial levels to encompass the civil and public service plus employees of Crown agencies and institutions such as liquor boards and workers compensation boards. (Note that Ontario excludes from this Crown-employee category the employees of the successor companies of Ontario Hydro and the Ontario

Northland Transportation Commission. But they may fairly be described as public-sector workers.)

claim

We never use claim to mean simply say or assert, because it is usually taken to imply that the reporter has reservations about whether the speaker is telling the truth.

Claim should be used only in the sense of demand as a matter of right (claim an inheritance), or claim damages in a civil suit. In stories about suits it can technically be used for any assertion covered in a statement of claim (he claimed the company was at fault), but to avoid any implication of disbelief it is better to use said or alleged.

Similarly, we do not use claim as a noun for statement, assertion or contention (his claim that the board is inefficient).

We do not use claim in the British sense of a union contract objective (a wage claim).

clamour

But drop u for **clamorous**.

clawback (noun).

cleanup, noun and adjective. The verb is **clean up**.

clear

Say made **it** clear that, not made clear that.

clear-cut

Hyphenated as both noun and adjective in all senses, including those pertaining to forestry.

Clerk of the Privy Council

client

Use for those served by lawyers, accountants and other professional advisers, and for those served by most social service agencies. But for

merchants and most commercial services, including fashion and hair design, the proper term is **customer**. For doctors and other health professionals, use **patient**.

cliffhanger

climactic and climatic

Climactic has to do with a climax; **climatic** pertains to the climate.

Climate refers to the prevailing or characteristic weather in a region. Do not use it for the actual weather at a particular time.

clinic

Do not use indiscriminately for any office offering health of referral services. Reserve for a regulated office that keeps records and employs professional staff.

closure

Reserve this for the parliamentary procedure used to end debate and for the psychological sense of acceptance, healing and recovery after bereavement or other loss. Do not use it as a synonym for closing.

CMA

For certified management accountant. The former title is registered industrial accountant.

CN, see Canadian National.

CNE

Acceptable in second reference for the Canadian National Exhibition. The Ex is also allowed. It is held annually in Toronto, ending on Labour Day.

co

This prefix always takes a hyphen.

coal oil

This name for kerosene is used in Canada in reference to lamps, lanterns and heating stoves.

coast

Lower-case for simple shorelines, such as the northern coast of Venezuela, but upper-case for geographic regions, e.g. the West Coast. See capitalization.

COBOL

Upper-case all letters in this short form of the programming language Common Business Oriented Language.

Cobourg, Ont., but **Coburg**, Germany.

Cocom

Use upper-and-lower in the acronym for the Paris-based Co-ordinating Committee for Multilateral Export Controls, set up in 1949 to maintain lists of strategic goods that should not be sold to East Bloc countries.

Members are Japan and all NATO members except Iceland. With the end of the Cold War, it has rescinded many of the restrictions against exporting high-technology goods to Eastern Europe.

code of conduct

See conduct, code of.

co-ed

Marginally acceptable in second reference to co-educational, but do not apply to women students.

co-equal. Just say **equal**.

co-exist

coffee cake

coho, lower-case. See salmon.

Coke

A trade name. Use it lower-case as a nickname for cocaine only in direct quotes.

Colborne, Port and Toronto street.

Do not confuse Port Colborne (in the Niagara area) with Colborne (near Cobourg, Ont.)

Cold War

Upper-case. It can be said to have wound down between 1989, when democracy movements in Soviet satellite states in Central and Eastern Europe culminated in the breaching of the Berlin Wall, and December of 1991, when Mikhail Gorbachev resigned as president and the Soviet Union was dissolved.

Coliseum

In North American arena names (Quebec, Vancouver, Hamilton, Edmonton, Long Island etc.). But the one in Rome is the **Colosseum**.

collectible

collective agreement

Do not say collective-bargaining agreement.

collective nouns

These words for groups of things, such as army, company, crowd, group, majority, number, party and population, can be either singular or plural, depending on whether we are considering the whole unit or the individual members. For example, we would say the family is the biggest on the block, but the family are eating their hamburgers; the orchestra is the most famous in Europe, but the orchestra are tuning their instruments. Our choice is often dictated by a modifier or pronoun that appears later in the sentence.

Trouble strikes when the thought spans both senses, and singular and plural verbs are attached to a single noun. (The orchestra, which is the most famous in Europe, were tuning their instruments.) Fowler says these clashes are as distasteful to the reader as being served with a dirty plate.

The solution is to recast. In some cases we can eliminate one of the verbs (The orchestra, the most famous in Europe, were . . .). In others we must introduce a second noun.

The pronoun **none** is a good example of a seemingly singular word that can be made plural by a subsequent modifier. We say none of the crop is rotten, but say none of the people are priests.

On the other hand, many seemingly plural words are sometimes construed as singular, particularly units of measurement. If we are considering a single block or entity, which just happens to be measured in those units, the verb and any pronouns should be singular, as in "This 640 acres is the best tobacco land in the province." It is clear we are speaking of an acreage (and indeed this same block could also have been described as one square mile). Similarly, say 10,000 hectares was burned, 10,000 barrels was spilled, $10,000 was stolen. But in this sentence, "These three acres were the first my grandfather sold off," we are clearly speaking of individual lots, and so the verb is plural.

Words expressing quantity such as plenty, heaps, lots and not enough also can be either singular or plural, depending on the context. (There are heaps of rifles, and there is also heaps of ammunition.)

Nouns of assemblage for animals and birds (herd etc.) are usually singular. We limit ourselves to those that are in common use, e.g. flock, school, pride, litter, brood, pod, swarm, hive, colony, troop. We do not inflict on the reader such products of an overwhimsical Victorian imagination as a clamour of rooks, a kindle of kittens, a muster of peafowl, a leap of leopards, an unkindness of ravens.

collision

For this word to apply, both things must be moving. A car does not collide with a tree; it hits it. A moving train does not collide with a stationary one. In describing road accidents, avoid wherever possible the expression **in collision with**; it is awkward police-blotter jargon. Collided with is better, but only if true; beware its connotation of fault.

collusion, collaboration

Collusion is always pejorative; it means a secret agreement for a wrongful purpose or for deception. **Collaboration**, from the Latin for work together, should be used only in reference to artistic pursuits (collaborate on a book, script etc.). In any other sphere, it carries the same load as collusion (collaborating with the enemy).

Colombia

Adjective and people: Colombian. Currency: peso. Capital: Bogota.

Panama adjoins it about midway along its coast, making Colombia the only South American country to front on both the Pacific and the Caribbean. The coastal lowlands are thinly populated; most of the 42 million people live on the Andean plateaus, at altitudes of 1,200 to 2,800 metres (4,000 to 9,000 feet). More than two-thirds are mestizos (a mixture of European and Indian); about 20 per cent are white, 7 per cent are Indian and 5 per cent are black. Colombia has oil, and is also rich in minerals, including iron, gold, silver, platinum and emeralds. The range in elevation allows the production of tropical crops (rubber, rice, various fibres), temperate crops (corn, potatoes) and mountainside crops (coffee). Colombia is the world's leading cultivator of coca, and the world's largest processor of that coca into cocaine. The production is illegal but economically important. A decades-old civil war continues between rebels and the government.

colon, see punctuation.

colonel, Col. See ranks.

Colosseum (in Rome).
But Coliseum for NHL rinks.

colour
But drop the u for **colorant**, **coloration**, **colorific**, **colorimeter**, Technicolor and **Colorize**.

coma
Profound and prolonged unconsciousness in which brain-wave activity is present but the person cannot be awakened by sensory stimulation. Causes include poisoning (including drug overdoses), head injury, diabetes and stroke.

combatted, combatting

come
It must reflect the location of the writer. For example, do not write that many children come to school without breakfast; say go to school, unless the story is a feature written as if the reporter were at the school. See bring and take.
Do not use come to refer to sexual climax. In those rare stories in which the subject is dealt with, use ejaculate or reach orgasm.

Come By Chance
No hyphens, upper-case B.

Comecon
Acronym, upper-and-lower, for the Council for Mutual Economic Assistance, set up in 1949 by Communist countries to co-ordinate the economic development of members, but largely moribund well before it was formally wound up in June, 1991. Members were the Soviet Union, Albania (non-active), Bulgaria, Cuba, Czechoslovakia, East Germany, Hungary, Mongolia, Poland, Romania and Vietnam.

comes/came
Avoid the journalese use of comes/came as all-purpose generic verbs, particularly favoured by wire services as devices for avoiding a passive, for relating one event to another or for bridging two parts of a story. For example: The ruling came more than four months after the inquiry began. The assault came as diplomats gathered in Damascus for talks to end the violence. The settlement comes as the company undertakes a major expansion.
Rulings do not come; they are made or announced or handed down or leaked etc. Assaults do not come; they begin or are launched or are carried out or flatten the neighbourhood or overwhelm the garrison etc. Settlements do not come; they are achieved or imposed or worked out or arrived at or announced etc.
Journalists are told to shun passive verbs in favour of their active counterparts, but this does not extend to removing altogether the most accurate verb just because it is passive, and replacing it with a generic mush-verb that is active in form but virtually catatonic in terms of conveying information. Unless something is actually arriving, good editors and writers will always replace comes/came, except in a few idiomatic expressions such as "came as a shock."

comma, see punctuation.

commander, Cdr. See ranks.
In describing someone as the commander of a vessel, make sure there is no impression that the person holds the military rank of commander if this is not the case.

commandos

commence
Begin or **start** is better.

commission

Lower case (the Hall commission) except where the formal name is cited: the Royal Commission on Health Services.

commitment

common-law

We do not use common-law wife or husband. It is better to describe the partner by name and age and add "with whom he (or she) is living." Terms such as housemate are also acceptable. But a word of caution: It is dangerous to assume, and to report either directly or by implication, that two people living under the same roof are sexually intimate.

Commons, the

Acceptable even in first reference in political stories for the House of Commons.

Common Sense Revolution

Upper case for the political platform on which the Ontario Progressive Conservatives ran in 1995 under leader Mike Harris.

Commonwealth

Although the term commonwealth was first used generically by Jan Smuts in 1917 to refer to the self-governing dominions of the British Empire, it did not enter formal use as the Commonwealth (British Commonwealth of Nations) until the Balfour Declaration adopted at the Imperial Conference of 1926. The declaration referred to "autonomous Communities within the British Empire, equal in status, in no way subordinate one to another in any aspect of their domestic or external affairs, though united by a common allegiance to the Crown, and freely associated as members of the British Commonwealth of Nations." The Commonwealth came into being in 1931 with the passage of the Statute of Westminster. It has not been called the British Commonwealth since 1946. In references before 1926, use the Empire or the British Empire, or "in what is now the Commonwealth."

Commonwealth of Independent States

May be called the CIS in second reference and in headlines.

Proclaimed on Dec. 8, 1991, by Russia, Belarus and Ukraine, which declared the Soviet government defunct, it was intended as a military and economic grouping of former Soviet republics. The Belarussian capital, Minsk, was made its administrative centre. By the end of 1993, it comprised 12 of the 15 former Soviet republics: Russia, Armenia, Azerbaijan, Belarus, Georgia, Kazakhstan, Kyrgyzstan, Moldova, Tajikistan, Turkmenistan, Ukraine and Uzbekistan. (The three that did not join were the Baltic states: Estonia, Latvia and Lithuania.) Nationalist protesters in some countries, notably Ukraine, agitated for withdrawal from the CIS, but economic (and sometimes military) necessity weakened their cause.

Russia was from the beginning the first among equals. The original military goal of a common defence force, particularly joint management of strategic weapons, was hampered by a dispute between Russia and Ukraine over ownership of former Soviet forces, notably the Black Sea Fleet, but was advanced by numerous internal disputes that brought Russian military intervention. (Russia was accused of fomenting some separatist movements as a way of bringing recalcitrant republics into line.) Russia's policy of "firm good neighbourliness" evolved quickly into a military doctrine announced in November of 1993 that it had a right of intervention in its "near abroad," a military sphere of influence conforming to former Soviet territory.

It claimed the right to protect the "rights, freedoms and legitimate interests" of Russians living in other republics (a declaration aimed particularly at the Baltic states). Most CIS members signed a common defence agreement in July of 1994.

The basic economic goal of a ruble zone for trade among the republics (though they could create their own currencies internally) developed into the creation in September of 1994 of a payments union to ensure mutual convertibility, and of a new economic co-ordinating committee. CIS leaders were expected to "abandon part of their national functions" to this new committee, the commonwealth's first supranational body. In 1996, Belarus and Russia signed a treaty reuniting them in a political and economic association, with a complete merger stated as the eventual goal.

See Soviet Union.

Communication Canada

Not Communications Canada, for the federal agency that took over from the Canadian Information Office on Sept. 1, 2001.

communism, Communist

Always lower-case **communism**.

Communist is upper-case when referring to a party of that name or an official member, but could be lower-case in such expressions as communist leanings. See capitalization.

Comoros

Adjective and people: Comorian. Currency: CFA franc. Capital: Moroni.

The Comoros are a group of islands in the Indian Ocean at the north end of the Mozambique Channel, between Madagascar and the southeastern African mainland. Three of them became fully independent of France in 1975 as Comoros (the official name is Federal and Islamic Republic of the Comoros), but a fourth island,

Mayotte, chose to remain a French protectorate. In 1997, the island of Anjouan declared its independence from the other two. There have been several attempts to overturn that decision through coups. Moroni is on the largest of the three islands, Grand Comoro. Most of the 673,000 people are Muslims, of mixed Arab and African ancestry.

company

Abbreviate to Co. in company names, but not in the names of theatrical organizations (the Canadian Opera Company) or when identifying military companies.

company names

It is important to get corporate identities straight. A slight change, such as the use of Inc. instead of Ltd. or Corp., could differentiate a holding company from a subsidiary, a Canadian company from a U.S. one. There are many sources available to Globe writers and editors. The alphabetical list kept up to date by Report on Business is particularly helpful.

compared with and to

If someone has compared things to determine their similarities and/or differences, or has contrasted them, say **compared with**. (He compared his piece of cake with his brother's. His sales topped $20-million, compared with $8-million by his closest competitor.)

If someone has simply stated without elaboration that two or more things are alike, say **compared to**. (He compared her to a spring flower. They compared the government's actions to those of Nazi Germany.)

See contrasted with and to.

compatible

compatriot, but expatriate

complacent and complaisant

Complacent means smug, self-satisfied. Complaisant means showing a desire to please, compliant.

complement and compliment

Complement, as both noun and verb, denotes completeness, fullness. A newsroom that is up to its allowable strength has its complement of 300 employees. Complement also applies to things that complete, reinforce or supplement another thing, or each other. (Her scarf complements her coat; the couple have complementary careers.)

Compliment, as both noun and verb, applies to expressions of praise or courtesy. (The editor complimented the reporter; the reporter was gratified by the compliment.) It is the connotation of courtesy that gives us the term complimentary for free, as in complimentary tickets.

compose, comprise, constitute

Compose means create, or put together from various parts, or make calm. (After he frantically composed the song, he composed himself.) It can be used in the passive when listing component parts. (The news team is composed of reporters, producers and technical staff.)

Comprise means include, contain, consist of. It is always the larger thing that does the comprising. (The orchestra comprises strings, brass, reeds and percussion.) It is virtually never encountered in the passive (for which the preposition would have to be comprised by).

The component parts do not comprise the whole; they constitute it. (Several types of instruments constitute or make up an orchestra.)

compunction and compulsion

Compunction is often misused to mean compulsion or pressure: He felt a compulsion (not compunction) or was under pressure to get the job done.

Compunction means a sense of guilt, remorse, regret or pity, and is more often encountered in the negative (He felt no compunction about foreclosing on her mortgage).

CONCACAF

The Confederation of North, Central American and Caribbean Associations of Football. It is an awkward acronym that should be used sparingly, and never in headlines.

concerned

It has two meanings, for which it takes different prepositions. If it means having to do with, the preposition is with (or occasionally in). If it means worried, the prepositions are about or for.

concertgoer

Concorde, the plane.

condemned

With buildings, it usually means declared unfit for use. But in the legal language of many U.S. states, it could mean that a property has been expropriated for public use, or declared forfeit. In such cases, use the Canadian equivalent.

conduct, code of

The Globe and Mail's comprehensive code of conduct for staff, covering such issues as journalistic practices, advocacy for outside organizations, political activity and personal investments, is printed at the back of this book.

confectionery

Confederation

This word has two meanings. The first is the Act of Union of July 1, 1867, that created the Dominion of Canada from four British North American colonies. The second is a synonym for the country created by Confederation.

In time references ("since Confederation"), it should always take the first meaning. Otherwise, the fact that many provinces joined Confederation after 1867 (Newfoundland joined in 1949) creates ambiguity. Do not, for instance, say that a Newfoundland and Labrador riding has been lost by the Liberals only twice "since Confederation."

Confederation Bridge

The bridge linking Prince Edward Island and New Brunswick across the Northumberland Strait opened on June 1, 1997. It may be referred to as the PEI bridge. In a 1988 plebiscite, 60 per cent of islanders had voted in favour of a fixed link, the generic term used before the choice was made to build a bridge rather than a tunnel.

Congo

There are two of them, which is inevitably awkward in news stories. The larger, which changed its name from Zaire in 1997, is officially called the Democratic Republic of the Congo, and the other is the Republic of the Congo; but descriptive accuracy aside, these are too similar to be useful for differentiating them. If a story deals with only one, a placeline from the capital is usually enough to signal which one we're talking about. In addition, the former Zaire can be identified as such in a high reference. If an article deals extensively with both, identify the capitals high in the story and then follow the local practice of differentiating the countries as Congo-Kinshasa and Congo-Brazzaville.

Congo, Democratic Republic of the

Adjective and people: Congolese. Currency: Congolese franc. Capital: Kinshasa.

It is the former Belgian Congo. At independence in 1960, it was called The Congo (as opposed to Congo, its

French counterpart), but in 1971 it changed its name to Zaire. In 1997, after the overthrow by Laurent Kabila of long-time leader Mobuto Sese Seko, the name was changed to Democratic Republic of the Congo. Call it simply Congo, except when the official name is at issue, but take pains to avoid confusion with its smaller neighbour, also called Congo (see the above entry on this issue). It is in central Africa straddling the equator, and is the continent's third-largest country (after Sudan and Algeria). It has an Atlantic coastline of only 40 kilometres, the end of a narrow westward corridor straddling the Congo River. There are about 200 languages, mostly Bantu, and French and Swahili are also spoken. The total population is 55 million. The largest group is the Kongo, whose language is Kikongo. There was a civil war after independence over the attempted secession of Katanga province. (It is now called Shaba, and its principal city of Elisabethville is now Lubumbashi.)

A civil war broke out in 1998 that within five years had claimed 2.5 million lives. Rwanda and Uganda backed two different rebel groups challenging Kabila's regime, but Zimbabwe, Angola and Namibia sent troops to support Kabila. A 1999 international ceasefire did not last. Kabila was assassinated on Jan. 16, 2001, and was succeeded by his son Joseph Kabila. Rwandan forces left eastern Congo in October, 2002. After 18 months of talks, all the parties signed a fragile peace agreement brokered by South Africa in April, 2003.

Congo, Republic of the

Adjective and people: Congolese. Currency: CFA franc. Capital: Brazzaville.

Official name is Republic of the Congo (until 1992, People's Republic . . .). Avoid the official name except when it is at issue, and take pains to avoid confusion with the larger neighbouring Congo (see the above entry on this issue). Congo was part of the ancient Kingdom of the Kongo, then part of French Equatorial Africa. (Its neighbour is the former Belgian Congo.) Congo is on the equator, between Congo-Kinshasa and Gabon, mostly inland but with a short Atlantic coast. (The port city is Pointe Noire.) Its three million people are mostly speakers of Bantu languages, but French is the official language. The 15 tribes of the Bakongo people make up about half the population.

congressional
Lower case unless part of a proper name. A congressional committee, the Congressional Record.

Connecticut

consensus

Constitution
Upper-case when referring to Canada's and to that of any other English-speaking country when that is the document's official name. But lower-case in translation, as in China's constitution. Lower-case for the constitutions of clubs, unions etc.

consult
A transitive verb, so it does not require the preposition "with."

contempt of court, see courts.

Continent, the
Europe as seen from Britain.

continual and continuous
Continuous means unbroken or uninterrupted. **Continual** means over and over again. If a baby cries continuously, its parents are continually getting out of bed.

contractions
Contractions formed from not, such as isn't, can't, won't, don't and their past tenses, are proper English words and shouldn't be automatically edited out if they help a phrase or headline, or properly convey a mood. But be aware that in many cases the negative is the very thing that is important in the sentence, so it should not be submerged into a contraction. (The judge said she would not allow the evidence.)

Contractions formed from other words are also proper English, found in the dictionary, but are often more awkward or less clear than the ones formed from not, and so should be used only sparingly, largely confined to direct quotes and short headlines. The ones formed from will and shall look awkward in type (I'll, he'll, she'll, they'll). The ones that end in 'd can be ambiguous because they may mean either had or would (she'd gone, she'd go, she'd a dark and a roving eye), and so might give the reader momentary pause.

contrasted with and to
If someone has pointed out the various differences between two or more things, say contrasted with (He contrasted the Canadian Constitution with its U.S. and French counterparts).

If someone has simply stated, without elaborating, that two things are radically different, say contrasted to (She contrasted the hectic pace of her life today to the peace of her small-town upbringing).

See compared with and to.

contretemps
It does not mean an argument; it means a mischance, an embarrassing or awkward occurrence. We might say a slight contretemps at the restaurant marred their evening, but not that he and the waiter had a slight contretemps over the bill.

contusions, say bruises.

convert

One does not convert to another religion; one is **converted** to it.

convince

From the Latin word for conquer, it means to win over or cause to believe. It can be followed by a phrase beginning with of (convinced of the rightness of his cause) or by a clause beginning with that (convinced that his cause is just). But it cannot be followed by to, because it does not mean to induce someone to do something. For that, we must use persuade (from the Latin word for advise). Persuade is suitable for all three uses, followed by of, that and to.

Coon Come, Matthew

No hyphen for the native leader.

co-op

This is acceptable, without elaboration, in informal references to various farmers' co-operative organizations and the stores they operate. (He shipped his grain to the co-op; he went to the co-op for some wire.)

chicken co-op

co-operate

co-ordinate

copter

Acceptable for helicopter in short headlines.

cord

See chord.

corn

In stories from countries with British colonial backgrounds, what we know as corn is often called maize. And when such stories do use the word corn, they often mean wheat. In both instances, we must translate, including such expressions as maize meal.

Corner Brook, Nfld.

Two words.

coronary

Do not use alone for coronary thrombosis. **Coronary**, from the Latin word for crown, is applied to the two major arteries that feed the heart. It is not the adjective that means pertaining to the heart as a whole. For that, use **cardiac**.

Correctional Service Canada

The name of the agency that runs the federal prison system. No "the," no plural, no "of."

There is no problem lapsing into the more informal Corrections Canada, particularly if the story has already quoted someone using it, but we should be sure to use the correct name at least once in the story.

Corrections, Clarifications

Serious factual errors are promptly acknowledged on Page A2, or on Page B2 of Report on Business. All must be cleared through the managing editor, the editor of ROB or the senior editor on duty. They are carried in all editions in which the error appeared.

In general, a Correction or Clarification does not repeat the error; it conveys the correct information concisely, and gives the date that incorrect information was published.

When errors appear, it is our priority to correct them, not to lay blame. But when errors have been introduced into a reporter's story without consultation, the correction should refer to "an editing error." Otherwise, readers will assume that the reporter whose name appears on the story is responsible. Any such correction should be discussed with the reporter and editors involved, including senior editors. It is also relevant to note that the error was conveyed by one of our wire services or by an official source, such as a company's press release or representative. After giving the correct information, say erroneous information was contained in an Associated Press story, for example, published on such-and-such a day.

All editors and reporters should read and note each Correction and Clarification, to prevent embarrassing repetition of errors we have already acknowledged.

correspondent and co-respondent

A **correspondent** is one who communicates by letter or who reports news from distant places. A **co-respondent**, in a divorce action, is one who is alleged to have committed adultery with one of the spouses.

Costa Brava

It is the Mediterranean coast of Catalonia in northeastern Spain, with Barcelona at its centre.

Costa Rica

Adjective and people: Costa Rican. Currency: colon. Capital: San Jose.

The democracy has not had armed forces since 1948, when they were abolished after a civil war. It separates Panama and Nicaragua. Its high central plateau, between two mountain ranges, is devoted almost exclusively to coffee production. Bananas are grown on the coastal plains. The population of four million is also unusual for Latin America, being overwhelmingly white, mostly of Spanish descent. There are about 15,000 blacks on the Caribbean coast.

Côte d'Azur

It originally meant only the eastern end of the French Riviera, from Cannes through Nice to Menton, but now it is taken to mean most if not all of it, including St-Tropez etc.

Côte d'Ivoire

See Ivory Coast.

cottage

A vacation retreat can be referred to variously across the country as a cottage, a cabin, a chalet, a camp or a shack. An Albertan, for example, goes to the cabin, no matter how large or luxurious. A national newspaper should beware using a word inappropriate to the locale, but must also keep in mind the perceptions of readers elsewhere, who may picture a cabin as being necessarily small and rustic.

couldn't care less

Shun the common but nonsensical corruption "could care less," although there is no need to explain in direct quotes.

coulee

No accent. In Western Canada, it means a deep gully or gulch carved by spring runoff. They are usually dry in summer.

counselled, counselling, counsellor

counter

This prefix does not take a hyphen (counterattack, counterintelligence) unless the root word begins with r (counter-revolutionary).

counterfeited

countervailing duty

This is an extra import duty, added to the normal duty when the importing country concludes that the export price contains a subsidy.

couple

Usually takes plural verbs and pronouns. (The couple are selling their house.)

Courage, Star of

See bravery decorations.

coureurs de bois

(Not courieurs.) Requires italics. This term should not be applied to all fur traders of New France. These woods-runners were renegade traders, competing illegally with the big licensed fur merchants and their sanctioned "voyageurs."

courthouse, courtroom

court-martial, courts-martial

The verb is court-martial, court-martialled.

courts, contempt, libel

The need for accuracy and fairness is particularly great in stories relating to crimes or civil proceedings, and in those that depict a person, corporation, municipality, union or any other legal entity in an unfavourable light. If a writer or editor has the least suspicion that a report might prejudice the rights of any party in a criminal or civil trial, or any doubt about the advisability of reporting certain unflattering information or opinions, the story must be reviewed by a senior editor, who may decide to seek legal advice.

Note that the two areas of concern are not separate. In worrying about whether a story prejudices a trial, we cannot lose sight of the fact that it may also be defamatory, the basis of a successful libel suit.

This summary deals with five areas:

court names; court terminology; restrictions on publication (what we can't print); contempt of court; and defamation. Of the references used to prepare it, two books were particularly useful and are available in the Globe library: *Martin's Annual Criminal Code*, an annotated version with case examples and index, updated annually; and *The Journalist's Legal Guide* by Michael Crawford. For more detailed information on defamation, consult *Canadian Libel Practice* by Julian Porter and David Potts.

Court names

Courts of the same level have various names in different provinces. For example, the Manitoba Court of Queen's Bench is the equivalent of the B.C. Supreme Court, Quebec Superior Court and Ontario Superior Court. These courts, called high courts of justice, conduct all criminal and civil trials beyond the jurisdiction of the lower Provincial Court (called this in all provinces except Ontario and Quebec, where the names are Ontario Court of Justice and Quebec Court).

Here is a brief rundown of court structures and formal names. **Federal:** Supreme Court of Canada, Federal Court of Appeal, Federal Court of Canada, Tax Court of Canada. **Alberta and Manitoba:** Court of Appeal, Court of Queen's Bench, Provincial Court. **B.C.:** Court of Appeal, Supreme Court, Provincial Court. **New Brunswick:** Court of Appeal, Court of Queen's Bench (divided into the trial division and family division), Provincial Court. **Newfoundland and Labrador:** Supreme Court (divided into the Court of Appeal and the trial division), Unified Family Court, Provincial Court. **N.S.:** The last province to have county courts, it passed legislation in 1992 to fold them into the Supreme Court, effective in 1993, giving it four levels: Court of Appeal, Supreme Court, Provincial

Court, Family Court. (Unique in Canada is Halifax City Court, municipally administered, which performs the functions of the Provincial Court within the city of Halifax.) **Ontario:** Court of Appeal, Superior Court of Justice, Ontario Court of Justice. We refer simply to the Superior Court and the Ontario Court except in stories dealing with appointments etc. Until April, 1999, Superior Court was known as the Ontario Court of Justice (General Division) and the Ontario Court of Justice was known as the Ontario Court of Justice (Provincial Division). It may be necessary to give the previous names in referring to past trials—or, in cases before 1990, the names Ontario Supreme Court, District Court and Provincial Court—but we should always insert a reference equating these with the new names. **PEI:** Supreme Court (appeal division and trial division), Provincial Court. We refer to rulings of the PEI Court of Appeal, unless the nature of the story (appointments to the bench etc.) requires that we use the actual name: the Supreme Court. **Quebec:** Court of Appeal, Superior Court, Quebec Court (Quebec's name for its provincial court). **Saskatchewan:** Court of Appeal, Court of Queen's Bench, Unified Family Court, Provincial Court. The Superior Courts in Quebec and Ontario are the equivalent of the Supreme Courts of B.C., Nova Scotia, PEI and Newfoundland and Labrador, and of the Court of Queen's Bench in the three Prairie provinces and New Brunswick.

We use lower case for divisions within a court (trial division, civil division, family division etc.), but use upper case for the Ontario Divisional Court; these three-judge courts, drawn from the Superior Court, hear appeals of decisions of quasi-judicial boards and commissions.

The top trial court in each province may be referred to as the "high court" in lower references and in headlines (from the traditional name High Court of Justice). This term must not be applied to appeal courts, or to the Supreme Court of Canada.

Provinces have chief justices of both their appeal court and their high court, and it is important that we be specific. It is the chief justice of the appeal court who is the chief justice of the province. We would refer to them, for example, as Ontario Chief Justice Roy McMurtry and as Chief Justice Heather Smith of Ontario's Superior Court. See capitalization, honorifics.

We speak of **Youth Court**, upper-case, for all provinces, although the formal name is the Youth Justice Court. The federal Youth Criminal Justice Act replaced the Young Offenders Act on April 1, 2003, and applies to young people from 12 to 17. Charges involving young people are dealt with in each province by the courts with jurisdiction over summary (low-level) offences, e.g. Provincial Court, criminal division. In most provinces, a judge who also tries adults will be assigned to sit as Youth Court when there are charges against young persons, although a judge of the family division might also sit as Youth Court for younger teenagers if the matter is more a family one.

Court terminology

In this description of procedures, the Ontario court system is used as the example.

Criminal proceedings

Criminal proceedings are begun either by the **preferring of an indictment** or by the issuing of a **summons**. The seriousness of the charge generally dictates the method, but many charges give the prosecution a choice of proceeding by indictment or by **summary conviction**. The choice is the responsibility of the **Crown attorney,** the official in each district responsible for directing prosecutions.

A charge in a summary-conviction offence, or one on which the Crown has chosen to proceed by this method, is heard in **Provincial Court** (Ontario Court). Its judges are called Judge John Blank of [name of court] in first reference, and Judge Blank in second reference.

A person charged with an **indictable offence** usually may choose whether to be tried by an Ontario Court judge, by a higher judge acting alone, or by a judge and jury. Certain serious indictable offences, such as murder, must be tried in the Superior Court (the **high court**, which in other provinces may be called the Supreme Court, Court of Queen's Bench or Quebec's Superior Court), where we refer to judges as Mr. Justice John Blank (or Madam Justice) in first reference, and as Judge Blank in second.

When the accused has chosen trial in a higher court by either judge and jury or judge alone, a **preliminary hearing** is held in the Ontario Court, at which a prosecutor must convince the judge that there is enough evidence to warrant a trial. The prosecutor may be the Crown attorney, an assistant Crown attorney (who is a lawyer employed in the Crown's office) or a lawyer in private practice retained for the case. The generic term encompassing all these is **Crown counsel** or simply **prosecutor**. (Do not use the word prosecutor if he or she is representing the Crown at a coroner's inquest or other proceeding in which there is no question of prosecution.)

In reporting guilty verdicts, we may say that the accused was either **convicted** or **found guilty**. If the verdict is otherwise, we say that the accused was either **acquitted** or **found not guilty**. We do not use the term "found innocent," because some acquittals are on a technicality.

Descriptions of charges must be specific and exact. Reporters should make a note of the section of the Criminal Code or other law cited in the charge, not necessarily for publication but for checking the exact nature of the alleged offence. This should be reported accurately but in standard English, not in the convoluted language of the statute or in the cryptic, ungrammatical language of the police blotter (break and enter, weapons dangerous).

Note that an **information** sworn by a justice of the peace, which can result in an arrest, does not become public until it is read in open court. We always take a calculated risk in giving the charge before then, because the Crown might alter or drop it. Publishing the wrong charge could be libellous, or ruled to be contempt of court.

The word **alleged** is no defence against defamation actions (see defamation, below), but it does have a real place in crime stories to make it clear that the suspect's guilt, or sometimes even the fact that there has been a crime, has yet to be established. Many actions do not become crimes until a court decides they fit the statutory definition, so we should speak of an alleged fraud, for example. When describing the specifics of charges, we can say they allege that the person did such and such. However, the term "police allege" cannot be used to give the force's version of events, in effect convicting the accused. When speaking of people, avoid such terms as alleged robber, alleged murderer, because these come too close to linking the person to a type of criminal. Our wording should make it clear that the person has merely been accused, not convicted.

Similarly, the adjective **accused** should not be used in such expressions as accused robber. This could well be taken to mean that the person is indeed a robber who has now been accused. We should say instead that the person is accused of robbery, or charged with robbery.

Someone charged under the Youth Criminal Justice Act should not be referred to as a **young offender** until he or she has actually been convicted.

The word **murder** should not be used to describe a slaying until a court verdict establishes that it applies. The verdict could well be that it was manslaughter, or even that there was no culpability at all, as in cases of self-defence. Stick to the facts, which are that a person has been charged with murder. Specify high in the story whether it is first-degree or second-degree murder.

For legal purposes, someone who is 11 or younger is called a **child** and cannot be charged with a crime. Someone aged 12 to 17 is called a **young person**. Someone 18 or older is an **adult** (but might be tried in Youth Court if the alleged offence took place when he or she was a young person). See child.

Recognizance should be kept singular, as in The five men were released on their own recognizance.

The **race or national origin** of an accused should not be included gratuitously. But it would be relevant if, for example, an assault was the result of racial taunts, or if a defendant says poor English created a misunderstanding.

Civil proceedings

Civil proceedings take place at various court levels, depending on the amount of damages claimed. The courts dealing with small amounts, handling trials quickly and without the requirement that the parties have lawyers, may be referred to as **small-claims court**, whatever their formal name (typically, Provincial Court, civil division). The dollar limits for small-claims courts vary by province.

Actions involving damage claims above the small-claims limit are dealt with by a province's high court (Supreme Court, Court of Queen's Bench, Quebec's Superior Court, Ontario's Superior Court).

The person, body or corporation starting the action is the **plaintiff**, and the party against which the action is brought is the **defendant**. A defendant may in turn allege damages at the hands of the plaintiff, in which case the defendant may make a **counterclaim**. If one defendant in an action alleges that another defendant was the one responsible for the damages to the plaintiff, this defendant may file a **crossclaim**. If a defendant alleges the damages were the fault of another party who has not been sued, the defendant would start a **third-party action**.

Verdicts in civil suits are described as **findings** for or against either party. Do not use such words as guilt, acquit or convict that imply criminal wrongdoing. A defendant in a civil case must never be called the accused.

See tort.

Appeals

Each province has an appeal court that is the court of last resort for matters arising in that province (subject to the possibility of an appeal to the Supreme Court of Canada). A court decision may be appealed by either party. The person, company or organization making the appeal is the **appellant**, and the party responding to it (asking that the lower court's decision stand) is the **respondent**. In many cases the appeal court has the option of deciding whether a case is worth hearing, and so the appellant must seek **leave to appeal**.

We may use the name **Court of Appeal** in all provinces, although in Prince Edward Island the proper term is **appeal division** of the Supreme Court, and should be preserved in stories dealing specifically with the distinction or with appointments to the bench. The term "appeal court," lower-case, is acceptable in heads and copy, except when giving a court's official name. A court of appeal may not be called "high court" even in headlines (this term is reserved for the next rung down, the senior trial courts) but the Supreme Court of Canada may be called "top court" if we are pressed in a short headline.

Other court terms

Two or more Canadian judges hearing a case jointly should usually be called a **court**, not a panel.

The **initial J.** appearing after the surname of a judge in court documents, as in Jones, J., is not that of a given name. It means Justice, and the initials J. A. mean Justice of Appeal. C. J. means Chief Justice. J. P. means Justice of the Peace.

The **prisoner's box** and **witness box** are distinctive physical features of Canadian courtrooms, and should be called that. Do not use misleading foreign terms such as witness stand and prisoner's dock, and such expressions as "took the stand." Take care when a trial is held in an unusual place, such as a hotel, school or Legion hall. The usual court furniture and trappings may be absent.

If a Canadian judge raps for silence, it might be with a pencil or other such instrument, but never with a **gavel**. Gavels are not found in Canadian courts.

In almost all instances, the word is **lawyer**. **Counsel** is also widely used in Canada. (Its plural is counsel.) Attorney is not the proper Canadian term for lawyer, except in the titles attorney-general and Crown attorney. And despite what it says on lawyers' shingles, barrister and solicitor are also not common Canadian usage, although they might arise in stories about trials in other Commonwealth countries.

A lawyer's opening or closing remarks in a Canadian court case are called an **address**, and a judge's instruction of the jury is called a **charge**. For lawyers' closing addresses, we may also use the word summation.

Adjourn is preferred to recess.

An order to appear before a court to answer a charge, to serve on a jury or to testify as a witness is called a **summons** (plural: summonses). But the verb is simply **summon** or summoned, never summonsed.

Latin legal terms are lawyers' jargon. As such they ill serve the reader and should be weeded out of news stories. If their use is essential, as in a story about what kind of writ could be used to end a strike, a translation or explanation must be provided. Even a common term such as **habeas corpus** might well need explanation, because there is widespread confusion about it. Such a writ does not demand that a prisoner be freed; it demands that the authorities acknowledge that a person is being held and deliver him or her to a court for a review of the lawfulness of the detention. Latin legal terms are deemed to have entered the English language and so need not be in italics.

Also see M'Naghten rule, maximum sentence.

Restrictions on publication

There are provisions in the Criminal Code, the Youth Criminal Justice Act and some other statutes, including the Narcotic Control Act, prohibiting the publication of certain names or evidence, or allowing a judge to impose a ban. (A notable example is a judge's power under the Canada Evidence Act to ban publication of confidential government information.) In addition, judges have some general powers to prohibit or limit publicity in other cases if they think it necessary to serve justice, including cases involving trade secrets. But the reasons for limiting press freedom must be weighty ones, and the news media have successfully challenged gag orders when the public's right to know or an accused's right to an open hearing transcended the arguments for secrecy. Such a decision to test a publication ban must be made by editors at the most senior level, since the newspaper's stand can put it at risk of criminal or contempt charges.

When to omit names:

Under the **Youth Criminal Justice Act**, there must be no publication of the name of a person sought by police, charged or convicted if he or she was under 18 when the offence was allegedly committed. (That is, the ban also applies to adults who were under 18 when the offence took place and are being tried in Youth Court.) The same restriction applies to the names of juvenile victims and witnesses in Youth Court cases.

The ban extends to any information that might serve to identify a young accused, victim or witness. The type of information is not specified, but possibly even naming the young person's school or an institution where he or she is a ward could be too big a clue. Anything beyond age, sex and community should be carefully considered.

Under the Youth Criminal Justice Act, the name of the accused cannot be published until he or she has received an adult sentence or unless the accused is over 14 and has been convicted of a serious violent offence. A judge can also allow use of the name if a young person being sought by police is a danger to society and publication of the name would aid in capture. Such an order is valid for five days.

It is also illegal to disclose the fact that anyone has a record as a young offender, but we can report a disclosure by others in a public setting. It is illegal to possess a copy of a juvenile record not obtained by authorized means.

Under the **Criminal Code**, a judge can prohibit publication of the names of complainants in cases of alleged sexual offences, and of the names of witnesses under 18 in such cases. On rare occasions, judges have also prohibited publication of the names of

adult witnesses or complainants in other types of cases if it would put them in danger or cause them extreme hardship.

There are also publication bans covering persons named as owners, occupants or suspects in search or eavesdropping warrants, unless the reporter obtains the permission of all those named or unless charges are subsequently laid.

Under provincial laws, it is illegal to publish the names of certain individuals of any age (for example, family members) in cases before **family courts** in such matters as adoptions and child welfare.

In Quebec, no person under 18 testifying or named at a coroner's inquest can be identified.

It is also illegal in almost all provinces to publish the name of someone who has a **sexually transmitted disease** or has been tested for one. The purpose of such laws is to aid prevention by removing a major disincentive to seeking tests. Recent experience indicates there is no danger in publishing someone's own acknowledgment, but beware quoting anyone about someone else's disease. This might be illegal as well as libellous.

Beyond bans imposed by statutes and by judges, The Globe considers it unfair to publish the name of a person charged with an offence if it does not plan to follow the case through to the trial and report whether the person was found guilty. Accordingly, the practice in most minor cases is to describe the accused by age, home town or neighbourhood and possibly occupation (e.g. A 23-year-old Rexdale labourer has been charged with public mischief).

Omitting the name increases slightly the scope for describing the details of an alleged criminal act, but there must be no implication that the person sought, arrested or charged is the perpetrator.

When to omit evidence

In addition to the general prohibition against publishing types of evidence that might prejudice a trial (summarized below under contempt of court), there are several specific bans imposed by statutes.

At **bail hearings**, the judge or justice of the peace can, and usually does, order a ban on publication of evidence and of the reasons for the decision on detention or release. We may still report that a hearing took place, the name of the accused, the specifics of the charge, whether release was granted and what conditions were attached to it.

At almost all **preliminary hearings**, the judge grants a request to impose a ban on publication of evidence. That means we can report only the name of the accused, the specifics contained in the charge and the fact that the person was committed to trial. The ban on publishing evidence from hearings holds until the person is discharged or a verdict is rendered at the subsequent trial (although similar evidence brought out at the trial may be reported). For this reason it is important that reporters assigned to a trial determine whether a publication ban was imposed at an earlier stage.

Even in those rare cases in which a publication ban is not imposed, we cannot publish any evidence at the preliminary hearing indicating that the accused made a confession to authorities or otherwise admitted guilt. This has been taken to include evidence that the accused led police to where loot or a body was buried. But if the accused actually testifies at a preliminary hearing at which no publication ban was imposed (a combination of two rare events), there is no restriction on reporting his or her testimony.

At **jury trials** in which jury members are allowed to go home each night (which is the usual case),

evidence heard while the jury was excluded, including evidence from a voir dire (the trial of an issue within a trial), cannot be reported unless the jury later hears it in court or unless the court on application (usually by the media) permits it. This publication ban ends if the jury is later sequestered, or when it retires to consider its verdict.

We must be mindful of the fact that the Criminal Code prohibits jurors from disclosing any details of the **jury's deliberations** while it was absent from the courtroom, even after the trial ends, unless these have been brought out in court.

At trials involving **sexual offences**, a judge almost always orders the media not to identify the complainant or any witness under 18, and we cannot report evidence from hearings within the trial held to determine whether evidence of the complainant's sexual conduct should be admitted.

We cannot report any evidence from trials in **Youth Court** that might identify the accused, unless the young person has received an adult sentence or is over 14 and has been convicted of a serious violent offence.

There is a criminal law against publishing evidence obtained by **electronic surveillance** until it is submitted at a trial.

In covering **Quebec coroner's inquests**, we cannot publish any evidence if a person has been charged in the same death, and the coroner has the power to ban publicity even if no one has been charged. We also are barred from publishing information in Quebec coroner's warrants, or photos of the dead person unless the coroner gives his permission.

In **Alberta lawsuits**, before a case comes to trial, we are allowed to print only the names of the parties involved and a concise summary of the statement of claim. The word concise is open to interpretation, so exercise caution.

Where we are considering publishing information related to indecent sexual or medical details, we must exercise sensitivity and judgment.

Contempt of court

In addition to outright defiance of a publication ban imposed by statute or by a judge, there are two categories of transgressions in published reports for which a journalist, publication or broadcast company can be charged with contempt of court: those prejudicing a person's right to a fair court hearing and those casting a particular judge or court or the entire justice system into disrepute.

The right to a fair trial

A journalist cannot say or imply that a person who has not yet been tried is guilty of an offence, or that one side is in the right in a civil case. Further, a journalist cannot reveal any information that might prejudice an impending trial or that might not be admissible at that trial.

The rules are designed to avoid prejudicing a jury, but if it turns out that the trial is before a judge alone there is little danger of contempt charges. However, although the judge might consider himself immune from prejudicial information, he or she could theoretically rule that the confidence of the public or a higher court in the trial's fairness was undermined.

The most dangerous published statements in a criminal case are those that imply guilt, that reveal to the public (i.e., prospective jurors) that a person has made a formal or implied confession to authorities, or reveal that an accused has a criminal record.

A media outlet might be charged with contempt over a wide range of transgressions, including: the publication of statements by police or witnesses that imply guilt or reveal inadmissible evidence; an incorrect description of the charges laid; stories linking an accused to the conviction of a co-accused at a separate trial; unfair juxtaposition of stories, such as a feature about insane killers that runs alongside a story about a person accused of murder; a published photo of the accused if identity will be a major issue at the trial.

A writer or editor is advised to come up with a theory, however improbable, to justify a notion that the wrong person has been charged. (The theory of the Evil Twin works well.) Read a story with this mindset, and any prejudicial information or implication of guilt fairly jumps out.

There is occasionally an argument made for revealing a criminal record by stating, for example, that the accused was on parole for the same sex offence, or was on a day pass. Globe senior editors might decide they must give precedence to the public service of pointing out a failure in the penal or treatment system. (But it would be difficult to justify revealing that a person charged with murder was on parole from a sentence for fraud. And a revelation that was justified at the time of arrest might be dangerous on the eve of the trial.)

Implying the existence of a criminal record is unavoidable in reporting on crimes committed in prison or on charges of escaping custody, but there is little danger here because the prison connection would not be kept from the jury in a subsequent trial. However, revealing the exact nature or extent of the criminal record as the trial approaches might be considered needlessly prejudicial.

Murderers serving life with no parole for 25 years can apply after 15 years to be considered for early parole. Since these are jury proceedings, the rules against influencing juries apply. In 1992, the Edmonton Journal's owner, publisher and editor and a reporter were found guilty of criminal contempt over a story that was prejudicial in tone, gave evidence that the jury had not yet heard, and was especially harmful because it appeared on the morning the hearing was to have begun.

In **civil cases**, juries are not allowed to know the **amount of damages sought** by the complainant, or whether the defendant has **insurance** to cover a damage award. And there can be no implication, however slight, that one side is right or wrong. If a company is being sued over pollution, for example, it might be dangerous close to the trial or during it to accompany the story with a picture of one of the company's plants belching smoke or spewing effluent.

Case law has established that there is considerable laxity in the ban on publishing the amount claimed, as long as the trial is still some weeks away. The amount can certainly be used safely on the day the suit is filed, but even then The Globe often omits it, because many complainants claim huge, unrealistic sums as a scare tactic or a publicity ploy.

A warning: Most journalists are aware that accurate reports of what happens in a trial, in a legislature and in some types of public meetings have protection against libel actions. But there is no such protection against contempt-of-court charges. If testimony at a trial or a statement in Parliament prejudices a pending court case or scandalizes the justice system, it is dangerous to report it.

Scandalizing the court

Scandalizing the court involves false allegations of prejudice or improper motives on the part of the justice system, a court or a judge. An editorial or a person quoted in a news story can disagree with a judgment or a sentence, but cannot imply falsely that it resulted from such things as dishonesty, prejudice or personal political or financial motives. The protection against this kind of criticism also extends to the members of juries.

Judges are not immune from criticism of their personal conduct and public actions, but it must be accurate and without malice.

The Ontario Court of Appeal increased the scope for critical comments when it ruled in the case of lawyer Harry Kopyto that the Charter of Rights and Freedoms protects statements of sincerely held personal belief on a matter of public interest. Such statements would constitute contempt in Ontario only if they were made recklessly, with no regard to whether they were true, and if they brought the justice system into sufficient disrepute to create "imminent danger to the fair and effective administration of justice."

Defamation

What follows is a synopsis of a very complex area, that of libel law. Its purpose is merely to offer broad guidelines on when a reporter or editor would be advised to tread carefully, and in most cases to seek an expert opinion. We must also keep in mind that libel law varies slightly from province to province. A national newspaper will often need to consult the statute of the appropriate province before deciding what may be published.

Any statement, broadcast or printed matter (including photographs) that might damage the reputation of a person, corporation, municipality, union or any other legal entity might be the basis of a successful defamation action. In particular, we must watch for statements that expose the subject to hatred, ridicule or contempt in the mind of the average member of the public; that allege criminal or immoral conduct; that impair the subject's pursuit of a business, trade or profession; or that harm the subject's financial reputation.

Pursuing a libel suit beyond the initial process of filing a notice is a long and expensive affair, and most of those who do so genuinely feel they have been unjustly defamed. Almost all such suits can be prevented by our obeying two basic rules of journalism: Don't publish information we have not verified, and give the other side the chance to present its version of the facts, or its explanation, in the same story. If a person or other entity is wrongly defamed nevertheless, we set the record straight as soon as possible and sincerely express regret. This satisfies many complainants, and greatly reduces the potential damage award to those who decide to launch a suit.

A newspaper can be sued not only for what it says in its own right, as in an editorial or headline, but also for what it quotes others as saying or permits them to say in an ad or letter to the editor. That is why such words as **alleged** and **reputed**, intended to indicate that the criticism is not being made by the newspaper or necessarily supported by it, are no defence against a libel action. Never use such expressions as an allegedly incompetent teacher or a reputedly insolvent businessman.

Defences

Details may vary from province to province, but in general there are three major defences against a libel action: The statement was true; it was fair comment; or it was privileged, meaning that its origin in a certain type of public body or forum gave it statutory immunity against libel actions.

The defence of **truth**, called "justification," is absolute in all provinces except Quebec, where the defendant must also prove the statement was published in the public interest and without malice. But proof of truth is often difficult to establish, and the onus is on the defendant. Reporters must be able to produce their research notes and documents, but these may well be insufficient. It may be that we know something is

true but our only proof is hearsay evidence that would be inadmissible in court, or evidence from a lawyer who must claim lawyer-client privilege and refuse to testify, or evidence from someone who is now abroad and cannot be subpoenaed. Editors should be aware of the documents or willing witnesses that might be used in mounting a defence.

The defence of **fair comment** applies to opinions, both those of our own editorial and news writers and those of others. To qualify for this defence, the statement must be on a subject of genuine public interest, must be based on provable facts that are included in the article (unless they are well-known facts), must be a fair expression of the person's opinion, and must not reflect any underlying malice. This is a defence that is applied to editorials, arts reviews and even letters to the editor, which may contain opinions with which the paper disagrees but that could reasonably be drawn from the known facts.

Privilege, which is immunity from liability for defamatory statements, falls into two categories: absolute and qualified. **Absolute privilege** depends on the occasion when the words were uttered; a libel action will not succeed if the law recognizes the occasion as one for which the public interest favours complete freedom of speech (such as a trial in open court). With **qualified privilege**, the publisher of the defamatory statement must be able to show that it was on an important matter of public interest and that there was a legal, social or moral duty to publish it, and the plaintiff must be unable to prove malice. (Malice would be involved if the defendant knew the statement was false, or published it out of ill will or some motive other than public duty.)

In the context of the media, some defences based on privilege will fail if the defendant refused to publish a reasonable contradiction or explanation from the party claiming to have been defamed.

In practical terms, **absolute** privilege for journalists applies only to reports from **courts of justice**. Even then, they must be fair, accurate and balanced reports of proceedings publicly heard, not sessions closed to the public, and they must be published contemporaneously.

Privilege also extends to such quasi-judicial entities as **coroner's inquests** and **judicial inquiries**, but we must be careful if the defamatory statement is not relevant to the proceedings. A witness's gratuitous comment that someone not involved in the issue is a crook may not be considered privileged. In reporting on inquest findings, we must be mindful of the fact that assigning fault is beyond the scope of inquests.

Note that sworn information does not become public until it is read in open court or otherwise submitted as evidence. Be especially wary of **examinations for discovery**, held as part of the preparations for a civil trial. We have no protection in quoting defamatory statements made under oath in these proceedings. We can safely print them only if the transcripts are publicly filed with the court, or if the case indeed goes to trial and the statements are presented in open court. Until then, defamatory information in pretrial examinations is useful only as background.

Members of Parliament and legislatures have absolute privilege while speaking in the House or in committees, as do their reports and other official documents. But journalists reporting on them have only qualified privilege, except in the rare event that they are quoting entire statements or papers verbatim.

A fair and accurate report of the following proceedings and documents has qualified privilege, as long as they were public and the publication of the report was not malicious:

- Proceedings of legislative bodies in the Commonwealth, including their committees;
- Proceedings of any public authority in Canada, any administrative body constituted by a public authority, and any commission of inquiry set up by a public authority;
- Proceedings of a public, lawful meeting held to discuss a matter of public concern;
- Reports, notices, press releases or other documents issued for public information on behalf of any such body or organization, or after such a meeting;
- The findings of certain organizations relating to their members or to persons under their jurisdiction. These organizations, which must be formed in Canada to qualify for immunity, include those established in the interests of professions, trades, businesses, industries, learning, arts, sciences and religions, and public sports or pastimes. A Canadian sport league's finding that a player under its jurisdiction is a goon would qualify for privilege.

Whether a meeting fits the statutory definition of a public one on a matter of public interest is not always easy to determine. If it has been advertised as a frankly partisan gathering, or if it is simply a lecture with no element of public discussion, such as a religious sermon, defamatory statements might not be privileged. A simple news conference could also qualify as a public meeting. Even if a meeting does fit the definition, gratuitous defamatory comments not related to the subject being discussed should not be reported.

Incorrect defamatory information about a company's product officially issued by a government consumer department would be privileged, but the comments of an individual civil servant or a report from a private consumer group might not be. Similarly, an official bulletin or release from a police force would be privileged, but defamatory oral elaboration by an individual officer would not.

Reports of shareholders' meetings are not immune from suits over defamatory statements, and neither are reports to shareholders until they become public documents by being officially filed with a provincial securities commission.

Public figures in Canada, including politicians and artists, may be criticized in their public activities, as long as this is fair comment, but unlike many of their U.S. counterparts they have as great a protection against defamation in their private lives as do members of the public. In fact, with a greater reputation at stake, they might well be awarded greater damages.

Most journalists know it is impossible to libel a **dead person**, but are unaware that it could be found that an untrue defamation blackened the person's family name to the extent that survivors suffered injury.

Finally, even a statement that is clearly safe if published **contemporaneously** might be made dangerous by the passage of time or by constant repetition. Something that causes grief and embarrassment when dredged up as irrelevant background from years ago might well lead a civil jury to suspect malice. So might continually repeating, in every story about a particular company, on any subject, that it was once investigated by a securities commission.

couscous

cousins

The children of our aunts and uncles are our first cousins. These first cousins' children and grandchildren are our first cousins once and twice removed. The children of our great-aunts and great-uncles (our parents' aunts and uncles, the sisters and brothers of our grandparents) are our

second cousins, and their children and grandchildren are our second cousins once and twice removed. However, unless the exact relationship is significant, we normally simply use the word cousin.

cover-up, noun. The verb is **cover up.**

coxswain

CP

See Canadian Pacific and Canadian Press. Take care there is no ambiguity about which is meant.

CPAC

Cable Public Affairs Channel. The public service of Canadian cable companies used to be called the Parliamentary Channel.

craft

In the sense of vehicles in the air or on water, the plural is craft. Say watercraft, not watercrafts.

credible and credulous

A **credible** person is one who can be believed. A **credulous** one is too ready to do the believing on slight evidence. The comparable nouns are credibility and credulity.

Cree

For the plural we use Crees, which is preferred by most of the people themselves and is included in the legal name of the Crees in Quebec. (This is an exception to the practice with most other Canadian native language groups and bands, for which the singular also serves as the plural.) See native people.

creole

This word has two uses. Lower-case, it means a pidgin language that has become the first language of the people who speak it. (See pidgin.) Upper-case, it refers to a group of people. In Louisiana, it means descendants of the original French settlers (as opposed to the Cajuns, whose ancestors arrived from Acadia). In Latin America and the Caribbean, Creole usually means someone of European descent. In some African countries, it may mean someone descended from black slaves who returned from the Americas. We should specify which meaning applies.

Cres.

The abbreviation for Crescent, used only in an address that includes the house number. See streets.

crescendo

We cannot speak of something "building to a crescendo," as if the crescendo were the end point in a process. The crescendo is the process itself, a gradual increase in sound, not the point of climax. Speak of "a crescendo of boos," but not of boos reaching a crescendo.

cretinism

It is a specific congenital disease in which a lack of thyroid hormone in the fetus and early infant interferes with development of the body and brain. (Hormone treatment can lessen or even prevent the mental retardation associated with cretinism.) Because of the sensitive nature of the subject, we should avoid the word **cretin**, which would create the image of a homogeneous class of people, and should not use the word cretinism without providing a definition.

crew

A collective noun. The singular is **crew member**.

crime, see courts.

criteria is plural. One is a criterion.

critical

It has two meanings, and we must take care that the reader knows whether we are using the sense derived from criticism or the one derived from crisis. If there is ambiguity, as in "a critical statement," consider using **crucial** for the second meaning. Crucial (from the Latin *crux*) refers to a turning point, not something that is merely important.

criticize

critique

In the literary sense, critique and criticism simply mean analysis and assessment. In stories of this type, do not assume they imply an unfavourable assessment. Do not use critique as a verb.

Croatia

Adjective and people: Croatian. Currency: kuna. Capital: Zagreb.

When Croatia declared independence from Yugoslavia in June of 1991, its Serb minority (about 11 per cent) and the republic of Serbia reacted by seizing control of a third of the territory and forcing Croats to flee in a program of "ethnic cleansing." The Croats, in turn, forced many Serbs to flee other regions. The authoritarian Zagreb regime of Franjo Tudjman became more repressive, purged Serbs from state-run enterprises, and tolerated the existence of the neo-Nazi Croatian Armed Force and its murder of Serbs. This group, known by its Croatian initials HOS (the Serbo-Croat name for Croatia is Hrvatska), included skinheads and other thugs, and used the swastika symbol and slogans of the Ustasha regime, which killed about 700,000 Serbs, Gypsies and Jews during the Second World War. The Zagreb regime also provided aid to secessionist Croats in neighbouring Bosnia-Herzegovina. A United Nations peacekeeping force was deployed in 1992, largely to observe a ceasefire agreed to in January of 1992 along existing battle lines and to help with aid convoys.

Croatia's population is 4.5 million, mostly Croat with Serb, Slovene, Muslim, Hungarian and other minorities. Croatia is mountainous and irregularly shaped. With a long, thin Dalmatian coast on the Adriatic and a curving inland arm in the north, it surrounds Bosnia-Herzegovina on two sides. It also borders on Slovenia, Hungary and Serbia. It was the most industrial of Yugoslavia's republics and also drew the bulk of the tourists, to its coastal resorts.

See Yugoslavia.

cross-country, the adjective.

But say **go across country**.

cross-examine, cross-examination

Cross-examinations in court cases do not always involve aggressive hectoring and badgering.

Crown

Upper-case except when referring to the headgear. See capitalization.

Crown employees, see civil service.

Crowsnest Pass

Use this spelling for both the pass and the grain-hauling agreement.

crucial, see critical.

CSIS, see Canadian Security Intelligence Service.

CT scan

The initials stand for computed tomography. This name has largely supplanted the older term, CAT scan (computerized axial tomography). The technique uses X-rays, but in a completely different way. A scanner emitting multiple X-ray beams is moved in a circle around the body. Sensors record differences in the rate of absorption by different tissues, and a computer uses the information to create an image of a cross-sectional "slice" of the patient.

CTV

Acceptable even in first reference for the CTV Television Network. See abbreviations.

Cuba

Adjective and people: Cuban. Currency: peso. Capital: Havana.

It is the largest island in the Caribbean, lying about 150 miles across the Straits of Florida from the Florida Keys and across the Yucatan Channel from Yucatan, and dividing the Caribbean from the Atlantic and the Gulf of Mexico. It is the most westerly of the West Indies and the Greater Antilles. It also owns the Isle of Youth (formerly called the Isle of Pines). About 70 per cent of its population of 11.2 million is white, of Spanish origin; the rest is black or of mixed race. Iron and other minerals abound, but sugar dominates the economy, accounting for almost half the value of all exports. Cuba became independent from Spain in 1898 (after the Spanish-American War). Fidel Castro's revolution began in 1953 (on July 26, now a national holiday), and achieved success in January of 1959 with the flight of Fulgencio Batista. The Bay of Pigs invaders landed on April 17, 1961, and were dealt with by April 20. The U.S. naval blockade of Cuba, during the Cuban missile crisis, lasted from Oct. 22 to Nov. 22, 1962.

cubical and cubicle

Cubical means cube-shaped. This spelling is often wrongly used when we mean a small enclosed area, which is spelled **cubicle**.

cupfuls

cure

Use with great care in stories about developments in medical research, to avoid raising false hopes among those with the disease. Consider less absolute words and phrases such as helps, improves, relieves, an advance in the treatment of.

currency

If there is a need to specify the country, brackets are required only for dollar amounts. (This is a result of the peculiar nature of the written form, in which the dollar symbol, $, appears before the amount but is pronounced after it.) Write $2-million (U.S.). For other currencies, we write amounts as they would be spoken (two million Swiss francs). This is also true of cents (it costs 50 U.S. cents) and of dollars if no amount is involved (he is paid in U.S. dollars).

In the interest of clarity, use the **pound symbol** only for British currency. For other countries, write out the word after the amount (200 Lebanese pounds).

We assume that an unadorned dollar figure in a story refers to Canadian dollars. This need be specified only if the reader is likely to suspect that the amount is in U.S. dollars, such as the price a Canadian company pays to buy a U.S. one. We write out the adjective in full—$2-million (Canadian), not Cdn.—unless it appears several times in a statistical story.

In most overseas stories, **convert local currency amounts to Canadian dollars**. We might occasionally leave out the local currency altogether, but then we must use a phrase such as **the equivalent of** $2,500, to prevent any impression that the transaction in question was conducted in Canadian dollars. With such conversions, the reader also usually requires that the amount be put into the **context of wages or buying power**. To say that a pound of meat in a particular country costs the equivalent of $15 is misleading until we add that this is about a week's wages for the average factory worker. In stories involving many amounts, it may be better to convert only the first one and relate it

to buying power, and leave the rest in the local currency.

If the subject is an international one for which U.S. dollars are the common standard, such as national debt, aid, gross national product etc., there is no need to convert to Canadian dollars. Simply specify (U.S.) for the first amount given.

The names of foreign currencies (krone, ruble etc.) do not require italics.

curriculums (not curricula).

CUSO

This is now the official name of the organization formerly called Canadian University Service Overseas. We should explain the origin of the name, or provide a thumbnail description of the organization's activities if the story does not make this clear.

customer

This is the preferred word for buyers of goods and most non-professional services, as opposed to client, patron. See client.

cut-off, noun and adjective. The verb is **cut off**.

cyber

This prefix does not take a hyphen (cyberpunk, cyberspace, cybersquatters).

cyclone

A weather system featuring strong winds spiralling toward a low-pressure centre, usually with heavy rains. In the Atlantic and Caribbean, the most concentrated (and therefore violent) ones are called hurricanes. In the western Pacific and the China Sea, they are called typhoons. See weather words.

Cyprus

Adjective and people: Cypriot. Currency: Cyprus pound, but the

Turkish lira is also used. Capital: Nicosia.

It is an island in the eastern Mediterranean, about 55 miles off Turkey and about 60 miles off Syria. It is nominally a single republic, with a population of 783,000 that is 80 per cent Greek and 20 per cent Turkish, independent from Britain since 1960. There was constant violence between Greek and Turkish Cypriots until a UN peacekeeping operation, with a significant Canadian contingent, was set up in 1964. (The operation continues, but Canada announced in 1992 that its contingent would be pulled out in 1993.) When a junta of Greek army officers favouring union with Greece (*enosis*) staged a coup against the president, Archbishop Makarios, in 1974 (it proved to be short-lived), Turkey invaded and set up the Turkish Cypriot Federated State in the northern third of the island. Its appointed president, Rauf Denktash, declared that it would not seek international recognition.

In 2002, Greek and Turkish Cypriots began direct talks on a proposal to bring the two sides under one central government, but the UN announced in March of 2003 that talks had broken off.

Cyprus is occasionally misspelled **Cypress**, a word which, in lower case, refers to a family of evergreens.

Czechoslovakia

The adjective for references to this former federal state, dissolved on Dec. 31, 1992, with the creation of the separate Czech and Slovak states, is Czechoslovak (never simply Czech). Its formal name was the Czech and Slovak Federative Republic (chosen in 1990 to replace Czechoslovak Socialist Republic). It lay to the north of Austria and Hungary, and to the south of eastern Germany and Poland, having been created in 1918 on the dissolution of Austria-Hungary. The Czechs (inhabiting the "Czech lands"

of Bohemia, Moravia and a portion of Silesia) made up 60 per cent of the population, and the Slovaks (in Slovakia) made up 30 per cent, the rest being of German, Hungarian, Polish or Ukrainian origin. Czechs and Slovaks speak western Slavonic languages related about as closely as Spanish and Portuguese. Originally a unitary state, it was converted to a two-state federation in 1968.

Student demonstrations beginning in the mid-1960s eroded the position of the Communist Party's hard-line Stalinist leaders, and leader Antonin Novotny was replaced by Alexander Dubcek as party leader, by war hero Gen. Ludvik Svoboda as president and by Oldrich Cernik as prime minister. Their program of liberalization begun in early 1968, dubbed the Prague Spring, had the stated goal of "socialism with a human face." Soviet troops (nominally, the Warsaw Pact countries as a group) invaded in August, and Dubcek was replaced by Gustav Husak in 1969 as part of a purge of party liberals. Cernik was replaced as prime minister by Lubomir Strougal in 1970, but Svoboda stayed on as president until 1975.

Student pro-democracy demonstrations in November, 1989, precipitated a lightning change, dubbed the "velvet revolution." Violent suppression of a rally on Nov. 17 at Prague's Wenceslas Square so angered the country that it swelled the protests there and at Bratislava, the Slovak capital. A new coalition, Civic Forum, was hastily formed under playwright Vaclav Havel. On Nov. 24, party leader Milos Jakes and his entire Politburo resigned, but protests continued, including a general strike. Within a week, the federal assembly removed the Communist political monopoly, on Dec. 10 a new coalition government was formed, Husak quit as president, and he was replaced by Havel on Dec. 29 after a unanimous assembly vote.

In 1992, differences over the pace of reforms (the Slovaks favoured a more gradual transition from a planned economy) led to the "velvet divorce." After their leaders' mutual agreement in June to split up, polls showed most citizens would have preferred to prevent this but saw it as inevitable. Legislators formally voted for the split on Nov. 25, setting the date of midnight Dec. 31.

See Czech Republic, Slovakia.

Czech Republic

Adjective and people: Czech. Currency: koruna. Capital: Prague.

It became independent at midnight on Dec. 31, 1992, through the peaceful breakup of the former Czechoslovakia. (It had come into being in 1968 when Czechoslovakia, until then a unitary state, was split into two federated components.) Its population of about 10 million is more than 90-per-cent Czech (including the Moravians, who speak in a slight dialect and consider themselves distinct), and there are German, Polish and Slovak minorities.

It comprises the Moravian and Bohemian regions and a small part of Silesia (the bulk of Silesia is in Poland, to the north). Other neighbours are Slovakia to the east, Germany to the west and Austria to the south. Its language, formerly called Bohemian, is of the western Slavonic family and about as closely related to Slovak as Spanish is to Portuguese. It is also closely related to Polish. In Czech, the republic's name is Ceska Republika, the language is Cestina and the capital is Praha.

The Czech Republic became a member of NATO in 1999, and in 2002 was invited to join the European Union in the near future.

Among the leading European economies even during the Soviet period, despite a relative scarcity of resources, it has a diverse and relatively efficient industrial sector, especially by Eastern European standards, although it suffered severe disruption after 1989 in the conversion from a planned economy. Products include sophisticated machinery, ceramics, glass and textiles. The agriculture sector is strong, timber is important in higher districts, and there is considerable tourism revenue in the Bohemian, Western Carpathian and Sudetes Mountains, with many spas, hot springs and both summer and winter resorts.

See Czechoslovakia, NATO, Warsaw Pact.

D

D-Day

To most people, it means June 6, 1944. Describe it as the day the Allies invaded Normandy, not invaded Europe. (They had taken Sicily in July of 1943 and were heavily engaged in Italy.) The operation itself was called Overlord, and we refer to landings, not landing. (The troops on five beaches code-named Omaha, Gold, Juno, Sword and Utah did not link up into a solid front until June 11. There were also landings by parachute and glider.)

If D-Day is used to refer to any other operation, we must be sure there is no confusion with the Normandy landings. D-Day and H-Hour, formed simply by repetition of the first letter, had long been standard terms for military planners. A still-undetermined date for the beginning of any large, complex operation would be called D-Day. Various preliminary operations (marshalling of troops, supplies and transport, preparatory bombing, deceptive manoeuvres etc.) would be scheduled for D minus 30, D minus 3 etc., while objectives and follow-up operations would be planned for D plus 2, D plus 20 etc. Later, when plans became final, these would all be converted to actual dates.

D-ring

dachshund

Dacron, a trade name.

dais, podium, stand, stage, lectern, pulpit, rostrum

A **dais** is a raised platform for speakers, head tables etc. A small dais for one speaker, an orchestra conductor etc. is usually called a **podium** (from the Latin for foot). Outdoors, both are usually called a **stand** (speaker's stand, reviewing stand). Stand is also often used for bands and orchestras not playing in a pit or on a theatre stage. A synonym for all of these is **platform**.

Stage is usually reserved for theatrical halls, in which the platform is equipped with wings, lighting and other equipment for performances.

A **lectern** is a reading desk that holds a speaker's notes or book. It is wrong to refer to it as a podium, or to imply this by saying the speaker stood at or behind the podium.

A useful word that is usually taken to mean podium and lectern combined, particularly as part of a pulpit or as a fairly permanent installation in an academic lecture hall, is **rostrum** (from the Latin for prow of a ship). Speak of someone being **on** the rostrum.

A **pulpit**, the place from which the congregation in a house of worship is addressed, is taken to mean not only the platform but also its various trappings such as a lectern and possibly railings. Accordingly, we speak of the preacher being **in** the pulpit, not on or behind it.

Dalmatian

A, not o. That goes for all 101 of them.

damage, damages

Confine use of the plural word to stories about civil litigation, and be aware that in this context it does not refer to the harm, wrong or injury done, but rather to the money ordered paid in compensation for it.

References to physical damage are always singular, even though it may involve several types of harm or loss. The storm caused $3-million in damage (not damages).

damn, damned

Prefer damned as the adjective.

Danish

Always upper-case, even for pastry. See Denmark.

Danzig is now Gdansk, Poland.

darnedest

Darwin, Charles

It is a distortion to call his theory one of "survival of the fittest." His *Origin of Species* describes evolution by means of natural selection.

dash, see punctuation.

Dash 7, Dash 8

The names of these planes contain no hyphen or dash. (The Dash was once an actual dash forming part of the name during design and initial production at de Havilland.)

data

Most Canadians still consider it a plural (of datum) that takes plural verbs and pronouns (these data are). Since this is jarring to many, and since the word is somewhat pretentious, consider substituting information, facts, figures etc.

database

dates

Be cautious when approaching dates written in the form 2/12/03 or 2-12-03. In general U.S. practice, the form represents Feb. 12, 2003, following that style of writing the date: month, day, year. In Europe, it represents Dec. 2, 2003, following the European style of day, month, year (2 December 2003). Canada's preference tends to be day, month, year, but it cannot be assumed that all Canadian sources use it this way.

Note that an increasingly popular standard of the International Organization for Standardization (ISO) is year, month, day, which, since it descends from the longest unit to the shortest, permits the addition of hour, minute, second: 2004-05-20 06:30:43. See numbers.

da Vinci

It means from Vinci, which was Leonardo's home town. It is not his surname. He should be called Leonardo in second reference, and his works should be called a Leonardo or Leonardos.

Davis Cup

It is a silver bowl awarded each year to a national tennis team. Countries in various areas of the world, called zones, play off against each other, after which the zone winners meet until all but one team is eliminated. (Each meeting involves four singles matches and one doubles match.) The surviving team then plays the previous year's winner for the cup, in what is called the challenge round. The trophy was donated by Dwight Davis, who organized the first tournament in 1900.

Dawson

It had 25,000 inhabitants in its gold-rush heyday, and although it now has only about 700 permanent residents, it is still an incorporated city, Canada's smallest. It is on the east bank of the Yukon River, at the confluence of the Klondike River.

Day, Stockwell

He led the Canadian Alliance from 2000, when the party was created as a successor to the Reform Party, until 2001, when he resigned as a result of turmoil within the Alliance. See Jet Ski.

daycare, noun and adjective.

daylight time (no **saving**).

It is lower-case in such expressions as switch to daylight time, but upper-case when we include the time zone, as in Pacific Daylight Time. The initials are upper-case, as in 3 p.m. EDT.

de and du

In names of Quebec organizations, agencies etc., those involving cities use **de**, and those involving the province use **du**.

deadly and deathly

Deadly means able to cause death (a deadly poison), while **deathly** means resembling death (a deathly pallor).

deaf, deaf-mute, see disabled.

death rate

Since we are all going to die one day, avoid writing sentences such as this: A rise of 0.6 millilitres of cholesterol per litre results in a 38 per cent increase in the death rate.

The death rate is 100 per cent. If you mean the rate of premature death or, more helpfully, the rate of death before the age of 40 or within five minutes or some other specific measurement, say so.

debate

People can debate issues, but they cannot debate one another. Use debate with in such instances.

debt and deficit

A **deficit** is a shortfall, specifically a failure of revenues to cover expenditures, obligations or expectations. The term is used in reference to a budget, either annual or drawn up for a specific occasion, such as a fundraising event. **Debt** is what is owed at a particular time, the accumulated result of deficits and borrowing.

Confine deficit to money matters. Avoid such sports expressions as a two-run deficit; substitute such words as handicap, disadvantage, shortfall.

debut, do not use as a verb.

decades, see numbers.

decision

In normal Canadian idiom, they are made, not taken.

decline

It means to refuse politely. We do not use it if there is an indication the refusal was brusque, violent or obscene.

Also note that decline takes a direct object only when it means to reject something that is offered, as in decline an invitation. When it means refuse to do something that has been requested, it must be followed by an infinitive, as in declined to comment (not declined comment).

Strictly speaking, decline does not mean to be reduced in size or number. Prefer the population is decreasing, falling, dropping, not declining.

decomposed

We can all imagine the state of a body discovered after more than a day or two. There is usually no need to inflict such words as **decomposed** on our breakfast-table readers. If the issue arises, we look for oblique wording, such as "the condition of the body made identification difficult."

However, it is relevant to comment on condition if it is other than what might be expected, as when a body unearthed after many years is remarkably well preserved. See taste.

deductible

deep-sea, the adjective.

defence

It is a noun. Use it as an adjective only in reference to the administration of national defence, as in defence spending, defence committee. Otherwise, the adjective is defensive (defensive weapons, defensive coach, defensive position).

In many cases, defence is a euphemism that is better replaced by military, arms, weapons etc.

defining and non-defining clauses

See punctuation (comma), that and which.

definite

It means known for certain (It is definite he is coming), and also clearly defined, precise. It does not mean firm, unalterable. Speak of definite plans or a definite decision only if we mean they are precise, spelled out in detail. Otherwise, say firm, final or some such.

defuse and diffuse

Defuse is a verb meaning to remove the fuse from, or figuratively to remove the danger of a confrontation. **Diffuse** as a verb means to spread in all directions; as an adjective it means dispersed, or wordy.

De Grassi Street, Toronto.

Note that the spelling was changed in the title of the long-running CBC television series. *Degrassi High* (successor to *The Kids of Degrassi Street* and then *Degrassi Junior High*) ended

with a feature-length episode in January of 1992.

degrees

For academic degrees, lower-case the full name (bachelor of arts) but upper-case the abbreviation (BA).

For degrees of temperature, arc, latitude, see Celsius, directions, measurement, numbers.

de Havilland Inc.

It is owned by Bombardier Inc. It was previously a division of Boeing of Canada Ltd., and before that was called de Havilland Aircraft of Canada Ltd.

de-ice, de-icer

deleterious

It means harmful, not unflattering.

De Laurentiis, Dino

demeanour

De Mille, Cecil B.

Democrat

A member of the Democratic Party. The party may also be called the Democrats, but the adjective is Democratic, as in the Democratic national convention, the Democratic candidate. In political stories with several references to party and state, we use brackets and the abbreviation D with no period, as in Sam Nunn (D, Georgia). Do not use this as a general practice in stories with only a few politicians, and never in the lead.

Dene

This word, referring to the northern Athapaskan-speaking peoples of the Mackenzie Valley and the Barrens, means "the people." The Dene Nation, which in 1978 officially replaced the Indian Brotherhood of the Northwest Territories, also includes many Crees along with the speakers of Athapaskan languages in the area: Chipewyan, Slavey, Dogrib, Loucheux. See native people.

Denendeh

This Athapaskan word, meaning Home of the People, is used by Dene to refer to what they consider their homeland. In constitutional negotiations, it is the name they give to a proposed self-governing Dene territory in the Western Arctic. It was to have been the counterpart of the new territory in the Central and Eastern Arctic (approved in 1992) called Nunavut (Inuktitut for Our Land), which has an Inuit majority. However, after Nunavut's creation, the remaining section of the old Northwest Territories retained the name Northwest Territories rather than adopt the name Denendeh. The size of the new NWT is 40 per cent that of the old NWT. See native people, Nunavut.

Denmark

Adjective and people: Danish. Currency: krone (plural kroner). Capital: Copenhagen.

Always upper-case Danish, even for the pastry. (In Denmark itself, such pastries are called Vienna bread.) Denmark is a constitutional monarchy comprising the peninsula called Jutland, 482 islands just off the peninsula (including Zealand, which contains Copenhagen), plus Greenland and the Faroe Islands. Although not residents of the Scandinavian Peninsula, Denmark's 5.3 million citizens may be referred to as Scandinavian. **Greenland**, a Danish possession since 1380, was granted home rule in 1979 and full internal self-government in 1981; constitutionally, it has the same rights as Danish counties. The Faroes, lying north of Scotland about midway between Norway and Iceland, have been a self-governing region since 1948.

Danish voters rejected the Maastricht Treaty on European union in a 1992 referendum. The country agreed to it only after being exempted from the requirement to join in the single European currency. In a 2002 referendum, voters again rejected the euro. See European Union.

dependant

Use this spelling for the noun meaning one who relies on another for support. The adjective is dependent. The abstract noun is dependence.

deportation

Not everyone ordered to leave Canada can be said to be deported. The generic terms are **removal** and **removal order**. There are three classes of removal order, of which a deportation order is the most severe. Next comes an exclusion order, while the least severe is a departure order.

Someone removed by means of a deportation order, whom we can accurately describe as having been deported, cannot legally return to Canada without the explicit consent of the immigration minister. An exclusion order allows the person to apply for readmission in 12 months. A departure order allows the person to reapply immediately.

deprecate

It means to express disapproval, to belittle. The adjective is deprecatory. Do not confuse with depreciate, although this word can also mean to speak ill of, in the sense of lower the value of. Both words are a bit highbrow for use in news stories.

Depression

Upper-case only when referring to the Depression of the 1930s. Otherwise lower-case, as in warnings of a coming depression, but be aware that it is not in the normal lexicon of economists. See recession.

deputy

Upper-case only for the cabinet position of Deputy Prime Minister or Deputy Premier. Otherwise, say deputy leader, deputy Speaker etc. See capitalization.

de rigueur (note the -gu-).

desalinate, desalination, not desalinize, desalinization.

desert and dessert

As a noun, **desert** means a region lacking in precipitation, and as an adjective also means uninhabited. (A desert island need not be dry.) Do not equate desert with sand, since low precipitation also qualifies the polar regions and some rocky or even mountainous areas as deserts. Desert is also a noun meaning what is deserved, usually used in the plural (just deserts).

Dessert means a sweet as the last course of a meal (from *desservir*, to clear the table).

deshabille

desiccate

designated hitter, DH

desirable

despite

This is often a loaded word, implying that the writer and The Globe are of the opinion that a more principled, just or intelligent person would have done something different. (Despite reports of wing cracks in many of the aircraft, the minister has refused to order them grounded for inspection.) It can easily be taken to carry the implication that the subject is showing defiance, even malice, flying in the face of what is obviously right. If its use creates the erroneous impression that we are making a moral judgment, the sentence must be recast.

diagnose

A condition or disease is diagnosed, not a patient.

dial, dialled, dialling, dialler

dialectic

It has several meanings in philosophy, having been used in different ways by Aristotle, Plato, Socrates, Kant and Hegel. (For Socrates, it was a method of argument in which an opponent is led into self-contradiction.) We should not use dialectic merely to mean a treatise, argument etc.

dialogue

It may be used for an exchange of ideas, not merely for theatrical lines, and it may involve more than two people. But good writers do not use it to mean mere conversation, and do not use it as a verb (I want to dialogue with you), although it appears as a verb in some dictionaries.

diarrhea

Dictaphone, a trade name.

dictionary

Ours is *The Canadian Oxford Dictionary*, but we make some style exceptions. See spelling.

dicey

diesel

dietitian

different

Usually followed by a phrase beginning with **from** when simply relating one thing to another (He is different from his brother). When it is followed by a clause, it usually takes **than**, as in The countryside is different than I remember it. (Fowler says this is now preferred to the more cumbersome

"different from that which" or
"different from what" etc.)

Like the adverb **successfully**, this
adjective is often redundant. The
Raptors dressed 23 different players
this season; we travelled to 12
different countries in Europe. Neither
example needs different.

differ from, differ with

Differ from indicates dissimilarity.
Differ with indicates a disagreement.

Digby chicken

This jocular name for a small salted
and smoked herring refers to Digby,
N.S. It requires a translation. (In
contrast, Digby scallops are indeed
scallops.)

dike

An embankment. Never use this
word, or dyke, to refer to a lesbian.
See gay.

dilatation and curettage, D and C

dilemma

It means a situation offering two
choices that are equally unpleasant.
We must not use it simply to mean a
serious problem, a seemingly insoluble
problem, or a tricky or difficult choice
(the lady or the tiger). If the choices
are not both unpleasant (leaving one's
spouse or losing one's children, for
example), find another word. The horns
of a dilemma are the two choices.

dilettante

dimwit

dinero

It is Spanish for money, and so can
be used only in the singular. Do not
say someone "was short a few dineros."

dingo, dingoes

Movie and novel plots aside, these
Australian dogs are mainly solitary,
rarely hunting in packs. They are true
dogs, descended from those taken to
Australia by the Aborigines.

dining room

Dion, Celine

The Quebec singer spells her first
name Céline on her French-language
CDs and Celine on her English-
language CDs and in Las Vegas. Use
Celine, no accent.

Dionne quintuplets

Contrary to what the anglophone
ear expects, Oliva Dionne was the
father (died 1979) and Elzire Dionne
was the mother (died 1986). The
quints, born on May 28, 1934, near
the villages of Corbeil and Callander,
Ont., were Annette, Cecile, Emilie
(died 1954), Marie (died 1970) and
Yvonne (died 2001). The surviving
quints, living in poverty in Montreal,
alleged that there had been
mismanagement of the millions in
revenue that their fame engendered,
and in 1998 won a financial
settlement from the Province of
Ontario.

diphtheria

diphthong

See spelling.

directions

Spell out the points of the
compass, such as northeast, north-
northeast, in most news stories, but
abbreviate in tabular matter or stories
with many directions, such as weather
reports and yachting stories.
Abbreviations are upper-case, without
periods, as in NE, NNE etc.

When referring to part of a
jurisdiction or region, use the
adjectives northern, southern,
northeastern etc. (northern France).
Upper-case for distinctive regions
(Northern Canada, Southwestern

Ontario). See capitalization. Use the nouns north, south, east and west as adjectives only when they are a part of the name, either formally or by long usage, and can therefore be in upper case (North Carolina, West Beirut). We would not say south Canada or southeast Canada, so we should not say south Lebanon or southeast Lebanon.

Latitude and **longitude** are spelled out in most news stories (at a latitude of 49 degrees north, a longitude of 34 degrees 30 minutes west). Abbreviate in later references only if there are many such readings, as in military or yachting stories. The style for degrees, minutes and 10ths of minutes (seconds) is 49 deg. 37.4 min. N, 24 deg. 38.2 min. W etc. There is no need in later references to use the words latitude and longitude if it has already been established in the story that readings of north or south indicate latitude and readings of east or west indicate longitude.

The words parallel and meridian are also usually enough to establish what we are referring to, as in: The troops moved south of the 37th parallel for the first time.

Do not use the words up and down when referring to north and south, or the words above and below when referring to parallels. (Say south of 60, not below 60.) Remember that Quebec is downstream from Montreal, and that the Mackenzie and the Nile flow down (as water has a habit of doing) northward to the sea.

dirt road
We usually mean gravel road, and there is a big difference.

disabled, disabilities
People with disabilities, and their support groups, prefer the words **disability** and **disabled** to the words handicap and handicapped, except when describing mental retardation (see below).

In writing about people with disabilities, we must take care not to use words that are demeaning or hurtful, or that serve to set them apart from society. In particular, avoid expressions that contain the definite article (**the** disabled, **the** deaf, **the** blind, **the** mentally ill), which imply that they are a separate class or that people with a particular disability are all the same. Many disabled people also dislike such expressions as victim, defect, afflicted, sufferer and suffers from, and they use the word patient only in a medical context. We should respect their wishes in this.

However, clarity is our first concern, and we do not go along with euphemisms advocated by some support groups if these words are misleading or are vague generalities that do not make it clear what is being discussed. The term exceptional, for example, is taken by most readers to mean greater than average, not merely an exception to the usual, and so the term exceptional child should not be used to mean a mentally retarded one, as some groups advocate. Another term, mentally disabled, is far too general, because mental disabilities can range from mild dyslexia or other perceptual problems to severe autism or retardation and to the whole range of mental illnesses. The term **mentally handicapped** seems to be clearer to readers, and so is more acceptable; another alternative is intellectually handicapped. Similarly, speech impairment can range from a lisp or a stammer to a cleft palate or even more severe physical conditions. If we know the specifics, we should state them.

Here are some specific suggestions that can be followed without sacrificing clarity:

Disabilities should be mentioned only if they are germane to the story.

Use **mental illness** or **mentally ill persons**, not crazy or insane, as a general description, and do not use the word sane as the opposite of mentally ill, although the word insanity may be used to describe the most severe classes of mental illness. When speaking of a specific person, be aware that any such description, including mentally ill, may well be libellous. Treatment by a psychiatrist and admission to a psychiatric hospital are by no means certain indications of mental illness, and there must be no implication that mental illness is beyond cure, or that a past episode indicates current condition. Consult a senior editor before describing any identifiable person as mentally ill.

The word **normal**, standing alone, should not be used as the general opposite of disabled, because it implies that disabled people have general differences beyond their specific disabilities, or that there is a single, ideal standard to which everyone else in society conforms. Lean toward such opposites as able-bodied, or even more specific opposites such as sighted, able to walk. When comparing people's degrees of ability, not the people themselves, the adjective normal may be used in such expressions as normal vision, normal hearing, implying a normal range.

The words **cripple** and **crippled** are offensive to the disabled and also too vague to be useful. If we know the specifics, say paraplegic, quadriplegic, walks with crutches etc. If we must use a vague term, make it disabled.

Do not use **hunchback**. Speak of a spinal deformity, or specify a bent spine, twisted spine, curved spine.

Say a person **uses a wheelchair**, not that he or she is confined to a wheelchair or is wheelchair-bound. A wheelchair is not confining; it provides mobility, including the capacity to participate in sports, to people who cannot walk, and many who use them also drive cars.

The words **blind** and **deaf**, standing alone, should be used only for those who have no vision or almost no vision, or a profound lack of hearing

from birth or shortly afterward. And we should come down on the side of the half-full cup rather than the half-empty one, saying that a person has impaired, partial or slight vision, not that he or she is partially blind.

Do not use **deaf and dumb** or **deaf-mute**; say a person uses sign language. If a person loses his or her hearing later in life and so speaks relatively normally, we should convey this, possibly by speaking of a profound hearing loss rather than deafness. A person with hearing loss not severe enough to prevent communication primarily by speech should be referred to as hard of hearing rather than deaf.

If a person cannot speak, a condition caused by many factors other than deafness, simply say so. We do not use the labels dumb and mute.

The expressions "turned a deaf ear" or "she was deaf to his entreaties" are marginally acceptable in copy, where it is clear we simply mean a refusal to listen. But we should be more circumspect in headlines, where saying something "fell on deaf ears," in the absence of context, could be taken to equate deafness with stubbornness or intransigence.

Instead of the noun **autistic** (an autistic, the autistic, autistics), which implies a class of people all with identical conditions, refer to a person with autism, and give its form and degree of severity if we know it. Autistic can be used as an adjective, as in an autistic child, but again, it is truly informative only if the form and degree of autism are added.

Instead of the noun **epileptic**, speak of a person with epilepsy. We say epileptic seizure or seizures, not fits or spells.

Avoid the word **defect**, as in birth defect, when speaking of congenital conditions. Use the specific expressions blind from birth, born without feet etc.

We say **brain-injured**, not brain-damaged. (The word damaged, used in connection with any part of the body, such as a damaged hand as opposed to an injured hand, conveys a destruction of tissue so extensive that recovery is impossible.)

We do not use the terms **Mongoloid** or Mongolism. Say Down syndrome, a child with Down syndrome.

In describing **amputations**, specify the location when this is known, because this greatly affects the degree of adaptability and the type of prosthesis available. Say at the shoulder or hip; above, at or below the elbow or knee; at the wrist or ankle etc. Avoid exaggeration in leads with such expressions as "lost an arm" if we must explain later that only half the forearm was involved.

Some support groups object to the words **retarded**, mentally retarded, retardation, although these are still used in most other countries and no shame is attached to them. (Retarded is itself a replacement for such words as idiot, moron, imbecile, mental defective, and has the advantage of implying that mental development, although slowed, is still possible.) Retarded may be used in the generic sense, particularly in an international context, but we should be sensitive to the prevailing mood in Canada and seeks synonyms, especially when discussing a recognizable individual or group. The two that are clearest to readers are mentally handicapped and intellectually handicapped. Two others, developmentally disabled and developmentally challenged, are too vague and general, failing to make it clear even that the subject is the mind; and the term disabled in particular does not convey that progress is possible. The expression learning-disabled is also too general, covering those who, for example, are extremely intelligent but have a perceptual problem.

As with other descriptions of disabilities, the words retarded and retardation are truly informative only

if the degree is included. For this reason, and because of sensitivity about the word retarded, when speaking of an individual we may be able to replace it with such expressions as "functions at a Grade 4 level" or "at the level of a 10-year-old," etc. See retarded.

disc

This is the spelling for all uses not involving computers, including compact disc, disc brakes, disc harrow, disc jockey.

For computers, use **disk**, as in disk drive, floppy disk. CD-ROM falls on the computer side: disk.

discolour

But drop the u for **discoloration**.

Discovery Day

In Newfoundland and Labrador, it is a statutory holiday observed on the closest Monday to June 24. It commemorates a landing (for which there is no firm evidence) by John Cabot in 1497. Discovery Day is also the name of a Yukon statutory holiday, on Aug. 17, the date in 1896 that gold was discovered at Bonanza Creek.

discreet and discrete

Discreet is by far the more usual, meaning tactful. **Discrete** means made up of distinct parts.

disease

It is a mistaken notion that the word disease applies only to an illness caused by a micro-organism. In addition to infectious diseases, there are deficiency diseases, metabolic diseases, occupational diseases, congenital diseases, vascular diseases, degenerative diseases etc. The word disease means any disruption of the normal functioning of a living thing, but it is usually understood to mean one that has been previously recognized and classified according to a certain set of symptoms. Cancers certainly qualify as diseases. Technically, so do poisonings, but it would be confusing to describe them as such. Psychiatric diseases are disorders that cannot be linked to known abnormalities of the brain; however, at least some are certain to be traced eventually to physical or chemical causes.

The set of symptoms that indicates the presence of a disease and its nature is called a **syndrome**. This word should not normally be used to mean the disease itself, although common usage allows this in certain cases, notably acquired immune deficiency syndrome. (AIDS is unusual in that it manifests itself as one or more of several rare diseases that the body can no longer fight.)

A disease tends to have a single cause. A disorder tends to have multiple possible causes. A syndrome has multiple manifestations.

disfavour

dishonour, dishonourable

disinterested and uninterested

did i say "uninterested"? no, no, of <u>course</u> i meant "disinterested."

Disinterested means having no stake in, not standing to lose or gain anything as a result of. A disinterested observer may be fascinated by a game, but has no stake in seeing either side win. **Uninterested** means taking no

interest in. An uninterested observer is bored by the game. The nouns are disinterest, lack of interest.

disk, see disc.

dispatch

Use this spelling for both the verb and the noun, as in dispatch a message, mentioned in dispatches.

disseminate

dissent, but **dissension**.

dissociate, not disassociate.
distemper

This term is applied to various diseases in animals, not just to the familiar viral disease that attacks unvaccinated dogs, usually as puppies. (It brings fever, runny nose and throat, and occasionally bronchial pneumonia.) If there is any chance of ambiguity, as in an outbreak at a farm, specify canine distemper etc.

dived, not dove.

DJ

Use this spelling, not deejay, both for radio disc jockeys and turntable artists.

Djibouti

Adjective for country: Djibouti. Refer to the people as citizens, residents, population etc. of Djibouti. Currency: Djibouti franc. Capital: Djibouti. (Locally, called Djiboutiville.)

It is in northeastern Africa, across from the southwestern corner of the Arabian Peninsula (Yemen) at the chokepoint between the Red Sea and the Gulf of Aden. It borders on Ethiopia and Somalia, and its 640,000 citizens are Issas from Somalia and Afars from Ethiopia. It is a desert, with negligible agriculture and no oil. The main economic activity is operation of the port.

do

Be on guard against the growing use of this word as an all-purpose transitive verb, as in do routine care, do a heart operation, do an assault, do an agreement. It has its place in some expressions, as in do my work, do your duty, do a good deed, do the washing, but in many cases it must be replaced by a more idiomatic, precise and descriptive verb, such as provide, perform, commit, achieve etc.

The idiomatic expression do business (let's do business, they did some business) means specifically to hatch or conclude a deal or deals, and pet owners know what it means to add a possessive (he did his business). But in other expressions involving business, we usually must find some other verb (He is in the oil business, he conducts business, he carries on business etc.).

In particular, eliminate do in reference to taking or using drugs, as in do drugs, did some crack, doing some reds. It is the jargon of the street drug culture, and could well be taken by readers as indicating the writer's acceptance of that culture or even participation in it.

Doberman pinscher

Upper-case. (But the developer of the breed is spelled Ludwig Dobermann.)

Doctors Without Borders

See *Médecins sans frontières*.

Dofasco Inc.

Dogma 95

Use this style, not Dogme 95, for the cinematic movement championed by Danish director Lars Von Trier.

d'oh!

Use this spelling for the interjection associated with cartoon patriarch Homer Simpson.

dole

This word is not used in Canada to mean any kind of government payment, including welfare, employment insurance or disability pensions. See pogey.

dolour

But drop the u for **dolorous**.

Domesday Book

Dominica and Dominican Republic

They are two different Caribbean states, on different islands. The adjective for both is Dominican (pronounced differently— Domi**nee**can and Do**min**ican—but this is no help in a written medium). Never use Dominican in first reference, before the country has been established. Instead say the president of the Dominican Republic, an immigrant from Dominica etc.

Dominica

Adjective and people: Dominican (but only after it is clear which country is meant, Dominica or the Dominican Republic). Currency: East Caribbean dollar. Capital: Roseau.

This former British possession, largest of the Windward Islands in the Lesser Antilles, has been an independent republic, a member of the Commonwealth, since 1978. It lies between the French islands (Overseas Departments) of Martinique and Guadeloupe. There are small white and Asian minorities, but most of the approximately 70,000 inhabitants are of black or mixed ancestry.

Dominican Republic

Adjective and people: Dominican (but use only if there is no chance of confusion with Dominica). Currency: peso. Capital: Santo Domingo.

It occupies the eastern two-thirds of the island of Hispaniola. (The rest is occupied by Haiti. Hispaniola, between Cuba and Puerto Rico, is one of the Greater Antilles, which define the northern limit of the Caribbean.) The population of about 8.3 million is mostly of mixed European and African blood, but there is a white minority, of Spanish descent. The capital, Santo Domingo, was called Ciudad Trujillo from 1936 to 1961. Sugar cultivation is the primary industry. Other products include bauxite, cement, silver, gold, textiles and tobacco.

Dominion
   Acceptable as both a noun and an adjective when referring to things Canadian. Always upper-case in this sense.

dominoes

Donegal, Ireland.
   But note Marquess of Donegall.

donnybrook

doppelganger

dot-com
   The phrase for Internet-related companies refers to the top-level domain name "com" (short for commercial) preceded by the dot (.) that separates components of a Net address. It is unnecessary to include the word "company": Investors got out of dot-coms as fast as they could.

double-cross, both noun and verb.

doughnut

Doukhobor
   Take care not to imply that all Doukhobors engage in the occasional violent or nude protests of some members of the Sons of Freedom sect.

Dow Jones (not Dow-Jones)

downhill

down payment

downplay, a non-word. Use **play down**.

Down syndrome
   Our style echoes the lack of possessive in the Canadian Down Syndrome Society. Do not use the terms Mongolism, Mongoloid. See disabled.

Downtown Eastside
   See Vancouver.

D'Oyly Carte Opera Company

Dr.
   Honorific for **doctor**, both MDs and PhDs. See honorifics.
   Also the abbreviation for **Drive**, but used only in actual street addresses in which the house number is given. See streets.

Draconian, upper-case.

draegerman
   Lower-case this name for a mine-rescue worker, despite its origin in the name of the company that made early rescue equipment, Draeger. Explain draegerman unless the context is clear.

draft
   Use this spelling (not draught) for all meanings, including a breeze, draft beer, bank drafts, ships' drafts and military or sports drafts.

DREE, DRIE
   These two extinct names for federal departments stood for Department of Regional Economic Expansion and Department of Regional Industrial Expansion. Neither contained the word and. The successor is the Department of Industry, Science and Technology.

dressing room

drive-in, noun.
The verb is **drive in**.

dropout, noun.
The verb is **drop out**.

drown

It can be either intransitive (He drowned; His cat drowned) or transitive (He drowned his cat; His cat was drowned). Accordingly, we never say He was drowned unless we really mean that he was a victim of foul play.

drugs

Be careful with the word **drug**. It once meant any substance other than food used for a medical purpose. Then the definition expanded to cover illegal substances used for pleasure or such purposes as cheating at sports. Now, this second definition has all but hijacked the word. People still speak of going to the drugstore, but say they are going to have a prescription filled, or name a specific medicine such as headache pills. They do not say they are buying drugs, are on drugs or are using drugs. These expressions mean only one thing to most readers.

Use the word drug in such general expressions as prescription drugs, over-the-counter drugs and generic drugs, but in specific references, if there is any chance the reader might infer that illegal substances are meant, consider such words as medicine, medication or remedy, or such adjectives as prescription, legal. Speak of drug manufacturers and the drug industry, but be careful not to defame legitimate manufacturers by using the word drug in a way that could be misconstrued. The drug companies have, for good reason, swung toward the word "pharmaceutical" now that the illegal drug trade is so pervasive it can truly be called an industry.

In stories about illegal drugs, we must not imply that a particular **brand** is involved if we are not sure this is

the case. Indeed, the drug was probably made in an illegal laboratory. Some drugs, known as designer drugs, are created solely for the illegal market. For clarity, however, it is legitimate when using an unfamiliar street or generic name to add that the drug is also sold legally under a particular brand name.

Avoid using **drug-culture jargon** and nicknames in such a way that it appears the writer is tolerant of, or even a participant in, the street-drug culture. There is some latitude in feature stories to establish atmosphere, and in indirect quotes from abusers or police, but in most news stories say hashish and hashish oil, not hash; say marijuana cigarette, not joint; say sniff rather than snort or blow. The word high is acceptable as the commonly used equivalent to drunk on alcohol, but do not use such terms as stoned, spaced, blasted, floating, flying, ozoned, coasting, amped (on amphetamines), overamped, overcharged. Do not use street names of drugs as if the reader should be familiar with them; always give the proper name as well, usually first.

Never use the verb "do" to mean use or take drugs, as in She doesn't do drugs; He did some crack.

Be aware that the street value of seized drugs is often inflated in police reports. Always attribute such amounts to police, and whenever possible use the estimate of our own crime reporters, who are up-to-date on street prices.

The Globe library has an array of source material on drugs, including the comprehensive reference text *Drugs and Drug Abuse*, from the Addiction Research Foundation. It covers all drugs found on the street, giving brand names, street names, effects and method of use, and also has a useful list of other street slang. For reporters and editors handling drug stories, this book should be considered habit-forming.

Here is a brief overview of the main street drugs:

opiates The juice from the seed pod of the Asian poppy yields **opium,** which appears as brown chunks or powder and is usually smoked or eaten. It can be broken down into several alkaloids, including **codeine** and **morphine** (morph, M, Miss Emma), which are found in pills, cough syrups etc. (In street jargon, opiate cough syrups are called juice.) Morphine is chemically modified to produce **heroin** (also called diamorphine and diacetylmorphine), a white or brownish powder that is dissolved in water over a flame (cooked) for injection. It can also be smoked on a cigarette, a method called ack-ack. Street names include dust, H, horse, Harry, junk, smack and China White (a specific type of heroin). It is also found in combination with amphetamines or with cocaine (bombita, dynamite, speedball, whizbang). A powerful semi-synthetic opiate is hydromorphone, sold as **Dilaudid** (dillies). Opiate-related synthetic drugs include **meperidine** (trade names Demerol, Demer-Idine) and **methadone**.

cocaine Extracted from the coca bush of the Andes slopes. It induces feelings of well-being and energy, and was an ingredient of Coca-Cola until 1903, but with prolonged use euphoria is replaced by restlessness, suspicion, insomnia. It is sold as a salt, cocaine hydrochloride, which is mainly sniffed but also can be injected. Street names include C, coke, candy (nose candy), Corine, snow, blow, flake. It is more potent when purified and altered into its free base, a form that can be vaporized and therefore smoked. **Crack** cocaine is the salt heated with baking soda to form a slab which is cracked into chunks (rocks, rock) to be smoked in a pipe. It is potent but wears off very quickly and leaves the

user depressed, which creates a demand for more frequent doses.

cannabis Marijuana, hashish and hashish oil are from *Cannabis sativa,* the hemp plant. The active ingredient is delta-9-tetrahydrocannabinol (THC). Marijuana is the leaves and flowers smoked in cigarettes (called joints, reefers) or in special pipes. A roach is the final nub of a joint held in a roach clip, usually a hairpin. Scores of street names range from general ones such as pot, grass, weed, boo, leaf and Mary Jane to such geographical references as Mex (Mexican Brown and Mexican Green), Acapulco Gold, Colombian Red and Maui Wowie. Hashish is the dried resin from the leaves and flowers of the female plant, sold in chunks and smoked, usually in pipes. Hashish oil, a dark, oily extract also called oil or honey oil, is the most potent. Methods of smoking include putting it on the paper before a cigarette is rolled, or on the end of a regular tobacco cigarette.

hallucinogens These substances, also called psychedelic or mind-expanding, are either synthetic chemicals or extracts from plants or mushrooms. Mescaline, from the peyote cactus, and psilocybin, from certain mushrooms, can also be made synthetically. The best-known street drugs are PCP (phencyclidine), LSD (lysergic acid diethylamide), MDA (methylenedioxyamphetamine) and DMT (dimethyltryptamine). PCP, declining in popularity because it can induce paranoia and violent behaviour, is a white powder usually smoked in a marijuana cigarette (supergrass) but also sniffed, swallowed or injected. Its main street name is angel dust; others are peace pill, crystal, elephant, hog. LSD, commonly called acid, is crystalline but usually mixed with or dissolved in other substances. It is usually taken orally, often on blotting paper or in almost invisible specks of only 50 to 100 micrograms, called microdots or dots. DMT, called the businessman's lunch because its effects last 30 to 60 minutes, is often used with marijuana, which is soaked in a DMT solution and then dried for smoking. MDA is usually taken orally, as is mescaline (sometimes in the natural form of peyote buttons). Psilocybin is usually eaten in the form of dried mushrooms. Morning glory seeds, which contain lysergic acid amide (a much less potent form), are known as flying saucers, pearly gates, heavenly blues.

amphetamines Known as uppers, they are stimulants that act like adrenalin. Mostly produced illegally, because legal pharmaceutical production has dropped markedly. The most common compounds are amphetamine, methamphetamine and methylphenidate. They are sold as pills, or as crystals that can be swallowed, sniffed, or dissolved and injected. Injectable methamphetamine is called speed, or occasionally stove top. Crystal methamphetamine, which is smoked and is considered highly addictive, is known as **ice**. Amphetamines are often combined with other drugs to heighten or alter their effects. In addition to uppers, street names of pills include bennies (from a former trade name, Benzedrine, also known as peaches or roses because of their colour), dexies (from Dexedrine), pep pills, eye openers, lid proppers, truck drivers, co-pilots, leapers. Methylphenidate, sold under the brand name Ritalin, is known on the street as Rits or crackers. The designer drug MDMA (methylene-dioxymethamphetamine) is an amphetamine base that has been altered in structure to make it a hallucinogen as well as a stimulant. It is known as **ecstasy** (short form is E, upper case).

Qat is a natural amphetamine-like drug introduced to Canada by Somali immigrants. The leaves of a shrub that grows in northern East Africa and in Yemen are chewed fresh.

barbiturates Known as downers, these sedatives are often taken by heavy drug users when their usual drug is not available, or used to counteract the agitation and other effects of large doses of stimulants. They are also combined with alcohol. Other generalized street names are goofballs and barbs. Nicknames from the colours of specific brands include reds, red devils, red birds, pinks (Seconal, also called secos, seggy); yellows, yellowjackets (Nembutal, also called nemmy, nimby); blues, blue devils, blue heavens (Amytal); purple hearts (Luminal); and rainbows, reds and blues, double trouble (Tuinal, also called tooies). Barbiturate substitutes include methaqualone, known as ludes (from a former brand name, Quaalude), soap or soaper (from the brand name Sopor), love drug, wallbanger; and Mandrax, called mandrakes, mandies.

Talwin Pentazocine, sold under the brand name Talwin, is classed as a narcotic agonist/antagonist, designed to relieve severe pain without the abuse danger of narcotic painkillers. But it has developed an abuse problem of its own as a heroin substitute, and is known on the street as Ts, T or Big T. An illegal combination with the antihistamine tripelennamine is called Ts and blues, Ts and Bs. An illegal combination with methylphenidate (Ritalin) is called Ts and Rs, Ts and Rits, or crackers.

drunkenness

Druze

Druze, found in Lebanon, Syria, Israel and the United States, are regarded as an Islamic sect because their eclectic beliefs come closest to Islam, but it is not correct to refer to them as Druze Muslims. Druze treat both the Bible and the Koran as inspired writings, but also have a scripture of their own, the Discourses on Wisdom, and believe in the divinity (and eventual return) of Hakim bi-Amr Allah, the sixth Fatimid caliph of Egypt (996 to 1021). Druze are known to be clannish and secretive about their beliefs, and are instructed to appear to blend with the society that surrounds them.

Drybones
This landmark case, called by some the court ruling of the century, was the first in which the Canadian Bill of Rights was shown to supersede federal statutes that violated it. J. Drybones was a status Indian who was fined $10 in 1967 after pleading guilty to a breach of the Indian Act by being an Indian unlawfully intoxicated off a reserve (in the lobby of a Yellowknife hotel). On appeal, the Supreme Court of Canada ruled in 1970 that Section 94 (b) of the Indian Act treated Indians differently from other Canadian residents, contrary to the Bill of Rights' guarantee of equality before the law, and was therefore invalid.

dryly

Dry Tortugas
This group of dry coral islands, west of the Florida Keys at the entrance to the Gulf of Mexico, belongs, like the keys, to Monroe County, Fla.

du and de, see de and du.

Dubai, see United Arab Emirates.

duchess
But note Dutchess County, N.Y. See honorifics.

due
This is an adjective, not a conjunction; thus, the sentence must contain a noun or pronoun that it modifies. We may say the decrease in sales was due to product shortages, but not that sales decreased due to product shortages. For this second construction, replace due to with because of or owing to.

Duesenberg
These cars were built in the United States, not Europe, and popularized the word doozy, meaning something of top rank or quality.

duet, duo, trio, quartet
We do not use these words for any two, three or four people who happen to be together at a particular time. They imply teamwork and long association. Their use is limited outside musical settings.

duffel bag, coat etc. Not duffle.

dumbfound

dummkopf, plural **dummkopfs**.

dump
When the subject is snow, use this word only if the snow is leaving trucks, not the sky.

dumping
In trade, it means selling something in a foreign country at less than fair value as defined by the foreign country. Among other definitions, this may mean (1) less than the going rate in the home market, (2) less than the cost of production (but note that selling and administration expenses and an arbitrary rate of profit may be included in the presumed cost, making it easier to prove dumping) or (3) less than the price in some third market, especially in cases involving exports from command economies.

dumpster
This is not a trade name in Canada, so it is lower-case. If the

context is clear, it is acceptable for referring to disposal containers. But garbage disposal bin is clearer.

duplex

Depending on region, it can mean either a place with two apartments, one up and one down, or two residences attached side by side. We should be clear which is meant.

Du Pont Canada Inc. (upper-case D). But the parent company is E. I. du Pont de Nemours & Co.

durum wheat, not Durham.

The name means hard, but note that the wheat itself is no longer considered particularly so. It has been eclipsed in hardness by the hard red spring varieties, which are now used for bread while durum is used mainly for pasta.

Dusseldorf

Dutch

Always upper-case, even in Dutch treat, Dutch courage, but avoid such expressions as insulting to people of that nationality or ancestry. Dutch is the proper adjective for people or things in, of or from the Netherlands.

Dutch East Indies

Now called Indonesia.

dwarfs, noun and verb.

dying and dyeing

Dying (he died) refers to death; **dyeing** (he dyed) refers to changing colours.

dynamite

This safe high explosive, as invented by Alfred Nobel, consisted of nitroglycerin soaked into an inert filler such as wood pulp or diatomaceous earth. In modern dynamite, about half the nitro is replaced by sodium nitrate. If it also contains some nitrocellulose,

it is known as **gelignite** (gelatin dynamite).

d'Youville, Marie-Marguerite

The first Canadian-born woman saint. See Youville.

dysentery

dysfunction

dyslexia

dyspepsia

E

e

Lower case for electronic, as in e-mail and e-commerce. The drug ecstasy is E.

earned-run average

earring

Earth

Upper-case when referring to the planet, but not when referring to soil, or in such expressions as down to earth. See capitalization.

The Earth takes a day to rotate on its axis, and a year to revolve around the sun.

earthquakes

The magnitude ranking issued by government or university seismologists is not based on the Richter or any other particular scale. It is largely issued for public consumption, to satisfy the public's desire to compare the size of a new quake to big ones of the past, using a familiar, Richter-like number. We report this ranking simply as "a magnitude of 7.6," without specifying any scale.

These rankings are often subjective, so attribute the number to the authority that issued it. As further information becomes available, add details of the amount of energy released (often expressed in terms of comparable atomic explosions) and the amount of earth movement (slippage, rise or fall). But remember that the most important numbers for the purposes of a news story are not these scientific ones but rather the number of people killed or injured, the degree of disruption of services and the amount of property damage. Help readers by translating magnitude numbers into potential for damage if the epicentre is in a heavily populated area. The smallest quake felt by nearby humans has a reading of 2, and its energy is less than that from the burning of 500 litres of gasoline. (Seismometers can now detect much smaller ones, even into the minus numbers on the old Richter scale.) Magnitude 3 in a populated area means rattling teacups, 3.5 means slight damage, 4 means moderate damage, 5 means considerable damage, 6 means severe damage, 7 means a major earthquake causing widespread heavy damage, and 8 means a "great" earthquake. The ranking scale is theoretically open-ended (it is not a "top-10 list"), although most scientists believe that a reading of about 10 is the largest we can reasonably expect.

The epicentre is not the underground focus of the quake; it is the point on the Earth's surface above the focus. (Epi- means above or close to.) Say a city is at the epicentre, not over it.

The terms magnitude, energy, intensity and severity may not be used interchangeably. For example, each successive whole number in the magnitude ranking indicates a tenfold increase in seismograph reading (what Charles Richter called magnitude), but roughly a 30-fold increase in energy release (measured on what seismologists commonly call a "seismic moment" scale). Severity and intensity depend on such factors as rock structure, soil conditions and the proximity of large cities.

Seismic magnitude is a poor measure of intensity (the damaging effects actually experienced). The 9.2 Alaskan quake of 1964 killed only 114 people because the epicentre was relatively remote, while the much smaller (7.6) quake near Tangshan, China, in 1976 killed more than 600,000 and injured almost 800,000, and one of 7.5 in Guatemala the same year killed more than 23,000. The modified Mercalli scale represents an attempt to rate intensity, based on observations at the scene (some of them necessarily subjective, such as degree of panic). It ranges from 1 (tremors felt by only a few) to 12 (folds in the earth, objects thrown into the air, damage total).

See Richter, San Andreas Fault.

east

Lower-case for simple directions (the troops moved east, the sun rises in the east) but upper-case for recognized regions (he went looking for a job in the East). See capitalization, directions.

East is a relative term. To Western Canadians, the East is everything east of Manitoba. To Central Canadians, the East is everything east of Quebec. Note also that the term Far East was coined from the perspective of Europe, and is now little used. (From the perspective of the Pacific Rim, the Americas are the East.) However, the term Mideast is still current and useful.

Eastern rite churches

Prefer this to the formal term **Uniate Church**, which see.

Eastern Townships

They were originally settled mainly by Loyalists and have many English place names, but are now predominantly French-Canadian. They are the 93 townships surveyed and opened to settlement in 1791 at the time of the Loyalist migrations, and intended primarily for groups whose loyalty was beyond question, since they are between the U.S. border and the St. Lawrence lowlands (they do not extend to the river). The name recalls the fact that there were comparable townships surveyed west of Montreal in Upper Canada (Ontario) known as the Western Townships, a name that has not survived. The Eastern Townships are in 15 present-day counties, from Missisquoi (note spelling) in the southwest to Dorchester in the northeast. The other counties are Arthabaska, Bagot, Beauce, Brome, Compton, Drummond, Frontenac, Megantic, Richmond, Shefford, Sherbrooke, Stanstead and Wolfe.

East Indian

An inaccurate term resented by people from India, and more so by people from Pakistan, Bangladesh, Sri Lanka, Nepal and Bhutan. It implies they are from a non-existent country or district called East India, or from the East Indies (the islands now called the Malay Archipelago). The term has been used to prevent confusion with aboriginal peoples of the Americas, but in most news stories about people from India or of Indian ancestry, the context is clear enough. If there is a chance of confusion but the actual country is unknown, or if two or more countries are involved, South Asian is the proper adjective for the subcontinent and the accepted name for the race of people found there.

In Canada, many use the term Indo-Canadian. It is acceptable provided the meaning is clear.

East Indies

They are now called the Malay Archipelago. They include Indonesia, which comprises the islands formerly known as the Dutch East Indies.

East Timor

Adjective and people: Timorese. Currency: U.S. dollar. Capital: Dili.

A republic in the Lesser Sunda Islands at the eastern end of the Indonesian archipelago, East Timor includes the eastern half of the island of Timor, a chunk of territory on the northern coast of the western (Indonesian) half of the island, and the islands of Pulau Atauro and Pulau Jaco. The official languages of its 950,000 people are Tetum, one of 16 indigenous languages spoken in the country, and Portuguese.

The former Portuguese colony declared its independence from Portugal on Nov. 28, 1975, and was invaded by Indonesia days later. There followed two decades of brutal Indonesian repression of the new province, called Timor Timur, in which at least 100,000 and as many as 250,000 people were killed. In a referendum supervised by the United Nations on Aug. 30, 1999, the people of the province voted for independence. Indonesian troops and militias opposed to the result promptly destroyed three-quarters of East Timor's economic infrastructure and drove a quarter of a million people onto the western side of the island. An international peacekeeping effort followed, which encouraged most of the refugees to return. The new country, East Timor, came into being on May 20, 2002.

Eaton's

The founder of the Canadian department store chain was Timothy Eaton, who opened his store on Toronto's Yonge Street in 1869. The Eaton's catalogue began in 1884 and was discontinued in 1976. The privately held T. Eaton Co. was briefly saved from bankruptcy in 1997 when creditors approved a restructuring plan. It went public in 1998, issuing 11.7 million common shares, but filed for protection from creditors again in 1999 under the Bankruptcy and Insolvency Act. At the end of the year, competitor Sears Canada Inc. bought all the company's shares and took over 19 of the Eaton's stores, seven of which it continued to operate under the name Eatons (without the apostrophe). In 2000, it converted the seven to Sears outlets and the Eaton's name died, except in the name Eaton Centre in such cities as Toronto and Calgary.

eavestrough

eBay

The on-line auction company. But upper-case EBay if it begins a sentence.

EC, for **European Community**

The former name of the grouping that since Nov. 1, 1993, has been called the European Union, which see.

E. coli

The short form of *Escheria coli*, a species of bacillus usually found in the large intestine. There are many distinct varieties.

ecology

It means the study of the relationship of living things to their environment. More loosely, it has come to mean the science studying how humankind is wrecking its environment. But it always means science or study, never the thing being studied. Speak of damage to the environment, not of damage to the ecology.

The combining form eco- does not take a hyphen (ecotourism).

ecstasy

Ecuador

Adjective and people: Ecuadorean. Currency: U.S. dollar (adopted in 2000; had been the sucro). Capital: Quito.

As its name implies, it is on the equator, on the Pacific coast of South America, with Peru to the east and south and Colombia to the north. It is one of only two countries on the continent that do not border on Brazil, the other being Chile. Ecuador also owns the Galapagos Islands. Its main port and largest city is Guayaquil. Quito, the oldest capital in South America, was a long-established Inca city at the time of the Spanish conquest in 1534. The population of 13 million is about 80 per cent Indian or mestizo (of Indian-white ancestry), 10 per cent white and 10 per cent black. Most of the people live on the coastal plain or on 10 very high plateaus between Andean ranges. Ecuador is one of Latin America's leading oil producers.

eczema

edema

Prefer fluid buildup, swelling.

edgy

The traditional meaning is nervous, agitated, impatient. More recently, it has become shorthand for on the edge or cutting-edge, and acquired the sense of daring, provocative, unsettling. Like feisty, it is a generalized word-for-all-occasions that is crowding out more precise terms, and should be avoided for that reason.

Edinburgh

editor-in-chief

Edmundston, N.B.

eerie

effect and affect, see affect.

effrontery

It means insolent boldness, audacity. Do not confuse its spelling with that of affront, meaning an insult or, as a verb, to insult openly.

e.g.

It means for example (*exempli gratia*). It is useful in textbooks, style books and other such works, but should not be used in news stories. The direct approach is clearer and more facile: Say such as, for example, Examples include: Here are some examples: etc.

Eglinton Avenue, Toronto.

Egypt

Adjective and people: Egyptian. Currency: Egyptian pound. Capital: Cairo.

Most of its 70 million people live in the area from Cairo north to the Mediterranean, in the great alluvial delta of the Nile. The principal ports are Alexandria and Port Said, on either side of the delta, and Suez on the Red Sea. The Nile Valley, running the full 1,500 kilometres from Sudan to the Mediterranean, supports most of the people of Egypt, which is 96 per cent desert. In giving directions, remember that south is up the Nile. Most Egyptians are Hamitic Arabs, but there are also Berbers and small Greek and Armenian communities. Most educated people speak English or French in addition to Arabic.

Eid al-Fitr, Eid al-Adha

Eiffel Tower

Einstein, Albert

Einstein, 1879-1955, has sufficient historical stature to be referred to without the honorific in second reference. He won the Nobel Prize for physics in 1921, but not for his special or his general theory of relativity. He won it for his early work on photoelectric emission, which he explained through Planck's quantum theory. In his special theory of relativity, e equals mc squared, e is energy, m is mass and c is the velocity of light.

Eire
Call it the **Irish Republic**. See Ireland.

Eisenhower, Dwight

elbow room

elderly
A subjective term. See aged.

election
Canadian usage requires the singular for any general vote, so we change such wire-service references as "the Brazilian presidential elections." We also use the singular when voters are marking multiple ballots (federal, state, local) on a single trip to the polling station. The plural applies when the races are entirely separate, as when all municipalities in a province hold their local elections on the same day.

election coverage
The writing and handling of election copy involve unusual requirements, and a newspaper should play to its strengths. Television's strength is raw numbers, which it can crank out in bulk and update as the night wears on. The newspaper's strength is meaning, context, a synthesis of event, interpretation, background, quotes and colour in a concise package that goes beyond what a viewer could absorb even by watching an entire night of results trickling in.

As a matter of policy, we strictly avoid giving specific incomplete figures, which in effect would freeze our story at that stage of the counting. ("Results from 15 of 193 polls showed so-and-so leading 1,657 votes to 824.") Being this specific would only emphasize the untimeliness of the figures, conveying the incorrect impression that our assessment and analysis are also dated. Depending on the number of polls, such sentences could be reworded to something like "In early counting," or "With counting well under way," or "With counting all but complete," so-and-so had a two-to-one lead, or the two leading candidates were virtually even, etc.

The more complete the results, and the surer we are that the percentages will stand up, the less need there is to specify the number of polls. Just say that so-and-so scored an overwhelming (or easy, or comfortable, or narrow etc.) victory. We can begin to use voting percentages in the late stages of counting, when they are unlikely to change much, but they should be rounded off. If we round off "63.2 per cent" to "about 63 per cent," does it matter that the final 10 polls change the figure to 63.1? For the purposes of a majority, occasionally even "more than 60 per cent" is more than sufficient to carry the story.

A word about time elements: We use "last night" in reference to the counting, the quotes, the rallies and other things that clearly happened at night, but not in reference to the election, the voting. For those, use "yesterday."

When incumbents are running in a general election or by-election, identify them first as competitors and only second as holders of whatever jobs they held in the previous government. The principle is one of fairness. All the candidates are competing for the right to form the government, and the story should not give certain ones an air of entitlement.

electro

This combining form does not take a hyphen (electromagnetic, electrocardiogram etc.)

Eliot, George

Female novelist, editor and translator (1819-1880). Real name Mary Ann Evans. Novels include *Adam Bede, Silas Marner* and *Middlemarch.*

Eliot, T. S. (Thomas Stearns)

This modernist poet and critic (1888-1965) was a resident of Britain, but note that he was U.S.-born. He is known for *Prufrock and Other Observations, The Waste Land, Murder in the Cathedral* etc., but among the modern public is known particularly for *Old Possum's Book of Practical Cats,* source for the musical *Cats.*

Elisabethville

Now called Lubumbashi, Congo (previously Zaire, and before that The Congo), but give its former name as well when recounting the civil war in The Congo over the attempted secession of the district of Katanga (now the province of Shaba).

ellipsis, see punctuation.

El Salvador

Adjective and people: Salvadoran. Currency: colon (plural: colones). Capital: San Salvador.

It is the smallest state in Central America, on the Pacific coast bounded by Guatemala and Honduras, and its population of 6.4 million is the densest, at 256 a square kilometre. About 89 per cent of the people are mestizo, 10 per cent Indian and 1 per cent white. El Salvador is one of only two Central American countries that do not front on both the Pacific and Caribbean (Belize is only on the Caribbean). There is long-standing antagonism toward

Honduras (there was a brief war in 1969).

In January of 1992 the Farabundo Marti National Liberation Front (FMLN) signed a peace accord with the government to end a 12-year civil war that claimed about 75,000 lives. As the FMLN began disarming in late 1992, the army disbanded its infamous Atlacatl Battalion, long a symbol of repression, but enmity continued over its reluctance to charge army officers accused of past abuses.

Mild coffee, grown on the slopes and plateaus of two parallel volcanic ranges, makes up almost two-thirds of exports.

Elsas, Ont.

e-mail

Electronic mail.

Emanuel Church, but **Emmanuel College**.

Embankment, the

embarrass

embassy

Always lower-case (the embassy of the Dominican Republic, the French embassy). By convention, the word means either the building or its staff and operations (The embassy screens applicants for refugee status).

embattled

Often misused. To embattle means to prepare or equip for battle, or form up in battle array, fortify. In the sense we most often seek, of beset, harassed, the correct word is beleaguered.

embed

Not **imbed**.

emcee

Marginally acceptable as a noun for master of ceremonies (m.c.) in stories with an entertainment angle, but spell out in most news stories. Do not use emcee as a verb (He emceed the telethon). Also see author, host.

emigrate and immigrate
Preserve the distinction. The migrants are doing both; whether they are described as emigrating or immigrating depends on whether the view is from the country of departure or the destination. Always speak of departing Canadians as emigrants.

Emmy, Emmys

emphysema
An enlargement of the tiny air sacs of the lungs (the alveoli) and the destruction of their walls. Emphysema can cause chronic obstructive pulmonary disorder, a persistent obstruction of the airways that results in the slow death of the lungs. Note that emphysema and COPD are not synonyms. One is cause, one is effect. Note too that the disorder, one of the leading causes of death in Canada, can have many underlying causes.

empire
Upper-case when giving the full name, but in second reference only the British is upper-case (the British Empire, the Empire; the Austro-Hungarian Empire, the empire).

employment insurance (EI)
Use this style in news stories about the government program and in headlines, rather than the old "unemployment insurance" and its short form UI.
The Unemployment Insurance Commission was created in 1940 with the passage of the Unemployment Insurance Act. It was replaced in 1977 by the Canada Employment and Immigration Commission. In 1993, the CEIC became the Canada Employment Insurance Commission,

part of Human Resources Development Canada. The act is the Employment Insurance Act; the Unemployment Insurance Act survives only for applications under the old act, grandfathered when the new act came in.

enamour

encase

encephalitis
Describe it as inflammation of the brain. It usually should not be called sleeping sickness. An acute viral form, encephalitis lethargica, is sometimes informally called that, and we may impart this, but strictly speaking, sleeping sickness is the fatal stage of a tropical African form of trypanosomiasis, a disease caused by various protozoan blood parasites called trypanosomes.

endeavour

end zone, the noun.
The adjective is **end-zone**, as in an end-zone catch.

enervate
It does not mean to galvanize; it means to sap the strength or vitality of.

en garde

English Canada
Not a good term when differentiating Quebec and the nine other provinces and three territories. Its implication is that everyone in Quebec speaks French, and everyone outside speaks English. Prefer such terms as the rest of Canada.

English Canadian
Hyphenate only as an adjective (an English-Canadian poet).

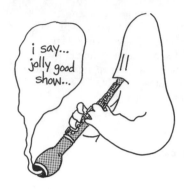

English horn
Not one of the brasses, but a woodwind, an alto oboe. See wind instruments.

enormity
It means heinousness, extreme wickedness or an outrageous or heinous offence. It has nothing to do with size, for which we would have to use the word enormousness or, preferably, a less awkward synonym such as immensity, vastness.

enroll, enrolled, enrolment

en route
Two words. Proper prepositions are en route **to** (not for) and en route **from**. But prefer the English phrases **on the way to**, **bound for** etc.

ensure and insure
Canadian usage dictates that **insure** be reserved for the buying and selling of insurance. For make sure or make certain, use **ensure**.

enthuse
Not an acceptable verb for express enthusiasm.

entombed
Overblown if we mean merely trapped, even underground. Confine it to the dead.

entomology and etymology
Entomology is the study of insects. **Etymology** is the history of a word, or the study of word derivations.

epidemic
There is no fixed definition of an epidemic, either in numbers or in percentage of the population affected. Use it to describe a rapidly spreading disease attacking or affecting many people simultaneously in a community. One definition in use in public-health circles is "a sudden increase in a disease considerably above that which had been occurring." If the initial spread of a disease has been contained, and if it is known how each person was infected, speak of an outbreak rather than an epidemic.

An epidemic that spreads across an entire country or to other countries may be called a pandemic.

epigram, epigraph, epitaph, epithet, expletive
An **epigram** is a short, witty saying. An **epigraph** is an inscription on any kind of monument (including a tomb), or at the front of a book. (It comes from the Greek word meaning to write upon.) An **epitaph** is an inscription on a tomb, or on a monument to the dead (from the Greek word for tomb). An **epithet** is a descriptive word or phrase added to a person's name, or used in place of the name, such as Lion Heart, Lackland, the Chief. It can also be any disparaging name, such as Egghead, Fishface, Four-eyes. But it is not an **expletive**, which is a profane exclamation.

equable and equitable
Equable means unvarying, steady (equable temperatures) or not easily upset, serene (equable temperament). **Equitable** (from equity) means just, fair, reasonable. There is also a word **equatable**, meaning capable of being considered equal.

equator

Lower-case. See capitalization.

Equatorial Guinea

Adjective and people: Equato-Guinean, but avoid as awkward. Currency: ekuele and CFA franc. Capital: Malabo.

This tiny state in West Africa on the Gulf of Guinea (Biafra Bight) consists of the mainland territory of Rio Muni and the island of Bioko (formerly called Fernando Po), which contains the capital. It is the least populated black African country, at about 500,000, and the only Spanish-speaking one. (It achieved full independence from Spain in 1968.) It is not to be confused with Guinea and Guinea-Bissau (which are on the Atlantic, far around the West African coast) or with the South American coastal region called Guiana.

equivocal, equivocate

Equivocate is too loaded a word for most news stories, meaning to use ambiguous language with an intent to deceive or confuse. **Equivocal** technically does not carry this burden (it may mean simply ambiguous or doubtful), but it is sufficiently tainted by the verb that readers would almost certainly draw the wrong inference if we were to use it.

Ericson, Leif.

Erieau, Ont.

Eritrea

Adjective and people: Eritrean. Currency: birr. Capital: Asmara.

It effectively won its 30-year independence campaign in 1991, when the Ethiopian regime fell to rebel groups from various regions, including the Eritrean People's Liberation Front. An independence plebiscite and admission to the United Nations followed in 1993. A bloody border conflict with Ethiopia from 1998 to 2000 left tens of thousands dead and displaced hundreds of thousands. A ceasefire agreement in June of 2000 was followed in December by a comprehensive agreement arranged by the United Nations. In April, 2002, the UN Permanent Court of Arbitration ruled on a new border between the countries, but relations between the countries remained strained. Eritrea is bounded on the northwest by Sudan, on the south by Ethiopia (including Tigray) and Djibouti, and on the east by the Red Sea. Asmara and the port of Massawa, once major Ethiopian economic centres, deteriorated badly during 17 years of full-scale civil war. The population of four million are mostly of mixed Semitic and Hamitic stock.

errant and arrant, see arrant.

escalate

It means to increase or advance gradually, in steps. The words sudden escalation would seem to cancel each other, so find another word that is more specific, such as sudden increase, sudden worsening, sudden intensification.

escape

Takes the preposition **from** when used for physical escapes, as in escape from jail. But it takes a direct object, with no preposition, when used in the figurative sense, as in escape criticism, escape notice.

Eskimo

Use Inuk (plural Inuit). See Inuit, native people. For the Eskimo breed of dog, see husky.

Establishment, the

Upper-case for the heavily traditional group exercising authority or influence in society.

Estonia

Adjective and people: Estonian. Currency: kroon. Capital: Tallinn.

It is one of the three Baltic states (along with Latvia and Lithuania), which were annexed by the Soviet Union in 1940 under a deal with Nazi Germany, and which were the first Soviet republics to gain independence, in September of 1991. Estonia had taken a leading role in the push for independence, adopting its own constitution in 1988 allowing private property, Estonian control of resources and a veto over Soviet legislation, and enduring severe Soviet economic pressure as a result.

Ethnic Estonians account for only 62 per cent of the population of 1.4 million. There is a large Russian population (30 per cent), and small Belarussian and Ukrainian minorities.

The smallest and most northerly of the Baltic states, it is on the Baltic Sea and the Gulf of Finland, and borders on Russia and Latvia. The climate is temperate but the land is mainly forests and lakes, ill suited to agriculture. Resources are scarce, mainly oil shale and phosphorite (used for fertilizers). Timber and wood products are important, and there is also production of mining and agricultural machinery, and products from cattle and pigs.

Refer to the Baltic states, not "the Baltics."

etc.

For **et cetera**, meaning and the rest, and so forth. Not a good construction for news stories. The reader has a better idea where the sentence is headed if we write "such as" in front of an example than if we follow it with an etc. If we are quoting someone as using this expression, write it out rather than use the abbreviation, and do not use a comma before it. It need not be in italics.

ethics, journalistic, see Globe and Mail code of conduct, at the back of this book.

Ethiopia

Adjective and people: Ethiopian. Currency: birr. Capital: Addis Ababa.

This ancient state between Sudan and Somalia is essentially highlands and plateaus, divided into eastern and western sections by the Great Rift Valley. Addis is in the centre of the western highlands, at about 2,500 metres (8,000 feet).

A Somali invasion in mid-1977 to capture the Ogaden desert plain was repelled in 1978 with Soviet and Cuban help. Autonomy movements in the provinces of Eritrea and Tigray ended in victory in 1991 when the national government fell to a loose coalition of rebel groups. The country's first multiparty elections were held in 1995. Eritrea achieved independence in 1993, leaving Ethiopia landlocked. A border war with Eritrea that began in 1998 ended on Dec. 12, 2000. See Eritrea. The largest racial group are the Gallas (also called the Oromos), at about 40 per cent of the population of 65 million, but they are divided among Christian, Muslim and pagan communities and so are too ethnically diverse to be politically dominant. The Amhara of the central highlands, of mixed Hamitic and Semitic stock, have been historically more important. Most Christians are of the Ethiopian Orthodox Church. There are also Muslim Somalis and Afars.

ethnic

Pertains to any racial, cultural or linguistic division of mankind—including white and English-speaking. We do not use the term ethnic standing alone to mean minority; if you cannot give the actual language, culture or country, say ethnic minority.

Use ethnic only as an adjective, never as a noun. Do not speak of a group of ethnics, a service for ethnics.

We do not gratuitously give ethnic information about a person in the news (his or her race, religion, language, origin). Use these only when they are pertinent to the story.

euro

Lower-case, the new European common currency, broken into 100 centimes. Agreed upon in 1991 for implementation beginning in 1999, it later ran into local resistance and was initially adopted by 11 of the 15 members of the European Union (Britain, Denmark and Sweden delayed joining, and Greece joined on Jan.1, 2001, when its economy was judged to be ready). Chronology of the change from local currencies: Jan. 1, 1999: The euro's exchange rate with local currencies becomes fixed; the euro becomes legal for paper and electronic transactions; stocks, bonds and other securities are issued in euros; businesses gradually begin converting for auditing and similar purposes; stores gradually begin listing prices in both local currency and euros to engender familiarity; massive printing and minting process begins in preparation for introduction of physical currency three years later. Jan. 1, 2002: New notes (5, 10, 20, 50, 100, 200, 500 euros) and coins (1, 2, 5, 10, 20, 50 centimes and 1 and 2 euros) become legal tender; banks convert accounts to euros for individuals. March 1, 2002: The old local currencies are no longer legal tender.

When giving amounts in euros, place the euro symbol before the amount, as with the dollar and British pound.

Eurodollar

Europe

A flexible term. Technically, the continent of Europe extends from the Atlantic to the Urals and from the Arctic Ocean to the Mediterranean and Black Seas and the Caucasus Mountains, and also includes many offshore islands, including the British Isles. However, many readers would not think to include the European part of Russia (the part west of the Urals); when we are using the term Europe to include this, we should say so. In stories set in Britain, Europe often means only continental Europe. Europe is also occasionally used to mean Western Europe, the countries of the European Union. We should be more specific in such references.

European Union, EU

We called it the European Community until Nov. 1, 1993, when the Maastricht Treaty on European unity took effect. (The EC still exists for legal purposes.) The EU is, in effect, the EC with the addition of two mechanisms: for a common foreign and security policy, and for co-operation in police and justice matters. Technically, the EU lacks legal status, and only the EC or its individual states can sign international agreements. But for the sake of simplicity, unless these legal arrangements are at issue in the story, we use the name European Union for all references.

The EC is commonly singular, but note that it is properly the European Communities, formed in 1967 through a merger of the executives of the European Economic Community, the European Atomic Energy Community (Euratom) and the European Coal and Steel Community. (These had been formed under the Treaty of Rome, signed in 1957.) There is now a single Commission of the European Communities, and a single executive, called the Council of Ministers. (This is not to be confused with the policy-making European Council, which is composed of the heads of state or government of the member countries. It meets three times a year.) The commission (a president, five vice-presidents and 14 members) may be referred to informally as the European Commissioners. The terms EC, European Common Market and Common Market are still widely used, and familiar enough that we need not explain them when quoting others. But when using our own words, we say European Union.

Membership increased to 15 in 1995 with the addition of Austria, Finland and Sweden to the existing 12 members: Belgium, Denmark, France, Germany, Greece, Ireland, Italy, Luxembourg, Portugal, Spain, the Netherlands and the United Kingdom. (The six originals were joined in 1973 by Denmark, Ireland and the U.K.; in 1981 by Greece; and in 1986 by Portugal and Spain.) In 2002, the European Commission, the EU's executive branch, said it would admit Poland, Hungary, the Czech Republic, Slovakia, Slovenia, Malta, Cyprus, Estonia, Latvia and Lithuania, perhaps within a year. Prospects were more distant for the admission of Romania and Bulgaria, and Turkey was told it would have to improve its human-rights record before it could join.

The Single Act, a treaty adopted by the European Council in 1985, committed the members to a gradual elimination of all internal barriers to the movement of people, goods, services and capital. See euro. In March of 1995, seven members (Belgium, France, Germany, Luxembourg, the Netherlands, Portugal and Spain) implemented the 1985 Schengen agreement on the free movement of people, and some others also planned to join this "Schengen zone" as their administrative setups were brought into line.

The EU also has trade arrangements with non-members Iceland, Liechtenstein, Norway (whose voters rejected EU membership in a 1994 referendum) and Switzerland.

euthanasia
It is not always active mercy killing. In the era of modern medicine, the decision not to use extraordinary mechanical or chemical means to keep a suffering person alive, or the decision to withdraw these, is often referred to as passive euthanasia. However, we should be wary of this term outside direct quotes, because the definition is impossibly murky even to medical ethicists. For example, taking an action (throwing a switch etc.) that is certain to result in the death of a person unable to survive without mechanical help may not be considered euthanasia by some if the person has not actually been in agony, and will even experience severe trauma (suffocation, for example) in the moments before death. In such cases, we should stick to the facts and use such terms as withdrawal of life support. This is especially important in cases in which death is by no means certain. Comatose Karen Ann Quinlan lived for 10 years in a New Jersey nursing home after her parents won the right to have her respirator turned off in 1976.

Keep clear the distinction between assisted suicide and euthanasia. In assisted suicide, another person supplies the means of suicide, which is then activated by the person who intends to die. Supplying pills, providing a suicide machine (injection or carbon monoxide), carrying someone to a car and closing the garage door, attaching a rope to the ceiling – all these fit the definition of assisting in a suicide. Assisting in a suicide is illegal in Canada, as is attempted suicide, although suicide itself is not.

In cases where the person is no longer capable of taking any active part in his or her death, however slight, a doctor or someone else who takes the person's life at the person's request is performing euthanasia.

Euthanasia is illegal in Canada, even if requested by the person (orally or in a living will).

Falling outside these considerations of suicide and mercy killing is the decision in hopeless cases not to begin life support in the first place, or to withhold other treatment (such as antibiotics when a bedridden patient contracts pneumonia). Sometimes the patient's preference in such circumstances has been made known, but most often the decision is merely made in accordance with widely accepted medical practice, usually with the family's concurrence. This should never be described as passive euthanasia.

eutrophication

This is the process of a body of water becoming choked with algae and plants because of a concentration of plant nutrients. The resulting oxygen depletion kills much of the animal life.

evacuate

It means to empty. A building or an area is evacuated, but people are not (except in the medical sense of emptying organs or cavities). As former editor-in-chief R. J. Doyle said in a memo after one of our stories about the eruption of Mount St. Helens, "I'm glad I wasn't there when they evacuated the scientists."

everybody

everyone and every one

Everyone means everybody, all those present or being discussed. **Every one** means each individual person or thing in a group, with no exceptions. (**Everyone** knows that **every one** of the workers is the mayor's relative. Tiny Tim said, "God bless us, **every one**!")

The colloquial impulse is to use they/them rather than he or she after "someone, "everyone" or "no one," to include both sexes: If someone feels the need to announce that they are creative, so be it. One day, this oral convenience may even be the norm in print. For now, it remains jarring to many readers who believe in the rule that singular must refer back to singular, and consider us at best sloppy and at worst incompetent if we ignore this basic grammatical rule. One way around the problem is to make the subject plural: If people feel the need to announce that they are creative, so be it.

every place (adv.)

evince

It means more than to display; it means to demonstrate clearly and convincingly (by argument etc.), or to present an outward sign of an interior quality (She evinced her defiance by staring down her captors). Rather obscure for most news stories.

ex- and former

Ex- is a proper prefix meaning former, as in ex-president. But it is awkward with a compound, as in ex-prime minister, and when it is attached to an adjective it can be downright ambiguous. Has an **ex-Liberal MP** lost his seat or merely left his party? A good rule of thumb is to attach ex- only to solo nouns. Use **former** in other constructions, but we still must make it clear whether we are discussing a former Liberal or a former MP. As for using ex- in headlines where space is at a premium, there is more tolerance of slight awkwardness there, but not of ambiguity.

exacerbate

No news writer should want to use a cumbersome, four-syllable Latinate word to replace a much simpler and more familiar one, such as worsen or heighten—even if it were a real synonym for these. It means to make more sharp or bitter (it is from the same root as acerbic). It can be used with such words as emotions, anger and resentment, and also with pain and diseases, but it is inappropriate with things that would not normally be described as sharp or bitter, such as flood damage, fuel consumption.

excel, excelled

execute

Reserve for killing performed in response to a judicial order from a civilian or military court. Do not use it for the acts of murderers, assassins, terrorists. It is possible, however, to speak of an execution-style slaying, meaning one performed in a cold-blooded, calculated manner with the victim prepared beforehand, possibly by being bound, blindfolded, forced to kneel etc.

exhaust, exhibit, exhilarate, exhort, exhume (all with an h). But exonerate, exorbitant, exuberant (with no h).

exotic

It means of foreign origin or, by extension, strangely different. Nude or scantily clad dancers have become so commonplace that they should be called that, not exotic dancers.

expatriate

explicit and implicit

Something **explicit** has been expressed directly, spelled out. Something **implicit** has been implied, with the meaning well understood but the actual words not used. (The order to disperse the students was explicit; the permission to shoot them was implicit.)

explode

Overused in reference to people and meetings.

Expo 67

No apostrophe for the 1967 world's fair in Montreal.

extra

As an adjective meaning additional, as a noun meaning something exceeding the normal, or as an adverb meaning unusually, it is a separate word. (He got an extra helping. He paid for a few extras. He is extra careful about his comfort.) If the modified adjective comes before the noun, it requires a hyphen: an extra-careful man.

When extra means outside the scope or limits of, it is a prefix forming an integral part of an adjective. It does not take a hyphen unless the root word begins with the letter a or with a capital letter (extramural, extraordinary, extrasensory, but extra-atmospheric).

extra-billing, the noun.

The verb is **extra-bill**. Always explain high in the story what these refer to: charges by a doctor or medical institution that exceed the amount covered by provincial medical insurance.

extraneous

eye of the storm

The person taking the worst buffeting is often wrongly described as being in the eye of the storm. In fact, the eye of a storm is an island of calm. See weather words.

eyeing

eyewitness

When describing people who have seen something, the word witness does nicely. But the word eyewitness is occasionally necessary in trial stories to differentiate between those who saw the alleged crime and those who are merely testifying about background to the case.

F

façade

face down, face up

face to face
Eye to eye, toe to toe, hand to hand, side by side, head to head etc. No hyphens except as adjectival phrases (a face-to-face meeting).

facility, facilities
Sometimes unavoidable, but it is an overused generalization that should be replaced whenever possible by a more specific, descriptive term. An educational facility could be a school, a university, a classroom, a laboratory.

facsimile
We use the term fax machine, and the verb fax, faxed, faxing.

FA Cup (no periods).
For Football Association Cup, symbolic of English (not British) soccer supremacy.

Fagin, character in *Oliver Twist*.

Fahrenheit
No need to write it out when giving a temperature; use the abbreviation F without a period (98.6 F).
Most temperatures in the paper will be in Celsius, and need not be so identified unless there is a chance of confusion, as when an American is being quoted.
For the sake of reader comprehension, always add the Fahrenheit equivalent in brackets when giving human body temperatures.

fair market value

Falange, Falangist

Falkland Islands
See Argentina.

Falconbridge Ltd.

fall
This is the preferred word in Canada to refer to autumn (in the fall, this fall, fall colours, fall planting). It is used less in the United States and only rarely in Britain.

fallacy, fallacious

Fallopian tubes
Upper-case, named for anatomist Gabriello Fallopio.

fallout, noun. The verb is **fall out**.

fall wheat
Refers to wheat sown in the fall, now more commonly called winter wheat in Canada. Both winter and spring wheat are harvested in the fall.

Falun Gong
Upper case, no italics, for this spiritual sect.

family allowance
Lower-case. It was paid under the Family Allowance Act, passed in 1944, and formally ended with the

introduction of a new system of child benefits on Jan. 1, 1993. Popularly called the baby bonus from its inception, it may be referred to as that even in first reference in less formal stories, and in headlines. But use the proper name at least once in more technical stories about the legislation itself or about taxation, the history of universal programs and similar matters. It was specifically paid to mothers, and so was often referred to as mothers' allowance.

Far North

In the eye of the beholder, but usually taken to refer to the Arctic and subarctic regions of Canada, not to forested regions.

Faroe Islands, see Denmark.

Farquharson, Charlie

The Don Harron character.

farther and further

Use **farther** and **farthest** when referring to physical distances. (He went farther north than any other explorer.) Use **further** when referring to extensions of degree or time. (He went further than any other opposition figure had dared. I won't detain you further.)

fascist

Upper-case only for the Italian party of Mussolini, its members and the government it formed. Lower-case for generalized descriptions of political systems, institutions and individuals (He denounced the police as fascist). A fascist government, system or philosophy is authoritarian and undemocratic, places the interests of the state above those of the individual, and equates the state with the ruling party and its glorified leader.

fatality

Refers to deaths, not dead people. See casualty.

Fathers of Confederation

Upper-case only when referring to the men who attended at least one of the three conferences (Charlottetown, Quebec and London) at which the terms of Confederation were agreed upon. Lower-case father in such informal terms as modern fathers of Confederation.

faults, see San Andreas.

favour

All variants retain the u.

faze and phase

Faze means to disturb or embarrass. A **phase** is a stage or an aspect.

federal building

Lower-case. The term is used throughout Canada for the building in a community that houses regional offices of federal departments.

Federal Bureau of Investigation

This U.S. agency is well enough known that the initials FBI may be used in first reference to simplify a complicated lead paragraph, but its full name should be used as soon afterward as possible.

Federal Reserve System

It is the central banking system of the United States, but it is not strictly correct to call it a central bank. It is made up of 12 Federal Reserve Banks that control 12 districts under the Federal Reserve Board in Washington. Both the system and the board are known colloquially as the Fed.

feedback

feel

Do not use this verb to read minds: The minister feels it would be dangerous to commit troops to this war. Did the minister say it would be dangerous? Do others say this is what the minister believes? Avoid in such cases as too subjective.

To feel is a copulative verb, like to be, and takes a predicate adjective rather than an adverb. Unless describing the way a person literally feels using hands or feet, say the person feels bad (not badly), strange (not strangely) etc.

feisty

This is a U.S. word that is quickly becoming accepted in Canada. But be aware that it is a generalized word-for-all-occasions that is crowding out a wide range of more specific and descriptive ones, such as tough, resilient, resourceful, spunky, argumentative, short-tempered. Each of these means something different, and they deserve better than to be homogenized into a single word, feisty. The reader also deserves the more precise term. Consider, too, whether our use implies admiration of a person's views, in which case it might be regarded as editorial comment. See no-nonsense.

fellow

Upper-case in the title of a person awarded a fellowship (a Southam Fellow, an Enrico Fermi Fellow).

Fernando Po

An extinct name. The island province of Equatorial Guinea is now called Bioko.

fervour

fewer and less

Use **fewer** to refer to the number of individual items, and **less** to refer to the quantity of a single thing or collective. Say fewer dollars, less money; fewer cookies, less dessert; fewer people, less of a crowd.

Do not use either with the actual word "number." For that, use smaller. (The number of cars is smaller than the number of drivers.)

FIA

For *Fédération internationale de l'automobile*. Always call it the International Automobile Association, and if there will be a second reference add that it is known by its French initials, FIA.

Fiberglas, a trade name of Fiberglas Canada Ltd. The generic terms are fibreglass (note the -re-) and glass fibre.

fibre

fiddleheads

The edible young, curled fronds of the ostrich fern. Lower-case.

fiddler

The Maritimes name for an Atlantic salmon under eight pounds. It is lower-case.

fief, not fiefdom.

FIFA

For the *Fédération internationale de football association*. Call it the International Association Football Federation, and add if necessary that it is known by its French initials, FIFA, and that association football is soccer.

Fife wheat

Not Fyfe. Upper-case, for developer David Fife of Canada West. It was the first Canadian rust-resistant strain, later called Red Fife.

fifth estate, the

The CBC current-affairs program. Keep the title in lower case, in italics, but upper-case The if the name begins the sentence.

figgy duff

Lower-case. The traditional Newfoundland raisin pudding.

figurative

It means metaphorical, constituting or based on a figure of

speech, not literal. If a metaphor or other such expression is sufficiently clear and apt to merit use in a news story, it should not be spoiled by insertion of the word figuratively. This word is occasionally misused to mean symbolically. See literally.

Fiji

Adjective and people: Fijian. Currency: Fiji dollar. Capital: Suva.

It is a republic comprising 332 islands and islets in the southwestern Pacific, in the part of Oceania known as Melanesia, with a total population of about 800,000. The largest of its approximately 110 inhabited islands are Viti Levu, which contains Suva, and Vanua Levu. (There is no island called Fiji.) Fiji gained full independence from Britain in 1970, as a member of the Commonwealth. Its ties with the Commonwealth were broken in 1987 after a coup, staged because candidates of Indian ancestry had won a majority. Fiji was readmitted to the Commonwealth in 1996, suspended after another coup in 2000 and readmitted as a full member in 2002 after holding a parliamentary election in 2001.

Note that all citizens are Fijians, and all born there are native Fijians. We should not use the term native Fijians to refer to those of Melanesian and Polynesian ancestry, as opposed to Indian ancestry.

filet and fillet

Make it fillet for fish, filet for meat. Filet mignon does not require italics.

Filipino, Filipina, Filipinos

The people of the Philippines.

filmmaker

The Council of Canadian Filmmakers.

Financial Post, The

Upper-case The for the newspaper that was absorbed into the National Post. The financial section of the National Post is the Financial Post; in both cases "the" is lower-case, since neither includes The in its official name.

Finland

Adjective: Finnish. Most of the people can be called Finns; all can be called citizens of Finland. Currency: euro (had been the markka). Capital: Helsinki.

The population of 5.2 million is more than 90 per cent Finnish, but be aware that there are Lapp and Swedish minorities. Finland, called Suomi in Finnish, was officially non-aligned during the Soviet era. It is a member of the World Trade Organization (WHO) and of the European Union (EU). Note that Finns consider the term Finlander incorrect, and find it insulting.

FIRA

Now extinct. The acronym stood for both the Foreign (not Federal) Investment Review Agency and the act that created the agency.

fired

Tread carefully when using this word, or such synonyms as pushed out, axed, dismissed, let go. They contain a suggestion that there was "cause" involved in the person's departure from the job, a characterization that could reflect on their reputation. If the person has not acknowledged on the record that he or she was actually fired, use the word "left." If the person is known to have left of his or her own accord, "resigned" is fine.

firefight

Avoid this confusing military jargon for a battle or skirmish primarily featuring small-arms fire.

firefighter

Preferable to the sex-specific fireman.

fire-reel

Hyphenated. A term still heard in older Canadian cities to refer to a pumper truck. It need not be explained in quotes. It is more common in the plural (I didn't know anything was wrong until the fire-reels woke me up).

firm

This is not a synonym for company, although its use in this sense is allowed in headlines. In copy, reserve it for such consultancies as legal, accounting and public-relations firms. Strictly speaking, it means a partnership, but it is also used to refer to solo practices (he has his own law firm).

first-degree murder

first lady

Lower-case, even before a name (a reception for first lady Hillary Rodham Clinton). A term not used in Canada.

first nation

A misleading term to most readers, because it implies much larger numbers than are in fact the case. They are status Indian bands, which might number only a few hundred in one or two villages. Prefer band, reserve, native community. When we do use first nation, it is lower-case unless we are giving a band's formal name: the Kettle Point First Nation.

The term applies to status Indian bands that belong to the Assembly of First Nations, not to other native peoples such as Métis, non-status Indians and Inuit.

See native people.

First World War

Use World War I only in direct quotes.

FIS

For *Fédération internationale du ski.* Call it the International Ski Federation, and add if necessary that it is known by its French initials, FIS.

FISA

For *Fédération internationale du sport automobile.* Call it the International Auto Sport Federation, adding if necessary that it is known by its French initials, FISA.

fiscal

In reference to governments, it has fairly wide use as a synonym for financial. (Its strict meaning is having to do with the public purse.) In the private sector, it should be used only in the narrow sense of doing the accounts, managing the assets, balancing the books. A broker would provide financial advice but not fiscal advice, which would come from an accountant. The term fiscal responsibility is heard in both the public and private sectors, but we use the term fiscal policy only in reference to governments.

fiscal year

For clarity, always give both calendar years spanned by a fiscal year, as in the 2003-04 fiscal year. Not all readers would be aware that when accountants speak of fiscal 2003 they are referring to the fiscal year that ends during that year. Both federal and provincial government fiscal years run from April 1 to March 31.

fish

It is useful to remember the distinction between the broad classes of fish caught by Canadian fishermen. The **groundfish** (e.g. cod, haddock, redfish, flatfish) feed near the bottom of the ocean. The **pelagic** species (herring, mackerel, tuna) swim in the mid-water depths in the open sea. The **anadromous** species (e.g. salmon) are born in fresh water, migrate to the ocean and return upriver to spawn. **Crustaceans** include lobster, crab, shrimp and prawns. **Mollusks** (shellfish) include scallops, clams, mussels, oysters, octopus and squid. See groundfish, salmon, trawler.

fish and brewis

No hyphens. It is the Newfoundland dish consisting of salt cod served with hard bread cooked in water and a topping of fried salt pork. It is pronounced to rhyme with stews.

fisherman

Avoid fisher, except in direct quotes. We encourage inclusive terms (see Women and language), but women in the fishing industry on both coasts have made it clear they call themselves fishermen and take strong exception to what they regard as a bureaucratic, politically correct term.

flack and flak

Flak is by far the more common. It means anti-aircraft fire (a German acronym from aircraft defence gun, *flieger abwehr kanone*), and is used figuratively to mean heavy criticism. **Flack** is slang for a press agent, and should not be used to mean an incompetent, slapdash or uninterested writer. That's a **hack**.

flair and flare

Flair means an aptitude or talent (a flair for music) or a sense of style. But for anything to do with a blaze or sudden burst, use **flare**, including flare guns, highway flares and the figurative sense of anger flaring. Flare also means to spread, as with clothing shapes and nostrils.

flamboyant (not -buoyant).

flammable

To avoid confusion, use this word instead of inflammable. Many people confuse inflammable, which means easily ignited or inflamed, with non-flammable.

Flanders Fields, In

Flanders is often misspelled with an apostrophe.

flatcar

flaunt and flout

Flout is by far the more common in news stories, meaning to defy contemptuously, scoff at, as in flout the law, flout tradition, flout convention. **Flaunt** means to display brazenly, as in flaunt one's wealth.

flavour

But drop the u for **flavorous**.

fleur-de-lis, fleurs-de-lis.

Note hyphens, and the spelling lis, not lys. Lower-case, except as the name of the flag (waving the Fleur-de-lis).

flex-time, not flexitime.

flier and flyer

Use **flier** for people, animals and things that fly through the air (frequent-flier program; he's a nervous flier; hens are not good fliers) or do so figuratively (he's a high flier). Use **flyer** for an advertising circular, for a financial gamble (take a flyer) or in the proper names of some express trains (Dixie Flyer).

flimflam, flimflammed

floe

Means a slab of floating ice. Ice floe is redundant. Often misspelled flow.

floor show

Flos Township, Ont.

Not Floss. One of three (Flos, Tiny and Tay) named in 1822 after the dogs of Lady Sarah, wife of the lieutenant-governor of Upper Canada, Sir Peregrine Maitland. The dogs are often wrongly described as belonging to Elizabeth Simcoe, wife of the first lieutenant-governor.

flounder and founder

To **flounder** means to struggle clumsily, either physically or in a speech, a job, an enterprise etc. Note also that flounder is not a single species of fish, but is the name for several species of edible flatfish. To **founder** means to sink (as with a ship), to cave in, to fail completely (as with a business) or to stumble and go lame (as with a horse).

A business might be described as floundering (if our legal advisers say this would not be libellous), but should not be described as foundering unless it has formally moved to wind up its affairs.

flu

Acceptable for influenza, even in first reference. Always lower-case, even when modified by an upper-case adjective (Asian flu). Do not confuse with flue, meaning a pipe in a stove, boiler or organ, or the vent of a fireplace.

fluoride, fluoridation

fluorocarbon

flutist

Use **flautist** only in direct quotes.

fly

The normal past tense of the verb is flew, but in baseball, referring to hitting a fly ball, the past tense is flied (he flied out, not he flew out).

fly-by

FM

For frequency modulation. No periods.

FN

No periods. The 7.62 mm military rifle used by Canada and some other NATO countries may be called simply the FN rifle. No need to spell out Fabrique Nationale, or to specify the FNC1 (semi-automatic) or FNC2 (fully automatic) models unless the distinction is germane to the story.

f.o.b.

Has periods. No need to spell out free on board, but there might be a need to explain what it means: free delivery of goods only as far as a shipper for forwarding. A price that is f.o.b. Vancouver means the buyer must pay freight charges from that city.

focused, focusing

-fold, see numbers.

Folies Bergère (not Follies).

folk

Folk art, folk dance, folk music, folk song, folk singer, folk tale, all two words. But folklore, folkways.

Folkestone, England.

following

It is an adjective meaning next (the following week), a participle (he is following her lead) and a noun (he has a large following). But it is not a preposition, and so it is not a synonym for after. Say a man was arrested after dinner, not following dinner.

Food and Drugs Act

Note plural.

foofaraw

It refers to foolish, trifling ornaments. It has come to mean a pointless flurry of concern and confusion, but should not be used for a real crisis or a serious disagreement.

foolscap

It is not a specific type or grade of writing paper but rather a size, 8 by 13 inches. (Actually, this is half a printer's full foolscap sheet, which is 13 by 16.) In Britain, sheets of a similar size (13½ by 17) were formerly identified by a watermark of a fool's cap and bells.

foot-and-mouth disease

Note the hyphens. We do not call it hoof-and-mouth disease. This highly contagious viral disease affects animals with cloven hooves (split hooves), such as cows, sheep, goats, pigs and deer. Horses are not affected. The disease is not fatal most of the time, but is extremely painful and has debilitating effects.

Foothills, the

When upper-case, it refers to the district comprising the grassy hill country in Alberta between the prairie flatland and the Rocky Mountains. Lower-case, it describes any hills on the approach to a mountain range.

forbear and forebear

Forbear is a verb (and a rather outmoded one) meaning to refrain from doing something, to stop doing something. It takes a direct object (he promised to forbear gambling). It is also an intransitive verb meaning to be patient, show forbearance. (We'll have to forbear a little longer.) The past and participle are forbore, forborne. **Forebear** is a noun, meaning an ancestor. It is used almost exclusively in the plural (his forebears). For some reason, forebears is often used wrongly to mean descendants.

forbid

The past is forbade, the participle is forbidden. When the object is a person, it is followed by an infinitive (They forbade him to see her), not by a phrase beginning with from, which is the construction used after such words as prohibit and prevent (They prohibited him from seeing her). An action or event can also be a direct object (They forbade the meeting).

Forces

Upper-case the Forces only when referring to Canada's military. For other countries, use upper case only in the full, formal name of a service (Israeli Defence Forces). In second reference to these foreign services, call them the military, the army, the police etc.

forego and forgo

Forgo is by far the more common, meaning to do without. (We will have to forgo a salary increase this year.) But the past tense and the participles (forwent, forgone, forgoing) are rather awkward and ambiguous; they should be used only in direct quotes. Say that he did without an increase, not that he forwent one.

Conversely, **forego**, meaning to precede or go before, is rarely used as the root word, but the past participle is alive and well in the expression foregone conclusion. The foregoing, meaning that which has already been said or written, is also still used, but in contexts more formal than the average news story.

foreign affairs, relations

When it comes to committees of the two houses in the U.S. Congress dealing with international issues, the representatives have foreign affairs and the senators have foreign relations.

foreign and French words

Globe writers and editors should assume readers to be intelligent and well informed, but unilingual. We expect them to know foreign or French words and phrases that have become a familiar part of Canadian English, such as coup de grâce, bagatelle, tête-à-tête. A good indication of whether a word or expression has entered the language is whether it appears in our English dictionary. But whether it has become a familiar part of the language, suitable for news stories, is a case of *caveat editor*. We must apply the same judgment that we use to weed out all obscure and pedantic words. If an unfamiliar expression can't be avoided, as in a story about a particular type of judicial writ, we provide an explanation.

We use the proper accents for words and expressions as they appear in our dictionary (café).

All foreign or French words must be in italics, unless they are proper names (see below), currencies or legal, scientific and musical terms, or are considered to have passed into English. And they must be accompanied by a translation, explanation or paraphrase. If we did not do this, the implication would be that the reader should know the meaning, and is somehow deficient if he or she does not. The explanation may be fairly simple, as in The sentry fingered his *kukri*, the Gurkhas' traditional curved knife. Such definitions might also begin the next sentence: The protester glanced nervously at the guard's *kukri*. These curved knives, worn by. . . . Short direct translations may be bracketed: Some are predicting a new *revanche du berceau* (Revenge of the Cradle).

Longer translations would have to be made a separate clause, beginning with "which means," "which translates as" or some such (but not with "or," which see), or made a separate sentence. If the translation slows or complicates the sentence or story to a degree far out of proportion to the foreign word's value in conveying information or adding colour, the foreign word should be dropped, or possibly used later.

Foreign words that gain currency for a time in connection with a continuing story, such as *intifada*, need not be explained immediately if they appear in the lead paragraph, provided the context makes the thought clear (The Palestinian *intifada* against Israel grew more violent yesterday as . . .). Translate the next time it appears,

unless the following sentence begins with the translation (The uprising, which has claimed . . .). The reader must be clearly told what a foreign word means; how this is done can be a matter of judgment.

An explanation need not always include a literal translation. It is enough, for example, that the readers are made aware that *mujahedeen* are Afghan rebels or guerrillas. They need not be told in every story that this translates as holy warriors.

Beware strictly literal translations of colloquial expressions. It is counterproductive to tell readers simply that the name of the Quebec TV show *Entre chien et loup* means "between dog and wolf," when in fact the idiomatic expression means "at twilight." Also, we do well to avoid some literal translations of more earthy Quebec expressions. It is enough to say that *pets de soeurs*, favourite treats in Quebec, are pastries; we need not add that the name means nuns' farts.

Proper names are already set off because they begin with upper case, so they are not put into italics. In particular, do not italicize people's names, street names, place names, political parties and names of companies. However, where not every word in the names of agencies, events and groups is upper-case, use italics for the sake of clarity (e.g., *Fédération internationale du ski*). As for translating the names of political parties, rebel groups, religious factions, etc., if the readers are told that Sendero Luminoso is a Marxist revolutionary group, they need not be told until later in the story that this translates as Shining Path. Political parties that are well known by name need not be translated. There is no need to say that Likud means unification or that Kuomintang translates as National People's Party, although there is no harm in enriching the occasional story by doing so.

The names of foreign provinces or other jurisdictions, and geographical features such as mountains, islands, rivers, lakes and seas, need not be translated, unless they are known in the English-speaking world by traditional English names. The significant discovery of prehistoric man was made in the Neanderthal (not Neandertal) valley. In Canada, we use the traditional English name whenever the official gazetteer offers the alternative. For example, we say Magdalen Islands, not Îles de la Madeleine. We also use available English names for countries (Germany, not Deutschland) and for cities (Florence, not Firenze; Rangoon, not Yangon; Kiev, not Kyiv).

We use **accents** on French words and names, as long as we are sure we have them right. We do not use accents on words and names in other languages unless there is a risk of confusion or ambiguity (if, for instance, an unaccented word would have a different meaning).

Quebec names

The names of **Quebec agencies and organizations** deserve special mention because they make up the majority of non-English words in our news pages. They are not exceptions to the rule that unilingual readers must know exactly what we are talking about. Readers must not be expected to know that *enseignants et enseignantes* are teachers, or that *hors* means outside, or that a *centrale* is a union, or that *langue* means language. There need not be a literal translation of the name, but the agency's or group's nature must be clear. We could speak, for example, of "the province's largest teachers union, the *Centrale des enseignants du Québec*."

If an agency's or organization's name also has an official English translation, the English version should be used (in the English style, with all principal words upper-case). But if the

translation is not on the agency's or group's own letterhead, incorporation papers or constitution as an alternative official name, stick to a generic description and the official French name. An exception is university names, which we always render in English (University of Montreal, University of Quebec at Montreal, Laval University).

Use only English for the names of **Quebec government departments** that are cabinet portfolios (the Labour Department), and also for the names of **legislative institutions** and officers (National Assembly, Speaker, whip, finance committee). Use English for the names of **courts**, the titles of judges (chief justice etc.) and the titles of **municipal officials and departments**.

Quebec community names should reflect local usage and spelling (Trois-Rivières, not Three Rivers; St-Basile, Que., but St. Basile, N.B.). Montreal and Quebec are deemed to have long-established English versions of their names, without accents, but we use accents if the name appears as part of an organization's French name. Use English for such words as County, Township, Region.

When naming **geographical features**, we generally use English for such words as Mount, Mountains, River, Lake and Bay if the name is an English word or an anglicized version (St. Lawrence River, Laurentian Highlands), but French if the name is a French word (Mont Tremblant, Baie des Chaleurs). There is room for latitude here if an English version is well known to English-Canadian readers, which is true of major features such as Mount Royal, the Gatineau Hills, the Saguenay River.

Note that **franco-** is an English prefix as well as a French one. Therefore, write franco-Manitoban and franco-Ontarian, not *franco-manitobain* or *franco-ontarien*, unless the word appears as part of an organization name we are giving in French. For guidelines on when we use the word **Québécois**, see Quebecker.

foreman

If an employer still uses this gender-specific title, the feminine is forewoman. Do not change it arbitrarily to a gender-neutral word such as supervisor, because this may be a different position in the company. The word forelady has a long tradition in the garment industry, and should be used in stories dealing with it.

forensic evidence

Forensic means having to do with the courts. By extension, it also means having to do with legal aspects, as in forensic medicine, or serving the needs of the legal system, as in forensic lab. But we state the obvious when we say a forensic lab produces forensic evidence, which after all simply means court evidence. A forensic lab produces **scientific evidence**. We may speak of testimony by an expert in forensic medicine, forensic chemistry, forensic accounting etc., but these should not be called simply a forensic (court) witness. Say medical witness etc.

foresee

forestall

foreword

A statement appearing before the text of a book. Commonly misspelled foreward or forward.

Forks, The

Upper-case the article when referring to the area of Winnipeg, which is built at the juncture of the Red and Assiniboine rivers.

Forks of the Credit, the

A hill district just northwest of Toronto. Note that the hamlet is simply Forks of the Credit.

former and ex-, see ex-.

former and latter

It is too much to expect a newspaper reader to sort back through a previous sentence to find the antecedents for a former-and-latter construction. It is better to repeat the nouns or names, or recast.

Formica

A trade name. The generic is plastic laminate, or plastic surface.

Formosa. Use Taiwan.

Forrest, Man.

forsake, forsook (not fore).

Fort

Do not abbreviate to Ft. in placelines or stories, although this is allowed in short headlines.

Fort Knox

This term may be used for the U.S. Gold Bullion Depository. However, be aware that Fort Knox is actually a large military reservation of more than 130 square kilometres in north-central Kentucky, a permanent army base and also the site of Godman Air Force Base. The gold depository was put there in 1936.

Fort Macleod

Fort McMurray

fortuitous

It means accidental, happening by chance. It cannot be used to mean fortunate.

49th parallel

South of the 49th parallel is a poor description of the United States. The 49th parallel forms the border only from Lake of the Woods to the Strait of Georgia. Lake Superior is entirely south of the 49th, as is almost all of the population of Eastern Canada.

forward, not forwards.

founder
Means sink, or fail completely. See flounder.

four allies, four victors
In stories about the postwar administration of Germany, do not speak of the United States, the Soviet Union, Britain and France as "the four wartime allies" or "the four Second World War victors." Both terms leave out several important contributors to the war effort, including Canada, and the term victor may not be applied unreservedly to France. The most accurate term here is the four postwar occupying powers, occupiers.

three horsemen of
the apocalypse

Four Horsemen
We should not be definite on the identity of the first rider, the one on the white horse, in the sixth chapter of Revelation (the Apocalypse). The red horse is ridden by war, the black by famine and the pale horse by Death. The rider of the white is called conquest in the 1916 novel by Vicente

Blasco Ibanez, *The Four Horsemen of the Apocalypse*, but in Revelation he is merely described as an armed, crowned rider who "went forth conquering," and most biblical scholars take this rider to be Christ. Use upper case only for Death, the only rider actually named.

Grantland Rice, in calling the 1924 Notre Dame backfield the Four Horsemen, did not use the word Apocalypse. He said the riders "of dramatic lore" were called Famine, Pestilence, Destruction and Death.

fourth estate
Use lower case. Strictly speaking, it refers to journalists who report on governments, strongly influencing political affairs by doing so. By extension it has come to mean the media they work for, and by a further extension to mean all journalists who cover or comment on news. It is dicey to extend the definition any further, to include advice columnists, fan and hobby magazines and other special-interest publications.

Thomas Carlyle was probably mistaken in saying Edmund Burke coined this expression about 1790. An early use in print was by William Hazlitt, in 1821, and the best known is that of Lord Macaulay in 1828. In a reference to the traditional orders (estates) of English society (the nobility, the clergy and the commons), he wrote that "the gallery in which the reporters sit has become a fourth estate of the realm."

Fox, Vicente
Not Vincente. Use this name for the Mexican President, rather than his full name Vicente Fox Quesada.

fraction
A fraction can range from a minute portion (a 1000th) to virtually all (999-1000ths). If we want to use the word fraction to mean a small portion, we must modify it to specify this (a

tiny fraction of his holdings). There is no need to do so, however, if the word is used in the sense of even less than a small unit of measurement, as in a fraction of an inch, a fraction of a second. For style and pitfalls involving fractions, see numbers, per cent, statistics.

France

Adjective and people: French. Currency: euro (had been the franc). Capital: Paris.

Metropolitan France has 22 regions, including Corsica, divided into 96 departments. Its population of about 59 million is overwhelmingly French-speaking, but Occitan (Provençal) is considered a distinct Romance language, and Basque is spoken in the extreme south. Most Corsicans speak standard French in addition to Corsican, a dialect similar to Tuscan. In addition, there are about four million foreigners, speaking Algerian, Portuguese, Moroccan, Italian and Spanish. Several overseas possessions are represented in the National Assembly, and four of them, Guadeloupe, French Guiana, Martinique and Réunion, have been classed as Overseas Departments since 1946, with the same status as the departments of Metropolitan France. Saint-Pierre and Miquelon held this status from 1976 to 1985, when it became a "territorial collectivity." (See Saint-Pierre.) The island of Marotte is also a collectivity. Status of "overseas territory" is held by New Caledonia, French Polynesia, Wallis and Futuna, and the French Southern and Antarctic Territories.

franchiser, franchisee

Franchiser for the entity selling a franchise, **franchisee** for the buyer.

francization

Awkward, and to be avoided if possible.

franco-

See foreign and French words.

francophile, francophobe

francophone, lower-case.
Also see allophone, anglophone.

Francophonie, la

Use upper case to refer to the French-speaking equivalent of the Commonwealth, set up in February of 1986 at a francophone summit of 38 countries. By 2003 it had 51 members and five observers. It does not require italics unless the full French name is used (*Organisation internationale de la Francophonie*), but it does need an explanation unless the context is clear. Canada and Belgium are members, and there is also specific representation for Quebec, New Brunswick and the Belgian French community. Louisiana is also represented. If *francophonie* is used in a quote to refer to the general fact of French language and culture, it is lower-case and in italics, and requires an explanation.

Frankenfood

This term, used by critics of genetically modified food to draw parallels with the creation of Frankenstein's monster, is too loaded for use in news stories and news headlines, except in direct quotes.

Frankfort, Ky.

Frankfurt, Germany.

Specify which of the Frankfurts we mean, the western one (on Main) or the eastern (on Oder). We do not use the German words *am Main* and *an der Oder*.

Fraser, Simon

Often misspelled as Frazer. This North West Company fur trader and explorer, whose name survives in that of the university, the Fraser River and the Fraser Canyon, may be described as a Canadian explorer, but we should note that he was born in Vermont, in 1776. The river was named in his honour by David Thompson, after Fraser had named the Thompson River for him.

free

Do not say for free.

freebie, freebies

Reserve for direct quotes.

freedom

In news stories, avoid this loaded word in references to votes or battles for secession, independence, altered federal systems and the like. We would never make such a leap into editorial opinion in connection with a secession movement or referendum in a Canadian province.

free-for-all

freelance

freestyle, noun and adjective.

A **freestyle** swimmer.

free trade

The Canada-U.S. free-trade agreement (FTA) went into effect on Jan. 1, 1989. The North American free-trade agreement (NAFTA) went into effect on Jan. 1, 1994. Negotiations continue on a free-trade area of the Americas, which would cover trade on both continents. Second reference is FTAA.

French

French must not be described as a foreign language. It is one of Canada's two official languages.

For style on French words and phrases, and Quebec titles and place names, see foreign and French words, and accents.

The word French is always upper-case, even in French cuffs, French fries, French-fried, French toast.

French Canada, French Canadian

Hyphenate French-Canadian only as an adjective. Avoid using French Canada to mean Quebec. It would imply that everyone in Quebec speaks French and that no one outside the province does so. See English Canada.

French Guiana

It is the French possession on the northeastern shoulder of South America, bounded on the west by Suriname and on the east and south by Brazil. It is on the Atlantic, not the Caribbean. Its main city and port is Cayenne. The penal colony on Devil's Island, just off the coast, was abolished in 1938. The population is 173,000.

Frisbee, a trade name.

No generic term would mean anything to the reader (throwing the disc?), so we use the trade name, upper-case.

from . . . to . . .

When reporting amounts before and after a change, avoid ambiguity. Say a budget rose to $4-million from $3-million, not that it rose from $3-million to $4-million, which might suggest to the reader that the budget rose by between $3-million and $4-million.

Front de libération du Québec, FLQ.

front line (noun).

front-runner

fuchsia

the f-word

In brief, don't use it. See obscene language.

fuddle-duddle

To keep the record straight, Pierre Trudeau did not officially utter an obscenity in the Commons on Feb. 16,

1971; he mouthed it. He reported outside that he had said fuddle-duddle.

fuelled

Fuhrer

fulfill, fulfilled, fulfilment

full-time

Hyphenate both the adjective and adverb.

fulsome

It does not mean merely effusive or generous. It means distastefully excessive in an insincere way. A fulsome compliment or fulsome praise is hypocritical bootlicking.

fund

Technically, fund as a verb has specific meanings connected with the creation of a fund, or conversion to long-term debt. If an organization or enterprise has been funded, a sum of money has been created from which it can draw. But Canadian idiom appears to regard a budget provided by a government as such a fund, from which the recipients draw during the year. They can be said to have been funded. The noun funding has become acceptable Canadian idiom for public funds provided through a yearly budget. But do not extend this to non-government financing unless an actual fund is created. Donors fund the United Way, and it funds its member charities, but a doting father finances a trip to Paris.

fundamentalism

In any religion, fundamentalism connotes belief in the literal truth of that religion's holy writings, and encompasses millions of moral and law-abiding people all over the world, including adherents of several faiths in Canada. On occasion, however, wire stories about terrorism in Egypt and at the World Trade Center in New York have used the term "Muslim fundamentalists" as if it were sufficient in itself to convey not only belief but also affiliation, motive and probable guilt.

There are zealots in every religion who are convinced they are justified in imposing their beliefs on others, and some who think that violence is justified in achieving this. Use other terms to avoid equating these people with the vast majority of fundamentalists. Possibilities include militants, fanatics, terrorists, depending on their statements and conduct.

Those who gather in mobs to stone embassies, for example, are certainly militants. Those who attack troops or police might be called guerrillas. Those who set bombs or fires that kill, injure or drive away innocent civilians are clearly terrorists.

fundraiser, fundraising

The nouns. The adjective is **fundraising**.

fungus, fungi

furl

When a flag or sail is furled, it is rolled up and lashed to the mast, spar or staff. The word is occasionally used mistakenly to mean flying free, which is unfurled.

furlough

In the U.S. military, a leave with official permission. Do not use it for a layoff.

further

For physical distance, use farther. See farther and further.

fusillade

A simultaneous discharge of firearms. Do not use it for sporadic shooting.

G

Gabon

Adjective and people: Gabonese. Currency: CFA franc. Capital: Libreville.

It is on the Atlantic coast of Africa, straddling the equator. The inland town of Lambarene is the site of Albert Schweitzer's hospital. Gabon is a large exporter of oil, a member of the Organization of Petroleum Exporting Countries (OPEC), and its small population (about 1.2 million) is the richest per capita in sub-Saharan Africa, and second only to the Libyans on the entire continent. It became an autonomous republic within the French Community in 1958, and achieved full independence in 1960. There are several tribal languages (the largest groups are the Fang, who are dominant politically and economically, the Eshira and the Adouma), but French is the official language.

gadfly

It does not mean a social butterfly, a gadabout. It means someone who is irritating, bothersome, like the gadflies (horseflies etc.) that bedevil cattle.

Gadhafi, Moammar

gaff and gaffe

A **gaff** is a pole with a hook for landing fish, or the hook itself, or a type of spar on a sailing ship. The word is contained in the expression stand the gaff (endure hardship). A **gaffe** is an embarrassing blunder or faux pas.

gag order

Do not use this pejorative term in news stories. Using it indicates to readers that we have taken sides, and believe the order is not legitimate. Use publication ban, or just ban, or order, if the following text explains it.

gaily

Unlike the adjective gay, the adverb gaily appears to have retained its meaning of in a happy, carefree manner. However, use with care, being wary of double meanings.

Gairdner Foundation

Gallic (French).

Gallup Poll

galop

The dance, or the musical form written for it.

galoshes

Not used in the singular in Canada. We would say, "I lost one of my galoshes." Overshoes is more generally used.

Gambia

Adjective and people: Gambian. Currency: dalasi. Capital: Banjul.

Also known as The Gambia. Smallest state in Africa, a narrow strip on both sides of the Gambia River, extending about 200 miles inland from the Atlantic coast. Enveloped by Senegal, which it almost bisects and with which it has formed the Confederation of Senegambia to co-ordinate security forces and communications networks and to work toward economic union. Gambia is a member of the Commonwealth. The Mandingo are the largest ethnic group, making up about a third of the population of 1.4 million.

gambit

Technically, it is an opening move in chess involving a sacrifice to gain a larger advantage. It may be used for any opening move, such as an initial position in negotiations, but should not be used merely to mean a tactic, or any tricky or deceptive move.

gambling, gaming

It may be in the interest of casinos and governments to portray gambling as fun and games, and to use gaming as a euphemism, but do not follow their lead in news stories. Use the word gaming only when it appears in direct quotes and in the formal titles of organizations (the Ontario Alcohol and Gaming Commission) or government departments (Alberta's Gaming Ministry). Otherwise, use gambling.

Gananoque, Ont.

Gandhi

Not Ghandi. Mohandas, Indira and Rajiv. Mohandas was called Mahatma, a title of respect (Great-Souled) given to holy men. See India.

garrote, garroted, garroting

gas

The form of matter that is neither solid nor liquid. The word may be used in Canada as an abbreviation of gasoline, as in gas station, but only if there is no chance of confusion with actual gases, particularly natural gas.

Gaspé Peninsula

May be called simply Gaspé or the Gaspé even in first reference.

Gatineau, City of

This western Quebec city was created through the amalgamation of the former city of Hull and the former municipalities of Aylmer, Buckingham, Gatineau and Masson-Angers, all of which sit on the Quebec side of the Ottawa River. The Quebec legislature approved the merger in December, 2001, along with mergers affecting Montreal, Quebec City and several other municipalities. The Gatineau merger took effect on Jan. 1, 2002.

In references and datelines, the city is now Gatineau, Que. Eventually we will drop the Que., but retain it for now to help familiarize readers with the new name. Where Gatineau is the focus of the story, it would help readers to mention that it was created on Jan. 1, 2002, out of the five former municipalities.

See Montreal, Quebec City, Trois-Rivières, Saguenay, Lévis.

Gatineau Hills, the Gatineaus

(Not -aux.) They are in Quebec, just north of Ottawa and Gatineau.

GATT

For General Agreement on Tariffs and Trade. See World Trade Organization.

gauge and gage

A **gauge** is a measuring device, or a size, as in shotguns. A **gage** is anything thrown down in a challenge, such as a glove.

gauntlet

Nelson, Oxford and *Gage* all agree that gauntlet, not gantlet, is now the most common spelling for the punishment in which the offender runs between two lines of men, being struck by both. Run the gauntlet is used figuratively to mean caught in the middle, assailed on all sides. **Gauntlet** is also a glove that flares over the wrist, used in industry and in hawking sports (also in hockey, although here it is called simply a glove). Figuratively, throw down or take up the gauntlet means to issue or accept a challenge.

gay

This word now may safely be used only to mean homosexual. It is the noun and adjective for both men and women, although when we are speaking only of women some prefer the word lesbian. Gay, lesbian and homosexual are the only terms to be used by The Globe. In direct quotes, such derogatory expressions as queer, fairy, fag and dyke should be allowed to stand only if they become the news, as when spoken by a senior politician or judge. Consult a senior editor.

We must never assume, or imply without proof, that two people of the same sex living under the same roof are sexually intimate. Unless both agree with this characterization, stick to the facts and say simply that they share a house or apartment.

Gaza Strip

A strip of land on the Mediterranean Sea, bordered on the south by Egypt and otherwise surrounded by Israel. Israel occupied it (and the West Bank) in 1967 after attacks by Egypt (and Jordan). Refer to the city as Gaza City. Both the strip and the city may be referred to as Gaza in headlines, and in second reference in copy if there is no risk of confusion. See Israel.

Gdansk and Gdynia, Poland.

GDP and GNP

The **gross domestic product** is now the commonly used broad measure of economic activity in a country or other jurisdiction. It measures total income from goods and services produced within the borders, whether by nationals or by outsiders, but not either group's earnings from activities abroad. The former common measure, **gross national product** (used by the United States until 1991), is the income from goods and services received only by nationals, both at home and abroad, minus the earnings that outsiders have removed from the country.

geezer

More offensive than humorous as a synonym for an old man. Best avoided.

gefilte fish

Geiger counter

Device for measuring radioactivity. Named for Hans Geiger.

geisha

Use the same form for the plural. We must not equate them with prostitutes, even by implication. The Japanese word means art person, but their role is best described as professional social entertainer or hostess. Their long apprenticeship includes art, music, dance and, particularly, the art of conversation, ranging from gossip to history and politics.

Geminis, Genies, Nellies

The **Genies**, for Canadian feature films, and the **Geminis**, for television (including TV movies), are both awarded by the Academy of Canadian Cinema and Television, in separate ceremonies. The **Nellies**, also called the National Radio Awards, are awarded by the Alliance of Canadian Cinema, Television and Radio Artists, and were formerly referred to as the ACTRA awards. The Genies were for a time called the Etrogs, after the statuette's sculptor, Sorel Etrog. The awards for French-language TV are the Prix Gémeaux.

gemutlichkeit

Said of a person or group, it means joviality, sociability. Of a place, it means snug coziness. Requires italics.

gene

Many reports about scientists "discovering the gene that causes" a certain disease imply that (1) some people in the world carry this gene and others do not, and (2) the existence of this gene makes people sick.

If journalists manage to understand only one thing about genetics, it should be this: Everyone has the same number of genes (with the exception of a few genes that determine male sexuality, found on the Y-chromosome). When scientists say they have isolated a disease gene, they are actually reporting that they have discovered what happens when that gene is defective.

In such stories we should speak not of a gene but of a genetic (or gene) defect or mutation. If necessary, we should insert in wire stories a brief explanation that the gene is universal, but the defect or mutation is not. When we know it, we should say what percentage of the population carries the defect, and possibly whether it is more common among certain racial, ethnic or geographic groups. This helps readers relate the risk to themselves.

genealogist (not -ologist).

general, Gen. See ranks.

-general

In double-barrelled titles that include the word general, The Globe hyphenates all those in which general comes second, as in Governor-General, attorney-general, secretary-general. It is not a style shared by many publications, but we consider it an aid to comprehension, indicating that an adjective has been placed in an unusual position, after the noun.

There is no hyphen if the word general comes first, as in general secretary.

In military ranks, the word general is the noun, and so it is the word made plural in speaking of several major-generals or lieutenant-generals. In non-military titles, the word general is an adjective, and so it is the other word that is made plural, as in governors-general, auditors-general, attorneys-general. See plurals.

General Electric Canada Inc.

GE on second reference.

General Motors of Canada Ltd.

GM on second reference.

Generation X, Gen X

Upper-case G for the generation of Canadians born from 1960 to 1966, in the second wave within the baby boom, which lasted in Canada from 1947 to 1966. (The boom started a year earlier in the United States, because more U.S. soldiers were in the Pacific and went home sooner.) As a group, Generation Xers didn't have the same job opportunities as the first wave of boomers.

Geneva Conventions

If a story refers to the 1864 international agreement, Geneva Convention is accurate. If, as is more likely, it refers to the document adopted in 1949, including the later protocols – that is, the document currently in force – use the official plural form, the Geneva Conventions, unless referring by name to one of the conventions.

The original Geneva Convention, approved at an international gathering convened by the Swiss government in 1864, was called the Convention for the Amelioration of the Wounded in Time of War. It said all establishments for the treatment of sick or wounded soldiers should be immune to capture or destruction. It set out rules for the humane treatment of combatants, the protection of civilians aiding the wounded and the recognition of the Red Cross as a source of information about people affected by war.

A 1929 treaty on the treatment of prisoners of war said belligerents must treat prisoners humanely, supply information about them and permit visits to prison camps.

In 1949, a Red Cross conference revised all the previous elements of the convention and called them the Geneva Conventions. There are four, all dated Aug. 12, 1949:

(a) The Geneva Convention for the Amelioration of the Condition of the Wounded and Sick in Armed Forces in the Field says belligerents must provide aid, care and protection for sick and wounded combatants regardless of their allegiance, and respect the red cross symbol as the identifying mark of humanitarian workers in the field.

(b) The Geneva Convention for the Amelioration of the Condition of Wounded, Sick and Shipwrecked Members of Armed Forces at Sea extends the rules of the first convention to combatants at sea.

(c) The Geneva Convention Relative to the Treatment of Prisoners of War requires belligerents to treat prisoners humanely, and not press them to reveal more than a minimum of information.

(d) The Geneva Convention Relative to the Protection of Civilian Persons in Time of War forbids belligerents to take hostages, torture civilians and deport individuals or groups.

That synopsis is necessarily brief; the third convention alone contains 143 articles and several annexes.

In 1977, an international conference added protocols dealing further with civilian populations and prisoners of war and the environment.

Genghis Khan
Not a name but a title, Universal Ruler, bestowed on the Mongol chieftain Temujin in 1206 after 20 years of tribal warfare. His wider conquests followed.

Genies
See Geminis.

geniuses

Gentleman Usher of the Black Rod
Upper-case. Ceremonial official of Canada's Senate who carries an ebony stick topped by a gold lion when he summons members of the House of Commons to the Senate chamber to hear the Speech from the Throne.

geographical adjectives
Use the same style internationally that we would follow for references in Canada. Just as we would say southern Manitoba or eastern Alberta (not south Manitoba, east Alberta), so we must say southern Lebanon, northern China. Just as we use the adjectival form in Irish prime minister and French election (not Ireland prime minister, France election), so we must say Taiwanese president, Bangladeshi election.

Avoid such shorthand as "Bhatinda in northern Punjab state," or "Kattankudy village in eastern Batticaloa district." First, the reader's obvious conclusion is that Bhatinda is in the northern part of Punjab, when in fact it is in the southern part. What the shorthand is trying to tell us, in too few words, is that Punjab is in the north of India, and Batticaloa is in eastern Sri Lanka. Second, normal people don't talk that way. If we wouldn't dream of saying "Campbellville village in Ontario province," we shouldn't expect our readers to plow through "Kattankudy village in Batticaloa district." Fix both the meaning and the idiom with one blow by changing such references to

"Bhatinda in the northern state of Punjab" and "the village of Kattankudy in the eastern district of Batticaloa."

Do not be misled by New York State and Washington State. These are exceptions made necessary by the risk of confusion with cities of the same name. No one speaks of New Hampshire state, Nevada state etc. That risks confusion with universities.

geographical placement

We should always check a map when we are bounding an area. Remember that the story will be read by people with detailed knowledge of almost any area we write about. Lapses such as saying the Rockies are visible from Vancouver (see mountains) or that Detroit is south of Windsor rather than north are embarrassing and unnecessary.

Locate smaller centres by reference to major cities. Readers probably are not sure of the location of a secondary city in another region, even if they know the name, so it may be necessary to use two cities as a reference. Say Taber is about 50 kilometres east of Lethbridge, 180 kilometres southeast of Calgary; Creemore is 65 kilometres west of Barrie, about 150 kilometres northwest of Toronto.

Take access into consideration when deciding on a description. Distance across a map as the crow flies is less useful to the reader than 35 kilometres by rail west of Kenora, or two hours drive by rough road east of Hay River.

Geographical features are useful references. We might say that Nipigon is on the northernmost hump of Lake Superior, 100 kilometres northeast of Thunder Bay, or that Moosonee is at the mouth of the Moose River, at the southern tip of James Bay. In foreign references, geographical regions are particularly important, such as in the coastal mangrove region, on the high central plateau, in the industrial north. (Canada's official geographical

regions are the Atlantic region, the Great Lakes-St. Lawrence plain, the Canadian Shield, the interior plains, the Western Cordillera and the Arctic. Except in stories specifically about geography, however, we would usually use more familiar local descriptions.)

Locate places in Canada's Far North by reference to geographical features (major islands, rivers, straits) and by distance from the most familiar communities in the area. As a reference point for the Western Arctic, use Inuvik, in the Mackenzie Delta. For the Eastern Arctic, use Iqaluit (formerly Frobisher Bay), on Baffin Island. Halfway between is Resolute Bay. Always state whether the distance is by air, by road or by sea.

For placement within cities, remember that uptown, downtown and midtown have different meanings in different communities, and are meaningless in some. It is better to use neighbourhood names, and better still to add the neighbourhood's relation to a landmark, such as along the CN tracks north of the river, or in the wealthy area on the south side of the harbour, or in the suburban neighbourhood surrounding the university.

In U.S. wire stories, references to an area being the size of a particular U.S. state should normally be converted to a Canadian equivalent, or possibly to a familiar European one. Also see capitalization, directions.

Georges Bank

No apostrophe, singular. It lies between Nova Scotia and Cape Cod. A World Court decision in 1984 gave the easternmost sixth of the bank to Canada, the other five-sixths to the United States. It is in the Fundy-Gulf of Maine tidal system, and the currents and tidal mixing of nutrients greatly increase its productivity. Canada's sixth is particularly rich in groundfish and scallops.

Georgia

Adjective and people: Georgian. Currency: ruble. Capital: Tbilisi.

The population of five million is about 70-per-cent Georgian, with Armenian, Russian, Azeri, Abkhazian, Adzhari and Ossetian minorities. It was made part of the Trans-Caucasian Soviet Socialist Republic in 1922 (along with Armenia and Azerbaijan), became a separate Soviet republic in 1936, and gained independence with the collapse of the Soviet Union in late 1991, having taken a lead in the process by declaring independence earlier in the year. Before and after independence, the South Ossetian, Abkhazi and Adzhari minorities were campaigning for autonomy.

Georgia is on the Black Sea, bordering on Russia, Turkey, Armenia and Azerbaijan, and is mostly mountains and forest. The small amount of agricultural land, essentially the Kolkhida plain, is used intensively for valuable cash crops, producing tea, citrus and orchard fruits, tobacco, grapes and silk. The climate is subtropical at lower elevations, and the Black Sea coast is noted for its resorts and spas. The mountains are rich in resources and hydroelectricity, which allows considerable heavy industry.

The Georgian Church was formerly part of the Russian Orthodox Church, but has been independent of it since 1917.

See Soviet Union.

germane

Germany

Adjective and people: German. Currency: euro (had been the mark). Capital: Berlin.

West Germany and East Germany formally merged on Oct. 3, 1990, keeping the name that had been used by the West, the Federal Republic of Germany. Germany is a federation of 16 states (*Länder*), including Berlin and the six states of the former East Germany. The states have wide powers, including administration of federal laws through their own civil services. The federal legislature consists of the elected Federal Assembly (the Bundestag) and the Federal Council (Bundesrat), appointed by the states. Executive power rests with the chancellor, the head of government, while the president is the formal head of state.

In 1989, agitation for reform in East Germany was expressed even within the Communist Party (officially, the Socialist Unity Party, SED), and attempts by Erich Honecker (leader since 1971) to forcefully suppress demonstrations led to his ouster from the party in October. The Berlin Wall crumbled in November when East Germany opened its borders in the face of internal political upheaval and an exodus of more than 30,000 East Germans through Hungary, which had opened its border with Austria in May. The Communist political monopoly was formally ended in November. Democratic elections on March 18, 1990, led to the formation in April of a non-Communist coalition government with a clear mandate to negotiate union with West Germany. An economic union was concluded in July, with formal unification on Oct. 3.

The first all-German election since 1932 was held on Dec. 2, 1990, won by a coalition under Chancellor Helmut Kohl. The financial strain of dismantling the inefficient state economy of the east, coupled with a worldwide recession and a wave of refugees from other countries, led to social unrest, including violence against foreigners. Throughout this difficult transition period, Germany continued to take a leading role in the process of wider European integration.

At the time of unification, East Germany's population was a little more than one-quarter that of West

Germany (17 million to 62 million). Germany's current population is 83 million.West Germany had become a sovereign country in May of 1955, after the United States, Britain and France revoked the Occupation Statute imposed after the Second World War. But international recognition was long delayed, largely because of West Germans' hope of unification. Conciliatory moves by Willy Brandt's government in West Germany led to a non-aggression pact with the Soviet Union in 1970 and mutual recognition by the two Germanys in 1972. Both were admitted to the UN in 1973.

If there is occasion to refer to the currencies before union, prefer West German and East German mark to deutsche mark and ostmark. There is rarely a need to use their formal names, Federal Republic of Germany and German Democratic Republic (Deutsche Demokratische Republik), except to explain the initials FRG, GDR or DDR in a quote.

gerrymander

The manipulation of riding boundaries to favour one party. Lower-case, despite its origin in the name of Elbridge Gerry, an early Massachusetts governor, and salamander, the strange shape of a constituency he created. However, upper-case Canada's Great Gerrymander (1882), in which Sir John A. Macdonald openly described the effect of his Redistribution Act as "hiving the Grits."

get-together, the noun.

The verb is **get together**.

Ghana

Adjective and people: Ghanaian (note spelling). Currency: cedi. Capital: Accra.

It is on the Gulf of Guinea, between Ivory Coast and Togo. As a colony of Britain, from which it gained independence in 1957 with Dominion status, it had been called the Gold Coast. It became a republic in 1960 with Kwame Nkruma as president, but remains a member of the Commonwealth. A military coup led by Jerry Rawlings in 1979 resulted, with one brief, early return to civilian rule, in a dictatorship that lasted until 1992, when a new-found if limited tolerance of democracy saw Rawlings become an elected head of state after a disputed election. He stepped down in 2000. An election that year saw his preferred candidate defeated, and John Kufuor elected.

Ghana is one of the most prosperous countries in Africa. Industrial development centres on the aluminum smelter at Tema. Other exports include cocoa, timber, gold, diamonds and manganese. Discovery of oil in commercial quantities was announced in 1978, but Ghana is still an importer of petroleum. Its population of 20 million is among the most literate in Africa, with 10 years of free, compulsory schooling.

gherkin

ghettos

GI

An enlisted man or woman in the U.S. Army. Short for General Issue.

gibe and jibe

Gibe, both noun and verb, has to do with taunts and jeers. Jibe is an intransitive verb meaning to be in accordance.

Gibraltar

An overseas territory of Britain, which received it from Spain under the Treaty of Utrecht in 1713. Spain has talked with Britain about the possibility of shared sovereignty over the colony, but a majority of Gibraltarians declared in plebiscites in 1967 and 2002 that they wished to remain British. See United Kingdom.

Gibraltar, Strait of (note singular).

gigolos

girl

In general, we do not use the word girl or girls to refer to adult women, as in the girls in the office, a shop girl. It carries two objectionable connotations—immaturity and servant status. Technically, girls are females under 18, but we refer to most who are 16 and 17 as young women, especially those who are holding down an adult job, shouldering family responsibilities or distinguishing themselves academically. However, a large group of whom only a few are 16 or 17 may be described as a group of girls. Also, a pom-pom girl or a bar girl (in foreign stories) might continue to be described in those terms well into their 20s. In feature stories with a lighter cast, girls may be used in expressions equivalent to boys' night out and the boys in the backroom.

Be mindful of the sensitivity of many readers to what they regard as demeaning distinctions when men and women are being described together. We would not speak of a cameraman and script girl, for example. See women and language.

girlfriend

Girl Guides of Canada, a Guide.

the Girls

Upper-case the Canadian art community's name for sculptors Frances Loring and Florence Wyle. Note that both were U.S.-born.

GIS

For guaranteed income supplement.

Giuseppe, not Guiseppe.

gizmos

Gjoa Haven, Nunavut

Named for the Gjoa, the first ship to navigate the Northwest Passage. Roald Amundsen took four summers, 1903 to 1906, to travel from Atlantic to Pacific. Gjoa Haven on King William Island, one of his wintering places, is now an Inuit hamlet, about 1,000 kilometres by air north of Yellowknife. See Northwest Passage.

glamour

But drop the u for **glamorize**, **glamorous**.

Glenbow Museum, Calgary.

It is now universally referred to as the Glenbow Museum, but be aware that it is actually a museum-archive-art gallery complex, and that its formal name is the Glenbow-Alberta Institute. The formal name should be used for the board and management. Glenbow, which grew out of the Glenbow Foundation of oil man Eric Harvie, celebrates Western Canada, but should not be described only in those terms. Many of its exhibitions are national in scope.

Global Television Network

For the purposes of most news stories, it may be referred to as Global Television, or simply Global if the context is clear. It is a division of Winnipeg-based CanWest Global Communications Corp., whose other assets include the former Southam newspaper group and the National Post, both acquired from Hollinger Inc. in November of 2000. Control of the National Post was shared with Hollinger owner Conrad Black until August of 2002, when CanWest acquired Black's share.

Globe and Mail, The

Upper-case the article in The Globe in second reference, except when Globe is an adjective, as in the Globe newsroom. See capitalization.

A brief history of The Globe and Mail appears at the back of this book.

Glooscap Trail

The scenic drive through Nova Scotia's Bay of Fundy and Minas Basin country, associated with Glooskap (note spelling), the Mi'kmaq creator figure and hero.

GNP, see GDP.

goalkeeper and goaltender

Ice hockey uses the word goaltender, and soccer uses goalkeeper. Both use goalie. In basketball, goaltending is the infraction of blocking a shot after it has reached the top of its arc. In the National Basketball Association, it means touching the ball when it is in the imaginary cylinder above the rim of the basket. (This rule does not apply in international play.)

God

Upper-case the deity in monotheistic religions, along with such pronouns as He and His, but lower-case deities and pronouns in pantheistic ones, both ancient and modern. See capitalization.

Upper-case God-fearing, Godhead, Godspeed, but lower-case godless, godlike, godfather, godmother, godson, goddaughter, godchild, godsend. (Godfather etc. would be upper-case if used as a name, as in Happy birthday, Godfather.) Godforsaken should be upper-case in references that are clearly religious, especially when modifying people, groups and institutions, but it is usually lower-case in reference to desolate places (a godforsaken wilderness).

God Save the Queen

In italics. Since 1967 it has been designated Canada's **royal anthem**. O Canada is the national anthem.

Goebbels and Goering

Joseph Goebbels was the Nazi minister of propaganda; Hermann Goering was head of the Luftwaffe, the German air force.

Golden Boy, the

Upper-case when referring to the Winnipeg landmark atop the legislature's dome. Cast in bronze, then gilded. He has a torch in one hand, a wheat sheaf in the other.

Golden Dog, the

Upper-case. A gilded dog chewing a bone, Le chien d'or, carved on a stone block believed to have been worked in the 1600s and now above the door of the main post office in Quebec City. The French inscription on the block ends with: "I will bite him who has bitten me."

Golden Horseshoe

Upper-case. Refers to the prosperous region enclosing the western end of Lake Ontario, including Toronto and Hamilton. The eastern ends of the horseshoe are Oshawa and St. Catharines.

golf terms

Use figures for identifying clubs (a 3-iron, a 4-wood), but write out numbers of shots and par values (an eagle-three, the par-four 18th hole, a nine-under-par 63).

goodbye

goodwill

One word, both for generous intent and for the established reputation of a business that enhances its value.

Gorky, Maxim

gospel

Upper-case in referring to the actual books of the Bible (the Four Gospels, the Gospel According to St.

Matthew, St. Luke's Gospel); but lower-case in general references to Christian teaching or as a synonym for religion, religious, biblical (preaching the gospel, gospel music, the gospel truth, don't take this as gospel).

GO Transit

GO stands for Government of Ontario (but is not spelled out). It is upper-case, with no periods or hyphen. Say GO train, GO bus, GO tracks, GO station.

government

Lower-case (except in such uses as Government House), never abbreviated. Say the federal government, the U.S. government. For style on government bodies, titles, commissions etc., see capitalization. When speaking of democratic countries, prefer governing party to ruling party. Similarly, prefer office to power in the constructions took office, has been in office.

Government House

Upper-case when referring to the official residence of a viceregal representative anywhere in the Commonwealth, including those of provincial lieutenant-governors. Also upper-case for residences of heads of state in other countries if that is the building's official name. However, note that we prefer the local or traditional name of a building, such as Rideau Hall, the Ottawa residence of Canada's governors-general.

governor

Do not abbreviate, even before a name. Say Governor George Pataki of New York, New York Governor George Pataki.

Governor-General

Hyphenated, and not abbreviated even before a name. Upper-case when referring to a specific person, even standing alone, but not when speaking

in general terms (he wants to be governor-general, a list of governors-general). Note that -general is the adjective, and it is the noun governor that is made plural. The hyphen is Globe style, but is not used by the government.

Governor-General's Horse Guards, Governor-General's Foot Guards

Not Guard. A militia armoured regiment based in Toronto and a militia infantry regiment based in Ottawa.

Governor-General's Literary Awards

May be referred to simply as the Governor-General's Awards.

grade

Like other nouns used as a label with a numeral, Grade 3 is upper-case. (See capitalization, numbers.) Do not use Roman numerals; say Grade 12, not Grade XII. Lower-case grade when not followed by a numeral, as in the first grade.

graduate

As a verb, it can be either intransitive (he graduated) or transitive (he was graduated). We prefer the intransitive.

graffiti

It is plural, so it takes plural verbs and pronouns (these graffiti are). The

graffiti artist

singular, graffito, is usually encountered only in stories about archeology; modern idiom usually refers to the singular as a piece of graffiti. Graffiti are words and drawings quickly and casually scrawled or sprayed on structures or natural rock faces. Do not use for more painstaking or elaborate writing, inscription and art, such as students' authorized decoration of a hoarding.

Grammys

Granada, Spain.

Grand & Toy Ltd.

Founded in Toronto in the 1880s by James Grand, who was soon joined by Samuel Toy, his brother-in-law. Sells office supplies, not toys.

Grand Bank, Nfld. A town. Singular.

Grand Banks

In the plural, it refers to the entire fishing area on Canada's continental shelf southeast of Newfoundland. In second reference, it may be called the banks, lower-case. It consists of several banks, the largest of which are Grand Bank, Green Bank and St. Pierre Bank. Others include LaHave, Sable, Banquereau. The individual banks need be mentioned only when relevant.

granddaughter

Grand-Mère, Que.

Note that French does not add an e to *grand-* when it is joined by a hyphen to feminine nouns, as in *grand-mère, grand-tante*.

grassroots, noun and adjective.

Gray Coach Lines

GRC

The French initials of the RCMP. They stand for *Gendarmerie royale du Canada*.

Great Divide

Upper-case when both words are used. This is the North American term for the continental divide that separates the Pacific drainage basin from the rest of the continent. The southern end of the Canadian divide forms the Alberta-B.C. boundary, in the Rocky Mountains. From the divide, water flows to the Pacific, to the Arctic Ocean or to Hudson Bay.

greater or less degree (not lesser).

Greater Toronto Area, GTA

Upper-case. As defined by the Ontario government, which includes the Office of the Greater Toronto Area within the Ministry of Municipal Affairs and Housing, the Greater Toronto Area is far larger than the City of Toronto. It includes Toronto and the four regional municipalities of Durham, Halton, Peel and York, containing 42 per cent of Ontario's population (5.1 million inhabitants) and stretching as far north as Lake Simcoe, as far west as the western boundaries of the local municipalities of Milton and Burlington and as far east as Lake Scugog and the eastern boundary of the local municipality of Clarington. Among the cities and towns that fall within the GTA are Burlington, Milton, Keswick and Newcastle. It does not include Guelph, Barrie and Port Hope.

The GTA contains what used to be simply described as the 416 and 905 area codes, but that description has been complicated by the addition of the area code 289 outside Toronto. The government and the regional municipalities consider the Greater Toronto Area to be a valuable promotional tool, but it should be used sparingly in copy unless explained, since its name might mislead readers into thinking it refers to Toronto and its immediate surroundings.

great-grandmother, great-great-grandfather

Hyphens. Resist the temptation to add any more greats. A person has 16 great-great-grandparents when both sides of each family are considered. Add a third great-, and we're into the realm of ancestors with fairly distant relationships. In expressions such as "his great-great-grandfather," consider saying "a" instead, or "one of his great-great-grandfathers," since there were eight: four paternal and four maternal.

Great-West Life Assurance Co.

Great Whale

This name may be used to refer in a general way to the place on James Bay about 1,200 kilometres north of Montreal, site of a giant hydro development. The name is used by Hydro-Québec, but it is not an official community name. Three other names define distinct municipal administrations: Whapmagoostui, a Cree community (not a reserve) with a chief and band council; Kuujjuarapik, an Inuit community with a mayor and council; and Poste-de-la-Baleine, a non-native community with a provincially appointed administrator.

Greece

Adjective and people: Greek. Currency: euro (had been the drachma). Capital: Athens.

This rugged country, 75 per cent mountainous, occupies the southern tip of the Balkan Peninsula and many islands in the Aegean, Ionian and Mediterranean seas. The islands, which make up almost a fifth of its land area, include Crete, Corfu, the Ionian Isles, the Cyclades, the Dodecanese and the Sporades. The narrow Isthmus of Corinth separates the Peloponnesus from the northern section of the mainland. The population is 10.6 million. After a military coup in April of 1967 and an unsuccessful countercoup later that year, King Constantine went abroad. After a referendum in 1973, the monarchy was abolished. Democracy was restored in 1974 after a bloodless coup in late 1973. Another referendum on the monarchy in late 1974 confirmed Greece's republican status.

Green

Use upper case for movements and political parties of that name, but lower case for generic descriptions denoting environmental activism. Such lower-case generic descriptions would be rare outside direct quotes, since they might be misinterpreted as meaning inexperienced (a green MP) or possibly even nauseous. Prefer environmentalist etc., or a description specifying the issue in question, such as anti-logging.

Green Chamber

Upper-case. A name for the House of Commons, from the colour of its carpet and upholstery. Rather affected and stilted in news stories, but still has its place, particularly in historical references.

Greenland, see Denmark.

green paper

A government paper tabled in the House to promote discussion on a subject, as an aid to forming policy. A white paper, in contrast, is presented as government policy that will be reflected in coming legislation. Upper-case when the full formal name is given, but lower-case in second reference, the green paper.

Greenpeace Foundation

May be referred to simply as Greenpeace, and described as an activist environmental group.

Greenwich Mean Time, GMT

Prefer this name as the one familiar to Canadian readers, but be aware that much of the world uses the name Co-ordinated Universal Time.

Grenada

Adjective and people: Grenadian. Currency: East Caribbean dollar. Capital: St. George's.

The most southerly of the Windward Islands, about 150 kilometres north of Trinidad. It is the smallest independent state in the Western Hemisphere, at 344 square kilometres, and a member of the Commonwealth, independent from Britain since 1974. The population is 90,000. Its spelling is occasionally confused with that of Granada, the Spanish city. The constitution was suspended after a revolution in 1979, and the army took control in October of 1983 after Prime Minister Maurice Bishop was killed in a power struggle. The United States invaded on Oct. 24 (officially, it was a U.S.-led invasion at the request of a group of Caribbean countries). Elections for the 15-seat House of Representatives were held on Dec. 3.

Gretzky, Wayne

grey

Grey County, Ont.

Grey Cup

Grey Owl

Archibald Stansfeld (Archie) Belaney became a guide in Ontario after immigrating from England in 1903, but most of his writing was done in Saskatchewan. Living among the Ojibwa and falsely describing himself as the son of a Scot and an Apache (his Grey Owl persona was an elaborate creation, a fact made public after his death), he became known as a naturalist after seeing service in the First World War. He was made an honorary ranger of Prince Albert National Park in 1931, the year of his first book, and lived there with the woman widely regarded as his wife, Anahareo. He died at 50 in 1938.

gridiron

A rather outmoded word for a football field (from its pattern of stripes), but it is alive and well as the headline-ese adjective **grid**.

grieve

Has come to be accepted in labour stories as a verb meaning to pursue a grievance. It also retains its original meaning, to feel sorrow or grief.

grippe

Prefer influenza, or flu.

grisly and grizzly

Grisly means gruesome, horrifying. It is the word we want for describing crimes, accident scenes etc., but only if they truly live up to the billing. **Grizzly** means grizzled, greyish, and is used nowadays only to describe bears. Grizzled is the word we may want for a greying person.

Grit

Acceptable in second reference, and in headlines, to refer to Liberals. Radical reformers in Canada West formed the Clear Grit Party, taking the name from Peter Perry's assertion that "only men of clear grit" were wanted.

groom

Acceptable Canadian idiom for a bridegroom.

Gros Morne National Park

The name means big hill. The park, on Newfoundland's western coast, is known for spectacular scenery, combining seascapes and the Long Range Mountains.

gross national product

See GDP and GNP.

groundfish

One word, the collective term used to describe species that feed near the ocean bottom. Principal species include cod, haddock, redfish (also known as ocean perch), pollock (Boston bluefish) and the various flatfish, such as halibut, flounder, sole, turbot. See fish.

Groundhog Day

According to myth in Canada and the United States, Feb. 2 signals the course of the weather over the next several weeks. If the groundhog emerges from its burrow and sees its shadow, winter weather will persist for six weeks; if it doesn't see its shadow, spring weather will arrive soon.

Since producing a groundhog on Groundhog Day can raise a town's profile and attract tourists, a number of towns in both countries have their annual rituals. Two high-profile examples are Wiarton, Ont. (with its Wiarton Willie), and Punxsutawney, Pa. (with its Punxsutawney Phil, celebrated in the movie *Groundhog Day*).

groundswell

group

Upper-case in commonly accepted names such as the Bloomsbury Group, the Group of Seven (artists and industrial countries).

Group of Seven, G7, Group of Eight, G8

The most accurate description of the G7 is a group of seven leading industrial countries: the United States, Japan, Germany, Britain, France, Italy and Canada. It began in 1975 with five members; Canada and Italy were added the next year.

After the appearance of Soviet President Mikhail Gorbachev at the 1991 meeting, and the participation of Russian President Boris Yeltsin in much of the 1994 meeting, Russia's involvement was officially recognized in 1997 with the meeting title The Summit of the Eight, though the body was still called the G7. The expanded body was named the Group of Eight, G8, at the Birmingham meeting in 1998.

The heads of government meet annually, with a ninth important participant being the president of the European Commission. Canada was host in 1981 (Montebello), 1988 (Toronto), 1995 (Halifax) and 2002 (Kananaskis, Alta.).

Group of Seven

A group began forming from 1911 to 1914 among Toronto artists, including Tom Thomson, but was not formally created until after the war, in 1920, three years after Thomson's death. The seven original members were Frank Carmichael, Lawren Harris, A. Y. Jackson, Frank Johnston, Arthur Lismer, J. E. H. MacDonald and F. H. Varley. Later members were A. J. Casson, LeMoine FitzGerald and Edwin Holgate. See Johnston.

grow

As a transitive verb, confine to plants and certain livestock. Shun such uses as "He wants to grow the company to 100 stores."

Guatemala

Adjective and people: Guatemalan. Currency: quetzal. Capital: Guatemala City.

Just south of Mexico, it is the second most northerly country in Central America after Belize. It is very mountainous, with the Pacific slopes and lowlands much more populous than the Caribbean side. Coffee dominates the economy, being grown on 1,500 large plantations and more than 10,000 smaller ones. Cotton, sugar, beef and petroleum are also exported, and Guatemala is the second-largest producer, after Mexico, of chicle, used in chewing gum. Pure

Indians, in 21 groups descended from the Maya, make up 53 per cent of the population of 12 million. About 4 per cent are white, and the rest are Indian-white mestizos, who in Guatemala are known as Ladinos. A destructive earthquake in 1976 left more than a million homeless. More than 30 years of civil war ended in 1996 when the government and leftist rebels signed a peace treaty.

guerrilla

It is taken to mean a fighter in an organized unit that uses hit-and-run tactics against military personnel and installations, avoiding head-on confrontations with a stronger enemy. Individuals and most urban groups that hit civilians are more accurately described as terrorist.

guinea

Lower-case guinea fowl, guinea hen, guinea pig.

Guinea

Adjective and people: Guinean. Currency: syli or Guinean franc. Capital: Conakry.

It is on the Atlantic just south of the extreme tip of the bulge of West Africa. It shares borders with, clockwise from the north, Guinea-Bissau, Senegal, Mali, Ivory Coast, Liberia and Sierra Leone. It became independent of France in 1958. Its population of 8 million, divided into about 16 ethnic groups dominated by the Fulani and Mandingo, is mainly agricultural, but its economy is heavily dependent on bauxite (58 per cent of exports) and alumina (30 per cent). There are also iron and diamond mines. The interior uplands are densely forested. Some of the estuaries and mangrove swamps of the coastal lowlands have been reclaimed for cultivation of bananas and rice.

Guinea held its first democratic election in 1993, electing Lansana Conté, who had been head of the military government, as president of the civilian government. He was re-elected in 1998.

Guinea-Bissau

No useful adjective for country or people; say "of Guinea-Bissau" or some such. Currency: peso. Capital: Bissau.

This tiny state on the Atlantic, formerly Portuguese Guinea, borders on Senegal and Guinea, and includes a large archipelago. A war of independence began in 1963, and Portugal eventually recognized the state in 1974. Its 1.3 million people, mainly Balante, Fulani and Mandingo, are agricultural; the main export crop is peanuts, and the main food crop is rice. Bauxite has been discovered but the resource is little developed.

Guinness

Family, brew and *Book of Records*. Note the double n.

Gulf Islands

These 225 islands between the mainland and Vancouver Island are called this because the Strait of Georgia was formerly called the Gulf of Georgia. The largest and most heavily populated is Saltspring. Others include Gabriola, Galiano, Kuper, Mayne, North and South Pender, Saturna, Thetis and Valdes.

Gulf of St. Lawrence

It is an extension of the Atlantic, to which it is linked by Cabot and Canso straits and by the Strait of Belle Isle. It is a sea in its own right, much of it deeper than the continental shelf.

Gulf Stream

Strictly speaking, we should say that the climate of northern Europe is moderated by warm seas or by ocean currents, not by the Gulf Stream. There are two reasons. First, this name applies only from the Straits of Florida to the Grand Banks, while the continuation northwestward to the Norwegian Sea is called the North Atlantic Current. The second and more fundamental reason is that the current is not a wide river of warm water, but rather a fast current, extremely narrow (60 to 100 kilometres), that prevents the cold and relatively fresh water on its left from mixing with the much warmer and more saline waters to its right. The division is so effective that the level on the warm Sargasso Sea side is about 80 centimetres (30 inches) higher than that of the "cold wall" on the left of the stream. The effect of the current is not that it carries warm water to northern Europe, but rather that it blocks colder water from reaching it.

gulls

Prefer this term to sea gulls; none of the approximately 40 species is called sea gull, and gulls are often found far from water in garbage dumps and plowed fields. Be aware that there are many varieties of similar sea birds that are not gulls (terns, frigate birds, skimmers, gannets, skuas, boobies, albatrosses etc.). We should be as specific as possible.

gunpoint

guns and calibres

Normally, use the word **gun** standing alone only for cannons, and be aware that, strictly speaking, guns are distinct from howitzers, which have a lower velocity and a higher trajectory than guns. The smaller cannons of the field artillery are usually howitzers. The word gun also appears in combination names of smaller weapons, such as handgun, shotgun, machine gun, submachine gun. If a wire story does not specify the type of weapons used by robbers, kidnappers etc., the word gun is preferable to the non-specific word weapon. Firearms is the non-specific

term of choice when speaking of small arms in general.

Calibre means the internal diameter of a barrel, or the diameter of the shell. Calibres are still expressed in decimals of inches for some small arms, but millimetres are used for all modern large weapons and many small arms. Use such expressions as 11-inch gun and six-pounder only in historical references.

Ordnance experts list the modern weapon types as guns, howitzers, mortars, recoilless rifles, rockets, guided missiles, tank/antitank guns, machine guns and small arms. Small arms, defined as those with calibres of 20 mm or less (.79 inches) that can be carried in combat or for hunting, include handguns, rifles, submachine guns, shotguns and some machine guns. Mortars are muzzle-loaded shell lobbers, with a very high trajectory. Recoilless rifles, combining high power with lightness, have perforated cartridge cases so the powder gases can escape to the rear rather than cause the breech to recoil. (They are mounted in place of guns on light armoured vehicles and some tanks. Do not confuse them with rifles, the much smaller weapons carried by hand.) Rockets can be large, but also include the small variety fired by the weapon commonly called the bazooka. Anti-tank guns have very high velocities and flat trajectories for accurate, close-range aiming.

Many small arms are classed as automatic, which means they continuously load and fire a stream of bullets as long as the trigger is kept pressed. They are the machine guns, submachine guns, machine rifles and machine pistols. Some of the powder gases drive mechanisms that eject the spent casing, load a new cartridge, recock the weapon and fire it again. (Machine pistols do this, but note that the vast majority of "automatic" pistols are misnamed. They have gas-operated autoloading, but fire a single shot with each pressing of the trigger, and are more accurately called semi-automatic.)

To be classed as a machine gun, a weapon must fire rifle-size ammunition with great accuracy over a sustained period without overheating. Some have a two-person loading/firing team. Submachine guns are much lighter weapons firing pistol-size ammunition with less range and accuracy. Machine rifles and pistols can fire only in bursts, not for sustained periods.

The words **handgun** and **pistol** are interchangeable for the purposes of news stories, but the word **revolver** refers to a specific type. It is the pistol seen in westerns, with its cartridges (usually six) loaded into a revolving cylinder. In contrast, the cartridges for a semi-automatic pistol are stored in a magazine, usually in the handgrip. Unless you know the type of weapon, say handgun or pistol.

The word **cartridge** refers to the entire unit of ammunition loaded into a small arm, consisting of the casing of powder plus the projectile (bullet). The word **shell** refers to the casing in small arms, but to the projectile in artillery pieces. (Speak of a ship firing shells, but a rifle firing bullets.)

Shotguns are sized by gauge or bore. Bore is a measurement of diameter equivalent to calibre, as in .410 bore. Gauge originally meant the number of lead balls of a given diameter that would make up a pound, and so 12 gauge describes a larger barrel than 16 gauge or 20 gauge. Do not hyphenate; say a 12 gauge shotgun. The size of pellets in shotgun shells varies according to what is being hunted. The most common sizes are referred to as buckshot and birdshot. Do not automatically refer to the load used by police as buckshot, which would kill rioters rather than merely disperse them.

Rifle and pistol calibres may be expressed in decimals of inches, as in .22 and .45, or in millimetres, as in

7.62 mm and 9 mm. Do not spell out figures under 10, and note that mm does not take a hyphen or period. Use a hyphen before the word calibre (a .22-calibre rifle). In such calibres as .30-06 and .30-30, the figure after the hyphen is not a decimal. If a pistol's calibre is followed by a word describing its design or load, the word is lower-case with no hyphen: .38 special; .45 semi-automatic; .357 magnum.

In 1995, Parliament created a national firearms registry, to be administered by the Justice Department's Canadian Firearms Centre. By Dec. 31, 2000, all gun owners in Canada were required to obtain a possession licence to retain the guns they owned and buy new ones. By Dec. 31, 2002, they were to register their individual guns. Opposition from Alberta and several other provinces led to a hearing before the Supreme Court of Canada, which ruled on June 15, 2000, that the federal government was within its rights to pass the law. Substantial cost overruns led Auditor-General Sheila Fraser to criticize the government's handling of the registry in her 2002 report.

Guns N' Roses

A formal commercial name. Our usual style for the abbreviation is 'n', as in rock 'n' roll.

Gurkha

The word does not describe a nation or race. Gurkhas are Nepalese mercenaries, from any of the several ethnic groups in Nepal. Most have served in their own units in the British or Indian armies. (The name derives from an ancient Nepalese principality, Gorkha.)

guttural (not gutteral).

Guyana

Adjective and people: Guyanese. Currency: Guyana dollar. Capital: Georgetown.

It is occasionally confused with the
three Guineas in Africa. Guyana,
which was called British Guiana (note
spelling) until it became independent
in 1966, is the largest of the three
jurisdictions in the Guiana region on
the northeastern shoulder of South
America. The others are Suriname
and French Guiana. All are on the
Atlantic, not the Caribbean. About
55 per cent of the population of about
760,000 trace their ancestry to India,
and 36 per cent are black. Education is
compulsory, and the literacy rate is
about 85 per cent. Exports include
sugar, rice, bauxite, alumina, shrimps,
rum and timber.

Guyana was the scene of the
poisoning of 911 members of the
People's Temple of Rev. Jim Jones in
1978. (The drink mix used to make
the beverage in which the poison and
sedatives were dissolved was not Kool-
Aid, as is popularly believed, but
Flavor Aid, no hyphen.)

Gwillimbury
East and West, north of Toronto in
York Region and Simcoe County.

Gypsy, Gypsies
See Roma. Use lower case for
gypsy moth. Do not use the word gyp,
meaning cheat.

Gzowski, Peter

H

h words

Words beginning with h take the article **a** if the h is pronounced (a hotel), but the article **an** if the h is silent (an heir, an honest man, an honour, an hour). Some treat the h in herb and historic as silent, but we use **a** for these. See a, an.

Haagen-Dazs

This ice cream has nothing to do with Scandinavia. Originating with Pillsbury Co., it is now owned by the Swiss food conglomerate Nestlé SA.

Haakon Fiord, Nunavut.

habeas corpus

As a legal term, it does not require italics. A writ of habeas corpus directs that authorities deliver a prisoner to a court for a ruling on the legality of the detention. It is not an order that the prisoner be freed. It is often misspelled habeus. See courts.

Habs

An acceptable second reference to the Montreal Canadiens. It stands for *les Habitants*.

hackmatack

A name used by some Maritimers for the tamarack tree. See tamarack.

Haggadah and Haganah

Haggadah is the name given to the story of the Exodus recited at the beginning of the Seder dinner on Passover. It is Hebrew for "narration,"

and in a broader sense means the branch of rabbinical literature dealing with non-legal matters, such as proverbs and legends. **Haganah**, which is Hebrew for "defence," was the Jewish volunteer militia established in Palestine after the First World War and outlawed by the British. It fought in the Second World War on the Allied side, and against the Arabs in 1947. In 1948, it became the national defence force of Israel.

Hague, The, see Netherlands.

Ha Ha Bay, Ha Ha River, Lake Ha Ha

They are physical features known to English-Canadian readers by these English names, not by their French ones (Baie des Ha! Ha!, Rivière des Ha! Ha!, Lac Ha! Ha!). But use French for the community name Saint-Louis-du-Ha! Ha! Note that Saint-Louis, near the New Brunswick border, is nowhere near the other Ha Has, which are north of the St. Lawrence. The Ha Ha River flows into the lower Saguenay at Ha Ha Bay and the town of La Baie.

Haida

Both singular and plural. The Haida, of the Queen Charlotte Islands, are renowned carvers of canoes, house pillars and totem poles. They numbered only about 2,000 in the 1986 census, but are considered to be a distinct language group. See native people.

hail and hale

Hail as a verb means to call to; to proclaim (All hail, Macbeth); or to fall either as ice or as a hail-like flurry of blows. It is found in the expressions hails from (born in or lives in) and hail fellow, a pleasant companion. **Hale** means robustly healthy (hale and hearty), and as a verb means to compel to go (a variation of haul), as in hale into court. This is often misspelled as hail into court.

hailstones, hailstorm

hair's-breadth

Haiti

Adjective and people: Haitian. Currency: gourde. Capital: Port-au-Prince.

It is not a separate island. It occupies the western third of the island of Hispaniola, with the other two-thirds occupied by the Dominican Republic. (Hispaniola is one of the Greater Antilles, which form the northern boundary of the Caribbean. See West Indies.) Most of the 8.7 million people are black, but there is a powerful mixed-race minority. Standard French is the official language and is used by the educated elite, but most people speak a creole dialect, called Creole. The United States occupied Haiti from 1915 to 1934. After a period of turmoil that included several uprisings, François Duvalier was elected president in 1957 and became president for life in 1964. His son, Jean-Claude, succeeded him on his death in 1971. Jean-Claude fled the country in February of 1986. The Duvaliers' secret police were the *tontons macoutes*. The nicknames Papa Doc and Baby Doc should be used sparingly, usually only in features. After a series of governments, the country's first democratically elected president, Jean-Bertrand Aristide, a leftist priest, was elected in December of 1990, inaugurated in February,

1991, and ousted in a coup in September, 1991. The Organization of American States imposed a trade embargo as part of an effort to force his reinstatement. In 1994, the U.S. military deposed the junta that had staged the coup, and Aristide briefly resumed the presidency. Prevented by Haitian law from running again until 2000, he made way for political ally René Preval after an election in late 1995. Aristide won the 2000 presidential election, amid continuing political turmoil.

halcyon days

Any calm and peaceful time. Literally, they are the seven days before and seven days after the winter solstice, when the legendary bird the halcyon was supposed to calm the seas so it could breed on the water. The expression is overused, often misused to indicate wealth, and often misspelled halycon.

half-and-half

half-breed

Do not use this to refer to humans. If the issue is relevant, specify the races of the parents, or use the expression **of mixed race**. Avoid such expressions as "part Indian" and "part black" if the reader might interpret an implication that white is the normal or the ideal.

half-mast

Use in all cases to describe the lowering of the flag to mark a person's death. The use of half-staff for mourning on land is the American convention, not the Canadian one. From Canadian Heritage's booklet Flag Etiquette in Canada: "The flag is brought to the half-mast position by first raising it to the top of the mast and then immediately lowering it slowly to the half-mast position."

half section
An expression used mainly in Western Canada for 320 acres. A section is one square mile, 640 acres.

half sole, the noun. The verb is half-sole.

half words
One word: halfback, halfpenny, halftime, halfway.
Hyphenated: half-baked, half-brother, half-caste, half-crown, half-empty (before the noun), half-full (before the noun), half-hearted, half-hour, half-life, half-mast, half-pint (the condescending name and adjective and the measure), half-sister, half-step, half-track.
Two words: half dollar, half empty (after the noun), half full (after the noun), half gainer, half hitch, half moon, half nelson, half note, half section, half wit.

Hall commission
Upper-case the word commission only when using the formal title, the Royal Commission on Health Services. Mr. Justice Emmett Hall's federal report in 1964 recommended universal medical, dental and drug benefits. A national insurance plan, limited to doctors' services, was approved in 1968.

hallelujah

Halley's comet
Lower-case comet. Edmond Halley wasn't the first to see it; he was the first to declare that past sightings were of the same periodic comet. It returns approximately every 76 years, and last appeared in 1986.

Hall of Fame
If it refers to a specific Hall of Fame, upper-case even when the full proper name isn't used, and upper-case the Hall standing alone in subsequent references.

Halloween

halvah

Hamelin, Pied Piper of

Hamtramck, a Detroit suburb.

Handel, George Frederick
He anglicized his names, from Georg Friedrich Haendel.

handfuls

handgun, see guns and calibres.

handlebar

handicapped, see disabled.

handmade

hand-me-down

handout, the noun. The verb is hand out.

hand-to-hand
Adjective, as in hand-to-hand fighting. But for the adverb, say fighting hand to hand.

hand-to-mouth
Adjective, as in a hand-to-mouth existence. For the adverb, say living hand to mouth.

hangar (for aircraft).

hangover

Hanlan
Hanlan's Point (not Hanlon's) on Toronto's Centre Island is named for world champion oarsman Edward (Ned) Hanlan.

Hansard
Hansard is acceptable as the name for the verbatim record of proceedings in Parliament or in legislatures. Note, however, that it is not the official name in Ottawa or in some provinces. (The name derives from the printing firm of Luke Hansard and his son, Thomas, which began printing Britain's parliamentary proceedings in 1774.) In Ottawa, the blues (lower-case) are the daily galley proofs, which are vetted by MPs for mistakes of sense and grammar before the printing of the official version, titled *House of Commons Debates: Official Reports.*

Hantzsch River, Nunavut.

Hanukkah

Happy Valley-Goose Bay, Nfld.
In Labrador, at the western end of Hamilton Inlet. Speak of the separate communities in stories dealing with events before their amalgamation in 1974. In stories about the airport only, say Goose Bay.

hara-kiri
Describe it as ceremonial suicide to avoid capture or dishonour. It did not involve stabbing or plunging. A short sword was used to cut the abdomen from left to right and then upward.

harass

harbour
Use this spelling except when the word appears in proper U.S. names.

harebrained (not hair).

Hare Krishnas
This name is acceptable even in first reference to the International Society for Krishna Consciousness, and to its members. Their orange robes, shaved heads, constant chanting in praise of Krishna, a Hindu god, and even their insistent begging are characteristics of this strict monastic order. Even stories featuring criticism of the movement's practices or financial affairs should contain no hint of ridicule or contempt. The order was founded in 1965 in New York by A. C. Bhaktivendanta Swami Prabhupada, but now is international in scope. They should not be confused with Buddhist monks, who are similar in appearance.

hark back
Not harken or hearken.

HarperCollins, HarperFlamingo (one word).

Harper's Magazine

Harrington Lake
This is the name of the summer home of Canada's prime ministers, but note that the name of the Quebec lake itself has been changed to Lac Mosseau.

Harrods, no apostrophe.

Harrogate, England.

Hart House, University of Toronto.
Named for Hart Massey, as is Toronto's Massey Hall. He was the father of Chester D. and grandfather of Vincent and Raymond.

Hartland Bridge
Crosses the Saint John River at Hartland, N.B. It is the world's longest covered bridge, at 390.75 metres (1,282 feet).

Hart Memorial Trophy

Note the word Memorial in the official name, although it may be referred to by its more common name, the Hart Trophy. For the NHL's most valuable player. Named for Cecil Hart, a former Canadiens manager-coach, donated by his father in 1923.

Hasidim, Hasidic

Hasty P's

The Hastings and Prince Edward Regiment.

hat trick

It may be used informally for any triple accomplishment. In hockey and soccer, it means three goals in a game. In cricket, where the term originated, it refers to a bowler taking wickets on three successive balls. Opinions differ on the meaning. The top contenders are that any bowler who accomplished this was entitled to a new hat at club expense, or that a hat was passed for contributions to reward him.

Hawaiian

Hawker Siddeley Canada Inc.

No hyphen.

Hayden Formula

Upper-case. Named for Senator Salter Hayden. Since 1969, it has allowed a Senate committee to study important bills that have not yet been passed by the Commons.

Haydn, Franz Joseph

hazel

H-bomb

headlines

A book of this type can outline the particulars of Globe headline style, but a broader examination of the arcane art of writing heads is beyond its scope. Various journalism texts lay down general rules and suggest techniques, but it is only in the crucible of day-to-day desk work, under time pressure and with instant acceptance or rejection of our efforts by finicky slot editors, that we begin to develop the art of writing great headlines that entice readers to the story while reflecting, indeed defining, the personality and values of our newspaper.

One general guideline worth mentioning is that a good headline is single-minded, dealing only with the main thread of the story. If there is space to fill, it normally should be used for elaboration or details of this angle, not to introduce a second one that might give readers the impression that the story is dauntingly complex. The place to introduce a second angle or detailed elaboration is the deck, the auxiliary line or lines in smaller type under the main head.

Here are some particular points about Globe headlines:

We use **upper case** for the first word of the first line of the head or deck, for proper names, for titles standing for an individual, and for the first word of a sentence within the head (NDP challenges Finance Minister: Ask the people).

Punctuation is kept to a minimum; we try to choose wording that does not require punctuation in the middle of a line. We do not use periods at the end of a head, but we follow the normal rules for use of commas and semi-colons. See punctuation. Exclamation points retain their effect only if used sparingly.

We may use **figures** for numerals under 10 if this is required for fit. The **per cent** symbol is allowed, but only after a numeral. Similarly, we never use the **dollar** symbol without a numeral. Use the **cents** symbol only if there is no alternative in very short headlines. Use the **ampersand** only if it is part of a proper name.

News headlines must have **both**

subject and verb. We do not use such lines as Accuses minister of dishonesty. Under extreme space pressure we may use the passive, Minister called corrupt, but in general the reader (and the minister) deserve the source of the charge. Witness the different tone of Rival calls minister corrupt, Activist calls minister corrupt, Judge calls minister corrupt, PM calls minister corrupt. The requirement for a verb is waived in label headlines on **news features** (Romania's secret nightmare).

Verbs are usually in the **present tense**. However, use the past or future when elements in the headline have different times, or when the story is not contemporary (Consulted Bush on NATO cuts, PM says; Stalin had plans to violate Nazi pact). For the future tense, we generally use the infinitive (PM to visit Germany), except when a statement is attributed (Will visit Germany, PM says).

We prefer the **active** voice to the passive, but we do not undertake elaborate contortions to avoid a passive if it is the most direct and conversational way of conveying the thought.

If a head has more than one line, a transitive verb may be **split** from its object if the headline is clear and cursive (PM to announce/ date for election). Splits that separate adjective from noun (PM gives tentative/ date for election) and adverb from verb or adjective are usually less cursive, but are allowed if there is no more elegant alternative and no confusion. Splitting a preposition from its object is almost always jarring, particularly in the case of short prepositions (of, at etc.), and is discouraged in all but the shortest of headlines.

Words that can be **more than one part of speech** are booby traps for the unwary headwriter, and the confusion they create is made even worse by splits (Steady decline/ in productivity/ gains baffles/ world experts).

We do not repeat words in headlines, and also make an effort to avoid using echo words in nearby heads.

Unfamiliar names, abbreviations and acronyms in headlines drive readers away from a story. It is far better to replace an unfamiliar specific term with a generic one. Instead of Abbott, say B.C. minister. Instead of ICAO, say aviation body or some such.

Abbreviate B.C. and PEI as a matter of course in headlines. Other provinces with initials may be abbreviated as adjectives (N.B. minister), but only rarely as nouns, if space is extremely limited (Changes by N.B. pose new challenge to Meech). We do not use provincial abbreviations that are not initials (Ont., Que. etc.), but allow Sask. or Nfld. if the full name standing alone will not fit on one line of a single-column head. See provinces. We never use abbreviated, often insulting nicknames for **national groups** (Brits, Japs, Yanks).

We do not use **honorifics** in headlines, but we may use royal titles (Prince Andrew) if required for clarity.

We normally use only the **surname**, but occasionally add the given name if this is how a person is known to the public, or if there is a chance of confusion with another person (Clifford Olson denied parole; Robert Kennedy knew of CIA link).

We do not use **obscure words** or ungrammatical constructions to save space in headlines (Wilson to ink bill upping taxes, MP avers).

Puns should be used sparingly, only when they are clever, clear and dead-on, and only when the subject matter is suitable for levity. **Rhyme** and **alliteration** should also be used sparingly, and only for lighter stories.

head of state, government

Reserve the term **head of state** for presidents and monarchs. Prime ministers are **heads of government**. In stories about international meetings, the word **leaders** covers both. Otherwise, we must say heads of state and heads of government, despite the awkwardness. Canada's governor-general represents the head of state (the Queen) in Canada, and is best referred to as the Queen's representative.

head-on

headquarters

The spelling is the same for both singular and plural. If we are speaking of only one, use singular pronouns and verbs (this headquarters is).

Health and Human Services, Department of.

It is the second-largest U.S. federal department, after Defence. The name dates from 1979, when education was removed from the Department of Health, Education and Welfare and made a separate department.

heavy water

It is deuterium oxide, which closely resembles water and occurs naturally in it (at levels of .014 per cent). In pure form, it freezes at 3.8 C and boils at 101.4. It is toxic only in high concentrations. It is used as a moderator (to slow down the neutrons) in some nuclear reactors. (Candu stands for Canadian deuterium uranium. Other designs use graphite or beryllium as moderators.) Heavy water is also used as a source of deuterium and its compounds. The term heavy water may also be encountered used loosely to refer to water containing tritium or heavy isotopes of oxygen.

hegemony

Heidelberg

heights

In giving heights of human beings, use feet and inches followed by the metric in brackets. For airplane altitudes, use feet, and add the metric equivalent only if relevant. See measurement.

heinous

Heligoland, the North Sea island.

Hells Angels (no apostrophe).

Helms-Burton act

Note the lower-case a. The formal name for the 1996 U.S. law that codified a trade and travel embargo against Cuba is the Cuban Liberty and Democratic Solidarity Act. The colloquial name derives from its Republican sponsors, Senator Jesse Helms and Representative Dan Burton. Canada and other affected countries criticized provisions in the law that penalized non-U.S.-based businesses for dealing with Cuba.

hemoglobin, hemophilia, hemorrhage. Not haem-. In most cases, replace hemorrhage with bleeding, bleed.

heparin, lower-case.

herculean

Lower-case for possessing or requiring great strength. Upper-case Herculean for pertaining to Hercules.

here

This word has the potential to confuse and inconvenience readers when used in copy to refer to the placeline at the top of the story. We serve readers better by repeating the name, or using such terms as "in the Austrian capital." Take care that the writer is referring to the placelined city and not the country in general.

Heritage
The federal Department of Canadian Heritage, which Prime Minister Kim Campbell created in 1993 by combining much of three former departments – Communications, Secretary of State, and Multiculturalism and Citizenship – should not be referred to as Heritage Canada. This risks confusion with the Heritage Canada Foundation, a non-governmental foundation active since the early seventies. In informal references or lists of departments, the federal department may be referred to as Canadian Heritage or simply Heritage (The Prime Minister is considering a cabinet shuffle involving Finance, Defence, Environment and Heritage).

Heritage Highways
Upper-case for the system of historical tourist routes in Ontario and Quebec.

heroes

heyday

hiccupped

hideout (noun).

hieroglyphics

high commissioner
The title of ambassadors exchanged by Commonwealth countries. Upper-case only as a title before a name, not as a regular noun (the Australian high commissioner).

highfalutin

high flier

high jinks

high jump

high-rise

high seas, see territorial waters.

highsticking

High Tor, Sask.

Highway, Tomson

hijab
Hijab has two meanings, related to each other. The hijab is the loose-fitting fabric (sometimes referred to as a head scarf or head covering) worn in public by some Muslim women to cover the head neck and shoulders. Hijab (no the) is the Islamic practice of obeying the Koran's rules on physical modesty, which have been widely interpreted in various countries and sects. Most orthodox Muslims say women and men alike should cover their head, and also their body as far as the wrists and ankles. Some say women's hair should be covered, and others say the head scarf should also drape across the face, or that a separate face veil is required. Liberal Western Muslims say they are required to dress and act in a manner that would be considered modest in the society in which they live. All these practices may be described as the observance of hijab.
It is acceptable to refer to the hijab, but clarity may dictate referring specifically to an Islamic head scarf, veil, robe and so on. For added colour we could add the local name, but be aware that these vary by country. The combination of coverings is called the abaya in most Arab countries, but it is the chador in Iran and the ohrni in Trinidad, for example.
See Islam.

hijack

hike
Canadian idiom for an increase in wages or prices, acceptable in headlines and less formal stories.

Hill, the

Upper-case referring to Parliament Hill.

Himalaya

Asia's great mountain system, running from northwestern Pakistan across northern India to Tibet, Nepal, Sikkim and Bhutan, is properly called the Himalaya, which means "home of snow" in Sanskrit. For the purpose of news stories the mountains may be called the Himalayas, but they cannot be called a mountain range. The Himalayan system, 2,550 kilometres long and up to 240 kilometres broad, has three parallel ranges that run its entire length (the Great Himalaya, the Lesser Himalaya and the Siwalik Range) and a fourth range, the Karakoram, in the northwest. Everest is in the Great Himalaya, and its nearest rival, K2, is in the Karakoram Range. See K2.

Hindi

The name refers both to the principal language group of northern India and to its written form, the official language of India. It is written in the Devanagari (Sanskrit) script.

Hinduism

It may be described as a religion, but it is more, the all-embracing culture of the Hindus, and is also less, lacking the doctrinaire centralism of other major faiths. As a religion it has no recorded beginning or founder, no central authority, no dogma and no hierarchy. There is a basic scripture, the Veda, believed to date from 1500 BC, and other works described as Vedic—the Brahmanas, Aranyakas and Upanishads. But Hinduism tolerates a wide range of beliefs, from near-monotheism to pantheism to animism, from abstract philosophy to physical magic, from severe asceticism to sensual cults, and considers none of these to be essential.

The overriding common belief is in the concept of Brahman, the essential self of all things, the All and One. There is also a common belief in a continuous cycle of transmigration of souls, with escape to become one with the Brahman finally achieved through duty, devotion and knowledge. (Yoga and meditation are two of the methods of acquiring knowledge.) The concept of Brahman is personified by many as the all-pervading god Brahma. Most would recognize the Trimurti, a sort of trinity with Brahma in the background combined with the gods Shiva and Vishnu, but this does not rule out the countless other gods of popular Hinduism. Devout Hindus respect all life, and many carry this through to vegetarianism. Most Hindus revere the cow, often referring to it as Go-Mata—the mother, or provider of milk and its byproducts, important to the early agricultural society. Even Hindus who eat other kinds of meat usually do not eat beef, and the tanning of cowhide is considered an occupation for people of low caste. Despite official disavowals, the caste system persists in modern Indian society, with the upper-caste Brahmin class demanding and accorded universal respect.

hippopotamus

The plural is hippos or, if we must, hippopotamuses.

Hispaniola

Between Cuba and Puerto Rico, it is shared by the Dominican Republic and Haiti. It is the second-largest island in the West Indies, after Cuba, and one of the Greater Antilles. See West Indies.

historic and historical

Historic means important, famous, significant. **Historical** means pertaining to history or the past, or detailed and accurate as opposed to legend, as in a historical account. The place where Archduke Franz

Ferdinand was assassinated might be called a historic site, but the location of the first distillery in Upper Canada is merely a historical one.

historical periods, centuries, decades etc. See capitalization.

hitchhike, hitchhiker

Hitler, Adolf

HIV
It means human immunodeficiency virus; thus, adding the word virus (the HIV virus) is redundant. In most references, the term AIDS virus is better. See AIDS.

HMCS
It means Her Majesty's Canadian Ship, so it must not be preceded by the article **the**. Say HMCS Haida. Use of HMCS, HMS, USS etc. is not mandatory if the nature of the ship is otherwise well established, as in the Canadian destroyer Haida, the U.S. carrier Coral Sea. In second reference, dropping the article is customary; say Haida.

Hnatyshyn, Ramon

hoard and horde
Hoard means to gather and store, and as a noun means that which has been gathered, as in a pirate's hoard. A **horde** is a multitude, particularly of people. It also means a nomadic tribe, as in the Mongol hordes.

hoarding, a temporary fence.

hobnob

Hobson's choice
It is not a difficult decision, or the lesser of two evils. It means no choice at all, take it or leave it. Hobson was a Cambridge liveryman who rested his horses by observing strict rotation in renting them out. Renters were

always obliged to take the one in the first stall.

Hodgkin's disease

hoi polloi
A jocular or dismissive term for all those not in the elite – the common herd, the great unwashed. Although it is colloquial to place "the" in front of it, be aware that "hoi" means "the" in Greek, and "polloi" means many. Use "the" if it would sound idiomatically awkward to do otherwise: He appealed to the hoi polloi to give him their blessing. In more general references, the article may be unnecessary: He has no truck with hoi polloi.

hoist with (or by) one's own petard
To be injured by one's own actions. Since the petard is an explosive device, not a lance or skewer, avoid the corruption "hoist on one's own petard" except in direct quotes.

holdup, noun and adjective. The verb is **hold up**.

holidays
Upper-case the formal names of religious and civic holidays, feast days and fast periods, and the names given to days, weeks and months for the purpose of education, fundraising etc., such as Apple Day, Heart Month, the Year of the Child. But lower-case nomination day, election day, payday etc. See capitalization.
Canada's national statutory holidays are New Year's Day, Good Friday, Easter Monday, Victoria Day (the Monday before May 25, which in Quebec is called Dollard des Ormeaux Day), Canada Day (July 1), Labour Day (first Monday in September), Thanksgiving Day (second Monday in October), Remembrance Day (Nov. 11) and Christmas Day. In addition, Boxing Day is observed in the provinces, although it does not

always restrict retail sales, and a civic holiday is observed on the first Monday in August under various names in Alberta (Heritage Day), Manitoba, Ontario (Simcoe Day), the Northwest Territories and Saskatchewan (Heritage Day). Newfoundland and Labrador, where July 1 is called Memorial Day, also celebrates Discovery Day (the Monday closest to June 24), St. Patrick's Day, St. George's Day and Orangemen's Day. Quebec observes its Fête Nationale on June 24 (also referred to as St. Jean Baptiste Day), and grants a day off work on the last Monday in June. Yukon has Discovery Day, Aug. 17. Major U.S. holidays in addition to those mentioned include Martin Luther King, Jr.'s birthday (Monday closest to Jan. 15), Washington's birthday (Monday closest to Feb. 22), Memorial Day (Monday closest to May 30), Independence Day (July 4), Election Day (first Tuesday after the first Monday in November) and Thanksgiving (fourth Thursday in November).

Holland Marsh, Ont.

This rich market-garden region south of Lake Simcoe did not, as many suppose, take its name from the Dutch immigrants who drained and developed it. The former swampy marsh, the Holland River and the community of Holland Landing, at the head of Yonge Street, were named much earlier, after prominent surveyor Samuel Holland, c.1728-1801, who surveyed the Loyalist settlements and was Britain's surveyor-general for the northern part of North America.

Holocaust

Upper-case when referring to Nazi genocide.

Holt Renfrew

The store, and the Holt Renfrew Centre. But note the comma in Holt, Renfrew & Co. Ltd.

Holy Land

Holy See

home and house

Home is where the heart is, be it a house, an apartment, a tent, an institution, or even a country or region. A house is a type of building. In stories dealing with physical property, as in sales, construction, destruction, expropriation, use house for single-family or row houses.

homeowner, but **home-owning**.

hometown, noun and adjective.

homicide

Homicide is the killing of another person, and a homicide is a killing. In types of writing too technical for news stories, a homicide is also the person who **commits** the act. But a homicide is never the victim. Say it is the city's 50th homicide of the year (meaning the killing), but never that he (the victim) is the 50th homicide.

Also note that not all homicides are murder. See courts.

homosexual, see gay.

Honduras

Adjective and people: Honduran. Currency: lempira. Capital: Tegucigalpa.

It is the most mountainous country in Central America, with only a few low-lying areas in river valleys and coastal plains, and is the second-largest after its southern neighbour, Nicaragua. It has a long northern coast on the Caribbean, but a very short one on the Pacific side, on the Gulf of Fonseca. About 90 per cent of its 6.5 million people are mestizo, people who are mostly Indian with some European (Spanish) in their makeup, and there are small minorities of whites, blacks and Indians (Miskito, Payas and

Xicaques). People of mixed Miskito and black makeup are called Sambos, but we should avoid this term. Most Hondurans live on small subsistence farms. Exports include bananas, coffee, timber, meat, sugar and cotton. Hurricane Mitch killed 6,000 people in 1998 and caused $1-billion (U.S.) in damage.

Hong Kong, see China.

honorifics

The courtesy titles Mr., Mrs., Ms. etc. are used in second reference to all persons 16 and older. (In first reference, use the given name or at least two initials.)

Plural honorifics appear awkward and stilted; if only a few names are involved, it is better to repeat the honorific (Mr. Brown, Mr. White and Mr. Green). If a sentence contains a very long list of names and cannot be recast, use the plurals Messrs., Mses., Drs. and Profs.

In view of the established practice in these fields, the **sports, arts and books sections** do not use the standard honorifics. Specialized honorifics that are more in the nature of job descriptions, such as Dr., Prof., Rev., Mr. Justice and Judge, are used in first reference along with the given name in these sections; thereafter, only the surname is used. However, if a husband and wife figure in the same story, the honorifics Mr. and Mrs. may be the most efficient way of keeping them straight in subsequent references.

Entertainment, arts and sports figures get honorifics whenever they appear in the news pages.

The fashion section indicates the great-figure status of top designers by using surnames without honorifics (Givenchy etc.), but uses honorifics for other persons, such as show organizers, store owners etc.

In the news section, significant figures in history and the arts are often referred to by a single name, such as Churchill, Hitler, Gandhi, Picasso, Pasteur. In some cases their given names are not needed even in first reference, and no honorific is used in second reference. For Canada, omit the honorifics for prime ministers from Confederation to Mackenzie King, for Fathers of Confederation, for explorers, for prominent colonial administrators, and for sports and arts figures prominent before the Second World War. However, an honorific might be necessary if a contemporary has been granted one in the same story. (Do not write King and Mr. Pearson.)

Children 15 and under are called by their first names in second reference. An exception might be a precocious 15-year-old engaged in an activity on an equal footing with adults, such as appearing as one of several speakers at a political convention. Conversely, it is sometimes necessary to call adults by their first names in second reference, if a story is dealing with two or more relatives of the same sex. A feature about the political Axworthy brothers, for example, could refer to Lloyd and Tom whenever there is a chance of confusion. There is no need to repeat the surname each time in such cases.

For women, the standard honorific is Ms., unless we know that a particular woman prefers and uses Mrs. or Miss.

The honorific Miss is used occasionally if a long-established stage name appears in the news pages, such as Miss Hepburn, Miss Taylor. This is a judgment call.

Use the title **Dr.** for all persons with an earned doctorate, be it in medicine, dentistry or history, unless the story is not about the person's professional capacity and the subject prefers that the title not be used in such contexts. Reporters should determine the subject's preference. Outside the professional context, we should not create the impression that a person is a medical doctor if this is not the case. Do not use Dr. for people with only honorary degrees. The title is often omitted in first reference, particularly if there is a description that indicates the doctorate, such as heart surgeon Mary Smith or paleontologist John Smith. They would be Dr. Smith in second reference. In first reference, Dr. and Prof. are abbreviated if used as honorifics, but are spelled out, lowercase, if they are used as descriptions, as in Vancouver doctor Peter Black, or history professor Alice White. If a person with a non-medical doctorate is expounding on medical matters, such as the benefits of vitamin C, specify the nature of the degree. In stories about mental treatment, differentiate between psychiatrists, who are MDs with an added specialty, and people with a PhD in psychology.

Use the English honorifics only, not M., Mlle, Herr etc. If such honorifics appear in direct quotes, follow the spelling custom of the language concerned. In French honorifics, for example, there is no period if the last letter of the honorific and the abbreviation are the same.

We do not use the **royal** honorifics HM, HRH etc. Simply say the Queen, Prince Charles. In second reference, members of the immediate Royal Family, with the exception of the Queen, are referred to either by their given names (Philip, Charles) or by their titles (the Duke, the Prince), but not both.

For duke or duchess, which may be a royal rank but is also the highest non-royal one, say the duke in second reference, using upper case only if the rank is royal. Lord is now commonly used in second reference to the next British ranks of marquess, earl, viscount and baron. For territorial titles, drop the "of" in second reference, as in the Marquess of Queensberry, Lord Queensberry. If only the rank is used, make it lower-case

(the earl said). The younger sons of dukes and marquesses attach Lord to their name, as in Lord Peter Wimsey, Lord Peter. Life peers choose their own names, but generally attach Lord to their surname, as in Lord Olivier. In second reference to knights and dames, say Sir Alec, Dame Wendy. In the arts and sports sections, however, we use surnames in second reference to peers, knights and dames (Olivier, Hiller).

Judges are called in first reference either Judge or Mr. Justice (Madam Justice), depending on the level of court, but we use the title Judge for all of them in second reference. The exceptions are chief justices at both the federal and provincial levels, who are called Chief Justice Smith etc. in second reference. Stories on both the Federal Court and the Federal Court of Appeal should use Mr. Justice or Madam Justice in first reference. Stories on the Tax Court of Canada should use Judge in first reference (or Chief Judge, if that's who is being mentioned). Retired judges (on commissions, in private life) are Mr. or Ms. on second reference. First reference to judges of the U.S. Supreme Court is Justice, not Mr. Justice or Madam Justice.

We do not use the **political** honorifics Rt. Hon. and Hon. Political officeholders and appointees in Canada or any other country become Mr., Ms. or Mrs. in second reference, or Dr. if they continue to use that title themselves in their political careers. We do not repeat the title, unless the second reference is far down in the story and the person is obscure. Say Mr. Chrétien, Mr. Bush and Ms. Fraser, not Prime Minister Chrétien, President Bush and Senator Fraser.

For the titles of clergy, see religious titles. For military and police titles, see ranks.

honoris causa
It means for the sake of honour, and cannot be pluralized.

honour

But drop the u for **honorarium, honorary, honoree, honorific**.

hoodoo

Lower-case, except for Hoodoo Valley and Hoodoo Lake, B.C. Found in several badland areas of the Canadian and American West, hoodoos are columns of earth formed by erosion, usually topped by a large boulder.

hoopla

hooves, not hoofs.

hopeful

As a noun meaning a person, it should be used sparingly, largely confined to the sense of a young person hoping to succeed or to be discovered. It is slightly precious when it refers to political candidates etc.

hopefully

It means in a hopeful manner, as in he held out his bowl hopefully. Do not use it to mean I hope, I am hopeful that, it is hoped, let us hope.

Hornepayne, Ont.

hors d'oeuvre

An appetizer or appetizers. The spelling does not change for the plural.

horsefly

horse race

hosanna

host

It is a noun. It should not be used as a verb in news stories, as in host a conference. It grates on the ear of most readers, and its connotation of hospitality does not really apply to the convening or organizing of meetings.

However, in the context of show business, and especially television talk shows, most well-educated readers would accept that host as a verb has become part of the language, especially in the passive form, hosted by. Purists will still seek to avoid it in entertainment stories, but this should not be done at the expense of clarity and simplicity. See author, emcee.

hostage crisis

Use this term, lower-case, for the taking of the U.S. Embassy in Tehran by Iranian militants on Nov. 4, 1979, and the imprisonment of 66 members of its diplomatic and military staff. Fourteen were released relatively early, but the other 52 were held until Jan. 20, 1981, minutes after Ronald Reagan assumed the presidency. Negotiations had been conducted with Algerian help. The crisis discredited Jimmy Carter, and an unsuccessful military rescue attempt on April 25, 1980, cost the lives of eight servicemen and resulted in the resignation of Secretary of State Cyrus Vance. The militants had stormed the embassy two weeks after Mr. Carter's decision to allow the former shah into the United States for medical treatment.

Hot Line, the

Upper-case when referring to the emergency link between the White House and the Kremlin, set up in 1963. Note that it was not a telephone line, but a telegraph and radio link.

house, see home.

House, the

Upper-case in second reference to the Commons or to a provincial legislative chamber. Upper-case House Leader, the three House leaders. Avoid the expression "the lower house" in reference to the Commons, but if it appears in a direct quote, make it lower-case.

housebroken

housefly

House of Assembly

The Newfoundland and Labrador legislature. Its members are MHAs. See legislature.

House of Lords

This chamber of the British Parliament can delay passage of money bills from the Commons by a month, and other bills by up to a year, and has provided a valued forum for second-look debates. Its members are divided into the Lords Temporal (the hereditary dukes, marquesses, earls, viscounts and barons, the persons made life peers, and the trial and appeal judges of the Supreme Court, who are known as the law lords and act as the country's highest court of appeal) and the Lords Spiritual (the two archbishops—Canterbury and York—the bishops of London, Durham and Winchester, and 21 other bishops holding English, not British, sees). Most of the 751 hereditary peers were stripped of their right to vote in 1999, under a plan which Prime Minister Tony Blair's Labour Party said would make the Lords "more representative and democratic." Ninety-two hereditary peers retained their vote, but are expected to lose it in the final stage of reform. In 2003, there were 610 life peers. The Labour government was divided over whether to make the House of Lords an elected body rather than an appointed one, as it has been.

Hovercraft

Upper-case. A trade name for a brand of air-cushion vehicle.

howitzer

A type of cannon with a higher trajectory and a lower muzzle velocity than a gun. See guns and calibres.

howls of protest

Avoid using this phrase in news stories. Reporting that a certain development "drew howls of protest" from teachers, nurses, doctors, the labour movement, provincial governments, seniors groups and so on is classic journalese. The hackneyed, habitual phrase reflexively brands legitimate protests as the caterwauling of brats or dumb animals, and may influence readers' perceptions accordingly.

hubbub

Hudson Bay

The body of water, and Hudson Bay Mining and Smelting Co. Ltd. But **Hudson's Bay Co.**, Hudson's Bay Centre. Note that Hudson Bay is not a bay, of either the Atlantic or Arctic oceans. It is classed as a sea (an epicontinental one), connected to the Atlantic by Hudson Strait and to the Arctic by Foxe Channel.

Hull

No longer exists as a separate city. See Gatineau.

Humane Society

Upper-case, even if the proper name of the group referred to in first reference was the Society for the Prevention of Cruelty to Animals.

Hummingbird Centre for the Performing Arts

The new name given to Toronto's O'Keefe Centre in 1996, after a large donation made by Toronto software company Hummingbird Communications Ltd.

hummus

humour

But drop the u for **humoresque, humorist, humorous**.

Hungary

Adjective and people: Hungarian. Currency: forint. Capital: Budapest.

When it is necessary to specify ethnic differences, the majority Hungarian stock should be called Magyars. The population of about 10 million also contains minority populations of Germans, Slovaks, Serbs, Croats and Romanians. Hungary's southern curve is cradled by Yugoslavia and Romania, but it is not considered to be on the Balkan Peninsula. The national language, which may be called Hungarian, is distinctive in Europe—it is not Slavic, Germanic or Romance—but it is considered to be distantly related to Finnish and Estonian. From 1867 until the end of the First World War, Hungary was part of Austria-Hungary, also called the Austro-Hungarian Empire. It joined NATO in 1999, and in 2002 was invited to join the European Union, perhaps within a year.

See NATO, Warsaw Pact.

Hungry Thirties, the

Huron

The Huron Indians of the 1600s should not be referred to as a tribe. They were a very loose confederation of agricultural villages in what is now Southern Ontario, possibly a mixture of several strains and commonly considered to have been roughly divided into four groups.

Huronia

The area of south-central Ontario once occupied by Huron villages, between Georgian Bay and Nottawasaga Bay on the west, and Lakes Simcoe and Couchiching on the east.

hurricane

A severe cyclonic storm originating in the Caribbean and tropical Atlantic. In the Pacific, they are called typhoons. See weather. Use lower case, even when accompanied by a person's name, as in hurricane Ronald. But upper-case the single-engine fighter in the Battle of Britain. Properly called the Hurricane X, it was manufactured in Fort William, now part of Thunder Bay.

hurting

Do not use as a synonym for suffer, as in He looks as though he's hurting. Say in pain, in agony etc.

husky

Lower-case. This term may be used for any working sled dog if the breed is mixed, unknown or irrelevant, but be aware that it is included in the proper name of only one of the four recognized breeds of northern dog, the Siberian husky. The others, all upper-case, are the Eskimo, the malamute and the Samoyed. (The Mahlemut are a group of Inuit in Alaska, and the Samoyed are a Siberian group. The Eskimo breed is thought to have originated in Labrador and Greenland.) Since there are several differences, always specify the breed in stories about dog shows, sales, breeders. The Inuk word for a sled dog is *qimmik*.

Husqvarna

Maker of chain saws, sewing machines, firearms.

Hussein, Saddam

Use the Westernized form Mr. Hussein, not Saddam, in second reference to the deposed Iraqi ruler.

Hutterites

There is no need to use their formal name, the Hutterian Brethren. They are a German-speaking Protestant sect that originated in the mid-1500s as a branch of the Swiss Anabaptist movement, and take their name from the martyred Jacob Hutter. They are pacifists, and believe in

communal ownership, but in many
details, such as dress and use of
automobiles, some colonies are more
traditional than others. Their colonies
are found in Alberta, Manitoba,
Saskatchewan and South Dakota.

hydroelectric, hydroelectricity
For the sake of accuracy, prefer the
word power as the generic term. In
Ontario, where the word hydro is
widely used, the bulk of electricity is
now generated by other means.

Hydro-Québec

hyper and hypo
Hyper means above, high, excess,
as in hypertension. **Hypo** means
below, low, insufficient, as in
hypothermia, hypoglycemia. They are
so alike that readers have to think
twice, which should make us think
twice about using them. Prefer high
blood pressure, low blood sugar etc.

hyperbole
It does not refer to just any type of
excessive language or exaggeration. It
is the type clearly not intended to be
taken literally, as in This book weighs
a ton.

hyphen, see punctuation.

hypocrisy

Hyundai Auto Canada Inc.
The manufacturing and sales
company. It and Hyundai Canada
Inc., which is essentially a parts
operation, are both subsidiaries of
Hyundai Motor Co., of South Korea.
It in turn is owned by Hyundai Corp.

I

I-beam

ice

    One word: iceberg, iceboat, icebound, icebox, icebreaker, icehouse, iceman. **Two words**: ice age, ice bag, ice cap, ice cream, ice field, ice pack, ice pick.

ice age

    Lower-case. There have been several of them, the last of which ended about 8,000 years ago, or is possibly still ending. (But upper-case Stone Age etc.; see capitalization.)

Iceland

    Adjective: Icelandic. People: Icelanders. Currency: krona (plural kronur). Capital: Reykjavik.

    The Althing is the world's oldest parliament, established in 930. Iceland, under the Danes since 1380, became fully self-governing in 1918, and an independent republic in 1944. It is geologically very young, still so volcanically active that many homes use geothermal heat. The island of Heimaey had to be evacuated in 1973 when Helgafell erupted, and the new island of Surtsey is still being formed, having emerged from the sea in 1963. The population of about 280,000 is heavily dependent on the sea, with fish accounting for two-thirds of exports. The "cod war" with Britain over Iceland's insistence on control within 200 miles of its coast culminated in a brief break in diplomatic relations in 1976. Iceland's most northerly point touches the Arctic circle.

iceworm

    Robert W. Service's *Ballad of the Ice-Worm Cocktail* was about a piece of dyed spaghetti with painted eyes, but iceworms are not mythical. There are at least three creatures in Canada (a worm, a caterpillar and a slim, wingless insect) that live in snow and melting ice and are referred to as iceworms.

idiosyncrasy

Iditarod

    The world's longest sled-dog race, a little more than 1,800 kilometres from Anchorage to Nome, Alaska. It may be called the Iditarod, although its official name is the Iditarod Trail Sled Dog Race. (The Yukon Quest, from Whitehorse to Fairbanks, is shorter, at about 1,600 kilometres, but is considered more gruelling because it passes through fewer villages.)

idle

    As a verb it is primarily intransitive, meaning to be lazy and unproductive. Use it transitively only in reference to engines running in neutral (She idled her car) or in the expression He idled away the time. Do not use it in the sense of make idle, as in a strike idling a plant, ships etc.

idyll

i.e.

    For *id est*. In news stories, we use it only in direct quotes. Otherwise, say "that is."

if and whether

When conveying a real or implied question, or uncertainty, use **whether**: I didn't know whether he would win. For clarity, confine **if** to its proper place, in conditional sentences. (If he is elected, I will emigrate. What would you do if I sang out of tune?)

igloo

Technically, this word (*igdlu* in Inuktitut) means any house, not just the familiar domed snow house, but in news stories igloo may be used for these. Do not imply that modern Inuit live in them, or even that all Inuit did so in the past. Many lived in dug-in shelters supported by whalebone or driftwood, using snow houses only when travelling. In summer they lived in skin tents (*tupek*, not *tuperk*).

Igloolik

A hamlet on an island in Foxe Basin, off the Melville Peninsula. The name means "it has houses." Note that one of the eight Inuit tribal groups is spelled **Iglulik**. See Inuit.

île

French for island; note there is no internal s. Use English geographic names if they are very familiar to anglophone readers (Magdalen Islands, not Îles-de-la-Madeleine), but Île for most French geographic names (Île d'Orléans) and for community names (Sept-Îles). See foreign and French words.

ill

Generally, it is a separate word as an adjective (ill wind, ill fame, ill humour), but hyphenated as an adverb (ill-mannered, ill-prepared, ill-equipped, ill-gotten).

illegal and illicit

Illegal means specifically against the law. (A synonym is **unlawful**, although Fowler says it is passing out of everyday speech. Reserve it for quoting charges: that he did unlawfully. . . .) **Illicit**, derived from the Latin for permit, is most often applied to activities that are permissible in some circumstances but are illegal or immoral in others: illicit sex, illicit gambling. Illegal is also widely used in this sense (an illegal tackle), but be wary of libel if it might be construed as meaning that a person or company has broken the law of the land when in fact only a contract rule or an unwritten standard of conduct has been breached (an illegal dismissal, an illegal worker). It is safer to refer to a contract violation etc.

illegitimate

There is no justification, legal or otherwise, to saddle a child with the label "illegitimate" in our pages. If the circumstances are relevant, and only if so, simply say the parents were not legally married, or the birth was out of wedlock, or the child was born of unmarried parents.

iMac

Use this style for the Apple computer unless the word begins a sentence, in which case it is IMac.

ill-used

It means mistreated, not misused.

Imax

The names Imax and Omnimax, connected with the process developed in Canada for movies on huge screens, are registered as all caps, but we follow our practice of using upper and lower for trade names.

imbroglio

IMF and World Bank

They are both affiliated with the United Nations, but are separate agencies. The **International Monetary Fund** provides funds to member countries if there is a need and if they commit themselves to certain policies.

The funds are usually for short-term use only, generally to deal with balance-of-payments problems. The IMF was set up by the 1944 Bretton Woods Agreement, which also established the **World Bank** (formally known as the International Bank for Reconstruction and Development). The World Bank is the main international body for directing funds to developing countries for specific projects, and its money, unlike that of the IMF, is usually medium-term. It can raise money by selling bonds on the world market, and can act as a channel for private capital in addition to making loans from its own resources. The **International Development Association** is an affiliate of the World Bank that lends money on easy terms (soft loans) to the poorest countries for specific projects. The **International Finance Corp.** is another World Bank affiliate that helps private companies in developing countries by mobilizing domestic and foreign capital, including its own.

Immaculate Conception

Upper-case. This does not describe the virgin conception of Jesus, but rather the conception of Mary. This Catholic dogma that Mary was conceived free from original sin, and therefore was perfectly sinless throughout her life, was officially adopted in 1854. See Assumption.

Immelmann

Upper-case the aerobatics manoeuvre for quickly gaining altitude and reversing direction. It begins as a backward loop, but is converted halfway through, when the plane is upside-down, into a half roll to right it.

immigrant, migrant

Someone who travels between two countries is a migrant, but not necessarily an immigrant. Refugee claimants, for instance, should be described as migrants rather than immigrants until the decision has been made whether they will in fact be allowed to immigrate.

imminent and eminent

Imminent means about to happen, impending. **Eminent** means famous, or of exalted standing or rank. (Also note **immanent**, which means dwelling within or, applied to God, pervading all creation.)

immolation

Immolate is a pretentious word meaning to kill a sacrificial victim, to sacrifice. Self-immolation is suicide for a political or other cause wider than personal reasons, and although burning is a method now in vogue, it is by no means the only one. (Throwing oneself under horses' hooves to win women the vote was another.) Since we must specify when self-immolation involves burning, why not ditch the word immolation and simply say a person burned himself or herself to death?

immovable

impact

It is primarily a noun; as a verb it has the narrow sense of pressing something against something else. We do not use it to mean have an impact (free trade will impact on employment).

Impact as a noun means powerful influence or effect, and should be used only in the singular. Do not speak of three major impacts; say three major effects, consequences, results etc.

impeccable

It means free of blame or sin, and so should be applied only to people or behaviour. It does not mean free of dirt, so do not speak of an impeccable house. There is justification for speaking of an impeccable suit, tie, outfit, furnishings etc. if the

rat a tat a
tat a -- ouch!

impeccable

implication is that a person or persons made a faultless selection, not that the item itself is without dirt, wrinkles, blemishes.

imperial

Lower-case for reference to empires in the abstract (imperial ambitions), and to actual empires other than the British (Rome's imperial allies; the Boer War involved both British and Imperial troops). This reflects the rule for upper-casing Empire.

But lower-case imperial for weights and measures, despite the fact that it is the British system that is referred to.

imperilling

implement

This is the spelling for both the noun (a tool etc.) and the verb (to put into effect).

implicit and explicit

If something is implicit, the meaning is clear but the actual words were not used. (Implicit does not refer to a hidden meaning.) Something explicit is plainly expressed, straightforward.

imply and infer

Both refer to a meaning beyond what is actually said or written. A

speaker or writer implies, or makes an implication; a listener or reader infers something from the words, or draws an inference.

impresario

inaccessible

in addition, in addition to

Also and besides are usually better.

inadmissible

inadvertent, -ence

Inc.

In company names, always use this abbreviation for Incorporated.

incense

Both the aromatic substance and to enrage.

incident

An incident is simply a happening. We should not say, for example, that there was a large protest meeting but "there were no incidents." The meeting itself was an incident, and so were all the minor happenings within it, including children being lost etc. If we mean there were no violent incidents, we should specify this. In that case, however, it would be more direct to say there was no violence. Depending on the story, incident might also be replaced by the more specific nouns fight, struggle, conflict, confrontation, disturbance.

including

When used to introduce a list, this word is interpreted by most readers to mean "including these prominent examples." If the list is all-inclusive, we should ensure that readers are not led to believe it is part of a larger one.

Inco Ltd.

incompatible

incredible and incredulous

Incredible means unbelievable; **incredulous** means unbelieving, skeptical.

Reserve incredible and incredibly for things that are truly beyond belief, or at least truly amazing. Speaking of an incredible meal or an incredible day, when we simply mean delicious, sumptuous, fun-filled, highly enjoyable or some such, debases the word.

increment

This is a fairly technical word involving adding quantities together. It does not stand easily for the simpler word increase.

independent, -ence

India

Adjective and people: Indian. Currency: rupee. Capital: New Delhi.

We do not use the term East Indian to refer to India or to people with roots there. (See East Indian.) India, a non-aligned member of the Commonwealth, remained a constitutional monarchy when it achieved independence with Dominion status in 1947, but became a republic in 1950. Its population is about one billion. India contains 22 states (including Sikkim, which became an Indian state in 1975) and nine union territories. Since English has official status, use upper case for India's Parliament, and describe the two houses as upper and lower or, when pressed, the Council of States and the House of the People. Their Hindi names, Rajya Sabha and Lok Sabha, may be used occasionally if we translate. There was a border war with China in 1962 and a war with Pakistan over Kashmir in 1965, and India invaded East Pakistan in 1971 to expel West Pakistani forces and allow creation of a separate Bangladesh. Tension between India and Pakistan over Kashmir continues. Prime Minister Indira Gandhi was

assassinated on Oct. 31, 1984. Her son, Rajiv, was defeated in the general election of 1989 and assassinated in 1991. Also see Hindi, Sikh, Kashmir.

India ink, rubber (not Indian).

Indian list

Do not use this term to refer to persons forbidden to buy or consume alcohol. The term interdict list is less objectionable, but awkward and obscure, requiring explanation if the context is not clear. Better simply to state the restriction.

Indians, see native people.

Indian summer

indictable

Indochina

This term applies to three countries: Cambodia, Laos and Vietnam.

Indonesia

Adjective and people: Indonesian. Currency: rupiah. Capital: Jakarta.

Its 13,600 islands, stretching 5,000 kilometres along the equator from New Guinea to Sumatra, occupy most of the Malay Archipelago. There are three main island groups. The Greater Sunda Islands include Java (which contains Jakarta and two-thirds of the national population of about 220 million), Sumatra, Celebes and Borneo, which Indonesia shares with Malaysia and Brunei. The Lesser Sundas include Bali, Flores and Timor. The Moluccas are the third major group. Indonesia also owns the western part of New Guinea, the rest being occupied by Papua New Guinea. The islands were called the Dutch East Indies until occupied by Japan in 1941-42. Sukarno declared an independent republic in 1945, and it was unconditionally recognized in 1949.

Indonesia was hit particularly hard by the financial crisis that swept East Asian economies beginning in 1997, which threw into sharp focus the corruption and cronyism throughout the government and financial sectors under the long, dictatorial regime of Suharto, who had deposed Sukarno in 1966. Student protests in early 1998 demanding financial and democratic reforms quickly turned violent and spread to the general public, and Suharto agreed to schedule new elections and resigned under pressure on May 21. His successor, B.J. Habibie, set in motion the referendum that led eventually to the independence of East Timor. In the 1999 election, the party of Megawati Sukarnoputri, Sukarno's daughter, won the most votes, but Indonesia's legislators selected Muslim cleric Abdurrahman Wahid as president. After a tumultuous 21 months, they replaced him with Megawati. See Suharto, East Timor.

On Oct. 12, 2002, two explosions in Bali's nightclub district killed almost 200 people. The bombings were widely attributed to Osama bin Laden's al-Qaeda network.

infer, see imply.

infinitives, split

If the Romans had been capable of splitting Latin infinitives, they probably would have. Fowler urges cocking an ear to the rhythm of English. Keep infinitives intact when possible, but come down on the side of splitting them when the alternative is awkwardness, ambiguity or artificiality. Instead of He rose to reject flatly increasing hostilities, say to flatly reject. Fowler says, "It does not add to a writer's readableness if readers are pulled up now and again to wonder— Why this distortion?"

Uncertain writers confuse infinitives (to go) with compound verbs (will go, has gone). Compound verbs are regularly split (will not

go, will gladly go, has often gone). See verbs.

inflammable

Avoid, because in- can easily be taken to mean not. Use **flammable**, the opposite of which is non-flammable.

inflammation

infrared, not infra-red.

innards (for entrails).

inner city

Avoid this term in Canadian references. In U.S. cities, inner city has a specific meaning that goes far beyond the sense of central or working-class or even poor. It connotes slum-ridden, hopeless, resentful and dangerous, and in most cases overwhelmingly black or Latino. Inner cities are the product of racial and economic migration patterns that are common to most big U.S. cities but not to those in Canada. Cities here have not seen a comparable flight of residents, businesses and jobs to the suburbs, with the resulting derelict buildings, economic stagnation, and schools and other services starved by the shrinking of the tax base. Most large Canadian cities retain pockets of affluence throughout their cores, and there are few central neighbourhoods that young professionals wouldn't consider suitable.

innocuous, but **inoculate**.

innovative

Innu

Do not confuse these people with Inuit. Innu are Indians who inhabit Labrador and northeastern Quebec. What they call the Innu nation is made up of four groups—the Montagnais, the Naskapi, the Atikamekw and a group in Labrador that calls itself the Innu. We also use Innu for the plural form.

innuendoes

input
A technical noun from science, industry and computers that has become accepted in the sense of a contribution to the process of making a decision or setting policy. We do not use it as a verb.

inquire, not enquire.

insignia
It is plural (these insignia are).

insistent, -ence

install, but **instalment**.

instigate
It goes beyond initiate, implying that the person is a provocateur, advocating and scheming to bring about a course of action that is drastic or even reprehensible. A word too loaded for most news stories.

instill

insure and ensure
Reserve **insure** for the actual buying and selling of insurance. For making certain, use **ensure**.

intelligentsia

inter and intra
Inter is a prefix meaning together, mutual, between (intercollegiate, international). It does not take a hyphen even when the root word begins with r (interracial). **Intra** means inside of. It takes a hyphen before an a (intra-abdominal) but not before any other vowel (intrauterine).

inter, interment
Use only in direct quotes. Say **bury, burial**.

interface
Reserve for technical and scientific references. In electronics, it is a device that links two others in such a way that they can communicate or work together. It also means a common ground or boundary, such as the boundary between two fluids. We do not use interface as a verb meaning to talk, communicate, reach an understanding.

interferon
Lower-case. It refers to any of several proteins produced by the cells of higher animals, including humans, to fight the growth of viruses within cells. The three known types are classed as alpha, beta and gamma. Beta is produced by many kinds of cells, while alpha and gamma are produced only by the type of white blood cells called lymphocytes.

International Court of Justice
May be called the World Court, even in first reference. The UN Charter describes it as "the principal judicial organ of the United Nations." Describe it as based in The Hague. Its seat is there, and most cases are heard there, but it can hold hearings anywhere.

International Date Line
The only one of Earth's imaginary lines that we run upper-case. (Say equator, tropic, meridian, but Tropic of Cancer.) See capitalization.

International Monetary Fund
See IMF and World Bank.

Internet, the Net
Upper case for this trademarked protocol and its short form. See World Wide Web.

interpreter

interpretive

intrauterine device

IUD on second reference.

Inuit

This is the only accepted name for the people formerly known by the pejorative Indian word Eskimo, meaning eaters of raw meat. Inuit means "the people," "humankind." The singular noun is **Inuk**. (We do not use the noun for two people, *inuuk*.) For the adjectival form, use Inuit even for one person (an Inuit mechanic, not an Inuk mechanic).

As a non-English plural, Inuit does not lend itself to creation of the plural possessive. Recast to avoid, either by using Inuit as an adjective or saying "of the Inuit" etc.

There are about 41,000 Inuit in Canada, strung out in small settlements from Labrador to Alaska (and indeed through Alaska into Siberia). They have been roughly classified into eight tribal groups, which are, from west to east, the Western Arctic Inuit (who call themselves Inuvialuit, and were migrants from the west who replaced the original inhabitants, the Mackenzie Inuit); the Copper Inuit; the Netsilik Inuit; the Caribou Inuit; the Iglulik Inuit; the Baffin Island Inuit; the Ungava Inuit; and the Labrador Inuit.

Globe style on the spelling of the language is Inuktitut (not Inuttituut). We should not refer to someone as "speaking Inuit," but we may refer to speaking "the Inuit language." (Note that in technical descriptions of Canada's native languages, Inuktitut is still classified under the name Eskimo-Aleut.) There are six Inuktitut dialects spoken in Canada.

We may use the word Inuit to refer to similar peoples across the North, but note that the Inuit of the Western Arctic call themselves Inuvialuit, those in Greenland call themselves Katladlit, and those in Siberia and western Alaska call themselves Yuit.

These regional words may be used for colour, or to differentiate between groups of Inuit, but always explain.

For the term Eskimo dog, see husky.

Inuit Tapiriit of Canada

No the. The Inuit organization's Inuktitut name (Inuit Tapiriit Kanatami) means "Inuit are united with Canada." The name was previously Inuit Tapirisat of Canada ("Inuit who will unite with Canada"), and before that the National Eskimo Brotherhood.

inukshuk

Lower-case, italics. A man-shaped pile of stones used by Inuit to create a landmark. Must be explained.

Inuvik, NWT.

It is in the Mackenzie Delta, about 150 kilometres north of the Arctic Circle on the river's East Channel. It is the main administrative, transport and service centre for the Western Arctic, and so should be used as the point from which to give distances to other communities in the area, including Tuktoyaktuk, Aklavik and Fort McPherson. See geographical location.

invigorating, but vigour.

IODE

This is now the official name of the organization. We should say somewhere in the story that the initials stand for Imperial Order Daughters of the Empire.

IOU, upper-case, no periods.

IQ

It stands for intelligence quotient, determined by various standard tests, notably the Wechsler scales and the Stanford-Binet Intelligence Scale, and is most relevant as a snapshot of the development of children at a particular age, and as a measure of the capabilities of below-average adults. An IQ figure we have for an average or above-average adult would almost certainly be left over from a childhood test. In any case, assigning specific IQs to individuals in news stories is a risky undertaking. Prefer such terms as highly intelligent, above-average intelligence, functions at a Grade 3 level, etc. When relevant, we should refer to the contention by racial and ethnic groups that the standard tests are culturally skewed. We might also refer to the different rates of development of different faculties, such as verbal and mathematical skills. In speaking of IQ levels, it is more accurate to refer to development or learning ability than to intelligence.

Note that references to mental age, once considered standard in rating children and deficient adults, are now little used by professionals (and were never relevant for average or above-average adults), but they are occasionally helpful in news stories if we have an authoritative estimate. In discussions of IQs, a level of 100 should be described as the **mean**, not the average. Average IQ is considered to be the range from 90 to 109. Levels of 69 or less are considered indications of defective mental functioning, retardation. Subjects at 70 to 79 are described as borderline, and those at 80 to 89 as dull average. Those at 110 to 119 are called bright average, those at 120 to 129 are superior, and those above 130 are very superior.

Iran

Adjective and people: Iranian. Currency: tuman, divided into 100 rials. Capital: Tehran (not Teheran).

It was called Persia until 1935. It is mostly a high, mountainous plateau, but also has sea-level districts, and so the climate ranges from subtropical to subpolar. Most Iranians are Shia Muslims. We cannot speak of an Iranian language. The majority language is Farsi (Persian), and there are also speakers of Kurdish, Luri, Turkish and Arabic among the population of about 74 million. A republic was declared in 1979 after the return of exiled Ayatollah Ruhollah Khomaini and the departure of the shah. War with Iraq, which began in September of 1980 with an Iraqi invasion and ended with a ceasefire on Aug. 20, 1988, arranged by the UN, seriously disrupted oil production. An earthquake in June of 1990, at 7.3 to 7.7 on the Richter scale, killed 35,000 to 50,000, injured 200,000 and left 500,000 homeless. Also see hostage crisis.

Iraq

Adjective and people: Iraqi. Currency: dinar. Capital: Baghdad.

It is a large oil producer and grows some cash crops, notably dates, but is mostly arid outside the plains of the Tigris and Euphrates rivers, which join in the south to form the Shatt al-Arab, flowing through vast salty marshes. Iraq occupies most of what was called Mesopotamia (Greek for between rivers) until the end of the First World War. Most of the approximately 24 million Iraqis are Shia or Sunni Muslim Arabs, speaking Arabic, but there is a large Kurdish minority, about 15 per cent, and some smaller ones, including ethnic Iranians. Oil accounts for almost 99 per cent of Iraq's exports. Saddam Hussein came to power in 1979. Under him, Iraq touched off the eight-year Gulf War the next year (see Iran) and invaded Kuwait in August of 1990 in a dispute over territory and oil production. Its refusal to withdraw in compliance with United Nations resolutions led to its expulsion in early 1991 by a U.S.-led coalition of 28 Western and Arab countries (including Canadian air and naval contingents) in an operation dubbed Desert Storm, now usually referred to as the Persian Gulf war. The bombing of Baghdad and Iraqi lines that began on Jan. 17 was a watershed in military history, showing the effectiveness of a new generation of aircraft, "smart" bombs, cruise missiles and surveillance systems.

Iraq's civilian population suffered greatly in the war and under the trade embargo that followed. Under the terms of the ceasefire, which took effect April 11, Iraq was to destroy its weapons of mass destruction, dismantle its nuclear-weapons program and observe "no-fly" zones in the north and south to prevent use of aircraft in its suppression of the Kurdish and Shia uprisings that followed the war. In early 1993, it engaged in a series of violations of the ceasefire agreement, provoking retaliatory air strikes by the United States, Britain and France. Its refusal to allow unfettered UN inspections of its disarmament compliance kept the embargo in place, except for limited oil sales to pay for food and medicine, and came close to provoking renewed U.S. air strikes in 1998.

At the particular urging of the United States, the UN Security Council adopted Resolution 1441 in November, 2002, which again called on Iraq to inform UN inspectors of the existence of any chemical, biological and nuclear weapons, so that the weapons might be destroyed. When members of the council disagreed over whether there were grounds to invade Iraq for not complying with the resolution, the United States and Britain attacked Iraq in March of 2003, with limited assistance from allies dubbed "the coalition of the willing." Canada said that it would not join the coalition, though elements of the Canadian Forces were present in the Persian Gulf. In early April, the Western troops reached Baghdad and the government fell.

Since the Iran-Iraq war was also a Gulf war, do not refer to the 2003 conflict as the second Persian Gulf war.

Ireland
Not Eire. Adjective and people: Irish. Currency: euro (formerly Irish pound, known as the punt). Capital: Dublin.

There is the potential for confusion of names in stories that also deal with Northern Ireland or the island called Ireland. To keep things clear, we can refer to the Irish Republic (the official name is the Republic of Ireland), while an unofficial alternative name for Northern Ireland is Ulster. Note, however, that Northern Ireland consists of only six of the nine counties that were in the old Irish province of Ulster: Londonderry, Antrim, Down, Armagh, Fermanagh and Tyrone, sometimes referred to as "the six counties." The three others – Donegal, Cavan and Monaghan – are in the Irish Republic. Do not speak of the republic as southern Ireland. Northern Ireland occupies the northeastern shoulder of the island, with Donegal lying to its west and extending its Inishowen Peninsula farther north than the most northerly point in Northern Ireland. The population of the republic is about four million, and that of Northern Ireland is about 1.6 million. See Northern Ireland.

iridescent
Note the single r. It does not mean gleaming or shining; it means showing an array of shifting colours, as in an oil slick or soap bubble. (It comes from *iris*, Greek for rainbow.)

Iron Curtain, the
Use only in direct quotes. Whether the term described reality or actually helped to shape it is open to argument. It is widely attributed to Winston Churchill from a speech in 1945, but it had been used in reference to the Soviet Union by an English traveller in 1920, and used by Hitler's finance minister, Count

Schwerin von Krosigk, and by propaganda minister Joseph Goebbels.

ironically, ironic

These words are rarely applicable in news stories. Confine them to references that truly involve irony, which can mean either the use of words to convey the opposite ("Isn't this nice" when we mean "Isn't this awful"), or an ending that is the opposite of what was expected. We should not use them when something is merely odd, strange, unusual, paradoxical, coincidental.

Iroquoian

Not the language of the Iroquois, but a large linguistic group comprising several languages and dialects, which in Canada alone include Cayuga, Huron, Mohawk, Oneida, Onondaga, Seneca and Tuscarora.

Irrawaddy River

irrelevant

Islam

The proper word for the religion of Muslims, it means "submission to God." Muslim means "one who submits." The holy book is the Koran (not Quran or Qur'an). The legal system is *sharia* (lower case, italics; not Shari'ah). It means a pathway, and is usually translated as "the path in which God wants men to walk." The major division is between the majority Sunni Muslims (the "traditionalists"), who believe the Prophet Mohammed designated no successor, and the Shiites, who believe he designated his son-in-law Ali. Shiism in turn has such sects as the Ismailis (whose spiritual leader is the Aga Khan) and the Druze, whose theology is different enough that they should not be called Druze Muslims. (See Druze.) Two other groups are the Ahmadiyah, begun by Ghulam Ahmad in the Punjab in the last century and now

split into two sects, both based in Pakistan; and the U.S. sect formerly known as the Black Muslims, whose official name now is the American Muslim Mission.

We should not say that Muslims face eastward when they pray. They face toward Mecca, from all directions. See hijab.

Islamicist, Islamist

An Islamicist is a scholar of or expert on Islam.

The term Islamist is still unfamiliar enough to many readers that it requires explanation if the context is unclear, but it is acceptable in reference to Muslim radicals/extremists, and is preferable to Muslim fundamentalists, which covers a far wider territory than intended. See fundamentalism.

The *Encyclopedia of The Orient* says Islamism is a group of ideologies in Islam that promote the fullest possible implementation of *sharia* law and see secular governments as foreign to a true Muslim society. It identifies as Islamism's four motifs (1) an imperative to alleviate poverty, (2) a concern that Western values are eroding Islamic culture, (3) a desire to return to an imagined strict, conservative golden age of Islam and (4) a belief in Islamism as a political alternative. To the third point, the encyclopedia says there "are no Muslim sources indicating that the Islam of the Golden Age was as strict and conservative as the Islamists believe. All indications show that it was the liberal Islam that paved the ground for cultural, social and military achievements of those days – values foreign to all major Islamist groups. Hence, there is reason to say that the Islamist idea of the Golden Age is a dramatic falsification of history."

To the fourth point, Iran and Sudan have implemented Islamist politics, as have Pakistan and Libya to a degree. Saudi Arabia may have had

Islamist politics for a long time, but is not seen that way by many people because it tolerates such a great gulf between rich and poor. During the past two decades, the encyclopedia adds, violence "seems to have become an intrinsic part of the Islamist ideology, and the will to use violence doesn't need much provocation any more. This seems to be the situation for some groups in Egypt, and some minor groups in Algeria."

Israel

Adjective and people: Israeli. Currency: (new) shekel. The officially designated capital is Jerusalem, but most countries have their embassies in Tel Aviv.

It is best described as a Jewish republic on the square eastern end of the Mediterranean. About 75 per cent of Israel's six million people are Jews; those who are not include Muslim and Christian Arabs, Samaritans, Circassians and Druze. The official language is Hebrew. Israel forms part of the area once called Palestine, taken from the Ottoman Empire during the First World War by the British, who allowed considerable Jewish immigration afterward. A 1947 UN declaration called for establishment of two states, Jewish and Arab, but the Arab one was never created. When Jewish leaders declared the state of Israel in 1948, neighbouring Arab states invaded and were defeated. There were wars to repel attacks by Egypt and Jordan in 1967 (the Six-Day War, which ended with Israel occupying the West Bank and Gaza Strip), and by Egypt and Syria in 1973. The Camp David accords in 1978, on a framework for peace, led to a treaty with Egypt in 1979. Israel invaded and occupied Lebanon in 1982; it withdrew in 1985, but continued to support a Lebanese Christian force there.

December of 1987 saw the beginning of violent protests, dubbed the *intifada* (uprising), by Palestinians in the West Bank and Gaza, and also the birth of Hamas, a radical group whose activities, along with those of the even more radical Islamic Jihad, eventually included suicide bombings of Israeli civilians. Agreements with Yasser Arafat's Palestine Liberation Organization signed in Washington in September of 1993, Cairo in May of 1994 and Washington in September of 1995, and the Oslo accords brokered by Norway in 1993, promised limited Palestinian self-rule in the occupied territories and set a schedule for gradual Israeli withdrawal. Subsequent detailed negotiations on the handover of administration and security to the Palestinian Authority produced the Hebron accord of 1997 but otherwise stalled, largely because of increased violence by those on both sides dedicated to preventing peace. (Many more were killed in suicide bombings in the years after Oslo than in the preceding *intifada*, and 29 worshippers at a mosque in Hebron were slaughtered by radical Jewish settler Baruch Goldstein in 1994. Prime Minister Yitzhak Rabin was assassinated by radical Jewish student Yigal Amir on Nov. 4, 1995.) Talks to decide the permanent status of the West Bank and Gaza Strip began in September of 1999, but broke off after a second *intifada* began in September of 2000.

Istanbul

Turkey's largest city, divided by the Bosporus.

italics

We use italics, in body type only, for titles of plays, films, books, short stories, poems, comic strips, dance works, musical works (including songs), works of art, records, videos and TV and radio shows. (We do not use them for holy books such as the Bible, the Koran etc., or for the names of periodicals, including newspapers and magazines, the titles of articles in them, the names of parts of larger works such as book chapter titles or symphony movements, or the names of ships or exhibitions and festivals.)

We use italics to flag foreign or French words. Italics are not necessary for proper nouns, which are already set apart by being upper-case; for currencies; or for words and phrases that have entered the English language, such as legerdemain, kismet, sotto voce. Legal, scientific and musical terms do not require italics (habeas corpus, allegro), but make an exception for Latin scientific names with upper-case genus (*Castor fiber canadensis*). See foreign and French words.

Avoid italics merely to flag a word as unusual, or to indicate it was stressed by the speaker. However, make an exception in sentences that are ambiguous or downright unintelligible unless the stress is indicated.

Italy

Adjective and people: Italian. Currency: euro (had been the lira, plural lire). Capital: Rome.

Italy includes Sicily, Sardinia and some smaller islands. It can be described as being in the Mediterranean, but note that the waters roughly bounded by Italy, Corsica, Sardinia and Sicily are called the Tyrrhenian Sea; the sleeve enclosed by Italy, Croatia, Montenegro and Albania is the Adriatic; and the sea between Italy and Greece, off the Italian peninsula's boot sole, is the Ionian. Italy's population is about 57 million.

its and it's

Commonly confused in copy, largely because the possessive form is the one without the apostrophe. **It's** is a contraction of it is or it has. It's a wise child that knows its mother.

ITT

Do not confuse this with the one that has an ampersand, AT&T. ITT stands for International Telephone and Telegraph Corp. AT&T stands for American Telephone and Telegraph Co.

Ivory Coast

Adjective and people: Ivoirien, but avoid as obscure. Prefer of or in Ivory Coast. Currency: CFA franc. Capital: Yamoussoukro, but the seat of government is Abidjan.

This former French colony on the Gulf of Guinea, bounded by Ghana, Burkina Faso, Mali, Guinea and Liberia, became fully independent in 1960. We continue to use the name Ivory Coast, but note that the French name, Côte d'Ivoire, was declared in 1986 to be the only official one. The population of about 17 million is divided into about 60 tribal groups, the largest being the Bete in the southwest at about 20 per cent. French is the official language. Petroleum is produced offshore, but cocoa and coffee each account for more export revenue.

A military coup in 1999 replaced elected president Henri Konan Bédié with General Robert Guéi. After Guéi declared himself the winner of a fraudulent 2000 election, a popular uprising forced him to flee to Benin. Opposition candidate Laurent Gbagbo was declared the genuine winner, and president.

Ivy League

Members are Brown University, Columbia University, Cornell University, Dartmouth College, Harvard University, Princeton University, the University of Pennsylvania and Yale University.

-ize

The creation of verbs by adding -ize to nouns and adjectives is a long-established practice in English.

(Jeremy Bentham gave us maximize and minimize.) In general, we should confine ourselves to those found in our dictionary, but we are open to particularly apt new coinages that arise out of social and technological change, are widely understood and save several other words. We should avoid such neo-verbs, however, if they are a solution to a non-existent problem. If there is already a perfectly good verb, we should use it. (Say initial a document, not initialize it.)

Be alert for easy ways to avoid the longer, inelegant -ize words in the dictionary, just as we seek to avoid all polysyllabic conglomerations. Sent or taken to hospital, or admitted to hospital, is an easier notion to grasp than hospitalized.

Izvestia

It was formerly the official daily newspaper of the Soviet government, while **Pravda** was the official daily of the Soviet Communist Party. Both became independent dailies with the death of the Soviet Union in 1989. The official Soviet news agency, **Tass**, became Itar-Tass.

J

Jack Daniel's, note possessive.

jack-in-the-boxes, jack-in-the-pulpits

jackknife

jackrabbit

jail, reformatory, prison
Preserve the distinction between these terms. A jail is a local city or county institution for people awaiting trial or serving very short sentences for such offences as being drunk or refusing to pay fines. A reformatory is a provincial institution generally reserved for people serving less than two years. A prison is a federal institution for terms of two years or more. The differences in conditions, services and location are very important to the prisoners and their chance for rehabilitation, and judges will often impose a sentence of "two years less a day" so it can be served in the provincial system.
Accordingly, do not write of someone receiving "14 years in jail." It is often enough to say someone received a sentence of 14 years.

Jakarta
Capital of Indonesia, on the island of Java.

Jamaica
Adjective and people: Jamaican. Currency: Jamaican dollar. Capital: Kingston.
It is one of the Greater Antilles,

south of the eastern tip of Cuba. A member of the Commonwealth, it achieved internal self-government in 1944 and complete independence in 1962. Like Canada, it remains a constitutional monarchy, with a governor-general. About 76 per cent of its 2.7 million people are of African descent, 3 per cent are white and the rest are of South Asian, Chinese or mixed ancestry. The literacy rate is high. Once heavily reliant on sugar, Jamaica has grown into the world's third-largest producer of bauxite and alumina, and also has valuable trade in silica sand, ceramic clays, gypsum and marble. Other major exports include rum, spices, cocoa and fruit.

James Norris Memorial Trophy
For the best defenceman in the National Hockey League. Named for a former owner of the Detroit Red Wings. May be called the Norris Trophy, the Norris.

Japan
Adjective and people: Japanese. Currency: yen. Capital: Tokyo.
There is no island called Japan. The Japanese archipelago includes about 3,500 islands stretching more than 3,000 kilometres. The largest is Honshu, containing most of the major cities (Tokyo, Yokohama, Osaka, Nagoya, Kyoto, Hiroshima). The other three major islands are Hokkaido (contains Sapporo), Kyushu (contains Nagasaki) and Shikoku. Between Japan and the Asian mainland (North and South Korea

and Russia) is the Sea of Japan. The islands, 80 per cent mountainous and 70 per cent forested, are geologically young and active. Earth tremors are frequent, and there are 190 active volcanoes. Only 16 per cent of the land is arable, giving Japan one of the world's smallest ratios of arable land to people. Its population of about 127 million is to a large extent ethnically homogeneous, except for about 15,000 aboriginal Ainu and about a million registered foreigners, two-thirds of them Koreans.

japan, japanned, japanning
Lower-case when referring to black enamel.

Japan Airlines
Until 1989 was Japan Air Lines, and may still be referred to as JAL.

Japan Alps, Japan Trench
Not Japanese Alps.

jargon
Avoid the obscure, specialized languages of specific professions, businesses, trades, crafts, sports and arts. Jargon words finding their way into print most often, usually through writers eager to make themselves appear to be insiders, are those of medicine, lawyers and the police. A rule of thumb is that if a well-informed layman would not use the expression in everyday conversation, it has no place in a news story. Speak of cuts, scrapes, bruises and swelling, not lacerations, abrasions, contusions and hematoma. Replace or translate Latin legal terms. Do not use police-blotter jargon, such as a charge of weapons dangerous. Avoid corporate financial jargon. Say an investor paid more or less than market price for a stake in a company, not paid a premium or a discount.

Be especially alert for the jargon most familiar to us, that of our own business. Say headline, not head; caption, not cutline; accompanying or companion story, not sidebar; send, not file, a story.

Some jargon or vogue words used in various fields might well enrich a story, adding colour and giving our readers an inside look, but they should be translated or explained.

Jasper National Park
The name derives from Jasper Hawes, whose trading post for the North West Company was called Jasper House. The park is on the Alberta side of the Rocky Mountains, along with Banff National Park adjoining it to the south. On the western (B.C.) side across from Jasper is Hamber Provincial Park, while across from Banff on the B.C. side are Yoho National Park and Kootenay National Park.

Jedi
In the *Star Wars* films, Jedi is both the singular and plural: one Jedi, two Jedi.

jeep
Acceptable in lower case as the generic term for a light, four-wheel-drive military or police reconnaissance vehicle of the type developed for the U.S. Army Quartermaster Corps (its name apparently derives from GP, for general purpose). It does not lend itself to any other generic term except the unnecessarily vague "vehicle," because it is halfway between a car and a truck (the Second World War version was classed as a quarter-ton truck).

But in civilian contexts, always put Jeep in upper case, to reflect its status as a trade name (now owned by Chrysler Corp.). If we are not sure of the make involved, particularly if the story involves a faulty vehicle or a vehicle used for unacceptable activities, say four-wheel-drive vehicle, off-road vehicle or sport utility vehicle (SUV).

Jeff Russel Memorial Trophy

Note spelling. It is for the most sportsmanlike player in the Canadian Football League's Eastern Conference.

Jehovah's Witnesses, a Witness

It should be described as a Christian movement or sect. Members had a long-time aversion to the terms church, minister and congregation, although this has moderated. Witness books and publications, notably Awake and The Watchtower, distributed around the world in many languages, are produced by the Watchtower Bible and Tract Society. Two corporations of that name (one in Pennsylvania and one in New York) direct Witnesses' activities, along with the International Bible Students Association. Witness buildings should be called halls (or Kingdom Halls). For clarity, use congregations, not the Witness term, companies. We normally refer only to "members," but note that all are considered ministers to the gentiles and, depending on the time devoted to meetings and doorstep missionary work, are called kingdom publishers, pioneer publishers or special pioneers (full-time employees of the society). Witnesses believe that Christ's Second Coming is imminent, that after Armageddon the enlightened will live forever on Earth under the Theocracy, and that secular governments are unwitting allies of the devil. (A major factor in the persecution they have faced in many countries is their refusal to salute any flag or perform military service.) They also believe that the Bible prohibits blood transfusions.

Jell-O

A trade name, so use upper case. If we are not sure of the brand involved in a story involving unpleasant circumstances, such as an allergic reaction, we use the generic term jelly or jelly dessert. See trade names.

jellybean, jellyfish

jeremiad

A tale of woe, a complaint. Lower-case, despite its origin in the name Jeremiah.

jerky

It is not a single type of meat, such as beef; the name refers to the method of curing, which is to cut into strips and then dry. Meat cured this way is said to be jerked. Specify beef jerky, venison jerky etc.

jerry-built, jury-rigged

Jerry-built means built shoddily and cheaply. Jury-rigged means improvised.

Jesuit martyrs

Lower-case martyrs. They were the first North American saints (although born in Europe), canonized in 1930 and proclaimed patron saints of Canada 10 years later. Although all eight were missionaries with the Society of Jesus, some were lay brothers rather than priests. They were killed by Indians in various clashes between 1642 and 1649, five of them in what is now Canada and three in what is now New York State.

jetsam

The word does not mean just any marine garbage; it specifically refers to goods thrown overboard (jettisoned) to lighten an endangered vessel.

Jet Ski

Upper-case for the registered trademark of Kawasaki. The generic term is personal watercraft or water scooter. The craft famously ridden to a lakeside news conference by wetsuit-wearing Canadian Alliance leader Stockwell Day – in Penticton, B.C., on Sept. 12, 2000, a day after he was first elected an MP in a by-election in Okanagan-Coquihalla – was a Wave Runner, made by competitor Yamaha.

jetsam

Jew

It means anyone who professes the Judaic faith. Be aware, however, that the word has been used pejoratively in the past. Although such offensive connotations appear to have dropped away from the adjective Jewish and the plural noun Jews, exercise care when using the singular word Jew. Its use is acceptable in copy, where context can make it clear no adverse implication is intended, but avoid the singular label Jew in headlines. Never use jew as a verb meaning to haggle or bargain.

The three major movements of Judaism are Orthodox, Conservative and Reform. The highest holy days are Rosh Hashanah and Yom Kippur. Others include Passover (Pesach), Shavuot and Sukkot. Hanukkah and Purim are better described as holidays; even the ultra-orthodox drive, cook etc. on them (and during the intermediate days of Passover and Sukkot).

The term anti-Semitic is generally taken to mean anti-Jewish, and may be used as such except when describing the attitude of an Arab, because technically the term Semite refers to both Jews and Arabs. Anti-Zionist means opposed to the movement to resettle Jews in Palestine, and anti-Israel means either opposed to the existence of the state of Israel or opposed to particular conduct or policies of Israel. Someone could have anti-Semitic motives in expressing views that are anti-Zionist or anti-Israel, but this must never be assumed. In fact, some Jews oppose the Zionist movement, and someone might be against Israel on an issue without being against Jews.

jeweller, jewellery

jibe and gibe. See gibe.

jigsaw

jihad

Lower-case, italics. A holy war waged by Muslims as a duty.

jimmy

Lower-case for a burglar's pry bar. Not jemmy.

jingoism, -ist, lower-case.

jockeys

The riders. But Jockey is upper case when referring to the shorts. It is a trademark of Jockey International, Inc. (The boxer in boxer shorts is lower case.)

jodhpurs

Johnny-come-lately, Johnny-on-the-spot

Upper-case, hyphens. The plurals are Johnny-come-latelies, Johnnies-on-the-spot.

Johnny-jump-up

Upper-case. The wild pansy. The plural is Johnny-jump-ups.

Johns Hopkins

Quaker merchant and financier Johns Hopkins, who died in 1873, left $7-million to be divided equally to found a university and a hospital. Both are in Baltimore.

Johns-Manville

Now reorganized as Manville Corp.

Johnson, Daniel

See Quebec premiers.

Johnston, Franz

When we are listing the original members of the Group of Seven, he should be called Frank. He resigned from the group in 1924, four years after its founding, and in 1927 changed his name to Franz.

join

Takes a direct object, so we do not say join with.

Joint Chiefs of Staff

Upper-case; also the Joint Chiefs. It is the committee at the top of the U.S. military chain of command, reporting to the secretary of defence and the president, and it is their principal military advisory body. It consists of a chairman, a vice-chairman, and the Chief of Staff of the Army, the Chief of Naval Operations, the Chief of Staff of the Air Force, and the Commandant of the Marine Corps. They are served by the Joint Staff.

Jolly Roger

Jordan

Adjective and people: Jordanian. Currency: dinar. Capital: Amman.

A monarchy, bordered by Israel on the west, Syria on the north, Iraq on the east and Saudi Arabia on the south. The West Bank, captured by Israel in the Six-Day War in 1967, accounted for only 6 per cent of Jordan's territory but more than half its population. Almost all Jordanians are Arab, speaking Arabic, but there are wide cultural differences between the agricultural or urban Palestinians and the traditionally nomadic Bedouin of the eastern desert plateau. Oil was discovered in 1982, and

Jordan is now an exporter of petroleum products in addition to phosphates, chemicals, cement and food and animal products. The population is six million.

Jordan was ruled from 1953 to 1999 by King Hussein, who signed a peace treaty with Israel in 1994. He was succeeded by his eldest son, King Abdullah II, under whom Jordan became part of the World Trade Organization in 2000.

joual

Lower-case, italics. We must not equate it with Quebec French in general, or say unadvisedly that a particular person speaks *joual*. The implication is that the person is uneducated and a lazy speaker, guilty of malapropisms, slang, mispronunciation, elisions and the wholesale dropping of consonants, syllables or even whole words. The name, coined by André Laurendeau in a Le Devoir editorial in 1959, is the supposed mispronunciation of the word *cheval*.

Jr.

Use the contraction as part of a name, with no comma (Hank Williams Jr.). But keep in mind that its use is far less common in Canada than in the United States. We attach Jr. to a name only if there is a genuine risk of confusion with the father, particularly if the wrong person's reputation might be harmed. If the person referred to is well known to the public and the father is not, or if we give the age, the name alone suffices. There is no need, for example, to say Rev. Martin Luther King Jr. or Donald Marshall Jr.

Juan de Fuca Strait (not Strait of).

Jubilee

Upper-case when referring to a significant anniversary, such as the Queen's Silver Jubilee, Queen

Victoria's Diamond Jubilee. Lower-case for general times of rejoicing.

judges, see courts, honorifics.

judgment

Judgment Day
Upper-case when referring to the time of the Last Judgment prophesied in the Bible, but lower-case for less cataclysmic days of reckoning, such as the day the credit-card bill arrives.

jugular
It is proper idiom to speak of "the jugular," meaning the throat or, figuratively, a vulnerable area, but note that there are two jugular veins, one on each side of the neck. Also note that they do not supply the head and brain with blood; like all veins, they return blood to the heart. The supply side is taken care of by the two carotid arteries, and it is these whose severing is most often fatal. If we don't know which has been severed, say a major blood vessel in the neck.

Juilliard School, New York.

jujitsu and judo
Jujitsu is a form of unarmed combat. Judo is a system of physical conditioning and a competitive sport based on jujitsu.

jujube

Junction, the
Upper-case for the area of West Toronto where railway lines intersect. The neighbourhood of homes and factories bounded by these tracks is the Junction Triangle.

jungle
Refers to a dense thicket or, figuratively, a cruel, dangerous or confusing environment (a consumer jungle). We should not apply it indiscriminately to tropical forests.

Much of the Amazon forest, for example, appears as a dense tangle only when viewed from a road, river or clearing, because these edges are the places where sunlight penetrates. Only a few yards in, the high canopy shades out most undergrowth, leaving open space between huge tree trunks, just as in temperate forests.

Junos
The Juno Awards are presented by the Canadian recording industry. They were named in honour of Pierre Juneau, who served as chairman of the Canadian Radio-Television Commission (which later became the Canadian Radio-television and Telecommunications Commission) from 1968 to 1975. While at the CRTC, he was instrumental in developing Canadian-content regulations for radio and television broadcasting, a policy that won him the recording industry's support.

jury-rigged, jerry-built
See jerry-built.

justice of the peace
Upper-case only before a name. Mr. or Ms. on second reference.

K

K2

No hyphen. At 8,611 metres (28,250 feet), it is the world's second-highest mountain, after Everest, which is 8,848 metres (29,028 feet). Both are in the Himalayan system, but K2, also unofficially called Dapsang or Mount Godwin Austen, is in the Karakoram Range in northern Kashmir, while Everest is on the Tibetan-Nepalese border in the Great Himalaya. See Himalaya.

kabloona

English rendering of the Inuktitut word for a white person, *qablunaaq*. We also use kabloona as the plural, not the Inuktitut plural *qablunaat*. The name is a reference to eyebrow (*qablu*) and belly (*naaq*). The English spelling does not require italics, but does need an explanation.

kabuki

Italics are not needed for the traditional popular Japanese theatre, a stylized but energetic dramatic form that features song, dance and mime.

Kahshe Lake, Ont.

Kakabeka Falls, Ont.

Kaladar, Ont.
But note that there is also a **Callander**, Ont.

kaleidoscope

Figuratively, the word denotes more than a beautiful scene; it refers to a swiftly changing one, like the patterns in the toy.

kamikaze

Lower-case. Avoid facetious use of this word. The Special Attack Force of the Japanese Naval Air Forces sank 34 ships and severely damaged hundreds more in the last year of the Second World War, and killed almost 5,000 U.S. sailors in the Battle of Okinawa alone. The force involved not only planes but also piloted missiles launched from planes. Speak of a kamikaze pilot, but be aware that he was referred to by the single name, a kamikaze, which compared him to the "divine wind" that dispersed a Mongol fleet in the 13th century.

kamiks

The skin boots of most Inuit. Only those of the extreme Western Arctic are called mukluks. Neither word should be italic, since we use the English plural.

Kampuchea, see Cambodia.

Kapuskasing, Ont.

karat and carat

Use **karat** for gold and **carat** for gems. **Karat** is the measure of the proportion by weight of gold in an alloy, expressed in 24ths, meaning that 24-karat gold is pure, and 18-karat gold is three-quarters gold. The **carat** is the unit of weight for measuring gems, equal to 200 milligrams (3.086 grains).

Karsh, Yousuf

Kashmir

This Muslim northern state, straddling India and Pakistan, has been the source of conflict between the two countries since the separation of British India into Muslim Pakistan and Hindu India in 1947. A ceasefire line drawn through Kashmir by 1949 was adjusted in 1965 and again in 1971 after Indo-Pakistani wars. Pakistan controls one-third of the territory, which it calls Azad (free) Kashmir. India controls the other two-thirds, which it includes in the twin state of Jammu and Kashmir; Jammu is largely Hindu.

Kathmandu

Katyn Forest

The Soviets killed about 4,000 Polish officers in the Katyn Forest in 1940. Soviet documents uncovered in the 1990s showed that Stalin ordered 14,700 elite Poles killed, to create a leadership vacuum that could be filled by Communists. Presumably the Katyn massacre of officers was only a part of this program.

Kawartha Lakes, Ont.

The City of Kawartha Lakes, Ont., was formed on Jan. 1, 2001, from the amalgamation of the Town of Lindsay, the Municipality of Bobcaygeon/ Verulam, the villages of Fenelon Falls, Omemee, Sturgeon Point and Woodville, the townships of Bexley, Eldon, Emily, Fenlon, Laxton, Digby and Longford, Manvers, Mariposa, Ops and Somerville. It replaced the County of Victoria, and covers so large an area that, where possible, stories should be located more precisely within it through the mention of the formerly independent parts.

kayak

The enclosed canoe of the Inuit and the sport craft patterned after it,
not a word for all Inuit vessels. The bigger, open boat for cargo or several passengers is an *umiak*. Kayak need not be italic.

Kazakhstan

Adjective and people: Kazakhstani (use Kazakh only for that ethnic group, a minority). Currency: tenge. Capital: Astana (the city's name, meaning capital, was changed in 1998 from Akmola).

This former Soviet republic is unusual in that the original Kazakh inhabitants, largely nomadic herders at the time, were swamped by an influx of outsiders sent in to exploit its abundant resources and rich agricultural land. The ethnic Russian population at its peak in 1991 was 41 per cent of the total of 17 million, but this dropped dramatically after independence as many Russians left and expatriate Kazakhs returned.

Kazakhstan, the largest of the former Soviet republics in Central Asia, stretches along Russia's southern border from the Caspian to Mongolia, and also borders on Turkmenistan, Uzbekistan, Kyrgyzstan and China. With the breakup of the Soviet Union in 1991, Kazakhstan was one of three republics left with nuclear weapons (along with Russia and Ukraine), having a major weapons-testing range near the Chinese border. It also contains the Soviet space-launch site, the Baikonur Cosmodrome near Leninsk. (It was given the name of the coal town of Baikonur, 300 kilometres away, in a bit of Cold War misdirection.)

Kazakhstan is second only to Ukraine in grain production among former Soviet republics, and also produces iron, steel, chemicals, fertilizers and cement.

The Kazakhs, related to the Kyrgyz and speaking a Turkic language, are Muslim, but retain many ancient pre-Islamic customs. They have shed their nomadic culture, their herds having been collectivized, and are now increasingly taking part in the industrial economy.

See Soviet Union.

Kejimkujik National Park

In western Nova Scotia about 170 kilometres southwest of Halifax; an inland park.

Kelligrews Soiree

No apostrophe; the song refers to the community of Kelligrews, not a family named Kelligrew. No accent on Soiree in this case.

Kensington Market, Toronto.

Upper-case Market, even though strictly speaking it is an area of small shops, in the area between College and Dundas Streets west of Spadina Avenue.

Kenya

Adjective and people: Kenyan. Currency: shilling. Capital: Nairobi.

It is in East Africa, straddling the equator, but only the climate of the Indian Ocean coast can be described as equatorial. Most of Kenya is a high plateau with moderate temperatures. Discontent before independence in 1963 spawned the Mau Mau terrorism. Kenya is a member of the Commonwealth. Its population is about 31 million. Kenya has a well-developed system of national parks, and tourism is a major source of revenue. The plateau is cleft north to south by the Great Rift Valley. The country was a one-party state under the Kenya African National Union from independence to 1992, when President Daniel arap Moi, successor to founding president Jomo Kenyatta, was forced by international pressure (in particular, a reduction in aid) to allow other parties. Kenya's first multiparty election was held in December of 1992, won by Mr. Moi and KANU. He won again in 1997. In

2002, KANU candidate Uhuru Kenyatta was defeated in the election by Mwai Kibaki of the Democratic Party of Kenya, who became president.

kerfuffle

Kermode bear

Upper-case; named after Francis Kermode of the B.C. Museum. It is a black bear subspecies on the northern Pacific coast.

ketchup (not catchup, catsup).

Keystone Kops

KGB

Acceptable in first reference. Explain somewhere that it was the Soviet secret police, security service or intelligence agency, as applicable.

Khachaturian, Aram

Khmer Rouge

Khomaini, Ruhollah

Khrushchev, Nikita

Khyber Pass

Historically important to the control of India, but has nothing to do with present-day India. It runs between Peshawar, Pakistan, and Kabul, Afghanistan.

kibbutz and kibitz

Neither needs italics. A **kibbutz** is an Israeli co-operative settlement. The plural is kibbutzim. Use resident, not kibbutznik. To **kibitz**, or to be a kibitzer, is to meddle in the affairs of others, especially with unwanted advice to workers, card players etc.

Kicking Horse Pass

No hyphen. The pass through the Rocky Mountains northwest of Banff that was used for the first trans-Canada railway. A geologist had been kicked by his horse there while working on the Palliser survey, 1857-60.

kid

Acceptable reference to a child only when used for atmosphere in lighter stories.

kiddie porn

Do not use this term in news stories. We do not write of kiddie killing or kiddie abduction. Child porn is acceptable as a short form of child pornography on second reference.

killer app

Slang term, short for killer application. This is the most popular or useful application for something, the one that can turn a new invention into an essential purchase. Elizabeth Reba Weise, U.S. reporter: "The killer application on-line is e-mail. It will always be e-mail."

kidnap

Means to abduct for ransom. If no ransom is demanded, as when a parent takes his or her own child, it is an abduction. Use kidnapper, kidnapped, kidnapping.

kilo

An acceptable short form for kilogram only in lighter stories. Do not use it in stories about drugs.

kilometres an hour (not per).

If there are more than one or two repetitions, contract second and subsequent references to **km/h**.

kilowatt-hours

In technical stories with several repetitions, use **kwh** on second and subsequent references.

kin

It means one's family, one's relatives collectively. Do not use it to refer to an individual relative.

King, Mackenzie

We need not use the full name of Canada's 10th prime minister, William Lyon Mackenzie King, except perhaps when referring to the fact that he was named for his grandfather, the revolutionary of 1837. We may consider him and his predecessors as prime minister to be historical figures, for whom the honorific Mr. is not required in second reference. See honorifics. King was born in 1874 in Berlin, Ont. (now Kitchener), and died in 1950. See prime ministers.

kingbird, but **king snake**.

King's English, Queen's English
Upper-case.

Kings Landing Historical Settlement
No apostrophe. The outdoor museum west of Fredericton.

Kinsmen Clubs
Not -men's. The only major service club to have originated in Canada.

Kiribati
No useful adjective or single word for its people; say citizens of Kiribati, or name their specific island. Currency: Australian dollar. Capital: Tarawa.
It is pronounced Kiribass. Kiribati, which became independent in 1979, consists of 33 coral islands spread across the equator in the central Pacific. It comprises Banaba (Ocean) Island, the 16 Gilbert Islands, the eight Phoenix Islands and eight of the 11 Line Islands. Most of the approximately 96,000 citizens are Micronesian. The official language is English. The capital, Tarawa, is one of the Gilberts.

Kitsilano (district in Vancouver).

Kitty Litter
It is a brand name, upper-case. The generic term is cat litter, cat-box filler.

Kiwanis Music Festival
Kiwanis Festival, the festival.

kiwi
Lower-case for the bird. Upper-case for a New Zealander, and use only in the frothiest of features.

Klondike
The Klondike, in the Dawson area of southwestern Yukon, is strictly speaking confined to the area of the Klondike River and its tributary streams. One of these, Rabbit Creek, was the scene of the strike in 1896 that started the Klondike gold rush. Note that Klondike Days are held each July in Edmonton, not Dawson.

Kluane National Park
In southwestern Yukon. It includes Mount Logan, Canada's highest at 5,959 metres (19,550 feet).

Knesset, the Israeli parliament.

knights and dames
In second reference, refer to each by his or her honorific and given name (Sir Ronald, Dame Wendy). See honorifics.

knockabout

knots
The number of nautical miles covered in an hour. Never say knots an hour.

knowledgeable

koala
A marsupial of eastern Australia that only superficially resembles a bear. Do not say koala bear.

komatik
Italics. The Inuktitut word for the most familiar type of dog sled.

Kootenay River
But note **Kootenai** River (U.S.).

kopeck, a hundredth of a ruble.

Koran
(Not Qur'an.) The sacred book of Islam.

Korea
See North Korea, South Korea.

Korean War
Korea, long occupied by Japan, was split between U.S. and Soviet

occupation forces in 1945, with the 38th parallel as the dividing line.

North Korea invaded the South in 1950, and UN forces, mainly U.S. but also including Canadians and others, were sent in to aid the South. The North continued its advance and took most of the country, including Seoul, until General Douglas MacArthur's brilliant end-run landing at Inchon turned the tide. By November of 1950 the UN forces had pushed the northern forces out of the south, across the 38th parallel and most of the way to the Chinese border, the Yalu River. But the tide turned again when 300,000 Chinese troops crossed the Yalu and pushed the UN forces south, back across the 38th. (MacArthur was fired in April of 1951 over his outspoken insistence that China be attacked directly.) Negotiations began in July of 1951 and lasted for two years, while inconclusive fighting continued. An armistice was signed at Panmunjom in July of 1953, restoring the status quo, but there has been no peace treaty.

Kosovo

Do not use Kosovar to refer to people living in, or events and issues connected to, Kosovo. Notwithstanding the 1999 bombing campaign and NATO peacekeeping mission, Kosovo is still a province of Serbia. Kosovar is a term used by the province's ethnic Albanians, and is politically freighted. The ethnic Albanians in Kosovo may be described as just that, or as Kosovo Albanians if we need something more concise.

Kouchibouguac National Park

In New Brunswick, a shoreline park along Northumberland Strait.

kowtow

Krakow, Poland.

Krazy Glue

A trade name. For a generic description, use instant glue.

Kremlin

In the new Russian democracy, confine Kremlin to the president, his ministers and staff, analogous to the term administration in the United States. Votes in the State Duma should not be shortened to "Kremlin decides" in headlines.

Krieghoff, Cornelius

Kriss Kringle

krona, krone

Krona is the name of the currencies of Iceland (plural kronur) and of Sweden (plural kronor). Krone is the name of the currencies in Denmark and Norway (plural for both, kroner).

'Ksan Indian Village

Note the initial apostrophe. A museum and model village on the Skeena River at Hazelton, B.C.

kudos

Pronounced Q-dose. It is singular, from the Greek word for glory, and means praise, credit. Never use plural verbs with it, as if there were such a thing as an individual "kudo."

Ku Klux Klan, the Klan.

Kuomintang

The governing party of Taiwan until it lost the 2000 election. Do not follow it with the word Party. Kuo Min Tang means National People's Party. The abbreviation KMT may be used if the context is clear.

Kuril Islands

Not Kurile, or Kuril'skiye Ostrova. We do not take sides on whether these 56 islands, which sweep from the Kamchatka Peninsula to Japan's northern Hokkaido Island, are Russian or Japanese. Russia occupies them; Japan claims them.

Kuskonook, B.C.
Avoid confusion with name of the well-known stern-wheeler, which was spelled Kuskanook.

Kuujjuarapik, see Great Whale.

Kuwait
Adjective and people: Kuwaiti. Currency: dinar. Capital: Kuwait.

This tiny sheikdom on the Persian Gulf, bounded by Iraq to the north and west and by Saudi Arabia to the south, has an estimated 20 per cent of the world's oil reserves and one of the highest per capita incomes in the world. Revenues from the oil industry, nationalized in 1975, finance a wide range of social benefits, including free medical care and education and subsidized housing. Almost 80 per cent of the people speak Arabic, with the rest speaking Kurdish or Farsi, but English is widely used as a second language. (Kuwait was a British protectorate from 1899 to 1961.) Involved in territorial disputes with both Saudi Arabia and Iraq, Kuwait was overrun by Iraq on Aug. 2, 1990. The Iraqis were expelled by a U.S.-led coalition of 28 Western and Arab countries in Operation Desert Storm (now usually called the Persian Gulf war), which began with a bombing campaign on Jan. 17, 1991, and ended with a ceasefire that took effect on April 11. The royal family resumed control, but promised more powers to the elected parliament.

The population of two million includes more than a million guest workers, including Iranians, Pakistanis and Palestinians.

Kwakiutl
These Indians of northeastern Vancouver Island are part of the Wakashan language group, along with the Haisla, Heiltsuk and Nootka. See native people.

Kyoto Protocol
Capitalize the P in the tentative environmental agreement on global warming and the control of carbon dioxide in the atmosphere. It was reached by 159 countries attending the Third Conference of Parties to the United Nations Framework Convention on Climate Change, in December, 1997. Other variations – Kyoto agreement, Kyoto accord – should be lower-case.

Kyrenia, Cyprus.

Kyrgyzstan
Adjective and people: Kyrgyzstani (use Kyrgyz for that ethnic group). Currency: som. Capital: Bishkek.

The population of 4.8 million is slightly more than half Kyrgyz (a Turkic, Sunni Muslim people of Mongolian-Tatar origin, related to the Kazakhs), and so Kyrgyzstani is a better term for the country and population as a whole. Other ethnic groups are Russians, Uzbek, Ukrainian and Tatar.

A mountainous former Soviet Central Asian republic, bordering on China, Kazakhstan, Uzbekistan and Tajikistan, it gained independence with the collapse of the Soviet Union in 1991. It had been annexed by Russia in 1864, and became part of the Soviet Union in 1924 after a brief period (from 1917) as part of an independent republic of Turkestan. Its economy, once largely herding, was broadened in the Soviet period to exploit its hydroelectric potential, coal, mercury and antimony. Crops include opium poppies, cotton and tobacco. It is a major manufacturer of farm equipment.
See Soviet Union.

L

Labatt

The company and most of its products carry the name Labatt. The possessive, Labatt's, is found only in the name of its U.S. subsidiary, Labatt's USA, and in the brands Labatt's IPA and (in Europe) Labatt's Canadian Lager. Note the Labatt Brier.

labour

But drop the u for **laborious**. Use the spelling Labor if it appears that way in a proper name in the United States, except Department of Labour, Labour Secretary and Labour Day.

Labrador

Labrador Current, Labrador Highlands, Labrador Plateau, Labrador Shelf, Labrador Trough, with both words upper-case. But Labrador duck, Labrador retriever, labradorite (a mineral).

labrusca

Lower-case for the native North American grape variety, also known as the fox grape.

lacerations, say cuts.

lachrymose

This is the spelling if we must, but prefer tearful, sad.

lackadaisical

It does not mean lazy, slow, careless or offhand, but it can mean listless. It literally means affectedly displaying melancholy (saying "lackaday").

lacklustre

laconic

It does not mean sad. It means brief and concise in speech. (It comes from the Greek word for a Spartan.) A laconic expression could emerge from a mouth, but could not be on a face.

lacquer

ladies' man

Lady

This title now is used informally for second reference to all British peeresses below the rank of duchess; that is, for a marchioness, countess or viscountess. Say the Marchioness of Queensberry, then Lady Queensberry. It is also used for the wives of peers, baronets and knights; but the wives of peers get the definite article (The Lady Hastings) while the wives of knights merely have Lady attached to their surnames (Sir John Jones and his wife, Lady Jones). Lady is also used as a courtesy title for the daughters of dukes, marquesses and earls, attached to their full names, as in Lady Diana Spencer.

Lady is always upper-case when referring to the Virgin Mary, as in Our Lady, and in Lady chapel (a chapel dedicated to her).

In general, we do not use the word lady in news stories to refer to women, except in such expressions as landlady, and forelady in the garment industry.

lady-in-waiting

laetrile, lower-case.

La Guardia Airport, New York.
Named for former mayor Fiorello
La Guardia.

Lahr
German city that was home to a
Canadian Forces air base.

laid-back
Avoid, except in direct quotes.

Lakehead, the
Refers not to the western end of
Lake Superior, at Duluth, but to the
head of navigation, almost 300
kilometres along the northwestern
shore at Thunder Bay. Viewed from
the west, it is the CN and CP railhead
for grain shipments. The Lakehead
can be used as a nickname for
Thunder Bay.

lakes
A lake is a body of water, either
fresh or salt, surrounded by land. The
largest is the Caspian Sea, followed by
Superior, Victoria, Aral (Kazakhstan/
Uzbekistan), Huron, Michigan,
Tanganyika, Great Bear, Baikal
(Russia), Malawi, Great Slave, Erie,
Winnipeg, Chad and Ontario.
Athabasca is 25th and Reindeer 29th.
The terms upper Great Lakes and
upper lakes are confusing to many, and
so should be avoided in favour of
naming the ones we mean. The terms
date from the early days of lake
navigation, when it was possible to
travel in one ship only as far as Lake
Ontario, because Niagara Falls was an
impassable obstacle. The upper lakes
are all the others—Erie, St. Clair,
Huron, Michigan and Superior.
Navigation between them is possible
because their elevations are in a very
narrow range, from 183 metres at Lake
Superior to 174 metres at Lake Erie.
Lake Ontario is just 75 metres, with
Niagara Falls accounting for 51 metres
of the drop.

In Newfoundland, many lakes,
even large ones, are called ponds.

Lakeshore, Lake Shore
It is Lake Shore Boulevard in
Toronto, but there is also a Lakeshore
Drive in the city and a Lakeshore
Avenue on the Toronto Islands. It is
Lakeshore Road in Mississauga,
Oakville and Burlington, and
Lakeshore Street in Oshawa.

lama and llama
A **lama** is a priest or monk in the
branch of Buddhism practised in
Mongolia and Tibet, known as
Lamaism (note upper case). Their
monasteries are called lamaseries.
Tibet's spiritual leader (now in exile)
is the Dalai Lama.
A **llama** is a South American
animal resembling a small camel with
no hump.

La Mauricie National Park
In the Laurentians between
Quebec and Montreal.

lame duck
This is a perfectly acceptable
phrase to describe a person or group
whose hold on a position of power is
about to end (in particular, people
serving out a term after an electoral
defeat) and whose influence is
therefore circumscribed (a lame-duck
president, council, Congress).
However, it is prone to overuse.
Reserve it for stories in which the
lameness of the duck is at issue, as
when a soon-to-depart official refrains
from (or embarks on) initiatives for
which the electorate has clearly not
granted a mandate.

lampreys
They are eel-like, but are actually
fish (rare jawless fish, parasites with a
suction-cup mouth lined with rasping
teeth that allow them to feed on the
flesh of their host). They should not
be called lamprey eels.

Lancaster, House of

Henry IV, V and VI, 1399 to 1471. The Lancastrians were deposed by the House of York, but Henry Tudor was heir to their line and re-established it when he defeated Richard III in the last battle of the Wars of the Roses (at Bosworth) and took the throne as Henry VII. He then united the two houses by marrying Elizabeth of York.

lance-corporal

A rank that no longer exists in the Canadian Forces. See ranks.

Lancet

The British medical journal has no The.

landed immigrant

Hyphenate the adjective, as in landed-immigrant status.

landlocked

Land of the Midnight Sun, caps.

Land-Rover, a trade name.

landscaper and landscapist

One designs or creates them; the other is an artist who paints them.

Langevin Block

Upper-case. Contains the federal government's central executive offices—the PMO and the PCO. It was built in the 1880s when the bureaucracy first outgrew the Parliament Buildings.

languor

L'Anse aux Meadows, Nfld.

A fishing village at the northern tip of Newfoundland, locally pronounced Lansy Meadows, a corruption of the French *L'anse aux méduses* (Jellyfish Cove). Remains of a Norse settlement dating from about 1000 have been found near there.

Laos

Adjective and people: Laotian. Currency: kip. Capital: Vientiane.

The official language is Lao (French is also common), and Lao is also the name of the predominant group, a Thai people. But use Laotian as the general noun for the entire population of about 5.8 million, because they also include Meo, Yao, Chinese and Vietnamese. Laos is mountainous and landlocked, surrounded by China, Vietnam, Cambodia, Thailand and Myanmar (formerly Burma). It was a component of French Indochina (along with Cambodia and Vietnam) until the Second World War. Laos became a constitutional monarchy in 1947. An insurgency by the Pathet Lao (Lao State) movement under Prince Souphanouvong (with North Vietnamese help) began in 1953 and ended with a protocol in 1973 under which the Pathet Lao became part of a coalition government. After the Communist victories in Cambodia and Vietnam in 1975, the Pathet Lao took over entirely. King Savang Vatthana abdicated on Nov. 29, 1975, and a republic was declared three days later. It was admitted to the Association of Southeast Asian Nations (see ASEAN) in 1977.

Lapland

Not a country, but the traditional homeland of the Lapps. It is north of the Arctic circle in Norway, Sweden, Finland and Russia, but the majority of the approximately 30,000 Lapps live in Norway. Their language is Lapp. Note that the people themselves prefer to be known as Sami.

La Prairie

Communities in Quebec and Nova Scotia, but note that the provincial Quebec riding is **Laprairie**.

largesse

larva, larvae, larval

larynx
Larynxes, laryngeal (not -ial); laryngitis.

La Salle
Put a space in the names of communities in Quebec, Ontario and Manitoba, and the name of the explorer. But note the federal riding of LaSalle-Émard, and the Ontario community of LaSalle Park, near Kingston. And it's De La Salle College in Toronto.

lascivious

laser, lower-case.
Acronym for light amplification by stimulated emission of radiation.

lasso, lassos
Also known as a lariat.

lassy tart
In Newfoundland, molasses pie.

last
It should not be used to mean the latter of two. Say the second half, not the last half.
When attached to a day, month or season, the word last means different things to different people, and so is often ambiguous. Many take it literally to mean the most recent one, but even these would be given pause if, in a story written in October, we were to use last September or last summer to refer to those that ended just a few days earlier. Most people would read these to refer to the previous year. For clarity, in references to the same calendar year simply say in March, in the spring etc. Early in the new year, we would also say simply in December, in November etc. After the first quarter has gone by, the danger of ambiguity fades and we may safely say last November, last fall, although this is not mandatory if the meaning is

clear. If there is any chance of confusion, resort to "in January of this year," of last year, of 2001.
Do not say in the last year (or month or week); say past.

this is definitely the last spike, so you'd better get it right this time.

Last Spike
Upper-case for the spike driven to complete the CPR in 1885 at Craigellachie, B.C. There were actually two of them; financier Donald A. Smith bent the first Last Spike, then drove another. Both were iron, not gold. (A golden spike had completed the Union Pacific in 1869.)

Last Supper

late
"The late" is the proper description for someone who is dead (never "the former"). However, it is appropriate only when readers are not likely to know the person is dead. We should not say the late Marilyn Monroe, the late Lester B. Pearson. We must always confirm that a person so described is indeed dead. Several people, such as long-time cabinet ministers who have been out of the limelight for several years, have proved to be embarrassingly healthy after being described by a careless journalist as "the late."

Latin America

This is the only expression that combines all the countries in the central and southern part of the Western Hemisphere in which Romance languages (Spanish, Portuguese, French and creoles of these) are spoken. Most are in Central or South America, but some are on Caribbean islands and one, Mexico, is in North America. Canada and Saint-Pierre and Miquelon are francophone, but readers would not consider them to be included in the term Latin America.

Latino, Chicano, Hispanic

People of Spanish-speaking heritage living in the United States tend to refer to themselves as Latino, and would prefer that others do so, too. "Hispanic" is no longer in favour because it has connotations of Spain, whereas the overwhelming majority have their origins in Latin America.

Accordingly, Latino is our word of choice when we want to be all-inclusive. When distinctions are relevant, use the more specific Mexican American, Cuban American, Puerto Rican etc. (hyphenated when used as adjectives). We retain the word "Spanish" in references to the language, and the word "Hispanic" undoubtedly will continue to pop up in references to Spain and in some organization names.

The word "Chicano" means a person born in the United States of Mexican heritage. As with Nisei/Issei/Sansei, use it only when the distinction is relevant and when the story explains the difference. Otherwise, refer to all people with Spanish-speaking roots, immigrants and native Americans alike, as Latino.

Latin remains a good all-purpose adjective for Latin Americans: the Latin influence, the Latin culture, a Latin celebration.

Latin Quarter, Paris.

latitude, see directions.

latter

A difficult word in news stories, forcing the reader to backtrack and sort out what is being referred to. It is usually worth recasting to eliminate the need for former and latter.

Latvia

Adjective and people: Latvian. Currency: lats. Capital: Riga.

Latvians, one of two remaining peoples speaking a Baltic language (Lithuanians are the other), make up only 55 per cent of Latvia's population of 2.4 million. Russians, sent in to industrialize the republic under Soviet rule, make up 33 per cent. Along with Lithuania and Estonia, it was annexed by the Soviet Union in 1940 (although it was occupied by the Germans from 1941 until the Soviets retook control in 1944), and it took a leading role in the eventual Soviet breakup. In 1988 it adopted its prewar flag and gave the Latvian language official status. It held multiparty elections in 1989, and unilaterally declared independence (subject to a transition period) in May of 1990, two months after Lithuania. The Soviets applied economic and military pressure, but Latvia achieved both Soviet and international recognition in September of 1991.

Latvia, the middle Baltic state in location, size and population, has no mineral resources. A third of its land is forest, and another third unsuited to agriculture except for grazing. Principal agricultural products are meat, milk and grains. Latvian industry, developed with a massive influx of Russian labour (and pollution), was assigned the production of ships, railway rolling stock, power generators and durable consumer goods such as refrigerators.

Refer to the Baltic states, not "the Baltics."

See Soviet Union.

laudable and laudatory

People and actions are **laudable** (deserving of praise); the words used to praise them are **laudatory**.

laughingstock

laundromat

It is a trade name, but is now considered to have become a generic word. See capitalization.

Laurentians

They are not really mountains, and are properly called the Laurentian Highlands, forming the southern edge of the Canadian Shield in Quebec. But we may avoid the issue altogether by simply calling them the Laurentians. The highest peaks, classed as scarps, are Mont Raoul-Blanchard, Mont Bleu, Mont des Conscrits, Mont Tremblant and Mont Sainte-Anne.

Laurier, Wilfrid

He became Canada's first francophone prime minister in 1896. After June of 1897, call him Sir Wilfrid Laurier. In second reference, Laurier.

Laval University

It should not be called the University of Laval. It is not in that community, but rather in Sainte-Foy.

Law of the Sea

See territorial waters.

laws, principles, effects

In general, upper-case proper names, but not the nouns they modify (Ohm's law, Archimedes' principle, Newton's first law of motion, Mach number).

lawyer

This is the usual word in Canada. We do not use barrister, solicitor (except in solicitor-general). Use attorney only for such positions as Crown attorney, attorney-general. See courts.

lay and lie

They are often confused, largely because lay is also the past tense of lie.

Lay is a transitive verb (except in the expression The hens have stopped laying). It describes what hens and masons do to eggs and bricks, and what people do to the groundwork, to plans, claims, tables, traps etc. Its other forms are laying and laid. (He is laying an egg. He laid the rumour to rest; he has laid it to rest. Bricks are laid, have been laid.)

Lie is an intransitive verb. In the sense of being recumbent, its other forms are lying, lay and lain. (He is lying in wait. He lay on the bed. He has lain on the bed.)

In the sense of telling an untruth, lie's other forms are lying and lied. (He is lying. He lied to me. He has lied. I have been lied to.) See lie.

layoff; the verb is **lay off**.

layout; the verb is **lay out**.

lazy Susan

lea and lee

A **lea** is a grassy meadow, usually a clearing in a wood.

Lee is a treacherous word for the nautical novice, because it can be defined in terms of either the sides of a vessel or the sides of a piece of land.

In references to land, it is a place sheltered from the wind, such as **the lee** of an island or headland, and for a ship this is a safe place to be.

Aboard ship, lee describes the side of a vessel opposite the one against which the wind is blowing. Confusion arises in the term **lee shore** because this is defined from the point of view of the vessel, being a shore that lies on the vessel's lee side. That means it is a shore toward which the wind is blowing, and a disabled vessel off a lee shore is in grave peril.

The word **leeward** is also defined by someone on a vessel. It is the direction off the lee side, which means it is the direction toward which the wind is blowing. A vessel running to leeward (pronounced looard) is running with the wind. A vessel beating to windward is working to move against the wind, toward the vessel's windward side.

leach and leech

Leach has to do with the percolation or filtering of a liquid. It is what toxic wastes do from dumps. A **leech** is a bloodsucking worm or, figuratively, a person who sponges off another.

Leacock Award

Upper-case, even though its proper name is the Stephen Leacock Medal for Humour. Awarded for the best humorous book published in Canada.

lead

Its past tense and participle, both led, are commonly misspelled in copy because they sound like the metal previously so central to our business, lead.

leader

We must be wary of describing someone as a leader or representative of any diverse group, such as an entire ethnic minority or profession, if the person has not been chosen through some form of broadly based democratic process. Splinter groups or special-interest committees often choose names that imply a universal constituency (the National Association of Such-and-such), when in fact they have no mandate to speak on behalf of anyone beyond their own limited membership. The head of such a group might fairly be described as a

vocal, prominent or even respected member of a particular community (if this is indeed the case), but members of the community at large often resent our going further and calling such people their leader or spokesman.

Leader, see capitalization.

leap year, leap second

Lower-case. The extra day added in a leap year has an impact on our calendar, while leap seconds have an impact on our clocks.

Leap seconds are added to a day approximately twice a year, whenever needed to ensure that UTC (Universal Time Co-ordinated, kept on the world's standard atomic clock in Paris and used to synchronize the world's clocks) stays in sync with actual solar time (GMT, for Greenwich Mean Time, kept in London).

For their part, leap years are more complex than most think. Everyone is familiar with the fact that, to prevent "date creep" because the Earth does not make an even number of day-night rotations in its year-long trip around the sun (it varies in the range of 365¼ days), an extra day is added to February in years divisible by four, known as leap years. Many may also be aware that leap years are skipped if the year is also divisible by 100. But few are aware that even this is not enough to keep things accurate, and that leap years are again observed in years divisible by 400, such as 2000. Even so, things will be out by about a day in another 2,000 years.

Learjet, a trade name.

Lebanon

Adjective and people: Lebanese. Currency: Lebanese pound. Capital: Beirut.

Not **The** Lebanon. It is on the square eastern end of the

Mediterranean, bordering on Israel and Syria, and has a wetter, more moderate climate than either. Its four main regions lie in north-south strips parallel to the sea: the fertile coastal area, the Lebanon Mountains, the fertile Bekaa Valley, and the Anti-Lebanon Mountains. The mountains were once forested by the Cedars of Lebanon, but only scattered groves are left. The population of about 3.7 million may be described as Arab, but only slightly above half are Muslim. Most of the rest are Christian, mainly Maronite. There is a small Druze minority that is militarily and politically significant. Lebanon has been effectively independent of France since 1944. A large U.S. force invaded in 1958, at the request of President Chamoun, to quell an insurrection that was largely Muslim and Nasserist. The presence of Palestinian guerrilla units was long a destabilizing factor, leading to unsuccessful government attempts to suppress them, intervention by Syria in 1976, and invasions by Israel in 1978 and 1982. Bachir Gemayel was elected president on Aug. 23, 1982, but was assassinated on Sept. 14 and succeeded by his brother, Amin. Israeli forces withdrew to the south, near their border, in 1985, and continued to equip a strong Christian militia as a buffer. They pulled out entirely in 2002. Fifteen years of civil war between various militias (Christian, Shia Muslim, Sunni Muslim and Druze) was ended in 1990 by Syrian military intervention, under terms of the Taif Agreement brokered by Syria and the Arab League at Taif, Saudi Arabia, in 1989. The country's first election in 20 years was held in September of 1992, despite a boycott by the Maronite Christians.

LeBlanc, Roméo
   The former governor-general.

lectern
   What speakers stand at or behind. It should not be confused with what they stand on, the podium. See dais.

Le Dain commission
   The colloquial name for the federal commission of inquiry into the non-medical use of drugs, which lasted from 1969 to 1973. The official name was the Royal Commission Inquiry on Drug Use; its chairman was Gerald Le Dain, later a justice of the Supreme Court of Canada. Among its recommendations was that simple possession of marijuana not result in a jail sentence.

leer, leery
   A **leer** is a sly, sideways look, now almost always with the connotation of carnal intent. (It is not a full-face stare, no matter how sexually suggestive.) Someone who is **leery** is also looking askance, but here the connotation is wariness, suspicion.

Left Bank, Paris.

left fielder, left-hander, left-winger

legal stories, see courts.

legerdemain, sleight of hand.

Legion
   Upper-case when referring to the Royal Canadian Legion or its counterparts in other countries, including the American Legion. A Legion hall, a Legion member. But lower-case legionnaire.

legislature
   In most provinces, use upper case when accompanied by the name of the province (the Alberta Legislature). We take this to be the proper name, even though the formal name might be Legislative Assembly etc. The two exceptions are the Quebec legislature,

called the National Assembly, and the Newfoundland and Labrador legislature, the House of Assembly.

Use lower case for legislature and assembly standing alone, but upper case for House when we mean the actual legislative chamber.

The members in seven provinces are called MLAs, the exceptions being Ontario (MPP), Quebec (MNA) and Newfoundland and Labrador (MHA).

The adjective **legislature** means pertaining to the legislature or the building; the adjective **legislative** means pertaining to legislation or the passage of laws. A committee may be legislative, considering proposed laws, but if it deals merely with members' privileges or similar administrative matters, call it a legislature committee.

Leif Ericson
Leif in second reference.

Leipzig

lengthwise (not -ways).

Leonardo da Vinci
He was from the Tuscan town of Vinci, the illegitimate son of a notary, and is properly Leonardo in second reference. His works are called Leonardos. He is the archetype of the Renaissance man: a naturalist, painter (the *Last Supper*, the *Mona Lisa*), sculptor, architect and engineer.

leprechaun

lesbian
Lower-case in references to homosexual women, except in organization names. Gay is acceptable to most, especially when referring to both sexes (the gay community), but when a point is made of mentioning the sexes separately, the expression gays and lesbians is more common than gay men and women.

lèse-majesté, italics.

Lesotho
No useful adjective for the country or for the people; use "of Lesotho" etc. Currency: loti (plural maloti), at par with the South African rand. Capital: Maseru.

Lesotho (formerly Basutoland) is a mountainous country surrounded by South Africa and heavily dependent on it economically. Its form of government is a constitutional monarchy. The Sotho people make up 85 per cent of the population of 2.2 million. Their own word for themselves is Basotho, but avoid this as confusing unless the context is clear and the word explained. It does not cover the minorities in the other 15 per cent of the population. Lesotho is a member of the Commonwealth.

less and fewer, see fewer and less.

letters
A single letter merely standing for itself as a letter of the alphabet is generally lower-case, and for clarity takes an apostrophe to form the plural, as in p's and q's; dot the i's and cross the t's. The exceptions are hyphenated nouns based on the shape of the letter, which are upper-case as in S-hook, T-shirt, I-beam.

Note that a single letter that is an abbreviation of a word, or is in a trade name, is upper-case, as in M Fund, H-bomb, Q-tip.

leukocyte, a white blood cell.

leveraged buyouts
Spell it out on first reference. The abbreviation LBOs appearing in a quote must be explained if the expression has not been used higher in the story. A leveraged buyout is one in which the purchase is financed, in part or in total, through the assets of the company being purchased. The assets

may be used as collateral for loans, or the buyer may plan to sell off some of the assets, such as subsidiaries or properties, to help finance the deal.

Lévis, Que.

A new, larger City of Lévis (population 125,000) was created on Jan. 1, 2002, through the amalgamation of 10 municipalities: Charny, Lévis, Pintendre, Sainte-Hélène-de-Breakeyville, Saint-Etienne-du-Lauzon, Saint-Jean-Chrysostome, Saint-Joseph-de-la-Pointe-de-Lévy, Saint-Nicholas, Saint-Rédempteur and Saint-Romuald. Lévis is on the south side of the St. Lawrence River, across from Quebec City.

See also Montreal, Quebec City, Gatineau, Longueuil and Trois-Rivières.

Levi's, a trade name.

Lhasa, Tibet, but **Lassa fever**.

liable

It should not be used to mean likely, apt. It means responsible or answerable for.

liaison (note the -iai-).

Liard Highway, Liard River, Fort Liard

Not Laird, as in Toronto's Laird Drive. The river is named for the poplars (French *liards*) that abound along it. It rises in Yukon, and flows into B.C. and then northeast to join the Mackenzie at Fort Simpson, NWT. The Liard Highway runs north from the Alaska Highway near Fort Nelson, B.C., 400 kilometres to the Mackenzie Highway near Fort Simpson.

libel, see courts.

Liberia

Adjective and people: Liberian. Currency: Liberian dollar. Capital: Monrovia.

On the northwestern corner of the Gulf of Guinea, bordered by Ivory Coast, Guinea and Sierra Leone, Liberia is Africa's oldest black republic, proclaimed in 1847. (The first settlement of freed slaves had been established in 1822, with the backing of several U.S. philanthropic societies. It was named Monrovia after President James Monroe.) Only 10 per cent of the population of about 3.3 million are the so-called Americo-Liberians, descended from freed slaves. The rest are divided into 16 major tribes. About 75 per cent of Liberians practise traditional African religions. About 15 per cent are Muslim and 10 per cent are Christian. A bitter civil war, largely tribal, resulted in the death of President Samuel Doe in 1990 and an invasion in August of that year by 15,000 troops of the six-member Economic Community of West African States in an attempt to lift the siege of Monrovia by Charles Taylor's National Patriotic Front of Liberia. As the carnage continued, a United Nations arms embargo was declared in November of 1992. In 2002, after the government refused to stop supporting rebels in Sierra Leone, the UN imposed sanctions on Liberian diamonds and on international travel by Taylor and those around him.

Many ships list their home port as Monrovia because of Liberia's lax rules for registering foreign vessels. The term Liberian freighter is misleading; we should always try to specify the country of ownership and, in stories involving the crew, give their nationality and that of the captain. If these are not known, we at least explain why they are not likely to be Liberians.

Libeskind, Daniel

The architect. Not Liebeskind.

Library of Parliament

Run by the Parliamentary Librarian, and may be called the Parliamentary Library, upper-case.

Libya

Adjective and people: Libyan. Currency: dinar. Capital: Tripoli.

It is bounded on the Mediterranean by Tunisia and Egypt, and in its Saharan southern part by Algeria, Niger, Chad and Sudan. About 90 per cent of the Libyan population of about 5.4 million is in the coastal strip. Most are Arab, but there are also Berbers, Bedouin and Tuareg. About half the work force is employed in agriculture (oranges, olives, almonds, dates, barley, wheat, millet, peanuts), and there are also leather and textile industries, but 99 per cent of export revenue comes from oil, of which enormous reserves were discovered in 1959. Libya is an ancient state, occupied in the past by the Romans, by the Turks from the 1500s to 1911 and by Italy from 1911 to the Second World War. In accordance with two UN resolutions it became a federal kingdom in 1951, under King Idris. He was deposed in 1969 by a group of army officers with Col. Moammar Gadhafi as chairman.

licence, noun, but **license**, verb.

All the variations are derived from the verb and should use the s: licensed, licensing, licensee, licensable. When the noun itself is used as an adjective, it retains the c: licence plate, licence number. See practice, practise.

lickety-split

licorice (not liquorice).

lie

(For a comparison with **lay**, see lay and lie.)

To lie, in the sense of telling an untruth, means to make a statement that the speaker knows is false, with an intent to deceive. It is a word that is far too subjective for a news story, and far too dangerous. Even when we are quoting someone else as alleging a lie by an identifiable person, the person referred to could well take libel action. If we know a statement is false, descriptions based on such words as untrue and inaccurate convey this without getting into speculation on the speaker's knowledge or intent. (Words such as mistaken go too far the other way, unless we are certain there was no intent to deceive.)

Liechtenstein

No useful English adjective or word for the people; say "of Liechtenstein" etc. (We avoid the German Liechtensteiner.) Currency: Swiss franc. Capital: Vaduz.

It is an independent, German-speaking principality of only 160 square kilometres, in the mountains between Switzerland and Austria, with a population of about 33,000. The reigning prince, Hans Adam, succeeded on the death of his father, Francis Joseph II, in November of 1989, but had been exercising the sovereign prerogatives since 1984. Thousands of companies list Liechtenstein as their nominal headquarters, because of its low taxes and bank secrecy. Liechtenstein has become highly industrialized since the Second World War, with only 3 per cent of its population now engaged in agriculture. Products include cloth, ceramics, precision instruments and pharmaceuticals.

lieutenant, Lt., see ranks.

lieutenant-colonel

Lieutenant-Governor

We do not abbreviate the title for the provincial viceregal office. It may be lower-case in generic references, such as Nova Scotia's past three lieutenant-governors. Note that lieutenant modifies the main word, governor, so it is governor that becomes plural.

For the lieutenant governor of a U.S. state, we do not use a hyphen.

life

One word: lifebelt, lifeblood, lifeboat, lifebuoy, lifeguard, lifelike, lifeline, lifelong, lifestyle, lifesaver, lifespan. (But note the trade name Life Savers; he ate a Life Saver.) Hyphenated: life-sized, life-support. Two words: life jacket, life net, life preserver, life raft.

lighthearted, lightweight, light heavyweight

light-year

Hyphenated. Note that a light-year is a measure of distance, not of time. We must not say, for example, that light from a certain star takes 35 light-years to reach Earth. A light-year is the distance that light traverses a vacuum in one Earth year, at nearly 300,000 kilometres a second (about 9.5 million million kilometres).

Note that among professional astronomers the light-year has been largely replaced by the parsec. Roughly speaking, two lines are drawn to a star, one from Earth and the other from our sun. If the angle these two lines create at the star equals one second of arc (one-360th of a degree), the star is one parsec away. A parsec equals about 3.26 light-years. Distances are commonly expressed in kiloparsecs and megaparsecs.

like

Can be used as a preposition (like a bird), an adjective (of like minds) or a noun (we won't see his like again). But it should not be used as a conjunction to begin a clause, meaning as, as if or in the manner that. Say things turned out **as** I hoped they would; it looks **as if** it will be sunny; she writes **as** a reporter should. Use "such as" if the intent is to give an example rather than make a comparison: great painters such as (not like) Renoir.

Lillooet, B.C.

Lillooet Glacier, Lake, River.

linage, lineage

Linage for the printed lines, lineage for the family tree.

Lindbergh, Charles

Not the first person to fly the Atlantic, but the first to do it solo and non-stop.

lineup, the noun. The verb is **line up**.

lingua franca, see pidgin. Does not require italics.

linked to

This is interpreted by most readers as meaning connected to. Its sole virtue in headlines is its length, because it is dangerously ambiguous out of context. If we write Businessman linked to organized crime, do we mean The Globe says he is connected to it, or merely that someone such as a judge or MP has linked him to it (expressed the conviction that such a connection exists)? Even if the headline includes an attribution (MP says, etc.), the source might merely be quoting others as having made the link. Use this term with extreme care, keeping aware of the impression it is creating.

Lions Gate Bridge

No apostrophe; it is named for the Lions, twin peaks on the North Shore. It links Vancouver to North Vancouver and West Vancouver, across Burrard Inlet's First Narrows.

Lipizzaner

Not Lippizaner. This breed of horse takes its name from the old imperial Austrian stud farm at Lipizza. Most are grey, but not all. A well-known string of greys is trained at Vienna's Spanish Riding School.

liquefaction (not -efication).

liquefied natural gas, LNG

Not to be confused with liquefied petroleum gas (LPG, or LP gas). LNG, made possible by fairly recent cooling and compression technology, has the same content as natural gas, primarily methane. LPG, which can be various mixtures of the heavy petroleum compounds propane, propene, butane and butene, is the "bottled gas" that has been used for more than a century as a portable fuel. Leaking LNG dissipates, the gas being lighter than air; but the heavier gas from an LPG leak collects in pools.

liquefy (not -ify).

lissome

Lissome does not mean beautiful of face. A lissome lass is flexible, agile, lithe.

Liszt, Franz

litany

It is a series of prayers or supplications, to each of which the congregation utters a fixed response. It is also used to mean a tediously long list or account. We should be careful here. Litany is fine if we mean that a list of woes or complaints is so long that reading it all is a tedious task, but not if we mean that the author or wording of the list is tedious.

literally

Often misused in place of virtually or figuratively. Literally means really, actually, in the strictest sense. We could stretch a point and say I'm literally exhausted, but not My heart was literally in my mouth.

It is best to avoid metaphors and other such non-literal expressions if they need to be qualified with a word such as figuratively or virtually. They lose their effect, clarity and usefulness if the reader does not instantly recognize them for what they are.

Lithuania

Adjective and people: Lithuanian. Currency: litas. Capital: Vilnius.

The most southerly, largest and most populous of the three Baltic states, bordering on Latvia, Belarus, Poland and the small Russian enclave of Kaliningrad (Koenigsberg), it was annexed by the Soviet Union in 1940, and occupied by the Germans from 1941 to 1944. It took a leading role in the breakup of the Soviet Union, being the first of the three Baltic states to declare independence (in March of 1990, subject to negotiations and a transition period). In November of 1989, under the leadership of the Lithuanian Restructuring Movement (Sajudis), it had adopted the prewar flag and declared Lithuanian the official language. In January of 1991, Soviet troops seized communications and political buildings in Vilnius, killing 13 civilians, but quickly withdrew in the face of Lithuanian and internal Soviet protests. Eight months later, in September, Lithuania received Soviet and international recognition as an independent state. The heavy industries set up under Soviet rule created devastating pollution, and were uncompetitive under free-market conditions, and unemployment soared. In November of 1992, Lithuania became the first former Soviet republic to democratically return Communists (renamed the Lithuanian Democratic Labour Party) to office.

Lithuanians, whose Baltic language retains many ancient Indo-European features, make up 80 per cent of the population of 3.7 million. Minorities include Russians (9 per cent), Poles (8 per cent) Belarussians and Ukrainians.

Refer to the Baltic states, not "the Baltics."

See Soviet Union.

litre (not liter).

We do not use the abbreviation, L.

little

As an adverb modifying an adjective, it is hyphenated when the two words precede the noun (a little-known fact), but a separate word if the adjective is used predicatively (He is little known outside Ottawa).

living room

LLD, for doctor of laws.
Usually an honorary degree.

Lloyd's

An apostrophe for the insurance association, but not in Lloyds Bank.

Lloyd's should not be called an insurance company. It is an association or pool of individuals, called underwriters, who assume unlimited personal liability for their share of a claim. They are grouped in about 300 syndicates.

loan

Use it only as a noun, as in a bank loan. The verb is **lend**, and its past tense is **lent**. The bank lends (not loans) money; the bank lent (not loaned) me money.

loan shark, loansharking

See usury.

loath and loathe

Loath is an adjective, meaning reluctant, unwilling (usually followed by an infinitive). **Loathe** is a verb, meaning to hate, detest. But note that the e drops in **loathing**, **loathsome**.

Loblaw, Loblaws

It is Loblaw Cos. Ltd. and Loblaw International Merchants, but **Loblaws Supermarkets Ltd.**, with an s but no apostrophe. Refer to a store as a Loblaws.

locker room

lockout, the noun. The verb is **lock out**.

locoweed

logarithmically

Shun this buzzword used to describe rapidly accelerating increases. The technically correct adverb for increases in which the figure is multiplied by itself is **exponentially** (an "exponent" is the figure in smaller type indicating how many times a number is to be multiplied by itself—squared, cubed etc.). However, this word is generally unsuitable for news stories because it is obscure to most readers, and is also vague (a number can be multiplied by itself once, twice, a million times etc.). Also, in such areas as cell division and the spread of AIDS, the number is continually multiplied by 2, not by itself. It is better to use a few extra words to make our meaning clear to readers unfamiliar with mathematics. It is often enough to say the number, amount, value etc. increases very rapidly by ever-larger amounts. If there is indeed a regular pattern, we might say that at each stage the amount doubles, triples, increases tenfold etc.

log-rolling

No need to explain if we mean birling, but we should translate if a person being quoted uses this U.S. term for trading influence and votes between politicians.

long

One word: longboat, longbow, longhair, longhand, longhorn, longhouse, longliner, longshoreman. **Hyphenated**: long-distance (adj. and adv.), long-lived, long-playing, long-range, long-standing (adj.), long-suffering, long-term (adj.), long-time, long-winded. **Two words**: long division, long shot.

longitude, see directions.

Longlac, Ont.

But the lake on which it is situated is Long Lake. Also the Long Lake Reserve.

Long Range Mountains

No hyphen. In western Newfoundland, part of the Appalachian system. See Appalachian.

Longueuil, Que.

A new, larger City of Longueuil was created on Jan. 1, 2002, through the amalgamation of eight municipalities: Boucherville, Brossard, Greenfield Park, LeMoyne, Longueuil, Saint-Bruno-de-Montarville, Saint-Hubert and Saint-Lambert. The city, just east of Montreal across the St. Lawrence River, has seven boroughs.

See also Montreal, Quebec City, Gatineau, Lévis and Trois-Rivières.

loofah

loonie

Lower-case. Acceptable reference to the Canadian dollar coin, but there is usually no need to specify coinage in such references as putting $2 into a vending machine.

Loop, the (Chicago). Upper-case.

loophole

This word has a specific application: a means of evading the intended purpose of the drafters of a law or contract. It always carries the pejorative connotation of cheating or at least sharp practice. Avoid it when referring to legitimate tax-reducing measures that conform to governments' intended tax policies, such as RRSPs, the exemption on capital-gains tax and deductions for business trips and meals. Reserve loophole for cases in which a practice was clearly not intended by the legislation.

lopsided, but **lop-eared**.

Lord's Cricket Ground, London.

Headquarters of the International Cricket Conference and of the two controlling bodies of English cricket; the site of important matches, including test matches between England and visiting national teams; and the home ground of the Marylebone Cricket Club. It is named for Yorkshireman Thomas Lord, who established the first ground (south of the current site) in the 1780s.

L'Orignal, Ont.

Loring Lion, the

The concrete lion in Toronto's Lakefront Park, the work of Frances Loring (see the Girls). It was moved there in 1973 to allow the widening of the Queen Elizabeth Way, whose eastern end it had guarded since 1939.

loudspeaker

Reserve for large, powerful speakers used for crowds. For a home stereo setup, prefer speaker.

Louisbourg

In Cape Breton, southeast of Sydney. The restored fortress is part of Fortress of Louisbourg National Historic Park (note the "of").

Lou Marsh Trophy

Awarded to Canada's top athlete, as chosen by a committee of sports editors. Named for a former sports editor of the Toronto Star.

loup-garou

Lower-case, italics. Werewolf, a popular subject in Quebec folklore. Use the French only for colour, and translate. The plural is *loups-garous*.

lover

An acceptable term, but often irrelevant and unprovable. We must not assume that two people living under the same roof are sexually intimate. Unless both agree this is the case and unless sexual intimacy is germane to the story, stick to the fact that they share a house or apartment.

Love's Labour's Lost

lower case, see upper case.

lower house
Lower-case in references to bicameral legislatures. But avoid it for Canada's House of Commons. It creates an inaccurate impression of the relationship between the Commons and Senate.

Loyalist
Upper-case for those who chose not to stay in the proposed or the newly independent United States. Attach "United Empire" to the front of Loyalist for those who arrived in British North America before or very shortly after the American Revolution ended in 1783. The governor-in-chief, Lord Dorchester, decreed that they and their descendants could add UE to their names, for the principle of Unity of Empire. Those who arrived after 1783 were the "late Loyalists," not UE. See Eastern Townships.

LSD
No need to spell out lysergic acid diethylamide in hard news stories. See drugs.

Lubumbashi, Congo (formerly Zaire).
Refer to its former name of Elisabethville, The Congo, when recounting the civil war over the secession of Katanga (now Shaba).

lustre

Lutz
The figure-skating move, upper-case.

Luxembourg
No useful adjective or single word for the people. Say "of Luxembourg"

etc. Currency: euro (had been the Luxembourg franc). Capital: Luxembourg.
It is a grand duchy about 90 by 60 kilometres, bounded on the north and west by Belgium, on the east by western Germany and on the south by France. The national language is Luxemburgish (we do not call it Letzburgesch), a German dialect, but German, French and English are common. The sovereign (Grand Duke Jean), of the House of Nassau, has the constitutional right to organize the government. The population is about 449,000. The southeast, along the Moselle River, is known for its wine and fruit. The more industrial southwest is rich in iron ore, and is a large producer of pig iron and steel. Luxembourg was one of the six founding countries of the European Economic Community (now the European Union) in 1957, and joined the euro currency area in 1999.

luxuriant
It means growing lushly and profusely, as in vegetation or hair. Not to be confused with luxurious.

luxury
The words luxury and luxurious are favoured in real estate and hotel promotions because they are one step removed from what is really meant: expensive. News stories need not wander from the strictly accurate in this way, to make an implied comment on quality. The best course is to avoid adjectives altogether and merely give the price: houses in the $2-million range, more than seven times the city's average house price.
Reserve luxurious for accurate descriptions of extreme comfort, opulence, sumptuousness.
We do not use luxury as an adjective. Use luxurious, or substitute expensive, opulent etc.

-ly adverbs

We do not use a hyphen after adverbs ending in -ly. Say a wholly owned subsidiary.

Lyme disease

Not lime or Lyme's. This bacterial infection is named not for a person but for Lyme, Conn., where it was first described in 1974. Spread by both the larval and adult stage of ticks whose preferred hosts are mice and deer, it causes fever, joint pain and a ring-like rash. It has become the most prevalent tick-borne disease in North America, surpassing Rocky Mountain spotted fever, whose vector (carrier) is a tick that habitually is a parasite of dogs.

lymphoma, see cancer.

Lynn, Lyn

Lynn Lake, Man., Lynn, N.S., Lynnville, Ont., but note Lyn, Ont.

lynx, both singular and plural.

Usually lives in northern forest regions. Its smaller cousin more common to Southern Canada is the bobcat.

Lyons, France.

M

m, mm
Abbreviations for metres, millimetres. No periods. We do not abbreviate metres in normal news stories, only in sports tabular matter. Spell out millimetres in first reference, except in gun calibres, which have figures and no hyphen (a 9 mm pistol). See guns and calibres.

MA, for master of arts.

Maastricht, see European Union.

Macau
The former Portuguese possession at the mouth of the Pearl River across from Hong Kong, 17 square kilometres made up of the Macau Peninsula and the islands of Taipa and Coloane, to which it is linked by a bridge and a causeway. Its population is 474,000. The city on the peninsula is called Nome de Deus de Macao. Macau was handed over to China in 1999. See Portugal.

Macbeth
Contrary to his bad press, in real life Macbeth did not gain the Scottish throne by murdering Duncan in his sleep. He defeated him in battle in 1040.

McCarthy, Senator Joseph
The U.S. senator left his name in history in McCarthyism, the demagogic strategy of making sensational but largely unsupported accusations of disloyalty or corruption, using damaging public inquisitions to intimidate or punish people against whom there is little or no evidence.

McClelland & Stewart Ltd.

M'Clintock
M'Clintock Channel and Inlet; Cape M'Clintock, Nunavut.

McClung, Nellie
Feminist writer, lecturer and suffrage campaigner, 1873-1951. Born in Ontario and raised in Manitoba, she was also an Alberta MLA for one term, and later lived in Victoria. She was one of the five women whose petition launched the Persons Case, which see.

M'Clure
Bay, Nunavut, and Strait, NWT.

McCrae, John
Doctor, soldier and poet, born in Guelph. *In Flanders Fields* was published in 1915. He died in France in 1918 (of pneumonia).

Macdonald College
At Sainte-Anne-de-Bellevue. The agricultural college of McGill University.

Macdonald, Sir John A.
Can be called Macdonald in second reference, or Sir John in colour pieces. Canada's first prime minister, associated with Kingston but born in Glasgow. The first Canadian-born PM was Sir John Abbott.

McDonald's

It is Mc-, despite the Big Mac.

Mace, mace

Upper-case for the disabling spray, a brand name. Lower-case for the ceremonial sceptre carried in and out of the House of Commons by the Sergeant-at-Arms.

Macedonia

Adjective and people: Macedonian. Currency: dinar. Capital: Skopje.

Use Macedonia, although Greek objections obliged the United Nations to admit it as "The Former Yugoslav Republic of Macedonia." It declared independence in November, 1991, with little Yugoslav opposition.

The ancient kingdom of Macedon covered a mountainous area of southeastern Europe on the Balkan Peninsula. Controlled by various conquering powers since the seventh century, including the Bulgars, Serbs and Turks, it was divided among Greece, Bulgaria and Serbia after the 1912-13 Balkan Wars.

The republic of Macedonia (Makedonija in Serbo-Croat) has a population of about 2.2 million. About 65 per cent are Macedonian, speaking a language akin to Bulgarian, and about 20 per cent are Albanian. There are also Turks (4 per cent) and other minorities. It is landlocked, bounded by Serbia, Albania, Greece and Bulgaria. Its mountains produce hydro power, minerals and timber, and industries include iron, steel, cement and cotton textiles. Its valleys produce grains, cotton, tobacco and livestock.

The northern Greek region of Macedonia (in Greek, Makhedonia) has a largely Greek population of about 2.2 million, producing such cash crops as olives, grapes and grain in the fertile mountain valleys (Mount Olympus is on the region's border with Thessaly). The main city is Thessaloniki.

See Yugoslavia.

Mach

Upper-case Mach number, named for Austrian physicist Ernst Mach. A Mach number can be roughly described in news stories as the speed of an aircraft expressed as a multiple of the speed of sound. In fact, it is the ratio of speed in any fluid (air, water etc.) to the local speed of sound in that fluid, which varies with temperature, pressure etc. Express Mach numbers in figures and decimals, with no hyphen: Mach 1, Mach 2.3.

Mach 1 in air is 1,192.6 km/h (741.1 mph) in air that is dry, at the freezing point and at sea-level pressure (1013.25 millibars, or 14.7 psi). For an aircraft at high altitude and extreme cold, we can say in news stories only that Mach 1 is about 1,100 km/h (about 680 mph).

Machiavellian

Note that Niccolo Machiavelli, a statesman, historian and political theorist, is considered to have been personally devoted to liberty and political morality. His name has been turned into an adjective applied to the unscrupulous political manipulation he describes in his work *The Prince*, but we should not go further and speak of someone acting "like a Machiavelli."

machine gun

See guns and calibres.

Machu Picchu

Ancient Peruvian city.

Macintosh computers, **McIntosh** apples.

Mackenzie Mountains

This range in the Northwest Territories is not named for the explorer Alexander Mackenzie, as are other things in the region, but for his namesake, the second prime minister, the Honest Mason from Lambton.

Mackenzie River

Canada's longest, at 4,421 kilometres, second only to the Mississippi in North America but 11th in the world. Upper-case Mackenzie Delta, Lowland, Valley, since these refer to well-known geographic areas in Canada, not merely to physical features. The Mackenzie Valley area is largely in the Northwest Territories, but is taken to extend as far south as northern Saskatchewan and Alberta (to include Lake Athabasca and the lower reaches of the Peace River). See rivers.

Mackinac, Straits of

Note plural. The channel connecting Lake Huron and Lake Michigan. It is spanned by the Mackinac Bridge, joining Michigan's Upper and Lower peninsulas. Including the main span and side spans, it is the longest suspension bridge in the world, at 2,255 metres (7,400 feet).

mackinaw

Lower-case for the blanket-weight woollen cloth, for coats made from it, and for the fur traders' mackinaw boat.

mackintosh

Lower-case for a rainproof coat, spelled differently from the inventor in 1823 of the process for rubberizing cloth, Scottish chemist Charles Macintosh.

McLauchlan, Murray, singer.

McLaughlin, Audrey

The former federal NDP leader.

Maclean Hunter Ltd.

No hyphen.

Maclean's magazine.

MacLennan, Hugh

Works include the novels *Barometer Rising, Two Solitudes, The Watch that Ends the Night*, and *Voices in Time*.

McLuhan, Marshall

Communications theorist and literary critic. His best-known works are *The Gutenberg Galaxy* and *Understanding Media*.

McMaster University, Hamilton.

Often misspelled MacMaster, McMasters.

MacMillan Bloedel Ltd.

No hyphen for the old Canadian forestry giant, which was acquired in 1999 by Weyerhaeuser Co. of Federal Way, Wash. Until 1966 it had been MacMillan, Bloedel and Powell River Ltd. When referring to its old nickname, spell it MacBlo.

Macmillan, Harold

British PM. Became Sir Harold, then Lord Stockton.

Mac-Paps

Well-known nickname of the Mackenzie-Papineau Battalion, Canadian volunteers on the Republican side against Franco in the Spanish Civil War.

Macphail, Agnes

Canada's first female MP, elected in 1921. Defeated in 1940, she became one of Ontario's first two female MPPs, in 1943. Primarily a supporter of farm interests and the co-operative movement, she was also a noted campaigner for prison reform.

McPherson, Aimee Semple

At one time the most publicized revivalist in the world, "Sister Aimee" was born Kennedy, in Ingersoll, Ont. Her first husband, clergyman Robert Semple, died in China in 1912 when they were missionaries there. Her huge Angelus Temple of the Four Square Gospel was in Los Angeles.

mad

May be used in lighter contexts to mean angry (mad as a hornet), but be careful that it is not interpreted as insane, psychotic (mad as a hatter).

Madagascar

No useful adjective for the country or single word for the people; say "of Madagascar" etc. Currency: franc. Capital: Tananarive.

The confusing adjective Malagasy should be used only if it is clearly defined. We do not use the local name for the capital, Antananarivo. Madagascar was called the Malagasy Republic from 1958 until it gained full independence from France in 1960. It is made up of the Indian Ocean island of Madagascar and several smaller islands, separated from mainland East Africa by the Mozambique Channel. The population of about 17 million is divided into two main groups, mutually antagonistic: the hill dwellers, of Indonesian/Polynesian stock, known as Merinas, and the coastal people, of Negroid stock, called *côtiers*. Both terms should be explained. Commerce is dominated by small communities of French, Chinese and Indian descent.

Madam

Lower-case for the term of respect (This way, madam) and for the keeper of a brothel. Upper-case in the title Madam Justice. The plural for the term of respect is mesdames, but for brothel keepers it is madams.

We use the French form, madame, only in direct quotes to indicate the speaker used the French pronunciation.

We use Mrs. or Ms. rather than the French honorific Mme. However, there is no alternative to Mme. for certain unmarried women in French-speaking countries who are called Madame as a sign of respect.

mad-cow disease

May be called that in first reference and in the headline, but explain early on that it is bovine spongiform encephalopathy and call it BSE thereafter.

Madding Crowd, Far from the

(Not maddening.)

Madison Square Garden

Singular, as is Boston Garden. But note Maple Leaf Gardens.

Mad Trapper, the

Upper-case for Albert Johnson, killed in a shootout in 1932 after an extensive RCMP manhunt in Yukon near the Alaska border.

maelstrom

Lower-case for any dangerous and irresistible force. Upper-case the Maelstrom for the whirlpool off northwestern Norway.

Mafia

Upper-case. It is a specific criminal organization in Italy and the United States. Do not use the name loosely for any sort of organized crime. Do not imply that any individual is a Mafioso without consulting senior editors, who may seek legal advice.

Magdalen Islands

We do not use the French name Îles-de-la-Madeleine except in direct quotes. This group of 12 major islands and some islets, totalling about 96 kilometres in length, is in the Gulf of St. Lawrence.

magi

Lower-case for the ancient Persian priestly caste. The singular is magus. Upper-case Magi only for the Three Wise Men of the New Testament.

Magna Carta

As a Latin term, it does not require the article the.

Magnetawan, Ont.

Magnetic Hill
Upper-case for the optical illusion just north of Moncton.

mahatma
Lower-case for the generic term, a holy one (literally great soul). Upper-case for the honorific, as in Mahatma Gandhi.

Main, The
Montreal's Boulevard St-Laurent, which splits Montreal Island, and street numbers, into east and west. It is the city's main north-south street.

mainframe

Maîtres chez nous
Upper-case only the first word in the Quebec nationalist slogan. Italics. It must be accompanied by a translation: masters in our own house.

maize
In wire stories, always change it to corn. Say cornmeal, not maize meal.

major-general, Maj.-Gen. See ranks.

majority
Most of is usually better, except in stories on votes in which a majority is required. Note that majority means simply 50 per cent plus one or more, and so it is not adequate, standing alone, to express a great preponderance. We must say a large majority, overwhelming majority etc. In reporting vote results, do not use majority if one candidate did not receive at least half the total votes cast. The word in that case is plurality. Also see collective nouns.

major leagues
The majors, a major-leaguer.

makeover, makeup; the verbs are make over, make up.

malamute
Lower-case for one of the four recognized breeds of northern dogs. See husky.

Malawi
Adjective and people: Malawian. Currency: kwacha. Capital: Lilongwe, but the major city is Blantyre.
It is in East Africa, on the western and southern shores of Lake Malawi, bounded on the north by Tanzania, on the west by Zambia and on the south by Mozambique. It is a member of the Commonwealth, called Nyasaland until it gained its independence in 1964. English is an official language, as is Chichewa, the most widespread tribal language, spoken by more than half the population of about 11 million. Malawi's economy is dominated by agriculture, mainly subsistence corn crops but also tea, tobacco and sugar.
Three decades of one-party rule after independence ended with a multiparty election in 1994.

Malay Archipelago
This vast string of islands, between the Indian and Pacific oceans off southeast Asia, was formerly called the East Indies. The largest island group in the world, it includes the 13,700 islands of Indonesia and the 7,000 of the Philippines.

Malaysia
Adjective and people: Malaysian. Currency: Malaysian dollar (ringgit). Capital: Kuala Lumpur.
It is a federation comprising the 11 states of West Malaysia (also known as Malaya), on the Malay Peninsula, and the two states (Sarawak and Sabah) of East Malaysia, 400 miles across the South China Sea on the island of Borneo. (Also sharing Borneo are the sultanate of Brunei and four provinces of Indonesia.) Malaysia is a member of the Commonwealth. Malay is the official language, but the population of

about 23 million is only about 47-per-cent Malay. It is 32-per-cent Chinese, 8-per-cent Indian and 13-per-cent of other ancestry. Malaysia's combined raw-material exports (rubber, crude petroleum, palm oil, saw logs, tin) are now almost equalled by manufactured goods.

Maldives

Adjective and people: Maldivian. Currency: rufiya. Capital: Male.

In the Indian Ocean about 400 miles southwest of Sri Lanka, the Republic of Maldives was formerly called the Maldive Islands, and may be referred to informally as the Maldives. There are about 2,000 islands, of which about 220 are inhabited. The total population is about 320,000. The language, Maldivian (Divehi), is related to old Sinhalese (see Sri Lanka). Maldives is a member of the Commonwealth, but does not normally attend summits.

Mali

Adjective and people: Malian. Currency: CFA franc. Capital: Bamako.

A landlocked state in northwestern Africa. Clockwise from the north, it is bounded by Algeria, Niger, Burkina Faso, Ivory Coast, Guinea, Senegal and Mauritania. From 1904 it was called the French Sudan, part of French West Africa, until it gained independence in 1960. (At independence, but for only a few weeks thereafter, it was joined to Senegal as the Federation of Mali.) Mali is largely desert, except for the Niger River marshes in the south, where some cotton and rice are grown, and has been hit hard by droughts. There is considerable ethnic and cultural diversity in the population of about 11 million, ranging from Negroid farmers in the south to Arabs, Moors and Tuareg in the north. In the days of the Mali Empire, through the 15th century, Timbuktu was an important centre of Islamic learning and culture.

Maliseet

For both the people and the Algonquian language they speak. Not Malecite.

Mallory, George

Tried to climb Everest "because it is there," dying in the attempt in 1924 along with Andrew Irvine. His remains were discovered in 1999. He was George Herbert Leigh Mallory, and it is incorrect to hyphenate Leigh-Mallory. However, the hyphen was used by his brother, Air Chief Marshal Sir Trafford Leigh-Mallory, a fighter pilot who became head of RAF Fighter Command in 1942.

Malta

Adjective and people: Maltese. Currency: Maltese lira. Capital: Valletta.

In the central Mediterranean, it comprises the islands of Malta, Gozo and Comino, and two islets. Its approximately 400,000 citizens speak Maltese, a Semitic language that has also borrowed extensively from other Mediterranean languages (Malta has been held by the Romans, the Arabs, Sicily and France). But English is also widely spoken, because the last colonial ruler (beginning in 1802) was Britain, and the republic is a member of the Commonwealth. (In 1942, the population as a whole was awarded the George Cross for bravery in the Second World War.)

mammoth

Lower-case. This term, for the extinct woolly, imperial and Columbian mammoths, should not be applied loosely to other extinct species of elephant.

Manchukuo (not Manchoukuo).

The name for Manchuria and Jehol under Japanese control.

Mandarin

Upper-case for the Chinese language. Lower-case for an important civil or military official in imperial China (there were nine grades of mandarins) and for high civil servants in Ottawa.

mandrel and mandrill

A **mandrel** is a shaft or spindle, or a bar over which various materials are bent or shaped. A **mandrill** is a large baboon found in West Africa.

Manila, Philippines

Also manila paper, envelope, folder, rope. But Manilla, Ont., Iowa and Australia.

Manitoba Schools Question

Upper-case for the national controversy of the 1890s.

manitou

Lower-case, italics, as the generic Algonquian word for a spirit, but upper-case Gitchi Manitou, Great Spirit. As a proper name it does not need italics.

mankind

Considered a sexist word by some readers. It is usually easily replaced by humanity, the human race, humankind. See women and language.

Mann Cup

Donated by Sir Donald Mann in 1910, for the Canadian senior amateur lacrosse championship. It is solid gold.

mannequin

manner and manor

"To the manner born," from Shakespeare's *Hamlet*, is often misquoted as "to the manor born."

manoeuvre, manoeuvring

man-of-war, men-of-war

For ships. But the horse was Man o' War. "Big Red" won 20 of 21 races, including the Preakness and Belmont in 1920, but was not entered in the Kentucky Derby, the third event of thoroughbred racing's Triple Crown.

manse, parsonage, rectory

A **manse** is the home of a Presbyterian minister; **parsonage** is the word used by Methodists; and **rectory** is the usual term for Catholic and Anglican residences. United Church congregations use either manse or parsonage, depending on the denomination of the congregation before union.

Mansouri, Lotfi (not Lofti).

mantel and mantle

A **mantel** is the shelf above a fireplace. A **mantle** is a cloak or covering.

Maori

Mao Zedong, not Tsetung.

Maple Leaf, the

Upper-case for the flag, or for the national symbol used on coins, crests etc. The plural in this sense is Maple Leaves.

Maple Leaf Gardens

Plural for the Toronto arena, which was the home of the Maple Leafs hockey team until they moved to the Air Canada Centre in February of 1999. But note Boston Garden, Madison Square Garden.

march past

marijuana, see drugs.

Marines

Upper-case the names of military services (the Royal Marines) and the adjective when standing for the service, as in a Marine investigation, a Marine officer. But lower-case the generic occupational description, as in three marines. See capitalization.

Maritime provinces, the Maritimes

There are three of them: New Brunswick, Nova Scotia and Prince Edward Island. When Newfoundland and Labrador is included, they are called the Atlantic provinces. Treat the Maritimes as a plural noun: The Maritimes have expressed concern over the policy.

Mark

Upper-case in model numbers, as in Mark 2. Do not abbreviate to Mk. Roman numerals are used only if they are part of a commercial name, as in Continental Mark IV.

marketplace, one word.

Marks & Spencer

Marquess of Queensberry, see Queensberry.

Marquis wheat

Upper-case. A fast-maturing variety, developed in 1907, that greatly expanded the area of the Prairies able to produce wheat.

Marseillaise, the (not la).

Marseilles

Not Marseille. France's second-largest city, and its major Mediterranean seaport.

marshal

Both noun and verb. Marshalled, marshalling.

marvellous

Marx Brothers, the

Upper-case for the vaudeville and film team—Groucho (Julius), Harpo (Arthur), Chico (Leonard), Gummo (Milton) and Zeppo (Herbert).

Marxist, Marxism

Karl Marx is best known for *Das Kapital* (*Capital*, in three volumes) and for the *Communist Manifesto*, co-written with his friend and benefactor Friedrich Engels. Lower-case the name of his philosophy, dialectical materialism. Beyond the realm of political action, Marxism has become the analytical core of a range of academic thought, from economics to history to literature. We must be careful, therefore, to avoid equating the Marxist methodology of a historian, for instance, with his or her political beliefs.

Mary Celeste

Not Marie. The famous mystery ship, found abandoned with cargo intact between Portugal and the Azores in 1872, was built in Nova Scotia 11 years earlier. Arthur Conan Doyle incorrectly called it the Marie Celeste in a short story, and the name stuck.

Maryknoll Fathers, Sisters

There is usually no need to use the formal name of these missionaries' organization, the Catholic Foreign Mission Society of America. (It is based in Maryknoll, N.Y.)

Marylebone, see Lord's.

Mary Queen of Scots (no comma).

Mason-Dixon Line

Masonite, Mason jar, trade names.

masonry (not -ary).

The work of a mason. Upper-case Masonry meaning Freemasonry, the Masonic movement.

mass

Lower-case for the various services in which communion is served, such as a requiem mass. See capitalization.

Massachusetts

massasauga rattlesnake, rattler

Lower-case; only three s's. One of three rattlesnakes in Canada, it is found in Southwestern Ontario and around Georgian Bay. The **timber rattlesnake** has the same range, but is believed to be nearly extinct in Canada. The **western rattlesnake** is found in southern B.C., Alberta and Saskatchewan. A fourth venomous snake, the more primitive **night snake**, extends north only as far as extreme southern B.C.

MasterCard

masterful and masterly

When we mean authoritative, bold, domineering, imperious, say **masterful**. If we mean highly skilled, say **masterly**. The adverbs are masterfully and masterly. Some performances can be both. A pianist may be highly skilled and also bold and authoritative.

Masters Tournament, golf.

masthead

This is the place in a newspaper or other periodical that gives its name, that of its owner, its address and often the names of its senior staff. It often appears on a newspaper's editorial page. What appears on the front page is called the **nameplate**.

Matachewan, Ont.

Matagami, Que.

But **Mattagami** Lake and River, in Ontario.

matronymic (not metronymic).

matte

matzo

Maugham, (W.) Somerset

Mau Mau

Maundy Thursday

The day of commemoration of the Last Supper, the day before Good Friday. In lower case, maundy is the ceremony of washing the feet of the poor. In Britain, the sovereign distributes maundy money on this day.

Mauritania

Adjective and people: Mauritanian. Currency: ouguiya. Capital: Nouakchott.

It is a former French colony on the Atlantic coast of Africa, bordering on Morocco, Algeria, Mali and Senegal, independent since 1960. It is almost entirely desert, and its population of about 2.8 million consists mainly of Moors engaged in nomadic herding. It exports iron ore and dried fish. See Western Sahara for an account of Mauritania's ambitions there.

Note that the two Cunard liners were spelled Mauretania, the name of the old Roman territory in north-western Africa.

Mauritius

Adjective and people: Mauritian. Currency: Mauritian rupee. Capital: Port Louis.

An archipelago in the Indian Ocean about 500 miles east of Madagascar, it comprises the islands of Mauritius, Rodrigues (a further 350 miles to the east) and Alalega, and the Brandon Group. It is a member of the Commonwealth and the Queen is still head of state, represented by a governor-general. About two-thirds of its population of 1.2 million is descended from Indian labourers who were indentured to the sugar plantations. There are also people of

European background (British and French), and of mixed ancestry, called Creoles. About 90 per cent of the cultivated land is devoted to sugar.

maximum and minimum

They are often pretentious, better replaced by greatest and least, except in such standard technical expressions as maximum and minimum sentence, maximum-security prison, minimum wage.

But **maximize** and **minimize** are not so easily replaced. They were coined by Jeremy Bentham to fill a gap in the language, and are still useful.

maximum sentence

It is misleading sensationalism to write, with no elaboration, that a person charged with a crime faces a maximum sentence of 10 years if such a sentence is highly unlikely in the case being reported. If it is a first offence and if the usual punishment of first offenders for that crime is two years less a day or a fine and probation, we should say so.

maxiskirt, the maxi

may and might

The standard present tense for the various meanings is **may**, to express a possibility (I may lose my deposit), or permission (you may come at noon), or a wish (long may she reign); or to emphasize a question (who may you be?).

Might is the past tense (I was afraid I might lose my deposit; I said you might come at noon; I hoped he might agree to an interview; he wondered who she might be).

Might is also the subjunctive, and should be used whenever we are expressing a possibility that is merely theoretical, contradicted by the facts: You **might** lend a hand (but you are not doing so). If I had been better at languages, I **might** be a foreign correspondent today.

The choice of a negative of may requires thought. Depending on the meaning, we could say either I **may not** lose my deposit (meaning perhaps I will not) or I **cannot** lose it (no possibility exists). In denying permission, we can say **may not**, **cannot** or **must not**, depending on our meaning or emphasis.

May adequately conveys that an alternative is also possible; there is rarely any need to say **may or may not**.

May Day

But a distress call is a **mayday**.

mayoralty

The noun. The adjective is **mayoral** (the mayoral race).

mazel tov, italics.

meagre

mean, median

The median is the point in a range at which half the items are on one side and half on the other. If the median salary of a group is $10,000, as many people make more than that as less than that. The mean is the average. In the previous example, it would be the sum of all the salaries divided by the number of earners.

meaningful

It means full of meaning. Use it for meaningful glances, pauses etc., but not in place of valuable, satisfying, rewarding, fulfilling, as in a meaningful experience, a meaningful relationship.

measurement

Our standard is the metric system, but with certain exceptions to aid reader comprehension, to conform to international usage or industry standards, or to avoid implying that a particular measurement was made or described in metric if it was not.

For measurements of **the human body,** use imperial first for heights and weights, followed by the metric. (It is usually simplest to supply the conversion in brackets.) If there are several such measurements in the story, supply the metric value for at least one, and for more than one if there is a wide range. For human body temperatures, use Celsius first, followed by Fahrenheit.

For **animals,** metric alone is usually sufficient, but supply the imperial, or use the imperial alone, if it is significant to the story, such as in comparisons between the sizes and weights of a child and the dog that attacked him. For comparing horses, give heights in hands, and mention in the story that a hand is four inches.

To conform to international usage, give **distances at sea** in nautical miles, but with at least one conversion into kilometres (multiply by 1.85; see mile). This includes the limits of territorial waters: 200 nautical miles (370 kilometres). See territorial waters. Give ship speeds in knots (nautical miles an hour), and give **aircraft heights** in thousands of feet.

Use hectares and square kilometres for general **land or water areas,** and for such things as floods and forest fires. But use acres for individual farms and fields that were surveyed originally in acres. Yields may be expressed either by the acre or the hectare, depending on the system the farmer or agency uses, but we do not mix them without translating one of them.

For **track events,** distances in metres are sufficient, although we should identify the mile run. In the field sports, give the lengths and heights of jumps in metric, but supply the imperial equivalent for at least one value in the story to give the reader a point of reference. In general, use imperial if it is the standard for a particular sport, as in yards for football, feet for baseball (e.g. the length of home runs).

Give **pressures** in kilopascals, but supply the equivalent in pounds per square inch.

---

conversion factors

From metric:

Centimetres to inches: multiply by .39
Metres to feet: multiply by 3.28
Metres to yards: multiply by 1.09
Kilometres to miles: multiply by .62
Square metres to square feet: multiply by 10.76
Square metres to square yards: multiply by 1.2
Hectares to acres: multiply by 2.47
Square kilometres to sq. miles: multiply by .38
Cubic metres to cubic feet: multiply by 35.3
Cubic metres to cubic yards: multiply by 1.3
Litres to gallons: multiply by .22
Litres to U.S. gallons, multiply by .26
Grams to ounces: multiply by .035
Kilograms to pounds: multiply by 2.2
Tonnes to short tons (2,000 lbs.): mult. by 1.1
Tonnes to long tons (2,240 lbs): mult. by .98
Kilopascals to pounds per sq. inch: mult. by .145

From imperial:

Inches to centimetres: multiply by 2.54
Feet to metres: multiply by .3
Yards to metres, multiply by .91
Miles to kilometres: multiply by 1.6
Square feet to square metres: multiply by .09
Square yards to square metres: multiply by .83
Acres to hectares: multiply by .4
Square miles to sq. kilometres: multiply by 2.58
Cubic feet to cubic metres: multiply by .03
Cubic yards to cubic metres: multiply by .76
Gallons to litres: multiply by 4.55
U.S. gallons to litres: multiply by 3.78
Ounces to grams: multiply by 28.3
Pounds to kilograms: multiply by .45
Short tons to tonnes: multiply by .91
Long tons to tonnes: multiply by 1.02
Pounds per sq. inch to kilopascals: mult. by 6.9

Vessel tonnages are in tons, not tonnes. It is a measure of volume or displacement, not weight.

We must never convey the impression that a speaker was using a particular system of measurement if this was not the case. Do not indirectly quote a U.S. policeman as saying a car was going 193.1 kilometres an hour, when in fact he said it was doing 120 miles an hour. Similarly, if a Canadian doctor gives a baby's weight in grams, we do not simply convert to pounds and ounces in an indirect quotation without indicating this. It is clearest to use the speaker's own figures first, then supply the conversion.

We make precise conversions only of figures we know were precise in the first place. If a source says a flood covers 350 acres, we can be fairly certain this is a rounded-off estimate. It would be misleading to say it covers 141.6 hectares. Round it off to 140, and use a qualifier such as about, approximately.

There is generally no need to supply conversions for approximate values given originally in metres (because of their similarity to yards), in kilometres or in kilometres an hour. There is no need to translate air or water temperatures given originally in Celsius, or to convert grams, millilitres etc. in scientific stories or those about blood-alcohol levels. But in stories about illegal drugs, convert at least one weight in the story as a point of reference. Supply the symbol C (no period) for Celsius only if the reader is likely to conclude a temperature is in Fahrenheit, as in stories about U.S. cold snaps. It is sufficient to use it for only the first temperature in the story.

We never convert colloquial expressions involving measurements, such as "going a mile a minute," or "give him an inch and he'll take a mile."

When giving a value in a single unit of measurement, we follow the normal rule of spelling out numbers under 10 and simple fractions (six metres, four pounds, half an ounce, two-thirds of a gram) but using figures for compound fractions and decimals (6.4 metres, 9½ pounds). However, use figures for temperatures (3 C). Also use figures when the value is in two units of measurement: 8 pounds 3 ounces; 6 feet 2 inches; he is 6 foot 2; a 6-foot-2 shortstop. Use figures for all gun calibres.

Except in tabular matter, we never abbreviate imperial units (do not say mi., ft., lb. etc.). In metric measurement, abbreviate km, cm, mm and some other familiar units (no periods) after the first of several references. The exception is gun calibres, which are abbreviated even in first reference (a 9 mm pistol). Note that these abbreviations serve as both the singular and plural. Say km, not kms.

Dollar figures, if unqualified, are taken to be in Canadian dollars. We add the word Canadian in brackets only if the reader might get the impression we are talking about U.S. dollars, as in a story about Americans or the United States. In stories involving huge sums normally expressed internationally in U.S. dollars, such as U.S. trade and budget figures or Third-World debt, there is no need to convert to Canadian dollars, but we must state high in the story that the figures are U.S. dollars. See currency.

Also see fraction, mile, numbers, oil, per cent, statistics.

It is inevitable that as pupils now learning metric in schools grow up to become the vast majority of our readers, the number of conversions we supply will taper off. But for some time to come, we must go the extra mile to make certain our current readers understand the significance of all measurements.

The **metric prefixes** for values less than a whole unit, ranging from a 10th to a trillionth, are deci, centi, milli, micro, nano and pico. The prefixes for multiples, ranging from 10 to a trillion, are deca, hecto, kilo, myria (10,000), mega, giga, tera. We do not use the less familiar prefixes without explaining.

Mecca

Upper-case for the Saudi Arabian city that is the birthplace of Mohammed and Islam's holiest city. Lower-case for a tourist mecca, a mecca for birders etc., but use this only in direct quotes. In our own writing, be sensitive to Muslims' objection to trivial references to their holy city. Muslims do not pray to Mecca; they pray to God, facing Mecca as a symbol of unity. The hajj is an annual pilgrimage to Mecca, which every Muslim is expected to join at least once in his or her life unless physically or financially unable to do so. The festival Eid al-Adha marks the end of the hajj. Another annual festival, the Eid al-Fitr, marks the end of the fast of Ramadan.

medalist

Medal of Honor

Use the U.S. spelling. This highest U.S. military decoration is indeed bestowed by Congress, but its name does not include the adjective Congressional.

Médecins sans frontières

Use this name, in italics, for the independent international medical relief organization founded in 1971, but add Doctors Without Borders in parentheses after the first reference. Second reference is MSF, no italics. The group was awarded the Nobel Peace Prize in 1999.

media

It is a plural noun taking in all the forms of communication, such as books, periodical publications, radio, TV, advertising, mass mailing. Use the singular medium to describe one of these forms, such as magazines, or even a category such as trade magazines, but not to describe an individual example of the form. Daily newspapers are a medium; The Globe and Mail is a newspaper.

Do not use "the media" to mean news organizations. Say the news media, the press, print and broadcast reporters etc.

medicare

Lower-case the informal word for government-run health insurance in Canada. In the United States, upper-case Medicare and Medicaid for the systems to aid the elderly and the poor.

Mediterranean

Meech Lake accord

Prime Minister Brian Mulroney and the 10 premiers of the day reached an agreement at Meech Lake, Que., on April 30, 1987, on a constitutional amendment in response to five demands presented by Quebec as prerequisites to its endorsing Constitution Act of 1982. They initialled the accord in Ottawa on June 3, and the Quebec National Assembly became the first legislature to ratify it, on June 23, starting the clock on the three-year deadline for ratification.

The federal Parliament and seven other legislatures followed suit, the only holdouts being Manitoba and New Brunswick, where new governments had been elected in the meantime. (In Manitoba it was a minority administration, and both opposition parties joined Gary Filmon's Conservatives in demanding improvements to protect minorities, women and native people, especially after Quebec used the notwithstanding clause in the constitutional Charter of Rights on Dec. 18, 1988, to override a Supreme

Court ruling against its prohibition of non-French commercial signs. Mr. Filmon withdrew his ratification motion the next day.) As the deadline neared in the spring of 1990, the year-old Liberal government of Clyde Wells in Newfoundland rescinded ratification, on April 6.

A companion resolution proposed by Liberal Premier Frank McKenna of New Brunswick formed the basis of nationwide hearings and a compromise proposal by a Commons committee, and led to a week-long meeting of the first ministers beginning on the evening of Sunday, June 3. By Saturday, June 9, they had reached a tentative agreement that could be put to the three holdout legislatures. New Brunswick ratified it, but obstructionist tactics by Indian MLA Elijah Harper prevented Manitoba from meeting the June 23 deadline. When this became clear, Mr. Wells adjourned the Newfoundland debate on June 22 without a vote, which he had predicted would have gone against the accord. With the failure of ratification, Premier Robert Bourassa of Quebec announced a select commission to draft options for a new relationship with the rest of Canada.

Demands outlined by various Quebec committees and proposals formulated in the rest of Canada led to cross-Canada consultation and negotiating sessions in 1991 and 1992, culminating in a package of proposed constitutional amendments dubbed the Charlottetown accord. It was defeated in a national vote on Oct. 26, 1992. See Charlottetown accord.

meet

To **meet** a person is understood by most readers to mean to make the acquaintance of, to encounter or to come together by appointment (meet me at the fair). If we are talking about conferring, having a meeting with, say **meet with**.

mega

As a prefix meaning large, it normally does not take a hyphen (megacity, megaproject, megastore), but insert one before a word beginning with a vowel.

Meighen, Arthur

Canada's ninth prime minister, who held office for 17 months beginning in July of 1920, and for 13 weeks in 1926. He died in 1960.

Melanesia

One of the three traditional groupings of the Pacific islands that make up Oceania (the others are Micronesia and Polynesia), Melanesia comprises those south of the equator and west of the International Date Line. It means black islands. It includes New Guinea, Fiji, Vanuatu (previously called the New Hebrides), Norfolk Island, the Admiralty, Santa Cruz and Loyalty islands, the Solomons, the Louisiades and the Bismarcks.

Ethnologists differ on the classification of a Melanesian race, with many holding that there is sufficient diversity that it should be defined only as a geographic race, a basic population. But general characteristics include dark skin, very strong jaws, large molars and wavy to kinky hair. Many hold that the Papuans of New Guinea belong to another racial group, that of the Australian Aborigines (Australoid).

There are about 400 Melanesian languages, some with only a few hundred speakers. The widely used common language is Melanesian Pidgin, based on English but with numerous consonant shifts (*dispela* for this fellow, *pinis* for finish). See pidgin.

mementoes

memoirs

The singular, memoir, may be used for a monograph or an article, but a longer narrative based on a person's personal experiences always requires the plural, his or her memoirs.

memorandums (not -da).

Memorial Day

The U.S. holiday for honouring the dead in all wars; the last Monday in May. It was originally called Decoration Day. In the South after the Civil War, both Confederate and Union graves were decorated. Memorial Day is also the July 1 holiday in Newfoundland and Labrador, commemorating the 1916 Battle of Beaumont Hamel.

Mendelssohn Choir

meningitis

Meningococcal meningitis is only one type, although it is most in the news in Canada because a fear of epidemics occasionally prompts mass meningococcal inoculation programs. Meningitis, which is an inflammation of the meninges, the covering membranes of the brain and spinal cord, can be caused by a variety of viruses (in viral [aseptic] meningitis) or bacteria (bacterial meningitis). The viruses are often those of the gut, spread by the oral-fecal route. In the bacterial category, three organisms account for 75 per cent of cases: meningococcus (most often in adolescents and young adults), pneumococcus (in older adults) and the influenza bacillus (a rare cause of meningitis except in the case of head injuries).

Mennonites

There is a wide range. Specify whether we are referring to Old Order Mennonites, who shun modern technology, or to more assimilated Mennonites. The church originated in Switzerland but is named for Menno Simons, a 16th-century Dutch Anabaptist reformer.

In Canada, there are 114,000 members in about 600 Mennonite churches, adhering to 27 different conferences. About 200,000 Canadians call themselves Mennonites, but not all are church members (children, for example, are not). The greatest concentration is in Manitoba. The Mennonite Central Committee engages in international relief work, while the Mennonite Disaster Service responds to disasters within Canada. Worldwide, Mennonite churches have about 850,000 members.

men's wear

But Menswear is allowed if it is part of a commercial name.

mental illness

Beware the possibility of libel in describing an identifiable individual as mentally ill. See courts, disabled, psychiatric terms.

Meo

Use this as both the singular and plural for the non-Chinese people of southwestern China and northern Vietnam, Laos and Thailand. They have little internal organization or contact with governments, and many grow opium as a cash crop.

Mercedes-Benz

Hyphenated. A Mercedes (but not the European term Merc, which in North America means a Mercury). The question does not often arise, but the manufacturer says the plural of Mercedes is Mercedes.

Merritton, Ont.

Mesopotamia, see Iraq.

Messerschmitt (not -schmidt).

Messrs.

Use this plural honorific only *in extremis*, either in a direct quote or when several surnames are given and there is no possibility of recasting. For a manageable number of people, it is far better to say Mr. White, Mr. Brown and Mr. Green.

mestizo

This is the term used throughout Central and South America for someone of mixed Indian and European ancestry. Requires italics and an explanation.

metallurgy

metaphor

This word should not be used loosely to describe all figurative language. A **metaphor** is a comparison, the kind in which the object is simply called something else, as in He is a brick, or This house is a millstone around my neck. (If we had said "like a millstone," that would have been a simile.)

The term **mixed metaphor** is looser. It usually involves a combining of metaphors (let's put our shoulders to the grindstone) or insertion of a clashing modifier (an unconscionable kettle of fish). The term may also be applied to figurative expressions that are not comparisons, if incompatible images are combined (We have to take the bull by the horns and run it up the flagpole), but there must be two or more images to a mix. A simple mangling of a familiar expression (up in thin smoke) is not a mixed metaphor.

In news stories, it is a rare metaphor that meets our standards of accuracy, fairness and brevity. It is occasionally apt to call someone a loose cannon, a spent force or a battering ram, or to say an MP has been a bulldog in Question Period, but beware triteness. Also beware libel: Calling a beleaguered company chairman a stag at bay is one thing; calling him a trapped weasel is quite another.

A metaphor should be apt enough to stand unqualified, without the insertion of such words as virtually or figuratively. See literally.

meteor, meteorite, meteoroid

Meteoroids are chunks of matter travelling around in our solar system. Those that enter Earth's atmosphere in a visible way are called **meteors**, also known as shooting stars or fireballs. If a meteor is so large that it is not completely consumed, the fragment that hits Earth is called a **meteorite**.

Normally there are about five meteors an hour, but there are up to thousands an hour during the approximately 20 meteor showers each year, some named for the constellations that seem to produce them (the Leonid shower, the Leonids; the Perseids).

meter and metre

A **meter** is a measuring instrument (a gas meter, a thermometer). A **metre** is a unit of length.

Métis, see native people.

metric conversions

See measurement.

metro

Lower-case to describe a city and its satellites, unless Metro is part of the proper name.

Mexico

Adjective and people: Mexican. Currency: peso. Capital: Mexico City.

Mexico is in North America, north of the isthmus of Central America. But it can be defined as part of Latin America, of which it is the third-largest country (after Brazil and Argentina). Mexico is divided into 32 states. Its population of 103 million is about 55-per-cent mestizo (a mixture of Indian and European), 29-per-cent Indian and 16-per-cent European.

Spanish is the first language of more than 92 per cent; the rest speak one of 59 Indian dialects. Crude oil accounts for almost two-thirds of exports, but there are also rich deposits of coal and uranium. Only 20 per cent of Mexico is suitable for agriculture. The North American free-trade agreement with the United States and Canada was signed in December of 1992 by the three national leaders and was implemented in 1994. A devaluation of the peso that year triggered a serious recession.

In the election of July 2, 2000, Vicente Fox of the opposition National Action Party defeated Francisco Labastida of the Institutional Revolutionary Party, known by its Spanish acronym PRI. This was the PRI's first presidential defeat in its 71 years of existence. In 2001, Mexico implemented free-trade agreements with Guatemala, Honduras, El Salvador and the European Free Trade Area.

MHA

For member of the House of Assembly, Newfoundland and Labrador.

MI-5, MI-6

The two British intelligence services. These informal titles are holdovers from the Second World War, when they were Sections 5 and 6 of military intelligence. MI-5, whose formal name now is the Security Service, deals with internal security and counterintelligence within the United Kingdom. MI-6, the Secret Intelligence Service, collects and analyzes foreign intelligence. It is MI-6 that was penetrated by "moles" working for the Soviet Union. The two services can trace their history, under various names and in various forms, back to the Secret Service formed in the 1500s under Elizabeth I.

micro

Does not take a hyphen unless the main word begins with o (microbiologist, microdot, microfilm, but micro-organism). Some new coinages take hold (microcomputer), but most should be avoided in favour of a separate adjective; creating a longer word that is hard to read is not good news writing. See mini.

As a metric prefix, micro means a millionth, as in a microsecond. See measurement.

Micronesia

Adjective and people: Micronesian. Currency: U.S. dollar. Capital: Kolonia (on the island of Ponape).

The Federated States of Micronesia was formerly part of the United Nations Trust Territory of the Pacific Islands, under U.S. administration. It has signed a Compact of Free Association (ratified by a U.S. law in 1985) under which it is an independent republic, but the United States supplies financial aid and is responsible for defence and internal security. It comprises about 600 tiny islands divided into four states grouped around the islands of Ponape, Truk, Yap and Kosrae. The population is about 136,000. Micronesia is north of the islands of Melanesia, and is separated from those of Polynesia by the International Date Line. All are part of Oceania.

microwaves

They are electromagnetic radiations with wavelengths between one millimetre and 30 centimetres and frequencies in the range of 1,000 to 30,000 megacycles. They are used not only for cooking but also for radar and telecommunications.

mid-

Most words take a hyphen with mid. But anatomical terms do not (midventral), nor do these common words: midday, midmorning, midafternoon, midevening, midlife, midnight, midweek, midmonth, midyear, midseason, midsummer, midautumn, midwinter, midway, midpoint, midsentence, midship, midterm, midtown, midwife.

Mid-Canada Line
Upper-case, the string of military radar stations across Canada approximately along the 55th parallel. They were comparable to those of the DEW Line, but were unmanned. They were dismantled in 1965.

Middle-earth
Use this spelling for J.R.R. Tolkien's imagined world, as he wrote it. The name of his trilogy begins with the definite article: *The Lord of the Rings*. The three books in the Rings trilogy are, in order: *The Fellowship of the Ring*, *The Two Towers* and *The Return of the King*.

Middle East, the Mideast
These terms refer to the area at the eastern end of the Mediterranean, covering countries in southwestern Asia, on the Arabian Peninsula and in northeastern Africa as far west as Libya, and also including Cyprus. They do not include the Islamic countries of northwestern Africa (Tunisia, Morocco and Algeria), but their involvement in the area's politics dictates that they be included in stories about the region.

Middle Island
This island in Lake Erie, south of Pelee Island, is the most southerly point in Canada.

Middlesbrough, England.
(Not -borough.)

Middle West, the Midwest
Taken to refer to the 12 north-central U.S. states from Ohio in the east to North and South Dakota in the west, and as far south as Missouri and Kansas. We never use this term to refer to Canada's Prairie provinces.

midget
A midget is a proportionate dwarf, but the term has fallen into disfavour and is considered offensive by most people of short stature. Prefer dwarf. The organization Little People of America also suggests the term little person, which presents the problem of ambiguity but may be used if the context is clear.

Mies van der Rohe, Ludwig
The German-born U.S. architect and designer may be referred to in first reference either by his full name or simply as Mies van der Rohe. Second reference is Mies, no honorific.

MiG
Note the lower-case i. There is no need to spell out the names of the designers who began this line of fighter-interceptor aircraft, Artem Mikoyan and Mikhail Gurevich. Several models are still in service in many countries, ranging from the subsonic MiG-15 of Korean War vintage to the MiG-27 (the Flogger) and the twin-tailed MiG-29 (the Fulcrum), capable of more than twice the speed of sound. For this reason, to say only that a country's air force is equipped with MiGs is not sufficiently informative. Always add the model number when available. They progress by twos: MiG-15, -17, -19, -21, -23, -25, -27, -29. The MiG-21, built in several configurations, can use relatively rough airfields and is easy to service; it is used by about two dozen countries.

might and may
See may and might.

migrant
See immigrant.

Mi'kmaq

For both the people and the Algonquian language they speak. Not Micmac.

milch

Giving milk, as in milch cow, milch goat.

mile

A statute mile (land mile) is 5,280 feet (1.6 kilometres). An air mile (and the traditional nautical mile) is 6,080.2 feet, one-60th of a degree of longitude at the equator (1.853 kilometres). The new international nautical mile is 6,076.103 feet (1.851 kilometres).

mileage

No need to add an explanation when others use this word to mean a vehicle's rate of fuel use, but in our own writing we lean toward such metric-friendly expressions as fuel consumption.

miles an hour

Preferred to miles per hour, but note the commonly accepted abbreviation mph (no periods). It still appears in U.S. stories about racing, wind speeds, baseball pitches etc., but should be accompanied by the km/h conversion. See measurement.

military, see ranks.

militate and mitigate

Militate means to have an effect or influence. It is usually used with the preposition against (His marital infidelity militates against his candidacy). **Mitigate** means to make less severe, or to become so. It is found most often in the expression mitigating circumstances.

Milky Way

Our galaxy, a flat pinwheel about 15 kiloparsecs (about 49,000 light-years) across, containing about 100 billion stars. The centre, toward Sagittarius, is about nine kiloparsecs from our sun, which is out on one of the spiral arms.

millennium

Lower-case, even when referring to the prophesied thousand-year rule by Christ. The question of whether this millennium started at the end of 1999 or 2000 may be of largely academic interest now, but most people whose business it is to worry about these things (historians, chronologists, theologians, some astronomers) deem that the last year "before Christ," 1 BC, was followed immediately by 1 AD (anno Domini, the first "year of the Lord"), with no intervening "zero year." Thus, the first year, century and millennium began on Jan. 1, 1 AD. And if a cycle of 10, 100 or 1,000 years begins on a year that ends in a 1, then the 10th, 100th or 1,000th year must end in a 0. The last day of the past century and millennium, they say, was Dec. 31, 2000, and the current one began on Jan. 1, 2001.

Some astronomers do interpose a zero year between 1 BC and 1 AD, and so say the last day of the past millennium was Dec. 31, 1999. And the world's understandable rush to celebrate that date – as the 19 clicked over to 20 – reflected its treatment of the decades. When people speak casually of the forties, they include 1940, which is technically the last year of the previous decade, and leave out 1950. In that spirit, it is perfectly acceptable to say informally that the 1990s began on Jan. 1, 1990. As for the millennium, should the question arise in a story, a line to this effect might suffice: "Academics say the current century/millennium began on Jan. 1, 2001."

millimetre, mm (no period).

See measurement, guns.

mineralogy (not -ology).

mini

This prefix meaning tiny should be used sparingly, especially when it takes on a vaguer meaning not strictly related to physical size. It is no service to the reader to turn a long word into a longer one by saying mini-revolution etc., when more accurate separate adjectives are available.

Use a hyphen after the prefix, except in these words: minibus, minicab, minicomputer, minigolf, miniseries, miniskirt, minivan. See micro.

minimum, see maximum.

ministries

Upper-case both the formal and the commonly used names of federal departments and provincial ministries, but lower-case the names of their branches, divisions, secretariats and offices. (Say the health-protection branch of the federal Health Department, or, for such well-known entities, simply the federal health-protection branch.) In general, the word "department" is used throughout the federal government, in seven provinces and in the territories. The word "ministry" is used in three provinces: British Columbia, Ontario and Quebec.

There are minor exceptions. Alberta has departments, but also uses the word "ministry" to identify certain small portfolios responsible for an area of policy or advice, such as the ministries responsible for occupational health and safety, seniors, recreation, women's issues. The Northwest Territories has a Ministry of Intergovernmental and Aboriginal Affairs. See capitalization.

minke whale, lower-case.

minor leagues, a minor-leaguer

Mint

Upper-case when standing for the legal entity, the Royal Canadian Mint, or for its administration (the Mint announced). Lower-case for the actual building or operation that turns out coins.

minuscule

Often misspelled miniscule.

MIRV

It is not enough to say the acronym stands for multiple independently targeted re-entry vehicle. We must translate. Re-entry vehicle is a euphemism for nuclear warhead. A ballistic missile is said to have been MIRV'd if its "bus" (final stage) contains several warheads that can be directed to different targets by varying their release times and trajectories.

misbehaviour

misdemeanour

missiles

The description "guided" is insufficient; most modern military missiles are guided, including some small anti-tank "bazooka" rockets that are steered by means of thin wires that play out behind them.

Classify missiles by their size and use, such as intercontinental, medium-range, short-range, tactical, anti-tank, surface-to-air missile (SAM), air-to-surface, surface-to-surface (SSM). When relevant, also note the type of guidance system. Ballistic missiles are guided only to the top of their arc, beyond which they follow a normal ballistic trajectory. The newer precision-guided missiles can be steered all the way to the target. Others guide themselves, once the target has been indicated, by means of radar or heat sensors. A cruise missile steers itself around and over obstacles. See MIRV.

Mississaga etc.

There is a **Mississaga** Street in Oakville and Orillia, Ont.

The river, bay, strait, island and provincial park in Ontario's Algoma District are spelled **Mississagi**, but the community in the same area, near Blind River, is **Mississauga**, the same as the big community in Peel Region.

The lake, river and Landing in Peterborough County north of the Kawarthas are spelled **Mississagua**.

References in Peel Region are **Mississauga**, except for **Mississaugua** Golf and Country Club. The Ojibway-speaking Indian band in the area is called the Mississaugas of the Credit.

The rattlesnake is spelled **massasauga**, which see.

Mississquoi, Missisquoi

The bay that forms the northern end of Lake Champlain is Baie Mississquoi. But the federal and Quebec ridings are both called Brome-Missisquoi, with an s dropped.

missus (not missis).

Mistake, Our, see Corrections and Clarifications.

mitigate, see militate.

mitochondria

It is plural. The singular is mitochondrion.

mitre

Mitterrand, François

MLA

The abbreviation for legislature members in all provinces except Ontario, Quebec and Newfoundland and Labrador.

MNA

For member of the National Assembly, Quebec.

M'Naghten rule

Long used in much of the English-speaking world as the test of legal insanity. The ruling in the British case of M'Naghten, killer of Sir Robert Peel's secretary in 1843, was that to establish the defence of insanity it must be proved that the accused did not "know the nature and quality of the act he was doing; or if he did know it, that he did not know he was doing what was wrong." It has been challenged as outmoded in some jurisdictions, but the Criminal Code of Canada sticks quite closely to it: "A person is insane when the person is in a state of natural imbecility or has disease of the mind to an extent that renders the person incapable of appreciating the nature and quality of an act or omission or of knowing that an act or omission is wrong."

mnemonics

Can be either singular, meaning the science or system of assisting or developing the memory; or plural, meaning the various aids to remembering specific things, such as sentences in which the initial letters match those of the planets, medical symptoms etc.

moccasin

mockingbird

Mohammed

Use this spelling for the Prophet and for names transliterated from Arabic. But follow the spelling used by individuals with this name in countries that use the Roman alphabet, such as Muhammad Ali.

Mojave

mold

Use **mould** instead.

Moldova

Adjective and people: Moldovan. Currency: leu. Capital: Kishinev.

Formerly part of Bessarabia and then a Soviet republic, bordering on Romania and Ukraine, it was known for many years by the name Moldavia. Moldovans, a branch of the Romanian people, make up 64 per cent of the population of 4.5 million. A campaign for unification with Romania was fiercely opposed by the Ukrainian and Russian minorities (14 and 13 per cent). There are also Gagauzi and Jewish minorities.

A popular front won official status for the Moldovan language in 1989 (this triggered riots by Russians in Kishinev) and a declaration of sovereignty by the Moldovan parliament in June of 1990. In May of 1991 the word Soviet was removed from the republic's name, and in August, after the failed Soviet coup, the Communist Party was outlawed.

Moldova is largely agricultural, with a warm climate and fertile soil. Sunflower seeds and oil are the main industrial crop. Wine, fruits and vegetables and tobacco are important products.

See Soviet Union.

molehill

mollusk, but **molluscoid**.

mollycoddle

Molotov cocktail

Upper-case; named for revolutionary veteran Vyacheslav Molotov (born Skriabin), who was Soviet premier throughout the thirties under Stalin and foreign minister for most of the period from 1939 until 1956. The generic term in North America is gasoline bomb (not petrol bomb), but Molotov cocktail is well understood by readers and need not be explained when used in quotes. A glass

who made this cocktail anyway?

bottle or other breakable container is filled with a flammable liquid, fitted with a flaming wick and then thrown.

molt

Use **moult** instead.

mom

Use this spelling, not mum, for the short form for mother. However, the Queen's late mother was the Queen Mum and to stay silent is to keep mum.

momentarily

Reserve this for describing actions or states that last only **for a moment**. It is not a synonym for soon, **in a moment**.

Monaco

Adjective and people: Monacan. Currency: euro (had been the French franc). Capital: Monaco.

We do not use the local adjective, Monegasque, except in a colour piece in which the reader has been properly prepared to understand the reference. Monaco is a principality on the Mediterranean, surrounded on three sides by the French department of Alpes Maritimes, and may be described as being on the French Riviera. Its area is 195 hectares, and its population about 32,000. It is divided into four districts—Monaco (Monaco-Ville), the capital; Monte Carlo, the casino area; la Condamine, the commercial centre; and Fontvieille, which has some light industry and some reclaimed land for offices and apartments. Prince Rainier (born May 31, 1923) succeeded his grandfather in 1949, and married Grace Kelly in 1956. She was killed in an auto crash on Sept. 14, 1982.

monarch butterfly, lower-case.

money, moneys, moneyed

money's worth

Mongolia

Adjective and people: Mongolian. Currency: tugrik. Capital: Ulan Bator.

Formerly a Chinese province called Outer Mongolia, it is now an independent republic whose independence was guaranteed by a Sino-Soviet treaty of 1950. Except for a Kazakh minority of about 5 per cent, the population of 2.7 million is entirely Mongol (three-quarters of them Khalkha Mongols and the rest split among eight Mongol minorities). The climate is extreme, with temperatures below freezing for six months of the year. The main exports are live cattle and horses, meat, wool and hides, but ore is gaining in importance, principally copper and molybdenum. There are also large deposits of other minerals, including nickel, zinc and tin.

Mongoloid

Do not use the terms Mongoloid and Mongolism to refer to persons with Down syndrome. See disabled.

But Mongoloid is the proper adjective to describe one of the major racial divisions of the human species. In addition to many Asian peoples, the Mongoloid division is also considered to include Inuit. Other aboriginal

peoples of the Americas were formerly classed as Mongoloid, as were Polynesians, but now both are classed as separate geographic races. See race.

mongooses

Monroe Doctrine

Issued to Congress in 1823 by the fifth U.S. president, James Monroe, it said the Americas were no longer to be considered areas of colonization or outside meddling. Theodore Roosevelt's "big stick" corollary to the doctrine in 1904, that the United States had the right to ensure acceptable governments in Latin America, was repudiated by the Clark Memorandum of 1928.

Monrovia

Always explain the Liberian flag of convenience when writing about ships that list Monrovia as their home port. We give the country of ownership and nationality of the crew when available. See Liberia.

monsoon, see weather.

Monte Carlo

In Monaco it is spelled with a hyphen, and it should appear that way in formal commercial or literary names in French. Monte Carlo, one of the four districts of Monaco, is the gambling resort on the French Riviera.

The **Monte Carlo fallacy** (lower-case) is the nickname statisticians give to many gamblers' notion that overall statistical probabilities also apply in the short run, in individual cases. In fact, if a coin has come up heads in several consecutive tosses, the odds for tails on the next toss are still even. The formal name of the fallacy is the doctrine of the maturity of the chances.

Monte Cassino

Two words. The monastery, which for centuries was the headquarters of the Benedictine orders, was not impregnable before its destruction in the Second World War. It had been destroyed three times since St. Benedict of Nursia established it in the sixth century. It has now been rebuilt a fourth time.

Montenegro

Adjective and people: Montenegrin. Currency: euro and dinar. Capital: Podgorica.

One of the two federal republics, along with Serbia, which continued to constitute Yugoslavia after the secession in 1991-92 of Bosnia-Herzegovina, Croatia, Macedonia and Slovenia. Its population of about 600,000 is two-thirds Montenegrin, with Muslim and Albanian minorities. In February, 2003, Serbia and Montenegro agreed to become a loosely federated country called Serbia and Montenegro, and to hold referendums in each republic in three years to decide whether the two parts should become fully independent. See Yugoslavia, Serbia.

Monterey and Monterrey

In California, it is Monterey, Monterey Bay and Monterey Park (a city near the centre of greater Los Angeles). But in Spain and Mexico, it is Monterrey. Monterrey is an important Mexican industrial city and capital of the northeastern state of Nuevo Leon.

months

Five of the months are never abbreviated, and they are consecutive: March, April, May, June and July. The others are abbreviated only for a specific date (I'll see you in September, on Sept. 4.) The abbreviations are Aug., Sept., Oct., Nov., Dec., Jan., Feb.

Upper-case the designations given to months for the purpose of fundraising, education etc., such as Cancer Month.

Montmartre

The highest hill in Paris, at 131 metres (432 feet), and a centre of the Right Bank's night life and artistic community.

Montpelier and Montpellier

The communities in Jamaica and the United States (in Idaho, Indiana, North Dakota, Ohio and Vermont) are spelled **Montpelier**. Those in France and in Quebec (about 60 kilometres northeast of Ottawa) are spelled **Montpellier**.

Montreal

No accent in English, but make it Montréal as part of an organization or agency name rendered in French.

The Island of Montreal is in the St. Lawrence at the confluence with the Ottawa, the largest in the Hochelaga Archipelago. It and the next-largest, Île Jésus to the north, divide the St. Lawrence into three channels. The name St. Lawrence River is retained by the southernmost channel, between the Island of Montreal and the South Shore. Between Montreal and Île Jésus is Rivière des Prairies, and the channel along the North Shore is Rivière des Mille-Îles. Some of the other islands in the group are Île Sainte-Hélène, Île Notre-Dame, Île Bizard, Île Dorval, Île Sainte-Thérèse, Îles de Boucherville.

A new, larger City of Montreal (population 1.8 million) was created on Jan. 1, 2002, through the amalgamation of the old city of Montreal and 28 other municipalities on the Island of Montreal. It replaced the old Montreal Urban Community, a body that had been composed of city mayors and had co-ordinated activities in the municipalities of L'Île-Bizard, Sainte-Geneviève, Pierrefonds, Senneville, Sainte-Anne-de-Bellevue, Baie-d'Urfé, Kirkland, Beaconsfield, Roxboro, Dollard-des-Ormeaux, Pointe-Claire, Saint-Laurent, Dorval, Dorval Island, Lachine, Côte-Saint-

Luc, Ville-Saint-Pierre, Montreal, Montreal East, Montreal West, Montreal North, LaSalle, Town of Mount Royal, Hampstead, Outremont, Westmount, Verdun, Saint-Léonard, Anjou. The new city has 27 boroughs.

The enabling provincial legislation, Quebec's Bill 170, resulted in other amalgamations as well, including Quebec City, Trois-Rivières, Lévis, Gatineau and Longueuil. See the individual entries.

Greater Montreal, a designation used by Statistics Canada, contains more than half the province's population. It comprises the Island of Montreal, communities on the South Shore, Laval (on Île Jésus), and several off-island suburbs as far west as Salaberry-de-Valleyfield.

Montserrat

A British colony, it is an island in the Leeward group in the northeastern corner of the Caribbean, just southwest of Antigua and southeast of St. Kitts-Nevis. Its capital is Plymouth. The name, meaning saw-toothed mountain, is also that of a mountain in Spain's Catalonia region, the site of a renowned Benedictine monastery.

Mont Tremblant, Mont-Tremblant

The Quebec community has a hyphen; the mountain itself does not.

moolah

moon, lower-case.

moral and morale

Moral has to do with right and wrong. **Morale** means state of mind, especially the spirits. However, help that is not physical but rather directed toward boosting morale is called moral support. Note that morale can be either high or low.

moribund

It means on the point of death or extinction. We should speak of a moribund company or enterprise only if it is inactive and in the process of being wound up, not if it is merely declining or ailing.

Mormons

There is usually no need to spell out the formal name of the Church of Jesus Christ of Latter-day Saints (note the lower-case d). It may be called the Mormon Church, or simply the Mormons. In addition to the Bible, its scriptures include the Book of Mormon, written by founder Joseph Smith and considered divinely inspired.

Morocco

Adjective and people: Moroccan. Currency: dirham. Capital: Rabat.

On the northwestern shoulder of Africa, on both the Atlantic and the Mediterranean, it cannot be described as part of the Middle East. It is a monarchy, officially called the Kingdom of Morocco. Its principal cities, which also include Tangier, Casablanca and Marrakesh, are all on the Atlantic side. The town directly opposite Gibraltar is Tetuan. The population of 31 million is about two-thirds Arab and one-third Berber, but there are also French and Spanish communities. Agriculture is a mainstay of the economy (grains, fruit, livestock, leather), but there are also minerals, with phosphates the chief revenue earner. See Western Sahara for an account of Morocco's ambitions there.

mortar, see guns.

mortgage

Strictly speaking, a mortgage is a conditional transfer of title, given by the owner or prospective buyer of a property in exchange for a loan, so it is the lender (a bank, for example) that receives the mortgage. Modern idiom allows us to refer to a mortgage loan as simply a mortgage, and to speak of the borrower as having sought or obtained a mortgage, but we must remain aware of the literal meaning if we are to sort out the terms mortgagor and mortgagee. See below.

mortgagor and mortgagee

They are often confused, and for this reason should usually be replaced by such expressions as the person or company receiving the mortgage loan, or the person or institution granting the loan. The party that receives the loan and in exchange gives a mortgage (a conditional transfer of title) is the mortgagor. The party from which the loan is obtained, and to which the mortgage is given, is the mortgagee. Remember it this way: Simon Legree is the mortgagee.

mosquitoes

mothball

mother-of-pearl

motor

One word: motorbike, motorboat, motorbus, motorcade, motorcycle, motorhome, motorman. Two words: motor scooter, motor vehicle, motor vessel.

mottoes

mould, moulder, moulding, mouldy

moult

Mount

Generally, do not abbreviate it to Mt. in place names, although this is acceptable in short headlines.

mountains

Mountains are one of the most treacherous areas into which writers and editors venture. Errors in the name or location of a particular range are all the more glaring in a national newspaper, because it is read by people who live in the area and in whose lives those mountains are a looming presence. The Globe library has numerous references, including topographical atlases, which should be consulted if there is the slightest doubt about which range is being referred to.

The **Western Cordillera**, the mass of mountain systems in western North America, merits special attention, because it is such a complex web of ranges. Its four largest systems in southern B.C. and Alberta are the **Rocky** and **Columbia Mountains**, divided from each other by the Rocky Mountain Trench; and, on the other side of B.C.'s Interior Plateau, the **Cascade** and **Coast Mountains**, divided by the Fraser River. Each of these systems comprises several ranges. It would be embarrassing in the extreme to imply, for example, that the Rockies are visible from Vancouver, since the Coast Mountains, the Cascades, the Interior Plateau and the Columbias intervene.

North of the Liard River, which is generally taken to be the northern limit of the Rockies, the Cordillera also includes the **Mackenzie Mountains** of the Northwest Territories and Yukon, and the **St. Elias Mountains** of B.C., Yukon and Alaska. The St. Elias range, much of it included in Kluane National Park, contains Canada's 15 highest mountains, the highest of which is **Mount Logan**. It stands at 5,959 metres (19,550 feet), and with its great breadth and three peaks it is one of the most massive mountains in the world. In North America, it is second in height only to Mount McKinley in the Alaska Range, at 6,193 metres. (McKinley is increasingly referred to by the native name Denali.)

From Alberta's Foothills, ranges deserving individual mention because of their importance in tourism or mining include the Rockies' **Continental Ranges** (containing the Main or Park Ranges visible from Banff and Jasper), the northern **Hart** and **Muskwa Ranges** and the southern **Border Ranges**. On the other side of the Rocky Mountain Trench are the Columbias' **Purcells, Selkirks, Monashees** and **Cariboos;** and, farther north, the **Cassiar Mountains** and **Omineca Mountains,** including the **Finlay, Swannell** and **Hogem Ranges**.

On the far western side of the Cordillera, the major ranges are, from north to south, the **Boundary, Kitimat** and **Pacific Ranges** of the Coast Mountains; and, offshore, the **Queen Charlotte Mountains** and the **Vancouver Island Ranges**. Inland in the south, east of the Fraser River, are the **Cascade Mountains**, and ranged across southwestern B.C. are the **Skagit, Hozameen** and **Okanagan Ranges**. Further north, inland from the Boundary Ranges separating B.C from the Alaska Panhandle, are the **Hazelton Mountains** (including the **Nass** and **Bulkley Ranges**) and the **Skeena Mountains**.

In **Eastern Canada**, geographers list such formal designations as the **Laurentian Highlands**, the **Mealy Mountains** of Labrador, and the **Newfoundland, Nova Scotia** and **New Brunswick Highlands**. But be aware of such locally prominent names as Newfoundland's **Long Range Mountains** and **the Topsails**; Nova Scotia's **Cobequid Mountains, Glenmore Mountain, North Mountain** and **South Mountain**; New Brunswick's **Black Mountains**; and the Gaspé's **Notre Dame** and **Shickshock** ranges. (Do not use the French name Monts Chic-Chocs.) The highlands of the Gaspé and the Atlantic provinces are part of the vast Appalachian system, stretching into the U.S. South. See Appalachian, Laurentians.

Mountain, the
Upper-case for the portion of the Niagara Escarpment that passes through Hamilton.

Mount Allison University
It is in Sackville, N.B., and made history in 1875 when Grace Ann Lockhart became the first woman BA in the British Empire.

Mountie, Mounties
Acceptable in all stories for members of the RCMP, and in most stories for the force itself in second reference.

mouse
The plural of the animal is mice. The plural of the computer peripheral is mouses. The computer mouse was invented in 1963 by engineer Douglas Engelbart with fellow engineer Bill English, and was so named because the wire looked like a tail.

moustache
Use mustache.

mousy

mouth, the verb (not mouthe).

movable

Mozambique
Adjective and people: Mozambican. Currency: metical. (Use the plural meticals, not the local meticais.) Capital: Maputo.

It is a former Portuguese colony, independent since 1975, on Africa's southeastern coast, lying between Tanzania and South Africa. Directly offshore is the Mozambique Channel, separating it from Madagascar and the Comoros. It is mainly low and humid, but has mountainous regions in the west and north. The official language is Portuguese, but several Bantu languages are spoken locally, and

Swahili is a trade language north of the Zambezi. The population is about 20 million. Mozambique signed a non-aggression pact with South Africa in 1984. The ruling Frelimo Party announced in July of 1989 that it was abandoning Marxism in favour of a mixed economy, and it opened negotiations with the Mozambican National Resistance (known by its Portuguese acronym, Renamo). A ceasefire aimed at ending the 16-year civil war was signed in Rome in October, 1992.

MPP

For members of the Ontario legislature. Do not use the full term member of the Provincial Parliament, a name the province no longer applies to its legislature.

Mr., Ms. etc. See honorifics.

MRI

It is magnetic resonance imaging, which, unlike X-rays, can show soft tissues. A part of the body is subjected to a magnetic field, and the image depicts differences in the way various tissues reflect the magnetic waves.

MSc, for master of science.

muckamucks

As in high muckamucks, the rich and powerful. In the Chinook Jargon, the trade pidgin of the West Coast, muckamuck meant food, and *hiu muckamuck* meant those with lots of it.

muckraker

mucus

This is the word for the substance, but the adjective, meaning something that secretes or resembles mucus, is **mucous** (mucous membrane).

mugwump

Lower-case the American term for someone who is politically independent. Upper-case it only for Republicans who would not support James Blaine for president against Democrat Grover Cleveland in 1884.

mujahedeen

Italics. It is a plural noun, requiring a plural verb: The *mujahedeen* are assembling in the mountains. One holy warrior is a *mujahed. Mu* means "one who" – in this case, one who undertakes *jihad.*

mukluk

Does not require italics. It is the Inuktitut word in Alaska and the Western Arctic for skin boots. In the rest of the North, they are called kamiks.

muktuk

Does not require italics. Should not be described simply as blubber. It is the Inuktitut word for the skin of bowhead whales. The skin of beluga whales and narwhals is *maktaaq.*

multi

Does not take a hyphen (multicoloured, multilingual, multimedia, multiparty) unless the main word begins with i (multi-insular).

mumps

Make every effort to recast a sentence to avoid the issue of whether this takes a singular or plural verb.

munch

To munch means to chew with considerable jaw action and a crunching sound, as cattle chew herbiage. We can describe human beings as munching on celery, potato chips, peanut brittle and similar crunchy stuff, but not on such things as cake and most sandwiches.

Musical Ride

Upper-case. The 32 Mounties and horses assigned to this ceremonial cavalry drill are the Troop of the Ride.

Muskoka

Just as the Finger Lakes district isn't called "the Fingers" and the Great Lakes region isn't known as "the Greats," neither is the Muskoka lakes region in Ontario known to anyone familiar with it as "the Muskokas." It is simply Muskoka, as reflected in the name of the regional municipality.

This creeping trend of using a plural to describe the region is an extension of the practice common in mountain resort districts (the Laurentians, the Adirondacks, the Poconos). It is rarely applied to lakes, although there are exceptions (the Kawarthas).

muskellunge, muskie

Muslim

Use this spelling, not Moslem, for a member of the Islamic faith. The Prophet Mohammed is not worshipped by Muslims; he is revered as the one to whom God revealed the words subsequently written in the Koran. See Mecca.

Note that a majority of Muslims are not Arabs and Arabs are not necessarily Muslims. See Arab.

mustache

The adjective is mustachioed.

muumuu

Muzak, a trade name.

Always upper-case when we use it, usually in quotes. In our own words, we should not use Muzak in a pejorative sense. Prefer such generic terms as taped music, background music, mood music, mall music, elevator music.

MV, for Motor Vessel.

Unlike HMCS and HMS, MV may take the definite article, as in the MV Maid of the Mist. HMCS is relevant when used to indicate military status, but MV is normally omitted.

Myanmar

Adjective and people: Myanmarese. Currency: kyat. Capital: Rangoon. (In quotes, it may be necessary to explain use of the official name, Yangon.)

Always mention as high as practicable that it was formerly called Burma. Myanmar is on the Bay of Bengal, bordering on Bangladesh, China, India, Laos and Thailand. Most of the population of 42 million is rural, and much of the land is watered by the Irrawaddy River and its extensive delta. Burmans make up about three-quarters of the population, and the official language may be referred to as Burmese. Other major groups are the Karens, Shans, Indians and Chinese.

A military junta nullified an election in 1990 in which the opposition National League for Democracy won a sweeping victory, and party leader Aung San Suu Kyi (in second reference, Ms. Suu Kyi; her father was Aung San) was placed under house arrest from 1989 to 1995, and again from September of 2000 to May of 2002. After clashes between her supporters and supporters of the junta, she was taken into custody on May 30, 2003, and held incommunicado. She was awarded the Nobel Peace Prize in 1991.

In such names as U Thant and U Nu, the U is an honorific.

mynah

myriad

It is both an adjective meaning innumerable and a noun meaning a large, indefinite number, so it is

correct to say either myriad stars or a
myriad of stars.

mystery

May be used as an adjective in
such familiar expressions as mystery
man, mystery novel, mystery ship,
things that involve a true mystery. But
for things that are merely uncanny or
puzzling, prefer **mysterious** (a
mysterious letter, not a mystery letter).

N

NAFO

See Northwest Atlantic Fisheries Organization.

Nahanni National Park

It is in the southwestern corner of the Northwest Territories, along the South Nahanni River. Note the different spelling, Nahani, of the informal name for the Kaska Indians of the Nahanni River area of northern B.C. and southern Yukon.

Naipaul, V. S.

He is known as an Indian writer, but note that he was born in Trinidad. The initials stand for Vidiadhar Surajprasad.

naiveté

nameplate, see masthead.

name words

The rule is not ironclad, but in general, words formed from people's names (eponyms) are lower-case when they are units of measurement (ampere, curie, hertz, ohm, pascal etc.) but upper-case as adjectives and possessives. The nouns they modify are lower-case (Mach number, Fallopian tubes, Newtonian method, Archimedes' principle, Ohm's law).

Namibia

Adjective and people: Namibian. Currency: dollar. Capital: Windhoek.

The former German territory, rich in such valuable minerals as diamonds and uranium, was put under South African mandate in 1920 as South-West Africa. The UN declared the mandate terminated in 1966, and in 1968 officially changed the name to Namibia. South Africa agreed in December 1988 to a UN independence plan. The process began on April 1, 1989, and Namibia declared its independence on March 21, 1990. Namibia contains both the Namib (on the coast) and Kalahari deserts. The population of about 1.8 million comprises several Bantu tribes, along with Bushmen, Europeans and people of mixed race.

nano

It means a billionth (nanosecond). Readers need a translation, so why not bypass nano in the first place?

napalm

Strictly speaking, it is a soap of aluminum salts, but the name is also given to the gel formed when it is added to gasoline, at a concentration of about 10 per cent. The gel is the fuel in flame-throwers and incendiary bombs (not to be confused with gasoline bombs; see Molotov cocktail).

naphtha

Napoleonic Code

Informal name for the Civil Code, the civil law in Quebec. (See courts.) Prefer Civil Code. Do not use the French names *Code civil* or *Code Napoléon*.

Narcotic Control Act
Note singular.

narwhal

NASA
For National Aeronautics and Space Administration.

Nasdaq
It was originally upper-case, for National Association of Securities Dealers Automated Quotations, but now is called the Nasdaq Stock Market. On second reference, drop the article (On Nasdaq yesterday . . .). It should no longer be described as the over-the-counter market.

Nashwaak-Miramichi Trail
Roughly following the Nashwaak and Miramichi rivers through the New Brunswick interior, from Fredericton to Point Escuminac on the Gulf of St. Lawrence, the trail is noted for its fishing and hunting.

Naskapi, see Innu.

nation
Not a good synonym for country or state, particularly in an age when groups of people within countries are asserting their status as nations (that is, a group of people who have a common heritage, language and cultural identity). When that group includes virtually all the people in a country (as in most countries in Europe, for example), the country is referred to as a nation-state. Shun the current careless use of the term nation-state to mean any sovereign country. Most countries that experienced historical immigration (such as Canada) are not nation-states, nor are the many African countries comprising many tribal groups.

National, The
The CBC television newscast. Italic, with the article upper-case.

National Action Committee on the Status of Women
May be called NAC in second reference. It is Canada's largest umbrella organization of women's groups, founded in 1971. It must not be confused with the Canadian Advisory Council on the Status of Women, which advises the federal government on women's concerns.

national anthem, lower-case.
O Canada is the national anthem. *God Save the Queen* is Canada's **royal anthem**.

National Assembly
The Quebec legislature. Its members are MNAs. See legislature.

National Battlefields Park
Note plural. This 95-hectare national historic park in Quebec City includes the Plains of Abraham.

National Capital Region
It is an area of 4,662 square kilometres taking in Ottawa, Gatineau and their environs, designated in 1958 for the purpose of developing and beautifying the federal capital. It should not be described as being similar to the U.S. capital region, the autonomous District of Columbia. Rather, the National Capital Commission works with area municipalities and with the two provincial governments.

National Citizens' Coalition

national debt, public debt
The **national debt** is the amount owed by the federal government. The total owed by the federal and provincial governments is usually referred to as the **public debt**, and this is often taken to include also the debts of Crown corporations, utility commissions and the like.
Also see debt and deficit.

National Defence Headquarters

Takes singular verbs and pronouns. It comprises the former civil and military branches of the Defence Department, merged in 1972.

national energy program

Lower-case, but NEP in second reference. Often misnamed national energy policy.

National Guard

These are the volunteer reserves of the U.S. Army and Air Force, organized in each state. They are administered federally, but members take double oaths of allegiance, to their state government and the federal government, and can be called out by either the governor or the president in times of emergency. The generic description is guardsman (lower-case), but prefer the gender-neutral term member of the National Guard.

National Organization for Women

Not of. This U.S. group was founded in 1966.

national origin

Should not be reported unless relevant, particularly in court stories. See courts.

National Policy

Upper-case for Macdonald's three-pronged development strategy of protective tariffs, a transcontinental railway and immigration to the West.

National Revenue, Department of

No longer exists by that name. See Canada Customs and Revenue Agency.

native people

Native people is the generally accepted term in Canada embracing the four categories of aboriginal or semi-aboriginal peoples: Inuit, Indians, non-status Indians and Métis.

Status Indians living on reserves are represented by the Assembly of First Nations. The Congress of Aboriginal Peoples represents the interests of non-status Indians, status Indians living off reserves, and many who call themselves Métis, particularly in Eastern Canada. The Métis National Council largely restricts its constituency to Métis in the West and Northwest who claim descent from the Red River Settlement. Inuit are represented by the Inuit Tapiriit of Canada.

In 1991 and 1992, these four groups negotiated as part of the Charlottetown accord a proposed constitutional amendment recognizing an inherent right to aboriginal self-government (a term that was to be precisely defined in later negotiations). When the accord was defeated in the national referendum of Oct. 26, 1992, they cited polls showing that this provision had broad public support, and said they would press for its implementation by other means.

Many native leaders advocate the terms "aboriginal" and "aboriginal person," but the terms "native" and "Indian" are still used by the vast majority of native people themselves, as well as by our readers, by governments and by various world bodies and academic disciplines. We should respect the wishes of the particular person being referred to whenever this is consistent with clarity, and in fact "aboriginal" is more useful than "native" as a worldwide generic term. But "Indian," despite its origin in a mistaken notion of the early explorers, is an acceptable term both in Canada and around the world, and indeed is the only practical term at present for distinguishing Indians from other native peoples.

(There is a theoretical chance of confusion with citizens of India, but in practical terms the context of the story usually precludes any mix-ups. If clarification is necessary, provide it in full, possibly by using the language group or band name. Do not use the ambiguous term "native Indian" or the erroneous term "East Indian," or expect the reader to divine the difference between "Canadian Indian" and "Indian Canadian." See East Indian.)

When identifying a native person, prefer the more informative nation or band name to the generic term Indian (a Haida, a Mi'kmaq, a Chippewa man, an Ermineskin woman).

Do not identify a person as an Indian, Métis etc. in a court story or other general news story unless this is relevant (as in the case of an assault stemming from racial taunts). Use the Canadian word "reserve" (upper-case when accompanied by the name), not the American term "reservation." Use igloo, *tupek*, *umiak*, teepee, hogan, longhouse, totem etc. only if you are sure the description is accurate. Do not use such insulting terms as squaw, buck, brave, papoose, Indian list, Indian-giver. Never imply, and normally do not quote anyone as implying, that all Indians are alcoholics or on welfare, but we should not shrink from a fair examination of the problems of alcoholism and poverty on reserves.

For the names of language groups, bands, reserves, Crown-land communities and northern settlements, we generally conform to the spelling of the federal government. The library has several references, including the Schedule of Indian Bands, Reserves and Settlements and lists of native organizations, chiefs and band offices. Several reserves and communities, which in some respects have a role similar to that of municipalities, have recently changed their names. We use these once they become official, but also provide the former name. Some are changing their basic name (St. Regis has become Akwesasne), and others are abandoning the description "Band" or "Reserve" in favour of "First Nation,"

as in the Kettle Point First Nation (an Ontario Chippewa band).

Standing alone, the term **first nation** is taken to be a synonym for status-Indian band or reserve, and is lower-case. It will be found most often in direct quotes.

As a general rule, language-group and band names are taken to serve as both singular and plural. Many are already plural in the language of the people themselves, and so it is incorrect to add an s to create a spurious English double plural. The corresponding singular in the native language would confuse most readers, and so by convention we make the one word do double duty. (A notable exception is Inuk/Inuit. See Inuit.) Even when a long-established name is English or French, tradition usually dictates that we not create a plural (we say five Blackfoot, two Dogrib). However, there are a handful of exceptions used by the government or preferred by the people themselves, and we conform. The traditional list has been Crees; Mohawks; Hurons; Algonquins; the Munceys of the Thames; the Mississaugas of the Credit; Chippewas; Oneidas; the Ojibways of Onegaming. For the names of individual bands that emerge from relative obscurity because of land-claim, resource or environmental disputes, we use English plurals if quotes in a story make it clear that the people themselves do so (the Lubicons, for example). This list will grow as native people continue to lose their traditional languages.

The Ojibways of Onegaming are also an exception to another general rule: We use **Ojibwa** for other members of this linguistic group (both singular and plural), and **Ojibway** only for their language.

Creation of a plural possessive is possible only when we use English plurals (the Mohawks' religion). For others, we must either treat the name as an adjective (the Gitksan religion) or resort to a phrase (the religion of the Gitksan, practised by the Gitksan etc.). See Inuit.

Population estimates for native people vary widely, and official census figures are usually described as low, since enumeration is difficult in remote areas and there are differences over the definition of Métis and non-status Indians. Native representatives put their numbers in the early 1990s at just under one million, but the 1996 census produced a number of about 800,000, made up of about 554,000 Indians (69 per cent of the total), 210,000 Métis (26 per cent) and 41,000 Inuit (5 per cent). There were another 6,400 who considered themselves members of more than one of these groups. We should not imply that any native population figure is exact, or join the battle over who is a Métis. This issue gained great importance when Métis, previously largely excluded from consideration, were included in the aboriginal-rights clause of the Constitution Act of 1982. Whether this will affect land claims is still uncertain, since Métis do not have as strong a legal claim as Indians and Inuit to be first-nation occupants of a particular tract. The broadest definition of Métis would include everyone of mixed race, the narrowest only those who took land scrip. A middle-ground position, and the one gaining widest acceptance, would include all the mixed-race francophones of the Northwest.

There is also a dispute over who holds official Indian status, entitling a person to what has been called citizenship-plus: the full legal and political rights of a Canadian citizen plus a package of extra benefits in such areas as health care, education and taxation while on a reserve. Such status is conferred by Ottawa, usually according to patrilineal bloodlines from the original treaty group. The landmark Bill C-31 reinstated the status of Indian women who married non-Indians, and conferred status on their children and grandchildren. Many bands want the right to determine their own membership, some using matrilineal, clan or other criteria, including traditional adoption practices.

About 35 per cent of native people live in urban areas; the other two-thirds live on about 2,240 reserves, in about 85 Crown-land communities or in numerous northern settlements. Most have small areas and populations, sometimes only a few families.

Racially, all the native peoples of the Americas were once considered to be part of the Mongoloid (Asian) biological division. However, modern analyses put only the Inuit in this category; American Indian is considered a separate biological and geographic race. (See race.)

Guide to native groups

Official lists of Canada's native people are usually broken down into 11 language groups, but we should not imply that languages within a group appear similar to anyone but language scholars. They can be as different as French and Finnish, and languages from diverse groups are as different as Greek and Cantonese. (Do not describe a person as speaking Indian.) It should also be remembered that up to half of native people no longer have any knowledge of their traditional languages, so we cannot automatically describe a particular Sarcee, for example, as a speaker of an Athapaskan language.

Also note that a large "tribe" spread over thousands of square miles was often the concept of white scholars and administrators. Most native peoples traditionally lived in small groups having little or no contact with the other bands that shared their language, and many have regarded their individual band or a handful of area settlements as their tribe or "nation." For example, the

Crees of the Lubicon Lake Reserve in Alberta call themselves Lubicons, and other Crees call themselves Ermineskin, O'Chiese, Sunchild, Peepeekisis, Star Blanket etc. Reserves of the Cowichan people in B.C. call their members Malahat, Nanoose, Musqueam etc. We use these names, but add the linguistic-group name whenever possible.

Distinguish between a band (usually reserve-based) of Indians and groups of bands (usually of the same native language or dialect) that act collectively, often for political purposes, and in that role cannot correctly be called a band. For instance, the Nisga'a are a distinct people of the Tsimshian language group, and comprise several bands. As with most native groups, our first choice when referring to them is simply the name itself, and "people" may also do in a pinch. Since the bands are combined under a Nisga'a Tribal Council, use of "tribal council" is valid when relevant, but the word "tribe" standing alone has no resonance in Canada.

Here is a brief rundown of the location of native linguistic groups (although it should be kept in mind that members of virtually all, including Inuit, can be found in large southern cities):

The two language heritages covering by far the largest number of reserve residents are the **Cree** (covering more than 120,000 on reserves in 1986) and the **Ojibway** (about 80,000). Both peoples, members of the diverse Algonquian language group, were eastern and central woodland dwellers who spread west with the fur trade, and are now represented on reserves from Quebec to the Rockies. Generally speaking, the Ojibwa were people of deciduous forests and the Crees were found in the northern coniferous forests, and today the Cree reserves are still the more northerly. There are six Cree

dialects (East, Moose, Woods, Swampy, Plains and Northern) and five Ojibway dialects that also correspond to band or tribal names (**Algonquin, Chippewa, Mississauga, Ottawa** and **Saulteau**).

Extreme southern Ontario and Quebec as far east as Quebec City also have reserves with a heritage of the Iroquoian language group (the six languages in Canada today are **Mohawk** and **Cayuga** in Quebec and Ontario, and **Oneida, Onondaga, Seneca** and **Tuscarora** in Ontario).

The Prairies, in addition to Crees and Ojibwa, have reserves with a heritage of Siouan languages in the south (**Dakota** in Manitoba, Saskatchewan and Alberta, and **Assiniboine** and **Sioux** in Saskatchewan); Blackfoot reserves in Alberta (**Blackfoot, Blood** and **Peigan**); and reserves of various Athapaskan languages in the north.

The diverse Athapaskan linguistic group, whose peoples are found not only in the northern Prairies but also in the Northwest Territories, Yukon, northern B.C. and Alaska, includes the **Chipewyan** language (note spelling) in the three Prairie provinces and NWT; **Slave** in B.C., Alberta and NWT; **Loucheux** in the NWT and Yukon; **Beaver** and **Sarcee** in Alberta; **Carrier, Chilcotin, Sekani** and **Tahltan** in B.C.; **Dogrib, Hare** and **Yellowknife** in NWT; and **Kutchin** and **Nahani** in Yukon. A common Athapaskan word for "the people" is **Dene**, and the former Indian Brotherhood of the Northwest Territories changed its name in 1978 to the Dene Nation. It represents various peoples of Athapaskan and Cree heritage, and has advocated the creation of an autonomous Indian jurisdiction in the Western Arctic to be called Denendeh (Home of the People). However, after the creation of the new territory of Nunavut in the Eastern Arctic, the remainder of the Northwest Territories retained the name Northwest Territories rather than adopting Denendeh. See Nunavut.

British Columbia, in addition to its Athapaskan peoples and one Ojibwa band (the **Saulteau**, near Prince George), has six separate language groups of its own: the **Haida** of the Queen Charlotte Islands; the Tlingit (**Tagish**) of the B.C.-Yukon border area; the **Kootenays** of the south-central region; the Tsimshian languages (**Tsimshian**, **Gitxsan** and **Nisga'a**) of the northern coast; the Wakashan languages of the northern and central coast and Vancouver Island (**Haisla**, **Heiltsuk**, **Kwakiutl** and **Nootka**); and the Salishan languages of the southern coast and Interior (**Bella Coola**, **Comox**, **Cowichan**, **Lillooet**, **Ntlakyapamuk**, **Okanagan**, **Puntlatch**, **Sechelt**, **Semiahmoo**, **Shuswap**, **Songish** and **Squamish**).

In Eastern Canada, all other native peoples except the Iroquoian and Inuit share the Algonquian language group with the Crees and Ojibwa. They are the **Mi'kmaq** in New Brunswick, Nova Scotia and Quebec; the **Delaware**, **Ottawa** and **Potowatomi** in Ontario; the **Montagnais**, **Naskapi** and **Atikamekw** in northeastern Quebec and Labrador (these three groups, plus a Labrador group calling itself the **Innu**, make up the Innu nation); the **Abenaki** in Quebec; and the **Maliseet** of New Brunswick and Quebec.

For a list of the eight main Inuit tribal groups, see Inuit.

NATO

The acronym may be used in a lead paragraph, but spell out the full name high in the story: the North Atlantic Treaty Organization. This mutual-defence group may also be called the Atlantic Alliance. The North Atlantic Treaty was signed in 1949 by Belgium, Britain, Canada, Denmark, France, Iceland, Italy, Luxembourg, the Netherlands, Norway, Portugal and the United States. Greece and Turkey joined in 1951, West Germany in 1954 and Spain in 1982 (it had been barred while Franco was alive). That raised the membership to 16. Poland, Hungary and the Czech Republic joined in 1999. France remains part of the alliance, but left the integrated military structure in 1966.

The collapse of Communist regimes in Eastern Europe in 1989 and 1990 created pressure for changes in NATO to accommodate a united Germany and to become more a political organization. A conference in July of 1990 did not bring an abandonment of NATO's military role, but did produce the London Declaration, on the use of nuclear weapons only as a last resort and the withdrawal of nuclear artillery shells. This represented a significant moderation of two keystone NATO strategies, those of flexible response and forward defence.

In another departure, NATO led a peace-implementation force in Bosnia in the late 1990s. Russia was also a participant in the Bosnia operation, and was included in many NATO meetings. In 1999, NATO undertook its first offensive military operation, bombing Yugoslavia for three months in the spring to end the Serbs' repression of ethnic Albanians in the Serbian province of Kosovo.

natural gas

Not to be confused with petroleum gas. See liquefied natural gas.

Nauru

Adjective and people: Nauruan. Currency: Australian dollar. No official capital.

An independent island republic of 21 square kilometres about 40 miles south of the equator in Polynesia. Surrendered by Germany in 1914, it was governed by the British Empire, then under joint UN mandate by

Australia, New Zealand and Britain until independence in 1968. It exports phosphate rock from its central plateau. It is a member of the Commonwealth, but does not attend summits. It joined the United Nations in 1999. Its population is 12,000.

nauseous

Confine to the sense of sick, queasy, affected by nausea. To describe things that cause this, use nauseating.

Navajo (singular and plural).

Nazi

Use upper case when referring to a party that actually bears that name, or to its members. Use lower case for the philosophy or movement, nazism (not naziism), and for descriptions of bullying or undemocratic people and things (the landlord was accused of using nazi tactics). Using this word in connection with any identifiable person or corporation, or quoting anyone else as doing so, is almost certainly defamatory. Consult a senior editor.

NBC

No need to spell out National Broadcasting Corp. if the context makes it clear we are talking about a broadcasting network.

NCAA

The National Collegiate Athletic Association (not College), U.S. equivalent of the Canadian Interuniversity Athletic Union.

Neanderthal

Use this widely accepted English word, not the German Neandertal.

nearby

nearsightedness

A long word, but preferable to myopia, except when used figuratively.

nebula, nebulas (not nebulae).

Formerly applied to any fuzzy object in the sky, this term is now properly used only for interstellar clouds of gas or dust.

née

Prefer such English words as formerly or born, as in Mary Brown, formerly Mary Green. If née is unavoidable, use it only with the surname, as in Mary Brown, née Green, and be sure it was actually the name the person was born with.

ne'er-do-well

negative growth

A dreadful oxymoron used by economists. Say the economy contracted or shrank. (We would never describe growth as a positive contraction.)

Negro, Negroes

Use only in direct quotes. Otherwise, use black, black men and women. Use "coloured" only for historical references to South Africans of mixed race, and explain. However, the expression "of colour" is used by some Canadian advocacy groups as a generic adjective to encompass all visible minorities, as in "women of colour." **Negroid** is the correct name for one of the racial divisions of humankind, but be aware of whom it covers. See race.

neighbour

neighbourhoods

The use of neighbourhood names enriches a story from any city, but we overreach ourselves if we do not have the boundaries exact. To say that a street is in Rockcliffe Park when it is in nearby New Edinburgh diminishes us in the eyes of every reader in Ottawa. For the benefit of readers in other cities, provide a thumbnail locator with each neighbourhood name (e.g. in Edmonton, describe Strathcona as the central part of the city south of the river).

Beware of automatically grabbing for labels that unfairly brand an entire neighbourhood, as in "beleaguered Parkdale" or "the crime-ridden Jane-Finch corridor," or that have become outdated, as in "wealthy Rosedale." The name Chinatown is acceptable in certain contexts to describe a designated business and tourist district, but in general we should not imply that any neighbourhood is inhabited entirely by people of a certain race or national origin, or entirely by gays, drug users, people on welfare etc. We should be sensitive to the concerns of residents fighting unfair generalizations. Do not shrink from giving the nearest major intersection as a way of pinpointing unfamiliar streets, but do not unfairly enlarge a neighbourhood's orbit. For example, Toronto's Yewtree Avenue and Wilmont Drive are properly identified as being near Jane Street and Finch Avenue, but Shoreham Drive is closer to Steeles Avenue than to Finch.

Nellies

The radio awards. See Geminis.

Nepal

Adjective and people: Nepalese. Currency: Nepalese rupee. Capital: Kathmandu.

Nepal, whose form of government is a constitutional monarchy, ranges from the Himalayas in the north through the temperate central Valley of Nepal to the swamps and forests of the southern Terai region. The adjective is Nepalese, but use Nepali for the language of the majority (about 52 per cent of the country's 24 million people). The Gurkha soldiers in the British and Indian armies are not drawn from a single Nepalese group. See Gurkha.

In 2001, Crown Prince Dipendra shot King Berendra, the queen and several other family members, and then shot himself; he died three days later. In 2002, the prime minister dissolved parliament but could not hold a new election because of continuing attacks by Maoist rebels, in an insurgency that began in 1996. The new king dismissed the prime minister and his cabinet, and appointed a cabinet to run the country until an election could be held.

nerve-racking

Nestlé SA

Remember the company's accent, from founder Henri Nestlé.

Net

Upper-case when used as a short form for the Internet.

Netherlands, the

Adjective and people: Dutch. Currency: euro (had been the guilder). Capital: Amsterdam is the official capital, but The Hague is the administrative capital and seat of government.

This monarchy is one of the most densely populated countries in the world, with 16 million people in an area of 41,863 square kilometres. Administratively, it also includes the **Netherlands Antilles** and **Aruba**, Caribbean islands that have internal self-government. The Netherlands Antilles comprise the southern Leeward group near Venezuela (Curaçao and Bonaire) and three islands 500 miles to the northeast, in the Windward group (Saba, St. Eustatius and the southern part of St. Maarten). Aruba, constitutionally separated from the southern group in 1986, is properly described as a separate entity within the Kingdom of the Netherlands. See Zuider Zee.

never

It means not ever. Avoid in expressing a simple negative. Say I never saw such a thing, but not I never saw the movie.

nevertheless

newborn

New Caledonia

A French Overseas Territory in the southwestern Pacific, comprising the island of New Caledonia, the Loyalty Islands, the Isle of Pines, the Belep Archipelago and smaller groups. The capital is Nouméa. New Caledonia is rich in nickel, chrome, iron and other minerals.

New Democratic Party

May be called the NDP even in first reference in political stories. In keeping with the party's own practice, its members may be called New Democrats, but do not use this as an adjective (say an NDP or a New Democratic initiative, not a New Democrat initiative). The NDP was formed in 1961 to succeed the Co-operative Commonwealth Federation. It is not correct to say it was formerly the CCF, or that the CCF merely changed its name. Call it the successor to the CCF. New Party clubs for discussing a new socialist party had been formed in 1958 by the CCF, the Canadian Labour Congress and other interested groups.

Newfoundland and Labrador

The Province of Newfoundland and Labrador is the official name of the province that used to be Newfoundland. A constitutional amendment to that effect was proclaimed by the Governor-General on Dec. 6, 2001, after separate votes of the Senate, the House of Commons and the Newfoundland House of Assembly, which had asked for the name change in a resolution adopted April 29, 1999. Although Quebec has never recognized a 1927 ruling by the Imperial Privy Council that confirmed the current boundaries of Labrador, it dropped its objections to the name change after being assured the change would have no impact on the border dispute.

As a rule, in headlines and in copy, use the short form Newfoundland. Continue to use the place line Nfld. after a city or town on the island or mainland, but if the story takes place in Labrador, mention the fact in copy. In those infrequent cases in which the official name of the province is at issue, give the full name: the Province of Newfoundland and Labrador. And do not be shy about using the full name if it aids reader comprehension: Quebec is in negotiations with Newfoundland and Labrador over the future of the Churchill Falls hydroelectric development.

Do not refer to Newfoundland and Labrador as an island province, since the island accounts for only one-third of its territory. Similarly, do not use the colloquial term "the rock" to refer to the entire province.

New France

Not La Nouvelle France. Do not equate it with Quebec. At its height in the early 1700s it comprised three-quarters of North America, including the entire Mississippi Valley.

New Hebrides, see Vanuatu.

news

No space or hyphen in such established combined forms as newspaper, newsagent, newsdealer, newscast, newsboy, newsman, newsmagazine, newsstand. But news organization, news media, news broadcast, news show, news reporter.

Newsworld

The CBC Television information channel, which began operations in 1989.

New World

New Year's Day

A New Year's party. But lower-case new year, as in We'll discuss that in the new year.

New York (not New York City).

New York Thruway

New Zealand

Adjective: New Zealand. People: New Zealanders. Currency: dollar. Capital: Wellington.

May be abbreviated to N.Z. in placelines. It comprises North Island, South Island, Stewart Island, the Chatham Islands and several minor islands. It also has two overseas territories (the Pacific island of Tokelau and the Ross Dependency in Antarctica) and two self-governing overseas territories (the Cook Islands and Niue). North Island, containing Wellington, Auckland and Hamilton, is separated by Cook Strait from South Island, which contains Christchurch and Dunedin. Stewart Island is farther south, across Foveaux Strait. The country's population is four million. Australia is about 1,200 nautical miles to the northwest, across the Tasman Sea. (Sydney is 1,983 kilometres from Wellington.)

Niagara Escarpment

Niagara-on-the-Lake

Nicaragua

Adjective and people: Nicaraguan. Currency: cordoba. Capital: Managua.

It is the largest country in Central America, stretching from the Pacific to the Caribbean and bounded by Honduras in the north and Costa Rica

in the south. All the major towns and 90 per cent of the population of five million are in the eastern lowland belt, which also contains Lake Nicaragua and Lake Managua. The leftist Sandinistas overthrew a dictatorial government in 1979, then fought an eight-year civil war against U.S.-backed counter-revolutionaries (known as contras) that eventually claimed an estimated 30,000 lives. The contras largely disbanded after the Sandinistas under Daniel Ortega were defeated in an election by Violeta Chamorro in April, 1990. The civil war spawned a major political scandal in the United States, where members of President Ronald Reagan's security staff hatched a scheme to supply the contras, in violation of a congressional ban, using profits from secret arms sales to Iran. It was dubbed the Iran-contra scandal, or Iran-gate.

nickel

Nickel Belt

Upper-case the electoral riding, but lower-case when referring to the rich streak of mineral deposits in the Sudbury area.

nickelodeon

This name for early movie theatres, to which admission was five cents, was later applied to coin-operated picture machines and then to jukeboxes. Explain which we mean.

nicknames

As a general rule, we do not use nicknames or contractions of given names in news stories, but allow them in sports and entertainment stories.

In news stories, full, correct names are important to lessen the chance of mistaken identity, and to eliminate any suspicion of bias (as in calling the prosecutor Joseph and the defendant Joe, or using a friendlier name for one side in a dispute). However, if only the nickname is available in a news story, and there is no practical way of discovering the formal name, never guess. It is preferable to live with Bert than to guess whether it stands for Bertram, Herbert, Norbert, Cuthbert etc. Not all Bobs are really Robert, and Jack is often a formal name.

We make exceptions in the cases of politicians and other prominent people who are known primarily by a nickname, such as Jimmy Carter. To do otherwise would be confusing to readers, who might see the formal name only in The Globe. Use the nickname alone if it appears as the formal entry in the *Parliamentary Guide*, as is the case with several members of the Alberta cabinet. We have also used only the nickname when other politicians have requested that we do so (Joe Clark and Bob Rae, for example). However, in general we are wary of appearing to be more friendly toward one side if we use a nickname for one person and a formal name for an opponent. Our usual style is to use the initials followed by the nickname in brackets (not quotes), as in J. A. (Bud) McDougald.

In campaign stories, use the name that appears on the ballot, even if this is a nickname. In stories from the New York Times Service, delete the ubiquitous second initial if the person has a given name.

niece

Nielsen ratings, the Nielsens
Named for market researcher A. C. Nielsen.

Nietzsche, Friedrich

Niger
No practical adjective or word for the people that would not create confusion with Nigerian. Say "of Niger" etc. Currency: CFA franc. Capital: Niamey.

Niger is the largest country in West Africa, but thinly populated. Its north is Saharan, but slightly higher rainfall in the south and the presence of the Niger River in the southwest allow some crops. More than half the 10.6 million citizens are Hausa. There are also Fulani and Tuareg in the north, and Beriberi-Manga and Djerma-Songhai in the south. Niger is landlocked, bordering on seven countries, including Algeria and Libya in the North and Nigeria in the south.

Nigeria
Adjective and people: Nigerian. Currency: naira. Capital: Abuja.

It is Africa's most populous country, with a population estimated at 130 million.

After 16 years of military rule, the country adopted a new constitution in 1999 and made a peaceful transition to a civilian government. Tensions remain between the central government and the Islamic states of northern Nigeria, where the enforcement of brutal versions of *sharia*, including stoning, has brought international protest. Its people are mainly Hausa and Fulani in the north, Yoruba in the south and Ibo in the east. Nigeria is on the Gulf of Guinea, with Benin to the west, Cameroon to the east and Niger to the north. Oil accounts for 95 per cent of exports, but most Nigerians are farmers, herders or fishermen. Nigeria is a member of the Commonwealth and of OPEC.

night
Night is necessarily a flexible concept in a country where sunrise and sunset vary so much during the year, or indeed may be absent for a time in the North. For time elements, consider **night** to be the period from after the average Canadian supper hour (about 7 p.m.) until midnight or shortly thereafter, in the time zone in which the event took place. (For overseas events, it is occasionally relevant to add in brackets the corresponding time period in Eastern

Time.) If the event begins after midnight, or if the pivotal action (such as a vote) takes place well after midnight, the time element usually should be **early today**. For events that take place about suppertime, consider such time elements as **late yesterday afternoon** or **early yesterday evening**, depending on the exact time and the season. See time elements.

One word: nightcap, nightclothes, nightclub, nightfall, nightgown, nighthawk, nightlong, nightshirt, nightspot, nightstand, nightstick, nighttime. **Hyphenated**: night-light. **Two words**: night blindness, night crawler, night owl, night school, night soil, night table, night watchman.

Nipawin, Sask.

Nisei

The Japanese word for second generation, applied to someone born in Canada or the United States of parents who were born in Japan. Immigrants who were born in Japan are **Issei** (first generation). Their grandchildren are **Sansei** (third generation). These words also serve as the plural. In view of the chance for confusion, prefer Japanese Canadian unless the story is specifically about the three groups.

Nixon, Richard Milhous

He was not convicted or impeached. The House of Representatives recommended impeachment over the Watergate scandal, but he resigned from office on Aug. 9, 1974, the only U.S. president to have done so. He was pardoned by Gerald Ford for any possible illegal acts while in office, but was barred from practising law. He died in 1994 at 81.

no, noes (as in the noes have it).

Nobel Prize

Upper-case, but not the categories (Nobel Prize for physics). An

exception is the Nobel Peace Prize. The prizes for peace, medicine, chemistry, physics and literature were first awarded in 1901. The prize for economics was added in 1969.

boot!

no-confidence

The correct parliamentary term in Canada, used in both the Index to Standing Orders and in Beauchesne's, is **no-confidence**, both as an adjective and as a noun (a no-confidence motion, a no-confidence vote, a motion of no-confidence). Do not use non-confidence, although this term is well understood and need not be corrected in direct quotes. The vote may be called by the less awkward name **confidence vote** (as in The government survived a confidence vote), but it may not be called a "vote of confidence" unless the motion was worded in that way. Similarly, do not say "confidence motion" unless that is its intent, as in a group expressing support for its leaders.

Noh (theatre).

noisome

It means offensive and disgusting, but to the nose, not the ear.

no man's land

non
Almost always takes a hyphen.
(Exceptions: nonplussed, nonentity.)
This prefix conveys either a simple
negation (non-alcoholic, non-
standard, non-functional) or an
absence of (non-attendance, non-
compliance). Other negative prefixes
(un, in, anti etc.) usually carry further
connotations or more emphasis, and
so should be used with care. For
example, compare non-American, un-
American and anti-American.
Similarly, non-edible simply describes
something that is not food (non-
edible oils), while inedible is often
applied to something that tastes bad,
such as food ruined in the preparation.

none
Fowler, Nelson, Oxford and others
agree that **none** may take either
singular or plural verbs, depending on
the meaning, and some hold that the
plural is the commoner construction.
Regard it as a sort of negative
collective, and decide whether the
things referred to are being considered
as individuals or as a unit. Say none of
the bills are counterfeit, but none of
the money is mine. None of the crowd
have abandoned their places, but none
of the crowd has spilled out of the
square. If the construction sounds
awkward, reword.

non-existent

non-flammable
Inflammable means the opposite,
capable of being ignited, but is too
confusing for our use. For the opposite
of non-flammable, use flammable.

no-nonsense
This journalese mush-word
displaces a wide range of more
accurate and descriptive adjectives
(stern, curt, businesslike, spartan,
practical, aggressive, efficient,

energetic etc.). Even worse, it is
usually a backhanded way of
editorializing, implying we approve of
whatever is so described. (See feisty.)
Its careless use is discouraged.

nonplussed

non-status Indian

noon, not 12 noon.

no one

normality, normalcy
Either is correct.

NORAD
All caps by convention, an
exception to the rule that acronyms
formed from syllables are written upper
and lower (see abbreviations). It means
the North American Aerospace
Defence Command. The acronym may
be used to shorten a lead paragraph, but
supply the full name high in the story.

Norris Trophy
See James Norris Memorial
Trophy.

north
Lower-case as a direction, but
upper-case for a recognizable region
(the Canadian North). See
capitalization, directions.

North Coast
Upper-case for the coast of British
Columbia north of Vancouver Island.

Northeast Passage
Upper-case for the sea route
between Atlantic and Pacific across
the Arctic coasts of Norway and the
Soviet Union. Swedish explorer Adolf
Nordenskjold was the first to make it
across, in 1878-79.

Northern Dancer
He was the most successful sire in
racing history (siring more than 100

winners of major stakes races) but he did not win the U.S. Triple Crown in 1964, finishing third in the Belmont Stakes. His last yearlings were sold in 1989. He had to be destroyed in 1990.

Northern Ireland

In the context of the frequently violent dispute over the future of Northern Ireland, republicans and nationalists are those (mainly Catholic) who want Northern Ireland united with the Irish Republic to the south, and loyalists and unionists are those (mainly Protestant) who want to keep Northern Ireland in Britain. However, avoid the term loyalists in news stories, as it suggests the other side is somehow disloyal. Most of those in the Republic of Ireland are Catholic; most of those in Northern Ireland are Protestant, though the proportion of Catholics has been steadily increasing.

The signing of the Good Friday peace accord in 1998 paved the way for the creation of a 108-seat power-sharing Northern Ireland Assembly, and a North-South Ministerial Council to pursue joint policy-making on certain issues between Northern Ireland and the Republic of Ireland. The accord was approved in a referendum on May 22 of that year by 71 per cent of voters in Northern Ireland and 94 per cent in the Irish Republic. Although terrorist violence has decreased, unresolved disagreements have several times led the British government to suspend the assembly's authority.

See United Kingdom, Ireland.

Northern Lights

It is upper-case, but lower-case aurora borealis, an aurora.

Northern Service

Upper-case for the CBC's radio and TV service to the North.

North Korea

Adjective and people: North Korean. Currency: won. Capital: Pyongyang.

There is usually no need to use its formal name, the Democratic People's Republic of Korea, except to explain the initials if they appear in a quote. It borders on China and Russia in the north, and is divided from South Korea by the 38th parallel. Its population is 23 million. It signed a non-aggression agreement with South Korea in 1991, and agreements on proposed economic, political, social and military co-operation in 1993, but tension, hostility and mistrust persisted, and it continued as a major arms supplier. Kim Il-sung, its Great Leader since 1948, died on July 4, 1994, and was succeeded by his son, Kim Jong-il, dubbed Dear Leader, although he did not actually assume the key office of general secretary of the Workers' Party until Oct. 8, 1997. A landmark nuclear agreement in 1994 called for replacement of North Korea's reactors with Western models less amenable to production of weapons-grade material, but North Korea repudiated that agreement in December, 2002, and expelled United Nations monitors. A series of disastrous harvests in the mid to late 1990s brought serious famine, massive food aid and further cracks in North Korea's self-imposed isolation.

North of Sixty

Upper-case, and by convention spell out Sixty. It refers to the 60th parallel, the northern boundary of Canada's four western provinces, and so is another way of saying Nunavut, the Northwest Territories and Yukon.

North Pole

Upper-case for the northern tip of Earth's rotational axis, in the Arctic Ocean about 700 kilometres north of Greenland, about 750 north of

Ellesmere Island and about 950 north of Russia's Komsomolets Island. But use lower case when you call it the north geographic pole, usually necessary only for comparison with the north magnetic pole, about 1,000 kilometres away (south) in Canada's Arctic islands. The magnetic pole wanders by several kilometres a year.

North Shore

Upper-case for the portion of Quebec north of the St. Lawrence River and Gulf of St. Lawrence; for New Brunswick's coast on the Gulf of St. Lawrence and Northumberland Strait (this shore faces more east than north); and for the shore of Burrard Inlet (West and North Vancouver) across from Vancouver.

North Warning System

This is the U.S.-Canadian continental defence system announced in 1985 to replace the old DEW Line and Pinetree Line. It incorporated some of the existing Pinetree air bases.

Northwest Atlantic Fisheries Organization

NAFO. It is the international body that regulates the fishery outside Canada's 200-mile limit on the Atlantic coast. The successor organization to the International Commission on the Northwest Atlantic Fisheries, it was set up after the extension of fisheries jurisdiction to 200 miles on Jan. 1, 1977.

The zones into which ICNAF had divided the waters off Canada's east coast are now known as NAFO areas. Stocks and quotas both inside and outside the 200-mile limit are defined officially with reference to these areas, which are identified by letter and number, but we would normally substitute, or at least add, more understandable geographic descriptions. For example, the

cod stock in NAFO areas 2J, 3K and 3L (commonly written as the combined area 2J3KL) would be referred to in most news stories simply as northern cod.

North West Company

No hyphen, and do not abbreviate Company. This group of trading partnerships was the major competitor of the Hudson's Bay Company for furs. Its traders may properly be called Nor'Westers.

North-West Mounted Police

Note hyphen. The NWMP was formed in 1873 to keep order in what is now Saskatchewan and Alberta (then part of the North-West Territories—note the different spelling from today's Northwest Territories). After 1904, when the word Royal was added, the correct initials are RNWMP. In 1919 it merged with the Dominion Police, whose main duty was to maintain the security of public buildings, to form the RCMP. See RCMP.

Northwest Passage

Upper-case. There are two routes for the leg between Baffin Island and the Beaufort, either through the intervening islands or south of them. The passage was first sailed by Roald Amundsen in 1903-06. RCMP Sgt. Henry Larsen took the St. Roch from west to east in 1940-42. The first non-stop passage was made in four days by the U.S. nuclear sub Nautilus, in 1958.

Northwest Territories

In March, 1999, the former Northwest Territories was divided into two new territories. The eastern one is Nunavut (which see), controlled by the Inuit. The western one, which there had been talk of calling Denendeh (Athapaskan for Home of the People) to reflect control by Dene, has retained the name Northwest Territories. It is roughly the size of Alberta and Saskatchewan combined.

We do not use periods in the abbreviation NWT. The title of the government leader is premier. See premier.

A number of communities in the old NWT have adopted Inuit names. The original six were Iqaluit (Frobisher Bay), which began the process in 1987; Arviat (Eskimo Point); Taloyoak (Spence Bay); Lutselk'e (Snowdrift); Deline (Fort Franklin); and Tsiigehtchic (Arctic Red River). The first three are in Nunavut; the second three are in the new NWT. Others in the new NWT: Tulita (Fort Norman) and Wha Ti (Lac La Martre). Others in Nunavut: Kugluktuk (Coppermine) and Kimmirut (Lake Harbour). Make some reference to the old name in a story from one of these places.

North Yemen, see Yemen.

Norway

Adjective and people: Norwegian. Currency: krone (plural kroner). Capital: Oslo.

This constitutional monarchy occupies the western (Atlantic) coast of the Scandinavian peninsula, but note that it also curves around the northern side of the peninsula to meet Russia, blocking both Sweden and Finland from access to the Arctic Ocean. The main language of its 4.5 million people is Norwegian, but Finnish and Lapp are spoken in the north. In referendums in 1972 and 1994, Norwegians voted not to join the European Union.

note

As a verb used in place of say, it is a loaded word, usually taken to mean that what has been offered as a reason or example is a given, universally accepted as not being open to dispute. Its use is acceptable if this really is the case, as in The minister, noting that Thursday is Canada Day, released the figures early. But it is inappropriate in this sentence: The union, noting that the company is notoriously unfair to its workers, said it was not surprised by the ruling. Change it to saying, alleging, charging or some such.

not only . . . but also

In the second half of this construction, the word also (or as well, besides, in addition etc.) seems to be falling out of favour. Follett writes that the omission of also "should probably be regarded as now unobjectionable, but if a writer has the habit of the full, balanced construction and cannot feel that a sentence is symmetrical without it," that is all to the good. The crucial point is to maintain a parallel construction. Do not say: I have not only a cat, but I also have a dog. The corrected sentence is: I have not only a cat, but also a dog.

notorious

It means widely known for misdeeds. If the reputation is a good one, or at least neutral, use well-known, noted, reputed for, famous etc. However, do not use such words in ways that make us appear to be fans.

Notre-Dame

In Montreal it is not a cathedral or a church, but a basilica. The Pope elevated it to a minor basilica in 1982.

noun invaders

The noun is constantly striving to enlarge its sphere, to take over the role of verbs and adjectives. In most cases when there is a proper verb or adjective available and in current use, or when a simple change such as the addition of a preposition would fix the grammar, a pushy noun is jarring and should be replaced, as in a fun date, to author or co-author a book, for economy reasons.

However, we should not be doctrinaire, because the ability of its words to serve as other parts of speech is one of the great strengths of English. The dictionary has many words that do not change form in their various roles. Many nouns are still gaining acceptance as other parts of speech (pocket the difference, paper over the cracks), especially in new areas of activity in which there is no long-familiar verb or adjective to be mourned (a propeller plane, to program a computer, to access a disk). In such cases, to use anything else sounds stilted (as in to gain access to the information on a disk). A particularly apt or clever coinage that gains acceptance for one adjectival use of a noun (the brain drain, the missile gap) soon confers acceptability by association on many similar expressions (the technology drain, the information gap).

Nova Corp.

When referring to the former company, do not use its upper-case style, NOVA. Nova Corp. ended in 1998. Its pipeline division merged with TransCanada PipeLines Ltd., and its chemical-making division continued as Nova Chemicals Corp.

Novascotian, The

The reform newspaper published in Halifax by Joseph Howe.

Novocain

A trade name for procaine hydrochloride. There are many other local anesthetics in use (hydrochlorides of bupivacaine, mepivacaine, prilocaine, lidocaine etc., with such trade names as Citanest, Xylocaine). We cannot simply assume that an injected local is Novocain, especially one that causes an allergic reaction or other problem.

nucleus, nuclei

nude

In reference to people, it means the same as naked, but nude is the word of choice when speaking of nakedness for reasons of art (a nude model, the play contains scenes of nudity). Nude is also the more common when applied to activities and places rather than to the participants (nude dancing, nude bathing, a nude beach).

Nude is an absolute. It must be replaced or qualified if the nudity is not complete (topless, partly nude etc.). When writing of nudity in films and plays, be aware that whether it is frontal makes a big difference to some readers.

number

Write "No. 9" when giving a label, an order or ranking. But when referring to the numeral itself, write "the number 9." See letters.

Number is singular if the article is "the" (the number of ridings is being increased) but plural if the article is "a" (a number of ridings are vacant).

The usual comparative words for number are "larger" and "smaller," not "higher" and "lower."

We consider the words "number" and "figure" to apply also to numerals that in our style contain letters or words (three-16ths, 25 million).

numbers

Numbers are the major pitfall in any story for the unwary reporter or editor. Many journalists chose their calling because their word skills outweighed their mathematical ones. They can compensate for this shortcoming only by giving every number their total attention. They cannot afford to adopt the habit of a casual reader, letting their eyes skip past large figures and complex arithmetic. The first commandment of newspaper writing and editing is never to read past any number without stopping, looking and looking again, to determine whether it indeed makes sense.

Subject every figure to these four tests: Is the figure factually accurate? Is it expressed in a clear, unequivocal way? Is it consistent with other figures in the story? And is it consistent with other facts or assertions in the story? Inconsistent figures are a strong clue that a story is wrong, that a source is mistaken, distorting, lying.

Is there some way for you to check the figure? If two or more figures purport to add up to some other number, do they? Do a string of percentages add up to 100? Should that "per cent" really be "percentage points"? (See per cent.) Did this take place in the 18th century, or was it the 1800s? Is there some way this metric conversion could have gone awry?

Finally, even when we are sure that we understand the number, that it is relevant and that it does what it purports to do, we are faced with the task of making it understandable to the reader. Assume the story is being read by two radically different people—someone with little knowledge of mathematics or statistics and with no inclination to do arithmetic, and someone who is highly knowledgeable and eager to catch us out.

Even when a number is written in figures, it is read as words. Take care to use the article "an" instead of "a" if the first word begins with a vowel sound, as in "an $18 ticket." Remember also that although the symbol $ precedes a figure, the reader pronounces it as a word and puts it after the figure. This necessitates some style peculiarities when we are dealing with money figures. These and other style points are outlined below, and related issues are dealt with in such separate articles as measurement, currency, fraction, per cent, statistics, Roman numerals, Mach numbers, golf terms.

Numbers 10 and above are written in figures, both cardinal (13) and ordinal (13th). But there are some general exceptions:

Huge numbers of a million or larger are spelled out (six million, 6.5 billion, 20 million; note that the introductory number is also spelled out if it is a whole number smaller than 10). Unless precision is of overriding importance, as in corporate reports in Report on Business published in tabular form, round off such numbers to one or two decimal places. Avoid the unfamiliar words higher than trillion (quadrillion, quintillion etc.); change them to a thousand trillion, a million trillion etc., and tell the reader how many zeros they contain. Determine which system is being used; in North America, each step (million, billion etc.) is 1,000 times the previous one, while in the British system it is a million times the previous one.

Indefinite amounts are spelled out (hundreds of onlookers), as are most **approximate ranges**, especially those that appear in quotes. If a person says "between three and four thousand," we write it that way. It would be ambiguous to write "between three and 4,000," and inaccurate to quote the person as saying "between 3,000 and 4,000," implying that the word "thousand" was used twice.

Spell out **figures of speech** not intended to be taken literally (a hundred and one reasons, a thousand thanks).

Numbers that begin a sentence are spelled out. If the sentence cannot be recast, or if it is a direct quote, we must simply bite the bullet and spell out the number. Do not avoid this by artificially preceding the number with "about" or some such, which is ridiculous if the figure is precise (About 263?). However, words such as about, more than and almost are legitimate if the number can safely be rounded off. Do not use commas (write Three thousand two hundred fifty-six), and do not use "and" except in a direct quote.

Spell out **numbers followed by "fold"** if they are factors of 10 (tenfold, a hundredfold, a thousandfold), but not if they are intervening numbers (write 16-fold, 50-fold).

Long-established **words formed from ten** are spelled out (tenpins, tenpenny).

Spell out **centuries** under 10 (the ninth century), and use figures otherwise (the 21st century).

Decades given without the century are spelled out (the sixties), but we use figures for the decades of a person's age (he is in his 40s). Use figures for decades if the century is also given (the 1960s), including sequences in which the century is given only once (the 1830s, 40s and 50s). Upper-case decades if they are being referred to as an era (the immorality of the Twenties, a Fifties party), but not as mere blocks of time (he built his business in the twenties and thirties). See capitalization.

Whole numbers nine and under are spelled out when simply expressing how many people or things are involved (three horses, the death toll rose to six, the eighth wonder), even when a list also contains larger numbers (18 cows, 60 chickens and three horses). We also spell out the commonest fractions (see below), and spell out values under 10 for heights, weights, speeds, distances and durations, provided they are expressed in a single unit of measurement (see below). But when we depart from these simple counts and measurements, and when the number is more a name or label than a value, numbers below 10 are expressed in the same way as larger ones, as figures, as specified in the following list of exceptions:

Money: Most of the style peculiarities involving money stem from the fact that the currency symbol appears at the start of an amount but is pronounced at the end. Use figures for amounts under 10 if the unit of currency appears as a preceding symbol ($2), but use words if the unit follows the number (three cents, five rubles). The same rule applies to millions etc. ($5-million, but five million rubles). Note the hyphen linking the dollar amount and the word million, creating a unit that cannot be momentarily misread as $5. This style also applies to headlines.

When expressing a range, we cannot count on a hyphen to prevent ambiguity; write between $3-million and $5-million, not between $3- and $5-million.

The difference between the way dollar amounts are written and spoken creates special problems in rendering quotes accurately. We are sometimes obliged to write out the word dollars rather than use the symbol if the person is giving a range ("I could lose between three and four million dollars," he said). If the person does not use the word dollars at all, we cannot include it as a symbol. (Write "This could cost me two million.")

Dollar amounts are usually singular, because they are considered as a lump sum, not as a pile of individual dollar coins. Say $150 is still owing, not are still owing.

Decimals: All numbers that include decimals are in figures (3.5 times the speed of sound; she walked 5.4 kilometres). Where the number is less than 1, place a zero before the decimal point: 0.23.

Fractions: We spell out simple fractions in which the denominator is nine or less, using hyphens to link the two halves (three-eighths of a mile, a third of a gram, a half of 1 per cent, half a kilometre). If the numerator is under 10 but the denominator is not, spell out the numerator and use figures for the denominator, adding the appropriate letters for the ordinal ending (three-16ths of a mile). If both are 10 or higher, use figures and a slash (15/32nds of an inch). Compound fractions, in which a whole number is completed by a fraction, always appear as figures (3½); and for clarity we add the ordinal ending to fractions not available in our typeface (write 4 15/16ths). However, this is still far from clear, and would be rare outside a direct quote. All fractions containing large numbers are awkward; unless precision is vital or we are quoting directly, it is better to convert them to a decimal. (A decimal is, in effect, a particular fraction, 100ths, and you can convert any fraction into 100ths by treating it as a conversion to a percentage: add two zeros to the numerator, then divide by the denominator. For instance, ½ = 100 divided by 2 = 50 per cent.)

Be careful with the words "larger" and "smaller" when speaking of fractions. The number 8 is smaller than 16, but one-eighth is a larger fraction than one-16th. Also see fraction.

Per cent: Use figures for all numbers followed by "per cent" (a rise of 5 per cent), but apply the normal criteria for use of words when giving numbers of percentage points (a rise of three percentage points, of 3.5 percentage points). For an explanation of the difference, see per cent and percentage. Use hyphens for adjectival expressions (a 7-per-cent solution; a three-percentage-point increase).

Measurements: Use figures for **temperatures** (5 degrees; 9 C), but spell out numbers of degrees that merely define a rise, a fall or a range rather than an actual thermometer reading (write five degrees above normal; the temperature rose by three degrees, to 8). The rules on decimals and compound fractions apply, however (write 5½ degrees above normal).

Use figures for readings on **specialized measurement scales** in such fields as seismology, oceanography,

physics and chemistry (the quake was magnitude 6; it flies at Mach 3; the lake has an acidity reading of 5).

Use figures for **time** (3 a.m., 3 o'clock in the morning, 3 in the morning). If minutes are added, use a colon (3:30 p.m.). For durations, spell out numbers under 10 provided they express a single unit of measurement (it lasted three hours; a two-minute pause; I have been here two years), but switch to figures if more than one unit of measurement is used (it lasted 3 hours 9 minutes 15 seconds). Do not use commas in such values, and use "and" only in quotes.

Times in sports that decide placings are spelled out in first reference, using numerals and eliminating commas: Silken Laumann finished her race in 15 minutes 7.35 seconds; Steve Bauer's time in yesterday's Tour de France stage was 2 hours 12 minutes 45 seconds. In second reference in a story, these times would be rendered 15:7.35 and 2:12:45.0.

In a sport such as downhill skiing or sprinting, where placings often are determined in fractions of seconds, say that an athlete finished "a mere 0.03 seconds" behind the winner, not "a mere three one-100ths of a second."

As always, we would not change a time in a quote.

Spell out other measurements under 10 (**distances**, **heights**, **weights**, **speeds**) only if they are in a single unit of measurement (he is six feet tall, she fell seven metres, it weighs four kilograms, he was going four kilometres an hour). If the value is expressed in two or more units of measurement, use figures (he is 6 feet 2 inches tall, he is 6 foot 4, it weighs 4 pounds 6 ounces). This exception does not apply, however, if two figures are measures of different properties, such as length and weight (write a five-foot, 90-pound woman). If a measurement is used as an adjective, hyphens are required, and the units of measurement are usually expressed in the singular (the 5-foot-3-inch gymnast, the 6-foot-3 contender). Hyphens are also required if no unit of measurement is given (she stands 5-11). See measurement.

Ages: Use figures for an age under 10 if it appears as a figure standing alone, without the word years (James White, 6, and his brother Jason, who is almost 3). But follow the normal rule by spelling out numbers under 10 if the unit of measurement is given (the baby, six weeks old; three-year-old Jason; a six-week strike; a two-year-old factory). Spell out the age in thirtysomething, fortysomething etc.

Names, grades and ranks: Use figures if a number is part of a name, rank or grade, including the names of highways, electoral districts, military units, planes, spacecraft and ships: Highway 2, Ward 5; Grade 3 (but spell out the third grade); 2nd Lieutenant; 3rd Battalion; 6th Fleet; a DC-9; the Dash 8; Canada 1; Apollo 10.

Component parts: Use figures for parts that are numbered, or can be numbered by the observer, since these numbers amount to a name or label. If the numbers are formally assigned, use upper case (Chapter 3, Verse 2; Section 6, Article 3; Act 1, Scene 1; Room 5; Gate 7). But by convention, lower-case "size," "row" and "seat," even if these are formally numbered (she wears a size 5 shoe; she is a size 10; we were in row 8, seats 5 and 6). Also by convention, upper-case "Page" when referring to newspapers (Page 7), but lower-case it for other periodicals and books. Note that commas are not used in page numbers; write page 1256. Lower-case the names of parts that are not formally numbered (paragraph 2, line 5, chute 1, bay 2).

Spell out ordinal numbers under 10 for component parts, and use lower case (the third chapter, second verse).

Votes, scores, odds and ratios: Write a score of 3-2; a vote of 16-7;

the court ruled 5-4; in a 5-4 ruling. However, include the word "to" if it is a ratio (2 to 1), refers to odds (of 8 to 5) or appears in a direct quote. ("The doctors put my chances at 10 to 1.")

Dates: Use figures for years and for days of the month (Jan. 5, 1989; he was killed in 4 BC). Do not use commas in years (the year 2001). In quotes, if a date is given as an ordinal number under 10, spell it out before the month (I will rule on the fifth of January). If the ordinal in the quote comes after the month, spell it out if the article "the" was included (January the fifth). However, if the person said "January fifth," this is taken to be the normal pronunciation of our conventional date style, Jan. 5, and so it may be written that way.

Street addresses: Use figures for street addresses under 10 (he lives at 8 Yonge St.). Note that we abbreviate St., Ave., Dr. etc. as part of an address, but not if merely naming the street (he lives on Sussex Drive; he lives at 24 Sussex Dr.). See streets. If a house number is followed by a letter, do not use a hyphen (221B Baker St.). Do not use commas in street addresses (write 5000 Yonge St.), but use a comma to set off apartment or office numbers, either before or after the address.

Gun calibres: Use figures even if the calibre is under 10. Use a hyphen if the unit of measurement is written in full, but not if it is abbreviated (a 6-inch gun, a 9 mm pistol). Spell out the number if it refers to the length of the weapon rather than the calibre (a four-foot musket; a four-inch derringer).

Latitude and longitude: Use figures for readings (5 degrees 9 minutes north) and also for ordinal numbers naming a parallel or meridian (the 6th parallel).

Recipes: Write 2 cups flour etc. if giving a complete recipe. Do not use abbreviations (tbsp, tsp etc.) unless forced to do so by space problems in tabular settings.

Exceptions for titles: Do not change the titles of books, plays, films etc. to conform to our style on numbers (write *Twelfth Night, The Ten Commandments* etc.).

numeral

A numeral is a symbol, a letter, a figure, a word or a group of words expressing a number. Ten, 10, X and many words and symbols in other languages are all numerals expressing the same thing. But we consider the words "number" and "figure" to be interchangeable for news stories, applying to any number of digits and to the numbers we write as words. Say he quoted a figure of six million.

numerals, Roman

See Roman numerals.

numskull

Nunavik

The name of a vast region of northern Quebec, covering almost one-third of the province. After eight years of negotiation, the Quebec Inuit (numbering 9,600 in 14 remote villages) signed a treaty with the Quebec government in 2002. They were to receive $475-million over 25 years and a measure of self-government, while Quebec was to be free to study hydroelectric development of the region. Not to be confused with Nunavut, the new Inuit territory in the central and eastern part of the former Northwest Territories (see below).

Nunavut

Means "Our Land" in Inuktitut. This territory, carved out of the Northwest Territories, was created on April 1, 1999, as a result of the Nunavut Land Claims Agreement that sought a homeland for the Inuit. The boundary between Nunavut and the new, smaller NWT was approved in 1992 in plebiscites in both Nunavut-to-be and the rest of the NWT.

Nunavut's two million square kilometres extend north and west of Hudson Bay, above the tree line to the North Pole. The capital is Iqaluit (called Frobisher Bay until 1987) on Baffin Island. None of the 26 communities is accessible by road or rail; people and supplies arrive by plane or sealift. The leader's title is premier and the elected body is the legislative assembly. Inuit constitute 85 per cent of the population of 29,000.

There is as yet no useful English noun for the people, and no adjective apart from Nunavut (the Nunavut government, the Nunavut people). The Inuktitut words are Nunavummiutaq (singular) and Nunavummiut (plural), and are used even in English documents by the Government of Nunavut, but are likely to be confusing to readers without explanation, and so are best avoided.

nunny-bag

Hyphen. In Newfoundland, a sealskin bag usually used to carry food.

Nuremberg

Do not use the German spelling, Nuernberg. Upper-case Nuremberg Trials.

nylon

Lower-case. It was a trade name, but is considered to have become a generic term. There are several nylons, because the name is applied to an entire group of polymers containing amide groups recurring in a chain. Nylons can be moulded into bearings, zippers etc., or drawn into several types of fibres.

O and Oh

O is the form used before a name as an invocation (O God, O *Canada*) and may be used in exclamations if there is no punctuation after the O (O for a cup of coffee!), though this use is being supplanted by oh. O is always upper-case.

Oh is upper-case only at the start of a sentence. It is usually used if the sense requires that it be followed by punctuation (Oh, what a ridiculous statement! Oh, is that so? She agreed to fix his mistake, but oh, was she angry!), and is now preferred to O in such expressions as oh boy, oh dear and oh yeah?

O Canada has been Canada's official national anthem since July 1, 1980, the day on which then-governor-general Edward Schreyer proclaimed into law the bill making it official. *God Save the Queen* is Canada's royal anthem.

Oh! Calcutta! is the proper spelling of the musical.

oak leaf cluster

Lower-case, no hyphen, as in Silver Star with oak leaf cluster. This bronze decoration indicates that the holder of a U.S. military medal has committed acts worthy of a second awarding of the same medal. It is similar to "and bar" in British and Commonwealth medals, as in DSO and bar.

OAS

The **Organization of American States.** The founding of the OAS in 1948 reflected acceptance of the principle of collective security, meaning an attack on one state would be an attack on all. The organization's other aims are to settle disputes between members and to encourage co-operation in economic, social and cultural matters. Its bureaucracy, the General Secretariat, is in Washington. Ambassadors from each member constitute the executive committee, called the Permanent Council. In addition, the General Assembly meets each year, and the executive body in the event of aggression is called the Meeting of Consultation of Foreign Ministers. The OAS comprises virtually all the independent states of the Western Hemisphere except Cuba, which was excluded from participation in 1962. Canada, long an official observer, announced in 1989 its decision to join, and did so formally on Jan. 8, 1990.

oat, oatcake, oatmeal.
But **oat bran, oat grain, oat grass**.

Oath of Allegiance

Upper-case as the name of Canada's official oath, administered to all new citizens, but lower-case the generic term when speaking of organizations or other countries. It should not be confused with the U.S. Pledge of Allegiance.

OAU

The **Organization of African Unity**, founded in 1963. It comprised virtually all the countries of Africa and nearby islands, and its 32 founding members had grown to 53 by the time it was replaced in 2002 by the African Union, which see.

obbligato

obdurate

It means more than stubborn or intractable. It means hardhearted, immune to human feelings or moral influence. It is too strong (and too obscure) a word for most news stories.

OBE

For officer (of the Order of the) British Empire. See Order of the British Empire.

obeisance

It is not obedience, but rather an act or expression of courtesy or homage, such as a bow.

obelisk

It does not mean any large monument. It means a shaft of stone with four equal sides, sharpened into a pyramid at the top, and often tapering slightly from bottom to top. The Washington Monument is an example.

obese, obesity

Fine in the abstract, but risky to apply to any recognizable individual unless we're reporting a medical evaluation. Best to state the height and weight and let the reader decide on the adjective.

obituaries

As a matter of style we do not say a dead person "is survived by" various family members; we say the person "leaves" them. It is often relevant to name offspring and give their cities in Canadian obituaries, but in most foreign obituaries, unless the children are also well known, it is sufficient to say something like: She leaves her husband, George, two daughters and a son.

objet d'art (not object).

Plural is objets d'art. Does not require italics.

obscene language

The fact that an obscenity is spoken in public does not constitute justification for including it in a story in any section of the newspaper, even in a sanitized form such as "f— off." There must be some overriding consideration that makes the obscenity news in itself, as in the Trudeau-era fuddle-duddle controversy in the Commons. (See fuddle-duddle.) In such cases, the decision whether to print the obscenity rests with the editor, deputy editor, associate editor, editor of Report on Business or their seconds-in-command. On those rare occasions when senior editors determine that use of the expression is warranted, we do not use a sanitized version, but rather spell it out in full. Writers who think it justified to include an obscenity should alert the desk as early as possible, preferably before starting to write, so that the process of obtaining a ruling can begin.

It is not easy these days to come up with a definition of what is offensive. Indeed, various people might find a certain profane, vulgar or disgusting word acceptable among close friends or when they hit their finger with a hammer at home, but deeply offensive and insulting when uttered to them in public by a clerk or other stranger. Our relationship with our readers is a public one, and in public everyone deserves, and expects, the courtesy of being considered capable of being offended by vulgarity.

Few stories lose by the deletion of such expressions. Our readers have vivid enough imaginations to fill in the blanks if we merely say that a crowd shouted obscenities, or that a speech featured salty, ribald or coarse language, sexual jokes, references to bodily functions etc. If it is the type of story that hinges on a particular quote, an offensive expression can usually be eliminated by casting part of the sentence into indirect. For example: He used several obscene expressions to denounce the police beyond the barricades, and warned that "if there is blood on this road tomorrow, it won't be ours."

Questions of taste also arise with photos and drawings. Those featuring frontal nudity, people holding vulgar signs, or images that a reader of a morning paper would find nauseating at the breakfast table, such as corpses, dismembered limbs or badly abused animals, must be submitted to senior editors for a decision on whether there is an overriding reason to run them. In some cases they can be cropped without losing much impact. For example, if the shocked face of an onlooker is the focus of the picture, we might crop out the horrible sight that caused the reaction, and then describe it in general terms in the cutline.

obscenity

This is a legal word. The Criminal Code (Section 163) says that "any publication, a dominant characteristic of which is the undue exploitation of sex, or of sex and any one of the following subjects, namely, crime, horror, cruelty and violence, shall be deemed to be obscene." We also use the word **pornography**. Since both involve value judgments, we should use them in reference to particular publications, movies or pictures only if such a determination has been made by a court, customs officials or an official censor. Otherwise, use such terms as violent, sexually explicit, portraying sex and horror, etc.

obstetrician

It literally means one who stands by (at a birth), but for clarity reserve it for medical doctors specializing in pregnancy and childbirth.

obverse

It means the principal side of anything, but usually refers to the "heads" side of a coin or medal. The "tails" side is the **reverse**. These words require explaining in all but specialized articles on minting and collecting. There is no need to add the word "side" to obverse and reverse.

OC

For officer (of the Order of) Canada. See Order of Canada.

Occidental

Western is usually better. Occidental is upper-case when referring to the non-Asian world, or to non-Oriental people, but in this racial sense it is too general to be useful (see race), and so should be confined to direct quotes. Lower-case occidental in technical references to sea routes and astronomical sightings.

occult

It means having to do with magic, things beyond human comprehension. Do not confuse it with the word "cult," and do not apply it to religions, including cults.

occur

Happen is usually better. Other forms double the r (occurring, occurred, occurrence).

Oceania

This name is applied to a huge, island-studded area of the southern Pacific, or to the islands themselves. Its western boundary begins just east of the Philippines, in the area of the Carolines and Marianas, and stretches east to Easter Island (which is farther east than California). From north to south, Oceania stretches from the Hawaiian Islands to New Zealand. The islands of Oceania are grouped into three regions. All those east of the International Date Line, including the Hawaiian Islands, are called

Polynesia. The islands west of the line are divided roughly by the equator into Micronesia to the north and Melanesia to the south.

ochre

o'clock

A proper word whose use is encouraged whenever the context makes it clear whether a time is before or after noon. Say The search began at dawn, shortly before 6 o'clock.

octagon

Not octo- .

octogenarian

It means someone who is 80, or in his or her 80s. It is usually better simply to say so, particularly if octogenarian is taken to imply a class of people who are all alike.

octopuses

octoroon

When these things were important to people, this word was applied to someone who was one-eighth black, the offspring of a quadroon and a white. Such labels today are irrelevant, insulting and virtually impossible to verify. In the rare cases in which race is relevant, simply say of mixed race.

Odd Fellows

Independent Order of, IOOF, established in England in the 18th century. Do not confuse it with the IOF (the Foresters).

odour

But drop the u for **odorous**.

odyssey

Upper-case only when referring to Homer's epic poem about the wanderings of Odysseus after the Trojan War. The generic term means a long, wandering journey, not a long story.

OECD

The **Organization for** (not of) **Economic Co-operation and Development**. Founded in 1960 and in operation since 1961, it is a consultative organization for co-ordinating economic policies to encourage growth and trade, and has also become a clearing-house for a variety of economic statistics. Its staff of more than 1,000, located in Paris, issues annual economic evaluations of member countries. Its 30 current full members are Australia, Austria, Belgium, Britain, Canada, the Czech Republic, Denmark, Finland, France, Germany, Greece, Hungary, Iceland, Ireland, Italy, Japan, Luxembourg, Mexico, the Netherlands, New Zealand, Norway, Poland, Portugal, Slovakia, South Korea, Spain, Sweden, Switzerland, Turkey and the United States.

oenology

The study of wine, but too obscure a word to be used without explanation in general news stories. Retain the diphthong.

of

Usually a useless addition to prepositions, as in outside of, off of.

off

One word: offbeat, offhand, offset, offshoot, offshore, offside, offstage. **Hyphenated**: off-Broadway (both adjective and adverb), off-centre, off-colour, off-line, off-season, off-white. **Two words**: off chance.

The following nouns ending in off become two words as verbs (e.g. My takeoff was delayed, but I'll take off in five minutes): blast-off, cut-off, faceoff, kickoff, layoff, payoff, playoff, runoff, send-off, standoff, stopoff (more commonly stopover), takeoff, writeoff.

offence, but **offensive**.

offing

It means the waters between the anchorage and the horizon. A ship in the offing is within sight, close to home. Figuratively, in the offing means about to happen.

Ogopogo

Variously described as a huge fish or a sea serpent in the waters of Okanagan Lake, principally near the southern end, south of Kelowna off Penticton and Summerland in B.C. It has also been reported in the upper reaches of the North Saskatchewan River near Rocky Mountain House, Alta. It was named by the Shuswap, the most northerly of the Interior Salish peoples, and has been reported frequently since the days of the early settlers.

OHIP

For Ontario Health Insurance Plan. We must not assume readers in other provinces are familiar with these initials; avoid in headlines in the National Edition.

OHMS

On Her (or His) Majesty's Service. Do not use periods. James Bond aside, this was a postal designation, formerly used on Canadian government mail. It was also painted on mailboxes well into the 1960s.

Ohsweken, Ont. (not Osh-).

oil

Barrels are the usual unit of measurement, but litres or cubic metres are used in some countries (Japan uses 1,000 litres: kilolitres). We would normally provide the barrel equivalent. A barrel equals 158.987 litres, 34.972 gallons (42 U.S. gallons), 5.6146 cubic feet, 0.1589 cubic metres. See barrels a day.

For conversion from volume to weight (tonnes), a rough factor is 7.33 barrels per tonne. To be more precise, we must know the specific gravity, which varies among grades of crude.

Ojibwa

Use Ojibwa for the people, and Ojibway for their language. The name, meaning puckered from roasting, is a reference to their puckered moccasin seams. See native people.

Oka cheese

Upper-case, from Oka, Que., site of the Trappist monastery where this brine-cured cheese is made.

Okanagan Lake

Not Lake Okanagan. This long, narrow lake (about 110 kilometres long and three wide), lying north-south in the **Okanagan Valley** in south-central B.C., has many communities along its shores. The major ones are Kelowna about midway on its eastern side, Summerland and Peachland on the western side, and Penticton surrounding the southern end. Vernon is a short distance east of the northern end.

The Okanagan River flows south from the lake about 70 kilometres and then briefly widens into Osoyoos Lake, straddling the U.S. border. In its further 115-kilometre course south to the Columbia, the river is spelled Okanogan.

The Okanagan Valley, known for its fruit production, is about 200 kilometres long in Canada, and about 20 kilometres wide, bounded by the Monashee range of the Columbia Mountains on the east and by the Fraser plateau on the west. It has the largest concentration of people in the Interior, about 8 per cent of the B.C. population.

okay

Confine it to quotes. If it appears as a verb in a quote, spell it okays, okayed. OK is permitted in headlines.

O'Keefe Centre (no "the").

The Toronto theatre was renamed the Hummingbird Centre for the Performing Arts in 1996, after the software company Hummingbird Communications Ltd.

Okefenokee Swamp

(Not Okee-.) It is in southeastern Georgia and northeastern Florida.

Oktoberfest

Old Age Security Pension

Upper-case the proper name for the pension, which took effect in 1952, and also the Guaranteed Income Supplement, approved in 1966. Note there is no hyphen in the pension's proper name. In most references, it may be called the **old-age pension**, lower-case and hyphenated. It should not be confused with the retirement fund to which workers contribute, the Canada Pension Plan.

Old Country, the

old-fashioned

old-timer

and it's got hands, and they move in a circle...

old-timer

old wives' tale

Avoid, as implying that only old women spread such stories. Use folk superstition, misconception etc. See women and language.

Old World

olympiad

It is a four-year period that concludes with Olympic Games. It is often wrongly taken to refer only to the period of the Games themselves.

Use our regular Arabic numerals for olympiads (the 12th Olympiad), not Roman numerals.

Olympic Games

They are officially called the Games of the -nth Olympiad, but we call them simply the Olympic Games. If we give their number, we use Arabic numbers, not Roman numerals. The winter events are properly called the Winter Olympics, but it is not usual to speak of the Summer Olympics; they are simply the Olympics. If it is necessary to differentiate in a story, call them the Winter Games and the Summer Games, or summer events and winter events. Also upper-case "the Games" standing alone when referring to the overall events or the official organization (Steroids everywhere, Games official says). Refer to the Olympic village and the athletes village (lower case, no apostrophe).

Here are the Olympic venues (the Winter Games began in 1924): 1896 Athens; 1900 Paris; 1904 St. Louis; 1906 Athens; 1908 London; 1912 Stockholm; 1916 cancelled (had been awarded to Berlin); 1920 Antwerp; 1924 Paris/Chamonix, France; 1928 Amsterdam/St. Moritz, Switzerland; 1932 Los Angeles/Lake Placid, N.Y.; 1936 Berlin/Garmisch-Partenkirchen, Germany; 1940 cancelled (had been awarded to Tokyo, then Helsinki); 1944 cancelled (had been awarded to London); 1948 London/St. Moritz; 1952 Helsinki/Oslo; 1956 Melbourne/Cortina d'Ampezzo, Italy; 1960 Rome/Squaw Valley, Calif.; 1964 Tokyo/Innsbruck, Austria;

1968 Mexico City/Grenoble, France;
1972 Munich/Sapporo, Japan;
1976 Montreal/Innsbruck;
1980 Moscow/Lake Placid;
1984 Los Angeles/Sarajevo, in
Yugoslavia at the time;
1988 Seoul/Calgary;
1992 Barcelona/Albertville, France.

The 1992 Winter and Summer
Games were the last held in the same
year. Thereafter they alternate every
two years:
1994 (W) Lillehammer, Norway;
1996 (S) Atlanta;
1998 (W) Nagano, Japan;
2000 (S) Sydney;
2002 (W) Salt Lake City;
2004 (S) Athens;
2006 (W) Turin, Italy;
2008 (S) Beijing;
2010 (W) Vancouver/Whistler.

See track and field.

Oman

Adjective and people: Omani.
Currency: Omani rial. Capital:
Muscat.

This independent Arab sultanate,
an absolute monarchy formerly called
Muscat and Oman, is a crescent
wrapped around the toe of the
Arabian Peninsula snowmobile boot.
Its northeastern curve fronts on the
Gulf of Oman, while its southeastern
curve faces the Arabian Sea. Inland, it
borders on the United Arab Emirates,
Saudi Arabia and Yemen. It also
includes a peninsula to the north
jutting into the Strait of Hormuz and
cut off from the rest of Oman by a
strip of the UAE. It is hot, dry and
mostly barren, but produces almost a
million barrels of oil every two days. It
is a moderate in Mideast affairs, and
has a long association with Britain.
The population is about 2.7 million.

Omar Khayyam, Rubaiyat of

ombudsman

Lower-case the plural and the
generic or informal term (Father

Green has acted as an ombudsman for
troubled teens), but upper-case the
title of individual provincial
ombudsmen, even when standing
without the name (. . . the
Ombudsman said in his report).

omelette

Omemee, Ont.

omni

This prefix does not take a hyphen,
except when the main word begins
with i (omni-ignorant). Except in
quotes or in technical and scientific
terms, it is clearer to use the prefix
"all-," an adverb such as "totally" or
"infinitely," or a phrase along the lines
of "in every way."

on account of, avoid.

on board (adv.).

oncoming and ongoing

The first is an acceptable word (an
oncoming train) but the second is less
so (an ongoing situation). Use
continuing, unresolved.

one of the only

Not only is this a weasel phrase,
but it is self-contradictory, stretching
the meaning of "only" out of shape.
Prefer one of the few, or one of a
specific number.

one of those

It takes a plural verb. (She has one
of those dogs that are covered in spots.
He is one of those who vote the party
line.)

oneself

onetime, one-time

If the meaning is former, the
adjective is onetime (a onetime
celebrity). If the meaning is only once,
the adjective is one-time (a one-time
offer). The adverb is **one time**.

Onley, Toni

on-line

Use this style for both the adjective and adverb in reference to the Internet. An on-line service, he worked on-line. However, the company that bought Time Warner Inc. in 2000 to form AOL Time Warner Inc. was America Online Inc., no hyphen.

only

Careless positioning of this word can significantly alter the meaning or emphasis of a sentence. For example, it could occupy five different positions in this sentence, indicated by the slashes: / They / asked / the province for / a temporary ruling / last week. In general, insert "only" immediately ahead of the element we wish to stress.

Beware backhanded editorializing with the word only. Saying a grant, payment, prison sentence etc. was "only" a certain amount reflects the writer's opinion that it should have been more.

on stream

Two words. Confine it to technical stories, and to something added to an existing larger operation. (The third unit will come on stream next year.)

Ontario Hydro

No longer exists under that name. The provincially owned power utility was split into five successor companies on April 1, 1999. They are: Ontario Hydro Services Co., known as Hydro One, which owns and operates Ontario's electrical transmission system; Ontario Power Generation, which owns the former Ontario Hydro's hydro dams, nuclear plants and fossil-fuelled generation stations, and continues to generate power; the Independent Electricity Marketing Organization, which oversees the wholesale purchase and sale of electricity in a deregulated trading system; the Ontario Electrical Financial Corp., which assumed $21-billion of the $38-billion in government-guaranteed debt left behind (stranded) by the old Ontario Hydro; and the Electrical Safety Authority. Plans to privatize Hydro One were cancelled in 2002 by Premier Ernie Eves.

on to and onto

When "on" is not a preposition but rather an adverb (often with a meaning other than physical location), "to" must be separate; it is a preposition introducing a subsequent phrase. For example: I'm **on** (wise) **to** your tricks. We travelled on (farther) to Uganda. He passed the formula on (along) to his heirs.

In such uses, either on or to often could be omitted without substantially changing the meaning. But in some cases, omission of either element would seriously alter the meaning, as in: He rolled onto the sidewalk. The sentence He rolled on the sidewalk would imply that he was already on it, while He rolled to the sidewalk would imply that he rolled to its edge and no farther. If both elements are indispensable to the meaning, **onto** is a preposition and should be spelled as one word.

Ookpik

Use upper case for the name of the souvenir doll, which is purported to mean "a happy little snowy owl" in Inuktitut.

OPEC

The **Organization of Petroleum Exporting Countries**. It was founded in 1961 by Iran, Iraq, Kuwait, Saudi Arabia and Venezuela. As of 1997 it also included Algeria, Indonesia, Libya, Nigeria, Qatar and the United Arab Emirates. OPEC headquarters, including a secretariat for administration and research, is in Vienna.

ophthalmology

opinion polls, see polls.

opossum

Use this word for the various species of carnivorous, tree-dwelling marsupials of North and South America, ranging from mouse-size to cat-size. The word **possum** now is used to distinguish the Australian species. However, it is not necessary to change quotes to reflect this.

opposites

Few words have true opposites. Just as there is no opposite of stone, mathematical or Dutch, we should not say that a desert is the opposite of a swamp, or that Labour is the opposite of Conservative, or that fascism is the opposite of communism. Some words with several meanings may have a variety of opposites. There are no opposites of most colours, but many colour words have other meanings for which there are true opposites (blue means sad, obscene, puritanical etc.). See progressive and regressive.

Opposition

Use upper case for the Official Opposition, which is the largest of the minority parties in Parliament or a legislature. Use lower case to refer to all non-government parties or members. See capitalization.

opprobrium and approbation

See approbation.

opuses (not opera for the plural of opus).

or

For clarity, avoid this conjunction to introduce a translation, synonym, definition or explanation, as in this sentence: He asked the court for a declaratory judgment, or a decision that would not order a remedy. The reader could easily take this to mean the judge was being asked for either of two things, when in fact the last part

of the sentence is merely a definition of "declaratory judgment." In many cases, as in this one, we can simply drop the "or." Otherwise, replace it with "which is," "which means," "which translates as," "which is Latin for" or some such.

oral and verbal

Verbal means in words, either spoken or written. The word we want for distinguishing spoken from written is **oral**.

Orangemen's Day, Parade

Prefer the gender-neutral Orange Parade. It commemorates the victory of William of Orange over the forces of James II in the Battle of the Boyne on July 12, 1690. For clarity and brevity, refer to this Protestant fraternal organization in Canada simply as the Orange Lodge. The Ulster organization, a very different animal, is called the Orange Order.

orangutan (not -tang).

order-in-council

Lower-case. The plural is orders-in-council. They are simply federal or provincial cabinet orders. Some have the force of law, enacted under powers delegated by Parliament or a legislature, and others are merely appointments. A common form of legislative order-in-council sets specific regulations and standards to flesh out the general intent of an act passed by Parliament.

Order of Canada

Appointments are made by the Governor-General, following the recommendations of the Advisory Council of the Order of Canada. Under the Chief Justice, it meets twice a year to consider nominations by the public. The three levels (lower-case when spelled out) are companion (CC after the person's name), officer (OC) and member (CM; MC was already in use for Military Cross). Companions are limited in absolute number, to 150. The other two ranks are limited only by a maximum number of appointments in any one year: 46 officers and 92 members. Foreigners can be admitted as honorary members at any level. The order was inaugurated on Canada's 100th birthday: July 1, 1967. The medal, a six-pointed stylized snowflake hanging from a white ribbon edged in red, is worn around the neck by companions and officers, and on the left breast by members.

The Order of Canada is not a prize. One does not win it, or receive it, though one receives the medal. Say a person is admitted to or invested in or named to the order. We may also simply say they are honoured.

Technically speaking, even the officers and companions are members of the order. However, be careful when reporting that a number of people have been made members. If 32 people are honoured, a few may be promotions to higher levels of people who were already members.

Order of Military Merit
Membership in this order, established in 1972 as a complement to the Order of Canada, is awarded to members of the Canadian Forces, on the recommendation of the Defence Minister. The three ranks are commander, officer and member (CMM, OMM, MMM). Appointments in any one year cannot exceed a 1000th of the strength of the Forces (0.1 per cent). The Forces had about 60,000 in uniform in 1998, which meant a maximum of about 60 admissions. The rules say a maximum of 6 per cent of these (three at 1998 levels) may be commanders, and 30 per cent (18 at 1998 levels) may be made officers. The medal (a blue cross, on a blue ribbon edged in gold) is worn around the neck by

commanders and on the left breast by officers and members.

Order of the British Empire
We omit the first three words of its formal name, The Most Excellent. . . . There are five classes, reflected in the initials a person is allowed to append to his or her name, and each has a civilian and a military division. The two highest carry with them admission to knighthood: knight or dame grand cross (GBE) and knight or dame commander (KBE or DBE). The others are commander (CBE), officer (OBE) and member (MBE). Note that we use lower case when spelling out the names of the various ranks. Meritorious service by persons not eligible for any of the five classes earns the British Empire Medal (BEM).

ordnance
In the narrowest sense, it means artillery. In a broader sense, it means all military weapons, ammunition and related equipment, or the people in charge of supplying and maintaining them (the Ordnance Corps, Ordnance). It can have an even broader meaning of military, as in ordnance map, ordnance survey.

It should not be confused with **ordinance**, which is an authoritative decree or, in U.S. parlance, a bylaw.

Organization for Security and Co-operation in Europe
OSCE. The largest regional security organization in the world, it has 55 members in Europe, Central Asia and North America, including Canada, which was a charter member in 1973. Its headquarters is in Vienna.

Organization of African Unity
The pan-African body was replaced in 2002 by the African Union. See African Union.

orient, the verb.

The noun created from this is **orientation**. Resist the temptation to transform the noun, in turn, into the verb orientate, and to transform this in turn into the adjective orientated. The proper adjective is **oriented**; its opposites, depending on meaning, are non-oriented and disoriented. The sport involving map-using is orienteering.

Orient, Oriental

Use upper case to refer to eastern Asia and its inhabitants, or those with roots there. Use lower case in the technical sense dealing with sea routes and astronomical sightings. Avoid using Oriental as a noun. To many readers, it conveys an archaic, stereotypical and ignorant image of a mystic and unknowable people. See Occident.

original six

Although the term is widely used, in hockey stories we shouldn't speak of "the original six." The original four National Hockey League clubs were the Toronto Arenas, Montreal Canadiens, Montreal Wanderers and Ottawa Senators. By 1926 there were 10 teams, six of them in the United States. These had shaken down by 1942 to the six that persisted until expansion in 1967. It is these clubs we refer to, and they are more accurately described as "the pre-expansion six" or possibly "the original six postwar clubs."

O-ring

Orlon

Trade name for fibres drawn from acrylic resins.

orthopedic (not -paedic).

Oscars

Acceptable first reference to the Academy Awards (i.e. the annual awards of the Academy of Motion Picture Arts and Sciences).

OSCE

See Organization for Security and Co-operation in Europe.

oscilloscope

Osgoode Hall

It is the building on Queen Street in Toronto that houses the Supreme Court of Ontario. Note that the building no longer houses Osgoode Hall Law School, which in 1968 moved to York University. William Osgoode was the first chief justice of Upper Canada.

Osservatore Romano

The Vatican newspaper.

Otello, Othello

The first is Verdi, the second Shakespeare.

Other Place, the

For clarity, upper-case the expression used by the Commons and the Senate to refer to each other.

Ottawa

Ottawa is a useful word to refer to the federal government, particularly in leads and headlines. However, we should beware any perceived implication that it is Ottawa against the people, that the provinces represent voters but the federal government does not.

Ottawa, City of

A new, larger City of Ottawa was created on Jan. 1, 2001, through the amalgamation of the Region of Ottawa-Carleton and 11 local municipalities: Cumberland, Gloucester, Goulbourn, Kanata, Nepean, Osgoode, Ottawa, Rideau, Rockcliffe Park, Vanier and West Carleton. When mentioning, say,

Kanata, do not leave the impression that it is separate from Ottawa. It is one of the city's 21 wards, along with West Carleton, Rideau-Rockcliffe, Rideau-Vanier etc.

Ottawa Rough Riders

But **Saskatchewan Roughriders**.

out

As a combining form, it does not take a hyphen even when the main word begins with t (she can outthink him any day). Note also outfielder, outpatient.

Several nouns ending in out become two words as verbs (fallout/fall out, hideout/hide out, pullout/pull out, shootout/shoot out, takeout/take out, walkout/walk out).

Outaouais

The French name of the Ottawa River is Rivière des Outaouais. Western Quebec, the entire district north of the river, is known as the Outaouais. In addition, the regional community that includes Gatineau is the Outaouais Regional Community (known as the CRO, for *Communauté régionale de l'Outaouais*), the counterpart to Ottawa-Carleton on the Ontario side.

outraged and enraged

An **outraged** person is one extremely angry over an outrage—an act of shocking violence or cruelty, or at least some sort of gross abuse. If someone is merely angry about something, we have a multitude of words at our disposal, depending on the type and degree of emotion. They range from vexed, miffed, cross and several other low-level words, through fuming, indignant, incensed and many other middle-level words, all the way to furious, **enraged**, foaming and apoplectic. Bring these big guns into play only when they are truly on target, not when someone is merely a little hot under the collar.

outside

Say a person is outside the country and outside the room, not outside of the country and outside of the room.

over

As a combining form, over does not take a hyphen. Most writers have no trouble with this when the main word is a verb (overthrow, overextend), but are sorely tempted to insert a hyphen when the main word is an adverb or adjective. Resist, even when the main word begins with r (overreligious, overrich). The adverb **overly**, hatched in the United States for use before adjectives and now having many converts in Canada, was a solution to a non-existent problem. Let's not be overzealous in weeding it out of quotes, but in our own writing let's do our bit to preserve the combining form of **over**.

overall

Use this word for the adjective (meaning all-embracing) and for the garment (usually in the plural, **overalls**). But the adverbial expression meaning "all things considered" is two words: Over all, I think it best to give my overalls an overall mending.

over and above. Pick one.

over and under

For numbers and quantities, most good writers use **more than** and either **fewer than** (numbers) or **less than** (quantities). They reserve **over** and **under** for position.

overly, see over.

overwhelm

A strong word, meaning to bury, to crush, to defeat by irresistible force or numbers. It is debased if we use it for surprise etc., or in reference to defeats and victories in votes or other such contests unless one side was utterly humiliated.

owing to

It is a proper preposition, while **due to** is not.

Owing to the fact that is grammatically correct but wordy; simply say **because**.

owner

In combination, usually a separate second word, as in car owner. But note homeowner, landowner.

ox

Oxen are not a particular bovine species. The term is used for any of several species around the world, including the buffalo and yak. In North America, it is applied to adult castrated bulls of various breeds of cattle used as draft animals.

oxford

Use lower case for shoes (those with laces) and for oxford cloth.

ozone

It is an allotrope (another form) of oxygen, being composed of three oxygen atoms as opposed to oxygen's two, but is very different from it. It is a blue gas with a pungent odour like chlorine, used as a bleach, sterilant and deodorant. It can be formed by passing electricity through oxygen, or by subjecting oxygen to ultraviolet radiation. Chlorine atoms, such as those released by sunlight from volcanic gases and from the aerosol propellants called chlorofluorocarbons, begin a chemical process that breaks down ozone into oxygen.

The Earth's **ozone layer**, at 50,000 to 120,000 feet, is not entirely ozone; the ozone is in concentrations of only five to 10 parts per million.

P

Pablum, a trade name.

Developed at Toronto's Hospital for Sick Children and first marketed by Mead Johnson in 1930, it was the first vitamin-enriched precooked cereal. The name comes from *pabulum*, Latin for food in the sense of nourishment.

pachyderm

It is not a synonym for elephant. It applies to any thick-skinned ungulate that does not chew a cud (non-ruminants), and so in addition to elephants, rhinos and hippos it describes horses, pigs and their relatives.

Pacific Northwest

Upper-case. It is a vague term. In the traditional, narrowest sense it means Washington and Oregon. In the broadest sense, it also takes in the other northern states partly or entirely west of the Rockies (Montana, Idaho and Wyoming), plus British Columbia and coastal Alaska.

Pacific Scandal

Use upper case for the corruption scandal of 1873 that forced the resignation of Macdonald. A royal commission established that Sir Hugh Allan got the charter to build the Canadian Pacific in return for a huge campaign contribution.

paddy wagon

Use police van or patrol van.

Pagliacci

It means clowns, buffoons or charlatans. Referring to an individual,

we would use the singular, and to lend weight to the allusion to the sad clown of the opera we would retain the upper case, as in the Pagliaccio of Parliament.

paid (often misspelled payed).

Pakistan

Adjective and people: Pakistani. Currency: rupee. Capital: Islamabad.

It is on the Arabian Sea, where its principal port is Karachi. It borders on Iran in the southwest, Afghanistan on the northwest and north, and India on the east. It claims part of the northern Indian state of Jammu and Kashmir, as does China. Its population is 148 million. Do not refer to a Pakistani language; the languages of Pakistan are Urdu, English, Punjabi, Sindhi, Pushtu and Baluchi. It is an Islamic republic, 97 per cent Muslim. The former East Pakistan seceded in 1971 and became Bangladesh; Pakistan recognized it in 1974. Tensions remain high in the dispute over Kashmir (which see). After India tested nuclear weapons in 1998, Pakistan responded the same year with its own nuclear tests.

palate, palette, pallet

The **palate** is the roof of the mouth, divided into the bony hard palate in front and the muscular soft palate in the rear. This word also refers to the sense of taste or to relish for food and drink. A **palette** is a board on which an artist lays and mixes paint. It also refers to his or her characteristic range of colours, and is found in the name palette knife. The flat wooden board used by potters is a **pallet**, which is also the spelling for a platform on which goods are stored and moved, and for a small, rough bed, sometimes only a blanket on the floor.

Palau

Adjective and people: Palauan. Currency: U.S. dollar. Capital: Koror.

This Pacific republic of about 200 islands, eight of them inhabited, comprises the westernmost of the Carolines. The largest island is Babelthuap, but most of the approximately 20,000 citizens live on Koror. They are Micronesians. Palau is a semi-independent, U.S.-protected territory.

paleology and paleontology

The first is the study of antiquity or antiquities; the second is the study of ancient life forms, especially fossils.

Palestine

This is the ancient Holy Land, which lay mostly in modern-day Israel but also extended into Jordan. Its boundaries are necessarily vague, and we should not be drawn into the game of defining the exact territory traditionally inhabited by the Palestinians. However, the ancient Palestine, also called Canaan, may be roughly described as being bounded by the Mediterranean on the west, the Jordan River and the Dead Sea on the east, the Sinai Peninsula on the south and the area of Mount Hermon on the north, on the present-day border of Syria and Lebanon.

Lower-case p for the president and the prime minister of the Palestinian Authority, or if the short form Palestinian is used. Thus, Palestinian Authority president Yasser Arafat said; Palestinian prime minister Mahmoud Abbas; it will be difficult for the prime minister to act. In headlines, PM remains upper-case: Palestinian PM upset by progress of talks.

pallbearer

palomino

Pampas

Upper-case the Pampas, the great plain of central Argentina. It is *la Pampa* in Spanish, but English uses the plural. Use lower case for pampas cat and pampas grass.

panache

Panama

Adjective and people: Panamanian. Currency: The monetary unit is the balboa, reflected in coins ranging from the half-balboa to one cent, but the only paper currency is the U.S. dollar, with which the balboa is at par. U.S. coins are also legal tender. Capital: Panama City.

The curve of Central America is such that the length of Panama is east-west; the canal runs north and south. About 25 per cent of the country's gross national product comes from the canal. The economy is mostly agricultural, but leans heavily to bananas, coffee and sugar, forcing Panama to import most of its food. The population of 2.8 million is about 70-per-cent mestizo (of mixed blood), 14-per-cent black, 12-per-cent European and 4-per-cent Indian. Panama City is at the southern (Pacific) end of the canal, on the Gulf of Panama, and the country's other major centre, Colon, is at the Caribbean end. U.S. forces invaded in 1989 to oust the dictatorial and corrupt General Manuel Noriega. He was arrested and taken to the United States to face drug charges, on which he was convicted in 1992. The Canal Zone, previously controlled by the United States, reverted to Panamanian sovereignty on Dec. 31, 1999.

Pan American Games

No hyphen. Held every four years, between Olympic Games.

panda, not panda bear.

panelist

Panmunjom, Korea.

The original village was about five kilometres south of the 38th parallel. However, the hall for the truce talks was built straddling the line, and the name now applies to the community that built up around it, on both sides of the parallel.

pantyhose

paparazzi

It is the plural of paparazzo. Neither requires italics.

paper

One word: paperback, paperboy, papergirl, paperhanger, paperweight, paperwork. **Two words**: paper birch, paper clip, paper gold, paper money, paper profit, paper wasp.

papier mâché

papoose

Do not use this word for an Indian baby. See native people. The word may be encountered in reference to the infant carrier used by Indians in some parts of North America, but prefer cradleboard. For colour, in reference to Crees we may use *tikinagan*, but translate if the meaning is not clear.

Pap smear

Upper-case. Properly called the Pap smear test, or the Papanicolaou test, it is a method of screening for cancer of the cervix.

Papua New Guinea

No useful adjective for the country or single word for the people; write "of Papua New Guinea." Currency: kina. Capital: Port Moresby.

It occupies the eastern half of the island of New Guinea, plus the islands of Bougainville and Buka, the Bismarcks to the northeast and several small islands to the southeast. The western half of the island of New Guinea is Irian Jaya, a province of Indonesia. Papua New Guinea became independent of Australian administration in 1975, and signed a treaty with Indonesia in 1979 that recognized the border, ending efforts by Papuans in Irian Jaya to join the new country. The population of five million, mainly Papuan and Melanesian, is divided into small groups that collectively speak 500 or more languages. English is an official language, and pidgin English is a lingua franca.

A secessionist rebellion on the island of Bougainville that began in 1988, and closed the Panguna copper mine there in 1989, led to years of war and the death of thousands of people. After a couple of failed ceasefires, the struggle largely ended with a peace agreement in 1998. In 2002, Papua New Guinea voted to grant autonomy to Bougainville.

para

This prefix does not take a hyphen: paramedic, paranormal, paramilitary, parapsychology.

paraffin

In overseas wire stories, it usually means kerosene, not wax.

Paraguay

Adjective and people: Paraguayan. Currency: guarani. Capital: Asuncion.

It is landlocked, between Brazil and Argentina and also bordering on Bolivia at its northwestern end. Most of the 5.6 million people live in the small but more fertile region east of the Paraguay River. The lower and less productive area west of the river is called the Chaco Boreal. Most Paraguayans are mestizo, a mixture of Guarani Indian and Spanish. General Alfred Stroessner, whose military dictatorship ruled Paraguay for 35 years, was overthrown by his daughter's father-in-law in 1989, and a measure of democracy was introduced.

parallel, paralleled, paralleling

An exception to the rule on the doubling of final consonants (see spelling). As an adjective, it takes the preposition to.

Use lower case when naming lines of latitude, as in the 49th parallel.

paralyze, but paralysis.

parameter

This is a buzzword borrowed from mathematics, to which it probably should be returned with a thanks but no thanks. It means a quantity that varies from case to case, but is a fixed value in any particular case under consideration. It also means the common factor in a series of variables, such as x in this sentence: If we produced x tons of garbage in 1950, we are producing 2x now and will generate 3x only 10 years from now. In the non-mathematical world it is usually used in the plural to mean limits, guidelines, rules, standards. With all these to choose from, who needs parameters?

paranoid, paranoia, paranoiac

These words have narrow scientific meanings, and are inappropriate in most non-medical news stories. See psychiatric terms.

paraphernalia

It takes plural verbs and pronouns (these paraphernalia are).

parasol

Reserve for one designed to keep off the sun (the counterpart to the French *parapluie* for rain). If it is for rain, use umbrella.

pariah

parishioner

Paris Commune

Upper-case the name of radical Parisians' insurrection against the royalist National Assembly in 1871 after the defeat by Prussia. Its participants are called Communards, not Communists.

Parkinson's disease, Parkinsonism

Parliament

It consists of the Queen, the House of Commons, whose members (members of Parliament, MPs) are elected from Canada's 301 federal ridings, and the Senate, whose members are appointed by the government. To become law, legislation needs the support of the Commons, the Senate (though for most legislation the Senate has the power only of delay, not of veto) and royal assent, which is routinely given by the Queen's representative in Canada, the governor-general.

Use upper case for the Parliament of Canada and of other English-speaking countries in which that is the assembly's proper name. But speak of Israel's parliament, the Knesset; Poland's parliament, the Sejm.

Lower-case **member** of Parliament, and the word **parliamentary**, except in such proper names as the Parliamentary Press Gallery and the Parliamentary Library. (We use this term, but the proper name is Library of Parliament.) See capitalization.

parlour

parole

First-degree murder carries a mandatory life sentence with little chance of parole for 25 years, but remember that word "little." There is a provision (known as the faint-hope clause) that, after 15 years, murderers may seek a jury review of their parole eligibility. Few are successful in their parole appeals, but all the same it would be inaccurate to speak of "no chance" of parole. Alternatives: "with almost no chance," "with virtually no chance."

parsec, see light-year.

parsonage
This is the name used by Methodist and some United congregations. See manse.

partially
Partly is preferred, unless the sense we wish to convey is favouritism.

ParticipAction
Upper-case the second a in the name of the private, non-profit organization that for three decades promoted exercise among Canadians.

Parti Québécois
May be called PQ in headlines and in second reference. The word for a member, Péquiste, is spelled the same for both men and women.

part-time, the adjective.
The adverb is **part time**.

partygoer

Passchendaele
Taking this Belgian village in the fall of 1917 cost 16,000 Canadian lives.

passerby, passersby

passive voice
The active voice (The pitcher threw the ball) is the reporter's most effective tool, summoning up the direct action that tells the story best. It is almost always worthwhile to recast a sentence to eliminate an unnecessary passive (The ball was thrown by the pitcher). In particular, we should avoid the impersonal passives, which weaken an entire sentence: it is felt that, it was believed that, it is thought to be, etc.

However, we need not go to elaborate lengths to avoid a natural passive, if in doing so we replace the true subject of the story with a contrived one. If Robert Black was convicted of first-degree murder yesterday and sentenced to life, say so. We do more harm than good in avoiding the passive by saying a jury convicted Robert Black of first-degree murder yesterday and a judge sentenced him to life.

In particular, avoid the journalese use of the generalized mush-verb comes/came simply to avoid a passive. To say that the new system comes at a time of increasing Protestant-Catholic animosity, for example, is far less informative and evocative than using the more descriptive, although passive, verbs "is being imposed" or "is being tried" or "is being forced on the school boards" etc.

pasteurize
Use lower case, despite its origin in a proper name.

patented
Even allowing for flexibility in language for the sake of colour, overuse has blunted the impact of "patented," as in a basketball star's "patented slam-dunk." Rather than use it to mean merely famous or spectacular, try to reserve it for unique accomplishments, especially ones that were originated by the person in question and have never been duplicated.

pathetic
Reserve it for things that arouse pity, sorrow, grief. Do not use it to mean inadequate, mediocre, small etc. (This hamburger is pathetic).

patronage and pork-barrelling
Political **patronage** is the conferring of a benefit on an

individual to reward or secure political loyalty. The widest definition of such benefits would include not only jobs, contracts and other material benefits, but also honorifics and any other form of preferential treatment. **Pork-barrelling** is the extension of patronage to whole **communities or regions**, usually in the form of discretionary works projects. A particular project might involve both: pork-barrelling to the community, and patronage to the contractor who gets the work.

As Jeffrey Simpson notes in *Spoils of Power*, patronage can be criminal (as in vote-buying, job-selling etc.), but usually is not, and often does not even fit the usual definition of corruption, which is private gain at public expense. If a salary must be paid anyway, there is no public expense involved, only private gain, in the partisan selection of who will receive it. Whether patronage of a certain sort is even considered immoral depends on the region of the country.

The term pork-barrelling is always pejorative toward the politician or party; the term patronage is not necessarily pejorative, at least in the abstract. However, note that an individual allegation of patronage might be found to be defamatory, if it carried the implication that the person who received it was criminal or corrupt, or so incompetent that he or she would never have been considered for the post otherwise. In reference to a recognizable individual, it is safest to say merely that he or she is a supporter of the party in power, and let the reader decide whether the appointment was inappropriate, or made for purely partisan considerations.

Pork barrel is two words as a noun (he makes masterly use of the pork barrel), but hyphenated as an adjective (a pork-barrel project) and as a verb and gerund (pork-barrelling).

pavilion

paycheque, payday, payroll.

pay equity
It is more complex than equal pay for equal work, because of the difficulty of comparing different jobs. For example, education and responsibility are not easily compared to hazard, discomfort and physical exertion. The most concise definition is "equal pay for work of equal value," as long as it has already been established in the story that the principal issue is parity for women. Note that Ontario's legislation benefits only people in female-dominated occupations.

The most accurate definition, when we have room, would be something like "matching the pay scales for jobs performed mostly by women to those for jobs of equal value performed mostly by men."

payoff, the noun.
The verb is **pay off**.

pay-television, pay-TV

PCBs
For **polychlorinated biphenyls**. The initials may be used to keep a lead paragraph short, but use the full name as high in the story as possible.

PCBs have been used as coolants in electrical equipment. They may be defined as toxic, but not as "highly toxic" and certainly not as "deadly." (Do not call them "toxins," a word reserved for poisons produced by animals, plants and fungi. See toxic.) They have been linked to tumours, liver disease, birth defects and brain and nerve disorders in laboratory animals, but have yet to be shown to have harmed humans in amounts usually encountered in spills. They produce dioxins and furans when burned improperly, but in concentrations that do not produce any immediate effect on humans. PCBs can be safely incinerated at high temperatures.

PCBs are often contaminants in oils, but are not oils themselves. These non-corrosive, non-conducting liquids were clear when manufactured, ranging from colourless to pale yellow, but are darker and cloudy after long service in electrical transformers and capacitors. They are heavier than water and have a bitter smell.

peace

One word: peacebreaker, peacekeeper, peacekeeping, peacemaking, peacemonger, peacetime.

Hyphenated: peace-abiding, peace-destroying, peace-giving, peace-inspiring, peace-lover, peace-minded, peace-preserver, peace-restoring, peace-seeker.

Two words: peace conference, peace congress, peace offer, peace officer, peace party, peace plan.

Peace River Country

Use upper case for the large fertile region on either side of the Peace River in northern Alberta and northeastern B.C. Peace River lowland is the name for the geographic land form, but do not use the misleading word "lowland" standing alone. It is about 1,000 feet above sea level, part of the high plains of northern Alberta, and slopes upward to triple that elevation in the Foothills.

The Peace flows about 1,800 kilometres from the confluence of the Finlay and Parsnip Rivers in central B.C. to join the Slave River near Lake Athabasca. From there its waters reach the Arctic Ocean by way of the Mackenzie system. B.C.'s Williston Lake is the creation of a hydro dam on the Peace.

Peace Tower

Upper-case. It is almost 90 metres high, rising above the Centre Block, with a 53-bell carillon near the top. Below is the Memorial Chamber, containing books with the names of the 111,542 Canadians killed in the First and Second World Wars.

peacock

Use for males only. The females are peahens, and the species is properly called peafowl.

peccadilloes

A peccadillo is a fault or a trifling sin, not necessarily sexual.

pedal and peddle

What we do on a cycle, piano etc. is **pedal** (pedalled, pedalling, pedaller, soft-pedalling). What an itinerant seller does is **peddle** (peddled, peddling, peddler).

pediatrician

Peggys Cove, N.S.

No apostrophe.

Pekingese (dog)

Pelee

Point Pelee, in Ontario, is the most southerly point in mainland Canada. But the most southerly point in Canada is Middle Island, in Lake Erie south of Pelee Island.

Pellatt, Sir Henry

He built Casa Loma in Toronto.

Peloponnesus

Greece's southern peninsula, joined to the north by the narrow

Isthmus of Corinth. Its major city and port is Patras.

pemmican

This staple food of the plains Indians was made by pounding dried meat (jerky) with berries and animal fat.

PEN

Acronym for the International Association of Poets, Playwrights, Editors, Essayists and Novelists, founded in 1922.

Penetanguishene, Ont.

May be called Penetang in second reference and in headlines.

Peninsular & Oriental, P&O

Pennsylvania Dutch

They are descended from German (Deutsch) religious refugees of the 17th and 18th centuries. They are mainly in the Lutheran and Reformed churches, but also include Amish, Mennonites, Moravians and Dunkers.

penultimate, next to last.

people and persons

People has gained acceptance even in literate circles as a substitute for **persons** in most instances, and it is pedantry to insist that it be reserved for a nation, a populace or a class. We normally say that the professor had some people to dinner, not some persons; and that six people were poisoned, not six persons. As Copperud says, if we depart from the normal language of our readers, we weaken our impact by sounding stilted and bookish. People takes a plural verb even when referring to a single race or nationality (The Canadian people are united).

Péquiste

per

In general, use only with Latin words (he gets $100 per diem, but he gets $100 a day, $100 a person). However, per is used in such technical expressions as parts per million, and in financial stories and charts for descriptions of currency and share conversions. Per may be used to improve the flow of such double constructions as "he gets $100 a day per person." Clarity might also require that we use such expressions as "for each," "for every."

per capita

It does not need italics or a hyphen. Use it in statistical contexts to mean of or for each person in a population or group, as in per capita spending, per capita debt (it means divided or calculated "according to heads"). Do not use it to mean "a head," as in The boatman charges $2 per capita. That would require the singular, *per caput.*

per cent and percentage

Differences between percentage **rates** (of interest, unemployment etc.) are normally expressed in **percentage points**. A jump in interest from 10 per cent to 15 per cent, for example, is an increase of five percentage points, not 5 per cent. (If for some reason we wanted to express it as a percentage, 10 to 15 is a rise of 50 per cent. However, per cent of a per cent is too complex for most news stories.)

Comparisons of different **amounts** (of money, things etc.) and different **measurements** are expressed as a **percentage**.

Beware the tendency of writers and their sources to toss off percentages when they are clearly inappropriate. Percentages are fractions (100ths) useful as a common denominator for comparing disparate things, such as increases in shopping hours and increases in shoplifting. They also are useful for making comparisons of huge numbers understandable, and have the added advantage of being divisible into decimal places, which makes them as exact as we wish. But if a number is small, especially if it is less than 100, a percentage is far less useful than the actual figure. Why say that of the 86 employees 55.8 per cent were ill, forcing the reader to do the arithmetic, when we can simply say that 48 were ill? If the percentage of a small number is important, as in a vote requiring a two-thirds majority, give both the actual vote and the percentage.

Sources often use percentages to hide concrete numbers, or to make small ones look more impressive. An interest group that surveyed only 20 people is being manipulative if it announces only that "85 per cent of those questioned" agreed with its position. That 85 per cent sounds much more impressive than 17 people, and cloaks a few minutes of questioning in the mantle of a national opinion poll. We must always determine the actual figure, and then make our own decision on whether it is more usefully expressed as a percentage. (See polls.)

Our style is per cent (two words and no point), and figures for numbers under 10 with per cent but not for numbers of percentage points (write 7 per cent, but seven percentage points). The symbol % should be used only in graphs and some tabular matter, or in headlines after a figure. Follow the normal rules of hyphenating compound adjectives, as in a 7-per-cent solution.

Avoid the word percentage when we are not giving a specific number. Instead of a large percentage, say most.

peregrine falcon, lower-case.

period, see punctuation.

perks
The short form is more familiar to readers than the full word, perquisites.

Persian
It is the language of Iran, also called Farsi. Also use upper case for Persian carpet, cat, lamb.

Persian Gulf, not Gulf of Arabia.

Persian Gulf war, see Iraq.

personnel
Jargon. Prefer staff, workers, employees, clerks, officers etc.

Persons Case
This case, the result of a petition to Ottawa by Judge Emily Murphy of Edmonton and four other Alberta feminists (Nellie McClung, Louise McKinney, Henrietta Muir Edwards and Irene Parlby), paved the way for the appointment of Canada's first female senator. In 1928, seven years after Agnes Macphail became Canada's first female member of Parliament, the Supreme Court of Canada ruled that women were not "persons" for the purpose of Section 24 of the British North America Act, which spoke of summoning "qualified persons" to the Senate, and were therefore ineligible to be senators. The ruling was appealed to the Judicial Committee of the Imperial Privy Council in Britain, which reversed the decision in October of 1929 and described the exclusion as "a relic of days more barbarous than ours." Prime Minister Mackenzie King appointed Cairine Wilson to the Senate on Feb. 15, 1930.

persuade
See convince.

Peru
Adjective and people: Peruvian. Currency: new sol. Capital: Lima.

About half its 27 million people are Quechua Indians, 40 per cent are mestizos and 10 per cent are white. Spanish and Quechua are both official languages, and Aymara is also spoken. The coastal plain, only about 60 kilometres wide but containing all the major cities and a third of the population, gets little rainfall but is irrigated in places by rivers from the Andes. The mountainous region, called the Sierra, contains half the population, despite its harshness. The other sixth live further inland in the region called the Montana, which is the eastern foothills of the Andes and the beginning of the Amazon forest. Peru is a significant supplier of coca to the Colombian cocaine trade. It also exports fishmeal for animal feed, cotton, sugar, coffee, petroleum and several minerals, including lead, copper, iron, silver, zinc and phosphates. Until 1972 it was the world's top fishing nation, but El Nino of that year and subsequent overfishing greatly reduced the catch of anchovetas. Fishmeal production is recovering.

Military rule in the country ended in 1980. Alberto Fujimori, elected president in 1990, fled to Japan in 2000 in the midst of a corruption scandal, and was removed from office in absentia by Peru's congress in November of that year on grounds of "permanent moral instability."

Peterborough, Ont.

May be shortened to Peterboro in headlines.

Petro-Canada

May be called Petrocan in second reference and in headlines.

pets de soeurs

Italic. Pastries, a favourite Quebec treat. See foreign and French words.

petty larceny (not petit).

The word larceny may be used in U.S. stories, but in Canadian ones say theft.

pewter

It is an alloy, and we should not be categorical about its content. It is mostly tin (about 80 per cent), originally hardened with copper but in Roman times also having a high lead content. In modern pewters the tin is hardened with copper and antimony, and most also contain some lead.

PGA

For **Professional Golfers Association**. The initials U.S. do not appear in the official name. The Canadian version is the CPGA.

pH

The p is lower-case, the H upper in this acidity scale. It progresses upward from extremely acid to extremely basic. That means that when measuring rain, for example, the smaller the number, the higher the acidity. A reading of 7 is neutral. (What is being measured is a solution's hydrogen ion concentration; the term pH stands for potential of Hydrogen. We need not go into this technical detail; merely explain that it is a measure of acidity.)

phalanges (fingers and toes).

phalanxes (military formations).

pharaoh

phase and faze

A **phase** is a stage or aspect. The noun has become acceptable as a verb meaning to plan or execute in orderly stages. The expressions **phase in** and **phase out** are also acceptable.

Faze means disconcert, worry or embarrass.

PhD

Lower-case the full name of the degree, doctor of philosophy, but there is little occasion to use it. It is less awkward, and less misleading, to say simply that someone has a PhD in chemistry, or a doctorate or doctoral degree in chemistry.

Phi Beta Kappa

The oldest U.S. Greek-letter society, founded at William and Mary College in 1776, and now the top honour society for humanities and science students.

philanthropy

Do not measure philanthropy solely by the amount given. The word refers to the effort to increase human well-being, as by charitable aid. The person who has $50-million and gives $5-million of it makes a larger splash, but the person who has $50,000 and gives $5,000 of it is no less generous, and the person who has $50-billion and gives $10-million might even, on this scale, be seen as stingy when the sum is measured against his means.

Philippines, the

The adjective for the country is Philippine; the words for the people are Filipino, Filipina. Currency: peso. Capital: Manila.

The article "the" is dropped in placelines. The country comprises more than 7,000 islands, but only 730 are inhabited and the 11 largest contain almost all the population of about 80 million. The largest islands are Luzon in the north and Mindanao in the south; other principal islands include Cebu, Leyte, Mindoro, Negros, Panay and Samar. Luzon contains the capital and also the two former U.S. military bases. The United States officially ended its military presence in late 1992 with the closing of the Subic Bay naval base, near the city of Olongapo. Clark Air Base, near Angeles City, had closed in

1991 because of damage from the eruption of Mount Pinatubo.

The country was ceded to the United States by Spain in 1898 after the Spanish-American War, and gained its independence in 1946. Popular opposition drove dictator Ferdinand Marcos (and wife Imelda) into exile in 1986 after he had ruled for 21 years.

The official national language is Tagalog (also called Filipino), but English is the official language of the courts and commerce, and also is dominant in education and the media. Many native languages are also spoken, but Spanish is not. A long communist insurgency died out in the early 1990s because of a loss of foreign support and offers of amnesty. A 26-year Muslim separatist campaign in the south, which cost 120,000 lives, was formally ended in September of 1996 with an agreement for increased autonomy, although some groups vowed continued opposition. See Quezon City.

Philistine, always upper-case.

Phnom Penh (not Pnom).

phony

phooey, not pfui.

phosphorus, phosphorescence

photo

It means light. As a combining form it does not take a hyphen (photostatic, photoelectric, photovoltaic, phototransistor).

photo finish

Two words for a close decision in a race, but one word for the business of developing and printing pictures: photofinishing.

Piccadilly

piccolos

picket
Both verb and noun (not picketer).

picnicker, picnicking

pidgin, creole, lingua franca
Use **lingua franca** for any compromise language that serves as a medium between different peoples. Some are simplified languages, or are concocted from two or more others, but the term may also be applied to English in the air and in India, French in diplomacy, and Latin in the Roman Catholic Church. Other notable examples are Swahili and Bazaar Malay.

A **pidgin** is a reduced lingua franca, having a very small vocabulary and simple grammar, usually based on the language of a European trading or colonial nation, and remaining the second language of all who speak it. Examples are the several varieties of pidgin English spoken in Melanesia, notably in New Guinea. (The word for I, for example, is *dispela*, a corruption of this fellow.)

If a pidgin eventually takes over as the first language of a people, often with subsequent increased borrowing from the European language, it is called a **creole**. Examples are the French creole of Haiti and the English creoles of the Antilles, Suriname and some islands off South Carolina (this one is called Gullah).

Upper-case **Creole** when referring to people, in which case it often has little to do with language. This word is used for the descendants of the original French settlers in Louisiana (distinguished from the Cajuns, who arrived later from Acadia) and people born in Latin America or the West Indies of European descent.

pied-à-terre

piffle, babbling nonsense.

pileup
The noun. The verb is **pile up**.

Pill, the
Upper-case P for the birth control pill.

pinch-hit, pinch hitter

Pinetree Line
Not Pine Tree. These were the Canadian and U.S. radar stations and interceptor bases roughly along the 49th parallel. The name is now obsolete.

For the tree itself, say pine tree or simply pine, and note the spelling of Maine's sobriquet, the Pine-Tree State.

Ping-Pong
A trade name. Prefer the generic term table tennis. In such expressions as Ping-Pong diplomacy, use caps.

pingo, pingos
These are hills with cores of ice, forced upward by subsoil pressure, found in permafrost areas of Canada, Alaska, Greenland and Russia. One notable example is Ibyuk, near Tuktoyaktuk in the Mackenzie Delta. It is thought to be 1,000 years old.

Pinyin
Upper-case. It is the official system introduced in China in 1958 for writing Chinese in the Roman alphabet, intended as a better guide to pronunciation than such older systems as Wade-Giles. For the sake of readers who might think Pinyin is a language, references to a Chinese word being written "in Pinyin" should be changed to "in the Roman alphabet" or even "in the Western alphabet." We need refer to Pinyin only when the system of transliteration is itself at issue.

pipeline

Pipeline Debate

Use upper case for what was nominally a Commons debate in May of 1956 over a loan to Trans-Canada Pipelines, but ballooned into a controversy over the Liberals' announcement before the debate had even begun that they would use closure at each stage of the bill. The incident discredited the St. Laurent government, particularly Trade and Commerce Minister C. D. Howe.

pissed off

Many of our readers find this expression objectionable, and the term is easy to write around. If we're quoting someone as saying "I was really pissed off when the owners proposed that we . . .", we do no damage by moving the quote marks a bit to the right, thus: He said he was angry "when the owners proposed that we . . ." This is our usual strategy for dealing with coarse language in quotes: throw the offending part of the sentence into indirect.

If "angry" isn't colourful enough in that example, the thesaurus is alive with alternatives: infuriated, enraged, apoplectic, furious, livid, disgusted, blew his top, hit the roof etc.

pistol

A suitable word for any type of handgun. See guns and calibres.

place-kicker

plain clothes

But a **plainclothes officer**.

planets

The order of the planets from the sun outward, based on the farthest point (aphelion) of their orbits: Mercury, Venus, Earth, Mars, Jupiter, Saturn, Uranus, Neptune, Pluto. In practice, Pluto and Neptune take turns as the most distant planet, because Pluto's orbit is a long ellipse and that of Neptune is much rounder.

Pluto, which takes almost 250 Earth years to complete one orbit, is closer to the sun at present, and will be until 1999. Some astronomers have said variations in the orbits of Neptune and Pluto could indicate the existence of a 10th planet, but a University of Toronto study published in 1991 cast doubt on this, showing that the reported wobbles could be explained by technological limitations of current telescopes.

plastics

Most plastics are synthetic, usually made from petroleum, but in fact a plastic is any substance that can be moulded into shapes, including such natural products as resins, rubber and bitumin. **Thermoplastics** are those that can later be softened again by heat, such as nylon, lucite, vinyl and polyethylene. In contrast, **thermosetting plastics** can be moulded only once, since heat and pressure convert them into an infusible form. These include polyesters, epoxies, silicones, urea formaldehyde and phenol resins, including bakelite.

Plastic Wood

A trade name. Prefer the generic, wood filler.

plateaus

play down (not downplay).

player

Bay Streeters speak of the "players" in various deals (plays), industries, resource projects etc. It is jargon, a sports term used to make their business sound a bit more glamorous. In business stories, it is a useful word in general, used to encompass the entire range of those involved in a takeover proposal, for example—the raiding and target companies, their top officials, investment bankers, lawyers etc. But it is necessarily vague, applied alike to allies and rivals, principals and fringe interests, staff and outside advisers. When speaking of any of these individually, we lean toward more specific words that accurately describe their role. In stories outside the realms of sports and business, dealing with political controversies etc., the word player is rarely appropriate, a journalese buzzword used by writers trying to appear to be insiders.

play on words

playwright

PLC

No periods. It means Public Limited Company, the British term for a limited company whose shares are publicly traded, as opposed to privately owned. The former term was Joint Stock Company. See Pty. Ltd.

plead

Use pleaded, not pled, for the past tense.

plebiscite and referendum

The difference between these words does not hinge, as some suppose, on whether a vote is binding. (A referendum is always binding, and a plebiscite might be.) Rather, the difference is a subtle one, and does not seem to be of much concern to those who call such votes. For example, the conscription vote of 1942, the Quebec sovereignty vote of 1980 and the national vote in 1992 on the Charlottetown accord were essentially of the same type, and according to the definitions below should all have been called plebiscites, but the 1980 and 1992 votes were called referendums. Practical considerations dictate that in specific cases in Canada we adopt the name used by the authority calling the vote.

In general discussions, we should reserve **referendum** for a vote in which the general public (or the general membership of an organization) is legally involved in the formal passage of a specific law or constitutional measure; a measure that has been passed or formally proposed is being referred for a binding general vote of ratification or rejection. True referendums are virtually unheard-of in Canada, but they are used in Switzerland and several other countries; in Australia, there is provision for them on constitutional measures. They are widely used in the United States at the state and local levels; many states require referendums on constitutional amendments, bond issues and some tax bills. By the process of "initiative," a specified number of voter signatures can force a referendum on other measures.

A **plebiscite** is on an issue or policy direction that is not a specific law or constitutional measure. In the conscription plebiscite of 1942, voters were asked not to approve or reject a law on the military draft, but rather to declare whether they favoured releasing the government from past commitments on the method of raising men for the military. In 1980, Quebeckers did not vote on a specific constitutional change, but rather on whether the Parti Québécois should have a mandate to negotiate sovereignty-association. In 1992, Canadians were asked to accept or reject a constitutional accord reached by their first ministers, but the formal wording and actual passage would have been left to the various legislatures.

A plebiscite can be binding if the authority calling for the vote declares it to be, such as votes on the legitimacy of a certain regime, on whether a people should secede from one country and join another, or on whether a local jurisdiction should add fluoride to its water. Some binding plebiscites are required by law, such as those on whether a municipality or neighbourhood should allow the sale of alcohol in various types of establishments. Some offer more than one choice, such as the name for a new amalgamated municipality. Plebiscites can also be non-binding, if the authority calling them declares that it merely wants to know the public mood on a course of action or policy direction it is considering, usually as a factor in drawing up specific laws in future. Such votes may bind a government morally and politically, but not legally; it still has the power to disregard the result, possibly declaring that conditions have changed.

When a vote is a choice between Yes and No, we use upper case for the sake of clarity (he will vote Yes, No voters, the Yes camp, Canada said No.) This is an exception to our normal style for yes and no in all other types of stories (the teacher said no). See Charlottetown accord.

A referendum is a process, like an election. Do not say "the referendum will be defeated" or "this move will increase support for the referendum." Say "the independence option in the referendum will be defeated" or "this move will increase support for the independence option in the referendum."

plethora
It is more than a lot. It is a superabundance, an excess.

plot
The verb and noun suggest a secret, devious scheme to achieve a hostile or illegal end. For more neutral purposes, use plan or, if the move is simply being considered, mull.

plow

plowman, plowshare, but **Project Ploughshares**

plummeted, plummeting
It must be a steep and severe fall. The price may plummet from $100 to $50, but not from $100 to $95.

plurality
In references to votes in which the winner did not receive a majority of the votes cast (that is, at least 50 per cent plus one), we encounter **plurality** used in two ways: as the total number of votes received by the winning candidate, and as the difference between the winner's vote and that of the runner-up. Make sure the reader knows which we mean. See majority.

plurals

Resist those who would lure us into inaccuracy by contriving false plurals. Do not say charges were laid when there was only one; do not say ceremonies or church services were held when in fact there was one ceremony or service. See election.

In general, we do not change the spelling of a **proper name** to create the plural, beyond adding s (or es if the name already ends in s, sh, ch, x or z, as in the Schultzes). For proper **names that end in y**, say the Emmys, the Grammys, the two Germanys, the Kennedys, 10 Hail Marys, three King Billys. However, note that the Rockies and the Alleghenies are exceptions, as are Tommies for British soldiers and Johnnies (stage-door Johnnies, Johnny-come-latelies). Also see possessives.

Words being treated as words form their plurals in the normal way; they do not take an apostrophe (ifs, ands or buts; dos and don'ts). **Two or more letters**, including acronyms, also do not take an apostrophe for a simple plural (PCBs, the DTs, his ABCs), nor do **figures** (two 747s, the 1830s, nine Grade 5s) or combinations of figures and letters (three F-18s). However, for the sake of clarity we use apostrophes to form the plurals of **single letters**

(dot the i's and cross the t's; mind your p's and q's, the three r's).

We use **English plurals** for words that were originally from other languages, including Latin or Greek, but are now regarded as English; hence appendixes, auditoriums, cherubs (not cherubim), curriculums, honorariums, hippopotamuses, impetuses, maximums, memorandums, millenniums, opuses, referendums, scrotums, sopranos, tableaus. The few exceptions are mostly **scientific and academic**, such as algae, alumni and alumnae, bacteria, fungi, gladioli, larvae, nuclei, radii, stimuli, and vertebrae; but also castrati, criteria, data, media and strata. Note that some words have a Latin or Greek plural for scientific meanings and an English plural otherwise. We use antennae for insects, but antennas for TV and radio aerials; phenomena for things that are directly observable, but phenomenons for marvels and for exceptional people. Also note that most **nouns ending in -is** still form the plural by changing the i to an e (basis/bases, crises, hypotheses, oases, theses).

On those rare occasions when we use **foreign words** that have not become accepted as English, we are obliged to use the plural of the same language: kibbutz/kibbutzim; goy/goyim; paesano/paesani. The chance of going astray on plurals is another good reason for sticking to English.

Follow the dictionary's lead for **words that do not change in the plural**, such as aircraft, chassis and sweepstakes, and many plurals of animals (salmon, elk, sheep, swine). The names of most **Indian groups** are also unchanged in the plural (several Blackfoot, Sarcee and Blood). See the section on native people for the few exceptions.

In **compound nouns** it is the principal word that is made plural (goings-on, governors-general, courts-martial, notaries public, passersby,

rights of way, sons-in-law), even when a modifying word is already plural (sergeants-at-arms). Note that sergeant-majors is an exception. (Note also that possessives move to the end, as in the notary public's office. See possessives.) Compound nouns that do not actually contain a noun or other clearly predominant word usually add the plural to the entire expression (hand-me-downs). The common one-word compounds ending in **ful** add s to the end (handfuls, spoonfuls).

Beware the **plural nouns** that are regularly **mistaken for singular**, including media, data, strata, criteria. These require plural verbs and pronouns (these data are), or a change to the singular form if that is what we mean (stratum, criterion). Also beware the occasional **singular** that is regularly **mistaken for a plural**, such as kudos, meaning praise, news and mews.

It is standard Canadian English to use the singular, not the plural, in adjectival expressions before the noun (a six-foot defenceman, a 10-cent price increase, a 50-cent-a-share dividend). It is also idiomatic to continue dropping the s when expressing a rate (a 50-mile-an-hour speed limit, an 800-barrel-a-day flow rate). This also applies to rates involving cents: A proposed 18-cent-a-gallon gasoline tax sank the Joe Clark government.

The plural is retained if an adjectival phrase follows the noun (a tax of 18 cents a gallon), and this is the preferred construction if the modifier is at all complicated. Better to say "an average owl population of 76.8 a square kilometre" than "a 76.8-owl-a-square-kilometre average population."

plus

In general, confine it to arithmetical contexts. It is grating as a conjunction (Plus, we can expect a rise in school taxes).

p.m., see time elements.

PMO

We use these initials in second reference to the Prime Minister's Office. However, PMO is rather obscure for headlines, and so should be avoided unless the context is clear.

The PMO, which has a strong political role and is staffed largely by political appointees rather than career civil servants, is officially part of the Privy Council Office, under which its budget falls, but the two should not be confused or equated. The PMO's role stems from the prime minister's responsibilities as leader of his party; the PCO serves him in his role as head of government, and is in effect the prime minister's department of government. The distinction is often blurry, with the potential for conflict between the two bodies, but the lines are there nevertheless.

PNE

Acceptable in second reference for Pacific National Exhibition, and in headlines if the context is clear. It is held annually in Vancouver, ending on Labour Day.

Pocahontas

She saved the life of Captain John Smith, but did not marry him. In 1614, at 19, she accepted Christian baptism and married John Rolfe. They went to England, where she died of smallpox three years later. The colony in question was Jamestown, Va., not the Plymouth Colony of the Pilgrim Fathers, which was not founded until 1620.

pocketbook

The term can mean either a purse or a wallet (for either sex, but now primarily for women), and is still current in the United States, but it is rarely encountered in Canada outside newspaper stories. It hasn't quite retreated into the realm of journalese, the arcane dialect that separates us from our readers, and there is no practical substitute for such expressions as "a pocketbook issue." But instead of automatically saying that smokers are worried the coming budget will "hit them in the pocketbook," once in a while try "whack them in the wallet" or some such alternative.

podium

It is not a lectern. See dais.

pogey

This is well-established Canadian slang for employment insurance, acceptable in lighter features and colour pieces. Pogey is no longer used to refer to welfare or handouts, as it was during the Depression.

poisonous and venomous

Something that is harmful when eaten or drunk is **poisonous**. Something that actively injects a poison as a means of hunting or defence is properly called **venomous**. There is no harm in using the idiomatic expression "poisonous snake," since the meaning is clear, but we should be aware of the distinction if there is any chance of ambiguity. For example, some fish and insects are poisonous, while others are venomous. See toxic and toxin.

poke-check, in hockey. Poke-checking.

Poland

Adjective for country: Polish. Name for people: Poles. Currency: zloty. Capital: Warsaw.

It is on the Baltic Sea, north of the Czech Republic and Slovakia, separated from them by the Carpathian and Silesian mountains. It also borders on Germany, Ukraine, Belarus, Lithuania and Russia's Kaliningrad enclave. Other main cities are Gdansk (Danzig), Krakow, Lodz, Poznan and

Wroclaw. About half of Poland's land is arable, and about half of the rest is forest. Its population is 39 million.

Polish workers can accurately be said to have ignited the liberal reforms that eventually swept all the countries of the Eastern Bloc. Strikes over prices in 1980 led worker groups in Gdansk, Gdynia and Sopot to form a joint strike committee led by Gdansk shipyard electrician Lech Walesa. He and the government signed the Gdansk Agreements on Aug. 31, 1980, permitting the formation of unions independent of the Communist Party, a first in the Soviet sphere. Trade unions formed the national federation Solidarity under Walesa, and on Oct. 24 it was granted legal status. The government under General Wojciech Jaruzelski banned Solidarity in 1981 and declared martial law, but popular protests, with the backing of the church, shook its authority. It resigned in September of 1988, Communists fared badly in the parliamentary election in June of 1989, and on Aug. 24 the Sejm chose Solidarity member Tadeusz Mazowiecki as prime minister. In 1990, Walesa was elected president. The government embarked on a Big Bang conversion to a capitalist market system; the resulting upheaval caused some splintering of Solidarity and, after Poland's first completely free parliamentary election in October of 1991, an era of coalition government. In 1999, Poland became a member of the North Atlantic Treaty Organization. In 2002, it was invited to join the European Union, probably within a year.

The argument over charges of Polish anti-Semitism raises strong emotions on both sides. We must take pains to maintain historical accuracy when dealing with the subject of Poland during the Second World War. Write "a Nazi concentration camp set up in German-occupied Poland," not "a Polish concentration camp." If we

speak of Treblinka as being a Nazi German extermination camp in occupied Poland, a subsequent reference to Sobibor should say that it was "also in occupied Poland," rather than simply "also in Poland." We should not expect all readers to know that the entire country was under occupation for the entire war; there was no puppet regime as in some other countries.

See NATO, Warsaw Pact.

pole, see North Pole.

pole vault (no hyphen).
The noun. The verb is **pole-vault**.

police
It is plural (the police are . . .). This is also true for organization names and their initials (the RCMP are, the OPP are). If the name ends in the word force or department, or if these words are used standing alone in second reference, the verb is singular.

police-blotter jargon
Do our readers the courtesy of assuming they have no firsthand knowledge of criminal charges but do have a close acquaintance with good English. Translate the shorthand and jargon of the police blotter into standard, grammatical English. Say breaking, entering and theft, or break-in and theft, not break, enter and theft. Translate "weapons dangerous" into "possession of a dangerous weapon." On the other hand, there is no need to use the formal "weapon dangerous to the public peace," on which the jargon is based. While we should not be overfamiliar and cryptic, we should not overcompensate by using the formal wording of the Criminal Code if it is unidiomatic or convoluted. Again, the reader deserves a translation.

Police use the word suspect in reference to unknown perpetrators, but we confine it to references to known persons who have been charged or are being sought. Even though the person is unknown, the crime is not, so we usually refer to fugitive criminals with such words as the thief, the robber, the assailant, the killer (but not murderer; see courts).

police officer

This is acceptable idiom in Canada for any rank. Police forces in Canada do not have the military's clear-cut distinction between commissioned officers and other ranks, and we should not try to impose one. See ranks.

polio

There is no need in most stories to call it poliomyelitis.

Politburo

Upper-case. It was the top policy-making secretariat of the Soviet Communist Party, in theory elected by the Central Committee but in fact dominating it. By convention, also use upper case for the comparable bodies in other Communist parties. The Politburos in the Soviet Union and Eastern Europe usually had about 15 members, headed by the party general secretary. (However, the beleaguered Soviet party voted in July of 1990 to expand the Politburo, which then had 12 members, to include the party chiefs of all 15 Soviet republics.) China's Politburo has about 24 members, but it is dominated by the powerful Standing Committee, of about seven members.

Control of the party traditionally meant control of the government, but with Mikhail Gorbachev's election as Soviet president, the Politburo was largely eclipsed in government by his body of appointed advisers, the Presidential Council.

Note that in 1952 the Soviet Politburo, then with only about five members and controlled by the ailing Stalin, was greatly enlarged in a move to restore collective leadership, and

was renamed the Presidium of the Central Committee. The name Politburo was restored in 1966.

polls

To a Canadian, a poll is an opinion sampling. For elections, we can say "go to the polls," polling booth, polling station, but we never call the election itself a poll or polls, and wire stories must be altered accordingly.

Stories on the results of opinion polls should contain the sample size, the margin of error, the method of interview (in-house, by telephone, on the street etc.), and, if they are known, the exact wording of the question and the method of selection if it is other than random dialling (it could be computerized random dialling by area, selection by such criteria as income or age, or a return to those questioned in a previous poll).

We must also compare the results to those of recent polls by other organizations, particularly The Globe's own polling. For example, a poll from a particular company might differ markedly from those of several other pollsters. If that company's next poll merely brings its figures into line with what the others had been saying all along, the readers must be told this. Otherwise, they might see a real political shift in what is really only the correcting of a previous bad poll. However, do not go as far as saying that agreement by two polls proves both are accurate.

In general, do not use decimal places when giving the opinion of the general population: The poll showed 64.7 per cent of Canadians want. . . . This sounds misleadingly precise, given the usual margin of error of three or four percentage points. Decimals are statistically meaningful in references to the actual number of people questioned: Of 2,550 teachers surveyed, 42.6 per cent said. . . . However, "more than 40 per cent" is easier to grasp and is fine for most stories. Revert to such precision when it is significant (as when a majority is required, and the respondents split 49.9 per cent to 50.1).

poltergeist, -s

It is now an English word, from the German words meaning a spirit that makes noises.

polyethylene

It is used for much more than wraps and bags. It is a thermoplastic (see plastic) that can be formulated in a wide range of forms, and so in the abstract should rightly be used in the plural, polyethylenes. They are opaque white in thicker slabs but translucent to clear in thin sheets, and are easily coloured. One type is an important electrical cable insulator, and polyethylenes are also found as pails, drums, pipes, toys, sporting goods and various other products.

polygamy

It is the condition of having taken more than one spouse at the same time, either male or female, or the practice of doing so. We should rarely use the relatively unfamiliar words that distinguish the taking of more than one wife (**polygyny**) from the taking of more than one husband (**polyandry**). But if only polygyny is permitted in a society, we should note this, usually by saying that polygamy is permitted only to men.

The term **bigamy** (taking two spouses) is almost certainly interpreted by the Canadian reader to mean the **illegal** taking of two spouses (or even more). A Muslim who has two wives in a country where this is legal should not be called a bigamist.

polymer

This name applies to any substance with large molecules built up by the linking of small molecules (monomers). Made-to-order synthetic polymers are the basis of the modern fibre and

plastics industries, but there are also many natural polymers, including rubber, resins, proteins, nucleic acids and such minerals as quartz.

Polynesia

It is the southern Pacific east of the International Date Line, and particularly the many islands there. (The entire southern Pacific, with its thousands of islands, is called Oceania. Its other half, west of the date line, is divided roughly by the equator into Micronesia in the north and Melanesia in the south.) The islands of Polynesia are arranged roughly in a triangle, formed by the Hawaiian Islands, New Zealand and Easter Island. Also included are French Polynesia (made up of the Tubuai Islands, the Tuamotu Archipelago, the Marquesas and the Society Islands, including Tahiti), the Samoa group, the Cook Islands, Tuvalu (the former Ellice Islands), Tonga, Pitcairn, Tokelau and Wallis and Futuna. New Zealand's Maoris are members of the Polynesian geographic race (see race).

pommel, pummel

A **pommel** is a knob, especially at the end of a sword, dagger or bayonet handle, or at the front of a saddle (in western-style riding, it's called a saddle horn). The verb **pummel** (pummelled, pummelling) means to beat with a sword or dagger knob, or to use one's fists to the same effect. (The verb is derived from the noun, to beat with the pommel of a sword, but Globe style favours the u in the verb.) Pummel should not be used in reference to throwing things; for this we need pelt, bombard etc.

Pompeii

pompom and pompon

Use **pompon** in reference to a ball or tuft on hats and clothing, such as the ball on a tuque or the exaggerated buttons on a clown suit. They can be made of yarn, but also of other materials such as feathers or ribbon. Also use this spelling for the facial-tissue flowers that decorate cars in wedding processions.

But use **pompom** for the large balls of crepe paper waved by cheerleaders, and also for a rapid-fire anti-aircraft cannon.

pontiff

It means any bishop, but the weight of current use virtually eliminates it as a useful reference to anyone but the Pope. As a generic term, it should be lower-case even when referring to the Pope.

pooh-pooh

pop

Acceptable Canadian idiom for a bubbly soft drink, as in a can or bottle of pop. It should not be used in reference to a dose of illegal drugs (see drugs), and should be used only rarely in lighter features as an informal reference to "apiece" or "a time" (he has had half a dozen tummy tucks, at up to $10,000 a pop). For soft drinks, avoid the regional U.S. term "soda," which in Canada is used almost exclusively for club soda or a drink made with ice cream.

Pope

Use upper case when referring to any individual, past or present, but lower case for the plural and for the generic (the Medici produced three popes; a new pope will be chosen today).

The term "the Pope," without the name attached, may be used in first reference in current stories about the present one (the Pope began his African tour yesterday). In subsequent references, he should be called at least once by his name (John Paul was welcomed by . . .). But in stories about the past, even those about the early

years of the current pope's tenure, the name must be added in first reference, because the general reader should not be expected to know the names of past popes or the date the current one was elected.

One does not kiss the Pope's hand, but rather his ring. We do not use His Holiness as an honorific, but capitalize it if it appears in quotes or as colour in stories.

Sources differ on the number of popes from Peter to John Paul II. Michael Valpy observes that the range, from 262 to 268, stems from "antipopes, Avignon popes, double-counted popes, popes-elected-but-not-consecrated and a confusion over how many Johns were pope between XV and XXI (the answer is not VI)." The most authoritative number (from the 2001 Pontifical Yearbook) is 264 popes – and 266 papacies. (Benedict IX reigned three times.) Thus, John Paul II is the 263rd successor to St. Peter as Bishop of Rome.

Popsicle

A trade name, which may be used generically, upper-case. ("Iced treat" and other such expressions sound fussy, and are vague.) However, it must not be used in stories about poisonings, allergic reactions etc. unless we are sure of the brand.

poring and pouring

Do not write of someone **pouring** over a book, unless the tome in question is getting wet.

pork barrel

Two words as a noun (he makes good use of the pork barrel), but hyphenated as an adjective or verb, including the gerund, pork-barrelling. It is patronage extended to an entire community or region rather than to an individual, and usually takes the form of works projects. See patronage.

pornography

Use this word for material intended solely to arouse sexual interest, with no redeeming artistic merit. (It is from the Grrek for writing by or about harlots.) For material that goes beyond the sexual into the areas of disgusting objects, violence, cruelty or horror, use the broader term **obscenity** (see obscenity). Since a value judgment is involved—and since obscenity has a particular meaning under the Criminal Code—do not use these words in reference to a particular publication, movie or picture unless the determination has been officially made by a court, customs authorities or official censor. Use such terms as "sexually explicit" instead.

Portage la Prairie

portentous (not -ious).

It means ominous or astonishing. Do not confuse it with pretentious.

porterhouse steak, lower-case.

Portugal

Adjective and people: Portuguese. Currency: euro (had been the escudo). Capital: Lisbon.

It occupies the southwestern corner of the Iberian Peninsula, being bounded on the west and south by the Atlantic and on the north and east by Spain, and also includes Madeira and the Azores, which are integral parts of the republic. Its sole remaining overseas territory, Macau, west of Hong Kong across the mouth of the Pearl River, was handed over to China in 1999. Portugal's major cities are Lisbon, Oporto (from which port wine gets its name), Coimbra and Setubal. Its population is 10 million.

Portuguese names

See Spanish and Portuguese names.

possessives

It is rarely good idiom to create possessives for inanimate things that are not capable of ownership, such as the heart's wall, the air's temperature, economics' rules. However, possessives are encountered in such idiomatic expressions as a hair's-breadth and a stone's throw, and are also acceptable (but not mandatory) for most inanimate things with proper names (Saturn's rings, Vancouver's mayor), although these are often swung into "of" phrases if they end in s (the canals of Mars, not Mars's canals). Possessives are also fine for things that are often personified (life's ironies; at death's door), and idiom also seems to make a blanket exception for conveyances (the car's windshield, the ship's anchor, the plane's crew).

The opposite is true of animate things, particularly people: putting them into an "of" phrase to convey the possessive (the bowl of the dog) is usually so stilted that even a possessive with many sibilants is preferable (the hostess's gown). Things made up of people or animals (team, club, organization, flock, herd) are usually regarded as animate for the purpose of possessives (the herd's pasture, not the pasture of the herd). See the notes below on compounds and double genitives.

Expressions that sound possessive but **do not involve true possession** are treated as merely descriptive, with no apostrophe (first ministers conference). These include common expressions involving lengths of time (two weeks vacation, five years imprisonment); however, idiom requires an apostrophe for the singular (a week's vacation). Other expressions considered descriptive are those that, if rewritten as phrases, would take the prepositions "for" or "by" rather than "of"—a hitchhikers guide, a teachers college, citizens band. (By convention, we use apostrophes for such historical events as the Seven Years' War.) We treat the names of sports teams as descriptive (a Jays outfielder).

Note that we follow commercial corporations' own style (McDonald's, but Diners Club) and the style used by organizations in their official names (the Department of Veterans Affairs, the Ontario Secondary School Teachers' Federation). The possessive is required if the plural is not formed by adding s (notably women, men, children, as in the International Longshoremen's Association). In addition, we do not suppress genuine possessives (the Teamsters' president, the Jays' starting lineup).

Compounds: Expressions such as attorney-general, even though the plural is created on the principal word (attorneys-general), are treated as an entire expression for the purpose of possessives (the attorney-general's order, the notary public's office). Plural possessives of compound expressions are so awkward that an "of" phrase becomes by far the lesser of two evils: "the conference of the attorneys-general." Some other expressions are treated as **compound units** for the purpose of possessives (the government of Alberta's lawyer, the Shah of Iran's family), but if they get any more complex (Jean Charest of Quebec's proposal), they are better recast.

Two or more names: Placing of the possessive depends on whether possession is shared or separate. For shared possession, idiom makes only the last name possessive, treating the owners as a compound unit (June and Bob's children, Mr. White and Mr. Green's partnership). If different things are attached to different people, all the names should be made possessive (Mr. White's and Mr. Green's families).

Pronouns: Particular care is warranted with the pronouns that have special possessive forms without

an apostrophe. Apostrophes are proper with some pronouns (nobody's baby, someone else's problem), which makes it all the easier for the contractions it's, there's, who's and you're to supplant the proper possessives **its**, **theirs**, **whose** and **your**. In addition, the possessives that end in s often acquire incorrect apostrophes (her's, their's).

Double genitive: We use a possessive pronoun in such expressions as "a colleague of mine" and "a quirk of his." Idiom requires these, even though the possessive is redundant after the preposition "of." When the pronoun is replaced by a noun or a name, the ear usually does not demand a possessive (a colleague of his aunt, a quirk of Mr. Trudeau). However, the double genitive would still be considered idiomatic here, and a writer might occasionally feel that it sounds better. Personal choice can prevail.

When do we add an s? Possessives are normally formed by adding an apostrophe and s to the singular, and an apostrophe alone to a plural. Questions arise when the singular ends in an s sound or a silent s, and when a plural ends in some letter other than s.

As a matter of policy, we add an apostrophe and s to create the possessive of all singular words and names that end in s (James's, Davis's, Copps's), and leave the reader to decide how to pronounce what we have written. This is also true of names in which the s is silent (Duplessis's, Louis's, Arkansas's, Illinois's), and names in which the final sibilant is created by some other letter (Schultz's, France's, Cox's).

Exceptions are singulars with a sibilant ending that are followed by the word sake. Idiom calls for an apostrophe but no s on the expression for goodness' sake.

Normal plurals ending in s do not add an extra sibilant for the possessive;

only an apostrophe is required (the Davises' house, the hounds' quarry). But if a word forms its plural by some means other than adding s, or does not change at all for the plural, add an apostrophe and an s: women's rights, the children's hour, the alumni's lounge, the deer's mating season. Exceptions are the Sox team names, which are pronounced as if they ended in ks, and merely add an apostrophe for the plural possessive (the White Sox' losing streak).

Companies and countries whose name contains a plural word are usually regarded as singular (General Motors is), but are treated as plural for the purpose of possessives (General Motors' new models, the Seychelles' new president).

post
As a combining form meaning after or later, it usually does not take a hyphen, as in postbellum, postdated, postelection, postgame, postgraduate, postmortem, postpartum, postprandial, postwar, except with a proper name (post-Darwinian). Use two words for post meridiem, after midday, abbreviated as p.m.

When post means mail, use one word for postcard, postman, postmaster and postpaid, but two words for post office.

Post-it notes

Poste-de-la-Baleine, Que.
See Great Whale.

poste restante

potash
It is not an element like iron or copper. The name is applied to a variety of potassium salts and often to a combination of these, but particularly to potassium carbonate, an alkali formed from a fusion of potassium and carbon dioxide, used as a fertilizer and in making glass. Other potassium salts used as fertilizer include potassium chloride (sylvite) and potassium nitrate (saltpetre), also used in explosives. Saskatchewan's potash deposits, which are among the world's largest, are primarily in the areas of Esterhazy, near the Manitoba border; Belle Plaine, midway between Regina and Moose Jaw; and Viscount, southwest of Saskatoon.

Potawatomi

potbelly

potluck
Both noun and adjective.

pot pie

pound-foolish

PoW, for prisoner of war; **PoWs**.

power
Reserve the expression "took power" for authoritarian regimes. For leaders and parties elected by democratic means, say "took office."

powwow
Do not use this for a political meeting of native leaders. It has a specific meaning in some parts of the country having to do with spirit dancing, or healing ceremonies often involving music and dance.

practical and practicable
Practicable means capable of being carried out. **Practical** has several meanings, including useful, real or virtual, and based or grounded in experience rather than theory. An idea or plan can be either or both (doable, and grounded in experience), but a person can be only practical.

practice (noun).
The verb is **practise, practising**. A practised golfer would take a practice shot.

Prairies

Use upper case for the plains of southwestern Manitoba, southern Saskatchewan and southeastern Alberta, and for the provinces themselves use the term Prairie provinces. Do not imply that any of the three is entirely prairie. Do not apply the U.S. term Midwest to these provinces.

Use lower case for prairies as the generic term for rolling grasslands, particularly those of central North America. The three types, depending on rainfall, are tallgrass, mixed-grass and shortgrass (the driest). The words steppes and veld mean the same as plain or prairie, and this should be pointed out.

Pravda, see Izvestia.

pre

As a combining form it takes a hyphen only if the main word begins with e (pre-election, pre-eminent) or a capital letter (pre-Roman; but note Precambrian).

Preakness, the

Precambrian Shield

Also known in Canada as the Canadian Shield, and occasionally referred to as the Laurentian Shield, it covers more than 40 per cent of Canada's land area, forming a crescent around Hudson Bay from Nunavut through northern Saskatchewan and Manitoba, Northern and Central Ontario and Quebec, to Labrador and Baffin Island. The name Precambrian means that its formation was complete before the beginning of the Cambrian period 600 million years ago, the beginning of significant fossil deposits.

precede, to go ahead of, but **proceed**, to advance.

precipitate, precipitous

Precipitate means hasty. **Precipitous** means steep.

preconditions

The pre goes without saying, and should.

predicative adjectives

Verbs that express a state of being are often followed by an adjective describing the subject, rather than by an adverb modifying the verb. These verbs include be (am, is, are, was, were), become, appear, seem, look, sound, taste and feel. Say that the orchestra plays badly, but that it sounds bad.

predominantly

Often misspelled predominately. The adjective is predominant, the verb predominate.

pre-eminent, pre-empt (see pre).

premier

Use for the head of a parliamentary government in a province or state (an Australian state, for example), to distinguish these from the head of a national parliament, the prime minister. The exception is China, where we still use the title Premier to conform to that government's own style. Use premier as well for those leaders of Yukon, Nunavut and the Northwest Territories who have chosen it.

premier-designate, president-elect

In Canada's parliamentary system, in which prime ministers and premiers are chosen by their parties rather than directly elected by the people, it is inaccurate to copy the style of countries that elect their leaders directly. Thus, an American presidential candidate who has been elected but has not yet taken over the job is properly a president-elect, but a prime minister or premier in Canada is a prime-minister-designate or premier-designate.

premiere

No accent. Can be used as a noun, adjective or verb in reference to a first performance or showing.

premises

The plural noun refers to land and the buildings on it, or to a building or part of a building. Do not drop the s when using these senses. Do not write of an unlicensed premise.

prepositions

Incorrect choice of prepositions is a certain giveaway that someone is not totally familiar with English, or else is overfamiliar to the point of carelessness. These words, whose role is to establish relationships (under the table, to the government, in the bag, from the people), require particular care, since idiom often departs from logical rules, and one word may take various prepositions depending on meaning. For example, we **part from** a person, but **part with** a thing. Use **angry at** or **with** or **toward** a person, organization or animal, but not an event or situation. For these, we need **angry over** or **about** or **because of**. This distinction also applies to the nouns anger, fury, alarm, disappointment etc. Say her anger toward her assistant, her anger over (not at) the mix-up.

We cannot force a preposition to do the work of a different one in such double constructions as "charged and convicted of murder." Make it charged with and convicted of, or reword.

"Of" is usually an unnecessary addition to other prepositions, as in off of, outside of. Use off, outside.

In an either/or or both/and construction, if a preposition comes after the first word there must also be one after the second. The prepositions

need not be the same. (He has worked both in government and in the private sector; she has worked both in government and for General Motors.) If a preposition comes before the introductory word, it is not repeated in the second half, but must logically apply to it. (He has experience in both government and business.)

As long as our sentences are fluid, clear and concise, the supposed rule against ending them with prepositions is not one we should lose any sleep over.

prerogative

Presbyterian Church in Canada

presently

It means in a little while. It does not mean now, at present, currently.

president

Upper-case as a political title (President Jacques Chirac) and when standing alone referring to a specific individual (the President announced), including historical references (the President was assassinated in Dallas). However, use lower-case with the word former or late (former president Bill Clinton) and in generic references to the office (the president has veto power; she is running for president). Use lower-case for presidents of companies, clubs etc. Lower-case president-elect even before the name: president-elect Chelsea Clinton. See capitalization.

presidium (not prae-).

Presqu'ile

Point and Provincial Park in Ontario, but **Presque Isle** in Maine and Michigan.

Press Gallery

Use upper-case for an organization representing parliamentary or legislature reporters, but lower-case for the balcony or other place in the chamber reserved for them.

pressure

Avoid as a verb. Use press, or put pressure on.

pressure cooker

But a **pressure-cooker** atmosphere.

pretense

prevalent, -ence

preventive (not preventative).

pricey

prima facie

Italics not required. It means by initial appearances. Best left to direct quotes in legal stories.

prime minister

Upper-case as a title (Prime Minister Tony Blair) and when standing alone referring to a specific individual (the Prime Minister's official residence), including historical references (the Prime Minister met President Roosevelt at Quebec). Use lower-case with the word former or late (former prime minister Brian Mulroney), and in generic references (the official residence of Canada's prime ministers), except when the generic term is part of a proper title (the Prime Minister's Office). (See PMO.)

Use this title for heads of national parliaments, and use premier for heads of provincial or state legislatures in parliamentary democracies (Premier Robert John Carr of the state of New South Wales). The exception is the Premier of China.

Here are Canada's prime ministers, with their party affiliation: **Sir John A. Macdonald**, C, July 1, 1867, to Nov. 5, 1873; and Oct. 17, 1878, to June 6, 1891. **Alexander Mackenzie**, L, Nov. 7, 1873, to Oct. 9, 1878. **Sir John Abbott**, C, June 16, 1891, to Nov. 24, 1892. **Sir John Thompson**, C, Dec. 5, 1892, to Dec. 12, 1894. **Sir Mackenzie Bowell**, C, Dec. 21, 1894, to April 27, 1896. **Sir Charles Tupper**, C, May 1, 1896, to July 8, 1896. **Sir Wilfrid Laurier**, L, July 11, 1896, to Oct. 6, 1911. **Sir Robert Borden**, C from Oct. 10, 1911, to Oct. 12, 1917, and then Unionist until July 10, 1920. **Arthur Meighen**, U from July 10, 1920, to Dec. 29, 1921; and C from June 29, 1926, to Sept. 25, 1926. **Mackenzie King**, L, Dec. 29, 1921, to June 28, 1926; Sept. 25, 1926, to Aug. 6, 1930; and Oct. 23, 1935, to Nov. 15, 1948. **R. B. (Richard Bedford) Bennett**, C, Aug. 7, 1930, to Oct. 23, 1935. **Louis St. Laurent**, L, Nov. 15, 1948, to June 21, 1957. **John Diefenbaker**, C, June 21, 1957, to April 22, 1963. **Lester Pearson**, L, April 22, 1963, to April 20, 1968. **Pierre Trudeau**, L, April 20, 1968, to June 4, 1979; and March 3, 1980, to June 30, 1984. **Joe Clark**, C, June 4, 1979, to March 3, 1980. **John Turner**, L, June 30, 1984, to Sept. 17, 1984. **Brian Mulroney**, C, Sept. 17, 1984, to June 25, 1993. **Kim Campbell**, C, June 25, 1993, to Nov. 4, 1993. **Jean Chrétien**, L, Nov. 4, 1993.

The record for the shortest term as prime minister is held not by John Turner but by Tupper.

Note that these dates are not the dates of elections, but rather the dates of swearing-in. Also, not all can be said to have been "elected" prime minister. Some, such as Mr. Turner, were chosen by their parties to complete an electoral mandate won under another leader.

When referring to the number of prime ministers Canada has had, count each leader only once, even those such as John A. Macdonald who have served non-consecutive terms. Thus, Jean Chrétien is Canada's 20th prime minister.

This differs from U.S. practice, which counts Grover Cleveland as two presidents (22nd and 24th) because he served non-consecutive terms. George W. Bush is the 43rd president of the United States.

Prince Edward Island

The abbreviation PEI, without points, may be used in headlines and in second reference in copy (in first reference if it appears as an adjective). PEI is in the Gulf of St. Lawrence, separated from New Brunswick and Nova Scotia by Northumberland Strait.

Princes' Gates (not Princess).

At the Canadian National Exhibition grounds, Toronto.

principal and principle

If it's an adjective, it must be **principal**. A noun can be either, depending on meaning. A **principal** is a head or leading figure (in a school, a group, a company, a deal) or the sum or property from which interest or income is derived. A **principle** is a rule, law, moral guideline or general truth. These words are always worth a second look.

priority

This word standing alone is taken to mean top priority; there is no need to use an adjective if so. Use an adjective for all other degrees (high, low etc). Use priority as a noun only, except in commercial names (Priority Post).

privatize, privatization

Acceptable new words for describing a new phenomenon, the transferring to the private sector of government companies or services. Note that such companies cannot usually be described as privately held, which means that their shares would not be publicly traded.

Privy Council

The Queen's Privy Council for Canada is not the equivalent of the cabinet, since it also includes all living former federal cabinet members, plus the governor-general, the premiers, the leader of the opposition, the chief justice, the speakers of the Commons and Senate, and other distinguished people whom the governor-general (on the cabinet's advice) decides to honour, such as long-time parliamentarians, former top civil servants and Commonwealth prime ministers. The cabinet, which has no basis in statute, acts as the Committee of the Privy Council, and issues its orders-in-council in the name of the governor-general.

In historical references, note that disputes in Canada were referred not to Britain's Privy Council (that country's cabinet), but to a special body set up for the purpose, called the Imperial Privy Council.

Privy Council Office

See PMO. The two should not be equated. Avoid the unfamiliar abbreviation PCO unless the context is clear and there are several repetitions. It is too obscure for most headlines.

pro

This prefix takes a hyphen in the sense of in favour of (pro-industry, pro-American, pro-democracy), but not in such senses as prorate.

pro-active

The adjective means taken in advance to avoid an undesired outcome, but it smacks of jargon. Resist its use outside direct quotations. The opposite of "reactive" is "active," or another word that better conveys the idea of initiating action, such as "causal," "aggressive." Usually, the thought requires a phrase: "He said they had to start setting the agenda, rather than simply being reactive."

problematic

It means questionable or contingent, or involving a problem or puzzle. Careful writers do not use is problematic to mean is or causes a problem, and news writers mindful of the likelihood of misinterpretation do not use it at all.

proceed

Even when there really is a formal procession involved, the verb **proceed** is pretentious as a substitute for walk, go, ride etc., and is objectionable also because it is a general word supplanting a more descriptive specific one. Translate such accounts from police notebooks as "the suspect was proceeding down the highway." Also avoid **proceeded to** as a replacement for "began" or "then," as in "the crowd proceeded to batter down the gate."

Procter & Gamble Inc.

But it's Proctor-Silex, Proctor & Redfern (Toronto consulting engineers).

profanity, see obscenity.

profit

Prefer this to earnings, the jargon of company reports.

programmer

Programmed, programming.

progressive and regressive

When describing taxes, **progressive** has two meanings—a technical one (having a rate that rises in stages according to amount) and a value judgment (contributing to the progress of society). The fact that most people regard technically progressive taxes, such as income tax, as also being socially progressive should not blind journalists to the fact that only one of these meanings is properly used outside quotes or opinion pieces. Given the ambiguity, we are better advised to refer to a

sliding scale or some such, rather than use the word progressive.

The two meanings also dictate two different contrasting terms. The term **regressive tax** should be confined to the sense of reversing social progress, and so should not appear outside quotes or opinion pieces. The contrasting term to progressive in the technical sense is simply non-progressive or, preferably, fixed-rate tax or flat tax. (These are different. A fixed-rate tax is at a constant percentage, with the payment rising according to gross amount, as in a sales tax. A flat tax is always the same, as in a set $25 airport tax regardless of ticket price.) See opposites.

Progressive Conservative (no hyphen).

The short form Conservative (Conservative Party) is acceptable even on first reference for the national and provincial Canadian parties, unless the formal name is at issue.

Prohibition

Use upper case for the period during which alcoholic drink was outlawed or severely restricted, but lower case for the act of doing so. Legal measures against alcohol have a long history in Canada, dating from the pre-Confederation Dunkin Act and the Canada Temperance Act of 1878, which gave provinces the power to ban alcohol. Nova Scotia and Prince Edward Island did so shortly before the First World War, and all other provinces except Quebec followed in 1916 and 1917. (Ontario continued to allow domestic wine. Quebec outlawed spirits from 1919 to 1921, but allowed beer and wine.) The western provinces began ending their restrictions soon after the war, but Ontario and New Brunswick held out until 1927, Nova Scotia until 1930 and PEI until 1948, and local option has kept some jurisdictions free of bars in otherwise wet provinces.

U.S. Prohibition began in 1920, under the 18th Amendment and the enforcement provisions of the Volstead Act. The amendment was repealed in 1933.

proletariat

In Marxist theory, this is the name given to wage earners as a social and economic class, exploited by their employers in the bourgeois class.

pro-life

Use anti-abortion instead. See abortion.

promissory

prone

Technically, it means lying face down, as does **prostrate**. Sunny-side up, you're **supine**. Unless the distinction is important, however, prone and prostrate can be used to mean lying flat in any attitude.

pronghorns

Should not be called antelopes. (Traditionally they have been so classed, but recent scholarship suggests they belong to the bovid family, which also includes sheep and goats.) Abundant in the western United States, they also extend into southeastern Alberta and southwestern Saskatchewan.

pronouns

The personal pronouns he, she, him, her, it, they and them are alive and thriving everywhere except in news writers' professional vocabularies. Reporters who would use "him" in speech or in a letter to a friend seem strangely compelled to write "the man" in an identical sentence in a news story. The result is that we bore readers with stilted prose, offend them with insulting overexplanation and occasionally baffle them with a string of increasingly inaccurate synonyms in subsequent references to avoid repeating the noun.

Shunning pronouns out of habit can also create confusion. If readers encounter a noun when they would normally expect a pronoun, they might well suspect that a second person or thing is being referred to. Consider this sentence: Guards seized Hans Exner after the official arrived at the border post. The pronoun "he" would have removed any doubt that Exner is being referred to. If the noun is intended as an economical means of conveying additional information (the official, the youth, the elderly man, the mother of four, the 20-year veteran, the charitable group), take care that it is not a false economy.

Pronouns are classified as **personal** (I, we, you, he, she, it and they, along with their objective and possessive cases), **demonstrative** (this, these, that, those), **relative** (who, whom, which, that), **indefinite** (all, any, both, each, either, everyone, one, somebody, such) and **interrogative** (who, whom, which, what). With the addition of self or selves, personal pronouns become emphatic (the man himself) or reflexive (he is fooling himself). Pronouns can also be used in conjunction with nouns, as pronominal adjectives (his assistant, my word).

Personal pronouns must match their antecedent in both number and gender, but their case (subjective/he, objective/him, possessive/his) depends on the construction of the sentence. We would never say police rescued he; it must be police rescued him. But some are sorely tempted to change the case when the object is enlarged, saying "rescued he and his family" when we should say "rescued him and his family." Remember that whether alone or as part of a list, I, we, he, she and they do something, while something is done to me, us, him, her and them.

The relatives who and whom deserve special mention. Writers usually have no trouble sorting out subject and object (the man who came to dinner; the man whom I invited to dinner), but many come to grief when adding such elements as "they reported" or "they said" or "I thought" or "we learned." Again, case is unaffected by any such addition. Say "the man who I learned later came to dinner." See who and whom.

It is sometimes awkward, confusing or ambiguous to use pronouns, and Fowler offers some simple rules: There must be a principal (a noun or name) for which the pronoun stands. This principal should be close by. There should not be another noun or name that the reader might mistake for the correct principal, even for a moment. A pronoun should seldom come before the principal.

For a discussion of the pitfalls of possessive pronouns (their, not they're), see possessives.

proof

As a suffix, it traditionally has not taken a hyphen (acidproof, leakproof, waterproof). But we make exceptions for recent coinages and those involving initials or proper names, since they would otherwise be awkward or obscure (inflation-proof, PCB-proof).

The expression "the exception that proves the rule" relies on an early, now archaic sense of the word prove: to test.

proof spirit

Can pure alcohol be called 200 proof? Not in Canada, where it is about 175 proof.

Various countries, for excise purposes, define a standard alcohol content against which liquors can be measured. (Their levels vary, as do their methods of measurement, such as weight, volume and specific gravity.) This theoretical beverage, or an actual one that matches it in alcohol content, is said to be a **proof spirit** in that country. Others are rated by percentage of the proof standard; thus, a proof spirit can also be

described as **100 proof**. One with more alcohol might be 130 proof, and one with less might be 70 proof.

Canada and Britain have each declared their proof spirit to be one that, measured on Sykes's hydrometer, is 12/13ths the weight of an equal measure of distilled water (both at a temperature of 11 C). That works out to 57.06 per cent alcohol by volume (48.24 per cent by weight). With 57.06 per cent alcohol being 100 proof, then, in Canada and Britain pure alcohol is about 175 proof. In the United States, the proof standard is 50 per cent alcohol by volume; so pure alcohol is 200 proof. When giving a liquor's proof rating, we must specify which country's standard applies.

Canadian distillers were restricted during the Second World War to a maximum of 70 proof (about 40 per cent alcohol by volume), and have continued to sell most of their products at that content after removal of the restriction. The same product sold in the United States can be labelled 80 proof by the U.S. standard.

The word "proof" should not be applied to beer and wine. Do not say that a U.S. beer with 5 per cent alcohol is 10 proof.

propellant and propellent

Propellant is the noun (this gas is a propellant). **Propellent** is the adjective (this is a propellent gas).

propeller

prophecy, noun. The verb is **prophesy**.

proportionally, proportionately

Proportionally means in proportion. Proportionately means in the right proportion.

prorate

It means to divide proportionally (pro rata).

prospectuses

prostate, prostrate

The first is short for the prostate gland, which is found in male mammals and surrounds the urethra at the base of the bladder and secretes a fluid that is a major constituent of semen. The second is a verb meaning to throw yourself down in humility, or an adjective that means lying face down. Try not to confuse them.

prosthesis, prostheses

It is more precise to say artificial arm, leg, hand etc.

protagonist

It rarely applies. It originally meant the leading actor in a Greek play, and now means a leading character or contestant. It should not be used in place of **proponent** to mean champion or advocate, nor as the opposite of **antagonist**, meaning opponent, adversary.

protégé

protest

As a verb meaning to express disapproval, it requires a preposition such as "against" or "over" (they were protesting against the rail cuts). However, if we are pressed to the wall on a very short headline, this requirement may be waived (MPs protest rail cuts). In copy, protest takes a direct object only when it means to declare solemnly and formally, as in protest one's innocence.

protester

prototype

It means the original from which something else is copied; an experimental car might be the prototype of a production run. This word should not be used to mean a perfect example, an archetype, as in "he is the prototype of the tough Hamilton lineman."

proved and proven

Proved is our choice as the past participle (he has proved his point). But **proven** is still acceptable as an adjective (a proven fact).

provided

This word (not **providing**) is the conjunction for conveying a formally stated condition, a stipulation. The clause it precedes properly begins with "that," but this is often omitted without ambiguity (We will end the strike, provided [that] there are no reprisals). For conveying a simple condition, stick to "if" (We will eat outdoors if it doesn't rain).

Province House

This is the name for the legislature buildings in both Halifax and Charlottetown.

provinces and states

The name of a province or state standing alone is not abbreviated in copy, except for the two provinces that Canadians regularly call by their initials: B.C. and PEI. (These should be spelled out in first reference, however, unless their first appearance is as an adjective.) In headlines, B.C. and PEI may be abbreviated as a matter of course. N.B., N.S. and NWT may be abbreviated in heads when used as adjectives and, when a fit is truly impossible otherwise, may also be abbreviated as nouns. Two provinces whose abbreviations are not initials, Saskatchewan and Newfoundland and Labrador, may be abbreviated in single-column heads, but only if there is no alternative. Never abbreviate Alberta, Manitoba, Nunavut, Ontario, Quebec or Yukon in a headline.

Abbreviate the names of provinces and most U.S. states when they follow the name of a community. But spell out the province or state when it is itself the issue and would be stressed in speech (I thought he meant

Windsor, Ontario, but it was Windsor, Nova Scotia).

The abbreviations for Canadian provinces and territories are B.C., Alta., Sask., Man., Ont., Que., N.B., N.S., PEI, Nfld. and NWT. Nunavut and Yukon are not abbreviated. Note that we use points if there are two initials (N.B.), but not if there are more than two (PEI).

We use the traditional abbreviations for U.S. states, not the less familiar two-letter forms used on mail. There are no abbreviations for Alaska, Hawaii, Idaho, Iowa, Ohio and Utah, and we do not abbreviate U.S. possessions. Here are the abbreviations for the other states: Ala., Ariz., Ark., Calif., Colo., Conn., Del., Fla., Ga., Ill., Ind., Kan., Ky., La., Me., Md., Mass., Mich., Minn., Miss., Mo., Mont., Neb., Nev., N.H., N.J., N.M., N.Y., N.C., N.D., Okla., Ore., Pa., R.I., S.C., S.D., Tenn., Tex., Vt., Va., Wash., W.Va., Wis., Wyo. There is little occasion to use D.C.

The name of a province or state modifying a community name is always surrounded by commas. This makes such constructions too awkward for use as adjectives (a Brantford, Ont., company), so these must be recast (a company in Brantford, Ont.), although there may be justification for leaving out the province or state entirely. This may be done if the context of the story has already established the jurisdiction (The new head of the Manitoba Federation of Labour is a Portage la Prairie rail worker), or if the city is well known to Canadian readers. In Canada, this applies to all capitals and to other major cities. A convenient definition is those non-capitals that have an NHL or CFL franchise: Montreal, Hamilton, Calgary, Vancouver. Some other cities are familiar to readers because they are important ports, railway points or industrial centres, or have a major prison or university, a distinctive name or historical significance. These are

Brandon, Corner Brook, Dartmouth, Gatineau, Kamloops, Kingston, Medicine Hat, Mississauga, Moncton, Moose Jaw, North Bay, Prince George, Prince Rupert, Rivière-du-Loup, Saskatoon, Sept-Îles, Saint John, Sherbrooke, Sudbury, Summerside, Thunder Bay and Trois-Rivières.

U.S. cities for which the name of the state is not required are the major centres Boston, Chicago, Cleveland, Dallas, Detroit, Houston, Los Angeles, Miami, New York, Philadelphia, San Francisco and Washington, and these other cities: Atlanta, Buffalo, Denver, Hollywood, Honolulu, Las Vegas, Nome, Orlando, Nashville, Phoenix, Pittsburgh, Reno, San Diego, Seattle, Tampa and Tucson. Unless they are on that list, U.S. state capitals should be followed with the name of the state. However, as with Canadian centres, the name of the state may also be omitted from other community names if the story has already established the location.

Note that while Ontario is Canada's most populous province, it is not the largest. That distinction goes to Quebec, which is 44 per cent larger: 1,540,680 square kilometres to Ontario's 1,068,582.

provincewide

psoriasis

psychedelic, see drugs.

psychiatric terms
It is best to steer clear of psychiatric terms unless a story is medical or scientific in nature, or unless we are quoting from formal reports or court testimony. It is almost certainly defamatory to refer to a recognizable individual as being mentally ill (see courts). In addition, it is a rare layman who can sort out the differences between the various kinds of psychological abnormalities: psychoneurotic disorders (neuroses),

psychotic disorders (psychoses), character disorders, disorders of intelligence, transient shock reactions and addiction disorders.

Be especially alert for the psychiatric terms that are misused in everyday speech. Paranoia, for example, has many symptoms, only one of which is an unreasoning fear. Do not use "paranoid" simply to convey great fear (it may be quite justified by an impending disaster, a rapist in the neighbourhood etc.). Extreme nervousness in itself is not neurotic; someone who is merely undecided is not schizophrenic.

psychic

For clarity, reserve this word for parapsychology, the field of alleged mental abilities that are not explainable by reference to the normal senses. "Psychic" is a general term, and we are more informative if we use more specific ones when these apply, such as clairvoyant, telepathic, telekinetic.

psychoanalysis

ptarmigan

These are the grouse that turn white in winter. They are found in the Arctic (the willow and rock ptarmigan) and in the higher elevations of the Rockies (the white-tailed ptarmigan).

Pty. Ltd.

This Australian company term means Proprietary Limited, denoting a private company, or a subsidiary of a publicly listed company. It cannot invite the public to buy its shares or take deposits from the public. Note the distinction with **Pty. Co. Ltd.**, which denotes that a firm's shares are listed. See PLC.

public service, see civil service.

publicly (not publically).

Publishers Clearing House

The direct-mail operation has no apostrophe.

Puerto Rico

It is classed as a self-governing commonwealth freely associated with the United States. Puerto Ricans are U.S. citizens, but pay no federal taxes and may not vote in federal elections. In plebiscites in 1967, 1993 and 1998, Puerto Ricans voted to remain a commonwealth. The island is the farthest east of the Greater Antilles, between Hispaniola (containing Haiti and the Dominican Republic) and the Leeward group. Its population is about four million.

pugnacious

puissance, equestrian term.

Pullman

Upper case for the railway sleeping car invented by George Mortimer Pullman.

pulpit

A clergyman is **in** the pulpit, not at, on or behind it. See dais.

pummel, see pommel.

punctilious

It means exact in observing forms, especially etiquette. It does not mean punctual.

punctuation

The goal of punctuation is to help readers read what writers write. Used properly, it guides the reader; used improperly, it confuses the reader and may distort the meaning. Simple, straightforward writing requires the least punctuation.

apostrophe Do not use an apostrophe to form plurals of words or numbers: B-52s, the ABCs, the ins and outs. However, if the discussion is about words as words, use an apostrophe to form the plurals: I prefer the's to a's and an's. Use an apostrophe to form the plural of single letters: dot the i's and cross the t's. Use it as well to indicate missing figures or letters: Cap'n Ahab. See the main entry on possessives.

brackets See parentheses, below.

colon The colon directs the reader's attention forward. Its principal use is in lists (Mary took the following: a knife, a fork, a spoon and a plate). Use the colon after an independent clause if what follows restates or expands on the clause. (There is only one thing in this world I value more than money: friendship. He knew one thing for sure: This would be a long night.) Note that the first word after the colon is upper-case if it begins a complete sentence.

Use the colon in transcripts, without quotation marks:

Judge Arthurs: Have you appeared in my court before?

Witness: Not that I recall.

Use a colon instead of a comma to introduce direct quotations more than a sentence in length, or at the end of one paragraph to introduce a direct quotation that occupies the next.

Use a colon when giving the time of day (3:42 p.m.) or the time elapsed (3:58:23.1).

The colon should be placed outside quotation marks.

comma The presence or absence of commas may radically change the meaning of a sentence. If a relative clause (beginning with such words as who, that and which) imparts information essential to our understanding of which person or thing is being discussed, it is a defining clause. Do not set it off with commas: The butcher who works on Selby Street is a friend of mine. If the clause merely provides information about someone who we already know is

under discussion, it is a non-defining clause and should be set off with commas: The butcher, who was out of town yesterday, came home today. (See the entry on that and which.)

The same rule applies to phrases. If one writes The minister in the blue car waved his hand, it means there are many ministers, and this one is unique in occupying a blue car. If one writes The minister, in the blue car, waved his hand, it means there is only one minister and he happens to be in a blue car.

Use a comma after an introductory clause or phrase: As the driver turned the corner, he saw the bridge. With a song in your heart, you're never alone. Use commas to surround a clause or phrase (unless it is a defining clause or phrase) in midsentence: When he whistles in the street, as he often does, people notice him.

If commas are used to set off qualifying words, numbers or initials, a comma must appear at each end: I live in Fredericton, N.B., and I speak two languages. She travelled on June 2, 1986, to a town near Toronto.

Commas may be omitted if a phrase is brief and there is no possibility of confusion: For a while I thought I was mad. I thought for a while about the problem. Use a comma if there is any chance of ambiguity: At the time, travel was not a possibility. He is, in a word, game.

If a clause immediately follows a conjunction, the first comma may be omitted: So far he has refused to alter his behaviour, but when his father returns from holiday in England and has a chance to talk to him, we may see a change in the boy's attitude.

As a rule, use a comma in sentences where such conjunctions as **and, but, as, for** and **while** join two independent clauses: The truck has arrived, but the car is still in Edmonton. No comma is necessary if the conjunction is **and**, if the subject of both clauses is the same and if the subject appears only in the first clause: He had come to see his daughter and would not be dissuaded.

Use commas to separate the ingredients in a list: Apples, oranges and plums are on the table. Note the absence of a comma before the "and"; this omission is Globe style. However, if one element in a series requires an internal conjunction, insert a final comma to remove ambiguity: He read poems about Jack and Jill, the man in the moon, and the owl and the pussycat. Make an exception as well if the series is unusually complex: She ordered the coach to pick her up in the morning, to drive her to the next village by the time the mail was delivered, and to take her home by dusk.

Do not use a comma before etc.: I bought apples, oranges, plums etc. However, the use of etc. usually suggests laziness on the writer's part and should be avoided.

If two or more adjectives precede a noun, use commas to separate them: This is a bright, cheery, wonderful day. If the adjective preceding the noun is integral to the noun, omit the comma before it: She returned home with a white, frisky toy poodle. Wilson Follett offers an example in which the adjectives integral to the noun are several, and argues persuasively against using any commas: He was wearing his battered old canvas fishing hat.

Use a comma to introduce a direct quotation of a complete sentence: Mr. Chrétien said, "I expect to be in Parliament today." If more than one sentence follows, introduce the quotation with a colon. If a quoted sentence is broken in two by the attribution, surround the attribution with commas: "There is much to do," she said, "but it can wait until tomorrow." If the attribution ends the sentence, place a comma after the quotation and follow the attribution

with a period: "There is nothing for me to do," he said. "I feel bored."

Do not use the closing comma in the quotation if it ends with a question mark or exclamation mark: "Do you understand?" she asked.

Do not use a comma to introduce an indirect quotation or a quotation in part: He said he felt bored. The doctor said there was "nothing to do to save his misspent life."

Where a comma or period ends a quotation, place it inside the quotation marks even in the case of partial quotations: He said it was a "scrumptious meal."

When the attribution falls in the middle of an indirect quotation, surround it with commas: When taking a shower, he said, he uses eucalytus soap. Note that if the comma after "said" were removed, the sentence's meaning would change significantly, indicating that he was taking a shower when he mentioned his favourite soap.

Use commas in figures above 999: There are 1,000 reasons not to do this. Exceptions include years (1993), addresses (2013 Sherbrooke St. W.), page numbers (She turned to page 1273) and telephone numbers.

Do not use commas before "of" indicating place or position if a person is mentioned for the first time (George Bennett of Toronto) or is being distinguished from others in the story with the same name (Mr. Bennett of Inco as opposed to Mr. Bennett of Ford). These are defining phrases. But use commas if we are merely providing additional information about someone under discussion (Mr. Bennett, of Toronto, added that he . . .). This is a non-defining expression, in the same category as "Mr. Bennett, a Liberal, said. . . ."

Strunk and White note that a comma may take the place of a conjunction in separating two independent sentences if they are short and alike in form: Man proposes,

God disposes. Be cautious here; push too hard and you will be guilty of a run-on sentence. The general rule requires a conjunction, a semi-colon, a colon or a division into two sentences.

dash The dash is used as default punctuation to cover the inevitable differences between spoken and formal written speech: the pauses, the changes in direction, the grammatical aberrations that defy the normal punctuation signposts. This use is legitimate, even encouraged, because it makes the quote easier to understand. For example: "There isn't any way to—it isn't in the province's interests to move in that direction," the Premier said.

The dash may be used in place of a comma to give strong emphasis to a particular thought within a sentence: The man swore—violently—that he knew no such thing. He had only one gun with him—and a good thing, too.

Dashes are routinely used by some writers, sometimes in great profusion throughout a story, as parentheses. That is, they insert an extraneous thought into the main grammatical thread of a sentence, and set it off with a pair of dashes rather than a pair of brackets: When he walked down the street—he enjoyed a morning stroll—the shopkeepers would call from their stores. Too often, such constructions are a crutch for lazy or sloppy writing, and are on the borderline of comprehensibility for the rushed reader of a daily paper. In most cases, strictly parenthetical inserts are best flagged with brackets.

The dash sets off a list within the sentence: By the end of the day, he had dealt with so many problems— broken machinery, a bad back, an angry boss—that he was ready to collapse. **Parentheses** are preferable for this purpose; their advantage is that the reader knows going in that the statement will be parenthetic. (See parentheses, below.)

If an author's name is cited after a quotation, lead into it with a dash: "It was the best of times, it was the worst of times."—Charles Dickens.

ellipsis An ellipsis is a series of three dots, separated by thin spaces, to indicate the omission of a word or words from a quotation. If any words are omitted from a direct quotation, whether for reasons of space or irrelevance, always insert an ellipsis. The original line: "I love your applause, I really, truly do, but please stop." As amended: "I love your applause . . . but please stop." The purpose, an important one, is to let the reader know that something is missing that might conceivably alter the tone or sense of the passage. A good reporter will not alter a quotation if the effect is distortive, but even the most thoughtful abridgments should not be passed off as the true quotation. (See also square brackets, under parentheses, below.)

There is no substitute for an ellipsis. Stopping a quotation to insert an attribution (the minister stated) does not entitle the writer to pick it up again two or three sentences later, unless the dots are added: "There is no reason to disbelieve me," the minister stated. ". . . I am an honest man."

Do not count a period at the end of a sentence as part of an ellipsis. As a matter of style, we place the period first, followed by a full space and then the ellipsis: "I was wrong. . . . Please forgive me."

The ellipsis is sometimes used to indicate an incomplete thought or a voice trailing off: "I thought that maybe . . ." In these cases, the number of periods is not crucial, but use this construction only if there is no possibility that it will be confused with the omission of words actually spoken.

When a partial quotation is used in a headline, deck or pull quote, the words appearing within quotation marks must be precisely as they appear in the text of the story. Excised words must be replaced with ellipses. The alternative is to drop the quotation marks. Any time an editor plays fast and loose with a quotation, the reader is given cause to mistrust us.

exclamation point Use sparingly, for expressions of rage, surprise and similar emotions: "How dare you!" he cried. Aha!

Often a comma or period will work as well: "How dare you," he cried. If a longer sentence needs an exclamation point to make the desired impression, it is probably a sentence in need of rewriting. (The same applies to italics, for which see the main entry.)

hyphen As a general rule, use a hyphen when two or more words modifying a noun are essential to each other, and when the absence of a hyphen might create misunderstanding: corn-coloured silk, small-arms dealers, free-trade pamphlet.

Use a hyphen if the prefix to a word ends in the same vowel that begins that word: co-operate, re-enact. Use it also if the same consonant is used three times in a row: shell-like.

Noun phrases create a special problem. One may speak of an ex-president, but to speak of an ex-prime minister suggests that the person is still a minister, but no longer prime. Try to find other constructions, in this case former prime minister. If the noun phrase is used adjectivally, and there is no way to recast the sentence, place hyphens between all parts of the phrase: then-prime-minister Pierre Trudeau. Similarly, use a hyphen between the prefix anti and already-hyphenated expressions (an anti-sales-tax demonstration).

If an adjectival expression stands alone, without its noun, in the role of a predicate adjective (after a "to be" verb or equivalent, such as is, was, will be, seems, appears, looks, sounds, smells, feels), there is no hyphen: This

artist is well known. That roast smells well done. If the expression precedes the noun it modifies, use a hyphen: a well-known artist.

The entire adjectival expression must be hyphenated: a 47-year-old man, not a 47-year old man. If the expression "first-degree murder" itself becomes an adjective modifying another noun, it gains another hyphen: a first-degree-murder charge. Often, a better option is to flop the sentence: a charge of first-degree murder.

Use a hyphen when writing of millions or billions of dollars: $2-million.

parentheses These are round brackets surrounding an incidental thought: He had a farm in Sherbrooke (in the Eastern Townships) to which he returned often. They also surround nicknames supplied with more formal names: R. T. (Arty) Jones.

Parentheses may clarify the meaning of a sentence, but they may also be a sign of a poorly worded sentence or one that should be broken in two.

If the parentheses contain a complete sentence, the closing punctuation goes inside the brackets. If the bracketed thought is part of a larger sentence, the punctuation goes outside: He told the crowd that he would do as he had done before (in dealing with the public service). An exception is made if a question mark or exclamation point applies to the bracketed material rather than to the sentence as a whole: He was shocked (who wouldn't be?) to find a ghost in his room.

Use parentheses when the Canadian equivalent of foreign money is given: She paid the driver 20 zlotys ($7) for the ride. Use them to specify which country's currency is meant: It costs $500 (U.S.). In the case of some proper names, parentheses may be necessary to distinguish between two cities: the London (Ont.) General Hospital.

If, for the sake of clarity, you insert your own words into a quotation, place those words in **square brackets**: "I had never seen him [Mr. Jones] before tonight." This will distinguish the insertion from any parenthetic comments that might be in the material quoted: "If I am right (and I believe I am), Mr. [Arthur] Jones is in the hall tonight."

period The period ends a declarative sentence: I walked to the door. It occasionally ends a rhetorical question: Why don't we stop here for the night.

The period ends most abbreviations: etc., Ltd., Inc. We make an exception for abbreviations of weights and measures (kg, C, km).

Use periods after people's initials (J. P. Smith) and in geographical terms with two letters (B.C.). Do not use periods in geographical terms of three letters or more (PEI), in the initials of organizations (CBC) or in acronyms (NATO, CIDA).

question mark Use a question mark at the end of a question, or to turn a declarative statement into a question: You turned the tap off? Do not use it for indirect questions: He wondered why his brother had not come home.

In sentences in which more than one question is being asked, use only one mark: Where was the soldier when he asked, "Who goes there?"

In sentences incorporating a partial quotation, the placement of the question mark depends on whether it applies to the entire sentence or only the quotation: How do you deal with "the man who has everything"? The look on his face suggested an attitude of "who cares?"

quotation marks Take care to close a quotation once you have opened it.

In direct quotations, the marks surround the words being quoted and any accompanying punctuation marks: He said, "I have no idea where we are. Do you?"

With quotations in part, place commas and periods inside the quotation marks whether or not they belong to the quotation: He always supplemented his coffee with "a wee touch of brandy." Semi-colons and colons remain outside the marks: I offered him a "wee touch of brandy"; he refused. The placement of question marks and exclamation points depends on whether they apply to the entire sentence or to the words being quoted: Do you seriously expect me to board a "ship of fools"? He sprang from his bath with a loud "Eureka!"

If one quotation falls within another, use single marks for the quotation inside, and double marks for any quotation inside that: "He asked me whether I ate meat, and I replied, 'Only chicken.'" (When a single mark

and a double mark abut, separate them with a thin space.)

Place foreign and French words in italics, not quotation marks.

Transcripts do not require quotation marks:

Judge Henry: And what did you do then?

Mr. Walters: I took the box back to the shed.

If a direct quotation from one person continues for more than one paragraph, omit the closing quotation marks at the end of the first paragraph, but retain the opening marks at the start of the next. When quoting two people in succession, make the second attribution before or soon after the second quotation begins, so as not to confuse the reader.

You may use quotation marks to introduce unfamiliar jargon, where possible with an accompanying explanation: The NATO leaders spoke of "MIRVable missiles." No quotation marks are necessary for subsequent references. Do not use quotation marks for a legitimate word merely because it may be unfamiliar to some readers; if you suspect it is exotic enough to confuse people, use another word or put the definition in parentheses.

Use italics, not quotation marks, to set off the titles of books, stories, plays, movies, works of music and poems: *The Iliad, How the West Was Won.* Do not use italics or quotation marks for headlines or the names of periodicals: Man lands on moon, The Globe and Mail, Maclean's. Use quotation marks for slogans, but upper-case only the initial letter of the first word: "Solidarity forever."

Use parentheses, not quotation marks, for nicknames supplied with formal names: J. F. (Tiny) Tinderbox.

semi-colon Use the semi-colon sparingly, without a conjunction, to join two sentences of equal weight: He walked into a store; it was empty.

Use it also instead of a comma, with a conjunction, if a sentence is already riddled with commas: He walked into the store, looked around and pulled a tin off the shelf; but the tin was empty, and he replaced it.

Use the semi-colon in lists that would be confusing without it: He ordered a cat with large, brown eyes; a goat, decorated with a sash; and five huge, ugly dogs.

Punjab

It is the name of both the state in India and the province in Pakistan. The fertile northern district called the Punjab, known for its wheat, was divided in the partition of 1947 into Punjab (India) and the larger Punjab (Pakistan). The Indian state was further divided in 1966, into Punjab and Haryana. (Haryana is primarily Hindi-speaking.)

About two-thirds of the people in India's Punjab speak Punjabi, while most of the rest speak Hindi. Sixty per cent of the people are Sikhs, some of whom want to make the state an independent country they call Khalistan.

The Pakistani province, which is almost entirely Punjabi-speaking, is the most densely populated and industrial in the country.

Punkeydoodles Corners

No apostrophe. This archetype of a tiny hamlet is in Ontario between Kitchener and Stratford, in the area of New Hamburg and Tavistock.

Punxsutawney, Pa.

Home of the meteorological groundhog Punxsutawney Phil. See Groundhog Day.

pupil and student

The difference involves an academic value judgment, but for our purposes all children in primary school should be called **pupils**. For high schools, colleges and universities, use **student**.

purdah

The system of secluding women; the screen used for doing so.

pure laine

Italics. This exclusionary expression, French for pure wool, describes descent from the founding families of Quebec, with no interbreeding along the way with Indians, anglophones or allophones. It should rarely make our pages, because, like WASP, it is almost always misused, is loaded with assumptions (most false), often implies superiority and is implicitly an insult to those who do not merit such a categorization.

Applying *pure laine* to a person implies that he or she accepts such a self-description. This is risky if the person has even a whiff of liberal leaning, because it finds favour almost exclusively with the few ultranationalists promoting a Quebec unsullied by *les autres*. We should treat this expression with the same circumspection that we give all comments on racial or cultural "purity."

purple prose

In regard to writing, "purple" means ornate, flowery. It does not mean sexually explicit. If we must label sex scenes with a colour, the usual one is blue.

purposely and purposefully

Use **purposely** to mean on purpose, intentionally. Use **purposefully** to mean motivated by a purpose or goal.

putdown

Pygmy

Use upper case for human groups and their members, but lower case to mean small, as in pygmy owl. Anthropologists apply the name Pygmy to any human group in which the average height of adult males is less than 150 centimetres (59 inches).

That means a taller-than-average member of the group is still called a Pygmy. Groups that are small in stature but slightly exceed the average height limit, such as most groups of Kalahari Bushmen, are called **pygmoid**. Several groups of true Pygmies are found in central Africa and in Asia. Those in Africa include the various Mbuti groups of Congo's (the former Zaire's) Ituri Forest, the Twa of the Lake Kivu area and the Tswa of the Congo River marshlands. The Pygmy groups of Asia, found in the Andaman Islands, Malaya and the Philippines, have their own names, but are also known by the generic term Negrito.

pyorrhea (not pya-).

It means any continuous discharge of pus, not just such a condition of the gums, which is called pyorrhea alveolaris.

Pyrenees

They are the mountains separating France and Spain. They are mainly forest and pasture land.

Pyrrhic victory, upper-case.

pythons

They are found in the Old World only, from Africa to Australia. The equivalent large constricting snakes in the New World are the boas.

Q-tips
A trade name. The generic term is cotton swab.

Qantas Airways Ltd.
Upper- and lower-case, with no u.

Qatar
Adjective and people: Qatari. Currency: riyal. Capital: Doha.

No u. It occupies the Qatar Peninsula, which juts into the Persian Gulf about halfway along its southern shore, at the conjunction of Saudi Arabia and the United Arab Emirates. It has a long association with Britain, which has continued since it declared its independence in 1971. Its other major centres include Dukham, the centre of oil production, and Umm Said, the oil terminal, principal port and industrial zone. In addition to oil, Qatar produces ammonia, urea, cement and some steel. It has a population of about 600,000. The long-time emir, Sheik Khalifa bin Hamad Thani, was overthrown by his son Sheik Hamad bin Khalifa Thani in a bloodless coup on June 27, 1995.

Qattara Depression
Note the double t. It is the large, low-lying desert in northwestern Egypt, as much as 130 metres below sea level.

qimmik
Not kimmik. No u. It is Inuktitut for dog. Requires italics and a translation.

quadraphonic, but **quadriplegic**.

quadrilateral group
The quad. The informal name for the trade ministers from the United States, Japan, the European Union and Canada, who meet every three months. The term requires an explanation if the context is unclear.

quadrillion
A thousand trillion; a 1 followed by 15 zeros (but in Britain it means a million trillion). Do not inflict spelled-out numbers larger than a trillion on the reader without explaining them as a multiple of trillions or giving the number of zeros. See numbers.

quadroon
Do not label a person with this word. If it is truly important to specify the racial mix, say the person has three white grandparents and one black, but be aware that in North America the black grandparent was almost certainly also of mixed race. See octoroon, race.

quadruple alliance
Four-country alliance is better. If "quadruple alliance" appears in a quote, use lower case in most instances, but upper case in historical references to the alliance of England, France, Austria and the Netherlands against Spain in 1718, and to that of England, Austria, Russia and Prussia against Napoleon in 1814.

Quai d'Orsay

Use to refer to the French foreign office only if the context is clear. The ministry is located at this quay, on the Left Bank.

Quakers

An acceptable name in all references to the Society of Friends, and to its members.

quality

To express degree of excellence, it requires an adjective, such as poor quality, low quality, good quality, top quality. It is a noun only, and so to become a modifier should properly be put into a phrase, as in material of good quality. Avoid using it as an adjective, as in a good-quality product, although this restriction may be relaxed in a very short headline. Never use standing alone as an adjective (a quality product), even in a head.

quandary

Qu'Appelle, Sask.

quarantine, isolation

People are placed in isolation if they are ill. Quarantine is for people who are (or appear to be) healthy so far, but who it is thought may become ill.

quarter horse

quarter section

No hyphen. These blocks of 160 acres, a quarter of a square-mile survey "section," are still common units of land sale in the Prairie provinces and in the western United States. It is unnecessary and possibly misleading to convert to 64.75 hectares.

quartet and quintet

Use these terms for musical groups or compositions, or for other formal groupings (a quartet of sonnets). Do not use them for any old four or five

people being referred to, as in a quartet of bank robbers. Also see duo, trio.

quash

This is the usual term (not squash) for putting down a rebellion or military resistance. It is also used in a legal sense to mean set aside or make void, as in quash an injunction.

quasi

Too ambiguous to be useful in most news contexts, except in direct quotes and in such well-established expressions as quasi-judicial, in reference to government tribunals. Before nouns, it can mean either resembling or not genuine (or, in law, resembling superficially but actually different, as in a quasi-corporation). Before adjectives, with a hyphen, it means nearly (as in quasi-human), partly (quasi-exempt) or slightly (quasi-humorous). An expression such as quasi-official could mean partly official, or almost official, or only seemingly official.

Quebec and the rest of Canada

Take care when using this expression in the context of the internal debate raging within Quebec. We must not be seen as having accepted the argument of one side that only the provincial government speaks for Quebeckers. They are also federal electors, with a strong say in the national government.

Quebec City

In placelines, make it simply Quebec. A new, larger Quebec City (population 515,000) was created on Jan. 1, 2002, with the amalgamation of 13 municipalities: Beauport, Cap-Rouge, Charlesbourg, Lac-Saint-Charles, L'Ancienne-Lorette, Loretteville, Quebec City, Saint-Augustin-de-Desmaures, Sainte-Foy, Saint-Emile, Sillery, Val-Bélair and Vanier. The new city has eight

boroughs, and is the second-largest in
Quebec, after Montreal.

See Montreal, Lévis, Trois-
Rivières, Longueuil and Gatineau.

Quebec Conference

Use upper case for the pre-
Confederation gathering of 1864, and
for two meetings of Churchill and
Roosevelt during the Second World
War, in August of 1943 and
September of 1944. The 1943 meeting
was also attended by King and the
Chinese foreign minister.

Quebec heater

A tall, cylindrical wood stove.

Quebecker

Use this for a resident of the
province, following the style of
frolic/frolicking, picnic/picnicking and
traffic/trafficking. However, if the
context demands that we stress we are
speaking of a French-speaking
resident, in contrast to others in the
story who are not, we may use the
word Québécois. The feminine is
Québécoise.

Quebec lieutenant

Lower-case. This term is usually
applied to a person of cabinet rank
who advises a prime minister on
Quebec matters and usually also runs
the federal party's organization in
Quebec. Leaders of opposition parties
also may have Quebec lieutenants.

Quebec premiers

Be aware that there have been two
premiers named Daniel Johnson. The
father, leader of the Union Nationale,
was premier from 1966 to 1968. The
son was premier from late 1993, when
he succeeded Robert Bourassa as
Liberal leader, to the general election
of September, 1994. Another son,
Pierre-Marc Johnson, was Parti
Québécois premier for just over two
months in 1985, after succeeding
René Lévesque as party leader.

Quebec provincial police

See *Sûreté du Québec*.

Quebec Winter Carnival

Upper-case. Note the spelling of
the French equivalent, Carnaval. Its
snowman mascot, Bonhomme
Carnaval, is also known as Jean
Bonhomme.

Queen

Use upper case when referring to a
specific monarch of any country (the
Queen began her visit). Use lower
case generically (three English
queens), and in references to chess,
cards and insects.

Canada's Queen should be called
simply the Queen, not Queen
Elizabeth (which was the reference for
her mother) or Queen Elizabeth II.
However, use names in first reference
to queens of other countries. See
Royal Family.

Queen Elizabeth 2, the ship.

May be called QE2 in second
reference and in headlines.

Queen Mother, the

Upper-case. The mother of
Elizabeth II, and wife of George VI,
was born on Aug. 4, 1900, and died on
March 30, 2002. Do not use the term
Queen Mum in news stories, and do
not write of Queen Mother Elizabeth.
Ontario's Queen Elizabeth Way was
named for her, not her daughter.

Queens

No apostrophe in the Prince
Edward Island provincial ridings (1st
Queens etc.), or in Queens Acres,
Ont.; Queens Bay, B.C.; the New York
borough.

Queen's Bench, Court of

This is the name given the highest
trial courts in Alberta, Manitoba, New
Brunswick and Saskatchewan. They
are the equivalent of the Supreme
Court's trial division in B.C.,

Newfoundland, Nova Scotia, PEI and the three territories, and of Quebec Superior Court and Ontario Superior Court, and also do the work of County Court in Nova Scotia. See courts.

Queensberry Rules

The sportsman under whose sponsorship these modern regulations for boxing (the three-minute round, the 10-second count etc.) were published in 1867 was the Marquess (not -quis) of Queensberry (not -bury). They were actually written by John Graham Chambers of the British Amateur Athletic Club.

Queen's Counsel, QC

An honorary status bestowed on senior lawyers.

Queen's (and King's) English.

Queen's Park

May be used as a sobriquet for the Ontario legislature building and for the Ontario government, if we are sure the context makes the meaning clear to readers in other provinces.

Queen's Printer

Upper-case for the apparatus in the federal government or in any provincial government responsible for publishing official documents and records.

Queens Quay

No apostrophe in the Toronto street name, but there is one in Queen's Quay Terminal.

Queen's University, Kingston.

question mark, see punctuation.

questionnaire

Question Period

Use upper case for the time near the beginning of a sitting day reserved for questions to ministers. Lower-case in other contexts, as in time set aside for questions after a discussion or speech.

Quetzalcoatl

Note the l in mid-word. This plumed serpent is said to have ruled the Toltec empire, which was pre-Aztec.

queue

Use this spelling (not cue) for a lineup and for a pigtail. Line and lineup, and the verb line up, are also acceptable.

Quezon City

Once 16 kilometres northeast of Manila but now surrounded by greater Manila, it was the capital of the Philippines from independence in 1946 until 1976. It is still the site of some government departments, most notably the defence headquarters and military academy.

Quiet Revolution

Upper-case for the period of the Quebec Liberal administration of Jean Lesage, 1960 to 1966, and for his major social and education reforms.

quintal

In Newfoundland, 122 pounds of fish, or a container that will hold that weight of dried salt cod.

quintet, see quartet.

quip

There is rarely any need to use it. To qualify as a quip, a remark or retort must be so sharp, clever or witty that adding such expressions as "he quipped" risks insulting the reader with overexplanation. If a person is exaggerating or being ironic, not intending to be taken literally, we usually need more explanation to ensure that no one is misled.

quisling

Lower-case for a traitor. Vidkun Quisling was the Norwegian fascist leader who aided the Nazi invasion in 1940 and led the subsequent puppet government. He was executed for treason in 1945.

quite

Quite legitimately, the adverb means either entirely (I'm quite exhausted; are you quite finished; not quite) or else to a large extent (I'm quite happy with my job). Take care the reader knows which meaning we intend, and guard against overuse.

quixotic

Lower-case, despite the allusion to Don Quixote. It should not be used to mean merely whimsical, or wandering among various places or interests. It means ridiculously chivalrous or romantic, or having impractically high ideals and goals; dreaming the impossible dream.

quoits

quota

A quota is that portion of a total that a person, body or group is entitled to receive, or is obligated to supply. It should not be used when there is no formal arrangement, no larger total or no question of giving or receiving, as in she has her quota of troubles. In such cases, use "share of troubles" or "all the troubles she can handle."

quotations

Direct quotations add authority to a report, and are our first choice when the speaker is clear and concise, particularly if he or she is also forceful or colourful. But if the speaker is long-winded and confusing, a paraphrase does a better job of conveying information; we can always use partial quotations for important or colourful passages. Here are some points to watch in both direct and indirect quotes:

If something is enclosed in quotation marks, it should be the speaker's exact words, with the exception of corrected mispronunciations and minor grammatical departures that are common in everyday speech. The spoken "gonna" and "o'" should be changed to "going to" and "of," for example, unless a particular flavour is sought for a feature. However, taking this too far can affect a newspaper's credibility, particularly since the reader may have already heard the statement on TV or radio. An "um" or "ah" may be left out, but we cannot omit such recognizable words as "like" and "you know" and pass off the quote as exact.

We usually retreat into paraphrase if grammatical and other spoken lapses make a quote rambling or confusing. In particular, do not include such lapses if it will appear that the intention is to hold the speaker up as an uneducated person or user of a quaint dialect, except in those very rare stories in which this is the point. Slang may be retained, especially when it is obviously being used for effect, as may regional words and such practices as referring to inanimate things as he or she, but regional pronunciation generally should not be reflected in spelling (pardnuh, de b'y dat builds de boat). This rule applies as well to quotations from people whose first language is not English. Do not retain profanity and vulgarity, even with letters removed, unless there are exceptional circumstances and approval is obtained from the editor-in-chief, deputy editor, Report on Business editor, associate editor or their deputies. See obscene language.

There is no way of inserting "[sic]" into a quote without implying that the speaker is misinformed or uneducated, and without bringing readers to an abrupt halt while they figure out the error. If a spoken slip is likely to mislead the reader (as when a person gives a wrong date, or says Second World War instead of First World War), our first choice is to use an

indirect quote to report this part of the sentence. If it is vital that the direct quote be used in full regardless of the error (rare indeed is the situation that justifies misleading or confusing the reader even for a moment), we would have to follow the quote immediately with an explanation. We should never call attention to grammatical errors in giving attribution, as in "Mr. Smith said, oblivious to the double negative."

One common and unacceptable form of straying from the speaker's exact words involves changing tenses and personal pronouns, in effect recasting the quotation into indirect but retaining the quotation marks. For example, if someone says "I will have your jobs," we cannot use quotation marks if we report him saying he would "have their jobs."

Can a person be misquoted even if we use the exact words? Yes, if we leave out nearby sentences that explain, modify or qualify the remark, or do not report facial expressions and gestures that might be important parts of the context. An ironic smile or a rolling of the eyes speaks volumes to the reporter, and these must be conveyed to the reader whenever they affect interpretation.

Do not place quotation marks around statements people "might" have made – a rhetorical device that

puts words in their mouths for satirical or argumentative purposes. You may have seen such "hypothetical quotes" elsewhere (in some popular biographies or histories, for example, and even in these their use is controversial). But they are extremely rare in newspapers, whose readers are typically rushed, reading primarily for information and not expecting this sort of nuance.

In the spirit of "never say never," there may arise some instance in which it is journalistically justifiable to use the device of hypothetical quotes, but we should take care to eliminate all confusion by tipping off the reader beforehand, not afterward, that the quote is not real, and we should set it off typographically (introduced by a colon, perhaps, or in italics if necessary), but not with quotation marks.

Translations of direct quotes from **other languages** pose a special problem for our foreign correspondents and for our reporters in Quebec and Ottawa. TV and radio reports can carry the original language at reduced volume as an undertone to the voice of the reporter or translator, a technique that clearly informs the listener that the words are not exactly those of the subject. In print journalism, the lack of a comparable handy device does not reduce our obligation to the reader and the person being quoted. It has become a convention that we may use quotation marks, presenting translations as if they were direct quotes rendered in English, but it should be clear that we have done this.

If a statement is made on Bulgarian TV, for example, our readers certainly know it was not in English. However, in reporting on interviews etc. when this is not as obvious, Globe writers should indicate that the interview was conducted in Spanish, that the news conference was conducted partly or mostly in French etc. It is then unnecessary to specify the language of each quote, unless this is significant, as when a politician gives conflicting messages to different audiences. (The requirement for indicating that the direct quotes we report are actually translations is relaxed for stories from other sources if it is impossible to determine the original language of the interview or statement.)

If a colloquial expression makes literal translation of a significant quote difficult, we should inform the reader of the problem and offer the conflicting interpretations. If we have any reason to doubt the accuracy of a translation done by others, we should tell the reader the source (said through an interpreter etc.).

Attribution should be clear, but not insultingly so. In a report on a speech or interview, or any other story in which extensive quotes are all from the same person, continual repetition of "she said" or "Mr. Green said" after direct quotes is pedantic and tiresome. The use of quotation marks alone is usually enough of an indication that these are the words of that person. A renewed attribution is usually necessary if we have interrupted the flow with paragraphs of background or colour, but can often be omitted if a series of direct quotes has merely been interrupted by an indirect one.

The best place for the verb of attribution (said etc.) is usually after the name or pronoun (not said he, said Ms. Brown). However, if the name is followed by a long modifier or description that would create an awkward separation of name and verb, we may place the verb first (said James Green, an economics professor and former adviser to the governor of the Bank of Canada).

Our usual verb in attributions is "said," but others are justified if the words spoken do not provide a clue to meaning or tone. For example, the simple quote "You'll hear from me" takes on various shades of meaning with various verbs—he vowed, he

promised, he warned, he shouted. We might also convey mood by augmenting "said" with such terms as menacingly, angrily, with a smirk, with a grin, with a chuckle, with a laugh, with a scowl. (Do not contract these to he grinned, he scowled etc.) We do not use such verbs as quipped and cracked unless the remark was truly funny, sharp or witty (see quip).

Avoid claimed and noted, and use admitted only if it truly applies. Admitted implies acknowledgment of a wrongdoing; claimed implies disbelief on our part; noted implies that the statement is universally considered true. See separate entries on these words.

Attributors are almost always in past tense (said, not says). See tenses.

An **ellipsis** (three dots) is our only way of indicating that material has been omitted from a direct quotation. It is not enough to end a paragraph with "he said," and then to pick up at a sentence from elsewhere in the speech or interview. We must either place an ellipsis at the start of the next sentence quoted, or introduce the sentence with an expression such as Earlier, Later or Elsewhere in the interview, or On the subject of, or Turning to etc. See ellipsis, under punctuation.

If we insert any of our own material in parentheses within a direct quote, we must use **square brackets**: He said, "I don't want you [the police] coming in here again."

We always flag to the reader that there has been a change of speaker, and we do not rely for this on the subtle fact that the previous quote ended with close-quote marks. It is annoying in the extreme to read a quoted sentence through in the belief that Ms. White is still speaking, only to have it end with "Mr. Brown said." The clearest and most economical solution is to put each new speaker at the start of the paragraph, before the material quoted. Exceptions are obvious changes in speaker in a question-and-answer context, such as a court examination in which lawyer and witness are easily differentiated, and in certain banter and repartee.

We enclose one or two words in quotation marks, in what is known as a **fragmentary quote**, only if the words are unusual or controversial (he called the building a "death trap"), if we are introducing an unfamiliar term (police are worried about a flood of "crank" on the Edmonton drug market) or if the reader requires an indication that words are being used ironically, not to be taken literally (the "little war" has claimed thousands of lives). In such ironic contexts, the quotation marks are a substitute for "so-called"; it is redundant to use both. If the quotes are used to flag an unfamiliar term, tipping readers that it is a term they are not expected to know, we explain the term immediately afterward, and do not use quotation marks in subsequent references.

We do not use quotation marks around commonplace words (he said the "raid" netted few drugs). If we were to do so, the reader would be confused, looking for irony or unusual meanings where none exist. We do not use quotation marks around slang or colloquial expressions; if they are worth using, they can stand on their own.

"Quote" is an acceptable word to mean "quotation" if the words were spoken by a contemporary individual, or possibly written in a note or letter, but it sounds jarring in contexts involving historical figures, literature, religious works, texts, law books etc. (Say quotes from the shortstop or the Prime Minister, but quotations from the Bible, Browning or Churchill.) "Quotes" is also an acceptable term to mean "quotation marks," if there is no ambiguity.

In reporting quotes secondhand, the verb "quote" does not stand alone in constructions like this: The leaders will be tried, the chairman was quoted. We must say was quoted as saying, arguing, ordering, demanding or some such.

For a discussion of punctuation in quotes, see punctuation.

qurunnamik

The common Inuktitut word for thank you (many thanks). Requires italics and a translation.

Quyon, Que.

R

R&B, R&D, R&R

Acceptable in second reference, and in headlines, for rhythm and blues, research and development, and rest and recreation. The ampersand is used without spaces when it is between letters. See ampersand.

rabies, singular.

race

It is better to identify people geographically, by continent or country, than by race, which is a biological term. If it is truly relevant to specify a race, we should be aware that science has moved far beyond differentiating races only on the basis of such things as colour, hair type and body measurement, a method that had first produced three "biological races," Caucasoid, Negroid and Mongoloid, and then five with the splitting off of Australoid and American Indian. Racial groups are now defined according to precisely measurable inherited traits, such as blood type, amino acids, enzyme deficiencies and the preponderance of certain congenital defects and disorders. The finding has been that all current racial groups are mixtures. They are broadly defined as eight to 10 **geographic races**, given the scientific names Caucasoid, Negroid, Indic, Mongoloid, American Indian, Australoid, Melanesian, Micronesian and Polynesian. (The last three are combined by some into Oceanic, while Negroid is divided by some into Capoid and Congoid.) For the purpose

of most non-scientific news stories, we replace Caucasoid with the more familiar terms Caucasian, white or European, depending on the context. For Negroid we use black, for Mongoloid we use Oriental, for Australoid we use Aborigine and for Indic we use South Asian. (However, it is better to say that a person or his forebears came from India, Pakistan, Bangladesh or Sri Lanka. We use the term South Asian only to group these peoples, or when the specific country is unknown.) In Canada, preserve the distinction between Indian and Inuit in stories specifically about race, since most scholars did not include the Inuit when they split American Indians from the Mongoloid race. If there is a chance of confusion with people from India, the term Indian may be replaced by the name of the language group, such as Cree, Sarcee, Blood. See native people.

In places where population groups are isolated, either physically or culturally, to the extent that they behave as distinct genetic groups, the geographic races have been divided further into **local races** and further still into **microraces**. These differentiate several Mediterranean local races from each other and from those in northern Europe, for example, and differentiate Welsh from Irish and the population of Oslo from that of Stockholm. However, for clarity we should not use the terms race, local race and microrace to refer to these subgroups, except in scientific stories on this subject. We should also not apply the word race to non-biological divisions such as national groups (the French, English or Scottish race), religious groups (the Jewish race) or language groups. For these, the word people makes the point without any spurious biological overtones. The term human race is also biologically meaningless but is acceptable, as an idiomatic holdover from the days when we also spoke of the avian race, the finny tribe. However, prefer the more accurate terms human species or humankind. Many of our readers object to the term mankind. See women and language.

Also be aware that an increasing number of people in the world, particularly in the Americas, are of mixed race, including such large groups as the various mestizo populations of Central and South America and the Métis in Canada. Some distinct mixed-race groups already qualify scientifically as genetic local races. We should not get into the game of measuring skin shade to declare that a person obviously of mixed race is either Caucasian or black, nor should we use such specific terms as mulatto, quadroon, octoroon, half-breed.

In stories in which physical distinctions are important, such as those about searches for missing children or fugitives, use racial names if the person has the dominant characteristics of that race (white, black, Oriental, South Asian etc.), or give a country of origin or ancestry. If a person is of mixed race, simply say so. It is helpful to add the races of the parents if these are known for certain (white and black, white and Cree etc.). Otherwise, simply describe the skin colour, hair, eyes and other salient features. Do not use such terms as part Indian, part black, which carry the implication that white is the standard.

race and national origin

These should be included only when truly relevant, as in stories about ethnic cultural events or about police searches for missing persons or fugitives, or in biographical stories in which background is an issue. We must be especially scrupulous about avoiding irrelevant references in stories about criminal charges or other matters in which identifying a person's race or national origin might unfairly associate an entire group with criminal or anti-social activity. However, we do not shy from such references when they are germane to the case, as when an assault was the result of racial taunts.

racetrack, raceway, racecourse, racehorse

All are one word, except in such proper names as Pimlico Race Course, The Woodlands Race Track. Use racetrack for thoroughbreds, raceway for harness racing. For other sports specify car track, stock car track, dog track.

rack

Rack one's brains, racked with pain. See wrack.

raconteur

racquet

Use this spelling for the racquets used in tennis and similar sports. Note that it is English. The French word, also used for snowshoe, has no c and a feminine ending: *raquette*.

radar

Lower-case. It is an acronym for radio detection and ranging. The two main types are pulsed radar and continuous-wave radar.

radio

As a combining form, its most common meanings are having to do with either radio or radiation. All the terms involving radiation are single words (radioactive, radiocarbon, radiochemistry). Most of the terms involving radio are two words (radio astronomy, radio beacon, radio phone, radio spectrum, radio station, radio telephone), but check the dictionary because there are some exceptions— radiolocation, radiogram.

Use upper case for an official government station (Radio Havana) but lower case to indicate that various broadcasts were monitored in a certain city (Beirut radio). Lower-case radio station, as in radio station CHML.

Radio-Canada

The French name for the CBC is confusing to some because it appears to deal only with radio. A better term in news stories is the French service of the CBC. However, Radio-Canada may be used for variety in a story that deals with both the English and French services, if there is a need to differentiate and the context is clear. (There is rarely any need to use the full name, Société Radio-Canada.) Note the hyphen, but also note the lack of one in Radio Canada International, the short-wave service. (Until 1972, it was called the International Service of the CBC.)

radiocarbon dating

This is a proper term for the method of determining the age of objects by measuring the radioactive decay of carbon 14. But this isotope has too short a half-life to date objects older than about 50,000 years, and so for older ones other radioactive decay series must be used, including potassium-argon, rubidium-strontium, ionium-thorium and various series that end in lead. The generic term covering all these methods, including radiocarbon dating, is radioisotope dating.

railway and railroad

Railway is the Canadian term. It should be used generically in stories

about other countries, including the United States, and to translate the names of railways and railway ministries from other languages. Use Railroad only in proper U.S. names (and note Long Island Rail Road).

rain forest

This is the correct term not only for the wet equatorial forests but also for forests in more temperate areas that have high annual rainfall. The word jungle means simply a tangle of vegetation. In most rain forests, jungle is found only where light penetrates the canopy along roads and rivers or in clearings. Elsewhere, these forests are mostly parklike, with relatively open space between huge tree trunks.

raise and rise

Raise is a verb, but idiom allows its use as a noun in regard to pay, wages, salary. For increases in other things, including prices, the noun is rise.

RAM and ROM

In the computer world, they mean random access memory and read only memory (no hyphens). For general news stories, we must explain that these indicate that the memory either is one on which the user can add, delete and change data, or is one used for the computer's control program and is unavailable to the user.

Ramadan

Upper-case. The ninth month of the Muslim calendar, during which devout Muslims abstain from food, drink and other pleasures in daylight hours to commemorate the revelation of the Koran to Mohammed.

ramp up

Avoid this jargon. Say the leader increased pressure, not ramped up pressure.

rancour

But drop the u for **rancorous**.

Rand Formula

Upper-case. It refers to the provision, widely accepted in collective agreements, that union dues will be automatically deducted from the pay of all members of a bargaining unit whether they join the union or not. The deduction is known as the compulsory checkoff. The formula was the major provision in a binding settlement imposed by arbitrator Ivan Rand, a judge of the Supreme Court of Canada, to end the 1945 strike by members of the United Auto Workers against Ford Motor Co. in Windsor.

ranks, police and military

Spell out all military and police ranks in first reference. Abbreviations may be used in subsequent references for most ranks, as indicated below. (In stories containing several police or military people, a rank that has already been spelled out for one person may be abbreviated for first references to subsequent holders of that rank.)

As a courtesy, holders of hyphenated versions of higher ranks are bumped up to the full rank in second reference unless the exact rank is an issue in the story (Lieutenant-Colonel or Major-General William White may become Col. White or Gen. White subsequently), but we do not follow this practice with deputy police and fire chiefs and deputy commissioners, since there is only one person who holds the higher rank. It is no courtesy to bump someone down a notch, so we do not turn a staff sergeant, master corporal etc. into a plain Sgt. or Cpl. in second reference. Use upper case for ranks before a name, but lower case generically (he is a major-general).

In the military, there is a wide gulf between commissioned officers and other ranks (Chief Warrant Officer and below), and there is a significant distinction between subalterns and officers of field rank (major and

above). However, there is no such distinction among police, and the term "police officer" is proper idiom in Canada to refer to any rank, including a constable. For higher police ranks, use the actual title or the generic terms senior officer, high-ranking officer etc.

Police ranks Here is the rank structure of the **Toronto Police**, which is comparable to those in many other large cities. In second reference we abbreviate only those ranks indicated: Chief, Deputy Chief, Staff Superintendent (Staff Supt.), Superintendent (Supt.), Staff Inspector (Staff Insp.), Inspector (Insp.), Staff Sergeant (Staff Sgt.), Sergeant (Sgt.), Constable. In the detective division, the rank of Detective Sergeant (Det. Sgt.) is equivalent to staff sergeant, and Detective (Det.) is equal to Sergeant. There is also a designation of Detective Constable (Det. Constable). For pay purposes, constables are graded from fourth to first class, but we do not indicate this unless it is an issue (as when a constable is disciplined by being dropped a grade).

Here are the ranks in the **Ontario Provincial Police** and **RCMP** (abbreviations match those given similar ranks in the Toronto force):

OPP: Commissioner, Deputy Commissioner, Chief Superintendent (Chief Supt.), Superintendent, Inspector, Sergeant-Major (Sgt.-Maj.), Staff Sergeant, Sergeant, Constable. (Constables begin as probationary, then progress from third to first class.)

RCMP: Commissioner, Deputy Commissioner, Assistant Commissioner, Chief Superintendent, Superintendent, Inspector, Sergeant-Major (plus equivalent ranks of Corps Sergeant-Major, Staff Sergeant-Major), Staff Sergeant, Sergeant, Corporal (Cpl.), Constable (three grades).

In Quebec, we use the loose English translation of chief or head for the titles of *Directeur* or *Directeur-général*, and we translate *Agent* as Constable. In general, Quebec forces do not have the ranks of staff superintendent and superintendent, and so the ranks of chief inspector and inspector have a higher status, below the chiefs and assistant chiefs. Below them are the ranks of captain and lieutenant. Between sergeants and constables, the provincial force (*Sûreté du Québec*) interposes a corporal.

Military ranks There is a single rank (pay and seniority) structure in the Canadian Forces, but Maritime Command has reverted to traditional naval ranks, each of which has an equivalent level in Land Forces Command (army) and Air Command.

The ranks in Land Forces and Air Commands, with our abbreviations, are: General (Gen.), Lieutenant-General (Lt.-Gen.), Major-General (Maj.-Gen.), Brigadier-General (Brig.-Gen.), Colonel (Col.), Lieutenant-Colonel (Lt.-Col.), Major (no abbreviation), Captain (Capt.), Lieutenant (Lt.), 2nd Lieutenant (2Lt.), Officer Cadet (OCdt.), Chief Warrant Officer (CWO), Master Warrant Officer (MWO), Warrant Officer (WO), Sergeant (Sgt.), Master Corporal (MCpl.), Corporal (Cpl.) or the artillery's Bombardier, Private (Pte.).

The highest-ranking privates wear a single chevron as a badge of rank, but are still called private (there is no longer a rank of lance-corporal). Depending on role, privates in Land Forces Command have a variety of titles, which we do not abbreviate on second reference. These include Craftsman, Guardsman, Gunner, Rifleman, Sapper, Signalman, Trooper. Holders of the various Warrant Officer ranks assigned to a particular regiment may also have titles reflecting their roles, such as regimental or company sergeant-major. These are awkward enough that they are best used after

the name as a lower-case job description, but their abbreviations (RSM, CSM) would be appropriate before the name in subsequent references in a detailed story about a regiment.

The Maritime Command ranks are: Admiral (Adm.), Vice-Admiral (Vice-Adm.), Rear Admiral (Rear Adm.), Commodore (Cmdre.), Captain (Capt.), Commander (Cdr.), Lieutenant-Commander (LCdr.), Lieutenant (Lt.), Sub-Lieutenant (SLt.), Acting Sub-Lieutenant (ASLt.), Naval Cadet (NCdt), Chief Petty Officer 1st Class (CPO1), Chief Petty Officer 2nd Class (CPO2), Petty Officer 1st Class (PO1), Petty Officer 2nd Class (PO2), Master Seaman (MS), Leading Seaman (LS), Able Seaman (AB), Ordinary Seaman (OS). A naval captain is equal in rank to a colonel, and a naval lieutenant is equal to an army or air force captain. If the context of the story does not clearly put them in Maritime Command, their ranks are written this way: Captain (N), Capt.(N), Lieutenant (N), Lt.(N). Generically, they may be called a naval captain, a naval lieutenant. An able seaman wears one chevron, being equal to a senior-grade private in the other commands. A leading seaman wears two chevrons, being equal to a corporal, and a master seaman wears two chevrons with maple leaf, being equal to a master corporal.

Our abbreviations closely match those of the Canadian Forces, but we have added periods and have made one or two other changes for the sake of clarity.

For differing ranks in other countries, we use abbreviations only if the meaning is clear, such as Col.-Gen., Group Capt. In the United States, Rear Admiral has no hyphen.

rapee pie
No accents. Popular in Quebec and the Maritimes, particularly in Acadian

areas, it contains chicken, pork or rabbit, and potatoes and onions.

rapprochement

rapt

This is the proper adjective for such expressions as rapt attention. (It comes from rapture). Not to be confused with rapped or wrapped.

rarefy, rarefied

raspberry, a Bronx cheer.

rationale, the noun.

rattlesnake, one word. See massasauga.

rat trap

raucous

ravage and ravish

Ravage means to destroy, lay waste. Ravish means to fill with strong emotion, or to rape. An army ravages a town or the countryside, not ravishes.

rayon, lower-case.

It is produced from cellulose, not petroleum.

razor blade

razzle-dazzle

razzmatazz

RBI

The plural, by convention, is RBIs, even though the plural properly belongs to the first letter (runs batted in).

RCMP

There is no need to write out the full name, the Royal Canadian Mounted Police, even in first reference. The term Mounties is also acceptable in first reference. RCMP is normally plural (the RCMP are investigating), but the ear may demand a singular verb if the verb leads into a singular noun (the RCMP is a force with a long history). See North-West Mounted Police.

re

As a prefix it normally takes a hyphen only before words that begin with e (reapply, but re-elect). However, use a hyphen for clarity when there is another word with the same spelling (the rifle recoiled, he re-coiled the rope; he recovered his senses, he re-covered the chair).

Reader's Digest, singular.

realize (not -ise).

realpolitik, lower-case. Needs italics.

Realtor

Upper-case. Use it only in real estate stories, and only in those that make an issue of membership in the Canadian Real Estate Association and the National Association of Realtors. These organizations describe the term as a registered trademark and run it all caps, but we upper-case only the first letter. In most stories, speak of a real estate broker, company or firm. Say of individuals that they are a real estate agent, salesman or saleswoman, sell real estate or are in real estate.

rear-view mirror

reason

Should not be followed by why or because. The reason we leave these out is that they are redundant. Also see cause and reason.

Rebekah Lodges

The women's section of the Odd Fellows.

recession

Economists consider that a recession has hit when there have been two consecutive quarters of decline in economic activity. (Prefer this description to the economists' own jargon, "negative growth.") Note that a recession requires a true decline, not merely a slowing in the rate of growth. The word depression is not a normal term among economists. Speak of a long, severe recession, and reserve depression for economic carnage equal to that of the thirties.

recipes

Use figures for all amounts in recipes. Do not use contractions (tbsp etc.) except when pressed for space in tabular matter. See numbers.

recognizance

Keep it singular, as in three suspects were released on their own recognizance. It means that their own promise to reappear was deemed to be sufficient, so no bail was required.

recoilless rifle, see guns.

recombinant DNA

This is DNA that has been produced by combining genetic material from two different organisms. The method, a form of genetic engineering, is to splice a gene from one organism into the DNA of a cell from another. There is rarely a need to write out the full name of DNA, deoxyribonucleic acid, but the context should make it clear that it contains the genetic code in all organisms and viruses.

reconnaissance

reconnoitre

record

Do not say a new record has been set. Every record is new until it is surpassed. At that point it becomes an old record.

rectory, see manse.

Red

Do not use this word as a noun meaning communist. It is proper as an adjective, upper-case, in such names as the former Red Army, in the expression Red Tory (meaning left-wing) and in historical allusions to such things as the Red Menace, the Red Scare. Do not use the expression Red China.

Upper-case Red Ensign for the flag of Ontario and the former flag of Canada, and Red Power, the slogan of the American Indian Movement.

red book

A reference to the campaign promises made by the federal Liberals under Jean Chrétien before the Liberals' election victory in 1993. It was indeed a red book, but that wasn't its title, so keep it lower-case. The clearest path is to refer to it in first reference as the Liberals' red book of campaign policies (or promises), and then as the red book.

Red Chamber

Upper-case this sobriquet for the Senate.

red-dog, to blitz the quarterback.

red Indian

Do not use this term for Indians. Like most light-skinned people of the world, Indians have red skin only if they have a sunburn. The terms red Indian, red man, redskin etc. are thought to date from the earliest encounter with native people in North America, the Beothuk of Newfoundland, who painted their skin with red ochre.

refer, does not need back.

referendums, see plebiscite.

reform, reformer

A reformer is taken to be one who seeks or brings about a change for the **better,** and so this is a risky term to apply to one side in a dispute, or to one faction on a city council, for example. It casts that side as the white knight, and the other side as causing, or at least condoning, the abuses in need of reform. It is in the interests of the outsiders or the minority to describe themselves as the reform caucus or reform faction, and in our interests as journalists to find a more neutral term.

Reform is also ambiguous, depending for its meaning on the point of view of the source, the writer or the reader. Does reforming drug laws mean charging more people or fewer? Does reform of abortion laws mean easier access or tighter? Stick to the more informative tighten, relax etc., or the more neutral change, rewrite.

Reformed churches

Strictly speaking, this term can be applied to all Protestant churches that grew out of the Reformation, that is, all except the Lutheran churches and the Church of England. For clarity, however, reserve the word Reformed for the Christian Reformed Church and others in which it appears as part of the name, such as the Free Reformed Church and the Canadian Reformed Church.

refugee

When does an immigrant become a refugee? The United Nations convention on refugees, which Canada signed in 1969, defines the refugees to whom Canada must give sanctuary in this way: people who, "by reason of a well-founded fear of persecution for reasons of race, religion, nationality, membership in a particular social group or political opinion," have left their countries of habitual residence and are unwilling or unable to return there. This distinguishes a refugee from other immigrants, who may have any number of reasons (economic hardship, family ties, a seeking of better opportunities) for leaving their native lands.

Some countries may establish more flexible rules for granting refugee status; to West Germany, for example, all who fled East Germany were entitled to refuge. Canada has often accepted refugee claimants on humanitarian grounds as well as under the stricter UN conditions.

In Canadian stories, reserve the term refugee for those passed by the refugee determination process. Others should be called refugee claimants, would-be refugees, people seeking or claiming refugee status etc.

refute

It means to prove a statement is false, or to prove a person wrong; its use involves an editorial judgment that the argument was successful. The same is true of **rebut**. If a person is merely challenging, questioning, arguing against or seeking to refute or rebut, we must say so.

regalia

It is plural (of *regalis*), and so requires plural verbs and pronouns (these regalia are). See insignia. Regalia are now any fancy trappings, not just those of royalty.

Regent Park

Not to be confused with the possessive Regent's Park, London. Canada's first public housing project, in central Toronto, runs from Parliament Street east to River Street, and is divided into northern and southern halves by Dundas Street. From Dundas north to Gerrard Street is the first phase, begun in 1948, which is a mixture of two-storey and six-storey buildings on the model of British public housing. From Dundas south to Shuter Street is the high-rise section, begun in 1957.

We must not imply that a person is of criminal inclination or a second-class citizen by virtue of residence in Regent Park.

reggae

Regina Manifesto

Upper-case for the platform adopted in Regina in 1933 by the Co-operative Commonwealth Federation, and by extension the guiding principle of the CCF's successor, the New Democratic Party.

registered retirement savings plan

Lower-case, but **RRSP**.

reign, rein and rule

A constitutional monarch reigns but does not rule. Reins are straps or lines used to control animals, but the word is also used as a symbol of authority (the reins of power). Someone who is allowed great leeway is given free rein.

Reign of Terror

Upper-case for the period 1793-94 when the fanatical Jacobins seized control of the French Revolution from the Girondins and guillotined more than 2,600 people described as counter-revolutionaries. It ended with the guillotining of the Jacobin leader, Robespierre. Use lower case for other periods of extreme violence and fear.

religious titles

The title Cardinal appears before the first name and surname, as in Cardinal Emmett Carter. In second reference, say Cardinal Carter.

Archbishops and bishops, in both the Roman Catholic and Anglican churches, get those titles before their name in first reference (Archbishop Desmond Tutu, Bishop Raymond

Roussin). They retain the titles in second reference (Archbishop Tutu said, the bishop said).

Catholic monsignors get that title in first reference, and Father in second reference. In Globe style, priests are called Rev. in first reference (not **the** Rev. or the Reverend) and Father in second reference.

Anglican deans are Very Rev. in first reference, and Dean in second. Archdeacons are Ven. in first reference and Archdeacon in second. Canons are Rev. in first reference, Canon in second. Lesser Anglican clergy are Rev. in first reference and Mr., Ms., Mrs. or Dr. in second.

In the United Church of Canada, on first reference the moderator is Right Rev. and former moderators are Very Rev., if they are ordained ministers. Moderators from the lay ranks would simply be called moderator Anne Squires, or past or former moderator Robert McClure. In second reference, both ordained and lay moderators are called Mr., Ms., Mrs. or Dr. (Both Squires and McClure are Dr.) Ministers are Rev., and in second reference are Mr., Ms., Mrs. or Dr.

In the Presbyterian Church in Canada, an ordained moderator and all ministers are simply Rev. in first reference and Mr., Ms., Mrs. or Dr. in second.

For all other Protestant denominations, we call clergy Rev. in first reference and Mr., Ms., Mrs. or Dr. in second.

For Judaism, use Rabbi as a title before the full name in first reference to rabbis of synagogues, then use Mr. or Dr. There are rabbis who are not connected with congregations, and these may be given the title if they habitually use it.

For Islam, use upper case for a title before a name indicating a spiritual leader (Imam or Sheik), a teacher (Mullah, Maulvi, Maulana), a religious adviser (Mufti), a religious judge

(Kazi) or a reciter in the mosque (Qari). We generally use Mr. in second reference, but note that the title Imam is given not only to a person chosen as the leader of a mosque but also to one elected or otherwise recognized as the leader of a sect or an entire national religious community. Repeat Imam (or Ayatollah, a term confined to Iran) with the surname in subsequent references if it denotes veneration so great that it amounts to national status. All titles are lower-case without the name (the ayatollah said), and most are better translated (the teacher, the judge).

For religions that lack a formal hierarchy, with spiritual leaders elected by the congregation or chosen by consensus, we use such generic (lower-case) terms as priest and holy man if they are used by the people and their followers, as in Sikh priest Jatinder Singh. Use Mr. etc. in second reference.

In animist and similar religions, we use such lower-case generic terms as shaman, medicine man or woman, spirit singer, spiritual leader, and in second reference use Mr. etc.

We follow the style used by new or fringe religions if they have formal organizations linking several congregations or have large numbers of followers (Rev. Sun Myung Moon). However, self-proclaimed new religious leaders who have only a handful of followers should generally get only the normal honorific.

We must tread carefully in stories about divided religions and congregations. Whether someone is entitled to be called a priest or leader, or merits a title that indicates a particular ancestry, caste or state of grace, is sometimes a highly political issue. In such cases involving disputes, we should stick to the fact that someone uses the title, calls himself, describes himself as, is referred to by his followers as, but we should also take care not to sound doubtful or ironic.

Also see capitalization.

remainder

Reserve this for stories involving arithmetic. Say the rest (not remainder) of the speech, and eight minutes left (not remaining) in the game.

Rembrandt

This was the great Dutch painter's given name. He was Rembrandt Harmenszoon van Rijn.

remuneration

Often misspelled renumeration. It means just or adequate payment, reward, recompense.

Renaissance

Use upper case for the period of transition between the Middle Ages and the modern era in Europe, roughly 1350 to 1650. Use lower case for other rebirths, revivals.

Rensselaer Polytechnic Institute

Troy, N.Y.

repellent

repentant

replica

Strictly speaking, it is a duplicate made by the original maker or artist. It has come to mean any duplicate, but we should make it clear which is meant.

Report on Business

No "the" for the daily section of The Globe and Mail, and ROB (no periods) on second reference. The magazine is Report on Business magazine (lower-case m, since it is not part of the title); it was formerly known as R.O.B. Magazine, and before that as Report on Business

Magazine. ROB magazine is acceptable shorthand in second reference. The cable channel is Report on Business Television.

representative

We do not describe someone as a representative or leader of a particular ethnic group, profession etc. if the broad membership has not shown that it accepts such a description. See leader.

Representative

We do not abbreviate it as the title for members of the U.S. House of Representatives.

reprieve

It isn't a discount or a cut or a break. It's a postponement.

Republican

In political stories involving several politicians, it may be abbreviated as R (with no period), as in Senator Alfonse D'Amato (R, N.Y.). However, most stories are improved if we forgo the shorthand and say Republican Senator Alfonse D'Amato of New York, or the New York Republican etc. Never use the shorthand form in a lead.

rescind

research and development, R&D.

reserve

This is the proper term in Canada for government land set aside for any purpose, such as Indian reserves, clergy reserves, timber reserves. In stories from the United States, use reservation.

resistance, but **resistible**.

respectively

Constructions using respectively are rarely appropriate in news stories. If the parallel is not so simple that use of

respectively risks insulting the reader (her sons James and Robert, a lawyer and an accountant), it is usually too complex to be helped by respectively, and should be recast. It is a rare newspaper reader who will brook being forced to backtrack in a sentence to sort out relative positions in two lists.

responsible

Limit this word to people. A storm or beavers are not responsible for damage; they cause it.

restaurateur (not -anteur).

restrictive clauses

Defining clauses. See comma (under punctuation), and also **that and which**.

resulted in

A lazy construction that should usually be replaced by a more specific transitive verb.

Resurrection

Use upper case only for that of Jesus and for the general Christian concept (in the hope of Resurrection). Use lower case for that of Lazarus and other people, or of things such as organizations, movements, ideas.

retarded, retardation

Acceptable in copy as general terms meaning born with intelligence below the normal range. But for specific individuals it is more informative to state the degree of retardation (mild, severe etc.) or, better still, to convey the level on which the person functions (on the level of a 10-year-old, at a Grade 3 level, able to support himself etc.). Be sensitive to support groups' objection to the word retarded, especially to any impression that it refers to a homogeneous class. Look for ways around using it in a headline, but use it if there is no alternative. In copy, the terms mentally handicapped and intellectually handicapped are reasonably clear to our readers and therefore acceptable. Specific learning disabilities (dyslexia, for example) should not be equated with retardation, nor should retarded be used to refer to mental disability caused by injury (use brain-injured) or to mental disturbance. Do not use **retard** as a noun. See disabled.

reticent and reluctant

Reserve **reticent** for quiet, uncommunicative, not given to speaking freely.

retro

As a prefix meaning back or backward, it does not take a hyphen (retroactive, retrograde, retrofire, retrofit, retrorocket).

Reuters Ltd.

In both credit lines and copy when referring to the news service, use Reuters, but the founder was Paul Julius, Baron de Reuter (1816-99).

Rev.

We use only the contraction, and only in first reference (Rev. Mary White). We do not use the full word or the article "the" (the Rev.). Second reference is Father or Mr. etc. See religious titles.

réveillon

Lower-case, italics. It is the meal traditionally served in Quebec early on Christmas Day, after midnight mass.

Revelation, Book of

Singular for the last book of the New Testament. It is not entirely made up of apocalyptic visions giving a Christian view of world history; it begins with seven letters to the churches of Asia Minor.

Revell, Viljo

The Finnish architect who designed Toronto City Hall. The spelling Rewell, while common during his lifetime, has generally fallen out of use.

Revenge of the Cradle

Use upper case for the notion, largely associated with the period before the First World War, that Quebec's high birth rate would allow it to exceed the population of English Canadians. It is a translation of *revanche du berceau*. Note that Quebec's birth rate is now among the lowest in the world, prompting the government to offer incentives for larger families.

revenue

Not to be confused with profit.

Revenue Canada

See Canada Customs and Revenue Agency.

reversible

revert back, tautology.

revolver

A specific type of pistol with several firing chambers arranged in a revolving cylinder. Most have six chambers (do not say six cylinders).

Rewell, Viljo

See Revell.

Rh factor

About 84 per cent of people have the Rhesus antigen in their blood (first discovered in rhesus monkeys). They are Rh positive (no hyphen), and those who lack the antigen are Rh negative.

rheumatism

Acceptable as a general term meaning a painful inflammation of muscles or joints, but is imprecise in specific cases. When we know the details, we specify rheumatoid arthritis etc.

rhinoceros

The two types in Africa are called black and white, but are both leaden grey in colour. White is a corruption of the Afrikaans word for wide, a reference to the square upper lip of this species. All other species (the black, the Great Indian, the Sumatran and the Javan) have pendulous, almost prehensile upper lips, useful for browsing on shrubs, while the white is largely confined to grazing. Rhino horns are made not of horn but of a fibrous protein called keratin, also found in hair, but it is not correct to say they are formed from hair.

Rhodesia

Northern Rhodesia became Zambia in 1964, under Kenneth Kaunda. Southern Rhodesia became the unsanctioned independent state of Rhodesia in 1965, under Ian Smith, and then Zimbabwe in 1980, under Robert Mugabe. See Zambia, Zimbabwe.

rhythm and blues, R&B.

Richter scale

Seismologists no longer use it to define the magnitude of quakes. For their own purposes, they measure a variety of factors, including energy release, amount of slippage and various kinds of seismic waves. For public consumption, they combine several of these factors and announce a ranking that allows comparisons with the magnitudes of previous quakes. We use this number to report simply that a quake had "a magnitude of 7.4," without specifying any scale.

When speaking of past quakes in terms of Richter readings, note that each successive whole number indicates a tenfold increase in earthquake magnitude (as measured on a standard type of seismometer, and corrected to assume that the machine was exactly 100 kilometres from the epicentre). A magnitude of 7.5 is 100

times one of 5.5, and one of 8.5 is a thousandfold increase on 5.5.

Always use the word "magnitude" when giving Richter readings, not "energy" or "severity" or "intensity." Each one-point Richter increase means a tenfold increase in magnitude but roughly a 30-fold increase in released energy. Severity and intensity depend on such factors as rock structure, soil conditions and proximity of large cities. The scale is theoretically open-ended, but a major reason it was abandoned was that it couldn't accurately measure large quakes.

We cannot put great faith in older recorded readings. The Richter numbers have been revised to reflect the new combined-scale magnitude rankings, and this brought a demotion of the San Francisco quake of 1906 to 7.9 from 8.3, and a promotion of the 1964 Alaska quake to 9.2 from 8.3.

See earthquakes, San Andreas Fault.

Richthofen, Baron Manfred von

The Red Baron.

rickets

This bone disease of children, caused by a shortage of vitamin D, is usually singular (rickets is). It should not be confused with the rickettsial diseases, caused by the micro-organisms classed as rickettsiae, which have some of the characteristics of both bacteria and viruses. Rickettsial diseases include typhus, Q fever, Rocky Mountain spotted fever and rickettsialpox.

rickshaw

Riel, Louis

Speak of the Riel rebellions, not of the Riel Rebellion. There were two: the Red River Rebellion of 1869-70 and the North-West Rebellion of 1885. Riel's occupation of Upper Fort Garry in late 1869 brought the issue of

Métis land concerns to national attention and hastened the creation of the province of Manitoba in 1870, but his ill-conceived execution of an Ontario Orangeman ruled out amnesty and Riel fled as troops approached in August. The North-West Rebellion of 1885, begun by Gabriel Dumont and others but later led by Riel, who returned from exile in Montana at their request, brought the death in action of 38 government troops and 72 Métis and Indians, the execution of Riel and 11 Indians, and three-year prison terms for the Cree leaders Poundmaker and Big Bear. The action in the North-West Rebellion took place in what is now Saskatchewan, notably the opening skirmish in late March at Duck Lake, the Indian attacks at Frog Lake and Fort Pitt, the battle of Fish Creek, and the decisive battle at Batoche, May 9-12.

rifle
Weapons of many sizes, including cannon, have rifled barrels, meaning they have spiral grooves that impart a spin to the projectile, increasing its range and accuracy. However, confine the word rifle to the personal weapon and to the heavier recoilless rifle mounted on vehicles. See guns and calibres.

rift valley
Use lower case in the generic term for land that has been thrust down between two parallel faults. Upper-case proper names, such as the Great Rift Valley of eastern Africa and the Rhine Rift Valley.

right fielder, right-hander, right winger.

right to life, right to work
But right-to-life movement, right-to-work laws.

rigour
But drop the u for **rigorism**, **rigorous** and **rigor mortis** and other medical and pathological meanings.

Rimsky-Korsakov (not -off), **Nicholas Andreievich**.

Rio
Never add the redundant word river, as in "the Rio Grande River" or "the Amazonian river Rio Negro."

Rio de Janeiro (not -iero).
It is not the capital of Brazil (that is Brasilia), or even the largest city (Sao Paulo).

rip-off. The verb is **rip off**.
Avoid except in direct quotes. Use steal, theft, cheat etc.

ritual
A ritual is a prescribed form for a religious ceremony or a similarly solemn observance. We do not speak of a ritual killing, for example, if the method is merely bizarre or heinous.

Ritz-Carlton Hotel, Montreal.
Not Carleton.

rivers
Rivers are major factors in the lives of people along their banks and indeed whole sections of the country. A mistake in a river's name, source, route or destination would be embarrassing in the extreme in a national newspaper, which has readers in the very area concerned. Editors and writers should make it their business to know, for example, that it is the North Saskatchewan that flows through Edmonton, and the Bow and Elbow that meet at Calgary; that the North and South Saskatchewan flow from Alberta to join just east of Prince Albert and form the Saskatchewan, their waters eventually reaching Hudson Bay via Manitoba and the Nelson. The Globe library has maps

showing the country's major drainage basins, and these should be consulted as a matter of course in stories dealing with rivers.

Rivers are classified according to the sea their waters eventually reach, and Canadian water drains into five: the Pacific, the Arctic, Hudson Bay, the Atlantic and the Gulf of Mexico. (Yes, the Gulf of Mexico. A small area of extreme southern Alberta drains into the Milk River, through which the water flows south to the Missouri and then the Mississippi.) About three-quarters of Canada's land area is drained northward, into the Arctic, Hudson Bay or Hudson Strait/Ungava Bay.

The country's three largest drainage systems are the Mackenzie, the St. Lawrence and the Nelson. The Mackenzie system, draining into the Arctic Ocean, comprises several other large systems: the Great Bear, Great Slave, Peace, Athabasca, Hay, Liard, Peel and Taltson. It is about equal to the St. Lawrence system in mean discharge to the sea, but could be considered Canada's largest system because it drains a larger area and, unlike the St. Lawrence, has its source waters entirely in Canada. These two systems, discharging about 10,000 cubic metres a second, rank second and third in North America (the Mississippi's flow is 75 per cent larger), but 16th and 17th in the world (the Amazon discharges 20 times as much).

The St. Lawrence system includes all the water flowing into the Great Lakes and into the St. Lawrence itself. In Canada, this includes Ontario's Nipigon, French, Trent, Severn, Grand and Thames systems, the Ottawa, and Quebec's Gatineau, Saint Maurice and Saguenay systems.

The Nelson system, flowing into Hudson Bay, drains a huge area covering the southern portions of all three Prairie provinces, drawing from such systems as the North and South Saskatchewan, Alberta's Battle, Red Deer, Bow and Oldman, the Qu'Appelle and Assiniboine, Manitoba's Red system and its giant lakes, and Ontario's Rainy and English. Also draining into Hudson or James Bays are the long Churchill system (extending as far as Alberta via the Beaver), three other systems in Nunavut and northern Manitoba, six in Ontario and eight in Quebec. One of these is Ontario's Severn, not to be confused with the other Severn in Southern Ontario, part of the St. Lawrence system.

rob

Robbery, strictly speaking, involves the taking of goods or money through the use of violence or the threat of violence. One may rob a person, a bank, a train etc., if people are confronted, but taking something when no one is around, including money from a bank vault, is theft, not robbery, and the verb is steal.

The direct object of rob is the person or institution, not the loot. Say three men robbed the bank of $50,000, not that they robbed $50,000 from the bank.

robin

This name is applied in different countries to various species of birds with red breasts. In stories from overseas, specify the European robin, Pekin robin, Indian robin etc., so that readers will not think the American robin is meant.

Rockcliffe Park

The neighbourhood of many diplomats and senior civil servants became part of the City of Ottawa in the amalgamation of Jan. 1, 2000. See Ottawa, City of.

rock 'n' roll

Use this term for the general style of music that began as the white version of rhythm and blues, and expanded to include such forms as rockabilly. But to encompass later forms as well, use the generic terms rock music or rock. In reference to individual performers, we use such specific terms as acid rock, punk rock, folk-rock, glitter rock, pop rock, heavy metal.

Rocky Mountains

They are the easternmost system of the Western Cordillera (the mass of mountain systems covering western North America), and the longest, stretching from Alaska to New Mexico. We must not give the impression that they are visible from Canada's Pacific coast (several other systems intervene). The Rockies should not be referred to as a range, because the system comprises several ranges and groups of ranges, including Canada's Continental Ranges, Hart Ranges and Border Ranges. See mountains.

rollback, the noun.

The verb is **roll back**.

roll call

Rollerblade

A registered trade name. If unsure of the make, use the generic equivalent: in-line skate. For the verb, follow *Canadian Oxford*'s style of lower-casing the word: She was rollerblading down the block.

roller coaster

roller skates

The verb is **roller-skate**.

roly-poly

Roma

Both singular and plural (not Romas). Use this term rather than Gypsy (Gypsies) for the people and their culture, but, until it becomes more fixed in the public's mind, it may help reader understanding to add a

reference after the first mention of Roma: often called Gypsies, sometimes called Gypsies, traditionally known as Gypsies.

A United Nations report in 2000 noted that there are as many as 10 million Roma in Europe, but that only 20 per cent are itinerant.

Roman Catholic

The word Roman may be dropped if the reference is obvious, as in Ontario's Catholic school boards.

Romance languages

In addition to the familiar Spanish, French, Portuguese and Italian, don't forget Romanian, Sardinian, Occitan (Provençal), Catalan (the official language of Andorra), the Raeto-Roman dialects of northern Italy and the southern Swiss Alps (including Romansch), and the various French, Spanish and Portuguese creoles of Africa and the Americas.

Romania

Adjective and people: Romanian. Currency: leu (plural lei). Capital: Bucharest.

The language is Romanian (we do not use the spellings Rumanian or Roumanian). Romania is the northernmost of the Balkans (the countries of the Balkan Peninsula), bordering on the Black Sea, with Hungary, Ukraine and Moldova to the north, Serbia and Montenegro and Bulgaria to the south. There are German and Hungarian minorities; the main religions are Romanian Orthodox and Roman Catholic. Romania's two distinct northern regions, Moldavia in the east and Transylvania in the west, are separated from each other by the Carpathian Mountains, and from southern Romania (the Walachian region) by the east-west Transylvanian Alps. The population is 22 million.

Long-time Communist dictator Nicolae Ceausescu resisted the reforms sweeping the rest of the Eastern Bloc in the late 1980s. He tried brutal suppression when a popular uprising began in Timisoara in 1989, but it quickly spread to the capital. He was toppled on Dec. 22 and executed by firing squad along with his wife, Elena, on Dec. 25, after being convicted of genocide.

Roman numerals

In general, we avoid them. We use them for monarchs and popes (George VI, John XXIII), in other names when the distinction between the current holder and a forebear is doubtful (John D. Rockefeller III), and in proper commercial names (*Rocky III*, Continental Mark IV). However, note that not all numbered movie titles use Roman numerals (it's *Halloween* 5), and usage also varies in ship names (Bluenose II, but Queen Elizabeth 2, Canada 1). In mere number labels and non-commercial names, we use normal Arabic numbers (Grade 13, Salt 2, Vatican 2, the 18th Amendment, the 23rd Olympiad); however, we conform to widespread usage in World War I and World War II when these appear in quotes. (Our normal style is First or Second World War.)

We also use Roman numerals on those rare occasions when we must formally cite a complex string of sections and subsections in such things as constitutions and contracts. In such cases, we must follow the document's use of upper or lower case for the Roman numerals.

The letters used as numerals in the Roman system are I, V (5), X (10), L (50), C (100), D (500) and M (1,000). If a letter appears before one of greater value, it is subtracted (XL means 40). If it appears after one of equal or greater value, it is added (LX means 60, and XXI means 21). We should take it for granted that few readers (or journalists) can decipher numerals above X, such as MDCCCLXVII.

Romanov (not -off).

The official name (although not always the family name) of the dynasty that ruled Russia from 1613 to 1917.

Roncesvalles Avenue, Toronto.

Roquefort cheese

Rorschach test

Rosebery, B.C. (one r).

Rose of Lima

This native of Lima, 1586-1617, became the New World's first canonized saint in 1671, and is the patron saint of South America. (The Jesuit martyrs were killed between 1642 and 1649, but were not canonized until 1930.) See Jesuit martyrs, saints.

Rosetta stone

Rosh Hashanah

Jewish New Year, celebrated on the first and second days of the Jewish month of Tishri, usually in September or early October. It begins 10 days of penitence that end on Yom Kippur, the Day of Atonement. (Do not call Tishri the first month on the Jewish calendar; it is actually the seventh. The agricultural or celestial year, reflected in the calendar, differs from the religious year.)

Ross Bay Cemetery, Victoria.

A virtual history lesson, it is the resting place of 10 B.C. premiers, Emily Carr, Sir James Douglas (the Father of British Columbia) and Sir Matthew Begbie, the "hanging judge" of the Fraser River gold rush and later chief justice.

Rotary Club

Rotary International, Rotarian. The location for meetings of the first club, in Chicago, rotated among members' offices.

ROTC and ROTP

There is a fundamental difference between the Canadian and U.S. plans for subsidizing education in return for military service. The Canadian plan is for regular officers (Regular Officer Training Plan) while the U.S. one is for reserve officers (Reserve Officer Training Corps).

Rothmans

No apostrophe, either in the brand or in company names such as Rothmans Benson & Hedges Inc.

Rothschild

rough-hewn

Rough Riders, Roughriders

The former Ottawa Rough Riders, but the Saskatchewan Roughriders, of the Canadian Football League.

Theodore Roosevelt's 1st Volunteer Cavalry were the Rough Riders, but the generic term for a fearless horseman is a roughrider.

round trip

rowing and sculling

Both can be called rowing, meaning propelling a boat by oars. In the sport of **sculling**, each person has two oars, while in **rowing** (also called sweep rowing) each has one. (All one-person boats are sculls.) Note that sculling is also a term for propelling a small boat with one oar swept side to side at the stern.

royal

Use upper case only for Royal Family and Royal Household, and only for that of Canada. Use lower case for royalty, royal couple and such things as royal assent, royal commission, royal tour, royal visit, royal car, royal yacht. (However, note that the vessel's full name was Royal Yacht Britannia.) We do not use the term Royals.

Upper-case "the Royal" as a reference to the Royal Agricultural Winter Fair, Toronto.

royal assent

Do not speak of a bill being "signed into law." Canada has no equivalent to the United States' separate executive function with the requirement that the president or a governor sign a bill. The process in Canada is royal assent, which is automatic and consists of a mere nod, not a signature.

Royal Canadian Legion, The

Use upper case for Legion, as in a Legion meeting, a Legion hall. The prefix Royal applies after 1959.

Royal Canadian Mounted Police

See RCMP.

Royal Family

In informal references, we use the term Royal Family to refer to a sovereign and his or her immediate family. In the case of Canada's sovereign, this includes the Queen, Prince Philip, their children and grandchildren and the children's spouses if they are not estranged. It also included the late Queen Mother and Princess Margaret, the Queen's late sister.

However, we should be aware that Royal Family also has a much narrower meaning: the sovereign, all lineal descendants, the queen-dowager (Queen Mother) and, if the sovereign is a king, the queen-consort. If the sovereign is a queen-regnant, as at present, her husband is not, as such, a member of the Royal Family. In a story specifically about who qualifies for official inclusion, we should add the Duke of Kent and his sister, Princess Alexandra, as members of the family of a former sovereign and the Queen's first cousins. (They hold appointments as colonels-in-chief of Canadian regiments, an honour restricted to members of the Royal Family.)

The sovereign is Her (or His) Majesty (although this issue does not arise in Globe style; we simply say the Queen or the King). The only other correct reference would be Queen Elizabeth II; the name Queen Elizabeth referred to the Queen Mother. The Queen of the United Kingdom should not be referred to as the Queen of England; no sovereign has officially borne that title since 1707.

Since 1917, the titles His or Her Royal Highness and Prince or Princess have been restricted to the children of a sovereign, the children of a sovereign's sons (which is why the Kents qualify), and the eldest living son of the eldest son of the Prince of Wales. That means that the late Diana, Princess of Wales, should not be referred to as Princess Diana. Note that since 1987 the proper title of Princess Anne has been the Princess Royal.

The family name of the Queen, the Prince of Wales and his sons is Windsor. Before the birth of her second son, the Queen adopted the family name of Mountbatten-Windsor for her descendants who are not in direct line of succession to the throne.

The Queen was born April 21, 1926, and succeeded to the crown on the death of her father, George VI, on Feb. 6, 1952. In 1947 she had married Lieutenant Philip Mountbatten (formerly Prince Philip of Greece), at which time he was created Duke of Edinburgh. In 1957, he was created Prince Philip, Duke of Edinburgh. Their children are Charles (born Nov. 14, 1948), Anne (Aug. 15, 1950), Andrew (Feb. 19, 1960), and Edward (March 10, 1964). Charles married Lady Diana Spencer in 1981; their children are Prince William (June 21, 1982) and Prince Henry, known as Harry (Sept. 15, 1984). They announced their separation on Dec. 9, 1992, and were divorced on Aug. 28, 1996. Diana was killed in a

car crash in Paris with companion Dodi Fayed and their driver on Aug. 31, 1997; she was 36. Anne married Captain Mark Phillips in 1973; their children are Peter and Zara. The marriage was formally dissolved in April of 1992, and Anne married Commander Timothy Laurence on Dec. 14, 1992. Andrew married Sarah Ferguson in 1986, and on the same day was created Duke of York; their daughters are Beatrice and Eugenie. They announced their separation in March of 1992, and were divorced on May 30, 1996. Edward married Sophie Rhys-Jones on June 19, 1999; he was named Earl of Wessex and Viscount Severn, and she became the Countess of Wessex.

The Queen Mother was born Aug. 4, 1900, and died March 30, 2002. Her second daughter, Princess Margaret, was born Aug. 12, 1930, and died Feb. 9, 2002. She married Antony Armstrong-Jones in 1960, and he was created Earl of Snowdon the next year. They divorced in 1978. Their children are David, Viscount Linley, and Lady Sarah Armstrong-Jones.

rpm
No periods. Use revolutions a minute in first reference.

ruble (not rouble).

rumba (not rhumba).

rumour

rundown
The noun. But the adjective is run-down.

runner-up, runners-up

running mate

Rupert's Land
Two words. This immense area was granted by Charles II in 1670 to the Hudson's Bay Company, formed by

Prince Rupert and 17 associates. It comprised all the land drained by rivers flowing into Hudson Bay. It became part of Canada in 1870.

Note that Rupertsland is one word for the provincial Manitoba riding and the Winnipeg avanue and boulevard.

rush to hospital

We can assume an ambulance doesn't dawdle.

Russia

Adjective and people: Russian. Currency: ruble. Capital: Moscow.

We normally call it simply Russia, but it is properly the Russian Federation, and may be called this if the story is dealing with relations between the various components. Similarly, refer to the people in general as Russian, but when relevant it will be necessary to distinguish between Russians and other peoples of the federation, such as Chechen, Ingush, Ossetian, Bashkir, Chuvash, Yakut. The vast region of Siberia, overrun by Russia during the 17th century, contains many peoples, and these are not normally referred to merely as Siberians. Prefer Siberian peoples.

The Russian language, a member of the Slavonic group, is referred to by Russians themselves as Great Russian, to distinguish it from Ukrainian (Little Russian) and Belarussian (White Russian).

Since it emerged from the defunct Soviet Union in 1991, the Russian Federation has changed the status of some of its members to reflect ethnic aspirations and other factors. It consists of 21 republics, one autonomous region (*oblast*), 49 administrative *oblasts*, six provinces (*krais*) and 10 autonomous districts (*okrugs*). The cities of Moscow and St. Petersburg also have special administrative status as federation members, for a total of 89 "federal territorial units" making up the federation.

At 17 million square kilometres it is still the largest country on Earth, but sixth in terms of population at 148 million, exceeded by China, India, the United States, Indonesia and Brazil. The former Soviet Union had been third, at 290 million.

Russia covers most of northeastern Europe and all of northern Asia, and a sixth of its land is classed as agricultural. Its economy is heavily weighted to agriculture, natural-resource extraction and heavy industry, at the expense of consumer-products industries.

The Russian parliament has two tiers, both elected. The upper chamber, the Federation Council, has 178 members, consisting of two from each of 89 federal territorial units. The lower house, the State Duma, has 450 deputies, some elected in local districts and others by proportional representation according to party votes. The word Duma standing alone is fine in second reference. The collective name for the two chambers is the Federal Assembly, but in most stories it is sufficient simply to refer to the Russian parliament, lower-case. As in Canada, the word government refers to the prime minister and cabinet. The prime minister (called the chairman) is appointed by the president with the consent of the Duma. Ministers are appointed with the consent of the president. The Duma, which approves the budget and legislation, can override the president's veto by a two-thirds majority with the Federation Council, but can in turn be dissolved by the president in certain emergencies. New elections would be held within a year.

After the republic of Chechnya declared its independence from Russia in 1991, fighting between Russian troops and Chechen rebels claimed tens of thousands of lives. Russian troops withdrew from the region in 1996, but returned in 1999.

See Kremlin, Soviet Union.

Rwanda

Adjective and people: Rwandan. Currency: franc. Capital: Kigali.

It is mountainous and landlocked, in eastern Africa, bordering on Uganda in the north, Burundi in the south, Tanzania in the east and Congo-Kinshasa in the west, with which it shares Lake Kivu. It ranks as one of the world's poorest and most overpopulated countries. The literacy rate is only about 10 per cent. About 90 per cent of its approximately eight million people are Hutu farmers, 9 per cent are Tutsi cattle herders (the Watusi, noted for their great height) and 1 per cent are Twa (Pygmy) hunters.

The government was dominated by Hutus after independence in 1962 (it had been a UN trust territory under Belgium). There was sporadic Hutu-Tutsi violence, and a civil war began in 1990 with an invasion from Uganda by Tutsi insurgents, the Rwandan Patriotic Front. A small UN force sent to implement a 1993 peace agreement was inadequate to stop continued fighting, or to prevent the slaughter (largely organized) of more than 500,000 Tutsis and moderate Hutus from April of 1994, after the Hutu president and his Burundian counterpart were killed in a plane crash, presumably assassinated. The RPF quickly won a military victory and took power, and an estimated 1.1 million Hutus fled into Zaire (now Congo) in fear of Tutsi reprisals, despite RPF assurances. France dispatched 2,000 troops in late June of 1994, and they maintained safe zones for refugees in the southwest. The RPF set up a government of national unity, with Hutus in the majority but the RPF holding several key posts, in July of 1994, and the French troops were withdrawn in August. About 700,000 Hutu refugees flowed back, in what was called history's largest such mass migration, in late 1996 after the fugitive Hutu extremists who dominated their refugee camps fled deeper into Zaire under military pressure, largely from Zairian rebel forces. Many thousands of their followers were believed subsequently slaughtered by Zairian rebels.

The new Rwandan government had arrested more than 80,000 suspected of leading the 1994 genocide of Tutsis. An international tribunal to try them, approved by the UN Security Council in late 1994, began operating in June of 1995. (It later merged with its counterpart trying similar crimes in the former Yugoslavia.) In March of 1996, the last UN troops departed.

rye

An acceptable term in Canada to refer to Canadian whisky. Note that elsewhere it is referred to as Canadian.

Ryerson University

The official name since 2002 of the former Ryerson Polytechnic University in Toronto. Before its change of status in 1993, it was Ryerson Polytechnic Institute.

S

S-bend, S-curve, S-hook

sabbatical

sabre

saccharin

The sweetener, lower-case. The adjective meaning cloyingly sweet is **saccharine**.

sackcloth

sackfuls

sacramental, but **sacrilegious**.

sacred cow

Be aware that this allusion is offensive to many Hindus, since it often carries the connotation of an unthinking, illogical or even ridiculous veneration. Where possible, it should be avoided except in direct quotes.

Sadler's Wells Theatre, Ballet

sadomasochism

safe haven

This term is used by United Nations peacekeepers and others to describe a protected district, and is fine for direct quotes. However, its redundancy makes it inappropriate for our own use. Just make it "haven."

Sagittarius

Saguenay

The City of Saguenay, north of Quebec City, was created on Feb. 18, 2002, as part of Quebec's program of municipal amalgamation. The first of its three wards includes the former cities of Chicoutimi and Laterrière, and part of the canton of Tremblay. The second includes the former city of Jonquière and the former municipalities Lac-Kénogami and Shipshaw. The third includes the former city of La Baie. If mentioning Chicoutimi or Jonquière as reference points, describe them as sections of or neighbourhoods in Saguenay rather than as separate municipalities.

Sahara

Desert is implicit in the name; there is no need to add it.

Saidye Bronfman Centre, Montreal.

saints

In 1969, the Roman Catholic Church removed from its liturgical calendar the feasts of saints whose universal appeal or even historical reality was in doubt. However, it says a feast day may still be observed in an area where a cult of that saint is still active, and we continue to use the title St. for long-familiar figures removed from the official list.

Saints' feast days are not those of their births but those of their deaths, considered the day of their birth into glory. An exception is that of St. Jean Baptiste (see below).

The patron saint of journalists, officially named by the church, is St. Francis de Sales. The traditional patron saint of editors is St. John Bosco. (The protector of computer-age journalists may well be St. Anthony of Padua, patron saint of searchers for lost articles.)

Saints are regarded as exemplars of virtue; canonization is the church's declaration that the person is in heaven, and is able to intercede with God on behalf of the faithful. There are also holy figures who are venerated in the Islamic communities in some countries (the *pir* in Pakistan, the *mir* in India, the direct descendants of the Prophet's family among Shiites), but their function is earthly assistance, not intercession with God. A figure in Buddhism similar to a saint is the *bodhisattva*, who qualifies for entry into the state of Nirvana but delays entry in order to assist others.

Use **St.** (not Ste., St-, San, Santo, Sao etc.) for the names of saints of any nationality, both male and female (St. Simeon, St. Jean Baptiste, St. Barbara, St. Marguerite Bourgeoys).

For place names, however, we follow the spelling the community uses (Santa Barbara). In Canada, our authority is the official federal gazetteer, in which we find that if the saint's name has a French spelling the place name is usually spelled St- or Ste- (hyphen, no period), or occasionally Ste. without a hyphen, as in Sault Ste. Marie and Ste. Elizabeth, Man. (We depart from the gazetteer in using a period if there is no hyphen.) The use of hyphens is universally true in Quebec and widely true in New Brunswick, but also note Ontario's St-Amour, St-Eugène, St-Onge, St-Pascal and Ste-Rose-de-Prescott, Manitoba's Ste-Geneviève and St-Lazare, and Saskatchewan's St-Denis, Ste-Marthe-Rocanville, St-Front, St-Julien and St-Laurent-Grandin.

It is worth checking the gazetteer on all place names containing saints with French spellings, rather than automatically using a hyphen. There is Saint-Adolphe, Que., but St. Adolphe, Man.; and Saskatchewan has St. Hippolyte. Even place names with other French words added can trip us up. Ontario, with its Ste-Rose-de-Prescott, also has a St. Isidore de Prescott, with no hyphens. Manitoba has St. Pierre Sud.

We always contract St. in giving saints' names. This is true also in most place names outside Quebec and in the names of geographic features (Mount St. Helens). But note Saint John, N.B., and Saint Joe, B.C., and the Saint John River in New Brunswick. For place names and geographic features in Quebec (except St. Lawrence River), the names of saints should be spelled out (Saint-Hyacinthe), in line with the Province of Quebec's 1987 gazetteer.

The use of apostrophes varies, and again our authority is the gazetteer. (St. Andrew's, Nfld., for example, but St. Andrews, Man., N.B., N.S., Ont. and PEI.) It is St. Marys, Ont. (and St. Marys Cement).

Be on the lookout for the occasional plural (Sts. Rest, N.S.).

Church names require particular care. For example, Metro Toronto has St. Andrews Catholic and Presbyterian churches, but two other Presbyterian churches spelled St. Andrew's. There are also a United church, Estonian Lutheran and Latvian Lutheran churches and a Japanese congregation all spelled St. Andrew's. There is an Anglican church spelled St. Anne's, and a Catholic one spelled St. Ann's.

St. or Saint-Ambroise

(Not Ambrose.) Place names in Manitoba and Quebec. St-Ambroise is also a popular brand of beer in Quebec.

St. Bernard
The breed of dog.

St. Catharines, Ont.
But note that all other place names in Canada are Catherines, Catherine's or Catherine. Even in St. Catharines, the cathedral is that of St. Catherine of Alexandria.

St. Elias Range
In southern Yukon and northern B.C., it is the most northerly range in the Coast Mountains. It contains Canada's 15 highest mountains (the top three are Logan, St. Elias and Lucania) and the country's largest mainland glacier fields. Kluane National Park covers much of the range.

St. George's Day
It is a holiday in Newfoundland and Labrador, observed on the Monday closest to April 23.

St. Helena
This British colony is in the Atlantic, 1,200 miles from the coast of Angola and Namibia. Napoleon died in exile at the capital, Jamestown, in 1821.

Saint-Hyacinthe, Que. (not Sainte-).

St. James's
In London, St. James's Palace and the Court of St. James's (which refers to the palace); in Montreal, St. James's Club. But it is St. James Street (Rue St-Jacques), Montreal.

St. James Town
Use this spelling for the Toronto housing development, as it appears in most official documents.

St. Jean Baptiste
Except in place names, use this spelling (period and spaces rather than hyphens) for the patron saint of Quebec. However, the Roman Catholic Church also considers him a patron saint of Canada, and if this is the focus of the story his name should be spelled St. John the Baptist. His feast day, which is a festive holiday in Quebec but also one with heavy political overtones, is on June 24, traditionally regarded as his birthday. (This is an exception; the feast days of other saints are those of their death. See saints.)

St. John Ambulance
(Not John's.)

St. John's, Nfld.
But **Saint John**, N.B., and the Saint John River in New Brunswick.

St. Kitts-Nevis
No useful adjective for the country, or single name for its 41,000 citizens. Say citizens of St. Kitts-Nevis, or inhabitants of either of the islands. Currency: East Caribbean dollar. Capital: Basseterre.

St. Kitts (there is usually no need to use the official name, St. Christopher) and Nevis are in the eastern Caribbean, in the northern (Leeward) group of the Lesser Antilles. The country became independent in 1983. St. Kitts is known to its Carib inhabitants as Liamuiga. A referendum was held in 1998 on whether Nevis should separate from St. Kitts, but supporters of separation failed to win the necessary two-thirds majority.

St. Laurent, Louis, but Saint-Laurent, Yves.

St. Lawrence Seaway
The Seaway. We refer to the entire system as the Seaway, not the official St. Lawrence Seaway and Great Lakes Waterway.

St. Lucia
Adjective and people: St. Lucian. Currency: East Caribbean dollar. Capital: Castries.

It is 250 miles north of Venezuela in the southern (Windward) group of the Lesser Antilles. Most of its 160,000 citizens are of African heritage. It became fully independent from Britain in 1979, and is a member of the Commonwealth.

St. Marguerite Bourgeoys

Canada's first woman saint was canonized in 1982. Mother Marguerite Bourgeoys, who died in Montreal in 1700, devoted her life to the poor and founded the first non-cloistered order of nuns in North America, the teaching congregation Sisters of Notre Dame.

St. Martin-in-the-Fields

Academy of, and the church near Trafalgar Square.

Saint Mary's University

Not St. for the Halifax university.

Saint-Pierre and Miquelon

There are eight islands in all, divided into the Saint-Pierre group and the Miquelon-Langlade group. Roughly 90 per cent of residents live on Saint-Pierre. Saint-Pierre and Miquelon was an Overseas Department, equal in status to the departments that make up Metropolitan France, from 1976 to 1985, when its status was changed to that of a Territorial Collectivity. However, even under its former status its population of about 6,000 entitled it to representation in Paris only by the minimum one deputy in the National Assembly, one senator and one member of the Economic and Social Council, and it retains these as a Collectivity. Its people elect a General Council of 14 members for a six-year term to run local affairs, and the French government is represented by an appointed commissioner.

St. Vincent and the Grenadines

No useful single adjective for the country or word for its 115,000 people. Say citizens of St. Vincent and the Grenadines, or inhabitants of the various islands. Currency: East Caribbean dollar. Capital: Kingstown.

This multi-island state is just north of Venezuela in the southern (Windward) group of the Lesser Antilles. St. Vincent is north of Grenada, from which it is separated by the Grenadines. Linked politically to St. Vincent are the Northern Grenadines, the largest of which are Bequia, Mustique, Canouan, Mayreau and Union. The state became fully independent from Britain in 1979, and is a member of the Commonwealth.

Salchow, in figure skating.

saleable

salmon

They are Canada's most economically important group of wild animals.

We may speak freely of Atlantic salmon, because all are of the same species (*Salmo salar*). But use the term Pacific salmon only in general, because there are five distinct species (all of the genus Oncorhynchus, different from the genus Salmo of the Atlantic). We use the popular names of the Pacific species, not their scientific ones, and all are lower-case: chinook (the name we use, although they are also known as the king or quinnat), chum (also known as dog), coho (silver, silversides, skowitz, kisutch or hoopid), pink (humpback) and sockeye (red or blueback).

The Pacific Coast steelhead is also popularly regarded as a salmon and we may refer to it informally as such, but it is technically a trout. Salmon, trout, char, grayling and several other fish are in the family Salmonidae. Other salmonids that are popularly called salmon include the red snapper and several English food fish, all called

WELCOME
BACK,
SAMANTHA!

rock salmon, and the walleyed pike, called the jack salmon.

True salmon all return to the place of their birth to breed (mostly in freshwater streams, but some pink salmon spawn on tidal flats). All the Pacific species then die, but Atlantic salmon return to the sea and often make it back for another spawn. (Note that some sockeye and Atlantic salmon are naturally landlocked, maturing in deep lakes rather than in the sea, and that coho have been successfully introduced into the Great Lakes.)

We may use the popular names for Atlantic salmon from certain rivers prized by aficionados, such as the Restigouche salmon, but we should not go further and imply they are of a separate species.

salmonella

It is a genus, which would normally be in upper case, but common usage dictates the use of lower case except when giving a scientific name, such as *Salmonella typhi*.

The bacteria that originate in poultry and cause mild to severe food poisoning in humans are only one of many types of salmonella. Various kinds are found in the intestinal tracts of specific animals, including man,

and while some are benign, others are severe pathogens. S. *typhi* causes typhoid, three others cause paratyphoid fever, and a type found in the intestinal tracts of swine can cause severe blood poisoning in humans.

SALT

It stands for Strategic Arms Limitation Talks, and so it is redundant to say SALT Talks. See START.

saltpetre

Saltspring Island

Use this style, not Salt Spring, for the B.C. island, in accordance with the official gazetteer.

Salvadoran, see El Salvador.

SAM

It means surface-to-air missile. We use the full expression in first reference, and SAM in second if the meaning is clear. SAM missile is redundant.

sambuca

The liqueur is lower case except in brand names.

Samoa

Adjective and people: Samoan. Currency: tala (pidgin for dollar). Capital: Apia.

This former German protectorate in the Pacific was administered by New Zealand until 1961, and became an independent country on Jan. 1, 1962, under the name Western Samoa. The name was changed to the Independent State of Samoa in July, 1997. Refer to it simply as Samoa. It is a member of the Commonwealth. The inhabited islands are Upolu, which contains the capital, Apolima, Monono and Savai'i. The population is 170,000, mostly Polynesian.

(The eastern islands of the Samoan group are called American Samoa, an unincorporated territory administered by the U.S. Interior Department. Their population is about 70,000.)

Samoyed, upper-case. See husky.

San Andreas Fault

There are several geological faults on the west coast of North America, including the San Andreas, the Triple Junction, the Juan de Fuca Plate, the Queen Charlotte Fault; by no means all quakes and tremors there involve the San Andreas. A fault is a point at which earth movement is evident, but it is incorrect to say the fault caused the movement. A more accurate explanation is that an earthquake is caused by the sudden release of elastic strain built up along a fault. Note, however, that some quakes are volcanic in origin, apparently unconnected to the movement of plates. Those in Eastern Canada are often far from faults or the edges of plates. See earthquakes, Richter scale.

sanction

An ambiguous word. As a noun, its most common meaning these days is an international declaration imposing measures to force a country to conform to stated conditions. But as a verb, to sanction, it almost always means to approve or allow (The mayor said she would be happy to sanction the outdoor concert). This makes the following sentence very confusing: "France has made every effort to denounce and sanction the actions of the Serbs in Bosnia-Herzegovina." To keep things straight, avoid using the verb sanction to mean impose sanctions or thwart by means of sanctions.

San Francisco 49ers (not '49ers).

San Marino

Adjective: San Marino. People: San Marino citizens. Currency: euro (had used the Italian lira). Capital: San Marino.

We may use the local name for the citizens, Sammarinesi, in a colour story if the name has been properly set up. San Marino, landlocked and surrounded by Italy (it is in the northeast, near the Adriatic coast), is considered the oldest independent state in Europe. Its population is 25,000. It lost its status as the world's smallest republic (at 61 square kilometres) when Nauru (21 square kilometres) gained independence in 1968. The smallest independent state, at only 195 hectares, is the principality of Monaco.

Sao Tome and Principe

No useful adjective for the country or single word for the people. Currency: dobra. Capital: Sao Tome.

This former Portuguese colony, comprising the two main islands and several islets, is in the Gulf of Guinea, off the west coast of Africa. Sao Tome Island, about 190 miles off Libreville, Gabon, is much larger than Principe, accounting for about 90 per cent of the republic's land area and population of 170,000.

sarcoma

It is a form of malignant tumour, but it is often distinguished from cancer because it may behave differently and have a different natural history. It is derived from connective tissue, and commonly appears in bone (osteosarcoma), cartilage (chondrosarcoma) or fibrous tissue (fibrosarcoma).

SARS

The acronym for severe acute respiratory syndrome, first known as atypical pneumonia. The first cases were reported in China's Guangdong province near the end of 2002, and the first Canadian cases were identified in March, 2003. SARS is caused by a coronavirus, so called because the virus looks like a crown.

sartorial

From the Italian word for tailor (*sarto*), it simply means having to do with tailoring, or with men's clothes. If we must use it, be aware that it carries no built-in connotation of elegance that would allow us to say simply that someone looks sartorial. We can have sartorial disrepute and ugliness as well as sartorial splendour.

Saskatchewan Roughriders

But the former **Ottawa Rough Riders**.

saskatoon

Use lower case for the purple berry of the shadbush, found on the prairies. Do not add the word berry. Eastern nurseries call it the serviceberry.

A resident of Saskatoon is a Saskatonian.

sasquatch

Use lower case for the hairy man-like creature that has been reported in British Columbia and the U.S. Pacific Northwest. Prefer this name (Salish for hairy men). In stories exclusively set in the United States we may use the term Bigfoot (not Big Foot), but explain that they are also called sasquatch. Both terms are the same in singular and plural.

satellite, often misspelled.

Saudi Arabia

Adjective and people: Saudi(s). Currency: riyal. Capital: Riyadh.

The 22 million people are almost all Arab and may be referred to as such, but this would not distinguish them from Arabs in other countries. Saudi Arabia, a kingdom covering most of the Arabian Peninsula, across the Red Sea from Africa, contains three major deserts: the An Nafud in the north and the Rub al Khali (Empty Quarter) in the southeast, both sand deserts, and the barren Nejd plateau in the centre. In the east are the oil-rich Hasa lowlands. In the west, the humid Red Sea coastal plain, the Tahimah, is separated from the interior by the steep Hejaz and Asir Mountains.

Sault Ste. Marie

May be called the Soo in second reference and in headlines.

sauternes

Use lower case for the wine, despite the reference to the French district of that name. Note the final s.

Savile Row

saviour

savour, savoury (the adjective).

But drop the u for **savorous** and **savory** (the plant).

saxophone

scab

Acceptable in direct quotes in labour stories to refer in general to outsiders or fellow union members who do the work of strikers. But it is a derogatory term that we must not use on our own, or use to refer to a recognizable individual. Prefer outside workers, replacement workers, strikebreakers.

scabies

It is singular, a skin disease caused by burrowing mites.

scam

It is a specific type of crime, namely a swindle or confidence game. It should not be used to refer to thefts etc.

Scandinavia

The Scandinavian Peninsula is occupied by Norway, Sweden and part of Finland. However, Denmark is usually included in the geographical concept of Scandinavia. In terms of people and culture, Scandinavian is also taken to include the people of Iceland and the Faroe Islands.

scared of
Make it scared by, or afraid of.

scarves

scenario
Use of this word in non-theatrical contexts has become political jargon and trite journalese.

sceptre, lower-case.
The one in the House of Commons is called a mace.

Scheherazade

Schenley Awards, football.

Schiaparelli, Elsa
Italian-born, but properly described as a French fashion designer.

schism

schizophrenia
Shy away from this word except in medical stories. In particular, do not use it (or schizophrenic, schizo, schizoid) to refer to a person who is merely uncertain, undecided or torn between loyalties. Schizophrenia is a true psychosis, the most serious class of mental illnesses. It manifests itself in one or more of the following: delusion, confusion of identity, paranoia accompanied by decline in intellect, illogical thought, hallucinations, withdrawal from reality, bizarre behaviour, self-neglect, autism, catatonia. See psychiatric terms.

schlemiel etc.
We use the sch- spelling for Yiddish words that have passed into English: **schlemiel** (bungler or dupe), **schlep** (to drag, or to walk heavily as if burdened), **schlock** (something cheap, shoddy), **schmaltz** (something

oversentimental), **schmo** (a pitiable person), **schmooze** (to chat), **schnook** (a dupe).
The exceptions to this spelling rule are **shemozzle** (a mess, muddle) and **shtick** (a gimmick, action or mannerism designed to impress).
Schmaltz is understood by most readers, but the other words should be used only if the meaning is clear and the subject matter appropriate.
Schmuck should not appear in The Globe without the approval of a senior editor. It means a fool, but its primary meaning is penis.

schmooze

schnauzer
Lower-case for the dog. It means growler.

school
Use upper case in the proper name of an institution, but lower case if referring merely to a faculty within an institution (University of Toronto law school, Queen's medical school, McMaster school of nursing).

Schumacher, Ont.

scientific terms, names
Scientific terms, such as plasmodium and aethelium, are lower-case and not italicized. Scientific names of biological organisms – Latin or Greek binomals in which the genus (upper-case) is followed by the specific name (almost always lower-case) – should be italicized on those rare occasions when we use them: e.g. *Cyanocitta cristata*, the blue jay.

Scot, Scottish, Scotch
Use **Scot** and **Scottish** to refer to the people, institutions and culture of Scotland (a Scot, the Scots, the Scottish Church, a Scottish village, Scottish soccer fans). **Scots** is the name of the old dialect of the Lowlands (based on English, not

Gaelic) that was made familiar by the poetry of Burns and Ramsay. Scots as an adjective should appear only in Scotsman, a word with limited use since Scot says the same thing.

Scotch is an English word that has come to be accepted as an adjective even in Scotland in a few non-human applications, such as Scotch whisky, Scotch plaid, Scotch egg, Scotch elm. Note that in Britain, Scotch whisky is referred to simply as whisky.

Scotch tape, a trade name.

Scotiabank
Acceptable in second reference to the Bank of Nova Scotia, and in headlines.

Scotland Yard
It refers not to all London Metropolitan Police, but to their Criminal Investigation Department (which also co-ordinates investigations throughout Britain). Its headquarters is now in New Scotland Yard.

Scout
Use upper case when referring to a member of the Boy Scouts: a Queen's Scout, a Scout.

Screech
Use upper case for the strong rum of Newfoundland, since the provincial liquor board markets a rum under that brand name. However, do not use the word in stories involving alcoholism, car crashes etc., unless we are sure of the brand involved, and unless the brand is relevant. The name probably derives from a Gaelic dialect word for whiskey, *screigh*.

Scripture
Use upper case when it is a synonym for the Bible.

scrotums (not scrota).

sculling, see rowing.

sculping
The term in Newfoundland for skinning a seal.

seal pup (not baby seal).

seasonal and seasonable
Seasonal means taking place in a certain season, characteristic of a season (seasonal rains, plants etc.). **Seasonable** means in keeping with the season (seasonable temperatures). It does not mean mild or pleasant, since snow and sleet are seasonable in winter.

SEATO
The Southeast Asia Treaty Organization, which terminated itself in 1977.

Second Coming
Upper-case for that of Christ.

second-degree murder

Second World War
Use Roman numerals if it appears in a direct quote as World War II.

secretary-general
Hyphen. Use upper-case as a title before a name.

sectarian
Apply it to strife between two sects of the same religion (Protestant against Catholic, for example) but not to strife between members of different religions (Hindu against Muslim etc.).

Seeing Eye dog
Upper case, for the registered name of The Seeing Eye Inc. The generic term is guide dog.

seigneur

seize

sellout

The noun. The verb is **sell out**.

semi

As a combining form it takes a hyphen (semi-conscious, semi-detached).

Semitic

This word applies to language (Arabic, Hebrew, Maltese) rather than to race. The term anti-Semitic, meaning hostile toward Jews, is acceptable in most instances, but we would have to refer to an Arab as being anti-Jewish or anti-Israel, not anti-Semitic. See Jew.

senate, Senate

The Senate is the appointed political body in Parliament, with 105 seats apportioned on a regional basis: six from Newfoundland and Labrador, 24 from the Maritimes (Nova Scotia 10, New Brunswick 10, Prince Edward Island four), 24 from Quebec, 24 from Ontario, 24 from the western provinces (six each for Manitoba, Saskatchewan, Albert and British Columbia) and one for each of the Northwest Territories, Nunavut and Yukon. On second reference, senators are Mr. or Ms., not Sen./Senator.

In the United States, both political bodies of the Congress are elected: the Senate and the House of Representatives. Except in political stories involving several politicians, avoid the abbreviations R and D for Republican and Democrat. (See Democrat, Republican.) Each state elects two senators. As with Canadian senators, the style on second reference is Mr./Ms. Smith.

Use lower case for the senates of non-political organizations, such as universities.

Senegal

Adjective and people: Senegalese. Currency: CFA franc. Capital: Dakar.

It is on the Atlantic, at the farthest point of the bulge of West Africa. This former French colony became part of the Federation of Mali in 1959, but separated the next year to become an independent state. It has a population of 10 million.

sensual and sensuous

Use **sensual** when the meaning is sexual, carnal. Use **sensuous** if the reference is to the five senses of perception, or to an appreciation of beauty, luxury.

Sept. 11, 2001

On this day, four airplanes were hijacked in the United States by 19 people affiliated with Osama bin Laden's al-Qaeda network.

American Airlines Flight 11 left Boston's Logan Airport (bound for Los Angeles) at 7:59 a.m., with 92 people aboard. At 8:48 a.m., it crashed into the north tower of New York's World Trade Center. The tower collapsed at 10:29 a.m.

United Airlines Flight 175 left Boston (bound for Los Angeles) at 8:14 a.m, with 65 people aboard. At 9:06 a.m., it crashed into the south tower of the World Trade Center. The tower collapsed at 9:55 a.m.

It was estimated a year later that 2,801 people were dead or still missing after the World Trade Center attacks, not counting the hijackers.

United Airlines Flight 93 left Newark Airport (bound for San Francisco) at 8:01 a.m. with 45 people aboard. The hijackers were overpowered by the passengers, but the plane crashed in a Pennsylvania field at 10:10 a.m. All aboard died.

American Airlines Flight 77 left Washington's Dulles Airport (bound for Los Angeles) at 8:10 a.m. with 64 people aboard. It crashed into the Pentagon at 9:43 a.m. Estimates a year after the attack were that 184 people died, not counting the hijackers.

The Federal Aviation Administration, which had closed airports in and around New York after the attacks on the World Trade Center, reacted to the attack on the Pentagon by forbidding aircraft to take off anywhere in the United States. A small number of flights, the first of them from Canada, were allowed to resume on Sept. 13. Also on Sept. 13, Secretary of State Colin Powell identified Osama bin Laden as the suspected mastermind of the attacks. Since he was said to be hiding in Afghanistan under the protection of the Taliban regime, the United States and Britain, with international support, invaded that country and ousted the Taliban. See Afghanistan, Taliban.

Although the phrase "Sept. 11" is burned into the memory, and in some incidental references may not need the addition of 2001, for most purposes the year should be included. Use the shorthand form 9/11 sparingly, since it may be read as frivolous or dismissive.

Sept-Îles (not Isles).

sepulchre, sepulchral

Serbia

By 1992 it was one of only two remaining republics in Yugoslavia (along with Montenegro), although it was campaigning to prevent the secession of Serb-held areas of Croatia and Bosnia-Herzegovina. (The dispute is an ancient one; Serbia controlled much of the Balkans area at various times, and its drive to annex Bosnia-Herzegovina in 1914, opposed by Austria but backed by Russia, touched off the First World War.) The intransigence of Yugoslav (and Serbian) leader Slobodan Milosevic and the complicity of the Serb-dominated Yugoslav army in the atrocities in Croatia and Bosnia-Herzegovina prompted an

international trade embargo against Serbia (and Montenegro) in 1992.

Serbia extends northward into the productive Danube plain, but is mountainous in the south. It borders on Albania in the southwest, and the predominantly Albanian population of its southern province of Kosovo (capital Pristina) has agitated for annexation by Albania.

The Yugoslav army's brutal expulsion of ethnic Albanians from Kosovo in 1998 and 1999, as part of a civil war with rebels known as the Kosovo Liberation Army, provoked an international military response. The North Atlantic Treaty Organization began air strikes against Yugoslav targets on March 24, 1999. In June of that year, NATO and Yugoslavia signed a peace agreement that saw NATO's peacekeeping force, KFOR, and Russian peacekeepers enter Kosovo the same month. Kosovo has since been governed under United Nations authority. In September of 1999, the population of Kosovo was half a million smaller than it had been the year before.

Milosevic was defeated in a 2000 election and forced by public protests to accept the result; Vojislav Kostunica replaced him as president. In 2001, Milosevic was arrested and transferred to the International Criminal Tribunal for the Former Yugoslavia in The Hague to be tried for crimes against humanity. In February, 2003, Yugoslavia renamed itself Serbia and Montenegro.

Serbs, whose Serbian Orthodox religion set them apart from others in Yugoslavia, speak the Serbian variant of Serbo-Croat. Both the Roman and Cyrillic alphabets are used.

See Serbia and Montenegro, Montenegro, Yugoslavia.

Serbia and Montenegro

No useful single adjective for the country or word for its people. Individually, Serbian and

Montenegrin. Currency: in Serbia, the dinar, though both the euro and dinar are legal currency in the southern province of Kosovo; in Montenegro, the euro. Capital: Belgrade.

Serbia and Montenegro is the new name, as of February, 2003, for the country formerly known as Yugoslavia. The two loosely federated republics of Serbia and Montenegro agreed in 2003 to hold a referendum in each republic within three years on full independence. The combined population is estimated at 10.7 million. The majority speak Serbian, and a relatively small minority speak Albanian.

On March 12, 2003, reformist prime minister Zoran Djindjic was assassinated by snipers in an apparent attempt to prepare the way for a coup.

See Serbia, Montenegro, Yugoslavia, Kosovo.

sergeant-at-arms, sergeant-major

Plurals are sergeants-at-arms, but sergeant-majors.

sergeant-at-law

serial killer

The important element in referring to a string of murders as the work of a serial killer is not the number of people killed, but the process. A serial killer murders repeatedly, often with no apparent motive but usually with a pattern. A bank robber who kills bank employees in the course of several robberies would not qualify as a serial killer, though he has indeed killed a series of people. It is imaginable that someone might be caught and convicted after killing the second person in what might have become a longer series and still be considered a serial killer, but in practice it requires at least three to detect a pattern.

serrated

service

It is a noun. It does not replace the verb **serve**, but it has become acceptable as a verb in the sense of repair or maintain, as in service a plane or car.

Avoid the hackneyed expression "without the services of." A simple "without" suffices.

seven deadly sins

Lower-case. We should not say that pride, lust, envy, anger, sloth, gluttony and covetousness were considered the most serious sins imaginable. Rather, they are vices that give rise to other sins. Theologians called them "deadly" because they were thought to be directly opposed to development of virtue.

seven seas

Lower-case. Acceptable idiom in informal references to mean all the seas and oceans of the world.

7-Eleven

7Up

The drink itself has a figure and no hyphen. However, the number is usually spelled out in company names, as in Pepsi-Cola & Seven-Up Bottling of Toronto.

Seven Wonders (of the World)

Upper-case.

Seven Years' War

sewage and sewerage

Sewerage is the system of sewers. **Sewage** is human, household and industrial waste that flows through sanitary and industrial sewers. (Readers would find it misleading if we referred to water in storm sewers as sewage.)

sexual abuse

This term has a wide variety of possible meanings. If we provide no elaboration, most readers would assume the classic, narrow meaning of sex involving a minor, or possibly degrading or violent sexual activity with a browbeaten partner. However, many professional groups regard any hint of sexuality involving a patient or client as sexual abuse under their codes of ethics, even such things as sexual remarks of the sort which, outside such professional relationships, would usually be defined as sexual harassment. It is not sufficient to say that a doctor, for example, has been accused of sexual abuse; we must specify the nature of the complaint.

Seychelles

Adjective: Seychelles. People: Seychelles citizens. Currency: rupee. Capital: Victoria.

We do not use the local French adjective, Seychellois, except perhaps in colour pieces. This republic of about 85 islands and islets in the Indian Ocean, close to the equator, was first settled by the French, and French and a French creole are still widely spoken. But it was controlled by the British for 182 years before it gained independence in 1976. About 90 per cent of the 80,000 people live on the island of Mahe, which contains the capital.

shakedown and shakeup

Noun and adjective. The verbs are **shake down** and **shake up**.

Shakespearean

shall and will

For the future tense, use shall for the first person (I or we shall come) and will for the second and third person (you, he, she, it or they will come). However, the roles are switched to achieve emphasis (I will not fail; they shall not pass).

shaman

In shamanism (also lower-case), a shaman is considered a medium to the

spirits or gods. The term medicine man is synonymous for some North American Indians, but for Inuit and many Indian tribes the word shaman (it is from a Siberian dialect) is more appropriate. An African witch doctor may also be a shaman if more than healing is involved.

Shangri-la

sharia

Italics. See Islam.

Sharif (not sherif).

Sheboygan, Wis.; **Cheboygan**, Mich.

Shediac oyster

sheik (not sheikh).

sheriff

In Canada, it is an official who executes orders of the court, including seizing and auctioning goods and conducting people to prison. In the United States, it is the chief administrative officer of a county, whose duties include executing court orders and, in some states, law enforcement. Second reference is Mr. or Ms. for both sheriffs and deputy sheriffs. In England and Wales, a sheriff is the Crown's chief representative in a shire (county), whose duties include the administration of justice and the overseeing of elections. In Scotland, a sheriff is a middle-level judge.

The Muslim title is spelled Sharif. See religious titles.

Shia, Shiite

Use Shia as the adjective (a Shia Muslim, Shia militia). Use Shiite (not Shi'ite) as the noun (he is a Shiite). Shiites, opposed to the orthodox Sunnites, reject the first three caliphs and recognize the descendants of Mohammed's son-in-law Ali as his rightful successors.

Shield, the

Use upper case when referring to the Precambrian (Canadian, Laurentian) Shield. See Precambrian.

shillelagh

shimbun

It means newspaper in Japanese, so we should try our best to avoid blatant redundancies such as "the Asahi Shimbun newspaper" unless these are unavoidable. If it is clear we are speaking of a publication, the word "daily" is often a suitable escape hatch (published in the daily Asahi Shimbun).

shingles

It is singular, a viral disorder of the nerve network. Also called herpes zoster.

shinny

Acceptable as a reference to an informal game of hockey, played without referees and perhaps without the full complement of players. (Shinny was the forerunner of hockey, played with a ball on either ice or grass.)

shinplaster

Lower-case for the 25-cent bills issued in Canada in 1870, 1900 and 1923. (In the United States, the word meant currency issued by private enterprise rather than the government.)

Shinto

It can be described as Japan's indigenous religion, although it absorbed much from Buddhism. Divine power (*kami*) is thought to be manifest in everything at every moment, and so attention paid to even what seems trivial leads to the realization of truth. Shinto means way of the gods.

ship

When speaking of sailing vessels, the word ship (also called a full-rigged ship) applies only to those with at least three masts and square-rigged sails on all three (fore, main and mizzen), although on the rear (mizzen) mast only the upper sails are square; the lowest is a fore-and-aft "spanker." There are also specific meanings for sloop, brig, brigantine, barque, barquentine and schooner, depending on number of masts and how each is rigged (square or fore-and-aft). Canada's Bluenose is not a ship but a two-masted schooner, both its masts being fore-and-aft rigged. See tall ships.

Shippegan, N.B.

But note Shippigan Station.

shivaree

Use this spelling for a singing party. The original charivari, meaning a mock serenade, is unfamiliar to readers.

shock

If we use it as a medical term, we should define it for the reader: the development of low blood pressure inadequate to sustain circulation, most commonly caused by blood loss or heart failure. We should not say someone was "in shock," which means experiencing this medical condition, when we mean he or she was shocked or stunned by a physical or mental battering.

shoo-in

shortchange

shortstop

Show Boat

Two words for the musical, though the lower-case noun and verb is showboat.

showroom

shrapnel

Lower-case, despite its origin in the name of a British (not German) ordnance officer.

Shubert

The theatrical promoters. Spelled differently from composer Franz Schubert.

Shultz, George

The former U.S. secretary of state. The *Peanuts* cartoonist was Charles Schulz.

shutout, the noun.

The verb is **shut out**.

SI

The proper name for the modern metric system, *Système international d'unités*, and the common English contraction, SI units, are not familiar to most Canadian readers. We may use them if we explain, but it is preferable just to say metric system. Note that "SI System" would be redundant.

Siamese twins

Prefer conjoined twins. The Siamese reference started with the famous conjoined twins Chang and Eng, born in what was then Siam and is now Thailand. Conjoined is the medical term preferred by twins and their families, who point out that they are not necessarily of Thai descent.

Siberian husky. See husky.

siege, but **seize**.

sierra

It means a mountain range or system; thus, adding the word mountains would be redundant, as in Sierra Madre Mountains. The Sierra Madre, the great mountain system of Mexico, has three major ranges (Sierra Madre Oriental, Occidental and de Sur). The Sierra Nevada, the mountain range in eastern California,

contains three national parks: Yosemite, Sequoia and King's Canyon.

Sierra Leone

Adjective and people: Sierra Leonean. Currency: leone. Capital: Freetown.

It is on the Atlantic, on the bulge of West Africa, bordering on Guinea and Liberia. It was named by the Portuguese in 1460 and was long a centre of the slave trade, but it became one of the earliest British colonies in Africa, in 1808. It gained independence in 1961 and was declared a republic in 1971. It has at least 18 indigenous tribes, plus the descendants of freed slaves from the Americas, called Creoles. The total population is five million.

Foday Sankoh and his 45,000-member Revolutionary United Front began a particularly vicious rebellion in 1991, supported by Liberia, largely to gain control of valuable diamond deposits in the east. A 1999 truce was widely flouted despite the presence of United Nations peacekeepers, but a 2000 truce proved more durable. The civil war formally ended in 2002, and a national election was held. Sankoh was captured in 2000 and indicted in 2003 by a UN special court for war crimes in Sierra Leone, a tribunal set up by the UN and the government.

Sikh

The Sikh religion combines elements of Hinduism and Islam. When boys and girls are initiated at puberty into the major order of Sikhism, the Khalsa, they adopt the additional name Singh (lion) or Kaur (lioness). We must be careful to use a Sikh's full name to avoid confusion of identities.

The kirpan should be described as a ceremonial dagger worn as a tenet of the Sikh faith. To say simply that someone was carrying a dagger or knife could draw an inference of violent or criminal intent. Wearing the kirpan is one of the five k's that Sikhs are sworn to observe, the others being refraining from cutting hair or beard (*kes*), and wearing a comb (*kanga*), shorts (*kach*) and iron bracelet (*kartha*).

The Sikh holy book, the Adi Granth, is a compilation of the writing of the early gurus. There is no professional priesthood; any man or woman is eligible to lead religious ceremonies, principally the reading of the Granth. There is one God, never represented by images, whom man serves by leading a good life and by praying, principally by repeating His name. A person's soul goes through various existences by means of transmigration until it ultimately becomes one with God.

silhouette

silicon and silicone
   Silicon is a non-metallic element, the second most abundant element on Earth after oxygen, found naturally as silica and in silicates. It is used in alloys and in making semi-conductors for the electronics industry, and lends its name to California's Silicon Valley. Carborundum is silicon carbide. Silicon tetrachloride is the basis of several other organic silicon compounds, including **silicones**. These are the familiar materials used as lubricants and moisture repellents, and in surgical implants.

silk-screen, silk-screen process.

silviculture
   Prefer tree planting, tree farming, reforestation.

Simcoe, John Graves
   Despite the name of the former hotel, he was not Lord Simcoe or even Sir John. He was the first lieutenant-governor of Upper Canada and founder of York (Toronto).

Simoniz, a trade name.

simpatico
   Probably too misleading to be useful in news stories. It does not mean in sympathy with, but rather congenial, pleasant, charming. Note spelling.

simper
   It is a silly, self-conscious smile. The word does not imply any sound.

SIN
   Acceptable in second reference for social insurance number, and in headlines if the context is clear and there is no unintended double meaning.

sine qua non
   Avoid. Use a condition, a prerequisite, an essential.

Singapore
   Adjective for the country: Singapore. People: Singaporean, citizens of Singapore, or Singapore Chinese, Malay etc. Currency: dollar. Capital: Singapore.
   This republic, consisting primarily of the island of Singapore but also about 60 nearby islets, is just north of the equator, by about 140 kilometres. Malaya lies northward across Johor Strait, while to the south, across the Strait of Singapore, lie several small Indonesian islands. Indonesia's giant island of Sumatra is southwest across the Strait of Malacca. The official languages are English, Malay, Mandarin and Tamil. The population is 4.2 million.

Sinhalese

sink, sank, sunk
   The boat sank; the boat has sunk.

sizable

skeet shooting, see trapshooting.

skeptic, skeptical

ski, skis, skier, skiing

Ski-Doo, a trade name.

The generic term is snowmobile. Note that the line of clothing is called Ski Doo Sports, no hyphen.

skid row

Use this version for the part of town inhabited by people down on their luck. It derives from **skid road**, a track used to haul logs.

skillful

skin diving, but **skydiving**.

Note that skin diving does not necessarily involve air tanks. That is scuba diving.

skookum

In the Chinook Jargon, it means big and powerful, as in Skookum Jim, one of the three men whose discovery touched off the Klondike Gold Rush. Skookumchuck means rapids or tides.

skulduggery

SkyDome

The Toronto stadium.

skyjack, skyjacker

Acceptable in headlines as an economical reference to the hijacking of an aircraft. In copy, prefer hijack.

slang

We avoid it in normal news stories, but it may be used to create a mood in lighter stories and in features. As with all departures from standard English or grammar, the trick is establishing an understanding between writer and reader that both know the rules and why they are being broken in this case. Slang is also permissible in direct quotes. In neither case is the slang set off by quotation marks, unless the expression is new to the reader and is

to be explained immediately afterward. See quotations.

Slavonic languages

We cannot refer to someone "speaking Slavonic," because many languages are involved, spoken by almost 250 million people in Central and Eastern Europe and in Siberia. The three groups are South Slavonic (Bulgarian, Croatian, Macedonian, Serbian and Slovene), East Slavonic (Russian, Belarussian and Ukrainian) and West Slavonic (Polish, Czech and Slovak).

sleight of hand

slipped disc

The term is acceptable in informal references, but note that the cushioning discs between vertebrae do not actually slip out of place. The soft inner portion bulges through the fibrous outer layer, causing pain and even paralysis by pressing on nerves.

slipstream

slough

On the Prairies, it means a pond or pothole, a low area where water gathers, often seasonally. On the West Coast and in Eastern Canada, it means a marsh. Westerners rhyme it with flue, while easterners rhyme it with cow.

When it means cast off, as with a snakeskin, all Canadians rhyme it with stuff. Write slough off, not sluff off.

Slovakia

Adjective and people: Slovak. Currency: koruna. Capital: Bratislava.

The official name is the Slovak Republic. A former constituent republic of Czechoslovakia, created when the formerly unitary state was split into a two-member federation in 1968, it became independent at midnight on Dec. 31, 1992. Slovakia was the driving force in the peaceful "velvet divorce," largely because of its opposition to the speed of conversion from a controlled economy to a market system. It is bounded by the Czech Republic to the west, Ukraine to the east, Poland to the north and Austria and Hungary to the south. Its population of about 5.4 million, almost 90-per-cent Slovak, includes a sizable Hungarian minority in the south, and there are also Czechs, Ukrainians, Germans, Russians and Poles. The Slovaks are a western Slavic people whose language, divided into three dialect groups, is closely related to Czech and Polish.

Slovakia is largely mountainous and comparatively sparsely populated, with more than 40 per cent of its territory forested. The Slovak Ore Mountains in the south, part of the Carpathians, are rich in minerals, particularly high-grade iron ore, copper, lead and zinc. There is also hydro power, and heavy industries predominate, with accompanying pollution problems in mill areas. Tourism is an important sector.

See Czechoslovakia.

Slovenia

Adjective and people: Slovenian, Slovene. Currency: tolar (Slovenian dinar). Capital: Ljubljana.

It declared independence from Yugoslavia in June of 1991, and faced only brief opposition from the Serb-led Yugoslav federal army (unlike Bosnia and Croatia). It was the northernmost and wealthiest of the Yugoslav republics, with only 7 per cent of the population but producing 15 per cent of the federation's economic output. It is also the most Central European, bordering on Italy, Austria, Hungary and Croatia and having long served as Yugoslavia's trade and cultural gateway to the north. The population of about 1.9 million is 90-per-cent Slovenes, whose Slavic language is akin to Serbo-

Croat. It is largely mountainous with little land suitable for farming, but extensive upland pastures support a large dairy industry. Its economy is well diversified, with mining, timber, steel, textiles, light industries and tourism.

See Yugoslavia.

slow-witted

smallpox

A disease caused by the variola major virus, marked by fever and blisters, fatal in about 30 per cent of cases. Eradicated worldwide by 1980, except in small stockpiles held in the United States and Russia.

small-time

smart aleck

Smiths Falls, Ont.

Smithsonian Institution (not Institute).

smithy

What stands under the chestnut tree, the village smithy, is the shop or forge. The mighty man who operates it is the smith.

smoulder

snakebite, snakeskin

But **snake eyes** (in craps), two words.

sneaked (not snuck).

snail's pace

snorkel

snow

One word: snowball, snowbank, snowbird, snowbound, snowcap, snowdrift, snowfall, snowflake, snowman, snowmobile, snowplow, snowshoe, snowslide, snowstorm, snowsuit. **Two words**: snow apple, snow blindness, snow blower, snow bunting, snow fence, snow flurry, snow goose, snow job, snow leopard, snow line, snow pellets, snow squall, snow thrower, snow tire. **Hyphenated**: snow-clad, snow-white.

s.o.b.

Use the initials only if the speaker does. The initials (note the periods) are acceptable in a quote, but if the speaker uses the full expression, son of a bitch, we must paraphrase. (There is a rare exception if the quote is unusually newsworthy; see obscene language.)

so-called

Avoid this expression if there is any chance that it will convey the impression that the following definition is not to be believed.

soccer

In overseas copy, substitute this word for references to football, association football.

Social Credit Party

We must not imply that modern Socreds apply, or even believe in, the principles of social credit developed by English engineer Major C. H. Douglas in the 1920s and seized upon by Alberta evangelist William Aberhart. In Quebec, the nickname Socred should be replaced with Créditiste.

socialist

Use lower case for socialist, socialism, if referring to a political philosophy. Use upper case if referring to a party called Socialist, or to its members.

social security

Use lower case in the generic term for U.S. government safety-net programs to help the poor, sick, disabled etc. (But note upper case in Social Security Act.) In Canada,

prefer social programs, social spending. See welfare.

Society of Friends. Prefer Quakers.

Society of Jesus. Prefer Jesuits.

soda

Reserve for bubbly water, or an ice cream drink made with it. In U.S. stories, the word soda usually refers to what Canadians call pop or a soft drink.

soft-pedal

solar system, see planets.

solomon gundy

In Atlantic Canada, pickled herring. (It is a whimsical corruption of salmagundi, a type of salad with meat and anchovies.)

Solomon Islands

People: Solomon Islanders, or citizens of the Solomon Islands. Currency: dollar. Capital: Honiara.

This mountainous archipelago, in the area of the southwestern Pacific known as Melanesia, gained full independence from Britain in 1978. Like Canada, it is a constitutional monarchy, with a locally named governor-general. The Solomons form part of the boundary of the Coral Sea, together with New Guinea and the Bismarcks to the west, the New Hebrides to the southeast and the east coast of Australia. The largest of the 21 major islands is Guadalcanal, which contains the capital. There are also many smaller islands. English is the official language; there is also a pidgin English lingua franca, and about 90 local languages. The population is 470,000.

Hundreds of islanders have been killed in factional fighting in past years. In June of 2003, the foreign ministers of 16 South Pacific nations endorsed a plan to send 2,000 troops and police, financed and organized largely by Australia with help from New Zealand, to restore and maintain order.

So long as

See as long as.

Solzhenitsyn, Alexander

Somalia

Adjective and people: Somali. Currency: shilling. Capital: Mogadishu.

Somalia is a republic occupying the entire coast of the Horn of Africa, its northern coast forming the southern shore of the Gulf of Aden, and the rest of its coast sweeping southwestward from the point of the Horn to just south of the equator. It borders on Ethiopia and Kenya. Formed from the former colonies British Somaliland and Italian Somaliland, it became independent in 1960. The national language, Somali, has no written form. Arabic is widely spoken, along with some English and Italian. The population is nine million.

The country descended into virtual anarchy after the ouster of dictator Mohamed Siad Barre in January of 1991, with local warlords and clans fighting for control of various areas and the violence turning a famine into a catastrophe. The north attempted to declare its secession in May of 1991, proposing to call itself Somaliland. In late 1992, the United Nations authorized a large-scale military intervention, led by U.S. troops but also involving smaller contingents from other countries, including Canada, to stop the banditry that was preventing a great proportion of international aid from reaching the starving.

The various UN contingents met with hostile receptions, and several were accused of racism in their treatment of Somalis, including some

Americans, Italians and Belgians and a few members of the Canadian Airborne Regiment. Canada was praised for its success in distributing aid and establishing civilian police in its area of responsibility, but Canadian soldiers also killed at least four Somali civilians, including teenager Shidane Arone, tortured to death at the Canadian camp at Belet Huen in March of 1993. (Private Kyle Brown, court-martialled in Canada, was convicted of manslaughter in 1994. Master Corporal Clayton Matchee was found unfit for trial because of brain damage from a suicide attempt in Somalia.) The last UN troops left on March 2, 1995.

In Canada, a growing scandal surrounding its Somalia tour led to the disbanding of the Airborne in February of 1995 (largely because of videotapes showing some members making racist comments and recruits taking part in degrading hazing rituals). A federal public inquiry began hearings in September of 1995, examining the Airborne's inadequate preparation for its Somalia tour and military efforts to suppress the videotapes and other damaging information, an effort that included the altering of documents. The inquiry far exceeded its deadline as it encountered new allegations and military stonewalling, and was ordered by the government to issue its final report, *Dishonoured Legacy*, in July of 1997 before it had completed its work.

sombre

some

Avoid as a synonym for approximately or about.

some day, some place, some time, some way

But as an adjective, **sometime** is one word (love is a sometime thing).

sonar

Lower-case. An acronym for sound navigation and ranging. The British and Canadian term during the Second World War was asdic, which see.

Soo, the

Acceptable in headlines and in second reference to Sault Ste. Marie.

SOS, no periods.

Sotheby's

Acceptable standing alone as a reference to the auctioneers, Sotheby's (Canada) Inc., or the British and U.S. firms.

sound, speed of, see Mach.

sound bite, not byte

soundtrack

sources

Readers deserve to know where their information is coming from. Even when we have good reasons for not naming people, we should describe them as closely as we dare. A quote attributed to "a source" appears in quite different lights if we expand the attribution to read a source at the top level of the department, a disgruntled employee, a member of the board, a lawyer for the opposing camp, a friend of the candidate, a party publicist. The reader needs such information to detect in the quote the background noise, however faint, of axe-grinding, the soft hissing of trial balloons.

sourdough

Not a name for just any prospector. This name for fermented bread dough was adopted for themselves by experienced prospectors in the Klondike. They called newcomers **cheechakos**.

south

See capitalization, directions.

South Africa

Adjective and people: South African. Currency: rand. Capital: Pretoria, but note that strictly speaking, there are three capitals. Pretoria is designated the administrative capital, Cape Town the legislative capital and Bloemfontein the judicial capital. This need be mentioned only in references to this issue.

It has been the Republic of South Africa since 1961. It had been called the Union of South Africa since 1910, when it was formed from the self-governing British colonies Cape of Good Hope, Natal, Orange Free State and Transvaal.

In 1961, National Party Prime Minister Hendrik Verwoerd announced his government's intention to create "homelands" for South African blacks in the name of apartheid, the policy of keeping the races apart and ensuring the continuation of white rule. Millions of blacks were forced to move to these territories, mostly rural and impoverished.

Apartheid laws were dismantled in stages by President F. W. de Klerk, who also freed black leader Nelson Mandela in 1990 and began negotiations on a democratic constitution. The last vestiges were eliminated in 1994 when the new constitution took effect, Mandela was elected president, and the black homelands were eliminated along with the four original provinces. They were replaced by nine new provinces, each with its own legislature: Gauteng, Northern Cape, Eastern Cape, Western Cape, Northern Province, Mpumalanga, KwaZulu-Natal, Free State and Northwest. The provinces are administratively equal, but Gauteng, which includes Johannesburg, dominates the business and industrial life of the country.

Mandela and de Klerk were awarded the Nobel Peace Price in 1993. South Africa was freed from international sanctions with the adoption of its new constitution, and also rejoined the Commonwealth in 1994.

South Africa is bounded on the northwest by Namibia, on the north by Botswana and Zimbabwe, on the northeast by Mozambique and on the east by Swaziland. Its territory surrounds the independent country of Lesotho.

The population of 44 million is roughly 70 per cent black, 18 per cent white, 9 per cent of mixed race and 3 per cent Asian.

Southam News
The news service once operated by Southam Inc. for its member newspapers no longer exists. CanWest Global Communications Corp., which bought Southam Inc. from Hollinger International Inc. in 2000, replaced the agency in 2003 with CanWest News Service.

Southern Cross
Upper-case. The four bright stars forming this constellation (also called Crux) near the south celestial pole are Alpha, Beta, Gamma and Delta, or Acrux, Mimosa, Gacrux and Delta Crucis.

South Korea
Adjective and people: South Korean. Currency: won. Capital: Seoul.

There is no need to use the full name Republic of Korea, except to explain the initials ROK in a quote. It is divided from North Korea (the Democratic People's Republic of Korea) by the demilitarized zone along the 38th parallel. It is separated from Japan by the Sea of Japan in the east and the Korea Strait in the south. In the west, it is separated from China by the Yellow Sea. (When relevant, we should note that the Sea of Japan is known to Koreans as the East Sea.) Its population is 48 million.

South Korea was long a virtual

one-party state that severely suppressed political dissent. Tentative liberalization began after 1993 under President Kim Young-sam, including the conviction on treason and corruption charges of his two predecessors as president, Chun Doo-huan and Roh Tai-woo, but he encountered fierce opposition after passing a new labour law in secret in December of 1996. In February of 1997 he was forced by widespread strikes and international pressure to agree to amend the law, and his power, based on a long-standing alliance between government and big business, was further eroded by the Asian financial crisis crippling Asian economies that year. A watershed was the election of former political prisoner Kim Dae-jung in December of 1997, the first member of an opposition party ever elected Korean president. In March of 1998 he declared an amnesty for 5.5 million prisoners. Another watershed saw Kim Dae-jung hold the first south-north summit in June, 2000, with North Korean leader Kim Jong-il, but relations soon stalled.

South Moresby
There is no South Moresby Island. South Moresby is a region in the Queen Charlottes that consists of the southern two-thirds or so of Moresby Island plus some of the larger neighbouring islands, notably Knight and Burnaby.

South Yemen, see Yemen.

sovereigntist, sovereignty-association

Soviet Union
The Soviet Union was formed in 1922, its constitution was adopted in 1923, and its driving force, Lenin, died in 1924. Joseph Stalin became the unquestioned leader after a power struggle with Leon Trotsky ended with

Trotsky's expulsion in 1927, and internal Communist Party democracy was replaced by a Stalinist personality cult. On his death in 1953 he was succeeded by a collective leadership, from which Nikita Khrushchev emerged dominant in 1957-58. He was ousted in 1964 and replaced by another collective leadership, which was gradually taken over in the late 1960s by Leonid Brezhnev. Yuri Andropov was elected leader on Brezhnev's death in 1982. He died in 1984 and was replaced by Konstantin Chernenko, who died 13 months later in March of 1985 and was replaced by Mikhail Gorbachev. As Soviet president as well as leader of the Soviet Communist Party, he held power until the Soviet Union dissolved at the end of 1991.

Eight Communist hard-liners, opposing Gorbachev's swift détente with the West, his headlong market and democratic reforms (*perestroika* and *glasnost*) and his plan to grant the restive republics more autonomy, staged a coup on Aug. 19, 1991. The coup collapsed on Aug. 21, largely because of the opposition of Russian President Boris Yeltsin, and Gorbachev virtually outlawed the Communist Party on Aug. 23.

The Soviet Union was at its largest, with 15 republics, with the annexation of the three Baltic states (Estonia, Latvia and Lithuania) in 1940 through a deal with Nazi Germany. These three also led off its disintegration, winning international and Soviet recognition as independent republics in September of 1991. Negotiations among the remaining 12 in October and November on a proposed economic union were inconclusive. On Dec. 8, 1991, the Slavic republics, Russia, Ukraine and Belarus, formed the Commonwealth of Independent States and declared Gorbachev's Soviet government dead. Several other republics joined the grouping, linked by economic and defence pacts. The population of the Soviet Union before it fell apart was 291 million.

The Trans-Caucasian Soviet Socialist Republic, which joined the union in 1922, was later split into Armenia, Azerbaijan and Georgia. These republics are still referred to as being in the Trans-Caucasian region.

See Armenia, Azerbaijan, Belarus, Commonwealth of Independent States, Estonia, Georgia, Kazakhstan, Kyrgyzstan, Latvia, Lithuania, Moldova, Russia, Tajikistan, Turkmenistan, Ukraine, Uzbekistan, USSR.

soybean, soy sauce (not soya).

space

Space begins where the atmosphere ends (or peters out). There is no exact boundary where the rarefied hydrogen and helium atoms of the exosphere give way to the particles of interplanetary space. For most purposes, space can be described as beginning about 1,600 kilometres from Earth's surface. However, for the purposes of flight, space is regarded as beginning much sooner, either where a craft can no longer rely on natural atmospheric gases for buoyancy and for combustion oxygen, or where it can achieve orbit (at about 200 kilometres).

The term outer space has no useful meaning. In general, we limit ourselves to the terms atmosphere and space, although we can divide space into several ever-larger spheres: that extending out about 10 Earth radii (65,000 kilometres), within which the Earth's gravitational and magnetic fields affect the density and motion of particles; that between Earth and the moon (cislunar space, but avoid the term); interplanetary space (within our solar system); interstellar space (beyond the solar system); and intergalactic space (beyond our galaxy, the Milky Way).

The minimum orbital altitude of about 200 kilometres should not be described as the point where Earth's gravity ends; the effects of Earth's gravity are felt to the moon and beyond, even affecting the motion of other planets. Rather, 200 kilometres is the point where, at a burnout speed of 28,800 kilometres an hour, a craft achieves a balance between gravity and centrifugal force. (To escape the Earth's gravitational attraction altogether, a craft must reach a speed of at least 40,000 kilometres an hour.) Another significant altitude is 41,600 kilometres, at which a stable orbit takes exactly one Earth day (24 hours and a bit). At this height a satellite is geostationary, staying above the same spot on the surface, useful for bouncing signals.

Spacecraft are always launched toward the east, to take advantage of the Earth's own rotational speed.

In general, we avoid the jargon of space agencies and astronomers (cislunar, perigee, apogee, perihelion, aphelion). We explain such terms as pulsar, quasar, black hole, nebula.

space-time

Hyphenate this way of describing the geometry of the universe as a continuum in which time is the fourth dimension rather than being separate from three-dimensional space. It arises from Einstein's special theory of relativity.

Spain

Adjective: Spanish. People: Spaniards. Currency: euro (had been the peseta). Capital: Madrid.

This constitutional monarchy is bounded on the north by the Pyrenees (separating it from France and Andorra) and by the Bay of Biscay, on the west by Portugal and the Atlantic, and on the east and south by the Mediterranean and the Strait of Gibraltar. It also includes the Canary Islands in the Atlantic (Tenerife,

Grand Canary, Palma, Gomera, Hierro, Fuertaventura, Lanzarote and several smaller islands) and the Balearic Islands in the Mediterranean (Majorca, Minorca, Ibiza and some smaller islands). Castilian Spanish is the official language of the state, but other languages also have official status in certain districts, namely Catalan, Galician (a Portuguese dialect) and Basque. The head of state is King Juan Carlos. Much of the interior consists of the Meseta, an arid plateau, but the Andalusian plains are fertile, and there are also narrow coastal plains. Oil was discovered in 1964, near Burgos. The country's population is 40 million.

There is ambiguity in the Spanish word for the country's political leader. The constitution, the press and people in polite conversation refer to the *presidente del gobierno*. However, since he serves within a constitutional monarchy, his position is equivalent to that of Canada's prime minister. Refer to him as a prime minister, not a president.

spam

Lower-case for the largely unwanted e-mail mass mailings, the electronic equivalent of junk mail. It derives its name indirectly from the lunch meat Spam made by Hormel Foods, and directly from a comedy sketch on the television show *Monty Python's Flying Circus*, in which a raucous group of Vikings in a restaurant repeatedly shouted the word "Spam!" Internet users seized on the word as a term of derision for unsolicited e-mails that crowded out other electronic conversation.

spandex

Lower-case. The brand name for du Pont's version of spandex is Lycra.

Spanish and Portuguese names

In Spanish-speaking countries, a person's full name includes both the father's and mother's surnames (in that order), and usage is quite predictable. Portuguese names appear similar but are a minefield for the unwary; the order of patronymic and matronymic is usually reversed, and there is a wide variety of informal practices. We must be at pains to determine the person's own usage.

When we know it, The Globe gives the full name in first reference for non-prominent persons, since identification is a problem in Latin countries where a great many people share relatively few surnames. But we drop the matronymic of prominent entertainers, top politicians and historical figures, such as Placido Domingo (Embil), Fidel Castro, Ernesto Zedillo and Juan Peron, and drop the patronymic of women known widely by their husband's surname, such as Isabel Peron. (However, these may be given in the course of a profile piece or obituary as enrichment.) We may also refer to a prominent woman by her maiden name after marriage if she continues to be known by that name.

Hispanic immigrants to Canada and other countries often do not observe the traditional practices in their names. Many drop the matronymic, for example, or hyphenate it. We must determine individual preference.

Spanish names: They are quite regular. If a man is named Juan Ortega Silva, his given name is Juan, his patronymic is Ortega and his matronymic is Silva. On second reference he is Mr. Ortega.

An unmarried woman, e.g. Josefina Hurtado Villa, also gets the patronymic in second reference: Ms. Hurtado. If she marries Mr. Ortega, she becomes Josefina Hurtado de Ortega (Josefina de Ortega is permissible if we can't determine her own patronymic). On second reference we call her Mrs. Ortega. If she had achieved status as a public figure under her maiden name,

we call her Josefina Hurtado in first reference, then Ms. Hurtado (never Mrs. Hurtado).

If Juan and Josefina have children, their names will be Alicia Ortega Hurtado, Felipe Ortega Hurtado etc.

There are occasions when both surnames are used in all references, mainly for well-known writers whose patronymics are common names, such as Garcia. Gabriel Garcia Marquez becomes Mr. Garcia Marquez to avoid confusion with other literary Garcias. In a headline he is Garcia Marquez— in a pinch Garcia, but never Marquez. The matronymic may also be used when two people in a story have the same patronymic, e.g. Ms. Camacho Torres and Ms. Camacho Reyes.

There are some compound surnames, and writers and editors must be sure of the patronymic if a second reference is required. For example, Carlos Torres y Torres Mantilla is the son of Mr. Torres y Torres and Ms. Mantilla. He would be Mr. Torres y Torres on second reference.

Also note that the particles de (of), del and la are integral parts of some surnames, e.g. Carlos Salinas de Gortari (father Mr. Salinas, mother Ms. de Gortari) and Miguel de la Madrid Hurtado (father Mr. de la Madrid, mother Ms. Hurtado). If Juana Palacios marries Mr. de la Madrid, she becomes Juana Palacios de de la Madrid (sic).

Portuguese names: Pitfalls abound. Not only is the order of patronymic and matronymic usually reversed, but usage in general is less predictable, especially in Brazil, where nicknames, diminutives and short forms are also ubiquitous.

The father's surname is usually the last in the sequence but not always the name by which a person chooses to be known; when in doubt, use both surnames in second reference. Former Brazilian president Fernando Collor de Mello is Mr. Collor (his mother's surname, which is less common than Mello).

Some married women use the husband's surname only for legal or official purposes.

There may be more than one given name, e.g. Ana Claudia Moreira, Fernando Henrique Cardoso. Particles such as de, do, da, dos and das may form part of a surname, but in Portuguese practice these need not be preserved on second reference. Mailson da Nobrega becomes Mr. Nobrega.

The words Filho (son) and Neto (grandson) are sometimes placed after Portuguese surnames; never call anyone Mr. Filho or Mr. Neto.

Spartan

spastic

Avoid this word as a noun or adjective to refer to someone with cerebral palsy. Describe cerebral palsy as being characterized by muscle spasms.

Speaker

Use upper case for the presiding officer in Parliament or a legislature. Lower-case the word deputy, but for clarity keep Speaker upper-case (deputy Speaker). See capitalization.

Special Forces

Capitalize the U.S. Special Forces. They are five groups commanded and controlled by the U.S. Army Special Forces Command. Each of the groups supports one of the five commanders-in-chief, of the U.S. European Command, U.S. Atlantic Command, U.S. Pacific Command, U.S. Southern Command and U.S. Central Command.

The U.S. Army Special Operations Command is the umbrella group governing special operations. Unless we are specifically referring to that body – which controls not only the Special Forces, but the Rangers, special aviation operations, psychological operations, civil affairs and signal and combat service support units – we should lower-case references to U.S. special operations forces.

The U.S. military has an overarching body – the Special Operations Command (Socom) – which looks after all the commandos, including the Army's Special Forces (a.k.a. the Green Berets), the Army's top-secret Delta Force, the Navy Seals (short for Sea-Air-Land) and the Air Force's search-and-rescue teams.

Socom was set up in 1987 at the end of the Cold War. It has 46,000 active-duty and reserve members, about 30,000 of them with the Army. The command has its headquarters in Tampa, Fla., based at MacDill Air Force Base.

specialty (prefer to speciality).

spectre

Speech from the Throne

Throne Speech.

speechwriter

speed skating

speedup, noun. The verb is **speed up**.

spell-check

Although spell-check computer programs will detect transposed or dropped letters or sheer garble (palce for place, ern for earn), more subtle mistakes will elude most of them. They pass no judgment on whether each word is appropriate in context, and would be oblivious to the misspelling of "mistake which we can't see" as "mistake witch wee cant sea."

To avoid being lulled into a false sense of security, edit the story first, and only then press the spell-check button to determine how well you did at one aspect (a fairly rudimentary one) of the task: spotting typos.

spelling

Since many English words have at least two "correct" spellings—usually conflicting British and U.S. versions, with Canadian versions playing the field—The Globe and Mail has developed its own style to maintain consistency in its pages.

For several years, The Globe has used *Nelson Canadian Dictionary* as its official spelling guide. Since the 1997 edition of that dictionary is not being updated, we will instead use the excellent *Canadian Oxford Dictionary* as our spelling dictionary. This means that, **unless a word appears in this entry as a spelling exception, it should be spelled the way *Canadian Oxford* spells it in the main entry for that word. If the main entry offers a choice of two or more spellings, use the first spelling.**

The Globe's preference is for spelling words such as humour and labour with the u. The following list of -our words indicates those variants that drop the u. If a variation on a root word is not included in the brackets, assume that it retains the u.

arbour (all variants are -or)
ardour
armour (armorial, armorist)
armoury
behaviour
belabour
candour
clamour (clamorous)
colour (colorant, coloration, colorific, colorimeter, Colorize)
demeanour
discolour (discoloration)
disfavour
dishonour
dolour (dolorous)
enamour
endeavour
favour
fervour

flavour (flavorous)
glamour (glamorize, glamorous)
harbour
honour (honorarium, honorary, honorific)
humour (humoresque, humorist, humorous)
labour (laborious)
misbehaviour
misdemeanour
neighbour
odour (odorous)
parlour
rancour (rancorous)
rigour (rigorism, rigorous, rigor mortis, rigor for other medical and pathological meanings)
rumour
saviour
savour (savorous, savory for the plant but savoury is the adjective)
splendour (splendorous)
succour
tumour (tumorous, tumoral)
valour (valorize, valorous)
vapour (vaporize, vaporizer, vaporous, vaporific, vaporimeter, vaporescent)
vigour (invigorating, vigorous)

We also spell such words as centre and litre with -re rather than -er. However, where a proper noun from an English-speaking country differs from our style, we should respect the difference if we are aware of it (e.g. Rockefeller Center). We make an exception to that rule for government departments and their officials: the U.S. Defence Department, the Secretary of Labour.

Our usual practice with diphthongs is to drop the first letter of the diphthong in words that have entered the English language, such as anesthetic (not anaesthetic) and archeologist (not archaeologist). Exceptions are proper names (Caesar, but note cesarean section), aegis, aerial, aeronautics, aesthetic, amoeba, oenology, onomatopoeia and certain words from legal or other jargon, such as subpoena.

Final consonants: When a word ending in a single-letter vowel followed by a single consonant takes the suffix **ed**, **er**, **or**, **ing**, **al**, **age**, **ish**, **ence** or **y**, follow this general rule: If the word has one syllable, or if the stress is on the final syllable, double the consonant (e.g. batted, preferred). If the final syllable is not stressed, do not double the consonant (altered, benefited, focused).

Exceptions: Do not double the consonant in bused or busing.

Do not double if the final consonant is h, w, x or y (oohed and ahed, plowed, boxed, annoyed). If the final consonant is c, add a k: panicked, picnicker, Quebecker.

Do not double the final consonant if it is silent (crocheted).

If the final consonant is l, g and sometimes m and p, our style is to double it with the suffixes above even when the final syllable is unstressed (traveller, counsellor, libellous, sandbagged, programming, eavesdropped, handicapped, kidnapped, worshipping, **but** developed, accustomed, ransomed). Exception: paralleled, devilish. The consonant should also be doubled for words ending in ial, ual and uel (dialled, initialled, equalled, fuelled, gruelling).

Rules of thumb: *Canadian Oxford*'s style on capitalization is not necessarily ours. At the same time, be aware that many words we take for granted are registered trade names in Canada, and should be capitalized in that context. (See trademark.)

Where the prefix to a word ends in the same vowel that begins the word, always insert a hyphen. Thus: co-operate, re-elect, anti-intellectual. Always insert a hyphen after a prefix if the main word begins with a capital letter.

Use hyphens after the following prefixes: anti, **co**, **extra** (in the sense of additional, not outside), mini, **non**, **pro** (in favour of), **semi**. There are a few exceptions to anti and mini; see their separate entries. Use a hyphen after **counter** only if the root word begins with r (counter-revolutionary).

Titles ending in the word general or beginning with vice use a hyphen. Thus: attorney-general, consul-general, director-general, governor-general, solicitor-general, surgeon-general, vice-admiral, vice-president. Exceptions: viceregal, viceroy.

Do not place an s at the end of such words as forward, toward and backward.

The plurals of words of Latin origin are formed in the main in the English rather than Latin or Greek style, with some exceptions for scientific, medical and academic terms. (See main entry on plurals.)

Individual exceptions: We have tried to keep this list as short as possible; editors and writers may wish to mark these exceptions (roughly 125 words) in their own copies of *Canadian Oxford* for ease of access. The spellings marked with an asterisk are expected to be the primary spellings in the 2004 edition of the dictionary:

abridgment
acknowledgment
anesthetic
animé (for Japanese animation)
any place
archeology
*audiotape
a while (not awhile)
BA (bachelor of arts)
B.C. (for British Columbia; BC for the date)
*bestseller
Big Bang (for the one that started it all)
*B'nai Brith
BSc (bachelor of science)
byproduct
cactuses

Candu reactor (not CANDU, though that is how Atomic Energy of Canada Ltd. spells its registered trademark)
capelin (not caplin)
*casbah (not kasbah)
cesarean section (not Caesarean)
*chequebook
citywide
*cliffhanger
*concertgoer
contra (for anti-Sandinista rebels, not Contra)
*copter (not 'copter)
*Crown land
darnedest (to match damnedest)
*deshabille (not déshabillé)
DJ
dialled, dialling, dialler, direct dialling
dimwit (but dim-witted)
*Dow Jones (not Dow-Jones)
Down syndrome
*dreaming in Technicolor (no u)
duffel
earned-run average
Earth, for the planet
Eid, Eid al-Fitr, Eid al-Adha (not Id)
e-mail
*English-Canadian (adj.)
enroll (enrolment)
every place
façade
*first minister (not First Minister)
first nation (not First Nation, except as part of proper names)
fleur-de-lis (not -lys)
flutist
flier (for people and things that fly; flyer for ads)
free-trade agreement (Canada-U.S. free-trade agreement, FTA, North American free-trade agreement, NAFTA)
franco-Canadian
French fry
fulfilment (fulfill)
gibe (a joke or taunt; to jibe is to be in accord with)
hallelujah (not alleluia, for the shout of joy)
high flier
hooves (not hoofs)
Hutus (plural, not Hutu)

interpretive (not interpretative)
*Jakarta (not Djakarta)
Khomaini, Ruhollah
Kim Il-sung (not Kim Il Sung)
Koran (not Quran, Qur'an)
*larynxes (not larynges)
*Lipizzaner (not Lippizaner)
*Macau (not Macao)
*makeover
medalist
Meech Lake accord (not Accord)
*megacity
men's wear
minister's permit (lower-case)
M'Naghten rule
mollusk
mom
mustache
*Noh (not No, for the theatre)
*okay (not OK)
*order-in-council (lower-case)
order paper (lower-case)
*O-ring
orthopedic
panelist
*partygoer
PhD
plowman, plowshare
*postgraduate
*postwar
protégé
*protester
provincewide
putdown
Quebecker
*representation by population, rep by pop (lower case)
*Salvadoran
sharia
skillful
sneaked (not snuck)
Solzhenitsyn, Alexander
some day, some place, some way
SOSes (should the plural ever be needed)
sovereigntist
speechwriter
Statscan (not StatsCan)
*stopgap
*theatregoer
tranquillize
*trendsetter

tuque (see style entry for tuque)
*under way
*V-chip
*videocassette
voiceover
Web, the (short for the World Wide Web)
*webcam, webcast, weblog, webmaster, website; web browser, web page, web ring, web server
*whir, whirring (not whirr)
*widescreen
willful
women's wear
word play
work force
writeoff
yogurt

Spider-Man

Not Spiderman, for the cartoon character and movie.

spiders

They should not be called insects (they have no larval or pupal stage, they lack antennae, they have a fused head and thorax, and their eyes are simple rather than compound). Not all are web spinners; there are also running, jumping, wolf, trap-door and aquatic spiders. They are found throughout Canada (there are even 13 species on Ellesmere Island, out of a total of about 1,300 species in the country). Black widows are found in Southern Ontario, Saskatchewan, Alberta and B.C. There are nine species of tarantulas in Ontario and B.C.

Spielberg, Steven

spinnaker

spinster

Avoid. It is grating to most women, is outdated and possibly misleading in this age of unsanctioned, informal unions, and is also vague (it means a woman of any age who has never married, but is usually equated with old maid). If marital status or domestic arrangements are truly relevant to the story, prefer single, unmarried.

spiritualism and spirituality

Spiritualism is a belief in communication with the dead; spirituality is concerned with matters of the soul or spirit.

spirituous (alcoholic), but avoid.

Spitsbergen, Norway.

Not a city but an Arctic island, part of the Svalbard Archipelago far to the north of mainland Norway.

Spitz (dog).

splendid isolation

It is quite possible to write the word isolation without splendid. Splendid isolation was a popular expression of British Empire solidarity in the early years of this century.

splendour

But drop the u for splendorous.

split-level

spoonfuls

sport fishing (not sports)

The Sport Fishing Institute of British Columbia, the American Sportfishing Association.

sportswriter

spree

It means a lighthearted romp. Never use it in the sense of a shooting spree or a killing spree. Substitute rampage, series of (killings) or some such.

spring

The season is lower-case. In a country such as Canada, we should not make too much of the vernal equinox being the official start of spring.

spruce beer

This is a soft drink popular in Quebec and the Maritimes, essentially a ginger beer that also contains spruce essence.

squaw

Avoid this derogatory term for an Indian woman. See native people.

Sri Lanka

Adjective and people: Sri Lankan (or ethnic names such as Sinhalese and Tamil when relevant). Currency: rupee. Capital: Colombo.

This island state became an independent member of the Commonwealth as Ceylon in 1948, with Dominion status, and became a republic as Sri Lanka in 1972. It has mountains in its centre, surrounded by a coastal plain that is widest in the north at about 160 kilometres. About 75 per cent of the population of 20 million are Buddhist Sinhalese, and Sinhala is the official language. Other ethnic groups are the mainly Hindu Tamils of the north and east (the Tamil language has status in these areas), the Veddas (forest people who were probably the island's original inhabitants), the Burghers (Christians of Dutch-Sinhalese ancestry) and Muslim Moors and Malays. Sri Lanka is separated from southeastern India by the Gulf of Mannar, Palk Strait and a 30-mile chain of shoals called Adam's Bridge.

Ethnic conflict and fighting between the separatist Liberation Tigers of Tamil Eelam and government forces killed an estimated 60,000 people in the 1980s and 90s. A ceasefire was signed in 2002.

SS

No periods in the initials for steamship or for Schutzstaffel (defence echelons), the elite corps commanded by Himmler. The SS included divisions of top combat troops in addition to the three more familiar branches: the Gestapo, camp guards and Hitler's personal bodyguard.

stadiums

staffer

Acceptable for staff member in political and media stories.

staff sergeant, Staff Sgt.

See ranks.

stage

One word for stagecraft and stagehand, but stage manager, stage door, stage fright, stage whisper, stage-struck.

stage, stand, see dais.

stagecoach

stalactite and stalagmite

Stalactites point down.

Stalin, Joseph

Not Josef or Josif. We spell his birth surname Dzhugashvili. Use lower case for destalinization.

stance

Reserve for posture or a way of standing, as in a golfer's stance, a batting stance. Do not use it for a non-physical stand, attitude, position.

standardbred

standard time

Lower-case the generic term (returning to standard time, the international system of standard time), but upper-case the particular, as in Eastern Standard Time. However, this rarely needs spelling out; EST or simply eastern time usually suffices after a figure.

Stanley Cup

It is the oldest trophy now competed for by North American professional athletes (a cagily worded

you'd think a watch this expensive would keep above-standard time.

definition that gets around America's Cup, first awarded in 1851), but it has been associated exclusively with the National Hockey League only since 1926. When Governor-General Lord Stanley donated it in 1896, it was for amateur hockey. The first professional team to win it was the Ottawa Senators, in 1909, and thereafter it fell under the effective control of the National Hockey League and came to symbolize professional supremacy.

staphylococcus

Use upper case only when giving the scientific name of one of the strains, as in *Staphylococcus aureus*. These are the bacteria most commonly associated with infected wounds and boils.

Starbucks

No apostrophe for the chain of coffee emporiums.

StarPhoenix, the Saskatoon daily.

START

It stands for Strategic Arms Reduction Treaty, so it is redundant to say START Treaty. There are two of them, START 1 signed in 1991 and START 2 in January of 1993 as one of the last acts of U.S. President George

Bush. START 2 called for elimination of almost three-quarters of all U.S. and Russian warheads by 2003.

Stars and Stripes

states, see provinces and states.

stationary and stationery

Unless it means materials used in writing, it is spelled **stationary**.

statistics

The word is both singular and plural (statistics is a science; statistics are figures). Reserve the singular, statistic, for a figure that is an element in a statistical analysis, or that at least contributes to an overall picture, such as a person's vital statistics or sports standings. Any figure all on its own (the height of a mountain) is simply a figure or measurement, not a statistic.

Statistics is the area of mathematics concerned with the manipulation of numerical information. To guard against the manipulation being taken any further, to include the media and the public, we never accept statistics unquestioned. The trick is knowing the right questions, but two that are always relevant are whether the statistics indeed prove what they are purported to, and whether the party offering the statistics has a stake in how they are presented. For example, a reported jump of 30 per cent in burglary arrests makes the police look good, but if we dig further and find that the number of reported burglaries is up by 60 per cent, it is clear that the force's arrest record is actually worse than last year's. We must always ask ourselves what is being omitted. Few sources would try to get away with releasing false statistics, but selective statistics seem to be regarded as par for the course.

Any statistics we print should be understandable to the reader, which means that first the writer and editor of the story must both understand them thoroughly enough to present them in the clearest, most unbiased form. Readers should be given not only the figures but also a brief explanation of their significance, or enough additional information to allow them to judge this for themselves. We should put statistics in context, citing past or parallel figures whenever these are relevant, and we should always flesh out percentages with the actual numbers. A 50-per-cent jump in a company's revenue sounds less spectacular if we add that the actual increase was only from $500 to $750, and that it included the proceeds from the sale of the owner's watch.

Be aware that statistics and economics are developing sciences, themselves groping with the issue of the right questions to ask as the nature of the economy changes. Economists are unwilling to interpret any particular monthly blip as an indicator of a trend, and we should use the same caution.

Do not shy from rounding off. We do not serve the reader by simply regurgitating reams of complex numbers, if exact figures are not the central issue in a story. It is much more understandable to say an amount "almost doubled" or "increased by two-thirds" than to say it increased by 96.3 or 64.9 per cent. About a million is easier to grasp than 1.13 million. The more general the treatment of a story, the more general (and therefore readable) the figures may be.

We also contribute to readability and comprehension if we limit ourselves to only the single most salient figure in the first few paragraphs, devoting the top of the story largely to explaining impact and significance. However, we must be as fair as we expect our sources to be. We do not haul a figure out of context because it makes a spectacular lead, and then water down the impact later with other figures.

Beware the arithmetical pitfalls of numbers and percentages, always asking whether they add up and otherwise make sense. For example, an increase of 200 per cent means a tripling of the original number, not a doubling. (An increase of 100 per cent is a doubling.) Also keep in mind the distinction between per cent and percentage points. A company that increases its ownership of another to 45 per cent from 30 has increased it by 15 percentage points, not 15 per cent. See per cent, numbers.

In deciding whether a statistic is newsworthy, we must keep the big picture in mind. Toronto averages about 50 homicides a year, but the number can vary greatly from year to year. It would be unprincipled hype to give big play to a 48-per-cent jump in the homicide rate when in fact there was a return from a very low 35 in one year to a nearly average 52 the next.

Statscan
Acceptable in second reference for Statistics Canada.

Statutes of Canada
Use upper case for the formal name of Canada's body of laws. Use lower case if the reference is worded otherwise, as in Canadian statutes.

Upper-case the full titles of statutes, and also titles from which only "Canadian," "of Canada" or some such has been dropped, e.g. the Criminal Code. Lower-case informal references, e.g. the traffic law. See bills, capitalization.

statutory rape
This term has no relevance in Canadian law. Use the specific charge, such as sexual interference with a child under 14, or with a young person under 18 over whom the accused was in a position of authority.

staunch

Use this spelling both for the verb (staunch the flow) and the adjective (a staunch ally).

Steel, Danielle

The author. Not Steele.

Stelco Inc.

stethoscope

Stetson, a trade name.

still lifes

stimuli

STOL

Acceptable in second reference and in headlines as the acronym for short takeoff and landing.

stomach ache

stomach flu

Avoid this term, which is a misnomer. Influenza, or flu, is a viral illness with specific symptoms that do not include gastrointestinal distress. There are hundreds of viruses and bacteria that circulate, particularly in the winter. Some cause stomach problems, and when they do so in large enough numbers to trigger a press conference, public health officials usually identify the specific bug. But it is never the "stomach flu."

Stone of Remembrance

Upper-case. This is the official name for the 12-foot, altar-shaped stone found in each cemetery for the Commonwealth war dead. They bear the inscription "Their name liveth for evermore." The monuments in parks and town squares across Canada are called cenotaphs, lower-case. The room in the Peace Tower containing books with the names of all Canada's war dead in the two world wars is the Memorial Chamber.

Stoney and Stony

The adjective is stony, and this is also the spelling for most place names in Canada, including Stony Beach, Sask.; Stony Hill, Man.; Stony Lake, Sask. and Ont.; Stony Mountain, Man.; Stony Plain, Alta.; Stony Point, B.C. and Man.; Stony Rapids, Sask.

But note Stoney Creek, Ont., B.C. and N.B.; Stoney Island, N.S.; Stoney Point, Ont. Note as well the Stoney Indians in Alberta.

stopgap

storey, storeys (of a building).

Stouffville, Ont.

straight and strait

Straight means without curve or bend, undiluted etc. **Strait** has to do with narrowness, restriction. It is the narrow water passage, and is also found in the expressions dire straits, straitjacket, strait-laced.

Straightened means having had bends or kinks removed. **Straitened** means distressed or embarrassed, particularly in finances.

Strait

The federal gazetteer is our authority on whether the word Strait comes before or after the name. There is no regional preference; the West Coast has its Strait of Georgia but also Juan de Fuca Strait, Haro Strait and Malaspina Strait, among others. The East Coast has its Northumberland Strait, but also the Strait of Belle Isle and Strait of Canso. Note the plural in Straits of Mackinac, joining Lakes Huron and Michigan.

straitjacket, straitlaced.

stranglehold

Strasbourg, France.

strata, the plural of stratum.

Stratford Festival of Canada

Although the festival celebrated its 50th season in 2002, that year marked the festival's 49th anniversary. The festival started in 1953 with its first season.

Stratford-on-Avon, England, **Stratford**, Ont.

streetcar

streets

Spell out Street, Avenue etc. when simply naming the street (a Main Street store; a collision on Eglinton Avenue; he lives on Sussex Drive). Use abbreviations when giving a specific address (24 Sussex Dr.). The acceptable abbreviations are St., Ave., Rd., Dr., Blvd., Cres., Ct. Do not abbreviate Lane or Mews, or less familiar words such as Rise, Ridge, Path.

We do not use commas for large numbers in street addresses (5500 Yonge St.). See numbers.

strewn

stripper

Prefer this to stripteaser. Nude dancer or topless dancer is acceptable, but they are now commonplace enough that we should not refer to them as exotic.

stroke

Prefer this short, well-understood word to the medical term cerebrovascular accident.

strontium 90

style book

Styrofoam

A trade name, so always upper-case. The generics are polystyrene or plastic foam, but usually simply foam is clear enough, as in foam cup, foam-slab insulation. Styrofoam is a

homogeneous product with many small bubbles. Coffee cups and low-priced rigid insulation are bead foam, formed by pressing hot beads into moulds.

sub

It is an acceptable short form for submarine in heads, and in second reference in copy. It is also acceptable in second reference for substitute.

As a prefix, it does not take a hyphen (subplot, subspecies, subcontractor). However, note that Latin expressions are two words (sub rosa, *sub judice*).

subarctic, subalpine, lower-case.

subjunctive mood

The subjunctive mood is on its last legs, but is still found in certain stock expressions: come what may, saints be praised, far be it from me, be that as it may, come summer. Its use is usually optional, to inject an air of formality or tradition, but the subjunctive is mandatory in some situations: expressing conditions that are contrary to fact (If Main Street were one-way, we wouldn't have these tie-ups); and expressing wishes or hypotheses that are unlikely to prove true (I wish I were smarter; If we were to win the lottery; If this rank outsider were to win the election). The subjunctive is also common in requests, demands, exhortations and formal motions (He asks that the city repaint his house; the union demands that the workers be rehired; I move that the board appoint him as treasurer).

Whether we choose the subjunctive or the normal indicative mood in sentences expressing a contingency or hypothesis is an indication to the reader of how likely such an outcome is. Contrast "If Canada cuts its defence spending" with "If Canada were to cut its defence spending." The first implies a real possibility, maybe under active consideration; the second merely throws out a hypothesis.

submachine gun

It is a hand-held weapon; a machine gun is not. See guns and calibres.

submarine

It is properly called a boat, not a ship. Those serving on them are submariners. See sub, U-boat.

subpoena, subpoenaed

subsequently

Prefer **afterward**, unless we are implying cause and effect.

successfully

This adverb is often redundant. He successfully overturned a publication ban; the bill has successfully cleared the hurdles in the Senate; police successfully defused a bomb. In all cases, the success is obvious without the need for successfully.

succour

Sudan

Adjective and people: Sudanese. Currency: dinar. Capital: Khartoum.

May also be called the Sudan, when we are speaking of its territory rather than its government (its official name is Democratic Republic of the Sudan). It is the largest country in Africa, lying south of Egypt and west of Ethiopia, and bulging between them to occupy part of the Red Sea coast. We must not imply that it is entirely desert. It has deserts and semi-deserts in the north, savannah grassland in the central zone, and rain forests and swamps in the south. Arab-speaking Muslims in the north make up about three-quarters of the population of 33 million. The black and Nilotic peoples of the south, mainly animist and Christian, were fighting for autonomy through the nineties under the Sudanese People's Liberation Army. The National Islamic Front, in power since a civilian government was overthrown in a military coup under Omar Bashir in June of 1989, also faced insurrection in the north by the National Democratic Alliance, a grouping of Muslim opponents of the regime.

In October of 2002, Calgary oil company Talisman Energy Inc. announced that it would sell its controversial stake in a Sudanese oil project, under pressure from critics who said the Sudanese government was using revenue from the deal to finance the civil war. The sale of its 25-per-cent stake in the Greater Nile Petroleum Operating Co., to India's Oil & Natural Gas Corp., was completed in 2003.

Suharto, Sukarno and Megawati

Indonesian presidents. As with many Javanese, only the given name (not the family name) is used.

sulpha drugs

The full generic term is sulphonamide, and the first to be synthesized is sulphanilamide.

sulphur, sulphuric

summons

This is the singular (it is a writ of summons). The plural is summonses. However, the verb is simply summon. Say he was summoned by the court, never summonsed.

sun, lower-case.

sunbathe, sunburn, suntan

super

As a prefix, it does not take a hyphen, even before an r (superrefined). But note such proper names as Super Continental, Super Chief.

superlatives

Unless they have ironclad proof, good writers and editors are wary of first, last, only, unique, none, never, and the superlative forms of adjectives. Our well-informed readers lie in wait for these words and take particular pleasure in skewering us upon them if we are wrong.

supersede

(Not -cede.) It originally meant to sit above, from the same root as sedentary.

supine

It means lying on one's back. See prone.

supply-side economics

This theory of economic management emphasizes stimulating production, rather than the traditional focus of manipulating demand through monetary, credit and tax measures. Supply-siders essentially want smaller governments. They call for drastic tax cuts to encourage investment in businesses, and greatly reduced government budgets and borrowing, to free credit for use by the private sector.

sure enough

Sûreté du Québec

The official name of Quebec's provincial police. Italics. The official translation is the Quebec Police Force, but it is rarely used, even by Quebec anglophones. In first reference, use the French name with an explanation, such as "the *Sûreté du Québec*, the provincial police." Brackets may be useful in some constructions. Subsequently, use SQ, the force, the provincial force, the provincial police etc.

surgery

Hospital jargon refers to "a surgery" or "surgeries." The practice of a vast majority of our readers (and therefore our practice) is to reserve "surgery" for the generic, collective sense, always rendered in the singular with no article preceding it. We say he underwent heart surgery, but he underwent a heart operation.

Suriname

Adjective and people: Surinamese. Currency: guilder. Capital: Paramaribo.

Formerly called Dutch Guiana (England gave it to the Dutch in 1667 in return for New Amsterdam, but it was briefly in British possession twice more), this republic on the northeast shoulder of South America became fully independent in 1975. The largest sector of the population of 444,000 (38 per cent) trace their ancestry to India, and 15 per cent to Java (formerly in the Dutch East Indies). Other groups include Creoles, Maroons (bush people descended from escaped African slaves), Europeans, Chinese and American Indians. Dutch and English are official languages, but a vernacular lingua franca called Sranan Tongo (also called Surinamese) is widely used. Bauxite dominates the economy, exported as ore or processed locally into alumina or aluminum, but there are also great timber resources. Guyana lies to the west, French Guiana to the east and Brazil to the south.

surreal

Suwannee

It is Suwannee River and Sound, Florida, and Suwannee Lake, in Manitoba. But the spelling of Stephen Foster's song is *Swanee River* (also called *Old Folks at Home*).

suzerainty

Prefer sovereignty, supremacy, control.

swastika

The bent-cross symbol was used by many peoples before the Nazis, including some American Indian tribes. The word *svastika* is Sanskrit. Note that the Nazis used the term *Hakenkreuze* (hooked cross), and rendered it with the bent arms radiating clockwise. It was also usually turned so the central cross was at 45 degrees, and certain religious groups strongly advocate that the Nazi symbol always be depicted this way, to differentiate it from their sacred symbols. The Jain symbol for the universe, for example, includes an upright, clockwise swastika enhanced by dots in the four quadrants. Practice varies even within some religions on whether the swastika is clockwise or anticlockwise, but it is generally clockwise among the Jains and Hindus, anticlockwise among Buddhists.

SWAT

Reserve this acronym, and the full name, special weapons and tactics team, for those that actually use this as their formal name. (Toronto's is called the emergency task force.) The generic terms that may be used for all forces are tactical squad or tactical team. For Toronto, prefer these to ETF.

Swaziland

Adjective: Swaziland. People: citizens of Swaziland. Currency: lilangeni, but the rand is also used. Capital: Mbabane.

Swazis are a tribal group, and although they predominate we should not refer to all citizens as Swazis. Others include Zulus, people of mixed race and Europeans. Swaziland is landlocked, surrounded mostly by South Africa but also bordering on Mozambique in the northeast. It is in a customs union with South Africa, and its currency is tied closely to the rand. It is a monarchy, under the Swazi king Mswati III, and has been fully independent since 1968. The population is 1.1 million.

sweatshirt

Sweden

Adjective: Swedish. People: Swedes. Currency: krona (plural kronor). Capital: Stockholm.

The population of nine million is almost entirely Swedish, but there are a few thousand Lapps in the north. Sweden is a constitutional monarchy, the reigning king being Carl XVI Gustaf (note word order), born on April 30, 1946. It is bounded on the west and north by Norway (with which it was united from 1815 to 1905) and on the northeast by Finland, and faces the Gulf of Bothnia, the Baltic and the Skagerrak and Kattegat. It has rich timber and metal resources in Norrland (the northland), but most of the people, cities and industries (iron, steel, paper, pulp and vehicles) are in the south. Sweden joined the European Union in 1995, but chose not to adopt the euro.

sweepstakes

Both singular and plural.

sweet potato and yam

They are the tuberous roots of two different tropical vines, and so should not be considered interchangeable in stories and headlines.

Swiss Guards

Upper-case. This name is acceptable for the Papal Swiss Guard at the Vatican Palace.

Switzerland

Adjective and people: Swiss. Currency: franc. Capital: Bern.

This country of 7.5 million people is called the Swiss Confederation, and its 23 cantons (states), which are also counted as 20 cantons and six half cantons, are highly autonomous. There are three official languages, but

German predominates, being the first language of 70 per cent of the population. About 19 per cent speak French, 10 per cent Italian and 1 per cent Romansch (in the southern Alps). Not all Swiss mountains are Alps. Those in the north are the Jura Mountains (noted for their fine meadows), and they are separated from the Alps by the central plateau, called the Mittelland. Switzerland has long been neutral, but became a member of the United Nations in 2002.

Sydney, N.S., but **Sidney**, B.C. and Man.

symposiums

synthetic

Its usual meaning is produced artificially by means of synthesis (combining of simpler substances), rather than occurring naturally. We maintain the distinction between synthetic and natural fibres, but in the case of plastics the word synthetic may be dropped, since the synthetics now are so predominant. Simply specify natural plastics (resins and bitumen) in the rare instances these arise.

Avoid the word synthetic as a general term for artificial or false.

syphilis (not -us).

See canker/chancre, Wassermann test.

Syria

Adjective and people: Syrian. Currency: pound. Capital: Damascus.

The coasts of Syria, Lebanon and Israel, north to south, form the square eastern end of the Mediterranean. Syria surrounds Lebanon on two sides, extending south of it to share a short border with Israel. It also adjoins Turkey, Iraq and Jordan. The Syrian Desert is in the south, but the north is much more fertile (the Euphrates River arises here, flowing southeast to meet the Tigris in southern Iraq).

Other major cities include Aleppo and the port of Latakia. More than 80 per cent of Syrians are Arab-speaking Muslims; there are also Bedouin, Kurds, Turks and Armenians. The population is about 17 million.

syringe

A syringe (from the Greek word for tube) is an instrument that can draw in a liquid and then squirt it out again. Not all are fitted with needles. In medicine, syringes are used to draw out unwanted fluids, to rinse wounds, body cavities, ears etc., and, when fitted with needles, to administer injections. Syringes used for injections are properly called hypodermic syringes (hypodermic means beneath skin), and the term includes the whole unit, both cylinder and needle. We may drop the word hypodermic when the type of syringe is obvious, as in drug stories, but we should specify the type of syringe in stories about medical wastes etc. We should speak of a government handing out syringes to addicts, not needles, although we may use the common term "sharing needles."

Szechuan

Reserve this spelling for the food and cooking style. Use **Sichuan** for the Chinese province.

T

T-bar, T-cell, T-shirt

table

Canadian parliamentary parlance uses this verb in its British meaning: to present or bring forward for discussion. Do not use it in its American sense of removing a document or issue from discussion, though that sense too is common in Canada. If that meaning is required, substitute such unambiguous words as shelve, postpone.

If the parliamentary usage is ambiguous, add a clarifying phrase, such as tabled for discussion, for debate, for action, for consideration.

tableaus (not -eaux).

table tennis

Prefer this generic term to the trade name Ping-Pong. Use upper case in such expressions as Ping-Pong diplomacy.

Tagalog

The official language of the Philippines, also called Filipino (note spelling), should not be called a national language. The Tagalog people make up only about a fifth of the country's population, but dominate business, the arts and the civil service, being in the majority in the Manila area.

Tahiti

Not a separate country. It is the largest of the Society Islands and the centre of French Polynesia, an Overseas Territory of France.

Tahltan

The traditional territory of these B.C. Indians is the mountain region inland from the Alaskan panhandle. Tahltan on reserves number about 1,000. See native people.

taiga

Use lower case for this word and the more common term in Canada, boreal forest, the giant arc of northern coniferous forest running from the Rockies to the Maritimes, north of the deciduous trees of the East and the prairies of the West. It is the third-largest continuous forest in the world, after the taiga of Siberia and the Amazonian rain forest, and is North America's biggest single ecological system.

tail first

Taiwan

Adjective and people: Taiwanese. Currency: dollar. Capital: Taipei.

We do not use the names Republic of China or Formosa. Taiwan, lying 120 miles off China across Taiwan Strait, also includes the Quemoy Islands, the Lan Hsu Islands and the Pescadores. The aboriginal people, of Polynesian-Malay origin, are now greatly outnumbered by immigrant Chinese (most from the province of Fukien) and their descendants. The total population is 23 million. Taiwan is tropical in the south and subtropical in the north, which allows two rice crops. It was the Portuguese who originally called the island Formosa (beautiful). The National People's Party (the translation of Kuomintang), driven out of China by the Communists in 1949, ran Taiwan as a virtual one-party state until the mid-nineties. In 1996, Lee Teng-hui became the first president directly elected by the people, rather than being chosen within the party. In 1999, he repudiated Taiwan's One-China Policy, said China and Taiwan should have state-to-state relations and rejected Beijing's view that Taiwan is a renegade province that must be reunited with the mainland. The opposition Democratic Progressive Party made big gains in the municipal elections of 1997, gaining a majority of seats for the first time. Chen Shui-ban, head of that party and a supporter of independence from China, was elected president of Taiwan on March 18, 2000. See Kuomintang.

The Republic of China was founded in 1912 after the fall of the Ch'ing dynasty, and fiscal years are officially counted in Taiwan from that base, with 1912 as year one. For instance, 1999-2000 is known as fiscal year 88-89. We do not follow that style, but take care not to mistake the discrepancy for a calendar system that lags the rest of the world by 11 years.

Tajikistan

Adjective and people: Tajikistani, or Tajik for that ethnic group. Currency: ruble. Capital: Dushanbe.

The Tajik people, Sunni Muslims with a language similar to Farsi (Persian, the language of Iran), make up the majority of the population of 6.2 million. The second-largest ethnic group are Uzbeks, and other minorities include Slavs with origins in Russia and Ukraine. Use Tajik to refer to the majority group, but Tajikistani for the population as a whole.

One of the former Soviet Central Asian republics, known for many years as Tadzhikistan, it borders on China,

Kyrgyzstan, Uzbekistan and Afghanistan. Ethnic violence erupted in 1990, along with rioting against the Communist Party headquarters in Dushanbe, and the violence increased after independence was declared with the collapse of the Soviet Union in late 1991. In the first year of independence alone, thousands were killed in fighting over ethnic, clan and political differences, and a quarter of a million were left homeless. After a long civil war, rival factions signed a peace agreement in 1997, which took effect in 2000.

It is mainly mountainous, with few areas below 11,000 feet, and the population is concentrated in the foothills and river valleys. It is subtropical at lower elevations, and irrigation has made cotton growing and textile manufacture the most important industries, although fruits, vegetables and grains are also grown and there is extensive cattle and sheep grazing. It has coal, oil and gas, and also produces lead and zinc.

See Soviet Union.

takedown

Except in direct quotes, avoid this police jargon for an operation in which police hope to make an arrest.

takeoff

The noun. The verb is **take off**.

takeover

The noun. The verb is **take over**.

take place

This is a mushy substitute for more specific verbs, often a greater drawback than the passive it seeks to avoid.

Taliban

Since the ousted Afghan faction derived its name from the plural of *talib* (divinity student, seeker of knowledge; *an* is the Arabic suffix for a plural group of males), follow it with a plural verb: The Taliban have decided, the Taliban are meeting. If the word is used as a noun-adjective, the verb will as always correspond with the main noun: Taliban members were meeting, the Taliban regime is no longer in place. See Afghanistan, *mujahedeen*.

talk

The usual preposition is talk to, not talk with.

tall ships

They are commonly and properly referred to generically as tall ships or sailing ships, but note that there are various types, determined by the number of masts and the choice of sail, and the term ship is technically used for only one of them. For our readers interested in such matters, we should be specific.

The two main types of sail are square and fore-and-aft (triangular). Fore-and-aft sails can be swung to either side, allowing better manoeuvring and beating against the wind, and so were favoured for coastal vessels. Square sails allow greater speed, but require more hands for hoisting, and were best suited to the major trade routes with reliable prevailing winds. The principal types of vessel:

Full-rigged ship: Three or more masts, all square-rigged.

Barque: Three or more masts, square-rigged on all but one, the aftermost, which is fore-and-aft-rigged.

Barquentine: Three or more masts, square-rigged on only one, the foremast, with all the others fore-and-aft-rigged.

Brig: Two masts, both square-rigged.

Brigantine: Two masts, square-rigged on the foremast, fore-and-aft-rigged on the mainmast.

Schooner: Two or more masts, all fore-and-aft-rigged. (Bluenose is a two-masted fishing schooner.)

See Bluenose.

Talmud

It is not the Jewish Bible (see Torah). Talmud, Hebrew for teaching, describes the compilation begun in the fifth century of Jewish law and rabbinical wisdom, including commentary on the Bible.

tamarack

This tree, found across Canada, is one of three native species of larch, the country's only deciduous conifers. In some areas of the Maritimes, it is called the hackmatack.

Tamil Nadu

This state in southern India was formerly called Madras. Its main language is Tamil, which is also spoken in northern and eastern Sri Lanka.

Tammany Hall

This term, recalling the corrupt Democratic machine in New York before the La Guardia reforms of the late 1930s, is too loaded to be used to refer to modern administrations.

tank, see armour.

Use a hyphen to separate letter from number, as in M-1.

Tanzania

Adjective and people: Tanzanian. Currency: shilling. Capital: Dodoma.

Tanganyika, in East Africa south of Kenya, became independent in 1961, and the Island of Zanzibar became independent in 1963. After the sultanate on Zanzibar was overthrown in January of 1964, the island combined with Tanganyika and the more northerly island of Pemba in April to form a united republic, which in October changed its name to Tanzania. The switch to Dodoma from the original capital, Dar es Salaam, began in 1975. Tanzania ranges from coastal mangroves and coral reefs to semi-deserts, the Rift Valley and the high East African plateau, including the Serengeti and Mount Kilimanjaro, Africa's highest peak. Its population of 37 million comprises more than 100 Bantu tribes, plus Arab, Indian and European minorities. Swahili and English have official status.

tape recorder

The verb is **tape-record**.

tarantula

The venom of tarantulas does not usually have any serious effect on humans, and so they should not be called deadly. The name is given to several different species around the world, all of them hairy, running hunters (not web-snarers) of insects and even small vertebrates. There are nine species of them in B.C. and Ontario. See spiders.

tariff

task force

Avoid this imprecise buzzword in non-military contexts, unless it appears in a formal name.

tassel, tasselled

taste

Bad taste is difficult to define but fairly easily recognized by a writer or editor sensitive to what others, particularly the reader, would find offensive or nauseating. It goes beyond the obscene to include such things as graphic descriptions of mutilated bodies or abused animals, and titillating but otherwise irrelevant details of private lives. Readers have a sense for what is necessary to convey the facts and what is added merely for its sensational effect. They usually have read all they need or care to when we have said that someone was run over by a train, or has been accused of bestiality, or is having marital difficulties. Knowing the difference between gut-smut sensationalism and what is truly

needed to inform the reader is a function of experience and judgment. When in doubt, consult a senior editor.

tattoo, tattooed

tawdry

It does not mean dirty, sleazy or ragged. It means cheap and tastelessly showy, gaudy (from the lace sold at St. Audrey's Fair).

taxpayer expense

When does something done at government or public expense become something done at "taxpayer expense"? Often when the writer wants to imply, without bothering to say so, that the spending is frivolous, unnecessary, wasteful, partisan.

There is a place for this expression, especially in the reporting of accusations levelled by others. In our own news stories, it is legitimate, useful for avoiding repetition and neutral enough in general or hypothetical discussions. However, we should be sure we have examined our own attitude toward the story and that we are not indulging, even unconsciously, in a bit of backhanded editorializing. If the spending is indeed unjustified, let's get somebody to say it.

tax shelters

There is no problem speaking of a tax shelter or a tax-sheltered investment, meaning one on which government regulations allow deferment, transfer or even forgiveness of taxes. However, unless we have clear knowledge of an individual investor's thinking, we should not take the extra step and ascribe motives, saying that he or she made a particular investment primarily for the sake of reducing taxes. Similarly, we should not imply that a person made a particular charitable or political donation for that reason.

Tbilisi

Use this spelling, not Tiflis, for the capital of Georgia.

Tchaikovsky, Peter Ilich.

TD Bank

Acceptable in second reference to Toronto-Dominion Bank. TD is acceptable in headlines.

Team Canada

Reserve this name for hockey teams representing Canada, principally at the Canada Cup or in the Olympics. A national team in any other sport should simply be called Canada, Canada's team, the Canadian team etc.

teammate

Teamsters union, a Teamster

These are acceptable in all references. There is no need to use the full name, the International Brotherhood of Teamsters, Chauffeurs, Warehousemen and Helpers of America.

teardrop, tear gas, tearjerker

Technicolor, a trade name.

Tecumseh

Use this spelling for the Indian chief and for the Windsor suburb, but note Tecumseth Street and Place, Toronto, and Tecumseth Township in Simcoe County.

Tecumseh was a Shawnee chief from the Ohio Valley, killed in 1813 fighting the Americans at the Battle of the Thames near Moraviantown, Upper Canada (close to modern Thamesville), after his British allies had retreated. Two years earlier, his brother Tenskwatawa, the Shawnee Prophet, had led their people to defeat at Tippecanoe. Tecumseh sought an Indian confederacy throughout what is now the U.S. Midwest to halt white expansion, arguing that, since the land was common to all tribes, no one tribe had the right to sign a treaty ceding any of it.

teen, teenager, teenybopper

teetotaller

Teflon, a trade name.

Tehran, not Teheran.

Tekahionwake

The Indian name of poet Pauline Johnson, who was born near Brantford, the child of a Mohawk hereditary chief and an English woman, and eventually retired to Vancouver. She used the name, and a buckskin costume, on her popular recital tours in North America and Britain.

Tekakwitha, Kateri

Not Tegakwitha. Kateri is the first North American Indian to be considered for sainthood; her beatification was begun in 1932 and proclaimed by Pope John Paul II in 1980. Stoned by her own Iroquois people in what is now New York State after her conversion by Jesuits (and baptism as Catharine), she fled to a mission near Montreal, at what is now Kahnawake, where her kindness and obvious faith brought her the sobriquet the Lily of the Mohawks. She died on April 17, 1680, at 24.

tele

As a combining form, meaning at a distance, it does not take a hyphen (telegraph, telekinesis).

telephone numbers

Since area codes are increasingly becoming an essential part of the number even when dialled locally, treat them as part of the number, and do not place brackets around them. Thus, 519-999-9999 or 1-800-999-9999.

Teleprompter

Upper-case only the first letter, not the two internal caps of the official trade name.

Teleran

Upper-case for the air navigation system that combines radar and television technology. It is a trade name, an acronym for television radar air navigation.

telescope

Specify optical telescope or radio telescope. If optical, it may be relevant to specify reflector or refractor.

Telex

Always upper-case, as in He sent a Telex to the Prime Minister. Avoid as a verb.

Temagami (not Tim-).

Témiscaming, Timiskaming etc.

The Quebec town is **Témiscaming**. The Quebec county and federal riding are **Témiscamingue**, and the provincial riding is Rouyn-Noranda-Témiscamingue. The Ontario district, lake and ridings, both federal and provincial, are **Timiskaming**.

tempera and tempura

Tempera is a painting medium, an emulsion of water and a binder, to which pigment is added to make a paint. Temperas may be made from egg yolks or various glues and gums. **Tempura** is Japanese for fried food, usually seafood and vegetables deep fried with an egg batter.

temperature

Speak of temperature or temperature readings as being high or low, not warm or cold. It is the air, water etc. that is warm or cold. See Celsius.

Ten Commandments, the

Not 10. Use upper case for this name, and also for First Commandment etc.

tendon, but tendinitis.

tenpin bowling (not 10-).

tenses

What is the reader to make of this sentence: Mr. Green said his company was the prime contender for the contract.

Is the company no longer in that position? Has he dropped from the running? Has the contract already been let to his company, or to another?

Ambiguity is the usual result when we slavishly throw the rest of the sentence into the past tense whenever we encounter such past-tense attributors as said, charged, stated etc. For clarity, when a continuing situation is being described, keep subsequent verbs in the simple present or future in which they were expressed (Mr. Green said his company is the prime contender). Reuters copy requires particular attention to weed out such ambiguity.

Our usual practice is to use past-tense narrative style, particularly for attribution of direct quotes. We make no claim that a person "says" specific words, as if it were habitual, but merely report what he or she "said" on one occasion, influenced by circumstances at the time. Exceptions are made for quotes from contemporary written matter (the report says, she says in the letter), certain colour pieces, brief present-tense scene-setters and curtain-closers on long features, and indirect quotes if they reflect the person's continuing belief. Present tense is suitable for certain straight interviews, provided we keep the contract with the reader implied by use of present tense: The quotes are exactly in chronological order, as if the reader is a witness to the interview as it is being conducted.

In headlines, the present tense is used for contemporary stories, but we use the past for historical references, and past or future for indirect quotes in which the source is speaking of those times: Churchill, Montgomery held stormy meeting; Trusted to luck, pilot says; Will meet Baker, Clark says.

In cutlines, use the present tense whenever the words "in this picture" are understood, but use the past for complementary information: Lottery winner kisses $22-million cheque in New York yesterday. She said she will donate most of it to charity.

terra cotta

territorial waters

The current internationally recognized jurisdiction is 12 miles, measured from the low-water mark. The United Nations Convention on the Law of the Sea, 1983, specified 12 nautical miles, or about 22 kilometres. This is four times the previous limit, also in nautical miles (one nautical league, 3.45 land miles, 5.5 kilometres). Commercial ships have the right of innocent passage in the 12-mile zone, but aircraft and submerged submarines do not. Waters beyond the zone are classed as the high seas for the purpose of the unrestricted passage of all vessels and aircraft. However, coastal countries can claim jurisdiction over the marine life extending 200 nautical miles (370 kilometres) from shore, and exclusive rights to petroleum and other resources in the first 200 miles (more if the continental shelf extends farther). Other provisions on seabed mining prevented several major countries from signing the treaty, but these countries supported most other provisions, including the 12-mile limit.

In keeping with international practice, refer to the limits in nautical miles, but add a metric conversion after at least one reference. One nautical mile is 1.85 kilometres.

terrorist

Use this term to describe groups or individuals who use violence against the innocent public, or the threat of it, to achieve political ends. The hijacking or bombing of planes, buses, public buildings etc. is terrorism, but for clarity we do not use this term to describe raids on military and police personnel or installations. They should simply be called guerrilla activity or some such, and government statements equating them with terrorism should be attributed. However, any group that commits terrorist acts, even if it also engages in guerrilla activity, may be called terrorist. When it comes to individuals, we must be more circumspect. Many present-day public figures were members of terrorist groups in their youth, including anti-colonial movements. It may be relevant in certain stories to refer to past terrorist connections of such figures as Menachem Begin and Nelson Mandela, but we should not imply they continued as terrorists.

Although the dictionaries accept terror as a synonym for violence committed to create terror, try to preserve the distinction in copy that terrorism and terrorists have as their aim to create terror, and that terror is the emotion created. In copy, prefer anti-terrorist or anti-terrorism to anti-terror. In headlines, given the limited space, anti-terror is acceptable.

Teutonic

Avoid this term as imprecise, except in such informal references as Teutonic good looks. The noun Teutons is taken to mean northern Germans, but in the realm of languages the adjective Teutonic is used to describe those of Austria, Belgium, the Netherlands and Scandinavia as well as that of Germany.

Thailand

Adjective and people: Thai. Currency: baht. Capital: Bangkok.

It is a large country (about the same area as France) in Southeast Asia, including a narrow southern extension that reaches halfway down the Malay Peninsula to form the western shore of the Gulf of Thailand. It is bounded on the west and northwest by Myanmar (formerly Burma), on the east and northeast by Laos, and on the southeast by Cambodia. It is not part of Indochina, this term referring only to Laos, Cambodia and Vietnam. Most of the 62 million Thais are Theravada Buddhists, but there are some Muslim Malays in the south. Thailand (Siam) was never a colony, providing a buffer between the French colonies to its east and the British in Burma.

The given name comes first in Thai names, equivalent to Joe or Joanna in Western names, but it is this name, not the family name, that takes the honorific in second reference. Thus: Weena Tipchindachaikul, later referred to as Ms. Weena.

thalidomide, lower-case.

Thanksgiving Day

This national holiday, as opposed to a religious service, was declared in Canada in 1879, but the day varied through several dates in October and November; the second Monday in October was fixed only in 1957. The U.S. holiday has been on the last Thursday in November since 1789.

The U.S. observance was the major inspiration for Canada's, largely via the Loyalists, but was not the only one. Thanksgiving services had a long tradition in Europe before the observance at the Plymouth Colony in 1621. North America's first recorded formal service of Thanksgiving was held more than 40 years earlier, in 1578, by Martin Frobisher in what is now Canada's Eastern Arctic, and autumn services have been held in Halifax since the 1750s.

thanks to

Reserve for things for which at least someone is grateful. Do not say a young family is homeless "thanks to a fire caused by faulty wiring."

that

If the structure and sense are straightforward, it is acceptable to drop the conjunction **that** from a clause introduced by the verb "said" (He said his son was arrested). Since parallel clauses should have the same form, we must decide whether two or more clauses dependent on the same verb should all have the conjunction or should all be without it. In the sentence "He said his son was arrested and that the family lawyer would file a protest," either drop the that from the second clause or insert one in the first. Since most alternatives to "said" may also be transitive, it is best to retain the **that** after these. Without it, the reader expects to be fed a direct object (he claimed his inheritance, asserted his rights, denied the request), and is given at least momentary pause.

that and which

A relative clause (one starting with where, when, who, whose, whom, or that or which) either imparts information that is needed to identify which person or thing, out of many possible, is being discussed (a defining clause), or else imparts additional information about the one person or thing we already know is under discussion (a non-defining clause). Defining clauses are not set off by commas, while non-defining clauses are, and these commas are often important clues to the meaning of a sentence. The words where, when, who, whose and whom are the same for both types of clause, but **that** is used for defining clauses (those without commas fore and aft) while

which is used for non-defining clauses (those with commas).

The difference in meaning can be considerable. Contrast these almost-identical sentences: Ottawa has announced tax breaks to spur construction of apartment buildings that contain tenants of all income levels. Ottawa has announced tax breaks to spur construction of apartment buildings, which contain tenants of all income levels. The first says this type of building is being singled out from many; the second says all buildings are affected, because all contain such a tenant mix.

See comma, under punctuation.

that that

This awkward combination of the same word in two roles, conjunction and pronoun, is sometimes a necessary evil, but it can be easily eliminated in most instances simply by using the pronoun **this** instead. For example, change "He acknowledged **that that** was his major concern" to "He acknowledged **that this** was his major concern." The slight difference in the two pronouns' meaning ("the thing we mentioned earlier" versus "the thing we are discussing") has no effect on the overall meaning of the sentence.

the

We follow the long-established journalistic practice of lower-casing the article in a proper name (the Taft Hotel, the Taft), and especially when a common noun has been promoted to the status of a proper one, as in the Strip, the Mall, the Wave. We also lower-case the article for those one-name casinos, hotels and resorts such as the Flamingo, the Mirage and the Ritz, and such sports palaces as the Saddledome. The practice also applies to theatres (the Royal Alexandra), to entertainment groups (the Beatles, the Grateful Dead, the Who, the Boston Pops, the Three Stooges), to businesses (the Bay, the Gap), and to

groups and organizations (the Loyal Order of Moose, the International Brotherhood of Teamsters), including military units (the Royal Regiment of Canada, the Big Red One).

There are exceptions for the names of newspapers and other periodicals, books, poems, songs and works of art, for The Sports Network (in view of its initials, TSN) and for The Hague in the Netherlands.

theatre

We use accents when it is pronounced in the French way, as in Théâtre du Nouveau Monde, but no accents if it is pronounced in the English way, as in Toronto's Theatre Passe Muraille.

Use the er spelling for the proper names of U.S. theatres (the Shubert Theater).

theatregoer

Theodore, Jose

No accents for the Montreal Canadiens player.

thesis, theses

Thibaudeau, Susan

The woman who challenged the rules on taxation of child-support payments told us her name is spelled Susan, not Suzanne. The Supreme Court of Canada spelled it the wrong way in its ruling of 1995.

think-tank

Third World

Upper-case. We do not use a hyphen in such adjectival expressions as a Third World country.

There is no First World or Second World. Third World is now virtually a synonym for poor, with an entirely economic meaning, but it originally had a purely political one: those countries, most of them newly independent, that were not part of either the capitalist or communist bloc. Even with this original meaning, we did not speak of a First or Second World. There is no precise level of per-capita income that is used to define Third World status, and even relatively poor countries can be disqualified by such factors as industrial capacity, location and political alliance. Most of Latin America qualifies, for example, but Mexico, Brazil, Argentina and Venezuela are usually classed as having middle-level industrial or resource economies, despite large pockets of poverty. European countries, no matter what their economic status, would not be referred to as Third World.

The expressions rich and poor, North and South, developed and undeveloped should be confined to the most general of discussions, since they imply two poles rather than a spectrum and do not cover the states with great oil wealth that is poorly distributed. The truly rich and truly poor countries are easily identified, but there are many others that should not be arbitrarily defined as being at one extreme or the other. Also note that the fortunes of oil prices, debt charges, war and insurrection can cause a particular country to slip in and out of Third World status.

The word developing should be used only for countries that are truly progressing, not those that are stagnant or regressing.

Thirty Years' War

Not one war but a series of European wars among various powers from 1618 to 1648, partly territorial and partly religious.

Thompson River

Named by Simon Fraser after geographer and explorer David Thompson, who in turn named the Fraser River after him.

Thomson

The Thomson family's private holding company is The Woodbridge Co. Ltd., which controls Thomson Corp., the electronic publishing giant. Thomson Corp. sold control of The Globe and Mail to BCE Inc. in 2000, and sold its interest in BCE subsidiary Bell Globemedia (which includes The Globe) to Woodbridge in 2003. BCE owns 68.5 per cent of Bell Globemedia; Woodbridge owns the other 31.5 per cent, and Kenneth R. Thomson is chairman of The Globe and Mail. Stories about the Thomson family or Woodbridge should inform readers about the Globe connection. See BCE Inc.

Thomson, Tom

He was a close associate, even a leader, of artists who would form the Group of Seven, but they did not do so until after his death. See Group of Seven.

Thorfinnson, Snorri

The first white person born in North America is properly called Snorri in second reference. He was born about 1005, possibly on the banks of the St. Lawrence, to a Norse couple on their way to help found a colony, possibly at Cape Cod. The colonists returned in about 1015 to Iceland, taking young Snorri with them.

Thorncliffe, Ont.

thoroughbred

Only for horses. Otherwise, it's **purebred**.

Thousand Islands

There are more than 1,500 of them, in the St. Lawrence just as it leaves Lake Ontario and crosses the Canadian Shield. Thousand Islands International Bridge is a chain of five bridges linking the two shores via successive islands.

3-D

360-degree turn

A frequent error is to refer to someone's change of mind as a 360-degree turn. That would describe a full circle, bringing the person back to the original position. The image sought is a 180-degree turn.

threepenny

The Threepenny Opera.

Three Wise Men

The Three Wise Men from Quebec, elected to the Commons as Liberals in 1965, were Pierre Trudeau, Jean Marchand and Gérard Pelletier.

St. Matthew speaks of "wise men from the east," but does not say there were three of them. This is a common assumption because their gifts are described as gold, frankincense and myrrh.

threshold

thrived

thrombosis

This is the forming of a clot in the heart (coronary thrombosis) or a blood vessel. The clot itself is called a **thrombus**, but prefer clot.

Throne Speech, Speech from the Throne

throughway

thunderbird

Lower-case. Belief in huge thunderbirds, which produced thunder by flapping their wings and generated lightning in their eyes, was not confined to West Coast totem carvers. The Ojibwa and other peoples of the central forests and plains also believed in them. Those with straight beaks were mild-tempered, those with hooked beaks bad-tempered.

Tiananmen Square

Tibet

Not an independent country, but the Tibetan Autonomous Region of China (we call it simply Tibet). It is a former independent Buddhist theocracy in mountainous central Asia, also bordering on India, Nepal and Bhutan. The regional capital is Lhasa. The spiritual leader, the Dalai Lama, is in exile in India.

tickle

In Newfoundland, it is a narrow strait, either between an island and the mainland or at the entrance to a harbour. It does not mean a small stream.

tic-tac-toe

tidal waves, see tsunami.

tiebreaker

Tierra del Fuego

It is an island group, consisting of one large island and many smaller ones. The eastern half of Isla Grande and about a third of the smaller islands belong to Argentina, while the western half and the rest of the smaller ones belong to Chile. Ushuaia, on the Argentine half of Isla Grande, is the most southerly city in the world. The big island is separated from the mainland by the Strait of Magellan, and from smaller islands to the south by Beagle Channel. Cape Horn, considered the most southerly point of land in the Western Hemisphere, is the rocky headland of the southernmost of the Tierra del Fuego islands, Horn Island (Isla Hornos), a Chilean possession. Separating it from Antarctica is Drake Passage (in which there is a more southerly group of small islands, the Diego Ramirez Islands).

Tierra del Fuego is also the name of the Argentine territory, as part of which Argentina also makes disputed claims to some other South Atlantic islands and about 2.5 million square kilometres of Antarctica.

tie-up, the noun. The verb is **tie up**.

Tiffany's

Acceptable for the stores of Tiffany and Co.

Tiger-Cats, Ticats

Tigray

Use this spelling, not Tigre, for the troubled Ethiopian province.

Ti-Jean

Ti is a contraction of Petit. Ti-Jean is the boy in numerous Quebec folk tales, and in later adventure tales for children.

till

This is a proper English word; in fact, it probably predates until. Do not write it as 'til.

Timbuktu, Mali (not Timbouctou).

time elements

The day of publication is referred to as today, and those bracketing it as yesterday and tomorrow. Wire copy must be altered to reflect this style.

In general, avoid use of dates if they fall in the week of publication or those immediately before or after it. In such cases, change a date, such as June 20, to on Wednesday, last Wednesday, next Wednesday.

The time element should fall where it would normally be placed in spoken English. In many wire stories it is placed awkwardly in front of the verb (MPs yesterday voted to . . .). It should usually go after the verb (MPs voted yesterday to . . .), or after verb and direct object (MPs questioned the Finance Minister yesterday about . . .).

However, written English does not always have the same structure as

spoken, and a subordinate clause or phrase might leave the reader uncertain about whether the time element goes with the main verb or with that of the clause, or even with the object. In such cases, we put up with the awkwardness of inserting the time element between the verb and its object, as in this example (with asterisks showing positions where the time element would be ambiguous): MPs challenged yesterday the Finance Minister's assertion (*) that he could not lower the rate of the new tax (*). (Alternatively, we might begin: MPs yesterday challenged. . . .) In an even more complex sentence, we may be forced to delay the time element to the next paragraph by making the verb progressive (is attempting, has warned).

If the paragraph is not the lead, and involves a switch in time, it is clearest to begin with the new time element (Earlier in the day, Last week etc.).

In overseas stories, we normally match the time element to the point of view of the placeline; that is, we would say an attack took place last night, even though it might be early afternoon Canadian time. However, to avoid confusion in stories from the Orient in which a different day of the week is involved, it may be necessary to add the equivalent Canadian time period, usually in brackets. If the exact time is crucial, particularly if Canadians are directly affected (as in the crash of a Canadian plane landing at Tokyo), relate it to Canada's eastern time zone. However, it is usually sufficient to relate it to a more general time period valid for all Canadians, such as "late last night Canadian time."

In deciding on a time element, keep the main story in mind. For example, say the Conservatives won a landslide election victory yesterday (the time period of the election), not last night (the time of the counting).

Use numbers to express times (10:30 rather than half-past 10).

However, do not tamper with the wording of direct quotes; if the source says quarter to five, do not change it to 4:45.

Watch for redundancies with a.m. and p.m., as in 2 p.m. Monday afternoon. Change it to 2 o'clock Monday afternoon or 2 p.m. Monday.

See months, night, numbers.

Time magazine

times greater than, less than

One of these terms leads to confusing arithmetic, the other to impossible arithmetic.

The proper term for expressing multiples is simply **times**, as in: His alcohol reading was three times the legal limit; The company's revenue was four times last year's.

The term "times greater than" (or higher than or more than) is usually taken to mean the stated multiple added to the original number; that is, "three times greater than 10" means the original number (10) plus three times that number (30), for a total of 40. Why leave readers in doubt about what we mean, and force them to do an extra arithmetical step, when "three times greater than" could simply be replaced by "four times"!

As for "three times less than," it is simply nonsense. "Times" is the word indicating multiplication, not division. Even if it could be used to indicate division or subtraction, one time less than a number would presumably equal zero. The proper way to express this thought is with a fraction: The count was half the legal limit; The profit level was a sixth of last year's. Instead of 1,000 times less than, say a 1000th of; instead of 165 times below, say one-165th of.

Tim Hortons

No apostrophe for the chain of restaurants.

Timiskaming, see Témiscaming.

tinfoil

Titanic

It sank on the night of April 14-15, 1912, off the Grand Banks with the loss of more than 1,500 of the 2,200 aboard. (It struck the ice just before midnight, and sank 2 hours 40 minutes later.) Discovery of the wreck in 1985 showed that it broke in two.

Titicaca, Lake

In the Andes on the border of Peru and Bolivia, it is the highest navigable lake in the world (at 3,800 metres) and the largest lake in South America.

titleholder

One word. Do not use the word titlist, which has unfortunate connotations when hyphenated.

title role

It does not mean merely the starring or central role. The work must be named after the character, as in *Macbeth, Hud*. We may stretch a point and include multiple-name titles (*Butch Cassidy and the Sundance Kid*), adjectival uses of the name (*Freddy's Nightmares, The Three Faces of Eve*), and single-person descriptions if the reference is clear (*The Hustler, The Phantom of the Opera*). But use starring role, not title role, for multiple descriptions (*The Witches of Eastwick*) or a reference not clearly related to the central character (*The Sterile Cuckoo*).

titles

Titles used before a name generally are not repeated before the surname. Say Mr. Blair, Mr. Bush, Mr. Klein, not Prime Minister Blair etc. However, the title may be used without the surname (the President, the Premier etc.).

The nobility are an exception; they keep a title, although possibly a different one, before their name in second reference (the Marquess of

Blank, then Lord Blank). See honorifics, capitalization.

Tlingit

This Indian language group, resembling the Haida in culture, numbered more than 7,000 in the early eighties. However, most are American, living along the Alaskan panhandle. In Canada, they are represented by four groups in northern B.C. and southern Yukon numbering about 700 in total: the Teslin, the Chilkat, the Carcross-Tagish and the Taku River Tlingit.

TNT

No need to write trinitrotoluene.

toboggan

today and yesterday, see time elements.

Togo

Adjective and people: Togolese. Currency: CFA franc. Capital: Lomé.

Togo, once the eastern part of the German protectorate of Togoland, was administered by France after the First World War, and gained independence in 1960. It is only about 100 kilometres wide, a narrow strip running northward for 550 kilometres from the Gulf of Guinea between Ghana and Benin. French is the official language, but the one most widely used is the tribal language Ewe. The population is five million.

tomatoes

Tonga

Adjective and people: Tongan. Currency: pa'anga. Capital: Nuku'alofa.

This Pacific kingdom of 106,000 people, formerly called the Friendly Islands, comprises about 170 islands and islets. Its western boundary is the eastern boundary of Fiji. The capital is on the island of Tongatapu. Tonga, a

British protectorate until 1970, is a member of the Commonwealth. The monarch is King Taufa'ahau Tupou IV, born July 4, 1918.

tonsil, tonsillectomy, tonsillitis

Tony Awards, the Tonys

These annual awards for achievement in U.S. theatre, named for actress and producer Antoinette Perry, were first awarded in 1947, the year after her death. The winners are named by several organizations, including the League of New York Theatres and various theatre arts unions.

toonie, toonies

Use this spelling for the two-dollar coin.

toque, see tuque.

Torah

It means the Law, but it may be called the Jewish Bible. In the narrowest sense, the name refers to the Pentateuch, the first five books of the Old Testament, those ascribed to Moses: Genesis, Exodus, Leviticus, Numbers and Deuteronomy. These books, handwritten on parchment scrolls, are found in every synagogue. In the broadest sense, Torah means all of God's law, His revealed guidance to mankind. Some would include laws and customs from the oral tradition of the Jewish people, and others would also include prominent rabbinic commentaries on both oral and written law.

tornadoes, see weather.

Toronto

A new, larger City of Toronto was created on Jan. 1, 1998, with the merger of the former cities of Toronto, North York, Etobicoke, Scarborough and York and the former borough of East York. It replaced Metropolitan

Toronto (known colloquially as Metro Toronto), which had been an overarching body with a chairperson and representatives from the five cities and one borough.

Toronto City Centre Airport

The official name of what used to be Toronto Island Airport. Use this name somewhere in the story if it is primarily about the airport itself, but, to avoid confusing readers outside Toronto, include the fact that what we are talking about is the airport located on one of the Toronto islands. First reference to "Toronto's island airport" (note lower case) would be fine, with the formal name noted later. If we use the formal name first, be sure to include a subsequent reference to "the island airport" or some such.

In short stories about other subjects in which the airport gets a passing reference, the formal name need not be used at all.

Toronto-Dominion Bank

TD Bank, TD Centre.

Toronto Islands

There is no island called Toronto Island; there are 15 named islands (and a few islets without separate names) that are referred to collectively as the Toronto Islands. The largest, a long boomerang that cradles the others, is Centre Island. Its sharp outside curve, facing southwest, is called Gibraltar Point. At its northwestern end is Hanlan's Point, Hanlan Memorial Park and the airport. Its eastern end is called Ward's Island, although this is not a separate island. The other named islands, east to west, are Algonquin, Snake, Snug Harbour (composed of three islands), North, South, Olympic, Island Park, Iroquois, Forestry, Mugg's, Donut and Jimmy's. The airport was renamed Toronto City Centre Airport in 1994, but we usually simply refer to "the island airport."

Houses are now found only on Ward's and Algonquin, which are administered and maintained by Toronto, owner of all the islands.

Centre Island Park takes in most of Centre Island plus the separate island called Island Park. The Royal Canadian Yacht Club takes in North, South and part of one of the Snug Harbour group; Island Yacht Club is on Mugg's; and the Queen City Yacht Club is on Algonquin.

Toronto Star, the

Toronto Sun, The

torque, torsion

Torsion is a term from mechanics that should not be used to mean mere twisting. Torsion is the strain produced by a twisting motion. The thing or force that causes twisting or rotation is called a torque. (Torque also refers to the efficiency with which reciprocating motion is converted to rotary motion, as in a car engine.)

tort

This is not an appropriate word for most news stories. Torts are one of three types of wrongs, the others being crimes and breaches of contract (dealt with under the law of torts, criminal law and contract law). A tort is a wrong (excluding breaches of contract) for which a civil suit for damages may be brought. A particular act should not be referred to as a tort until a lawsuit has established the existence of a wrongful act or omission, and established that compensable damage resulted.

tortuous and torturous

Tortuous means bent or twisted, and by extension devious, not straightforward or morally warped. **Torturous**, from torture, means causing pain or suffering, agonizing.

Tory

May be used in second reference, and headlines, to refer to Conservatives in both Canada and Britain. It has no pejorative connotation.

totalled

Use only in lighter stories in the sense of destroyed totally, damaged beyond repair.

totem

It means a spirit, either natural or ancestral, that watches over and often provides the identity of a people, a tribe, a clan. The word also refers to a carved or painted representation of such a spirit, in the form of a person, animal, plant or mythological being. Totems are found among many peoples of the world, including most Indian groups; the totem poles of the West Coast are one example.

touch football

Toulouse-Lautrec, Henri de

tour operator, see travel agency.

tourtière

This name for a type of meat pie has been absorbed into English. It is made principally from potatoes and ground pork.

toward (not towards).

Tower of London

It is not a tower, but rather a fortress on the Thames comprising a group of buildings surrounded by a wall and moat.

townie

This Newfoundland term refers to a resident of St. John's, as opposed to a bayman.

toxic and toxin

Toxic means poisonous. **Toxins** are a specific type of poison, those produced by a living organism (plant, animal, fungus or micro-organism). Arsenic and lead, for example, can be described as toxic substances, but they are metallic and therefore cannot be called toxins. Similarly, synthetic toxic substances are not toxins.

Use of the unmodified word toxic will be interpreted by most readers as meaning immediately very poisonous to humans. Like poisonous, toxic covers a wide range, and so should be modified with such words as mildly, moderately, extremely, lethally. In addition, we must say whether the effects are immediate or long-term. We must also specify what dose is toxic or lethal (either a specific amount or large, minute etc.). For example, 100 cups of strong coffee will supply a lethal dose of caffeine to an adult, but we would not describe coffee as toxic, and would not normally call caffeine toxic unless we also specified the dose. Since effects vary greatly even among very similar species, we must never draw uninformed parallels. The form of dioxin that has been called the most deadly manufactured poison was given this status because of the minute dose that will kill a guinea pig, but this dose must be multiplied by 5,000 before it is lethal to a hamster, and the lethal dose for humans is not known.

If the primary concern about a substance is that it does not break down in the environment, and therefore builds up in the food chain, the word toxic is usually misleading to the reader. Simply say in the lead that the substance is of concern to environmentalists, or is considered harmful to the environment, and later explain exactly why. See PCBs.

Toys "R" Us

track and field

The term **track** covers the running and walking events, both individual and relay, including those that involve some jumping (hurdles and steeple-chase). The **field** events are those that involve jumping for height or distance (high, long and triple jump and pole vault) and throwing or putting the shot, javelin, discus and hammer.

The decathlon (it means 10 contests) involves the 100, 400 and 1,500 metres, the 110-metre hurdles, high jump, long jump, pole vault, javelin, discus and shot. The women's heptathlon (seven) features the 200 and 800 metres, the 100-metre hurdles, the high and long jumps, javelin and shot. The men's pentathlon (five) is no longer an Olympic event.

track record

Except when referring to a record actually set on a track, prefer simply record.

trademark, but **trade name**.

We are careful to recognize proprietary interest in a trade name by beginning the name with a capital letter. We do so in the interest of accuracy and fairness. A brand name is a commercial asset, and to reduce it to the status of an ordinary word by using lower case has the effect of reducing its potential value to its owner. However, we do not go further and copy any stylized capitalization style in the rest of the word. Write Teleprompter, not TelePrompTer. However, use another capital after a hyphen (Band-Aid, Jell-O). We do follow the capitalization style in the names of corporations (as opposed to the brands they sell), as in TransCanada PipeLines.

There is no bar to using trade names in a general sense, in such idiomatic expressions as a Band-Aid solution, as long as we use upper case. We do not normally give such gratuitous publicity to trade names in news stories outside quotes, but a feature story may sound less stilted if we say someone stopped off for a

Coke, or was curled up with a sad novel and a box of Kleenex, rather than use the generic terms cola and tissues. In sports stories, it is difficult to avoid all publicity for a company sponsoring an event, but we should keep the name out of headlines as much as possible, and we prefer the corporation name to the brand name.

We should not use trade names in a pejorative way if we are not sure of the brand involved, and if the brand is not relevant to the story. Speak of a sports fan with a Thermos of coffee, but if he clubs someone with it, make it a vacuum bottle. If someone attempts suicide using ASA, there is no reason to specify Aspirin even if this was the brand used.

The process by which a trade name becomes a generic term is called debasement. U.S. court cases have determined that this has taken place with a handful of names in that country, and we should be aware of names that appear as generic terms in a U.S. wire story but are still actively protected in Canada (Kleenex and Aspirin are two examples). In Canada, we consider only a few former trade names to have become generic terms (nylon, rayon, laundromat, photostat, celluloid, melamine, bakelite, linoleum, mimeograph, escalator).

Our standard source for trade names in Canada is the *Canadian Trade Index*, available in the Report on Business library. For drug names, our authority for sorting generic names from brand names is the *Compendium of Pharmaceuticals and Specialties*, commonly known as the CPS. Both are updated annually.

trade-off

trafficker, trafficking

Traill, Catherine Parr

Note the double l in the married name of the Upper Canada pioneer remembered for her books describing her natural surroundings and offering advice to prospective immigrants. She was the sister of Susanna Moodie. Their maiden name was Strickland.

tranquillize, tranquillizer, tranquillity

trans

It takes a hyphen with most proper names (trans-Canada, trans-Siberian), but note these words established as lower-case by long use: transatlantic, transpacific, transarctic, transalpine, Transcaucasian, Transvaal.

Trans does not take a hyphen with lower-case adjectives (transcontinental) or with common nouns (transmountain), but its use with nouns often appears stilted or jarring. Prefer a trip across the desert to a transdesert trip.

Trans-Canada Highway

It is most accurately described as a federal-provincial highway system linking the 10 provinces, rather than as a single road. The Trans-Canada Highway Act was passed in 1948; the system was officially declared open in 1962 and completed in 1965.

TransCanada PipeLines, TCPL

Note the lack of hyphen, and the mid-word capitals.

transcendentalism

This philosophical movement of the mid-19th century, which had a strong effect on literature and the movements for women's rights and the abolition of slavery, stressed the unity of man and nature, and held that intuition was a better source of knowledge than reason and the senses. This word should not be used as a generic term for the unconnected modern movement **Transcendental Meditation** (TM), taught by Maharishi Mahesh Yogi. Clearing the mind of thought by chanting a phrase (mantra) during 20-minute periods of meditation

is intended to induce relaxation and a sense of transcending daily cares.

Transfiguration

Use upper case for the supernatural transformation of Christ, reported in Chapter 17 of Matthew, and the Aug. 6 church festival marking this.

translation

In general, we do not use non-English words without providing a translation, unless the meaning is crystal clear from the context. We assume our readers to be intelligent and erudite but unilingual. For style on translations, see foreign and French words.

translator

translucent and transparent

Translucent means allowing light through, as waxed paper does. **Transparent** means allowing images through, as clear glass does. Transparent and clear do not imply colourless.

Trans Mountain Pipe Line Co. Ltd.

transpire

To be emitted as a vapour, and by extension to become known by leaking out. It cannot be used as a fancy word for happen.

Transvaal

It is the northeastern province of South Africa, lying between the Vaal and Limpopo Rivers.

trap door

Trappists

There is rarely any need to use the formal title, the Cistercians of the Strict Observance. This order, stressing silence, prayer and physical work, was founded at La Trappe, in Normandy, but the abbot-general now lives in Rome.

trapshooting

But **skeet shooting**, two words. Trapshooting is the general word for the sport of shooting at clay targets thrown up by a spring device called a trap, and it is also the name of the original sport as opposed to the much newer variation, skeet. In trap, targets are thrown from behind or beside the shooter out toward the front, to simulate a bird flying away from the shooter. In skeet, two traps 40 yards apart throw targets toward each other, to simulate the flight of a bird across the shooter's field of view. One trap is set to deliver a high trajectory, the other a lower, flatter one. In both trap and skeet, the targets are thrown either one at a time or in pairs (doubles).

travel agency, tour operator

The travel industry makes a distinction between the terms tour operator (a wholesale operation) and travel agency (a retail operation).

Generally, a **tour operator** (or a tour firm or tour wholesaler) does not deal directly with the public. It is a company that puts together tours for sale through travel agencies. **Travel agencies** are the point of contact for members of the public. They sell the tours of any tour operator, the airline seats of any airline, the rooms of any hotel etc.

While there are exceptions (some tour operators do take bookings from the public and some travel agencies do put together their own tours), most travel companies define themselves as one or the other depending on their primary emphasis.

travelled, traveller

traveller's cheque

trawler and troller

A **trawler** drags a net along the sea bottom. A **troller** drags a line, or several lines, fitted with hooks.

A **wetfish trawler** preserves its catch by stowing it in ice for up to 10 days. A **freezer trawler** freezes its catch on board to preserve it. Fish are typically headed and gutted, then frozen in large blocks, to be thawed and filleted ashore. A **factory trawler** is similar to a freezer trawler, but the catch is usually processed (e.g. filleted) at sea and then frozen in its final product form. It is a floating fish plant.

The inshore (as opposed to deep-sea) fishery on the East Coast is conducted by relatively small vessels known as longliners.

treasury bill

Lower case for all countries except the United States, where it is Treasury bill.

Treasury Board

The federal government's central management agency has had its own minister (called the president) since 1966, but it is still formally a Privy Council committee, the only committee that the cabinet is required by statute to form. It consists of the president as chairman, the finance minister and four other ministers. The staff it administers is called the secretariat, and the deputy minister in charge carries the title secretary of the Treasury Board. The board advises the cabinet on which programs merit financing; sets administrative policy for the various departments on such matters as personnel, financial management, contracts and office space; negotiates with public service unions; and generally controls spending. The office of the comptroller-general, charged with improving financial administration and program evaluation within departments, was created in 1978.

tree line

Generally speaking, it is the limit beyond which trees will not grow in that form, although the same species may continue to grow as shrubs. The limit of even these shrub forms is called the tree-species line. Tree lines are created not only by latitude but also by altitude. (On a mountain, the tree line is also called the timber line or timber limit.) We should not imply a sharp division, or a static one, since the shelter and soil conditions of depressions and valleys can extend the tree line far to the north in places, and climatic cycles can cause it to ebb and flow.

trek

It need not necessarily mean a journey by ox cart with all one's belongings, but it still must connote a long, slow and arduous journey by foot or beast. It is not a synonym for trudge or tramp.

trendsetter

Tribal Class

Upper-case. There were 27 of these British-designed naval destroyers built, named for various native peoples from Commonwealth countries. The eight that served with Canada's navy during or after the Second World War were Athabaskan (1 and 2), Cayuga, Haida, Huron, Iroquois, Micmac and Nootka.

tribe

This word is marginally acceptable, but be aware that peoples to whom it is applied are alert to any implication of primitiveness. Speak in general of the Bantu tribes, the problem of African tribalism etc., but in reference to a particular group, prefer the Shona people, the Kikuyu people etc. In reference to native people of the Americas, beware any false impression that there was widespread organization or even communication between the many isolated bands speaking the same language (Cree, for example). See native people.

Tricolour

Upper-case for the French flag. Do not use *Tricouleur*.

Trinidad and Tobago

The combined adjective and noun Trinibagian may be used if the name of the country has already been set up. Residents of the individual islands may be called Trinidadian or Tobagonian. Currency: dollar. Capital: Port of Spain.

This two-island state off the coast of Venezuela is one of the most prosperous in the Caribbean; it is rich in oil, gas and asphalt, and in 1981 opened the Caribbean's first integrated iron and steel works. It is a member of the Commonwealth, independent since 1962 and a republic since 1976. Of its population of 1.4 million, about 45 per cent are black and about 35 per cent trace their families to India.

trio

This word implies organization and co-ordinated effort. We do not use it for any three who happen to get together.

Triple Alliance

Use upper case for several past European alliances: England-Sweden-Netherlands, 1668; England-France-Netherlands, 1717; Germany-Austria-Italy, 1882 (this one was also called the League of the Three Emperors, *Dreikaiserbund*, balanced by an informal diplomatic understanding between Britain, France and Russia called the Triple Entente). For modern groupings, prefer three-country alliance. See quadruple alliance.

Triple Crown

Upper-case. The original is that of thoroughbred racing in Britain, consisting of victories in the 2,000 Guineas, the Derby Stakes (pronounced Darby, and known in North America as the Epsom Derby) and the St. Leger. For U.S.

thoroughbreds, it is the Kentucky Derby, the Preakness Stakes and the Belmont Stakes. In Canada, it is the Queen's Plate, the Prince of Wales Stakes and the Breeders Stakes.

For pacers in the United States it is the Cane Pace, the Little Brown Jug and the Messenger Stakes. For U.S. trotters, it is the Kentucky Futurity, the Hambletonian and the Yonkers Trot. A less formal Triple Crown for Canadian pacers is the North America Cup, the Confederation Cup and the Prix d'Été.

TRIPS

The short term used for the Agreement on Trade Related Aspects of Intellectual Property Rights, annex 1C of the World Trade Organization's Uruguay Round, the agreement that established the WTO. All letters are upper-case as though it were an acronym.

Trivial Pursuit (singular).

trod

This is the past tense of tread, and the participle is either trod or trodden, with trodden preferred for the passive. You tread the boards; your father trod the boards, he has trod the boards, the boards have been trodden by him. It is either transitive or intransitive (he trod the boards, he trod upon the boards).

Trois-Rivières

Sits on the north shore of the St. Lawrence River halfway between Montreal and Quebec City. A new, larger City of Trois-Rivières was created on Jan. 1, 2002, through the amalgamation of Trois-Rivières, Trois-Rivières West, Cap-de-la-Madeleine, Saint-Louis-de-France, Sainte-Marthe du Cap and the Municipality of Pointe-du-Lac.

See also Montreal, Quebec City, Gatineau, Longueuil and Lévis.

trompe l'oeil

troop and troupe

Troop, troops and trooper are military; troupe and trouper are theatrical.

trooping the colour

There is no of in the formal name of the ceremony, but the preposition is required when the verb becomes a gerund, in such sentences as The Queen viewed the trooping of the colour.

tropics

This applies to the area between the Tropics of Cancer and Capricorn, which are imaginary lines 23½ degrees north and south of the equator.

Trudeau, Pierre

We normally do not use his middle name, Elliott. He was born in Montreal on Oct. 18, 1919, and died on Sept. 28, 2000. He was first elected to the Commons (Mount Royal) in 1965 as one of the Three Wise Men from Quebec (the others were unionist Jean Marchand and journalist Gérard Pelletier). He was made justice minister in 1967, and became prime minister in 1968. His government was defeated by Joe Clark's Conservatives in 1979, but regained office in 1980. He retired from politics in 1984. He married Margaret Sinclair in 1971; they separated in 1977 and divorced in 1984. (She has since married and divorced Fried Kemper, and may be called Margaret Trudeau Kemper.) Pierre and Margaret Trudeau had three sons together: Justin, Sacha (Alexandre) and Michel. Michel was killed in a back-country skiing accident on Nov. 13, 1998, swept by an avalanche into Kokanee Lake, B.C. After leaving public life, Pierre Trudeau also had a daughter, Sarah, with lawyer Deborah Coyne.

True North

Upper-case to mean Canada, an allusion to a line in the national anthem. Stanley Weir, who wrote the English words, borrowed the phrase from Tennyson, who referred to Canada as "That True North whereof we lately heard."

Truman, Harry S

The S has no period; it does not stand for a name.

try to (not try and).

Tsawwassen, B.C.

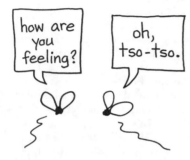

tsetse

There are 20 species of these flies, whose mouth parts are adapted to pierce the skin and suck blood. Only some are carriers of the organism that causes sleeping sickness.

Tsimshian

This Indian linguistic group, covering about 11,000 people in Canada and about 3,000 in Alaska, includes three languages in Canada, spoken on the northern B.C. coast as far south as Milbanke Sound and on the Skeena and Nass Rivers: Coast Tsimshian, Southern Tsimshian (Niska) and Nass-Gitksan.

tsunami

Prefer this to tidal wave, since they have nothing to do with tides, but where necessary include an explanation in brackets (i.e. formerly known as tidal waves). They are caused by underwater quakes or eruptions, and may also be called seismic ocean waves. In mid-ocean

they are less than one metre high, but move extremely quickly, at about 750 kilometres an hour. Near the shore, slowed by friction with the sea bottom, they increase in height to 25 metres or more. The word does not require italics. The plural is tsunamis.

Tuaregs

They are not Arabs but Berbers, fair-skinned people of the Sahara and of the savannahs on its southern fringe whose society also includes black labourers (until recently, slaves). Adult men wear a blue veil in the presence of women, strangers and in-laws, but women do not.

tugboat

For the large ocean-going variety, say tug.

tug(s) of war

tumour

But drop the u for **tumorous, tumoral**.

We must specify whether they are benign or malignant. If we know the details, we should also specify cancer, lymphoma or sarcoma, since these can behave differently.

tump

In Canada a tump, also called a tumpline, is a broad strap, tapering toward its ends, that is passed across the forehead or chest to help support loads carried on the back or for pulling canal barges.

tundra

This is the Barrens, the area north of the tree line to the Arctic coast, and including the unglaciated parts of the Arctic islands. It is mostly wet or otherwise unstable ground in summer, underlain by permafrost, having many rocky outcrops and abundant vegetation, both flowering and of the lichen type. There is also a wide variety of animal life. It includes much of the Northwest Territories and Nunavut, plus northern Yukon, far northern Quebec and northern Labrador.

Tunisia

Adjective and people: Tunisian. Currency: dinar. Capital: Tunis.

It is on the Mediterranean, flanked by Algeria to the west and Libya to the southeast. It is too far west to be called part of the Middle East, but its politics, religion and oil wealth earn it inclusion in stories about the area. Its population of about 9.5 million, mostly Berber and Arab, makes it the most densely populated of the countries of North Africa. More than 50 per cent of its people are urban, the other major cities being Bizerta, Kairouan, Sfax and Sousse. It became independent from France under Habib Bourguiba in 1956.

tupek

Not tuperk. Inuktitut for skin tent, summer replacement for the snow house, it requires italics and a translation or explanation. We should not imply that they are widely used in this era of government settlements. See igloo.

tuque

Use this spelling for the knitted cap familiar from many a Canadian winter. Reserve **toque** for a conical or plumed hat of earlier centuries, a chef's hat or a modern close-fitting hat of high fashion.

Turkey

Adjective: Turkish. People: Turks. Currency: lira. Capital: Ankara.

It has a small European section (Trakya) separated from Asian Turkey (Anadolu) by the highly strategic waterway made up, from north to south, of the Bosporus, the Sea of Marmara and the Dardanelles, the only route from the Black Sea to the Mediterranean (Aegean). Istanbul is on the European side of the Bosporus. The northern shore of the Dardanelles (formerly called the Hellespont) is the Gallipoli Peninsula. Ankara is inland in the region called Anatolia, which corresponds to the peninsula of Asia Minor. The languages are Turkish in the west, Kurdish in the east. Most Turks are Muslim, but Islam ceased to be the state religion in 1928, and women got the vote in 1934. The population is about 68 million.

Turk is also encountered as a general term covering all the Turkic-speaking peoples, extending from southeastern Soviet Europe to western China, and from the Mediterranean to Siberia, but it would be confusing to readers if used without an explanation. The Turkic languages include Turkish, Azerbaijani, Chuvash, Kazakh, Kyrgyz, Tatar, Turkoman and Uzbek.

In 1984, the Kurdistan Workers Party (PKK) began a fight in southeastern Turkey to create an independent Kurdish homeland called Kurdistan. PKK leader Abullah Ocalan was captured in Kenya in 1999, and urged his followers to make peace with Turkey. The party announced a ceasefire, though several thousand armed PKK militants continued to engage in sporadic fights with the Turkish military from a Kurdish base in northern Iraq. In 2002, the PKK changed its name to the Kurdistan Freedom and Democracy Congress (Kadek). In the same year, a Turkish court commuted Ocalan's death sentence to life imprisonment.

See Cyprus.

Turkmenistan

Adjective and people: Turkmenian. Currency: manat. Capital: Ashkhabad.

Made one of the Soviet Central Asian republics in 1924, it gained independence with the disintegration of the Soviet Union in late 1991. Most of its territory is the Kara Kum

(Black Sands) Desert, broken by occasional oases, but the land rises to foothills suitable for grazing in the south. It has a substantial coast on the Caspian Sea to the east, and borders on Iran, Afghanistan and Uzbekistan. Its population of five million is about 70-per-cent Turkmenian (of various tribes known as Turkmen or Turkoman), Sunni Muslims whose language, West Turkic, is closely related to Turkish. Minorities brought in for Soviet economic development, including Russians (13 per cent), Uzbeks and Kazakhs, are in the majority in urban centres. Intensive irrigation under the Soviets allowed development of an important cotton industry. Other products are oil, chemicals, carpets and sheep products, including astrakhan lamb pelts.

See Soviet Union.

Turks and Caicos Islands, the

They are included in the West Indies, lying southeast of the Bahamas, but are too far north to be called Caribbean. The two island groups consist of six inhabited islands and about 24 smaller ones. The largest are Grand Caicos, 50 kilometres long but only four or five wide, and Grand Turk, seat of the capital, about 11 kilometres long by two wide. Associated at various times with the Bahamas or Jamaica, the islands became a separate British colony in 1973. The population is 12,000. There have been overtures about an association with Canada.

turncoat

Tussaud's

The waxworks in London is Madame Tussaud's; the one in Niagara Falls, Ont., is Louis Tussaud's. Marie Tussaud was originally Swiss, not French.

Tutankhamen

Tuvalu

Adjective and people: Tuvaluan. Currency: Australian dollar, but with Tuvaluan coins. Capital: Funafuti.

This Pacific state, formerly called the Ellice Islands, separated from the Gilberts in 1975 and became independent in 1978 as a member of the Commonwealth. Funafuti is one of nine small atolls with an aggregate land area of only 24 square kilometres, spread over 1.3 million square kilometres of ocean. No point rises more than five metres above sea level, and the islands are at increasing risk of being swamped. The approximately 11,000 inhabitants are Polynesian, and about a third of them live on Funafuti. The mainstays of the economy are coconut palms, sale of stamps and remittances from Tuvaluans working abroad.

tuvavouteet

The Eastern Arctic word for goodbye literally means stay as you are. It requires italics.

TVOntario, TVO

Twentieth Century Fox Film Corp.

But the onscreen logo is 20th Century-Fox.

24 Sussex Dr.

It was built in Confederation year for Joseph Currier, and remained a private home until the federal government bought it in 1949 as the official prime ministerial residence. Louis St. Laurent moved in in 1951.

twister, see weather words.

two cents worth (no apostrophe).

tying

type

It is a noun and a verb, but not an adjective in the sense of new-type

parents, multiple-occupancy-type
housing. Make it a new type of parent.

typhoid fever and typhus

They are quite different. **Typhoid
fever**, caused by a species of
salmonella bacteria, is usually spread
in contaminated water or food. It
attacks the lymphatic system and
gastrointestinal tract. **Typhus** has less
spectacular symptoms (rash, severe
headache, a mild cough) but is fatal to
most untreated adults, although
antibiotics are effective treatments. It
is caused by rickettsiae (organisms
comparable to bacteria and viruses),
and is spread by fleas.

typhoon, see weather words.

Tyrrhenian Sea

It is that part of the northwestern
Mediterranean bounded by Italy,
Corsica, Sardinia and Sicily.

U

U

As in U Ne Win, U Thant. In Myanmar (Burma) it is not a given name but a title, conveying more respect than Mr. It should be retained in second reference.

U and non-U

No periods in these lighthearted British expressions distinguishing the in crowd from the rest.

U-boat, U-bolt, U-turn

U-boat is **English** for a German submarine. The German is *U-boot*, for *Unterseeboot*.

UCI

Avoid these initials for the French name of the world cycling body, the International Cycling Union (*Union cycliste internationale*).

UEFA

These are the initials of the French name for the European soccer body, the European Union of Association Football (*Union européenne de football association*). We avoid the initials as obscure and confusing, especially in headlines.

UFO

No periods. Use lower case when spelling out unidentified flying object.

Uganda

Adjective and people: Ugandan. Currency: shilling. Capital: Kampala.

Uganda, landlocked in East Africa, is on the equator but has a moderate climate because of its elevation, averaging 1,200 metres (4,000 feet). Clockwise from the north, it borders on Sudan, Kenya, Tanzania, Rwanda and Congo (formerly Zaire), and shares Lake Victoria with Kenya and Tanzania. Tanzania invaded it in 1979 to end the regime of Idi Amin, who had ousted Milton Obote in a coup in 1971. Obote (Dr. on second reference) regained the presidency in an election in 1980, but was overthrown by another coup in 1985 under Lieutenant-General Tito Okello. Okello's regime met with strong resistance from the opposition National Resistance Movement and its armed wing, the National Resistance Army under Yoweri Museveni. The NRA overwhelmed government forces, and on Jan. 27, 1986, Museveni was installed as president. He maintained a one-party state that permitted no opposition parties (he called it a "no-party state" in which all were free to join the NRM), but it was far removed from the brutal Amin and Obote regimes. He told his army its job was to protect Uganda's citizens, not oppress them, allowed considerable freedom of speech, fostered enviable economic growth and met the serious AIDS epidemic with a strong public-health effort. He won wide praise in the West for his enlightened policies and in Africa for his strong Afrocentric stand.

The population is about 24 million.

UHF

If it is clear we are speaking of one of the two TV frequency ranges, it is not necessary to write out ultrahigh frequency.

Ukraine

Adjective and people: Ukrainian. Currency: hryvnya. Capital: Kiev.

One of the original members of the Soviet Union (in 1920), it declared its sovereignty in July of 1990, aiming for a confederation of equals among Soviet republics. With complete independence in the fall of 1991, after the failed Soviet coup, it became one of the three founding members of the Commonwealth of Independent States. It was one of three former Soviet republics left with nuclear weapons, and was involved in a bitter dispute with Russia over division of former Soviet military forces, particularly the Black Sea Fleet.

Its population of 49 million is 75-per-cent Ukrainian, with most of the rest being Russian. Its language is known in Russia as Little Russian (as opposed to Great Russian in Russia and White Russian in Belarus).

About two-thirds of its area is extremely fertile "black earth" plain, making it a major agricultural producer. It also contains oil and gas and vast coal deposits; they made up 60 per cent of the total Soviet coal reserves. It is perhaps the republic best suited for independence in a free market, with a well-established industrial base in mining, metals, machinery and chemicals.

Ukraine has undergone considerable suffering in this century, including the death of 7.5 million people in the famine of 1932-33. There are more than 750,000 people of Ukrainian descent in Canada, and twice that number in the United States.

See Soviet Union.

ukulele

ultimatums

ultra

The prefix does not take a hyphen (ultrahigh) unless the primary word begins with an a (ultra-ambitious) or a capital (ultra-Christian).

ultrasonic and supersonic

Ultrasonic means having a frequency higher than the maximum detectable by human ears. The noun is ultrasound. Ultrasonic must not be used to mean **supersonic**, meaning moving faster than sound. See Mach.

ultrasound physician

The term ultrasonologist is not used in Canada. An ultrasound technologist may be called an ultrasonographer, but we would do so only in direct quotes, and should provide a translation.

Ultrasuede, a trade name.

ultraviolet

Electromagnetic radiation with a wavelength beyond that of visible light at the violet end of the spectrum cannot properly be called light. Speak of ultraviolet radiation or rays, not light.

ulu

This Inuktitut word for a woman's knife refers to one with a handle across a shaft that is attached to the centre of a crescent-shaped blade, used for cutting, skinning, chopping. It requires italics and an explanation. The man's knife, like a conventional butcher knife, is a *suvik*.

umiak

This is the large Inuit skin boat for cargo and passengers, traditionally paddled by women, as opposed to the one-man kayak used by hunters. It requires italics and an explanation (but kayak does not).

umlaut

To indicate an umlaut in a German word or name, English writers insert an e (Hermann Goering). This rule does not apply to other languages. See accents.

un

It takes a hyphen only before a capital (unnerving, but un-American). For a comparison with other negative prefixes (non, in, anti), see non.

unchristian, non-Christian

Unchristian means uncharitable, unbecoming to a Christian, against Christian precepts, but it is obviously risky in news stories, implying that Christianity has a lock on virtue. A **non-Christian** is a person not of the Christian religion.

unco-operative, unco-ordinated

unctuous

A highly pejorative term when used to refer to a recognizable individual.

Underground Railroad (not Railway).

undersecretary

undertaker

Prefer this to funeral director, mortician.

under way

unemployment, unemployed

For the purposes of economists and statisticians, unemployed is taken to mean willing to work and seeking a job, but unable to find one. We conform to this definition (with an explanation) in stories about employment statistics and the economy, but need not do so when writing about an individual. A capable, non-wealthy adult who does not have a paying job and does not perform any alternative function (running a home etc.) may be described in general news stories as unemployed, regardless of whether he or she is discouraged from seeking a job at the moment.

Statisticians divide the working-age population (those 15 to 64 and not in school) between the labour force and those "not in the labour force." (Those outside the labour force do not want a paying job at present, or are incapable of working, or are "discouraged workers" who have given up trying to find a job.) The labour force, in turn, is divided between those who have a job (the employed) and those looking for one (the unemployed).

The percentage of unemployed in the labour force is the **unemployment rate**. The percentage of labour-force members (employed or not) in the entire working-age population is called the **participation rate**. A third percentage that economists find a good gauge of an economy is that of employed people in the entire working-age population.

To make the monthly job figures useful as an economic barometer, statisticians provide a **seasonal adjustment** to discount the ups and downs that are normal at certain times each year (as when various fishing seasons end, and when students leave the labour force at summer's end). These adjusted rates are the proper focus of stories on unemployment figures, but we should also provide the actual numbers of working and unemployed, compare these with previous totals, and explain seasonal adjustment.

unemployment insurance

See employment insurance.

unforeseen

Uniate Church

Prefer **Eastern rite church**. These churches consider the term Uniate to have negative connotations (it was bestowed on them by the Eastern Orthodox churches, and was taken as an implication that they were becoming too Latinized). Eastern rite churches recognize Roman Catholic doctrines and the authority of the pope, but retain their own language, canon laws and rites, including marriage of the clergy, administration of wine at communion and baptism by immersion. There are five distinct Eastern rite traditions, but most Eastern rite churches in Canada (those from Eastern Europe and the Balkans) are of the Byzantine rite.

Unicef

Upper-and-lower. This is an old acronym now used on its own in the names of such organizations as Unicef Canada. The UN agency now called the United Nations Children's Fund was originally called the United Nations International Children's Emergency Fund.

Unification Church

This is the Christian religious movement of Rev. Sun Myung Moon, which generates intense dedication among its members in fundraising, business and missionary activities and has become a considerable economic force, owning many businesses and much real estate. The term Moonies was a derisive one that is now used by the members themselves, but we should be careful not to use it in a way that implies they are mindless cultists. They now number more than three million in 100 countries, but only about 10,000 in the U.S. branch, which has a high turnover. There is usually no need to use the full name, Holy Spirit Association for the Unification of World Christianity.

uninterested and disinterested

See disinterested.

Union Jack

Upper-case for the flag of the United Kingdom. Use lower case for jack if we mean a smaller version of a flag used as part of an ensign (as the upper quadrant on the staff side).

Note two potentially confusing factors: The U.K. flag is technically called the Union Flag unless it is being flown from the jack staff at the rear of a vessel; and the blue jack with stars in the corner of the Stars and Stripes is also called the Union Jack when flown on a U.S. Navy vessel's jack staff. We avoid both these usages as confusing, unless the story is specifically about this issue.

Union Nationale

The Quebec party founded in 1935 by Maurice Duplessis as a coalition of Conservatives and disaffected Liberals opposed to the corrupt Taschereau Liberal regime held office from 1936 to 1939 and from 1944 to 1960 (Duplessis died in 1959), and again from 1966 (under Daniel Johnson and Jean-Jacques Bertrand) until 1970.

unique

It is an absolute, meaning one of a kind. We may detract from it in certain ways (all but unique), but may not use modifiers that purport to augment it (very unique, most unique etc.).

Unitarianism

It may be called a Protestant faith, although its members reject the doctrine of the Trinity (the deity of Christ) and advocate freedom of religious opinion.

United Airlines

United Arab Emirates

Adjective and noun in second reference: UAE. Currency: dirham. Capital: Abu Dhabi.

The coasts of these seven oil-rich emirates on the Arabian Peninsula form the southern base of the Persian Gulf, what is known as the Trucial Coast, and until their union in 1971-72 they were known as the Trucial States. They are Abu Dhabi, Ajman, Dubai, Fujairah, Ras al-Khaimah, Sharjah and Umm al Qawain. The indigenous people are Sunni Muslim Arabs, but they are outnumbered in the population of 2.4 million by immigrant minorities (Iranians, Indians, Pakistanis, Africans and Europeans). The emirates have a long, friendly association with Britain, which was formally responsible for their defence and foreign relations until 1971. The federation is governed by the seven rulers, sitting as the Supreme Council. They all bear the title Sheik, not Emir.

United Church of Canada

Canada's largest Protestant denomination was formed in 1925 through a union of four groups: the Methodist Church, most of the Congregational Churches of Canada, about two-thirds of the congregations in the Presbyterian Church in Canada, and the General Council of Local Union Churches (a group of congregations, mainly in Saskatchewan, that had led the way in forming a union). A fifth group joined in 1968—the Eastern Canada congregations of the Evangelical United Brethren Church.

United Empire Loyalists

UE applies only to some Loyalists. See Loyalist.

United Kingdom

This name refers to the United Kingdom of Great Britain and Northern Ireland, with a population of 60 million. The initials U.K. are useful in headlines, and may be used in copy as an adjective or (on second reference) a noun. Except in a story

specifically about the history or state of the union, prefer Britain, British.

However, this shorthand cannot be used when we are specifically referring to the inclusion of Northern Ireland; in those references, it will often be necessary to fall back on United Kingdom. Strictly speaking, Britain refers to the peoples of the island of Great Britain (England, Scotland and Wales) and its smaller satellite islands. As a two-letter geographical abbreviation, U.K. takes periods. See Britain.

Until 1921, it was called the United Kingdom of Great Britain and Ireland. The adjective Great once distinguished the island (containing England, Scotland and Wales) from Little Britain (Brittany).

The Channel Islands (Jersey, Guernsey, Alderney, Brechou, Great Sark, Little Sark, Herm, Jethou and Lithou) belong to the Crown of England, its last remnants from the Duchy of Normandy, but are not, strictly speaking, part of the United Kingdom. The Isle of Man has a very different status, largely independent in laws and taxes but with a governor appointed by the Crown. The Isles of Scilly are also British.

Also excluded from the term United Kingdom are the dependent territories (the new term for colony) of Britain: Gibraltar, Bermuda, Anguilla, the British Antarctic Territory, the British Indian Ocean Territory, the British Virgin Islands, the Cayman Islands, the Falkland Islands, Montserrat, the Pitcairn Islands, St. Helena and Ascension, Tristan da Cunha, South Georgia and the South Sandwich Islands, and the Turks and Caicos Islands. Hong Kong, a former dependent territory, was handed over to China on July 1, 1997.

United Nations, UN

It has six central organs: the General Assembly, the Security Council, the Secretariat (the administrative body, headed by the secretary-general), the Economic and Social Council, the Trusteeship Council (now inactive) and the International Court of Justice (which meets in The Hague).

The General Assembly has established several funds and programs. They include the United Nations Children's Fund (Unicef), Office of the UN High Commissioner for Refugees, UN Conference on Trade and Development (UNCTAD), UN Development Program, UN Environment Program and UN Population Fund. Other bodies include five regional economic commissions and several committees overseeing compliance with international treaties.

Specialized UN agencies include the Food and Agriculture Organization, the UN Educational, Scientific and Cultural Organization (UNESCO) and the International Civil Aviation Organization. The International Monetary Fund, World Bank and World Trade Organization are theoretically affiliated to the UN, but in practice the link is weak.

United Service Organizations, USO

Note the plural in the name of this grouping of organizations (YMCA, Salvation Army etc.) that serve the needs of U.S. military personnel.

United States

U.S. is acceptable as an adjective in first reference. It may be used as a noun in headlines and in second reference in copy, if there is no better way of crafting the sentence. Do not use it at the end of a sentence if the first word of the next might be misread as a continuation: He visited the U.S. Army officials welcomed him. (Also see America, American.)

The United States is the world's fourth-largest country, after Russia, Canada and China. It has a population of 281 million.

In addition to the 50 states, Puerto Rico is classed as a commonwealth (see Puerto Rico). Other island possessions are classed as unincorporated territories of the United States: Guam, American Samoa, the U.S. Virgin Islands, Johnston Atoll, the Midway Islands and Wake Island.

The Republic of Palau was a U.S. trust territory, part of the Trust Territory of the Pacific Islands. Like the other three parts—the Northern Mariana Islands, the Marshall Islands and the Federated States of Micronesia (Yap, Truk, Kosrae and Pohnpei)—it has progressed to the status of a "freely associated state."

After terrorist attacks on New York and Washington on Sept. 11, 2001, the United States significantly increased security at airports, borders and other sites considered particularly vulnerable to attack. See Sept. 11.

On Nov. 25, 2002, President George W. Bush signed into law the Homeland Security Act of 2002, creating a Department of Homeland Security, which succeeded the White House Office of Homeland Security he had established in October of 2001. Tom Ridge was sworn in as the first Secretary of Homeland Security on Jan. 23, 2003.

The department assumed responsibility for 22 domestic agencies grouped under five directorates: Border and Transportation Security (including the U.S. Customs Service), Emergency Preparedness and Response, Science and Technology, Information Analysis and Infrastructure Protection, and Management (to manage the department). The Secret Service and the Coast Guard, though separate from the directorates, report directly to the secretary. The Office of Inspector-General audits the department's operations to promote economy and detect abuse.

United Steelworkers of America

Steelworkers in second reference is preferable to the less familiar and less obvious USW.

United Way

At the movement's inception after the First World War (it began at various times in various cities) it was called the Red Feather campaign of the Community Chest. The name United Appeal was adopted in 1956, and this was changed to United Way in 1975.

universities

We use English for the names of universities in Quebec and abroad (University of Montreal, not Université de Montréal).

The University of Saskatchewan is in Saskatoon. There is no University of Saskatoon, but there is a University of Regina.

unmistakable, unshakable (no internal e).

-up

One word for breakup, holdup and markup, but note hyphen in cover-up, cut-up, mix-up, set-up and warm-up. Our dictionary generally uses a hyphen when the root word ends in e, as in booze-up, frame-up, tie-up, tune-up, but note the exceptions lineup, makeup.

up-and-coming

upcoming

It is recognized in some dictionaries, but is inelegant telegraphese, in the same class as ongoing, downplaying. Prefer coming, approaching, impending.

up for grabs

It is a properly idiomatic expression, but much overused. Reserve it for true scrambles.

upfront

Avoid as an adjective in the sense of honest, straightforward.

It is less objectionable as an adjective or adverb in the sense of a prerequisite for a deal or agreement (an upfront payment; he demanded half a million up front), but it should be reserved for lighter stories. In most cases, use advance or in advance.

upgrade

Reserve for actual increases in grade, rank, status or responsibility. For inanimate things (roads, etc.) use improve, repair.

Uplands

Uplands Air Field became Uplands Airport in 1938, Ottawa Airport in 1960 and Ottawa International Airport in 1964.

Upper Canada

It may be used sparingly as a whimsical reference to Ontario. This name applied from 1791 until 1841, when it was changed to Canada West. The name Ontario was adopted in 1867. For references before 1791, use British North America.

upper case, lower case

They take a hyphen as an adjective or verb, but not as a noun (put it in lower case; an upper-case letter; we must upper-case that word). Consider using capital and capitalize as more familiar to readers who are not in our business, and small letters as an alternative to lower case. See capitalization.

upper chamber, upper house

Use lower case to refer to a legislative body. Do not use it to refer to Canada's Senate, since this would give an inaccurate impression of its relationship with the Commons.

upper lakes, upper Great Lakes

A vague expression, confusing to those who wrongly equate north with up and leaving the reader in doubt about exactly which lakes are meant. In fact, upper lakes was coined in the days before the building of the Welland Canal to refer to all the lakes above Niagara Falls, that is, all except Ontario. See lakes.

Upper Volta, now Burkina Faso.

and you'll play your next scene with a cute little dog and a darling baby...

upstage manager

upstage

Upstage is toward the scenery; downstage is toward the audience. To upstage, meaning to steal the scene, does not mean to stand between another actor and the audience. It means to move upstage, forcing the other actor to turn away from the audience to deliver his part of the dialogue.

upstream and downstream

We must never be led astray by considerations of north and south. Quebec City is downstream from Montreal; Moosonee is downstream from Kapuskasing; Khartoum is upstream from Cairo.

Ural Mountains

They are not merely a range but a mountain system 2,000 kilometres long, comprising several ranges. Running from the Kara Sea in the north to Kazakhstan, the Urals are the traditional dividing line between Europe and Asia. They are rich in minerals and timber, and are relatively low; the highest is Mount Narodnaya at 1,894 metres (6,214 feet).

Ursa Major, Minor

In most non-technical stories, prefer the most familiar English names, Big Dipper and Little Dipper. Ursa Major (Great Bear) has several other names, including the Plow. The two stars forming the outer edge of its bowl point past the rim toward Polaris, which is at the end of the handle of the Little Dipper.

Uruguay

Adjective and people: Uruguayan. Currency: peso. Capital: Montevideo.

It is on the east coast of South America (its official name is the Oriental Republic of Uruguay), bounded on the west and southwest by Argentina, on the northeast by Brazil, and on the south by the Rio de la Plata. Its population of 3.4 million, mostly of Spanish and Italian extraction, is about 80-per-cent urban, but the economy is largely pastoral, particularly reliant on exports of meat and other animal products such as wool.

usher

Use for both men and women (not usherette).

USSR

There is little occasion to use these initials for the defunct Soviet Union, except to avoid repetition of the word Soviet in head and deck. In copy, prefer Soviet Union, Soviet. If the initials appear in a quote, they take no periods. If we use the cyrillic initials of the Russian-language name, CCCP, we should explain that they represent the letters SSSR in our alphabet (Soyuz Sovyetskikh Sotsialisticheskikh Respublik). See Soviet Union.

usury

A word to steer clear of in referring to a recognizable individual or corporation, unless criminal charges are proved. Usury is usually taken to mean charging more than the legal interest rate. A person who is convicted of doing this may be called a loan shark, but be aware that the Criminal Code of Canada does not use the terms usury or loansharking. The offence, under Section 347, is that of charging a criminal interest rate, which is defined in the section as a rate exceeding 60 per cent a year.

utilidor

This term is common in the North to refer to aboveground conduits for water and sewer lines in communities built on rock or permafrost. If the meaning is not clear from the context, the term should be explained.

utility pole

Prefer this term to telephone pole or hydro pole if it carries both types of cable (as most do). Larger structures should be referred to as towers, not poles.

Uzbekistan

Adjective and people: Uzbek (for the majority ethnic group) or Uzbekistani. Currency: sum. Capital: Tashkent.

One of the former Soviet Central Asian republics, it is the only one that borders on all the others: Kazakhstan, Turkmenistan, Tajikistan and Kyrgyzstan. It also borders on Afghanistan.

It was absorbed into the Soviet Union in 1925, and gained independence with the disintegration of the Soviet Union in 1991. Its population of 25 million is 70 per cent Uzbek and 11 per cent Russian, with other minorities including Tajiks, Tatars and Mesketian Turks (forcibly transported from Georgia in 1944). It is largely a dry plain, and its major cities, Tashkent and Samarkand, are ancient oasis trading cities. But its land is very fertile when irrigated, and there is ample water for this (and for hydro power) in the southern mountains, which also contain oil, gas, coal and metals. Soviet development included irrigation schemes to allow production of cotton, fruit and rice, and factories to produce heavy equipment and farm machinery, but also left some areas severely polluted.

See Soviet Union.

V

V-chip

The V in the name of this software, capable of screening out television shows that viewers want blocked because of nudity, violence or bad language, originally stood for view-control, according to Tim Collings, the Simon Fraser University professor of engineering science who invented it. Popular (mis)use has it that the V stands for violence.

V-E Day, V-J Day

Hyphens. The official dates in 1945 of the Allied victories in the Second World War: in Europe, May 8; over Japan, Aug. 15 Japanese time (surrender announced), and Sept. 2 (formal signing of the surrender aboard the Missouri in Tokyo Bay).

V-neck

V-1, V-2

Use hyphens for the German self-propelled bombs of the Second World War. The V-1, used against Britain and Belgium, was a small ramjet airplane with no pilot, carrying a 2,000-pound bomb at about 360 mph. The V-2, used against Britain in 1944, was the first self-contained ballistic missile, powered by ethanol and liquid oxygen and reaching 3,500 mph.

V-6, V-8 engines.

vaccination, but vacillation.

vacuum

valentine

Use lower case for the greeting card, and for the person to whom it is sent.

vale of tears

Not veil, for the poetic phrase for earthly existence.

Valhalla

Upper-case. It should not be called the Norse heaven, nor should we say that only warriors went to heaven. They merely got the best seats. The realm of the gods was Asgard, which was believed to contain many halls and palaces, the foremost of which was Valhalla (Hall of the Slain). Those who had died in battle were entertained there by Odin until the day of doom, when they would follow him to fight the giants.

Valium

A trade name for **diazepam**.

Valkyries

Upper-case for the Norse "choosers of the slain." They conducted to Valhalla those they had selected in battle as being worthy. Wagner's opera (the second work of *Der Ring des Nibelungen*) is *Die Walkuere* (The Valkyrie, singular). The title refers to Brunnhilde.

valour

But drop the u for **valorize**, **valorous**.

Valour, Cross of

See bravery decorations.

Valuation Day

Use upper case for Dec. 31, 1971, known to lawyers as Fiscal VD, the date from which Canadians count increases in value for the purpose of capital gains tax.

Van Allen belts

Belts of highly charged particles discovered in 1958 by William Van Allen.

Vancouver

It is on the Strait of Georgia at the mouth of the Fraser River, across from Vancouver Island (at Nanaimo). The City of Vancouver proper is on a peninsula ending where the University of British Columbia Endowment Lands jut into the strait. Defining the southern side of the peninsula is the Fraser (its North Arm, to be exact). On the northern side of the peninsula are English Bay and Burrard Inlet, which are separated by a northward-thrusting sub-peninsula with Stanley Park at its tip and False Creek (an inlet of English Bay) at its base.

Vancouver is combined with various suburbs into the Greater Vancouver Regional District for garbage disposal, watershed management, water supply, sewage, hospital planning, social housing and regional parks. Here are the main suburbs:

Sharing the north shore of the Fraser with Vancouver, moving inland, are **Burnaby** (adjacent to the city, site of Simon Fraser University), **New Westminster**, **Port Moody** (which surrounds the landward end of Burrard Inlet), **Coquitlam** and **Port Coquitlam**.

To the north, across the bay and inlet, are the City and District of **West Vancouver**, the City and District of **North Vancouver** and the Village of **Belcarra**.

South of the city, across the North Arm of the Fraser, is **Richmond**, on a group of islands at the mouth of the river. The main island is Lulu, and Vancouver International Airport is on Sea Island.

Across the Fraser River proper, along its south shore from west to east, are **Delta** (including Tsawwassen), **Surrey** (with **White Rock** on its southern edge) and **Langley**. Tsawwassen is at the neck of a southward-jutting peninsula whose eastern (landward) side creates Boundary Bay. The southern tip of the peninsula is U.S. territory, containing Point Roberts, Wash.

Use the style Downtown Eastside for the Vancouver neighbourhood centred around Main and Hastings, notorious for its drug-ravaged streets and its status as the poorest postal code in Canada. It does not refer generally to the east side of Vancouver.

The name began to be used in the early 1970s by area activists as a way to distance it from the name it then had, Vancouver's skid row, and to give it a neighbourhood identity. Now it is as much a part of Vancouver's landscape as the West End, Strathcona, False Creek or North Vancouver. All the activist and social community groups in the area refer to it as the Downtown Eastside, and it is written that way in their titles. As with other neighbourhoods, when referring to the area locate it for our readers elsewhere in Canada.

Vandoos

One word. Acceptable in second reference, and in headlines, for the Royal 22nd Regiment. The nickname is from the French word for 22nd, *vingt-deuxième*.

van Gogh, Vincent

The Dutch postimpressionist, who cut off his ear in 1889, the year before his suicide at 37, signed his works Vincent.

Vanier, Georges

He was governor-general from 1959 until his death in 1967. He was a soldier and diplomat, a former commander of the Vandoos who rose to the rank of major-general. Use the French spelling of his given name, although he was known as George until late in his career. (His mother was an anglophone, born Margaret Maloney.)

Vanuatu

Adjective for the country: Vanuatu. No useful noun for the people. Currency: vatu. Capital: Vila.

This republic of Pacific islands, formerly called the New Hebrides, gained independence in 1980. The group is part of Micronesia, lying west of Fiji and northeast of New Caledonia. The largest is Espiritu Santo, but the capital is on the second-largest island, Efate. The national language is Bislama, but English and French also have official status. The population is about 196,000. Three of the smaller islands have active volcanoes.

vapour

But drop the u for **vaporize, vaporizer, vaporous, vaporific, vaporimeter, vaporescent.**

variegated

Varley, F. H.

This English-born member of the Group of Seven was as well known for his portraits as for his landscapes. He died in Toronto in 1969.

Vaseline

A trade name. The generic term is petroleum jelly.

Vatican City State

The central 44 hectares (including St. Peter's Square, St. Peter's Basilica and the Vatican Palace) is usually called simply Vatican City. In addition, there are 11 other buildings in Rome that enjoy extraterritorial status, including three other basilicas (St. John Lateran, St. Mary Major and St. Paul's Beyond the Walls) and a radio station. This status also applies to the Pope's summer residence outside Rome, Castel Gandolfo. The Pope is sovereign of the city state, with absolute executive, legislative and judicial power.

Vaughan Williams, Ralph

VC, for **Victoria Cross**.

It is the highest military decoration in the Commonwealth.

VD

It is misleading to speak of venereal disease or VD as if there were a single disease. Speak of a venereal disease, venereal diseases. Prefer the term sexually transmitted.

Veda

Upper-case. This is the basic scripture of Hinduism, believed to date from 1500 BC. Included in the term Vedic literature are the Veda and three other works—the Brahmanas, Aranyakas and Upanishads.

vein, but **venous**.

Velcro, a trade name.

It comes from the French words for hooked velvet, *velours crochet.*

veld

Explain that this open grassland is the equivalent of a prairie.

venal and venial

Venal means corrupt, willing to sell out, open to bribery, mercenary, a dangerous word in news stories. **Venial**, a theological term, means readily pardoned or forgiven, minor, as in a venial sin.

vendetta

Reserve it for a blood feud between families or, by extension, between rival gangs. More than simply a bitter enmity, it implies an endless trading of acts of revenge.

Venezuela

Adjective and people: Venezuelan. Currency: bolivar. Capital: Caracas.

It is the most urbanized country in Latin America, with 86 per cent of its approximately 24 million people living in cities and towns. About 70 per cent are mestizo. Venezuela has huge oil reserves both offshore and underground (in the region around Maracaibo, plus tar sands and heavy oil around the Orinoco). Venezuela's coast, on the Caribbean, is farther north than all of Panama and Costa Rica and half of Nicaragua. Colombia (with which it was once united) lies to the west, Guyana to the east and Brazil to the south.

Former army officer Hugo Chavez, who led a failed coup attempt in 1992, was elected president in 1998. His sweeping political reforms ignited fears of a slide toward dictatorship.

venomous and poisonous

See poisonous.

venue

It is best to reserve this for the legal sense, which is the jurisdiction where a crime was committed, or where the trial must be held. It should not be used for any old place, such as a concert location.

Venus de Milo

Not of Milo or of Melos. This armless statue was found on the Greek island of Melos.

Venus flytrap (not Venus's).

veranda (not -ah).

verbal, see oral and verbal.

trials of a venus flytrap

verbatim

verbs

See infinitives, noun invaders, passive voice, subjunctive mood, tenses.

Many writers and editors have an unfounded aversion to splitting **compound verbs** (have been, will go), usually springing from their phobia about split infinitives or from their insistence that any expression appearing as a single word in Latin must also be kept solid in English. However, even a simple negative puts the lie to this (I will go, I will not go). The most natural place for an adverb is between the parts of a compound verb (I **have recently been** to France; I **will gladly go** again), and Fowler says there must be special justification if we are to put the adverb anywhere else.

In parallel constructions, a verb part may do double duty if it would be in exactly the same form in each place (I cannot and will not **do** such a thing). However, if there is a change in form, the verb must be repeated (I have not **done** and will not **do** such a thing; this is the amount I have **given** and will continue to **give**). We must also use both verbs if they are spelled the same but pronounced differently (I have not **read** and will not **read** those gossip sheets).

Sentences without verbs can be effective, but only if used seldom enough that they keep their allure. Four examples: Awkward. Some chicken, some neck. Almost, but not quite. The fourth example was the anticipatory sentence, Four examples. This is perhaps the most common use of the verbless sentence in news stories, to introduce a set of bullets or other list of points or examples. Much more effective than adding the weak and obvious "Here are." (That last sentence was a fifth example.)

vermilion

Verrazano-Narrows Bridge

Note the hyphen in the name of this suspension bridge across New York Bay, at the narrows forming the harbour entrance. Its main span is the longest in the world, at 1,298 metres.

versus

In general, prefer against. Use the contraction v. (not vs) only in sports agate and in giving the formal title of court cases.

vertebra, vertebrae

very

It is overused, particularly when attached to adjectives that are already strong. In such cases it is at best wordy, and at worst weakens the word it is intended to magnify. To call someone a great man has an absoluteness to it. Calling him a very great man reduces the word great to an ordinary adjective, and the reader is left to wonder why our man is only very great rather than most great or absolutely great.

However, the insistence of some journalists that very never be used is difficult to justify. Vaguer adjectives that vary in degree usually benefit from being modified, and very is one of a range of adverbs available (slightly drunk, very drunk, extremely drunk).

veteran

Reserve for people of long service. Do not refer to "a two-year veteran of the force."

Veuve Cliquot

Vézina Trophy

Named for Georges Vézina, the cool Canadiens goalie known as the Chicoutimi Cucumber. He died of tuberculosis in 1926, a few months after collapsing during a game. The trophy goes to the top NHL goaltender, selected by a vote of team managers. The other award for goalies is the Jennings Trophy, awarded to the goalie(s) of the team with the best goals-against record. This used to be the criterion for the Vézina.

via

It means the direction of the journey, not the conveyance. Say He went to Montreal via Ottawa, but He went to Montreal by train or on the train, not via train (or via Via).

viable

It means capable of staying alive. A solution or an alternative may be feasible, practicable, workable, but not viable. A living organism, and by extension a company, a sports franchise etc., may be viable.

Viagra

The brand name of the drug used to treat erectile dysfunction in men. The generic name is sildenafil. Viagra does not increase the libido. It works mechanically, helping to produce a male erection by opening the body's blood vessels.

vice and vise

If it clamps things, spell it **vise**.

Vicente

The Spanish form of the name, often misspelled Vincente.

vice-president

viceregal

Commonwealth governors-general and lieutenant-governors may not be called viceroys, but the adjective viceregal is still used.

vichyssoise

This leek-and-potato soup was invented by Louis Diat, a chef at the Ritz-Carlton Hotel in New York, and named after his home town of Vichy, France. It can be either cold or hot.

vicious

Use it for people and animals, and for their actions (blows, bites, lies etc.), but not for inanimate things such as poisons, storms.

victim

Disabled people object to the word victim, and also to sufferer and afflicted, as reinforcing an erroneous public perception that they are necessarily helpless and passive. Say, for example, that someone has cerebral palsy, not that he or she is a victim of cerebral palsy. See disabled.

In crime stories, be wary of the word victim if the central issue is whether there has been a crime. If fraud is alleged, for example, it is not usually the action that is at issue but rather the interpretation of it. To call the complainant the victim before we hear the verdict constitutes prejudgment of the case. See courts.

videocassette, videotape, but video game.

vie, vying

It must involve a competition with another (vying with someone for something), not mere individual striving.

Vietnam

Adjective and people: Vietnamese. Currency: dong. Capital: Hanoi.

Vietnamese is acceptable as a general word for all citizens, but it is also used to differentiate the ethnic Vietnamese (Kinh), who make up 84 per cent of the population, from more than 60 ethnic minorities, including Chinese in the cities and numerous hill tribes, such as the Meo. The total population is 81 million. The economy is almost entirely agricultural, but there is widespread malnutrition; self-sufficiency in food is a major national goal. Vietnam is bounded on the west by Laos and Cambodia (with which it constitutes Indochina), on the north by China, and on the east and south by the South China Sea. The Communist Party of Vietnam was known until 1976 as the Workers Party of Vietnam. Do not call it the Viet Cong, which is taken to mean southern Communists (usually equipped by the North and often trained there) who fought southern and U.S. troops. The term Viet Cong is short for Viet Nam Cong San, which may be translated simply as the Vietnamese Communists.

As with Chinese names, in Vietnam the family name comes first, followed by the person's given name(s). However, unlike the Chinese, the Vietnamese refer to themselves on second reference by their given name, not their family name. Follow that style, using the honorific with the given name. For example, Phan Van Khai is Mr. Khai on second reference and Tran Duc Luong is Mr. Luong, just as during the Vietnam War South Vietnamese President Nguyen Van Thieu was President Thieu and Premier Nguyen Cao Ky was Premier Ky. Since the great majority of Vietnamese people have Nguyen, Le or Tran as family names, calling someone Ms. Nguyen or Mr. Tran would mean little.

Ho Chi Minh was an exception – everyone called him Ho – but his was a *nom de guerre* in any case.

Vietnam War

When it began and ended depends on what we perceive it was about. The usual definition is that it was an unsuccessful effort to prevent the union of North and South Vietnam under a Communist government, and the dates are 1955 to 1975. If it is judged to be an anti-colonial struggle, it began much earlier.

The Viet Minh (League for the Independence of Vietnam) was founded in 1941, and began its armed conflict against the French in 1946. In 1954, after the French defeat that year at Dien Bien Phu, an international conference in Geneva separated the two sides along the 17th parallel, pending national elections promised for 1956. With a Viet Minh electoral victory predicted, the Diem regime in the south, with U.S. support, refused to agree to the elections, and the Viet Minh renewed its military activity. Diem called for the help of U.S. forces in 1961, and by 1968 they were at a peak of 550,000. A ceasefire was signed in Paris in January of 1973, all U.S. forces pulled out a few months later, and Saigon fell in May of 1975.

vigour

But drop the u for **invigorating**, **vigorous**.

vilify

Villa-Lobos, Heitor (not Hector).

Brazilian composer.

VIP, VIPs

No periods. There is no need to write out very important person.

virgin birth, lower-case.

Virgin Islands

They are just east of Puerto Rico, and mark the beginning of the Lesser Antilles. The eastern group have been the British Virgin Islands since the 1600s. The western group were the Danish Virgin Islands until 1917, when the United States took them over. They may be called the U.S. Virgin Islands (the official name is The Virgin Islands of the United States). The two groups, divided by a channel called The Narrows, may be described as dependent territories (the modern word for colony). The largest of the British group, Tortola, contains the capital, Road Town. The capital of the U.S. group is Charlotte Amalie, on the island of St. Thomas. The other two large U.S. islands are St. John and St. Croix. The total population is about 100,000.

virtual and virtually

The adjective and adverb have slightly different meanings.

Virtual means in effect but not in form or title, as in She is the virtual supervisor of her department, but her position is only that of clerk. Virtual cannot be used to mean near, as in This is a virtual disaster. However, virtually can have the meaning of nearly, in the sense of all but, almost entirely, in effect, practically speaking (We have been virtually wiped out).

virtuosos

viruses

They are micro-organisms too small to be seen by a normal microscope. They are not cells, but resemble cell nuclei, being nucleic acid (either DNA or RNA) contained in a sheath composed of protein or lipoprotein. They can enter animal or plant cells or even bacteria and reproduce using pirated material, and in doing so some of them cause viral diseases. Viruses that invade bacteria are called bacteriophages.

vis-à-vis

Accent, but no italics.

viscous, but **viscosity**.

visionary

As both noun and adjective it has to do with impractical dreaming, impossible fantasies, and it is no compliment. Do not use it in place of farsighted, imaginative, prophetic.

visitation

Essentially a theological term involving appearances by a deity, an angel, the Virgin Mary or a saint. In child-custody cases, for example, speak of visiting rights.

vitamin

Lower-case, as in vitamin A, vitamin E.

vitreous

vittles, victuals

The word for food is pronounced vittles, but is properly spelled victuals.

voiceover

voir dire

Does not need italics. It is a legal term best omitted from most stories; say simply that a hearing was held with the jury absent, or that a hearing was held on the admissibility of certain evidence. Things a jury has been prevented from hearing may not be published until the trial is over or the jury has been sequestered. See courts.

Voisey's Bay

For the company, the town, the development and the body of water. This is an exception to the gazetteer, dictated by local usage, the company's practice and the advantages of consistency.

volcanoes

Volstead Act

It did not order U.S. Prohibition, but rather implemented it. It consisted of measures to implement and enforce the ban called for in the 18th Amendment to the Constitution. The act was passed in 1919 (over Wilson's veto) and was repealed in 1933. See Prohibition.

von Braun, Wernher

He designed the V-2, then led the team that first put a U.S. satellite in orbit, in 1958.

voodoo, voodooism

Lower-case. It describes any one of several local folk religions of West African origin. Haiti's voodooism is a blend of mysticism, sorcery and Roman Catholicism, in which the spirits of saints and ancestors are worshipped and believed capable of possessing believers.

vortexes (not vortices).

vow

To take a solemn oath. A promise or warning must have this added dimension of solemnity and irrevocable commitment if it is to merit the word vow.

voyageur

It does not need italics. This name is usually taken to mean a paddler in the big freight canoes of the Montreal fur companies, whose season-long journeys spanned half a continent, not a solitary canoeman doing some personal trapping or trading. These unlicensed individuals engaging illegally in the fur trade were the woods runners, the *coureurs de bois*.

VTOL

Vertical takeoff and landing. Britain's Hawker Harrier jump jet is an example, but don't forget helicopters.

vulgar language

See obscene language, taste.

Vulgate

Upper-case for the Latin Bible, established in its present form by about 800 and declared by the Council of Trent in 1546 to be the Roman Catholic Church's only official version. Its name has nothing to do with the quality of its Latin; its Old Testament translations were the work of the noted classical scholar St. Jerome. *Vulgatus* simply means made generally accessible; in other words, published.

W

W-Five

No hyphen. The public-affairs show on CTV began in September of 1966. The official spelling is *W-FIVE*, but following Globe style, we upper-case only the first letters. (See capitalization: arts and publishing.)

Waffle, the

Upper-case. Nationalist New Democrats formed this group in the spring of 1969, and disbanded in the summer of 1972 after a party convention rejected their Manifesto for an Independent Socialist Canada. Prominent members included Mel Watkins and James Laxer. Edward Broadbent, who helped draft the manifesto but broke with the group because he found it too radical, coined the name by saying in the manifesto that if the group waffled on any issue it would waffle to the left.

Wailing Wall

Prefer Western Wall.

Wakashan

This linguistic family takes in peoples on both the B.C. mainland and Vancouver Island. They speak the Haisla, Heiltsuk, Kwakiutl and Nootka languages, and number more than 12,000 on reserves.

walkout

The verb is **walk out.**

Walloons

These are the French-speaking people of southern Belgium. The Flemish (a Dutch dialect) speakers in the north are the Flemings.

wampum

These tiny white and purple shells strung as beads were used as currency and for ceremonial embroidery by the woodland Indians of eastern North America. (Wampum is the Algonquian word for them, meaning white string, but is also generally acceptable in references to other language groups.) It was also a treaty instrument, notably the Two-Row Wampum that served as a treaty between the Iroquois and the British Crown. The word is demeaning if used in modern references to the pay of a native person.

wapiti waiting for its antlers to dry

wapiti

In most references, prefer the more familiar term elk, or American elk. (Beware of confusion in stories from Europe, where elk means what we call moose.) Wapiti are actually an American subspecies of the European red deer, having a larger frame and a different antler shape.

war

Warhead, warhorse, warlord, warmonger, warship, but war games.

war crimes

The Nuremberg Trials established the principle of individual responsibility, and defined three categories—the conventional war crimes (murder of civilians or prisoners, plunder etc.); crimes against peace (planning and waging aggressive war); and crimes against humanity (genocide or enslavement of whole population groups).

Canada's war-crimes legislation, passed in 1987 as amendments to the Criminal Code and the Immigration and Citizenship Acts (listed as Chapter 37 of the Statutes of Canada for that year), mentions only war crimes and crimes against humanity. A war crime is defined as a criminal act or omission that is committed during an international armed conflict. A crime against humanity "means murder, extermination, enslavement, deportation, persecution or any other inhumane act or omission that is committed against any civilian population or any identifiable group of persons." In both cases, the act need not be against local laws in force at the time; it is enough that it "constitutes a contravention of customary international law or is criminal according to the general principles of law recognized by the community of nations."

-ward

Use this ending (not wards) for both adverbs (he fell forward) and adjectives (a backward step).

warrant officer, WO. See ranks.

warrants

The term Canada-wide warrant indicates that the jurisdiction issuing the warrant is willing to pay the cost of arresting, holding and transporting the subject no matter where in Canada he or she is arrested. (Warrants for lesser offences may specify 100 kilometres, within the province etc.) In a serious matter we need not specify that the warrant is Canada-wide, since this can be taken for granted. The rare exceptions are worth noting, however.

war resister

This is the inclusive term for those who fled to Canada to avoid service in the Vietnam War. (About 25,000 applied for landed-immigrant status between 1965 and 1975, when limited amnesty was offered.) It takes in the more specific terms draft evader/dodger, conscientious objector and deserter, which may be used if we are sure of the details.

Warsaw Pact

Those who gathered in Warsaw in 1955 to sign the Warsaw Treaty of Friendship, Co-operation and Mutual Assistance, in response to the formation of NATO, were the Soviet Union, Albania, Bulgaria, Czechoslovakia, East Germany, Hungary, Poland and Romania. Albania formally withdrew in 1968, but it had been boycotting the organization's activities and had severed diplomatic relations with Moscow in 1961. The group was formally named the Warsaw Treaty Organization, but in most references Warsaw Pact may be used for both the treaty and the organization. Leaders of the member countries declared the organization's military role obsolete in 1990, and ended it in February, 1991. They said it should seek a new role for itself, and look for ways to co-operate with NATO. However, it was formally disbanded a few months later, on

July 1, 1991. Poland, Hungary and the Czech Republic joined NATO in 1999.

Wascana Centre

This large park in central Regina contains Wascana Lake (created by a dam on Wascana Creek), the legislature, a museum, an art gallery, a performing-arts centre and the University of Regina. Wascana comes from the Cree word for Pile of Bones, the original name of the city site.

wash-and-wear

Washington's Birthday

It is a holiday in most states, celebrated on the third Monday in February. (The same holiday also honours Lincoln, born on Feb. 12, 1809.) Washington's birthday is Feb. 22, even though he was born on Feb. 11, 1732. That's no lie. When he was 20, in 1752, the Gregorian calendar reforms were finally adopted by England and its American colonies. There was a discrepancy of 11 days to be overcome, and Feb. 11 suddenly became Feb. 22.

WASP

A largely outmoded expression that should not be used as a mere synonym for white, especially when we are not sure the ethnic background is Anglo-Saxon and the religion Protestant. Note that Britain contains Irish, Scottish, Welsh and several other indigenous ethnic groups that by no means regard themselves as Saxon or English, and should not be referred to as such.

Wassermann test

It may be called a screening test for syphilis. In fact, it is a more general screening test for a group of organisms that cause such things as syphilis, yaws and several types of immune disorders. Those with a positive Wassermann reading are then given more specific tests to pinpoint their malady.

waste

In most combinations, use two words (waste disposal, waste heap, waste trap). But note wastebasket, wasteland. Use two words for waste paper as a noun (we are saving waste paper), but one word as an adjective (a wastepaper basket).

waste and wastage

Waste is the act of wasting or squandering. Use wastage only for what is wasted. Say the shortfall was the result of waste, not of wastage.

waterbed

watercolour

water polo

water-ski, water-skiing

Waterton Lakes National Park

This park on Alberta's southern border abuts Glacier National Park in Montana, and since 1932 they have been combined as Waterton-Glacier International Peace Park. Waterton differs from Canada's other national parks in the Rockies, such as Banff, Jasper and Yoho, in that it also contains prairie.

Watusi

Prefer Tutsi. Watusi is the English version of the Swahili word Watutsi, applied to the tall Tutsi peoples of Burundi and Rwanda. Tutsis may reach a height of seven feet.

wave and waive

Waive, meaning to dispense with, relinquish, forgo, is often misspelled wave. Say waive the requirement, obtain a waiver.

wax

As a verb meaning to increase in size, it is archaic except in references to the moon. It is occasionally used as a poetic word meaning to become.

Note that in this sense, like become, it is followed by an adjective, not an adverb. Say he waxed indignant about the poor service, not waxed indignantly.

ways

It is fine in ways and means, but use **way** in such expressions as a long way to go.

we

The first-person plural is fine in the mouth of the Queen (the royal we) or editorial boards (the collective editorial we), but columnists and critics writing as individuals should avoid it. Do not write "We have never seen a worse production" unless your friends were with you and have co-signed the review.

weather words

blizzard: It means a fierce winter storm. We need not be so categorical as to insist on the classic requirements of winds above 40 km/h, temperature below -10 and visibility less than 500 metres in falling or blowing snow, but readers who regularly experience true blizzards would resent our applying the term to a mere heavy snowfall in relatively mild temperatures and calm air.

chinook: It is a warm, dry, southwest wind regularly experienced in southern Alberta when Pacific winds are warmed by dropping their moisture as they rise over the mountains, and are heated further as they descend the lee side. Chinooks can raise the temperature by 25 degrees Celsius in an hour. They are common in Calgary (Calgary and Pincher Creek get 30 to 35 chinook days a year) but are seldom experienced as far north as Edmonton. Chinooks, similar to the *fohns* in the mountains of Switzerland, also arrive in summer, but are less noticeable then.

cyclone or **cyclonic disturbance:** These systems of winds are relatively non-destructive when spread over many thousands of square kilometres; they become dangerous when compressed into a small area. North of the equator, they circulate counterclockwise and the whole system tends to move eastward, although the direction of the wind at any particular place and time depends on the position on the spiral. The most severely compressed cyclones are called either **hurricanes** (those originating east of the International Date Line, particularly in the Caribbean) or **typhoons** (those originating west of the line, particularly in the China Sea). See wind, below. The stage below a hurricane or typhoon is a **tropical storm**, and the stage below that (winds of 61 kilometres an hour or less) is a **tropical depression**. We do not use cyclone to mean tornado, and prefer the more specific terms for the various categories of cyclones.

eye of the storm: We must never use this term to indicate the area with the worst conditions. In fact, the eye is the calm, low-pressure area around which the winds revolve.

floods: Reserve the term flash flood for those that are truly sudden and unexpected, such as those from a burst ice jam. Give the crests of river floods (the maximum height the water reaches) in metres, and don't forget the other piece of vital information— the number of metres by which this crest exceeds the height of the banks.

flurry: A flurry is a light, brief snowfall accompanied by small gusts of wind. There is rarely a need to use the word snow; if we do, make it two words, snow flurry.

freezing rain, ice storm: These terms should be used only for precipitation that falls as rain, then freezes on contact with the ground, trees, power lines etc. They should not be used to refer to **ice pellets** or to **sleet**, which is a mixture of rain and a frozen form (snow, snow pellets, ice pellets or hail), unless the sleet freezes on contact.

inversion: This is the phenomenon of a warmer layer(s) of air lying above a cooler layer(s), rather than the normal temperature drop. The effect is that pollutants are trapped near the ground.

monsoon: This term applies to any wind system that changes direction with the seasons because of the temperature differences between large bodies of water and land masses. Best known are the monsoons of southern Asia. Northwestern India gets warm, wet winds in summer, cool, dry winds in winter. Monsoon is also used to describe the summer wind alone, with its vital but frequently destructive rains.

precipitation: We should use this word only when speaking generally or theoretically. Prefer rain, snow, rain and snow, rain or snow etc.

shower: This term is used when the rain lasts less than 15 minutes.

storm: It has three meanings. We may use it in a general sense to mean any severe weather, particularly when modified as in rainstorm, snowstorm, ice storm, dust storm. In reference to tropical disturbances, a tropical storm involves winds of between 61 and 116 kilometres an hour. (Below that range it is a tropical depression; above, it is a hurricane.) In the Beaufort scale of wind force, used by sailors and others, storm means winds of 88 km/h to 116 km/h, usually accompanied by precipitation but not necessarily. See wind, below.

tornado: We reserve judgment until the weather office declares there has been one. The official definition is a highly destructive funnel-shaped column of rotating air that touches the ground. A violent storm can cause widespread heavy damage, but there is no weather phenomenon as destructive as a tornado in a concentrated area. Tornadoes are usually spotted on the southeastern fringe of a cyclonic system. The word **twister** should be reserved for a very small tornado, with damage limited to about 100 metres of ground. If a column does not touch down, it is called a **funnel cloud**. One that touches down on water is called a **water spout**.

weather advisories, warnings: An advisory alerts the public that the weather is expected to cause inconvenience. A warning raises the possibility of a danger to life and property.

wind: The direction indicates the origin of the wind. A north wind blows from the north, toward the south. **Wind speed** is generally given in kilometres an hour, but we may also encounter descriptions taken from the Beaufort scale, such as near gale, Force 9. In this scale, force ranges from 0 (calm) to 12 (hurricane).

The following Beaufort descriptions are converted from knots to the nearest kilometre an hour: Calm, Force 0, means wind of less than 1 km/h. Force 1 is **light air**, up to 5 km/h. Force 2 is a **light breeze**, 6 to 11 km/h. Force 3 is a **gentle breeze**, 12 to 20 km/h. Force 4 is a **moderate breeze**, 21 to 29 km/h. Force 5 is a **fresh breeze**, 30 to 39 km/h. Force 6 is a **strong breeze**, 40 to 50 km/h. Force 7 is a **near gale**, 51 to 61 km/h. Force 8 is a **gale**, 62 to 74 km/h. Force 9 is a **strong gale**, 75 to 87 km/h. Force 10 is a **storm**, 88 to 101 km/h. Force 11 is a **violent storm** (very rarely experienced on land), 102 to 116 km/h. Force 12 is a **hurricane** (called a typhoon in the western Pacific), more than 117 km/h. The force may be incorporated in the description; for example, a strong gale may be called a Force 9 gale. Note that the word wind does not appear in the Beaufort descriptions.

If only a general, non-technical indication of wind speed is called for, especially if the story is not about the sea, these six categories from The Canadian Press are acceptable: light wind (up to 20 km/h), moderate (21 to 40 km/h), strong (41 to 60 km/h), gale (61 to 90 km/h), storm (91 to 116 km/h), hurricane (above 117 km/h). We should not refer to actual wind speed when using these informal categories.

wind chill: This is a convention for describing the combined effect of cold and wind on humans. It sometimes appears as a **factor** on the meteorologists' wind-chill **index** (a factor of 1600 means exposed skin may freeze; a factor of 2700 means that exposed flesh freezes within 30 seconds). However, the most understandable form for the reader is the **wind-chill equivalent**—a theoretical lower temperature in calm winds that would have the same effect as the existing combination of temperature and wind. This equivalent should not be called a factor or an index. Note that wind chill should not be related to inanimate objects. A thermometer's reading of the air temperature stays the same regardless of wind speed. A car cools much more quickly in a strong wind, but its temperature stops falling when it reaches that of the air.

Web
Upper-case the short form for the World Wide Web. But lower-case the combining form: website, webcast. See World Wide Web.

weekend
Canadian idiom favours on or during the weekend, not at or over.

weigh
In nautical terms, weigh is used only in reference to the anchor. It means to raise it. (However, the adjective aweigh has a narrower meaning—raised just enough that the flukes hang clear of the bottom.) In all other expressions, the spelling is way (get under way, gangway).

weights, see measurement.

weird, but **wield**.

welfare
It refers to a direct payment from a government to an individual, but in Canadian idiom it has come to mean just one type—payments from municipalities and provinces to the poor. For clarity, use a specific term for any other form of direct payment, such as a disability pension. If a generic term is required, use social programs or payments (not social welfare). Social Security is the official name of a U.S. program, but it may also be used generically, lower-case, to mean the entire U.S. social safety net.

well
As an adverb it takes a hyphen in an adjectival expression that precedes the noun (a well-liked executive), but is a separate word when the expression is used predicatively (that executive is well liked).

Welland Canal
There is no need to call it the Welland Ship Canal. It runs about 44 kilometres, contains eight locks and rises 99 metres (326 feet) from its Lake Ontario end (Port Weller) to its Lake Erie end (Port Colborne). The present canal, built between 1912 and 1932 and modernized in 1972, is the fourth built across the Niagara

Peninsula to bypass Niagara Falls. The earlier versions were completed in 1829, 1845 and 1887.

well-known

Avoid it. If someone truly is well known, there is no need for the description, as in well-known artist Pablo Picasso. If we must use it, it has a hyphen before the noun or name, but is two words as a predicative adjective (This well-known artist is well known).

welsh

An ethnic slur against the people of Wales when used as a verb meaning to refuse to pay a betting loss, or in the noun welsher.

The adjective for Wales is Welsh. The adjective in most military regiments is Welch, but note the Welsh Guards.

Wenceslaus, Saint

The carol calls him a good king, but he was the Duke of Bohemia, revered for his efforts to Christianize his people. He died in 929, aged about 22. (Four others called Wenceslaus, reigning between 1230 and 1419, were true kings of Bohemia, and this probably confused the composer of the carol.) Note that we use the local English spelling of the Prague landmark, Wenceslas Square. Also note, however, that the Czech version of the name is Vaclav. The Polish is Waclaw, the German Wenzel and the Hungarian Vencel.

west

Use lower case for the direction, upper case for a distinct geographic or political region. Western is upper-case in reference to the developed non-communist world, and in combinations naming a distinct district, such as Western Canada, but it is lower-case as a normal adjective (western farmers, western novel). See capitalization, directions.

West Bank

This upland region to the west of the Jordan River and the Dead Sea was part of Jordan until occupied by Israel in 1967, and it is the focus of Palestinian political aspirations. The population is about one million. It contains the Old City of Jerusalem, and other historically significant communities such as Bethlehem, Hebron and Jericho. In ancient times it was known as Judea and Samaria.

West Coast

In upper case, it is a geographical and political region of Canada or the United States, or occasionally both. In Canada, it includes the B.C. coastal mainland (as opposed to the Interior), Vancouver Island, the Gulf Islands and the Queen Charlottes. Lower-case, it refers to the shore of the mainland (the inner coast) or the western shores of the outer islands (the outer coast).

West End

The London theatre district.

Western Australia

Upper-case for Australia's largest state. Its capital is Perth.

Western Sahara

This is the former Spanish province known as Spanish Sahara, fought over by Morocco and by Polisario, a guerrilla movement of the indigenous Saharawis. (Polisario is a contracted acronym for the Popular Front for the Liberation of Saguia el-Hamra and Rio de Oro.) When Spain withdrew in 1976, Morocco claimed the northern two-thirds and Mauritania the rest. When Mauritania reached a peace accord with Polisario in 1979, Morocco laid claim to Mauritania's share as well. A peace accord signed in 1991 called for a United Nations-supervised referendum on whether the 275,000 inhabitants wanted an independent country or incorporation into Morocco. Political unrest in Morocco delayed the vote far beyond the 1992 target, and talks between Rabat and Polisario dragged on intermittently through the decade.

Western Samoa, see Samoa.

West Germany, see Germany.

West Indies

This term has had different meanings in the past, but now takes in all the islands off the eastern coasts of North and Central America, from southeast of Florida to the north coast of South America. In addition to the Caribbean Islands, it includes Barbados to the east, and the Bahamas and the Turks and Caicos to the north. The Caribbean islands are also called the Antilles, divided into the larger islands across the north called the Greater Antilles (Cuba, Hispaniola, Jamaica and Puerto Rico) and the smaller islands sweeping from northeast to southwest (the Leewards and Windwards, Trinidad and Tobago, Barbados, and the islands off northern Venezuela, including the Netherlands Antilles). Barbados, while outside the Caribbean, is considered one of the Lesser Antilles.

Westminster (not -minister).

Westmorland

This is the spelling of the county, the earl and the former New Brunswick riding of Westmorland-Kent. (It is now Beauséjour.) But note that the U.S. commander in Vietnam (1964-68) and army chief of staff (1968-72) was William Westmoreland.

Westmount

This district of Montreal (built around a western spur of Mount Royal) is indeed a bastion of English, but we should not imply that all its inhabitants are rich.

West Point

Acceptable in all references as the informal name for the U.S. Military Academy, at West Point, N.Y.

Whapmagoostui, see Great Whale.

wharves

what

It can also be plural (This city has few good restaurants, and what there are seem overpriced; what are of greater concern are the lax health standards). As a subject, what may stand either for that which/the thing which, or those which/the things which.

whence

It means from where, and so "from whence" is redundant. In any case, avoid it as archaic.

whereabouts

It is usually singular, meaning a position, location, place (his whereabouts is unknown). However, if more than one place is meant, make it plural (The three escapers scattered, and their whereabouts are unknown).

wherefore

As in the Shakespearean line "Wherefore art thou Romeo?" wherefore means why, not where.

whether

Does not usually require "or not" (I don't care whether you reach the house), but the words are essential in such constructions as: I will call you whether I reach the house or not.

whether and if

See if and whether.

which and that

See that and which.

while

As a conjunction, its standard, temporal meaning is "as long as" or "during the time that" (Not while I'm in charge; she collected the mail while he walked the dog). It is also acceptable meaning "although" (While I don't normally drink, this is a special occasion) and "whereas" (She is a Liberal worker, while her husband is a staunch Tory). However, if the sentence is such that the meaning of while is not clear, we must fall back on although or whereas.

whir

Not whirr, for a whir of wings; but a whirring sound.

whisky, whiskies

White Mountains

This is the section of the Appalachian system in Maine and New Hampshire (see Appalachian). It contains four principal ranges—the Carter-Moriah, Franconia, Presidential and Sandwich. The highest peak is Mount Washington, in the Presidential Range, at 1,916 metres (6,288 feet).

white paper

Use upper case only when giving the full proper name of a document. Use lower case when giving a description (the white paper on defence) and in second reference (the white paper). A **white paper** presents, for discussion, legislation that the government plans to introduce essentially in the form outlined. A **green paper** merely outlines a problem and proposes some solutions, inviting discussion that will aid the government in drafting legislation.

whiz kid

who and whom

Grammarians say that when pronouns are the objects of verbs or prepositions but precede them at the start of a sentence, **who** is standard idiom and **whom** often sounds fussy

and pompous. Say Who will the Tories choose? Who is she talking to?

We still use whom when the pronoun follows the verb or preposition (Who am I speaking to? but To whom am I speaking?).

When who or whom introduces a clause, it is the entire clause that is the object of a verb or preposition, and the choice between who and whom hinges on the pronoun's role within the clause (I wondered who he might be, but I wondered whom the Tories would choose).

Take particular care in sentences in which who is followed by such expressions as he said, it seems, it appears, he thinks, we hope. It is a common error to change who to whom, as if it were the object of one of these verbs, particularly when the verb also has a transitive meaning. Write "There is a warrant out for the suspect, who police believe has eluded several roadblocks." Who is not the object of believe; it is the subject of has eluded.

whodunit

Not whodoneit, whodunnit.

whopping

Give the reader some credit in judging whether a percentage or amount is surprisingly large or small in context. References to a "whopping" 57 per cent mean nothing. If there is genuinely a reason to be astounded by the figure, the story should make it explicit: the largest amount ever paid for whatever, the highest percentage seen since whenever.

whose

It may be used for inanimate things if this prevents an awkward or stilted construction. Instead of "He drives an old car, the most endearing feature of which is its tendency to wheeze during the hay-fever season," write ". . . car, whose most endearing feature is . . ."

wide

Countrywide, nationwide, worldwide, provincewide, citywide.

These words are more common as adjectives (a worldwide problem) than as adverbs. Most writers would say that an international terrorist is being sought around the world, not sought worldwide.

widescreen

wield, but **weird**.

wiener

It means of Vienna (Wien in German).

Wiesenthal, Simon

This Nazi-hunter was born in Poland. His Jewish Documentation Centre is in Vienna. The Simon Wiesenthal Center is in Los Angeles.

wild

It is usually a separate word when modifying a plant or animal (wild boar, wild cherry, wild oats, wild rice). But note wildcat, wildfire, wildflower, wildfowl.

wildcat, wildcatter

A wildcat driller or company is one that is usually independent of the industry giants and is seeking resources in unproven areas. We must be careful not to use this word to convey unwittingly that a company's shares are a reckless investment.

A wildcat strike is one that is not sanctioned by the strikers' union. If a union itself calls a walkout before the end of a contract, it may be an illegal strike but it is not a wildcat one.

wildebeest

Not -beast. Prefer this name to gnu for Africa's most numerous antelope. The plural is also wildebeest.

Wile E. Coyote

The cartoon character who chases the Road Runner.

Wilfrid Laurier University

Until Nov. 1, 1973, the Ontario postsecondary institution was Waterloo Lutheran University.

will and shall, see shall and will.

willful, willfulness, willfully

Wimbledon

win big

Shun it, in both copy and headlines.

wind instruments

In the standard orchestra, they are divided into woodwinds and brass. The woodwinds (which need not be made of wood) comprise those in which the breath strikes a sharp edge (flute, piccolo, recorder) and those in which the breath vibrates a reed (bassoon, clarinet, English horn, oboe and saxophone). In brass instruments (cornet, French horn, sousaphone, trombone, trumpet and tuba), the vibration is made by the lips compressed in the mouthpiece.

There are many other wind instruments that do not appear in orchestras, particularly various kinds of pipes and such folk instruments as the pennywhistle, pan flute and ocarina.

Windsor, House of

The Queen has declared that the name Windsor is restricted to those on the throne or in direct line of succession (the sovereign, the Prince of Wales and his sons). For the others, she has adopted the family name Mountbatten-Windsor. See Royal Family.

windward, see lea and lee.

Windward Islands

These are the southeastern group of the Lesser Antilles stretching north from Venezuela—Grenada, St. Vincent and the Grenadines, St. Lucia and Martinique. They do not include the islands closest to Venezuela—Trinidad and Tobago in the east, the Netherlands Antilles to the west and several Venezuelan possessions in between.

wine

Grape varieties are lower-case when standing alone (chardonnay, semillon, cabernet sauvignon, pinot noir, merlot) and upper-case when part of a brand name (Sonoma Cabernet, Cave Springs Riesling).

Winnipeg

Do not use the unfamiliar expression Unicity, coined in 1972 when all the municipalities of the greater Winnipeg area were united into a single city. Refer to the original city as central Winnipeg. The other 11 districts that joined it in 1972 are Charleswood, Fort Garry, the four Kildonans (East, North, Old and West), St. Boniface, St. James-Assiniboia, St. Vital, Transcona and Tuxedo. Winnipeg is at the confluence of the Assiniboine and the Red, 100 kilometres north of the Minnesota border, 65 kilometres south of Lake Winnipeg and about the same distance southeast of Lake Manitoba. Winnipeg is in the transition zone where the Canadian Shield yields to prairie. The city contains both the University of Winnipeg and the University of Manitoba, which must not be confused.

winos

wiretapping

Use this for the interception of conversations on conventional telephones, regardless of whether this is done by the physical tapping of lines. For listening to cellular and other radio telephones and for other forms of snooping (hidden or parabolic microphones etc.) use the more inclusive expression eavesdropping, electronic eavesdropping.

witch doctor

This is an acceptable expression if the person has the added religious and mystic role of a shaman, a tribal priest. (For North American native peoples, use shaman or medicine man, woman.) If the person's role is limited to healing, use such expressions as folk healer or doctor, native healer.

witch hazel (not wych).

Wite-Out

No h in the brand name of the correcting fluid.

withhold

wits' end

Wolseley, Viscount

Also Wolseley, Ont. and Sask., Wolseley Barracks. But it was Thomas Cardinal **Wolsey**.

woman

Woman is a noun, female is an adjective (and a noun). There is an increasing tendency to use woman as an adjective, but just as we would write of a male actor rather than a man actor, we should write of a female writer rather than a woman writer.

Woman's Christian Temperance Union

Not Women's. The WCTU was founded in the United States in 1874 but quickly became a worldwide organization (the first Canadian group was formed in Owen Sound in 1875). We should not describe it only as an anti-alcohol group; it also campaigns against smoking and drugs, and promotes social programs and sexual hygiene.

women and language

Our principal job as journalists is to convey information clearly and accurately. This means keeping a watching brief on the language and grammar we use.

Using any loaded term unwittingly, merely out of habit, with no sensitivity to the message being received by the reader, is bad journalism. To use the word "man" as a generic term to describe men and women, or sometimes women alone, is inaccurate, offensive to some and unnecessary when such words as people, humans, human beings and individuals are available.

For the same reason, the **pronouns** he, him and his should not be used as generic references to both sexes, as in: The reader wants his news in a concise form. It is usually a simple matter to recast the sentence, either to eliminate the pronoun (The reader wants news; the reader wants the news) or to make the subject plural (Readers want their news). If the sentence cannot reasonably be recast, as a last resort use "he or she" and "his or her."

Do not use such forms as s/he and he-she. Although the pronouns they and their are increasingly heard in spoken English to refer back to a singular subject (Someone has lost their wallet), avoid this usage in written form.

Avoid such expressions as manpower, the common man and man in the street. (At the same time, do not carry this to extremes by avoiding such terms as boycott and manufactured, which have different roots.) Avoid manned, as in "a hospital manned by temporary workers." The expression "manned space flight" is acceptable in a pinch, there being no ready alternative.

The term man-made may be inaccurate and is certainly vague. Where appropriate, substitute the word engineered, manufactured, artificial, synthetic, simulated, imitation, counterfeit, custom-made, handmade etc. Accuracy may require the term machine-made, factory-built or fabricated.

Be gender-free or gender-specific: Words such as policeman, fireman, salesman and postman should be replaced, wherever possible, by gender-neutral terms such as police officer, firefighter, salesclerk and letter carrier.

Terms such as manager, aviator and author cover both sexes; do not use such tortured forms as manageress, aviatrix or authoress. (An exception is actress, which is well entrenched in the language and in awards ceremonies. See actor, actress. The word waitress is also widely used by these workers themselves, server having made slight inroads only as a generic term when there is a need to cover both sexes.) Women who fish commercially on both coasts have made it clear they refer to themselves as fishermen, and resent the term fisher.

We do not go out of our way to point out the sex if this is not relevant, as in female doctor, female judge, male nurse and male model. These are loaded terms, suggesting that the individuals are interlopers in a male or female profession. Similarly, do not use such expressions as "pioneers and their wives" or "farmers and their wives," making the likely erroneous assumption that the women were or are not themselves pioneers or farmers. Do not speak of city fathers.

If you cannot be gender-free, be gender-specific. Spokesman and spokeswoman are acceptable if the sex of the particular individual is known, though spokesperson is appropriate to all uses. The same applies to other words with the suffix -man or -woman, including chairman and chairwoman, though chair is preferable, and chairperson is permissible if there is a risk of confusing chair with a piece of furniture. Use horseman or sportswoman if necessary, but not if a gender-free term would do as well (rider, athlete).

The word **master** has lost its gender connotations in such expressions as masterpiece, master list, master key, master plan and masterstroke, but words such as harbourmaster and taskmaster pose a problem with no easy solution. Use them if there is no way of reworking the sentence.

Many object to the word **maid** (milkmaid, barmaid, chambermaid) because it formerly conveyed sexual status and now implies at least servant status. Reserve it for domestic servants whose primary role is personal attendant. For other occupations, use such generic terms as dairy worker, cleaner, room attendant, housekeeper, bartender, bar worker.

No double standard, please: Do not remark on the presence of women in a group where the distinction has no particular point. Do not report that 12 people were massacred, three of them women, unless it is somehow startling that women were in the vicinity.

It is occasionally relevant to make special note of a trailblazing achievement by a woman, but we should take it for granted thereafter that such a feat, office or occupation is open to both sexes. We should not continually imply that other women who achieve the same thing are merely further exceptions to some unwritten male-only rule. However, wishful thinking should not lead us to imply that large numbers of women are engaged in certain occupations if this is not the case.

Balanced pairs: If you refer to equals, make sure your words reflect this. Say a cameraman and a makeup woman, not a makeup girl; if the sex is not relevant, refer to a camera operator and a makeup artist. Say an advertising man and his assistant, not his girl Friday. Refer to husband and wife, not man and wife. Speak of a man and a girl only if the girl is under 16. For those 16 and 17, say young woman.

Gratuitous descriptions: We must be balanced in what characteristics we choose to describe. If it would not be relevant to describe a man's height, weight, figure, hair, dress or family status, we should not do so for a woman in the same circumstances. We should not refer to a female athlete as a grandmother, for example, if we would not refer to a comparable male athlete as a grandfather.

We should also avoid such **sexual stereotypes** as grandmotherly, manly, unwomanly, masculine, feminine, unfeminine and tomboy. These imply wrongly that there is a single standard or ideal in appearance and behaviour against which men and women should be judged, and that people in certain occupations or with certain physical and character traits or interests are not real men or women.

The word we should use for a prostitute, whether male or female, is prostitute—not call girl, hooker etc. (Hookers is allowed only in very short headlines.) However, beware libel. Never refer to a recognizable individual as a prostitute without incontrovertible proof that could be presented in court, and consult a senior editor. Those who buy the services of prostitutes are customers or, for variety in longer stories, clients— not johns or dates.

Such offensive words as slut, bimbo, bitch, broad, bastard, pansy and queer have no place in our newspaper; there is no lack of more specific, less offensive descriptions. If the words appear in quoted remarks, the quotation should be permitted only if a crucial point would be lost without it.

Animals and things: In general, use the neuter pronoun "it" when referring to an animal unless the sex is relevant, but "he" and "she" are permissible for pets and animals that have been given human names (e.g. a popular zoo animal). Do not assign gender to inanimate objects such as ships, countries and objects in space.

Time-worn expressions: Such traditional expressions as old wives' tales, woman driver and woman's work perpetuate stereotypes that do injury to women as a class, are inaccurate as a general characterization and are hackneyed to boot. There are many substitutes available: for old wives' tale, say superstition or popular misconception.

women's suffrage
   Not woman suffrage. Canadian women got the federal vote in 1918; their right to sit in the Commons was guaranteed in 1920, and their right to be senators was decided by the Privy Council in London in 1929 (in the Persons Case, which see). The provincial vote was won first in Manitoba (in 1916) and last in Quebec (in 1940).

women's wear
   But permit Womenswear if it appears in a corporate name.

wonder-struck

wont
   It is archaic. For the adjective, use accustomed. For the noun, use habit, custom, practice.

Woodbine Race Track

Wood Buffalo National Park
   It is the world's largest national park, about 45,000 square kilometres of grassland, forested uplands, lakes and marshes in Alberta and the Northwest Territories between Great Slave Lake and Lake Athabasca. It contains the breeding grounds of the whooping crane, and has the largest remaining bison herd, now mainly a hybrid population of prairie and wood bison.

Woods Hole Oceanographic Institution

Woolf, Virginia

woollen, woolly

word play

work
   Work force, but workday, workload, workout, workplace, workshop, workweek.

work-to-rule, noun.
   And a work-to-rule campaign.

World Bank
   There is little occasion to use the official name, the International Bank for Reconstruction and Development. It should not be confused with the International Monetary Fund. See IMF and World Bank.

World Series, the Series.

world's fair

Use upper case if the term is part of a formal name.

World Trade Center

See Sept. 11, 2001.

World Trade Organization

It was formally created by the members of the General Agreement on Tariffs and Trade at Marrakesh in April of 1994, and began operations on Jan. 1, 1995, gradually absorbing the 48-year-old GATT. The WTO began with 81 founding members, including the Big Four: the European Union, the United States, Japan and Canada. More members were added as their legislatures passed the necessary domestic legislation and ratified the Uruguay Round agreement (formal name: the Final Act Embodying the Results of the Uruguay Round of Multilateral Trade Negotiations). The WTO administration was largely created from the old GATT secretariat, and the headquarters remains in Geneva.

World War I, II

Do not use this form except in direct quotations. Prefer First World War, Second World War.

See Roman numerals.

worldwide

See wide.

World Wide Web

Upper case, as is the short form the Web. But lower-case compound words formed from the Web, including webcam, webcast, weblog (an on-line journal, short form blog), webmaster, website and the expressions web browser, web page and web server. This is a change from our previous style, and, except for the capitalization of Web standing alone, will be consistent with changes expected in the 2004 edition of *The Canadian Oxford Dictionary*.

World Wide Web is a trademarked protocol. Tim Berners-Lee wrote the original link software in 1980 while employed by the European physics laboratory CERN, which agreed to release the intellectual property rights. The non-profit World Wide Web Consortium helps set technical standards for the Web. Its 160 or so members include Apple, IBM, Microsoft, Netscape and Sun.

The system that links documents in the Web is HTTP (hypertext transfer protocol). HTML (hypertext markup language) is used to encode documents on the Web. The URL (universal resource locator) is the Web address—www.whatever.wherever—used to address documents. A search engine is a website that enables a user to find other sites on the Internet.

See Internet.

World Wildlife Fund, WWF

This is the official name of the Canadian and U.S. branches of the environmental organization, and should be used in stories about them. The international headquarters in Switzerland changed its name in 1989 to the World Wide Fund for Nature (but kept the WWF logo), but since then has decided to use only the original initials as its name: WWF.

On May 6, 2002, the World Wrestling Federation, which had been locked in a battle with the environmental group over the use of WWF, announced that it would change its name to World Wrestling Entertainment (WWE, but the logo has two jagged Ws).

World Youth Day

Indicate high up in stories that it is a Roman Catholic festival. It was created by Pope John Paul II in 1985 as a way to inspire young Catholics around the world, and may be referred

to as the Roman Catholic Church's
World Youth Day. Despite the name,
the festivities last a week.

worshipped, worshipper

worthwhile

wrack

Use it only as a noun, and only to
mean ruin, wreckage, destruction,
usually in the expression wrack and
ruin. Otherwise, the spelling is rack
(racked with pain, rack one's brains).

wreak

The past tense and participle are
wreaked (the storm wreaked havoc).
Wrought is an archaic past tense and
participle of work (What hath God
wrought?) that clings to life in
wrought iron.

wrist shot

write-off, the noun.
The verb is **write off**.

Wyandot

For the Indians. But it is
Wyandotte for the breed of chickens
and for the community in Michigan.

Wyle, Florence

Sculptor. See Girls.

X

x

Use lower case for an unknown or theoretical quantity (she said that if they have x amount of money, the need is always 2x). Use lower case for the letter of the alphabet (x's and o's), but upper case for a mark or sign (make your X; X marks the spot).

Do not use x in copy to indicate multiplication (5 times 3, not 5 x 3) or to give dimensions (the room is 12 by 16, not 12 x 16).

X and Y chromosomes

Upper-case. When speaking of them individually, use hyphens— X-chromosomes, Y-chromosomes. These are properly called the sex chromosomes, even though they also carry some other genetic information. Normal individuals are either XX (female) or XY (male). Do not say that Y-chromosomes produce the male sexual characteristics; in fact, they carry little genetic information.

X-rated, upper-case.

X-ray, X-rayed

xenophobia, xenophobe

Unless the context makes the meaning clear, it is better to refer to fear or hatred of strangers or foreigners.

Xerox

A trade name, upper-case. Prefer the generic terms photocopy and photocopier, unless the brand is at issue. Use lower case for the process, xerography, from the Greek words meaning dry writing. (In this process, the ink is a dry powder.)

Xinhua

The name of the Chinese news agency means New China. For added colour, provide the translation occasionally.

Xmas

Avoid in both copy and headlines.

Sorry, no room on this side of the page. we're allll full up. boy, is it crowded.

xenophobia

Y

Y-chromosomes, see X and Y.

Y-Flyer
A small yacht with a crew of two.

Y-front

yahoo
Lower-case for a backward, brutish person. Use upper case only for the race of beings described by Swift in *Gulliver's Travels* and for the Internet search engine.

Yangtze River
It is the longest in Asia, flowing from Tibet's Kunlun highlands to the East China Sea at Shanghai, about 5,500 kilometres. It can take ocean-going ships as far as Wuhan, about 1,000 kilometres. The country along its lower reaches is China's richest agricultural land.

Yankee
Use in historical contexts, meaning of New England (Yankee trader, Yankee clipper) or of the North in the U.S. Civil War. It may be used for colour in paraphrasing people or describing their attitudes (He said he distrusts the Yankees but doesn't mind buying their gasoline), as long as it is clear that the attitude is not our own.

yarmulke
Translate (skullcap) for readers unfamiliar with the term.

years
Readers know that 2015 and 2030 refer to years. There is no more need to write "the year 2015" than there is "the year 1999."

Yellowhead Highway
Its formal name is the Yellowhead Interprovincial Highway, also known as the Yellowhead Route. It runs between southern Manitoba and eastern British Columbia via Saskatoon, Edmonton and Jasper National Park.

Yellowhead Pass
It is the route of the CN main line and the Yellowhead Highway through the Rockies, west of Jasper, Alta.

yellow journalism
It does not mean inaccurate, although this may be an element. It means sensational, with the primary aim of attracting readers. The term originated not with yellow paper but with yellow ink used for the popular cartoon strip *The Yellow Kid*, which began in 1896 in the Sunday supplement of Pulitzer's New York World.

Yellowknife
It began with a gold rush in 1934, became the capital of the Northwest Territories in 1967, and became a city in 1970. (Until 1967, the territorial commissioner and staff were based in Ottawa.) Yellowknife is on Yellowknife Bay off the North Arm of

Great Slave Lake, with the older part of the city cradling Back Bay.

Yellow Pages, upper-case.

Yellow River and Yalu River

The **Yellow River**, named for its rich silt, flows eastward about 4,700 kilometres from the Kunlun highlands of Tibet to the northwestern bulge of the Yellow Sea, the Gulf of Chihli. Prefer this more familiar name to the Chinese name Hwang Ho. The **Yalu** also flows to the Yellow Sea, but southwesterly into the northeastern side. It forms part of the boundary between China and North Korea, and the crossing of the Yalu by about 300,000 Chinese troops in November of 1950 was a major intensification of the Korean War.

Yemen

Adjective and people: Yemeni. Currency: riyal. Capital: Sanaa.

The Yemen Republic is the result of a merger in 1990 between the Yemen Arab Republic (the pro-Western North Yemen) and the People's Democratic Republic of Yemen (South Yemen, which was strongly Marxist until the wave of reform swept the Communist world). Yemen held a multiparty, universal-suffrage election in 1993, and held largely peaceful parliamentary elections again in 1997 and 2003.

Yemen forms the heel at the southwestern corner of the snowmobile-boot-shaped Arabian Peninsula, lying at the southern choke point of the Red Sea across from Ethiopia and Djibouti. It borders on Saudi Arabia to the north and Oman to the west. The total population is 18 million. The former North Yemen, with the most fertile soil on the peninsula, is about evenly split between Shia and Sunni Muslims, while the former South Yemen is mostly desert and almost entirely Sunni. Sanaa was the northern capital, while the southern capital was Aden.

yesterday and today

See time elements.

yeti

Prefer this name when speaking of the abominable snowman of the Himalayas. The plural is yetis. Explain that the reports are similar to those on the sasquatch of the Pacific Northwest. See sasquatch.

Yiddish

Use the word only in reference to a language, and by extension to Yiddish writing, Yiddish theatre. Refer to people as Jewish or as European Jews, not Yiddish. The language developed in medieval Germany, and is classed among the Germanic tongues.

yin and yang

Not ying. Lower-case, no italics. In Chinese philosophy, all things exist through the interaction of these two elements, representing the passive and active forces in the universe. Their symbol is two comma-shaped forms, light and dark, nesting into each other to form a circle. Yin is perceived as standing for earth, dark, passive, female, and yang for heaven, light, active, male.

yoga and yogi

Yoga is Hindu philosophical meditation. A **yogi** is a practitioner of it.

yogurt

Yoho National Park

It is on the B.C. side of the Rockies (in the area of Golden and Field), bounded on the east by Banff National Park and on the south by Kootenay National Park. With its spectacular peaks (28 higher than 3,000 metres), steep valleys and strange hoodoos, it was named with

yogurt with live culture

the Cree word meaning awe. It contains Takakkaw Falls, the highest in Canada at 380 metres (and 16th highest in the world).

Yom Kippur

It may be described as the most sacred day of the Jewish calendar, the Day of Atonement, 10th day after the Jewish New Year. See Rosh Hashanah.

York boat

Upper-case for the backbone of the Hudson's Bay Co. transportation system, named after its York Factory trading post, where the Hayes River enters Hudson Bay in northern Manitoba. They were used across the North and West from about 1749 until after the First World War.

York, House of

This branch of the Plantagenets produced three English kings— Edward IV, his son Edward V and Richard III. Richard's defeat at Bosworth Field by Henry Tudor (Henry VII) in 1485 marked the beginning of the Tudor line.

York Redoubt

This fortified battery of coastal guns near Halifax, built in 1796 and in use through the Second World War, is now a national historic site.

Yoruba

This culture of southwestern Nigeria and southeastern Benin, comprising many traditional kingdoms and tribes, is also found in Brazil and Cuba.

Yosemite National Park

It is in eastern California, on the western slopes of the Sierra Nevada. Its attractions include the Yosemite Valley, with rock walls more than 1,000 metres high, and the 200 giant sequoias of the Mariposa Grove.

you

It is generally frowned on in formal writing as an impersonal pronoun, but should not be banned outright. It is much better than the awkward "one" in such sentences as You never know; You can't get there from here; You know what they say about Liberals.

Young, Cy

This pitching great's first name was not Cyrus or anything like it; it was Denton. Cy was short for Cyclone, a reference to his blinding fastball.

Young People's Theatre

yours

It often acquires an erroneous apostrophe.

youth

In reference to people of a certain age, particularly males, it is largely a journalese and bureaucratic expression, not heard in the real world. Most say young people, adolescents, teenagers, high-school students, 16-year-olds etc. It is too useful in short headlines to be abandoned altogether, however.

Use it to describe males aged 16 and 17. For those 15 and under, say boy. Some latitude is allowed when describing a group with a large majority in that age range; the term youths may be taken to include a few members who are slightly younger or older.

There is no equivalent word for females of that age; we must say young woman. For a balanced reference when both sexes are concerned, say young men and women or simply young people, not youths and young women.

Youville, Marie-Marguerite d'

The first Canadian-born woman saint, canonized in 1990. She was born at Varennes, in Quebec, in 1701, with the family surname Dufrost de la Jemmerais, and died at Montreal in 1771. Her husband, François d'Youville, died in 1730. She and four other women formed a lay charity group they called the Grey Sisters in 1737, and from 1747 they were in charge of the Hôpital Général. The Order of the Sisters of Charity (usually called the Grey Nuns) was given legal status as an official order, under Mère d'Youville, by Louis XV in 1753. She gained a reputation as having miraculous healing powers and prophetic ability.

Yucatan, the

There is no need to add the word peninsula unless there is a risk of confusion with the state. This spur jutting northward from southeastern Mexico divides the Gulf of Mexico from the Caribbean. It comprises not only three Mexican states (Campeche, Yucatan and Quintana Roo) but also Belize and part of Guatemala. The Mayan site Chichen Itza is found here, and the population is still largely of Mayan stock.

Yugoslavia

Formerly a federation of six republics, sharing the Balkan Peninsula with Albania and Greece, Yugoslavia was reduced by secessions in 1991 and 1992 to a rump consisting of the republics of Serbia and Montenegro, whose current total population is 10.7 million. In 2003, it changed its name to Serbia and Montenegro, which see.

Formed as a monarchy at the end of the First World War from parts of the dismantled Austro-Hungarian and Ottoman Empires, the country was originally called the Kingdom of the Serbs, Croats and Slovenes. The monarch Alexander set up a military dictatorship in 1929, and in 1931 renamed the country Yugoslavia (land of the southern Slavs). The Communists under Josip Broz (*nom de guerre* Marshal Tito), a Croat, emerged dominant from the Second World War, getting Soviet help to subdue the Serbian royalist Chetniks. Tito set up the Communist federal republic and led it until his death in 1980. He broke with the Soviet Union in 1948, and led in the formation of the non-aligned movement in 1961. After his death, ancient rivalries and resentments, a crippling foreign debt and mounting inflation and unemployment made Yugoslavia ripe for fracture in the anti-communist and nationalist wave that swept Eastern Europe in 1989 and afterward.

Slovenia and Croatia declared independence in June of 1991, Macedonia in November of 1991, and Bosnia-Herzegovina in February of 1992. The Serb-dominated Yugoslav federal army made only a brief, half-hearted attempt to prevent Slovenia's departure, but mounted a major operation in Croatia because of its large Serb minority, and took control of several areas. Macedonia's departure was largely unopposed, but Bosnia-Herzegovina was torn apart by violent resistance from its Serb minority, with heavy assistance from Serbia. International revulsion over Serb atrocities prompted a United Nations peacekeeping operation, begun in 1992, and a trade embargo against Yugoslavia (Serbia and Montenegro), including a naval blockade. Tens of thousands of citizens of former Yugoslav republics, mostly Bosnia and Croatia, were killed and millions were displaced.

See Bosnia, Croatia, Macedonia, Slovenia, Serbia and Montenegro.

Yukon

The government officially calls itself the Government of Yukon (or Yukon Government), rather than "the Yukon," and that is the way the official name should be written. However, in practice even the government uses "the Yukon" at least as often as it does "Yukon" in reference to the territory, and most territorial leaders, when pressed on which version is preferred, insist it doesn't matter. To further confuse matters, the title of the Government of Canada's representative in the territory is Commissioner of the Yukon. When using official names and titles, respect the official style. Elsewhere, favour Yukon in news stories, but either form is acceptable in features, lighter pieces and opinion pieces. Whichever form is chosen, it should be consistent within the article.

After a community name in placelines, say Yukon, not Y.T. A resident of Yukon is a Yukoner or Yukon resident, and the title of the government leader is premier.

Yukon Quest

This sled-dog race is 1,600 kilometres, from Whitehorse to Fairbanks. It is slightly shorter than the Iditarod, but is considered more gruelling because it goes through fewer settlements. See Iditarod.

Yukon River

It is one of North America's major rivers. It flows across Yukon, but it arises in northern British Columbia and most of its length is in Alaska. It flows into the Bering Sea.

Yule

It is marginally acceptable in very short headlines. Avoid it in copy.

yuppie

It is spurious as a sociological term. It may be used in lighter stories describing a certain type of consumer, but only if the consumers are truly young, urban and professional. One-word labels tend to discourage more apt descriptions, such as free-spending, image-conscious, hedonistic, self-indulgent, self-absorbed.

Z

Z-car

Zaire, see Congo.

Zambezi River

Not Zambesi. It flows south from northwestern Zambia, then eastward to the Indian Ocean via Mozambique and the Mozambique Channel. Victoria Falls is on the stretch where the river forms the border between Zambia and Zimbabwe. About 1.5 kilometres wide at that point, the river falls about 120 metres into a narrow fissure. (Niagara's drop is about 50 metres.)

Zambia

Adjective and people: Zambian. Currency: kwacha. Capital: Lusaka.

This landlocked state in southern Africa was formerly called Northern Rhodesia. From 1953 to 1963 it was part of the Federation of Rhodesia and Nyasaland, along with Southern Rhodesia (which became Rhodesia and then Zimbabwe) and Nyasaland (which became Malawi). Zambia became independent in 1964 under Kenneth Kaunda, who ruled as head of the country's sole political party, the United National Independence Party, until he was defeated by Frederick Chiluba in Zambia's first democratic election in 1991. English is spoken along with several Bantu languages, notably Bemba, Nyanja and Tonga. Zambia is one of the world's top exporters of copper, which accounts for about 95 per cent of its export earnings. It has a population of 10 million and is a member of the Commonwealth.

Zarathustra

Except when naming Richard Strauss's *Also Sprach Zarathustra* (Thus Spake Zarathustra), use the more familiar name Zoroaster. See Zoroastrianism.

Zechariah

This is the spelling (not Zachariah) of the second-last book of the Old Testament, between Haggai and Malachi.

zed

We must always keep in mind the Canadian pronunciation of the last letter of the alphabet, which does not allow for such expressions as E-Z payments, in the unlikely event such a term appeared outside a company name or a quoted slogan. If the pronunciation is at issue, write zed or zee.

Zellers

No apostrophe. Zellers, with about 300 stores in all provinces, is owned by Hudson's Bay Co.

Zen

Upper-case. Zen Buddhism developed in China, but now is identified most strongly with Japan, where it greatly influenced the culture after 1300 and now has about nine million adherents. Zen (the word means meditation) differs from traditional Buddhism in its aversion to ritual, scriptures and images. Its two sects in Japan are Soto Zen, which emphasizes contemplation, and Rinzai Zen, in which paradoxical riddles are used to produce sudden enlightenment.

zeppelin

Lower-case for the German dirigibles, despite the word's origin in the name of the designer, Count Ferdinand von Zeppelin. The rock group is Led Zeppelin.

zero, zeros

The word is usually spelled out (visibility was close to zero), but use the figure 0 when giving temperatures.

zero hour

zero-zero

Has a hyphen. If this expression appears in a quote in an aviation story, explain that it means zero visibility and zero ceiling.

Zhou Enlai

Use this form, not Chou Enlai, for the former Chinese prime minister.

Ziegfeld, Florenz

The Ziegfeld (not Zigfield) *Follies.*

ziggurat

Not zikkurat. These were the stepped-pyramid temples of ancient Mesopotamia, and the word is occasionally used to describe modern terraced designs.

zigzag

Zimbabwe

Adjective and people: Zimbabwean. Currency: dollar. Capital: Harare.

Zimbabwe was formerly Southern Rhodesia, then became part of the Federation of Rhodesia and Nyasaland along with Northern Rhodesia (now Zambia) and Nyasaland (now Malawi). In 1965 it became Rhodesia,

after Ian Smith's unilateral declaration of independence to prevent black majority rule. It became legally independent as Zimbabwe, a member of the Commonwealth, in 1980 under Robert Mugabe. In 2000, Mugabe inaugurated a program of land redistribution whose effect was to evict white farmers and transfer their lands to his supporters. While pursuing a campaign of violence and intimidation against farmers, opposition politicians, judges and journalists, Mugabe rigged the 2002 election to ensure he remained president. The country has been severely affected by the AIDS pandemic.

The 12 million people are mostly Bantu, with the dominant groups being the Shona and Ndebele.

zinfandel

Lower-case for the type of California wine, both red and white.

Zion

It now symbolizes Jerusalem, Jews and their national aspirations. Originally, it was David's citadel, on a hill in southeastern Jerusalem. Distinguish between anti-Zionism (opposition to a Jewish state or its expansion) and anti-Semitism (hostility toward Jews).

Zip code

Use upper and lower case for Zip, though it is an acronym for Zoning Improvement Plan. This does not need to be spelled out; postal code explains it.

zipper

Use lower case. The trademark has become a generic term.

zodiac

Lower-case. It is an imaginary belt around the sky, divided into 12 sections, called signs. It is no longer correct to say that the names of these

sections are those of the principal constellation found in them. Precession of the equinoxes over the centuries since the signs were named has put each of these constellations into the sign after the one that bears its name.

We must not indicate in a news story, however obliquely, that The Globe or any member of its staff believes in astrology.

zombie

Use lower case for all meanings: the living dead, the voodoo snake god, the rum drink and the Canadian conscripts who refused overseas service in the Second World War. (In the last sense, the term should always be attributed and not in The Globe's language.)

zones

Upper-case the Torrid Zone, the North and South Temperate Zones and the Frigid Zones. The dividing lines are the Tropics of Cancer and Capricorn, the Arctic Circle and the Antarctic Circle.

zoology, zoologist

zoom

It means to move with a loud, low humming sound. In photography, it

means to move a movie or TV camera in for a close-up shot, or to change the magnification of a lens to achieve that effect in either moving or still pictures. In aviation, it means to climb sharply.

Zoroastrianism

This is the ancient religion that survives among the Parsees of India, who fled there from Persia in the eighth century to escape Muslim persecution. It is based on the teachings of the Persian sage Zoroaster in the sixth century BC, as recorded in scriptures called the Zend-Avesta. It teaches that there are two forces, one good and one evil, that good will eventually triumph, and that a person's actions in life bring eternal reward or punishment after death.

zucchetto

Prefer skullcap, or at least translate. The word does not require italics, and takes the English plural zucchettos. These are the caps worn by Roman Catholic clergy—white for the pope, red for cardinals, purple for bishops and black for priests.

zucchini

Zuider Zee

Not Zuyder. It means southern sea, but it is no longer a body of water; it is a northern district of the Netherlands. It was an inlet of the North Sea, but a 30-kilometre dam completed in 1932 divided it into the inner Lake Ijssel (Ijsselmeer) and the outer Waddenzee, which is open to the sea. Lake Ijssel is now largely fresh water, and greatly reduced in size as canals, dikes and pumping stations create five planned areas of dry land called polders.

Globe and Mail code of conduct

This code is the product of several committees of senior Globe editors and writers.

The newspaper's greatest assets are its integrity and credibility. The first aim of this document is to ensure that The Globe and Mail and its editorial staff conduct themselves honourably in all circumstances and are seen to do so. The second is to interfere in staffers' lives no more than is clearly necessary for the purpose.

Journalistic practices

The credibility of the news, analysis and opinion in The Globe and Mail rests on solid research and clear, intelligent writing, and on working to maintain a reputation for honesty, accuracy, objectivity and balance. To these ends, the following rules and principles apply.

Integrity: The Globe and Mail will ask no one to slant an article, column, feature, headline or other item to suit any interest or opinion. Staffers may decline to write what they believe is untrue or unfair. A strict separation will be maintained between the editorial views of The Globe and Mail and the coverage, selection, editing and play of the news.

Fairness: The Globe and Mail will seek to provide reasonable accounts of competing views in any controversy so as to enable readers to make up their own minds.

Truth: It is unacceptable at The Globe and Mail to invent or falsify a quote, source, anecdote, detail or anything else pertaining to the news. News pictures must be real images captured by a camera, not created or combined in a computer. The rule is relaxed for feature illustrations, but careful judgment is required. Whenever a photograph has been staged, altered or otherwise faked, this must be made clear to readers.

Quotes: Quotation marks are the newspaper's warranty that what is printed between them is what was said. Exceptions to this rule are few and relate chiefly to the difference between written and spoken language.

Writers may sometimes fix lapses in grammar or pronunciation of the ordinary sort that go unnoticed in conversation, but the changes must be minimal and carry no risk of altered meaning.

Hesitations, repetitions and false starts may be overlooked. This does not mean that quotes may be tightened or smoothed or otherwise recast for the writer's convenience or any other reason.

A writer may not weave separate parts of an interview or speech into a seamless passage of direct quotation. If material is omitted, ellipsis is indicated by three dots (. . .) plus normal punctuation where the break ends a sentence. When in doubt, paraphrase.

See also the entry on quotations in this Style Book.

Attribution: Although verified facts need no attribution, The Globe and Mail identifies sources of less-than-obviously-factual information in most circumstances. The same goes for opinions, only more so.

Writers must minimize the use of unattributed quotes, keeping in mind that the justification for omitting attribution is to get the fullest story possible, not to let people dodge accountability or take anonymous potshots. Sometimes an important story cannot be obtained without protecting a source who risks retribution if identified, but quotes with names attached carry far more weight.

In routine matters, sources must be pressed to speak on the record, and pressed again if they refuse. When such efforts fail, writers must decide whether to proceed with the interview. If they do, they must ensure mutual understanding of such terms as "off the record," "background" and "not for attribution," and keep track of what elements of each conversation are subject to restrictions.

Not for attribution means the source will not be named. Background means the source will not be referred to at all. Off the record is often used sloppily to mean not for attribution, but this cannot be assumed.

Writers must be extremely wary of accepting information on a strict off-the-record basis, meaning they can know but not publish it. If they accept such information, they must be clear on whether it can be used to get the same information on the record elsewhere.

When writers undertake to protect sources, they must establish how far the protection goes: Is it understood that the writer could be compelled to identify the source in court? Will the source come forward and testify if The Globe is sued? In the meantime, the newspaper will respect writers' pledges not to name sources unless the sources themselves speak for attribution or senior editors determine that special circumstances exist.

Writers are not obliged to honour after-the-fact pleas for anonymity from people they interview, but may occasionally do so for the unsophisticated or those with a legitimate fear of reprisal.

When sources are unnamed, they must be characterized as clearly and accurately as possible without actually identifying them, so as to give the reader an idea of their motivations for speaking. Reasons must be given why they cannot be named. Care must be taken to distinguish them from nearby named sources so as not to cast unfair suspicion on the latter.

Official spokesmen are rarely, if ever, entitled to anonymity, and it is better to specify their titles or job functions than to call them spokesmen.

Information should almost never be attributed merely to "sources" or "reliable sources" and rarely hung on the quaint construction "The Globe and Mail has learned."

Plagiarism: Excerpts from other people's prose must be attributed so as to avoid even a suspicion of copying. Although it is sometimes reasonable to adopt a few words without attribution (in a technical definition, for example), careful judgment is required. When in doubt, consult a senior editor.

Any extensive unacknowledged use of another's words, structure or ideas may constitute plagiarism. Exception: Background from previously published Globe staff and news-service items may be recycled, verbatim or otherwise, without credit, although it is best to avoid borrowing someone's distinctive prose style in doing so. News services must always be given credit for fresh information.

Fact-checking: Plagiarism aside, information from other publications must be checked before it is used. This does not apply to material supplied by news services to which proper credit is given. It is usually safe to trust an encyclopedia or other authoritative reference work for background facts, and not normally necessary to give it credit. No one is infallible, however. When in doubt about information from any source, even The Globe and Mail itself, double-check.

Civility: In dealing with people who are emotionally vulnerable and unaccustomed to talking to reporters, The Globe and Mail will take extra care to respect their dignity and feelings.

Identifying ourselves: In the usual circumstances of the job, Globe writers will identify themselves and make it clear they are working on stories for the newspaper. There are times when it is best to remain unidentified, however. Writers must consult their editors if there is doubt about the legitimacy of any proposed news-gathering tactic.

Showing drafts: Except as specified below, no one may show an article to an outsider before publication. On occasion, it may be permissible to ask one or more experts to review a draft. This applies most obviously to complex scientific, medical, legal and financial matters. It does not mean The Globe will accede to any request from the subject of a story to read it in advance. Writers may occasionally read quotes and other directly attributed material to the source for comment. This courtesy confers no right to dictate changes.

Publication dates: As far as is practical, writers should avoid giving outsiders more than a general idea of when their stories might run, especially when the knowledge might be of financial, commercial or political advantage. (This does not apply to special reports for which schedules are published.) No one may pass on information about news schedules, coverage plans or colleagues' work in progress to anyone outside the newspaper.

News embargoes: Embargoes can be useful (giving writers extra time to digest complex reports, for example) or manipulative. The Globe and Mail will be bound only by restrictions to which it has agreed and may choose to ignore release dates on unsolicited material, except news-service items.

There may be occasions when material received under embargo is also obtained independently by the newspaper. Whether this justifies breaking the embargo is a matter for discussion with senior editors. If an embargo is broken elsewhere, all deals are off.

Telephone taping: Reporters are free to record their ordinary two-way phone conversations without notice to anyone. Consent is required only on one side. The rule is not as neat for conference calls and speaker-phone calls, however. It may be illegal to tape crosstalk between other parties without their permission.

Corrections: Substantial errors of fact will be acknowledged and corrected on Page A2 or B2. Trivial slips should be corrected in the Info Globe database to prevent repetition. This is done through the chief librarian, who will consult senior editors if necessary.

Gifts, junkets, discounts, free items, lunches: The guiding principle: Editorial staff members may accept no benefit of more than token value offered to them because they work for the newspaper.

Review copies of books, recordings and similar items may be kept for reference, sent to the library, passed on to colleagues for whom they may be of professional use or donated to a charity sale. Staffers may not sell them. Those who keep such items for personal enjoyment should make an appropriate charitable donation.

Other free items of substantial value (sample merchandise, bottles of liquor and so on) must be returned or given to charity.

Staffers must not use their connection with the newspaper to obtain free or discounted goods or services, including travel, or any other advantage not available to the general public. In no case may they use the name or letterhead of The Globe and Mail to advance their personal interests.

Free admission to sports and entertainment may be accepted for review purposes. In business entertaining, it is seldom important who pays for lunch, but The Globe and Mail pays whenever possible. Staffers may accept invitations to sport and entertainment events only for work-related purposes, such as the chance to talk to people they may have occasion to write about. At receptions, parties and so on, staffers may accept customary hospitality, meaning food and drink consumed on the spot.

When staffers travel for The Globe and Mail, they pay full price, subject to whatever discounts are available on an ordinary commercial basis. The same applies to freelancers on direct assignment for the newspaper. The custom of accepting press rates persists in limited areas of coverage. It will be phased out. The practice of accepting freelance material from contributors who do not comply with these rules will be phased out. In publishing copy from any source with looser standards than are applicable to its own staff, The Globe and Mail will make appropriate disclosure whenever possible.

Radio and television work: Broadcast appearances by editorial staffers are subject to these conditions:

Writers and editors routinely involved in coverage affecting a broadcaster may take no payment from the broadcaster.

Columnists with wide-ranging mandates are not automatically barred from paid on-air work merely because they write about broadcasting from time to time, but careful judgment is required. A columnist making frequent appearances may face a choice of refusing payment or not writing about matters affecting the broadcaster. When it is relevant, columnists may be required to disclose in their columns that they have received payment from specific organizations.

There is no restriction on unpaid appearances. Whatever the financial terms, however, staffers must keep in mind that their first duty is to the newspaper and its readers (see the section on freelance writing and editing). They must also be careful not to taint their Globe coverage by drawing conclusions or taking sides in ways that would be barred to them by newspaper practice.

Speeches, seminars and other appearances: Editorial staffers may make paid speeches and other paid appearances subject to these conditions:

(1) Any staff member wishing to accept payment for a speech or other appearance must notify his or her masthead editor or a person designated by that editor, leaving time to cancel the appearance if it is deemed inappropriate. The staffer must specify the payment and any expense reimbursement he or she would receive. Honorariums and gifts of substantial value are payments.

(2) Permission will generally be denied to any writer or editor routinely involved in coverage affecting the organization offering the payment.

(3) Columnists with wide-ranging mandates are not automatically barred from accepting paid engagements from every organization about which they may have occasion to write, but careful judgment is required. When it is relevant, columnists may be required to disclose in their columns that they have received payment from specific organizations.

These rules do not generally apply to unpaid appearances, but staffers must notify their superiors of plans to appear before groups they are routinely involved in covering. When unpaid appearances require out-of-town travel, staffers may accept reimbursement of reasonable expenses: airfare, meals and necessary hotel accommodation, for example, but not an extended stay at a resort. No one listed on the masthead will accept payment from any outside party.

Freelance writing and editing: All rules applicable to paid speeches apply equally to paid work for captive publications, meaning those published by or for groups or corporations that may be subjects of coverage. Examples include association journals, in-flight magazines, game programs, annual reports and promotional inserts. Staffers generally are barred from taking any sort of payment from an entity they are involved in covering.

The right to engage in freelance work for publications that compete with The Globe and Mail is subject to management policy and union contract. For the purposes of this document, the only other rule is that staffers' first duty is to the newspaper and its readers. Thus, for example, they may not withhold or suppress material in their Globe and Mail coverage for use in freelance articles or books. Nor may they scoop The Globe on subjects related to their regular work without first offering the story to the newspaper. These points also apply to broadcast work.

Community, charitable and advocacy groups, public institutions, for-profit companies: Staff members' outside interests will not be restricted without reason, but certain rules apply:

(1) Boards of directors and comparable decision-making bodies.

These are off-limits to writers and editors routinely involved in coverage affecting the organization in question, and to everyone listed on the masthead. For example, the editor-in-chief cannot sit on a hospital board, nor can a health-policy reporter or an editor who assigns health stories. Even where no clear conflict exists, staffers must inform their superiors before accepting board appointments.

Being a director implies keeping secrets. Thus, a Globe staffer serving on a board may know things he or she cannot report. At a minimum, the staffer must take no part in coverage of such matters, and do nothing to influence the coverage, declaring a conflict if necessary. In some cases it may be advisable not to take part in board discussions of touchy items.

It is hard to imagine a case in which a Globe staffer could appropriately serve as the chairman, spokesman or primary public face of an outside board. Staffers should be prepared to resign from boards when serious conflicts arise. Those involved in private ventures in any capacity must be particularly careful to do nothing to influence coverage of their business or stock-market prospects or those of their competitors.

It may be acceptable for columnists to sit on boards of charitable or community organizations provided they make appropriate disclosure in all columns touching the interests of the organizations. News stories making more than cursory reference to any board on which a Globe employee sits must note the employee's involvement.

Staffers who find themselves in violation of these rules may complete board terms to which they were committed before the rules took effect. The rules do not apply to newspaper industry associations, journalism groups or labour bodies representing Globe employees.

(2) Fundraising.

Writers and editors must keep their distance from organizations they take part in covering, which rules out raising money for them. Otherwise, staffers are free to help their chosen causes by any means from tag days to telephone campaigns, provided they do so as private citizens without identifying themselves as Globe employees. The newspaper connection must not be exploited even implicitly; for example, writers and editors must not solicit donations from anyone who might recognize them as such and hope to gain The Globe's favour.

These rules do not apply to charitable campaigns conducted within The Globe itself.

(3) Lobbying.

Again, the newspaper connection must not be exploited. Staffers generally are free to make submissions to government agencies (for example, school boards and municipal committees) on their own behalf or for groups of fellow parents, residents or whatever, assuming they do not routinely take part in coverage of the agency or subject matter involved. On the other hand, it is almost certainly inappropriate for anyone recognizable as a Globe employee to lobby the provincial or federal government on behalf of a group likely to be a subject of coverage.

In all cases, careful judgment is called for. Staffers thinking of taking part in lobbying efforts should consult their colleagues and superiors.

These rules do not apply to newspaper associations, journalism groups or labour bodies representing Globe employees.

(4) Membership and financial contributions.

As private citizens, Globe staffers may give money to almost any cause they wish. (Note, however, the discussion of political contributions and other partisan activity elsewhere in this document.) They may also be dues-paying, rank-and-file members of just about any organization they choose, assuming they do not routinely take part in related coverage. They should consult their colleagues and superiors before taking more prominent positions in groups likely to be in the news.

Staffers must not permit their association with the newspaper to be exploited by any outside group.

Award juries and advisory committees: Staff members may sit on award juries and advisory committees that serve worthwhile public or journalistic purposes and do not blatantly promote commercial or institutional interests. They may not take pay for doing so, but may accept reimbursement of reasonable expenses if travel is required. Honorariums, if any, must be declined.

In considering invitations to join such bodies, staffers should be aware of practical problems that may arise and the danger of being co-opted or appearing to be co-opted by the sponsoring group.

Writers and editors cannot be involved in coverage of awards for which they serve as judges. They must consult their superiors on whether this restriction would complicate assignments unreasonably. Nor can staffers agree to keep secret things they learn while serving on juries or advisory committees, except to the extent of not leaking award decisions before they are announced. In the interests of free discussion, they may agree not to attribute statements to other participants without their permission.

Staffers who serve on juries should avoid taking prominent roles in promoting or presenting the awards and in most circumstances should not serve as chairman. They are not barred from taking part in coverage of the awards in subsequent years, however.

Those who serve on advisory committees must keep in mind the distinction between helping groups understand what makes news and coaching them on manipulation of the press. They must avoid the latter.

Political activity: To the extent possible, the news operations of The Globe and Mail must be and seem to be impartial.

This goal must be balanced against the fact that staff members have rights and responsibilities as citizens, and the fact that The Globe, through its editorial page, exercises its own right to take political stands. Staffers' rights should not be restricted unreasonably. What is reasonable may depend on the individual's job or assignment.

Reporters and columnists who routinely write on political issues must avoid being identified in their private lives with any party or political tendency. They are barred from most political activity other than voting. The same goes for editors who direct political coverage or take part in news selection and for everyone listed on the masthead. For these people, such things as political contributions, party membership, marches, demonstrations, lapel buttons, lawn signs (see below) and campaign work are out.

Copy editors who may be called on to handle political copy must notify their superiors of any political activity. Whenever possible, they should avoid dealing with stories relating to areas of politics in which they are active.

In other cases, there may be little risk of shaking anyone's faith in The Globe. For example, a sports reporter could probably manage a neighbour's campaign for school trustee without affecting the newspaper. In general, staffers whose work does not relate to political coverage are free to engage in political activity in a private capacity, taking care not to appear to represent The Globe.

Even so, they are urged to avoid high-profile positions (riding association president, for example). When in doubt, they should consult their colleagues and superiors. The question is whether the proposed activity would tend to promote doubt about The Globe's impartiality.

Staffers who engage in political activity must stop doing so if appointed to jobs relating to political coverage. The fact that their impartiality is in doubt may affect their chances for such appointments.

Although it is desirable that certain staffers avoid any hint of partiality, nothing in this policy affects the right of those with whom they share dwellings, including their spouses, children and tenants, to display lawn signs or otherwise exercise their political rights.

Personal interests: As a general rule, reporters and columnists should avoid taking part in coverage of matters in which they have or may be perceived to have significant personal interests, and editors should do nothing to influence the selection, wording, approach or play of stories in which they have or may be perceived to have such interests.

In this context, personal interest means a financial stake in a matter being covered, an outside involvement with a group or association being covered, a close friendship, romantic attachment or near family relationship to someone whose career or other interests may be affected, or any other entanglement that could lead to less than evenhanded treatment.

The Globe and Mail relies on staffers' integrity and common sense in the application of this rule. In some cases, the necessities of daily newspaper production may make strict adherence impractical. Some personal interests may be too general or trivial to count. For example, it might be hard to cover a teachers strike if everyone related to a teacher were disqualified. On the other hand, close relatives of bargainers on either side could not take part in the coverage.

Similarly, it may be a bad idea for a writer whose spouse is an official of a company, association or government department to cover that body, or for an editor in the same position to direct the coverage, to cite just one possible source of conflict. In columns and feature stories, significant personal interests may be noted either in the text or in italics at the end. This gives the reader an even break and generally takes care of the problem. The news format does not lend itself to such disclosure, however.

At a minimum, writers must inform their editors and seek guidance when they have significant personal interests in matters they may have occasion to write about. When editors face comparable situations, they must inform their superiors and seek guidance. When they cannot avoid taking part in the assigning or handling of stories in which they have interests, they must notify the writers of the situation and take extra care not to let their views intrude.

Investments: All employees must honour the general principle of the Report on Business policy on staff investing, to wit:

No one should benefit personally from knowledge obtained as a Globe and Mail employee until that knowledge is in the public domain. . . . In general, staff members should not write about securities they own. And they should not trade on information they know is going to appear in the newspaper.

The policy sets out specific rules for ROB staffers, who are further asked to disclose their investments annually to an independent adviser. In all departments, employees with doubts about investment situations are encouraged to seek guidance from their superiors. ROB staffers may also consult the independent adviser.

Record-keeping: This document will be maintained in a box or binder in the editorial library along with background material and notes of decisions flowing from it. Masthead editors should write brief case summaries after significant decisions, omitting names as they see fit. Staffers may consult this material at any time.

Report on Business policy on staff investment

Why we need a policy: The purpose of this policy is to protect the reputation, credibility and integrity of our newspaper by preventing real or perceived conflicts of interest among our staff.

We also want to protect ROB staff from possible charges of bias or conflict of interest. The best way to do this is to have a policy on investment by staff that is clear and public.

This policy has been devised with input from many staff members. It applies to all ROB staff.

In addition to our written policy, we have a system of investment disclosure to a third party. We strongly encourage everyone in the department to participate in the disclosure process.

How it works: You will be required to be familiar with our policy on the personal investments you should and should not be making. A breach of the policy may result in a disciplinary response.

You will also be encouraged to make an annual disclosure of your investments to our independent adviser, and to update him when you make changes.

This information is confidential. It is not shared with ROB editors. The only exception is when our independent adviser perceives an instance of conflict or bias in the paper (e.g., in the most obvious case, a columnist hyping a stock he or she has just purchased).

If he spots a problem, he will contact both the staff member and the ROB editor. It's up to the ROB editor to decide whether the policy has been breached and what measures to take.

How it will be communicated: To staff: You will get a copy of the policy once a year. New staff will be asked to review the policy with their editors.

To readers: ROB readers will be informed of the policy from time to time in the newspaper. We'll also mention the fact that we have a policy every day on Page B2, along with other department information.

What about grey areas? If you're uncertain about whether you have an investing (or any other) conflict, talk to your editor. We recognize that not every circumstance can be covered in this policy.

You can also call the independent adviser on a confidential basis for his opinion.

The general principle: No one should benefit personally from knowledge obtained as a Globe and Mail employee until that knowledge is in the public domain. In situations of doubt, you are asked to discuss the issue with your editor or with the independent adviser.

In general, staff members should not write about securities they own. And they should not trade on information they know is going to appear in the newspaper.

A breach of this policy may result in a disciplinary response.

Specifics:
• ROB reporters are not permitted to make personal investments in companies they are likely to write about as part of their usual assignments. For example, an ROB reporter who writes regularly about the beer industry should not own Molson shares. In the case of a beat change, a reasonable period (normally three months) will be given to divest holdings.
• If an ROB reporter owning stock in a company outside his or her regular beat is assigned a story concerning that company, he or she should discuss the matter with a senior editor before undertaking the assignment. The editor may decide that another reporter should do the story.
• ROB staff members are not permitted to engage in speculative short-selling of stocks. However, short-selling—or using derivatives such as options or warrants—is allowed for hedging purposes (that is, to protect an existing investment or portfolio).

- Staff members are not permitted to buy shares in an initial public offering. They must wait until the shares begin trading on the secondary market. Abuses can arise in an IPO when the stock is limited and doled out to favoured investors.
- Staff members who write investment columns and also hold securities mentioned in the column will state their ownership clearly. The disclosure format will be determined between the columnist and a senior editor.

Freelance investment columnists who hold securities—or who work for firms that hold positions in securities—will also abide by this disclosure rule.

- Generally exempt are investments in broadly diversified mutual funds, money-market funds, treasury bills and government debt securities of all kinds, as well as investment accounts in which all trading decisions are made by an independent money manager. Beat reporters, however, should not invest in specialty equity funds that offer a play on companies on their beat, such as precious metals, energy or real-estate funds.

A reporter or columnist writing a major feature about a mutual fund that he or she owns, as well as a mutual-fund company where he or she has invested money, should discuss the matter with a senior editor before undertaking the assignment.

- Staff members who become aware of specific investment news should not make a securities transaction related to that news until it has appeared in the newspaper.

Similarly, staff members should not buy or sell any securities or otherwise make investments in anticipation of forthcoming articles in The Globe and Mail.

- Staff members should not alert people outside the Globe and Mail newsroom, including family and friends, to any investment-related information they have learned before it is published.
- There is no intention of interfering with independent decision-making by members of employees' families. However, any attempt to evade these guidelines by trading or holding securities in the names of family members or others will be treated as a breach of these guidelines.
- All freelancers for Report on Business will be advised annually of our conflict guidelines and will be requested to advise their editor of any potential conflicts that may arise from a story assignment.

The disclosure letter: For your guidance, a sample of a formal disclosure letter to the independent adviser is available from your editor.

A history of The Globe and Mail

The history of The Globe begins in Toronto in 1843 with the arrival of George Brown, a tall, angular Edinburgh Scot of 25. He had come to North America in 1837 with his father, and helped the family run the British Chronicle in New York, an anti-slavery paper directed at British immigrants. It was while drumming up circulation for the Chronicle that Brown visited Toronto and, sensing a fertile market, persuaded his father to dispose of the New York paper and move to Toronto with him.

In August, 1843, they established The Banner, a four-page weekly designed to promote the interests of the Presbyterian Church; but the younger Brown had more secular aims, and founded The Globe on March 5, 1844, as a political vehicle. It began as a weekly with a circulation of 300, and by Oct. 1, 1853, had become a daily with a circulation of 6,000.

By 1858 Brown had become a dominant figure in the Reform Party in Canada West (previously Upper Canada), and was briefly head of the Brown-Dorion government. He fought fiercely for political union in British North America, becoming in the process one of the Fathers of Confederation.

In 1880, Brown was shot in the leg by a disgruntled former employee, one George Bennett, and died weeks later from an infection in the wound. The Globe was bought by a syndicate whose members included Senator Robert Jaffray. In 1888, the Jaffray family obtained control and kept it until 1936, during which time the newspaper adopted the slogan Canada's National Newspaper as its influence and circulation grew.

In 1936, the paper (with a circulation of 78,000) was sold to a young financier named George McCullagh. Mr. McCullagh acquired The Mail and Empire (circulation 118,000) a few weeks later, and absorbed it into The Globe under the new name, The Globe and Mail. The first issue appeared on Nov. 23, 1936. (The Mail had been established by Conservative backers in 1872, at the urging of Sir John A. Macdonald, to counter the influence of Brown's Globe, and had merged with another Conservative paper, The Empire, in 1895.)

Three years after Mr. McCullagh's death in 1952, the executors of his estate sold the paper to Montreal financier R. Howard Webster. Oakley Dalgleish, who had been the paper's editor for some years, was made editor and publisher in 1957. It was during Mr. Dalgleish's tenure, in 1962, that the newspaper added Report on Business, distributed as a separate publication outside Ontario and as a distinct section of the newspaper within the province. In 1967, Report on Business appeared on a daily basis, becoming Canada's first national daily business newspaper.

When Mr. Dalgleish died in 1963, Mr. Webster assumed the post of publisher; in 1965, he appointed James L. Cooper as publisher and editor-in-chief. Later that year, through an exchange of shares, Mr. Webster associated The Globe and Mail with a newspaper group, FP Publications Ltd. of Toronto, headed by John Sifton, Richard S. Malone and Max Bell. In 1974, Mr. Cooper retired and Mr. Malone became publisher and editor-in-chief.

In 1978, A. Roy Megarry succeeded Mr. Malone as publisher, and Richard J. Doyle, who had been editor of the newspaper since 1963, assumed the post of editor-in-chief.

In 1980, Thomson Newspapers Ltd. of Toronto acquired control of FP Publications and The Globe and Mail. Mr. Doyle (who was later appointed to the Senate) was succeeded as editor-in-chief in 1983 by Norman Webster, who was in turn succeeded by William Thorsell in 1989. In 1992, Mr. Megarry was succeeded as publisher by David Clark. Mr. Megarry returned as interim publisher in November, 1993. In May, 1994, Roger P. Parkinson was named publisher and chief executive. He was succeeded in 1999 by Phillip Crawley. Richard Addis was hired later the same year to succeed Mr. Thorsell, and was himself succeeded as editor-in-chief in 2002 by Edward Greenspon. In 2000, The Globe and Mail was purchased by BCE Inc. It has operated since Jan. 9, 2001, as part of the BCE subsidiary Bell Globemedia, alongside the CTV television network and the Internet content provider Globe Interactive. As a result of a reorganization in February of 2003, which saw Thomson Corp. sell its remaining shares to The Woodbridge Co. Ltd., which is the Thomson family's private holding company, BCE owns 68.5 per cent of Bell Globemedia, and Woodbridge owns 31.5 per cent.

One of the newspaper's strengths has long been its coverage of national and international news. In 1900, The Globe had its own correspondent in South Africa covering the Boer War. The Globe and Mail was the first North American newspaper after the Communist takeover of China in 1949 to establish a resident correspondent in that country, in 1959. It was the first Canadian newspaper to open permanent news bureaus in Africa and Latin America. The Globe had a correspondent in Quebec City in the 1850s when it was the capital of the Province of Canada, and a correspondent telegraphing regular news from Ottawa as of 1867. A full Ottawa bureau followed in time, and in 1954 The Globe and Mail became the first Ontario newspaper to open a Quebec news bureau. Beginning in 1959 with British Columbia, the newspaper established news bureaus in other regions of Canada.

In 1979, The Globe became the first newspaper in the world to produce a full text commercial database containing every story from each issue (dating back to 1977), and the first to publish electronically and in print on the same day. An electronic information division called Info Globe was established to offer on-line access to this database and a variety of other information sources. Info Globe changed its name in 1992 to Globe Information Services. The Globe and Mail's website, www.globeandmail.com, began early in 1995 by offering a few of The Globe's regular features on-line. On June 19, 2000, the real-time site began, offering news and columns written specifically for the site as events unfolded during the day.

In 1980, The Globe and Mail became Canada's first space-age newspaper. It printed a national edition in Montreal, including general news, features and Report on Business, with the contents transmitted from the main publishing centre in Toronto to the Montreal printing plant via the Anik satellite. Since then, additional satellite printing plants have been established across the country, permitting rapid same-day distribution of the newspaper in the 10 provinces and the three territories.

In 1985, The Globe and Mail entered the consumer magazine field in a major way with the publication of Report on Business Magazine (which has since dropped the word Magazine from the title), a high-quality colour magazine distributed with the newspaper.

The Globe and Mail underwent a major redesign in 1990, both graphically and editorially, beginning with the issue dated June 12. It was as part of this redesign that the newspaper's editorial style book was completely revised and first published in its current form, and that The Globe produced its first visual style guide. The Globe underwent a further editorial and graphic redesign on July 9, 1998, a major feature of which was the introduction of colour to the front page and several other parts of the newspaper.

The newspaper's motto was selected by George Brown in 1844, and will be found at the top of the editorial page: "The subject who is truly loyal to the Chief Magistrate will neither advise nor submit to arbitrary measures." The quotation is from Junius, the pseudonym of an English writer of the 18th century. The Globe and Mail believes, as Brown did when he founded the newspaper, that only an informed public can defend itself against power seekers who threaten its freedoms.

British Columbia

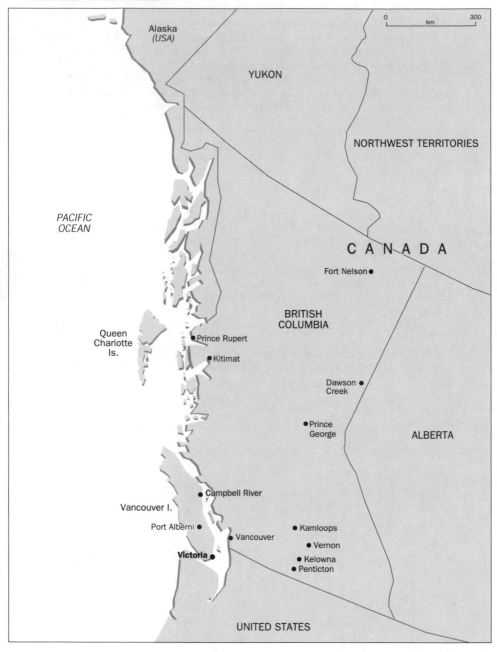

Alaska
(USA)

YUKON

NORTHWEST TERRITORIES

PACIFIC
OCEAN

C A N A D A

Fort Nelson ●

BRITISH
COLUMBIA

Queen
Charlotte
Is.

● Prince Rupert

● Kitimat

Dawson ●
Creek

● Prince
George

ALBERTA

● Campbell River

Vancouver I.

Port Alberni ●

● Kamloops

● Vancouver

● Vernon

Victoria ●

● Kelowna
● Penticton

UNITED STATES

0   km   300

Alberta, Saskatchewan & Manitoba

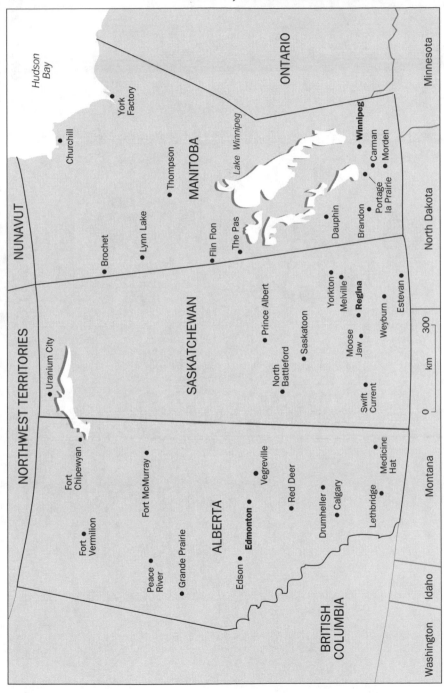

Yukon, Northwest Territories & Arctic Islands

Ontario

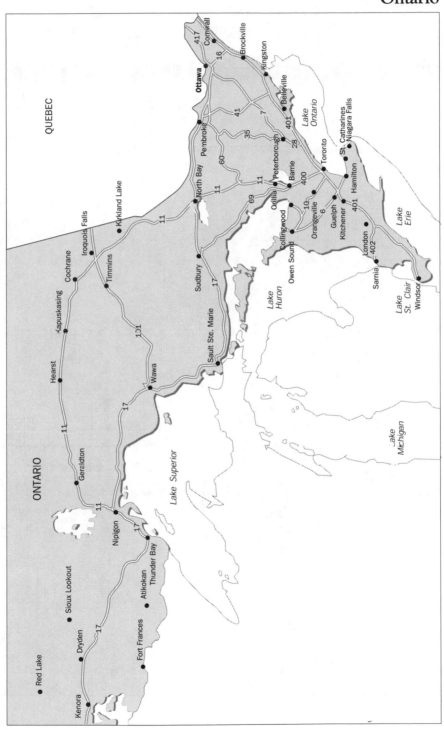

Quebec

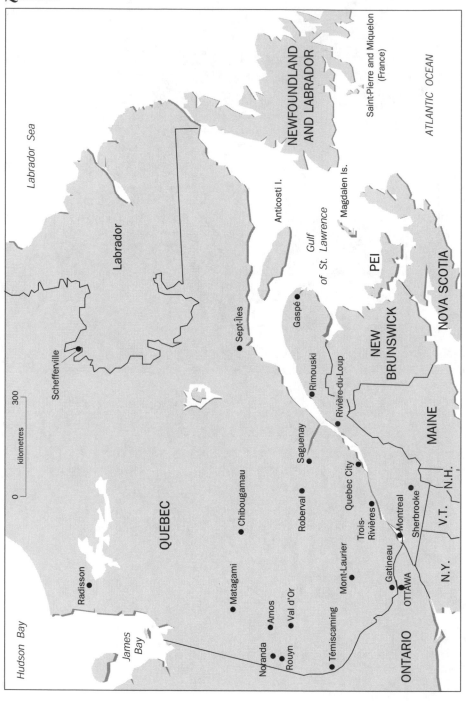

Atlantic Canada

0   KILOMETRES   300

Labrador Sea

QUEBEC

Labrador

NEWFOUNDLAND AND LABRADOR

Nain ●

Hopedale ●

Churchill ● Happy Valley-
Falls   Goose Bay

Labrador City ●
● Wabush

St. Anthony ●

● Baie Verte

Deer Lake ●   Grand   ● Gander
Corner Brook ●   Falls ●   ● Bonavista
Stephenville ●   Buchans   **St. John's**

Gulf of
St. Lawrence   Harbour Grace

Campbellton ●   Port aux Basques ●

Edmundston ●   Bathurst ●   Saint-Pierre and Miquelon
   Newcastle ●   Summerside ●   *(France)*
N.B.   Chatham ●   **Charlottetown**
   Moncton ●   PEI   ● Glace Bay
Fredericton ●   ● Sydney
Saint John ●   Pictou ●
St. Stephen ●   Amherst ●   NOVA SCOTIA
   Windsor ●   Dartmouth ●
   Lunenburg ●   **Halifax**   Sable Island

Yarmouth ●

ATLANTIC OCEAN

United States of America

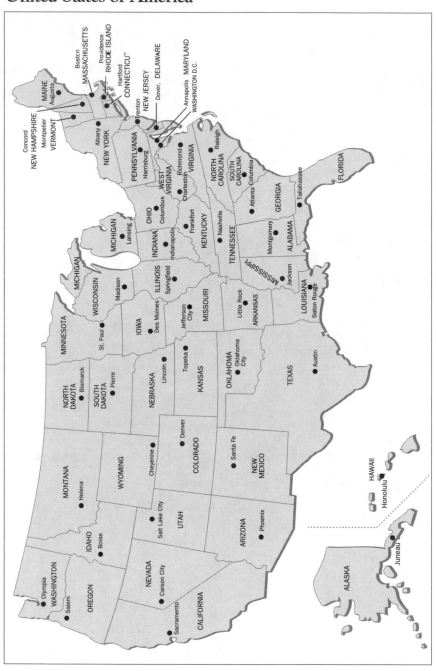

West Indies

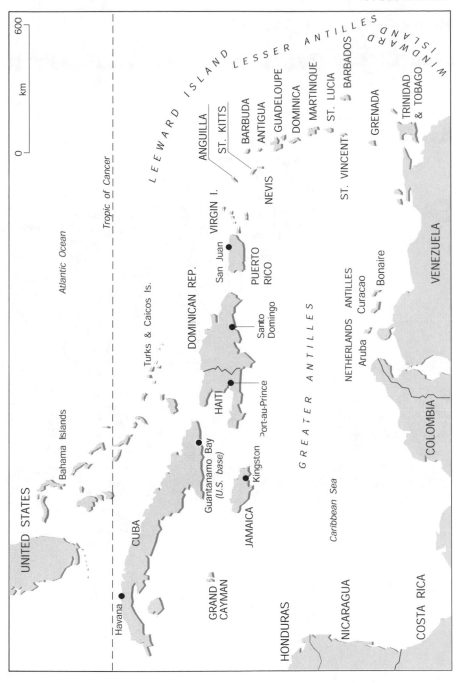

km
0
600

UNITED STATES

Atlantic Ocean

Tropic of Cancer

Bahama Islands

Turks & Caicos Is.

Havana

CUBA

Guantanamo Bay
(U.S. base)

GRAND
CAYMAN

JAMAICA

Kingston

DOMINICAN REP.

HAITI

Port-au-Prince

Santo
Domingo

San Juan

PUERTO
RICO

VIRGIN I.

GREATER ANTILLES

Caribbean Sea

L E E W A R D   I S L A N D

LESSER ANTILLES

ANGUILLA

ST. KITTS

BARBUDA

ANTIGUA

NEVIS

GUADELOUPE

DOMINICA

MARTINIQUE

ST. LUCIA

BARBADOS

ST. VINCENT

GRENADA

TRINIDAD
& TOBAGO

W
I
N
D
W
A
R
D

I
S
L
A
N
D

NETHERLANDS ANTILLES

Curacao

Aruba

Bonaire

VENEZUELA

COLOMBIA

HONDURAS

NICARAGUA

COSTA RICA

Central & South America

UNITED STATES

ATLANTIC OCEAN

Gulf
of Mexico

MEXICO

BELIZE
HONDURAS

Caribbean
Sea

NICARAGUA

GUATEMALA

GUYANA

EL SALVADOR

VENEZUELA

SURINAME

COSTA RICA

COLOMBIA

FRENCH GUIANA

PANAMA

ECUADOR

BRAZIL

PERU

BOLIVIA

PARAGUAY

CHILE

URUGUAY

ARGENTINA

PACIFIC OCEAN

ATLANTIC OCEAN

FALKLAND
ISLANDS
(Britain)

Picton, Nueva and Lennox Islands
(Chile)

0   km   1,000

Africa

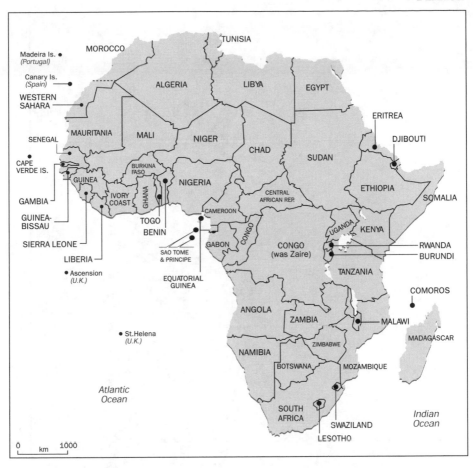

Madeira Is. ●
(Portugal)

Canary Is. ●
(Spain)

WESTERN
SAHARA

CAPE ●
VERDE IS.

GAMBIA

GUINEA-
BISSAU

SIERRA LEONE

LIBERIA

Ascension ●
(U.K.)

St.Helena ●
(U.K.)

MOROCCO

TUNISIA

ALGERIA

LIBYA

EGYPT

ERITREA

DJIBOUTI

MAURITANIA

MALI

NIGER

CHAD

SUDAN

SENEGAL

GUINEA

IVORY
COAST

GHANA

BURKINA
FASO

NIGERIA

CENTRAL
AFRICAN REP.

ETHIOPIA

SOMALIA

TOGO

BENIN

CAMEROON

SAO TOME
& PRINCIPE

GABON

EQUATORIAL
GUINEA

CONGO

CONGO
(was Zaire)

UGANDA

KENYA

RWANDA

BURUNDI

TANZANIA

COMOROS

ANGOLA

ZAMBIA

MALAWI

MADAGASCAR

St.Helena
(U.K.)

ZIMBABWE

NAMIBIA

BOTSWANA

MOZAMBIQUE

Atlantic
Ocean

Indian
Ocean

SOUTH
AFRICA

SWAZILAND

LESOTHO

0   1000
  km

Europe, northern part

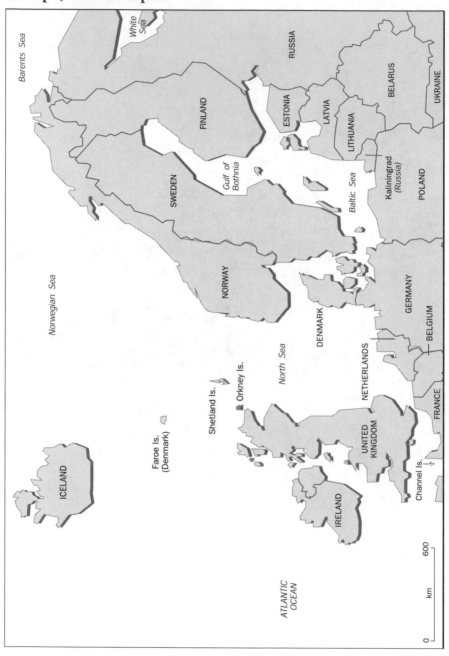

Europe, southern part

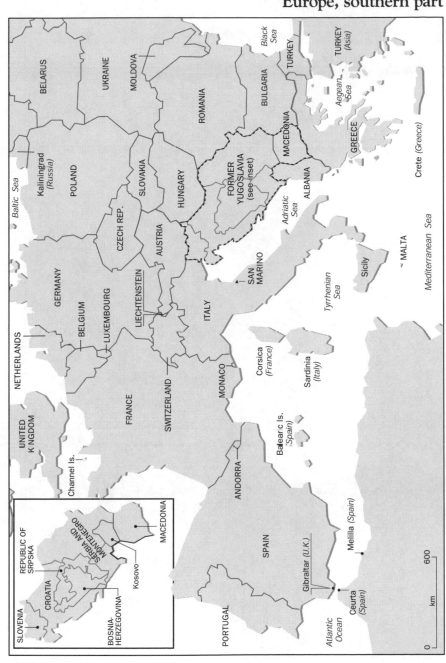

Russia and its neighbours

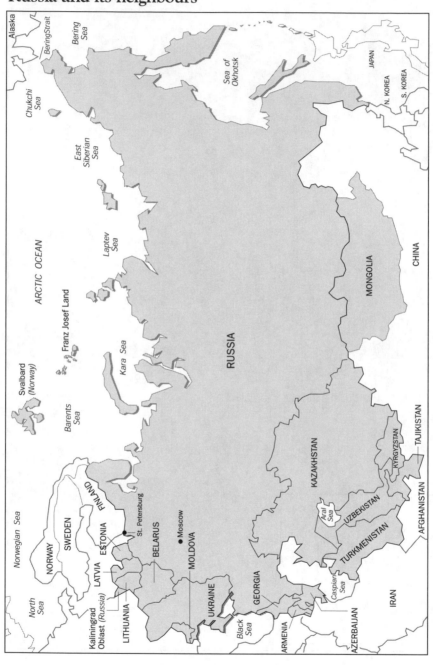

Middle East

GREECE
BLACK SEA
RUSSIA
0   km   650
TURKEY
GEORGIA
UZBEKISTAN
AZERBAIJAN
ARMENIA
Dardanelles
TURKEY
TURKMENISTAN
Caspian Sea
MEDITERRANEAN SEA
SYRIA
CYPRUS
AFGHANISTAN
LEBANON
ISRAEL
IRAQ
IRAN
Suez Canal
JORDAN
Sinai Peninsula *(Egypt)*
PAKISTAN
EGYPT
KUWAIT
Strait of Hormuz
BAHRAIN
Persian Gulf
QATAR
Gulf of Oman
SAUDI ARABIA
•Mecca
UNITED ARAB EMIRATES
OMAN
Arabian Sea
Red Sea
Boundary undefined
SUDAN
ERITREA
YEMEN
Gulf of Aden
INDIAN OCEAN
DJIBOUTI
ETHIOPIA
SOMALIA

Indian Subcontinent & Afghanistan

Southeast Asia

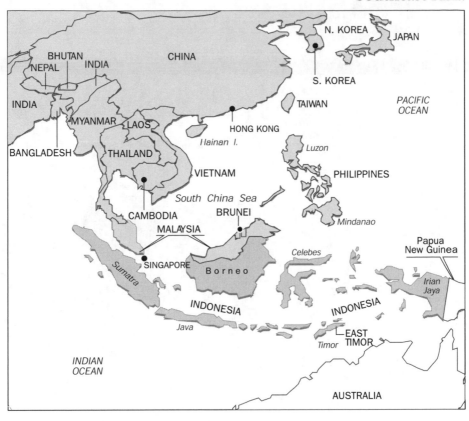